The Cambridge Companion to Newton

Sir Isaac Newton (1642–1727) was one of the greatest scientists of all time, a thinker of extraordinary range and creativity who has left enduring le for his *Princi*... of the calculus, New... chemistry and alchem..., and to stud... history, and ancient chronology. This new edition of *The Cambridge Companion to Newton* provides authoritative introductions to these further dimensions of his endeavors as well as to many aspects of his physics and mathematics. It includes a revised bibliography, a new introduction, and six new chapters: three replacing previous chapters on Newton's mathematics, his chemistry and alchemy, and the reception of his religious views; and three on entirely new subjects, namely his religion, his ancient chronology, and the treatment of continuous and discontinuous forces in his second law of motion.

ROB ILIFFE is Professor of History of Science at the University of Oxford.

GEORGE E. SMITH is Professor of Philosophy at Tufts University.

Other Volumes in The Series of Cambridge Companions

ABELARD *Edited by* JEFFREY E. BROWER *and* KEVIN GUILFOY

ADORNO *Edited by* THOMAS HUHN

ANCIENT SCEPTICISM *Edited by* RICHARD BETT

ANSELM *Edited by* BRIAN DAVIES *and* BRIAN LEFTOW

AQUINAS *Edited by* NORMAN KRETZMANN *and* ELEONORE STUMP

ARABIC PHILOSOPHY *Edited by* PETER ADAMSON *and* RICHARD C. TAYLOR

HANNAH ARENDT *Edited by* DANA VILLA

ARISTOTLE *Edited by* JONATHAN BARNES

ARISTOTLE'S POLITICS *Edited by* MARGUERITE DESLAURIERS *and* PAUL DESTRÉE

ATHEISM *Edited by* MICHAEL MARTIN

AUGUSTINE 2ND EDITION *Edited by* DAVID MECONI *and* ELEONORE STUMP

BACON *Edited by* MARKKU PELTONEN

BERKELEY *Edited by* KENNETH P. WINKLER

BOETHIUS *Edited by* JOHN MARENBON

BRENTANO *Edited by* DALE JACQUETTE

CARNAP *Edited by* MICHAEL FRIEDMAN *and* RICHARD CREATH

CONSTANT *Edited by* HELENA ROSENBLATT

CRITICAL THEORY *Edited by* FRED RUSH

DARWIN 2ND EDITION *Edited by* JONATHAN HODGE *and* GREGORY RADICK

SIMONE DE BEAUVOIR *Edited by* CLAUDIA CARD

DELEUZE *Edited by* DANIEL W. SMITH *and* HENRY SOMERS-HALL

DESCARTES *Edited by* JOHN COTTINGHAM

DESCARTES' MEDITATIONS *Edited by* DAVID CUNNING

DEWEY *Edited by* MOLLY COCHRAN

DUNS SCOTUS *Edited by* THOMAS WILLIAMS

EARLY GREEK PHILOSOPHY *Edited by* A. A. LONG

EARLY MODERN PHILOSOPHY *Edited by* DONALD RUTHERFORD

EPICUREANISM *Edited by* JAMES WARREN

EXISTENTIALISM *Edited by* STEVEN CROWELL

FEMINISM IN PHILOSOPHY *Edited by* MIRANDA FRICKER *and* JENNIFER HORNSBY

FOUCAULT 2ND EDITION *Edited by* GARY GUTTING

FREGE *Edited by* TOM RICKETTS *and* MICHAEL POTTER

FREUD *Edited by* JEROME NEU

GADAMER *Edited by* ROBERT J. DOSTAL

GALEN *Edited by* R. J. HANKINSON

The Cambridge
Companion to Newton

SECOND EDITION

Edited by

ROB ILIFFE
University of Oxford

GEORGE E. SMITH
Tufts University

CAMBRIDGE
UNIVERSITY PRESS

CAMBRIDGE
UNIVERSITY PRESS

University Printing House, Cambridge CB2 8BS, United Kingdom

Cambridge University Press is part of the University of Cambridge.

It furthers the University's mission by disseminating knowledge in the pursuit of education, learning and research at the highest international levels of excellence.

www.cambridge.org
Information on this title: www.cambridge.org/9781107601741

© Cambridge University Press 2002, 2016

This publication is in copyright. Subject to statutory exception and to the provisions of relevant collective licensing agreements, no reproduction of any part may take place without the written permission of Cambridge University Press.

First edition first published 2002

Second edition first published 2016

Printed in the United Kingdom by Clays, St Ives plc

A catalog record for this publication is available from the British Library

Library of Congress Cataloging in Publication data

Names: Iliffe, Rob, editor. | Smith, George E. (George Edwin), 1938—editor.
Title: The Cambridge companion to Newton / edited by Rob Iliffe and George E. Smith.
Description: Second edition. | Cambridge : Cambridge University Press, 2016.|
Includes bibliographical references and index.
Identifiers: LCCN 2015040735 | ISBN 9781107601741 (pbk. : alk. paper)
Subjects: LCSH: Newton, Isaac, 1642-1727. | Physics—Europe—History—17th century. | Physics—Europe—History—18th century. |Science—Europe—History—17th century. | Science—Europe—History—18th century.
Classification: LCC QC16.N7 C35 2016 | DDC 530.092—dc23 LC record available at http://lccn.loc.gov/2015040735

ISBN   978-1-107-01546-3 Hardback
ISBN   978-1-107-60174-1 Paperback

Cambridge University Press has no responsibility for the persistence or accuracy of URLs for external or third-party internet websites referred to in this publication, and does not guarantee that any content on such websites is, or will remain, accurate or appropriate.

Contents

Figures

Contributors

DOMENICO BERTOLONI MELI is a professor in the Department of History and Philosophy of Science at Indiana University. He specializes in seventeenth- and eighteenth-century science and medicine and is the author of a number of books, including *Equivalence and Priority: Newton versus Leibniz*.

I. BERNARD COHEN was Victor S. Thomas Professor of the History of Science Emeritus at Harvard University. He is the author of numerous books in the history of science generally and on Newton in particular, including *The Newtonian Revolution*, and is co-editor of the Variorum Latin edition of Newton's *Principia* and co-author of the new English translation.

ROBERT DISALLE is a professor in the Department of History and Philosophy of Science at the University of Western Ontario. He has published several papers on Newton, Einstein, and Mach, especially on their respective treatments of space, time, and motion.

MORDECHAI FEINGOLD is Professor of History at Caltech. He is the editor of the journal *History of Universities* and author of a number of books including *The Mathematicians' Apprenticeship: Science, Universities and Society in England, 1560–1640* (Cambridge, 1984), *The Newtonian Moment: Isaac Newton and the Making of Modern Culture* (2004), and *Isaac Newton and the Origin of Civilization* (2013), written with Jed Buchwald.

ALAN GABBEY is Professor of Philosophy at Barnard College, New York. He has published numerous papers on seventeenth-century mechanics and philosophy.

NICCOLÒ GUICCIARDINI teaches history of science at the University of Bergamo. He is author of *The Development of Newtonian Calculus in Britain, 1700–1800* and *Reading the Principia: The Debate on Newton's Mathematical Methods for Natural Philosophy from 1687 to 1736, and Isaac Newton on Mathematical Certainty and Method.*

WILLIAM HARPER is Professor of Philosophy at Western Ontario University. He has written extensively on Newton's methodology and the relationship between Newton's and Einstein's theories of gravity, as well as on Kant and on causal decision theory.

ROB ILIFFE is Professor of History of Science at the University of Oxford. He is author of the *Very Short Introduction to Newton* (Oxford, 2007) and *Priest of Nature: the Religious Life of Isaac Newton* (Oxford, 2016). He was director of the AHRC Newton Theological Papers Project from 1999 to 2014, is a General Editor of the Newton Project, and is currently co-editor of the journal *Annals of Science*.

SCOTT MANDELBROTE is Official Fellow and Director of Studies in History at Peterhouse, Cambridge. He is the author of many articles in the history of early modern scholarship, and is a General Editor of the Newton Project.

WILLIAM R. NEWMAN is a professor in the Department of History and Philosophy of Science at Indiana University. His work on early chemistry and alchemy includes *The "Summa Perfectionis" of Pseudo-Geber: A Critical Edition, Translation, and Study*, and *Gehennical Fire: The Lives of George Starkey, An American Alchemist in the Scientific Revolution.*

BRUCE POURCIAU is Professor of Mathematics at Lawrence University, Appleton, Wisconsin. His research has focused on optimization theory and global analysis in mathematics, the mathematical and logical foundations of Newton's *Principia* and Newton's mathematical work more generally, as well as the philosophy of mathematics, particularly Brouwer's intuitionism and Bishop's constructivism.

ALAN E. SHAPIRO is Professor of the History of Science and Technology at the University of Minnesota. He is author of *Fits, Passions, and Paroxysms: Physics, Method, and Chemistry* and *Newton's Theories of Colored Bodies and Fits of Easy Reflection*, and is the editor of Newton's optical papers.

GEORGE E. SMITH is Professor of Philosophy at Tufts University. He specializes in the development of evidence in the advanced sciences and engineering and is the author of several papers on Newton.

HOWARD STEIN is a professor emeritus in the Department of Philosophy of the University of Chicago. His research has focused on the philosophical foundations of physics and mathematics, and he has published several highly influential papers on Newton, as well as on Huygens, Maxwell, and Einstein.

CURTIS WILSON was a tutor at St. John's College, Annapolis. His writings on the history of science reach from the Middle Ages through the nineteenth century, most extensively on astronomy; he was co-editor of the two parts of *Planetary Astronomy from the Renaissance to the Rise of Astrophysics*, the second volume of *The General History of Astronomy*.

Preface to the second edition

The task of compiling *The Cambridge Companion to Newton* was originally taken on by Richard S. Westfall. After he died in 1996, it fell to the late I. Bernard Cohen and George E. Smith, who started it afresh. The first edition was published in 2002 and has received wide circulation. In the case of several of its chapters, research since then has not yielded sufficient reasons to make substantial revision to them. In several other cases, however, subsequent research has greatly advanced our knowledge of Newton, rendering the original chapters out of date. The goal of the second edition is to correct this situation, bringing *The Companion to Newton* more up to date.

Most notable in this regard has been research on Newton's extensive manuscripts concerning theology, many of which had scarcely been examined at all at the time of the first edition. Scott Mandelbrote's chapter in that edition focused largely on the reaction among theologians to Newton's conception of Christianity as it emerged in snippets during the years after he died. Mandelbrote has updated that chapter by incorporating new research carried out over the last decade. Rob Iliffe has added a new chapter surveying Newton's efforts in theology, while Mordechai Feingold has added an essay on Newton's efforts in chronology that extends the critical analysis of *The Chronology of Ancient Kingdoms Amended* that he and Jed Buchwald present in their book *Newton and the Origin of Civilization*.

Another area in which research during the last decade has greatly expanded and refined our understanding of what Newton was up to is the effort he devoted to alchemy and chemistry. William Newman has been analyzing the experiments Newton recorded in his notes, even reproducing some of them, and he, along with others, has continued his systematic study of alchemy

in the period. On the basis of this work, Newman has supplied an
entirely new chapter on Newton's efforts in alchemy and chemistry,
replacing the essays in the first edition by him and the late
Karin Figala.

Niccolò Guicciardini's chapter on Newton's mathematics in
the first edition, "Analysis and synthesis in Newton's mathematical
work," centered on the topic announced in its title, and hence
provided readers with a perspective of Newton's efforts in the area,
but not a comprehensive overview of efforts that stretched over
four decades. In the meantime Guicciardini has continued his
research on the subject, producing his recent book *Isaac Newton
on Mathematical Certainty and Method* that focuses heavily on
Newton's conception of truth and certainty in mathematics. This
has also led to an entirely new essay in this edition, which provides
a comprehensive overview of Newton's efforts in mathematics and
the significance he attached to it.

Finally, a new chapter by Bruce Pourciau has been added on a
long-time controversial issue within the foundations of Newton's
mechanics in the *Principia*, namely his appearing to go back and
forth between discrete (or impulse) forces and continuous forces
without laying a foundation for doing so. On the one hand, the
phrasing of the statement of his second law of motion in all editions
of the *Principia* appears to limit it to discrete forces, and this is
consistent with such initial applications of it as the first corollary
to the laws of motion and Propositions 1 and 2; on the other hand,
the second law is cited repeatedly throughout the *Principia* in
conjunction with continuous forces that are characterized in terms
of an incremental displacement from uniform motion in a straight
line and the square of an increment of time inversely – a claim that
makes no sense in the case of discrete forces. In a series of articles
since the first edition of this *Companion*, Pourciau has argued that
Newton himself provided a way of resolving this conflict in an
unpublished manuscript from the early 1690s that lays out "the

meaning of the law." Under this meaning of the law, it clearly applies to both discrete and continuous forces and hence makes it consistent with all the applications and citations of the law in the *Principia*. There nevertheless appears to be no textually authorized way to reconcile this unpublished statement of the meaning of the law with its express statement in all editions.

Bernard Cohen, who was fully aware of the manuscript from the early 1690s, elected to ignore it in his chapter in the first edition of this *Companion* and chose instead to restrict himself to the actual statement of the law in the *Principia*, leaving him with the difficult task of explaining how Newton thought of continuous forces as derivative from discrete ones. In his new chapter, Pourciau makes the case that Newton always understood his second law in the way he explicated it in the early 1690s, so that the only source of confusion has been the unfortunate phrasing of the law in the *Principia*. This leaves him with the difficult task of reconciling the explication from the early 1690s with the statement of the law not only in the 1687 edition of the *Principia*, but in the 1713 and 1726 editions as well. We decided that the appropriate way to deal with this situation is to include both Cohen's and Pourciau's chapters in the second edition, thereby enabling readers to see the complexity of the issue raised by the second law, as regards both Newton and the subsequent history of mechanics.

The addition of three completely new chapters by Pourciau, Iliffe, and Feingold has unfortunately necessitated our dropping of three chapters from the first edition, "Curvature in Newton's dynamics" by the late Bruce Brackenridge and Michael Nauenberg, "Newton versus Leibniz: from geometry to metaphysics" by the late A. Rupert Hall and "Newton on prophecy and the Apocalypse" by the late Maurizio Mamiani. Hall's chapter was to a large extent a summary of his book *Philosophers at War: The quarrel between Newton and Leibniz*, and hence readers can always turn to it if they want to go beyond the discussion of the priority dispute in

Guicciardini's chapter. The real loss, therefore, is the long chapter by Brackenridge and Nauenberg and its account of how Newton's investigations into curvature informed his writing of the *Principia* in ways not readily evident in the book itself. Our choice in this case reflects both the length of the paper and its more technically demanding analysis (in comparison with the other chapters in the *Companion*), but we encourage readers interested in the evolution of Newton's approach to curvilinear motion to turn to it.

Introduction

Rob Iliffe and George E. Smith

Isaac Newton was *the* giant of science in the seventeenth and eighteenth centuries, just as James Clerk Maxwell was *the* giant of science during the latter nineteenth century. By providing a completely novel cosmology, in which a taxonomy of interactive forces among particles of matter was fundamental, his *Principia Mathematica* of 1687 constituted an exemplary scientific revolution. This supplanted not only the Aristotelian system, but also that of the so-called "mechanical philosophy" espoused by moderns such as Descartes. Conceptions such as "mass" and "force" were quickly recognized by Newton's contemporaries as powerful concepts for representing aspects of bodies that allowed them to be measured and their dynamical interactions calculated. Newton's claim that almost all of the cosmos (including the internal structure of bodies) was entirely empty of matter, however, was deeply unpalatable to those committed to plenist and vortical accounts. Worst of all, many found Newton's great doctrine of universal gravitation, and the notion of "attraction" that underlay it, wholly unacceptable. It was easy for his most adept commentators to reject the idea of objects attracting each other immediately over vast distances as a return to the objectionable occult qualities of the scholastics.

The problems with accepting the reality of universal gravitation were linked to criticisms of the new conception of theory that Newton offered. The standard view, accepted both by scholastic natural philosophy and the mechanical philosophy, was that such phenomena were to be explicated in terms of known physical causes. Newton launched repeated attacks on the way that many of his contemporaries explained natural phenomena by means of what he called "hypothetical" metaphysical or physical entities such as "corpuscles" or the "aether," many of which formed central parts of great

1

(but, to Newton, fictitious) cosmological systems. It should be said that this remained Newton's official public position only, for in private, and over more than six decades, he had a firm conviction about the existence of corpuscles and aethers. Occasionally these views became more widely known, notably in the "Hypothesis" read out to the Royal Society in the winter of 1675–6 and in the "Queries" added to his *Optice* of 1706 and to the second edition of *Opticks* in 1717.

Most importantly, however, Newton brought together an empiricist, inductivist and anti-hypotheticalist sensibility from his immersion in the writings of Hooke and Boyle with a commitment to a mathematical approach to nature inspired by writers such as Galileo and Christiaan Huygens. Propositions were to be inferred from phenomena, Newton proclaimed, and made more general by induction until one arrived at the most general laws of nature. These laws, which were mathematical, could then be used to explain phenomena in the relevant domain of their application. This was enough to count as explanation within natural philosophy, with no need to have recourse to as yet unconfirmed underlying entities. Newton left open the possibility, however, that future empirical research would confirm the existence of entities that were currently undetectable.

Nothing about Newton is better known than the story that he came upon his theory of gravity while contemplating the fall of an apple in his mother's garden when away from Cambridge during the plague. Newton definitely did give careful thought at some point during the late 1660s to the possibility that terrestrial gravity extends, in an inverse-square proportion, to the Moon. From his papers and correspondence, however, we can clearly see that the earliest date that can be assigned to his theory of universal gravity is late 1684 or early 1685, during the course of his revision of the tract "De motu." As I. B. Cohen shows in his chapter, a necessary precondition for his conception of universal gravitation was his creation of the new concepts of *mass* and *force*, which were also required for his laws of motion, a topic examined in Bruce Pourciau's chapter as well as Cohen's. The theory of gravity did not arise as a "eureka" moment in a Lincolnshire garden, but was a product of thoughts about orbital motion extending over many years.

From the point of view of his contemporaries, Newton's theory consisted of a sequence of progressively more controversial claims: from the inverse-square centripetal acceleration of orbiting bodies to interactive forces not merely between orbiting and central bodies, but among the different orbiting bodies as well; then, to the law of gravity according to which the forces on orbiting bodies are proportional to the masses of the distant bodies toward which these forces are directed; and finally to the sweeping claim that there are gravitational forces between every two particles of matter in the universe. William Harper's chapter on Newton's "deduction" of his theory of gravity examines how Newton put this sequence forward, invoking specific evidence for each claim in turn. Even the most outspoken critics of universal gravitation thought Newton had established some of the claims in the sequence. Though they balked at different points, the common feature was where they thought concession of a claim was tantamount to conceding action at a distance. Newton himself was troubled by action at a distance – so much so that it seems to have driven him into thinking through and then laying out a new, elaborate approach to how empirical science ought to be done, an approach that the *Principia* was expressly intended to illustrate.

Curtis Wilson's chapter shows that Newton's important achievement in celestial mechanics involved two seemingly incompatible points. On the one hand, the *Principia* raised Kepler's rules, especially the area rule, from the status of one among several competing approaches to calculating orbits, to the status where they came to be thought of as laws, *the* laws of planetary motion. On the other hand, the *Principia* concluded that none of Kepler's "laws" is in fact exactly true of the actual system of planets or their satellites, and this in turn shifted the focus of orbital mechanics to deviations from Keplerian motion. With the exception of a few results on the lunar orbit, the *Principia* made no attempt to derive these deviations, and even in the case of the lunar orbit it left one major loose end that became a celebrated issue during the 1740s. The difficult task of reconciling Newtonian theory with observation occupied the remainder of the eighteenth century following Newton's death. This effort culminated with Laplace's *Celestial Mechanics*, the first volumes of which appeared in the last years of the century. It was in these volumes that what physicists now speak of as Newtonian physics first appeared comprehensively in print, more than a hundred years after the first edition of the *Principia*.

Robert DiSalle's chapter shows that the relationship between Einstein's theories of special and general relativity and Newton's theories of motion and gravity is an intricate one. Still, one point that is certain is that Einstein did not show that Leibniz had been correct in his claims about the relativity of space. For Leibniz denied that there can be any fact of the matter about whether the Earth is orbiting the Sun, or the Sun the Earth, and Einstein's theories do not show this. Newtonian gravity holds in the static, weak-field limit of Einsteinian gravity, so that the former bears the same sort of relationship to the latter that Galilean uniform gravity bears to Newtonian gravity, allowing the evidence for the earlier theory in each case to carry over, with suitable qualifications about levels of accuracy, to the later theory. Moreover, as Euler showed in the late 1740s, and as Kant learned from Euler,[1] Newton's approach to space and time is inextricably tied to his laws of motion, in particular to the law of inertia. Abandoning Newtonian space and time in the manner Leibniz called for would entail abandoning the law of inertia as formulated in the seventeenth century, a law at the heart of Leibniz's dynamics. In gaining ascendancy over Leibniz's objections, Newton did not set physics down a dead-end path from which it was finally rescued by Einstein; rather, Einstein's theories of relativity represent a further major step along the path initiated by Newton.

A BRIEF BIOGRAPHICAL SKETCH

Newton's pre-Cambridge youth spans the period from the start of the Civil War to the Restoration of Charles II. He was born in Woolsthorpe, a tiny village near Grantham, on Christmas Day 1642, a little short of twelve months after Galileo had died.[2] Newton's father, who had died the previous October, was a farmer. Three years after Newton's birth, his mother Hannah married a well-to-do clergyman, 63-year-old Barnabas Smith, rector of the neighboring village of North Witham. She moved to her new husband's residence, leaving young Isaac behind, to be raised in the family home, Woolsthorpe Manor, by his maternal grandparents.[3] When Smith died in 1653, Hannah returned to the family farm with three new children in tow. Less than two years later Newton was sent to the Grantham Free School, returning to Woolsthorpe in the winter of 1659–60. The family expected that he would manage his father's farm, but it soon became evident that – to put it mildly – he was not cut out for the job. Henry Stokes, the head-master of Newton's school, and Hannah's brother William Aiscough, who had received an M.A. from Cambridge, persuaded her that her son's destiny lay elsewhere and he returned to Grantham to prepare for a university education. In the summer of 1661 he entered Trinity, his uncle's Cambridge college, as an undergraduate.

Newton's years at Trinity College, as a student and Fellow and then as a professor, were spent predominantly in solitary intellectual pursuits. As an undergraduate he read the works of Aristotle and later commentators and some scientific works such as Kepler on optics. At some point towards the end of his third year as a student, he began reading widely on his own. In early 1664 he appears to have abruptly ended his interest in scholastic texts and ideas, and turned to the contemporary writings of such figures as René Descartes, Henry More, Robert Boyle, and Robert Hooke. His undergraduate notebook, which contains his scholastic notes on natural philosophy, his notes on modern natural philosophers, and his very first scientific experiments, reveals how Newton very quickly spotted serious problems with the views of such authors. The research program that led to his discovery of the heterogeneity of white light and the construction of the reflecting telescope emerged from a number of different ideas and approaches. These included theoretical speculations about the speed of globules constituting different colored lights, the anatomical dissection of the optic nerve of a sheep, the examination of variously colored threads through a prism, and the insertion of a bodkin and a brass plate underneath his eyeball to test the power of his imagination. His notes show how he repeatedly turned questions into research projects by devising innovative empirical tests.[4]

Restoration Cambridge also boasted one of the leading British mathematicians, Isaac Barrow, whose lectures he attended. Barrow happened to be at Newton's college, and the two men communicated with each other on various topics in mathematics and optics over the next few years. It is highly likely that Newton's first forays into mathematics and natural philosophy were guided by Barrow but the evidence from Newton's two student mathematical notebooks shows that, early on, he engaged in entirely independent and path-breaking research in a series of areas in mathematics. This was carried out through extensive reading of recent publications, most notably the second edition of van Schooten's Latin translation, with added commentary, of Descartes's *Géometrie*.[5]

Within an incredibly short period of less than two years, Newton had mastered the subject of mathematics, becoming de facto the leading mathematician in the world. He reached this status during the inaccurately styled "annus mirabilis" of 1664–6, when the university was closed because of the great plague and he returned to the family farm in Woolsthorpe. It was during this period that Newton developed the basic results of the differential and integral calculus, including the fundamental theorem relating the two. At the same time, he also made experiments on refraction and color that similarly put him at the forefront in optics. His notebooks from the mid 1660s show him working out answers to questions about motion, most notably uniform circular motion, that were undoubtedly provoked by his engagement with the ideas of Galileo and especially Descartes (from whom, among much else, he learned the law of inertia). It was also during this early period that Newton independently discovered the v^2/r rule for uniform circular motion, a few years before Christiaan

Huygens, who had discovered it in 1659, published it in his renowned *Horologium Oscillatorium*.

On his return to Cambridge following the plague years, Newton was elected a Fellow of Trinity College, receiving his M.A. in 1668. During these years, he continued his work in mathematics and optics, and he became immersed in chemical and alchemical research. At some point in the summer of 1669 he wrote a tract, "De Analysi," or "On Analysis by Infinite Series," in which he presented his key discoveries in the calculus. This work was circulated among British mathematicians and, notably, a copy was sent to the 'intelligencer' John Collins in London. It was undoubtedly because of this tract that Barrow recommended the youthful Newton to succeed him as Lucasian Professor of Mathematics. Newton occupied this chair from 1669 until he formally resigned in 1701, five years after moving to London.

Newton's publications before the *Principia* amounted to the series of letters on the theory of light and colors, including the invention of a reflecting telescope, published in the *Philosophical Transactions of the Royal Society* from 1672 to 1676. He was so embittered by the controversies that were engendered by these publications that he vowed to publish no further results from his research in natural philosophy. The statutes of his Lucasian chair did require him to deposit annually a copy of his lectures in the University Library. Among these are his Optical Lectures of 1670–2, which present an enormous range of experiments bolstering and complementing those described in his publications, and a series of Lectures on Algebra given from 1673 to 1683. The technical proficiency reached in these lectures makes it plain that – on the assumption that the surviving texts represent something similar to what was delivered in class – very few students could have handled the material.

In late 1679, in an effort to reinvigorate the activities of the Royal Society, Robert Hooke wrote to Newton concerning his "hypothesis" that curved or orbital motion could be analyzed by supposing two components: an inertial tangential motion and an accelerated motion directed toward a center of force. He also raised the question of the precise trajectory described by a body under an inverse-square force directed toward a central point in space. During the course of this brief correspondence, Newton discovered the relation between inverse-square centripetal forces and Keplerian motion that comprises the initial stepping-stone of the *Principia*. Yet whatever further conclusions he reached at the time, universal gravity was not one of them. This is clear from his correspondence with the Astronomer Royal John Flamsteed, following the appearance of the "Great Comet" at the end of 1680. Flamsteed initially suggested that two objects seen in December 1680 and January 1681 were the same celestial object, first attracted and then repelled in front of the Sun by a magnetic force. In response, Newton argued that if it had really been one object then it had inexplicably slowed down during the phase where its direction was reversed. Moreover, no magnet-type mechanism could explain this sudden cometary *volte face*. Putting both of these insights together, Newton suggested that if it was really the same comet then it must have gone around the back of the Sun, and he also noted that the Sun must have continually exercised an attractive force during the whole episode. It is clear from his remarks that, although he had effectively demolished the idea that the force was magnetic, he had as yet no alternative to put in its place.[6]

In the summer of 1684 Edmond Halley visited Newton in Cambridge in order to ask him a question that the London savants could not answer: what curved path results from an inverse-square force directed toward a center? Newton is reported to have replied without any hesitation: the curve is an ellipse. Although he could not lay his hands on a demonstration he had allegedly already written out, he promised Halley that he would send the proof on to London. In November, Halley duly received the proof as part of a longer (though still short) tract entitled "De motu corporum in gyrum." He was so impressed by the magnitude of Newton's achievement that he hastened to Cambridge for a second visit. On arrival, he learned that the reclusive professor was continuing research on orbital motion, and having ascertained that the tract was going to be expanded into a book, Halley agreed to supervise its publication on behalf of the Royal Society. The manuscript of Book 1 of the *Principia* arrived in London in spring of 1686, prompting a bitter dispute with Hooke, who claimed priority for the concept of an inverse-square solar force. Halley managed to keep Newton working in spite of the controversy, finally receiving Book 2 in March and Book 3 in April 1687.[7]

Publication of the *Principia* in 1687, which ended Newton's life of comparative isolation, led to adulation in Britain and intense opposition to his theory of gravity elsewhere. Other events also impinged on his life of donnish retirement. As early as February 1687, before he had even sent Halley Book 2, Newton became embroiled in efforts to defend the University of Cambridge from having to obey an order issued by the Roman Catholic King James II compelling them to award degrees to Catholics. He was one of eight dons who appeared before Judge Jeffreys to argue the university's case a few months later, and it was because of this, as much as his acknowledged intellectual and personal merits, that in the immediate wake of the Glorious Revolution he was elected to the Convention Parliament as a representative of the university. During his time as an MP, Newton did a great deal of committee work on business relating to religious toleration and the statutes of the two English universities, but he decided not to seek immediate re-election after the Parliamentary session was ended by William III in January 1690.

Newton now threw himself into a wide range of intellectual projects with a degree of intensity that matched that of the plague years. Freed from the demands of political life, he initiated work on a radically restructured second edition of the *Principia* and a never-finished comprehensive treatise on geometry, and he undertook sustained research projects on theological topics. In 1691 he did some remarkable work on integration in a paper entitled "De Quadratura Curvarum," although this was only published in 1704 (in order to assert his priority in the area) as an addition to the first edition of *Opticks*.

He also continued experimental research in alchemy and performed novel experiments on diffraction phenomena, laying out the basic structure of what would become *Opticks*. His best scientific work in this period was on the theory of the Moon's motion, carried out in the middle of the 1690s. This was the last piece of innovative work in the natural sciences that he undertook, though it ultimately ended in failure. It also triggered over two decades of hostilities with John Flamsteed, who would write a searing and by no means inaccurate account of Newton's morals and behavior in a private reminiscence.

Chronic overwork, coupled with the emergence of an ever-simmering paranoia that was fueled by his failure to land a plum job in London, both contributed to the catastrophic breakdown that he experienced in late summer 1693. These troubles soon abated, however, and with the support of his patron and erstwhile Trinity colleague Charles Montagu, he was appointed Warden of the Mint in 1696, and Master of the Mint three years later. By the first decade of the eighteenth century he was renowned in the Republic of Letters as a man of the highest intellectual abilities, as well as being a politician and a senior government administrator. He was elected President of the Royal Society in 1703, a post he held until his death, and he was knighted for his services to the government in 1705. Catherine Barton, the vivacious teenage daughter of his half-sister, moved in with him not long after he became Warden of the Mint, gaining great prominence in London social circles. She continued to reside with him until he died, even after she married John Conduitt (who succeeded Newton as Master of the Mint) in 1717.

The first decade of the new century witnessed the publication of the first edition of his *Opticks*, a work written in English rather than in Latin. In addition to "De Quadratura Curvarum" (which exhibited Newton's dot-notation for differentials), the appendix contained "Enumeratio Linearum Tertii Ordinis." In quick succession he published *Optice* (1706), translated from English by his confidant Samuel Clarke, and he authorized the publication of his lectures on algebra.

These appeared in 1707 under the editorship of William Whiston, his successor as Lucasian Professor, as *Arithmetica Unversalis: sive de Compositione et Resolutione Arithmetica liber.* During the last years of the decade Newton began work in earnest on a second edition of the *Principia,* which was finally published under the editorship of Roger Cotes in 1713. Although this edition was not radically restructured, 397 of its 494 pages involved changes from the first edition – sometimes mere changes in wording, but in places he completely rewrote passages or added new material. One important feature of the second edition was the concluding General Scholium with its slogan, "Hypotheses non fingo." This famous phrase had its origin in Newton's inveterate suspicion of the products of the human imagination. As he stated it clearly in his anonymous review of the Royal Society Report on the priority dispute over the calculus, ". . . and it is not the Business of Experimental Philosophy to teach the Causes of things any further than they can be proved by Experiments. We are not to fill this Philosophy with Opinions which cannot be proved by Phaenomena. In this Philosophy Hypotheses have no place, unless as Conjectures or Questions proposed to be examined by Experiments."[8]

It is well known that most continental natural philosophers found it impossible to accept Newton's concept of universal gravitation. Leibniz and Huygens, for example, were strongly opposed to Newton's theory of gravity from the time it first appeared. Leibniz's response was to publish an alternative account of Keplerian motion in 1689, followed by important papers in dynamics. The relationship between the two was certainly distant, if not frosty, in the 1690s and early years of the next century, but it only turned nasty when the mathematician and natural philosopher John Keill declared in 1709 that Leibniz had stolen the calculus from Newton. The ensuing priority dispute, which lasted beyond Leibniz's death in November 1716, was complicated by the fact that Leibniz had been in England and had visited John Collins in the early 1670s, before publishing his own fundamental results in calculus in 1684. Leibniz was shown a copy of "De Analysi" by Collins on his second visit to England in October 1676, but by then he had already discovered the fundamental algorithms of the differential and integral calculus. In the early eighteenth century, the priority dispute spilled over into arguments about the theory of gravity and its philosophical and theological implications, leading to the Leibniz–Clarke correspondence of 1715–16 (discussed in the chapter by Domenico Bertoloni Meli). Newton's calculus differed in key respects from Leibniz's, and we are now aware that the two men made their breakthroughs independently.[9]

Newton remained intellectually engaged during the last ten years of his life, though less in science and mathematics than in theology, chronology, and prophecy. Further editions of his *Opticks* appeared in 1717/18 (and posthumously in 1730). He also produced a third edition of the *Principia*, when he was 83 years old. It does not differ in essentials from the second edition, the main change being some new text based on recent data. Though his theory of gravity remained still largely unaccepted on the Continent, Newton had achieved the status of legend throughout the educated world. He died on March 20, 1727.

NEWTON THE SCIENTIST

Newton occupies a singular place in the history of science, having contributed far more than any other single individual to the transformation of natural philosophy into modern science. An obvious question is: why him rather than someone else? What was it about Newton that enabled him to have such an extraordinary impact on empirical inquiry? The answer involves at least three factors: the historical situation in which he found himself, the attitude with which he approached empirical research, and the breadth as well as the depth of his genius.

Newton's famous remark to Robert Hooke, that if he had seen further, it was by standing on the shoulders of giants, was not a straightforward expression of humility, and indeed Newton's point was (at least in part) to let Hooke know that he really had seen further than anyone else.[10]

Yet although he was conscious and even proud of his own intellectual gifts, Newton knew better than anyone the extent to which he proceeded from the work of others before him. The two giants who are invariably invoked as his precursors are Kepler and Galileo, but he had intellectual debts to a much wider range of individuals. Newton learned his orbital astronomy not from reading Kepler, but from the generation that followed him, in particular Thomas Streete, Vincent Wing, Ishmael Boulliau, G. A. Borelli, Jeremiah Horrocks, and Nicolaus Mercator. Most of these figures departed from Kepler in one respect or another, but in doing so they gave rise to questions that would have had far less force than without these departures. In his own generation, as well, Newton relied on John Flamsteed and, less directly, on members of the French Academy for astronomical observations of increasingly high quality. Without this body of research in astronomy over the century before the *Principia*, Newton could never have made the enormous advances that he presented to the world in that book.

The situation is similar in physics. Christiaan Huygens extended Galileo's work on motion in important ways, including a superb analysis of pendulum motion and an extraordinarily precise measurement of the strength of surface gravity. This research is presented in his *Horologium Oscillatorium* of 1673, a work Newton greatly admired – and appropriately so, for it would have been the most important work in the science of motion in the seventeenth century had it not been eclipsed by the *Principia*. Huygens's work was the culmination of a tradition represented not just by Galileo, but also by Marin Mersenne and Descartes. Huygens, not Newton, was the first to publish a mathematical account of the force required for a body to move uniformly in a circle, a force to which Descartes had first called attention. Huygens, John Wallis and Christopher Wren were the first in print with modern laws of impact, and the Royal Society, for which Robert Hooke was curator of experiments, confirmed these laws experimentally. Much the same can be said of advances made in theoretical and practical optics by figures preceding Newton, starting with Kepler and Snel and including Descartes, Barrow, Huygens, and others.

A central factor enabling Newton to produce his extraordinary impact was the depth of his commitment to empiricism. The view that the empirical world should be the ultimate arbiter was a hallmark of the era, whether voiced by Tycho and Kepler, by Galileo, by Bacon and Boyle, or by Mersenne and Gassendi. Those engaged in empirical research were quick to realize, however, that it was one thing to express a belief in this tenet and quite another to find ways in which the world would provide conclusive answers to theoretical questions. This realization led to a widespread guardedness, if not skepticism, toward theoretical claims. Perhaps all that could be hoped for, as Robert Boyle proposed, was to describe the world accurately in the manner of a natural history, with purely theoretical claims never rising above the status of conjectural hypotheses not incompatible with the so-far observed world.

Newton, by contrast, pursued ways in which Nature could be made to yield definite answers to theoretical questions. Throughout his career he maintained a sharper distinction than any of his contemporaries between conjectural hypotheses and experimentally established results. Whether in alchemy and chemistry, in optics, or in orbital mechanics, the challenge was to design sequences of experiments or to marshal complexes of observations that would warrant taking theoretical claims to be established. He saw himself as having met this challenge in the case of orbital mechanics, to a lesser extent in the case of optics in so far as he never thought he had established the corpuscular character of light, and to almost no extent at all in the case of alchemy and chemistry, despite years of effort and hundreds of experiments. The important point, however, is that the depth of his commitment to having the empirical world settle questions kept him going along lines of research, asking further questions and looking for further evidence that went far beyond where anyone else would have stopped.

Being unusually demanding and dogged in empirical research, even during exceptionally propitious times, means little by itself. The most important factor enabling Newton to have his extraordinary impact on contemporary science was the sheer range of topics on which he worked, in each of which he went far beyond his contemporaries. It goes without saying that he ranks among the two or three greatest theoretical scientists ever – one thinks of Maxwell and Einstein as well – where the skill involved is taking an initial line of thought and elaborating it into a full, detailed theory with a wide range of ramifications. Newton is also listed with Gauss as the greatest mathematicians in history, if not for his success in developing theoretical edifices, then for his ability to solve individual problems, first identifying the core difficulty of the problem, then devising apparatus to surmount this difficulty, and finally seeing the further potential of this approach.

Less widely recognized is the fact that Newton was among the most skillful experimental scientists in history. This is largely because such a large fraction of Newton's experimental effort is not well known. His experiments in alchemy and chemistry have only recently been published, the experiments in the *Principia* are mostly in the rarely read Book 2, and even the experiments that occupy much of the *Opticks*, which have indeed been widely heralded as examples of experimental science at its best, are rarely seen as the culminations of a much wider range of experiments that complement and support them. Great skill in experimental research is something that gets developed through extended practice over time. It involves more than just painstaking care, perseverance in the face of practical difficulties, and ingenuity in the schematic design of experiments. Telling experiments entail designing and carrying out a large number of preliminary and complementary experiments in order to obtain well-behaved results and to foreclose alternative interpretations of these results. Newton belongs in the first rank of experimentalists because his experimental research displays mastery of all of these aspects.

To be among the first rank of experimentalists, mathematicians, and theoreticians is more than enough to put Newton in a class by himself among empirical scientists, for one has trouble thinking of any other candidate who was in the first rank of even two of these categories. Moreover, we have not emphasized enough the extent to which each of these dimensions of Newton's genius fed off and informed the other two in the way he approached empirical inquiry. Even granting all of this, however, we have yet to capture the full breadth of Newton's genius. At least in comparison to subsequent scientists, Newton was also exceptional in his ability to put his scientific effort in much wider perspective.[11]

The philosophical dimension of Newton's science shows up in the present volume in three ways. First, he framed a conception of the natural world that, in addition to forming the core of our own current conception, contrasted in interesting and often radical ways with those put forward by other seventeenth- and eighteenth-century philosophers. This is the main topic of Alan Gabbey's chapter. Second, his pursuit of this conception forced him to be much more attentive to and careful about "metaphysical" aspects of his science than is at first apparent from reading this science. Howard Stein's chapter makes the metaphysics of Newtonian science explicit, a metaphysics that has been crucial to subsequent science; in the process Stein reveals how skillful a philosopher, in the grand sense of the word, Newton was. Third, Newton engaged in profound critical reflection on what was required to establish scientific results. Few, if any, successful scientists have given so much thought to questions of methodology. From both the point of view of understanding his science as he saw it and the point of view of philosophy of science generally, Newton's views about how science should be done are important. While this subject surfaces in many of the chapters in this volume, for example those by DiSalle, Cohen, Pourciau, Shapiro, and Stein, it is the central topic in the chapters by William Harper and George Smith.

NEWTON THE MATHEMATICIAN

Newton's achievements in mathematics were extraordinary, yet his impact on the history of theoretical mathematics, and consequently on aspects of mathematics of greatest interest to philosophers, is not in proportion to these achievements. Some reasons for this are less interesting than others. Although he circulated some manuscripts, he did not publish any of his work on the calculus until the first decade of the eighteenth century. By then the remarkable Leibniz "school" had been going strong, with frequent publications, for over ten years. Moreover, many of his mathematical results were never published in his lifetime. Whatever inkling Newton's contemporaries may have gained of the scope of his mathematics from his publication of individual solved problems in the *Principia*, their lack of access to the systematic development of the methods he had used in these solutions limited their ability to build a growing body of Newtonian mathematics. Instead, time and again, areas in which Newton made breakthroughs, such as differential geometry and the calculus of variations, had to be independently developed by later mathematicians – most often Euler – who then had the impact on the history of the subject.

Newton's style as a mathematician also helps account for his disproportionately limited impact on the history of the field. His approach to mathematics – especially during the early periods – tended to be primarily that of a problem solver, taking on the challenge of specific unsolved problems. As remarked above, he had an uncanny knack for identifying the core difficulty of a problem and then devising means for overcoming it, often adapting ideas and methods of others, but putting them to novel use. Thus, for example, his initial algorithms for derivatives combined techniques from Cartesian geometry with the idea of an indefinitely small, vanishing increment. Similarly, his initial algorithms for integrals adapted a method Wallis had devised for algebraic curves, first reconceptualizing it to represent an integral that grows as the curve extends incrementally and then combining this with the binomial series to obtain solutions for integrals of a much wider range of curves. Once he had these results and found, from geometric representations of them, the relationship between differentiation and integration, he adapted Barrow's way of treating curves as arising from the motion of a point to recast his results on derivatives in terms of quantities that change with time and their increments of change, "fluents" and "fluxions." (His first full tract on fluxions, dated 1666, was called "To Resolve Problems by Motion.") He continued to extend his methods over the next thirty years, applying them to a growing range of problems. For Newton, however, the calculus was always a collection of interrelated methods for solving problems, not a radically new, superior approach to mathematics.[12]

This view of the calculus is symptomatic of the factor that was probably most responsible for limiting Newton's impact on the history of mathematics, namely his mathematical conservatism. Leibniz and his school saw the calculus as opening the way to doing all mathematics purely through the manipulation of symbols. To this end they put great effort into devising a suitable notation for the calculus, resulting in the form familiar to us. With the exception of the dot-notation (representing derivatives with respect to time), which dates from the mid 1690s, the notations Newton devised were not at all perspicuous. Given the range of his talents, this reflects not so much an inability on his part to come up with good notations as a lack of interest in, if not opposition to, a revolutionary new mathematics dominated by symbol manipulation. Following an intense re-examination of classical mathematics during the early 1680s, Newton appears to have concluded that the true roots of all mathematics lay in classical geometry. Regardless, as Niccolò Guicciardini stresses in his chapter and recent book, the wide range of Newton's contributions to mathematics is perhaps matched only by the complexity of his views concerning the subject.[13]

Newton's conservatism is apparent in the mathematics of the *Principia*. Contrary to a myth endorsed by Newton himself, there is no evidence whatever that he first derived his results on celestial orbits by using the symbolic calculus and then recast them in geometric form. The differential calculus does appear in Book 2, where Newton was unable to find a geometric solution to problems of motion with resistance forces varying as velocity squared; and in a handful of places solutions for integrals are given, without derivations, that he surely obtained symbolically. Everywhere else, however, the mathematics of the *Principia* is his "method of first and last ratios," a quite elegant extension of synthetic geometry that incorporates limits in a way that avoids the extensive use of *reductio ad absurdum* proofs that others were resorting to when working with infinitesimals. It was left to individuals within the Leibnizian tradition to recast the *Principia* into the symbolic calculus. What became clear in this process was the superiority of purely symbolic methods in attacking perturbation problems in celestial mechanics. With this realization the fundamental step in problems of physics ceased being one of finding an adequate geometric representation of the quantities involved, and instead became one of formulating appropriate differential equations in purely symbolic form. In a real sense, then, it was Newton's physics that gave the greatest impetus to the Leibnizian approach to mathematics, disproportionately limiting the impact Newton's work in mathematics had on the history of the field.

THE "OTHER" NEWTON: THEOLOGY, ALCHEMY AND THE MINT

Newton's work on mathematics and physics, spectacular and expansive as it was, formed only a minor part of his intellectual life. Indeed, at times, his work in the natural sciences seems to have been an unwelcome diversion from what he considered to be the more important study of alchemy and theology. The publication of millions of words from his writings in these areas since the appearance of the first *Companion* has allowed historians for the first time to assess this work in its full extent, and to examine in minute detail its evolution over many decades.[14]

The growth in our understanding of Newton's non-scientific work is perhaps most striking in the area of his religious studies. He was a deeply devout man, and his worship took the form of the protracted study of the Bible and of sacred history. At some point in the 1670s, apparently unprompted by personal contact with any heterodox thinker, he arrived at a radically subordinationist position regarding the relationship between the Son and the Father. Jesus Christ was not God, he argued, and it was the most abject form of idolatry to say or believe that he was. His wrath was accordingly directed towards the doctrine of the Trinity, which he believed was an incomprehensible, polytheistic and diabolical notion that polluted all orthodox forms of Christianity. Since there were legal penalties and social costs associated with voicing such opinions, Newton kept these views to himself throughout his life, though from the early 1690s a handful of trusted colleagues were made privy to them. Nothing of his great research program on the history of the Church was made available to the general public during his lifetime. However, his brief references to the divine "sensorium" in his *Optice* of 1706, and to the nature of God in his "General Scholium" to the second edition of the *Principia* in 1713, served as the theological focus for the famous correspondence between Clarke and Leibniz.

Newton worked on many theological topics with a phenomenal seriousness of purpose and energy, although he completely ignored other areas, such as the nature of Christ's atonement, that had no basis (as he saw it) in Scripture. He believed that God had revealed truth to Mankind through the actions and sayings of his son, Jesus Christ, but he also held that very soon after the Christian revelation, authentic Christian beliefs and practices had been corrupted by idolatrous evildoers. All of sacred history was structured like this, for Moses had previously rescued his fellow Israelites from their enslavement and their idolatry and had returned them to the true religion of Noah and his predecessors. From the dawn of Christianity there had been many heresies, but Newton believed that the worst of them was the version of Roman Catholicism that had become the state religion of the Roman empire by the end of the fourth century. In his private writings Newton was confident that he had corrected the most depraved elements of Christianity, but to the consternation of followers like William Whiston and his Mint colleague Hopton Haynes, he could not bring himself to divulge these views to the wider public.

As Rob Iliffe points out in his chapter, most of Newton's energies were consumed by the study of prophecy and Church history, which he saw as intimately interlinked. The significance of the images in Revelation was drilled into him as a young boy in the turbulent times of the 1640s and 50s, and his deep interest in prophetic visions never waned. He began the serious study of prophecy in the 1670s, and had arrived at his mature position on the historical meaning of Revelation by the late 1680s, but he never stopped trying to locate historical evidence that showed how prophecy had been fulfilled in the past. All this work, both prophetic and historical, was fueled and shaped by his detestation of both Roman Catholicism and the doctrine of the Trinity. Like many of his contemporaries, Newton believed that the mysterious internal order of the apocalyptic images could be decoded by recourse to the right sort of "key." There were ready exegetical techniques for doing this provided by previous interpreters, the most important of which was the assumption (perfected by Newton's hero Joseph Mede) that certain groups of images referred to the same events and periods in the prophetic narrative. Once this order had been divined to Newton's satisfaction, then the visions had to be "applied" to real events in the past. The exact meaning of those visions that referred to future events remained conjectural. Newton refused to assign dates to future prophetic events with any certainty, professing that he did not deal in conjectures in his religious studies any more than he did in his scientific work.

In the mid 1680s Newton began a new and major research project that linked the ancient religion with the true (Newtonian) account of the cosmos. Early on in his research, he had decided that Noah and the first post-diluvian peoples had believed in a religion that combined an injunction to obey the cardinal virtues with the cultivation of ceremonies that respected the heliocentric cosmos. By the early eighteenth century Newton had abandoned this project, yet he dramatically expanded his research on one particular aspect of it. This was the correlation of histories written by different peoples in such a way that false accounts of antiquity were removed, and the remainder brought into one coherent form. Newton deployed standard interpretive techniques, employed by previous Christian chronologers, to argue that many individuals and events described in different histories were actually reports of the same people and incidents. By incorporating novel approaches drawn from astronomy, he also assigned what he took to be highly probable dates to the ancient events. In his chapter in this volume, Mordechai Feingold sheds new light on the techniques he used to do this, and points to the immense skill Newton required to concoct a consistent history of the world from a vast bank of information. Although the dates Newton had assigned to various events in history had leaked into the public sphere a few years earlier, the reasoning behind them only became known in a book that appeared soon after his death. Indeed, the great effort he expended on this topic in the last three decades of his life is only visible in the surviving manuscripts.[15]

As is well known, Newton also devoted much of his life at Cambridge to the study of alchemy. He seems to have begun the serious study of alchemy, rather than what he knew as "vulgar" chemistry, soon after he developed his reflecting telescope (in 1667–8), probably because he needed to find a good reflecting but non-tarnishing amalgam for its mirror. Unused to doing anything by halves, he scoured the writings of all the great names of the field using both printed and manuscript sources (the identity of his supplier/s remains mysterious). The vast majority of the one million or so words that survive from his alchemical endeavors are made up of notes from alchemical authors, and there is also a great deal of evidence of laborious and meticulous efforts to discern the chemical referents of the often lurid terms used by alchemists to describe the objects of their art. Newton took his alchemical pursuits seriously, and he compared the credibility of various authors and their endeavors just as he did in other areas. At the same time as he took notes he also did an extensive amount of alchemical experimentation, and there is evidence that he continued to work intensively at his furnace until the middle of the 1690s.[16]

Newton seems to have had similar aims to those of other alchemists, and he believed that there was (almost certainly) important knowledge about the natural world contained in the writings of the true adepts. Remarkably, only one short essay (now known from its first line "Of nature's obvious laws and processes in vegetation") survives from his alchemical career, a fact that has yet to be adequately explained.[17] In his chapter in this volume, William Newman sheds new light on this important document and draws on his recent studies of Newton's alchemical manuscripts to offer a new view of his alchemical research. He argues that Newton's discovery that he could resynthesize the spectral colors produced by refracting a ray of light through a prism was inspired by his reading about the chemical resynthesis of experimentally separated components. Notably, in his optical lectures he referred to the process as "redintegration," exactly the same word used by Robert Boyle to describe the chemical resynthesis of various substances in his *Origin of Formes and Qualityes* of 1666. Newman also lays to rest a series of myths about the nature of Newton's "chymical" research, including the claim that his ideas of chemical force were the basis of his theory of universal gravitation; the belief that the conceptual elements of his alchemical program were closely related to his heterodox religious beliefs; and the view that Newton's alchemical research was really pure scientific enquiry pursued under the guise of a baroque terminology. Newman had previously shown that the assumption that Newton was a consummate scientist ahead of his time had led Richard Westfall and Betty Jo Teeter Dobbs to attribute to Newton the authorship of an alchemical letter actually composed by the American chymist George Starkey in 1652. Here he also notes that, in experiments described in his chemical notebook, Newton was committed to chrysopoeia (transmutation into gold) en route to discovering the philosopher's stone.[18]

Finally, mention should be made of the last great unexplored territory of Newton's intellectual life, namely his administrative work. After five years of sometimes intensive lobbying by his friends and by Newton himself, he was appointed as Warden of

the Mint in the spring of 1696. One of three senior positions in the
Mint (along with the Comptroller and the master worker), the Warden
was notionally the agent of the Crown, who contracted with
(i.e., paid) the Master to produce coin. As Richard Westfall points out, by
Newton's time the prestige and salary of the Warden had fallen behind
that of the Master, and the position had been treated as a sinecure before
Newton arrived. Typically, Newton immediately sought to rectify
this situation, envisioning his role as a sort of *pantokrator* overseeing
the moral economy of the workers in the various English Mints. The
Master, however, distributed the salary of the Mint workers (including the Warden's), took a percentage of the income received for the
coinage, and effectively exercised control in the institution. Newton
was not slow to accept the position when it became vacant at the
end of 1699.[19]

Newton was employed just as England experienced the most
extraordinary financial revolution in its history. Drawing to some
extent on practices already common in the Netherlands, post-
revolutionary London witnessed the development of a number of new
schemes for making money, involving innovations in banking, insur-
ance, stock-jobbing and debt purchase. The most important desid-
eratum was to create mechanisms for raising money to build a navy
adequate for prosecuting the war against France. Parliament backed
various ruses to raise money, including the institution of the first
National Lottery in England, but the most successful project by far was
the creation of a national bank, which lent money to the government
to prosecute the war. The Bank of England was founded in 1694
for this purpose, being funded by loans from various grandees who
received a healthy annual interest rate, guaranteed by taxes raised by
parliament. Thus the National Debt was created, allowing the government to successfully raise money to fight wars for over a century.[20]

The government faced another serious problem. For some time,
the older "hammered" silver coin that was used as legal tender had
been degraded, having been "clipped," melted, and reconstituted with
a lower silver content. Good-quality coin, which was either hoarded,

or melted to be sold as bullion in Amsterdam (because the value of
the metal had risen above the face value of the coinage), was constantly taken out of circulation in favor of devalued currency. By the
early 1690s the government feared that there was insufficient good-
quality currency to fund day-to-day transactions. As a result, the
older money was called in, and a major effort was instituted to ramp
up the production of new silver coins. To preserve what was termed
"publick credit," these were minted with the old proportion of silver,
and with milled edges that contained writing that guaranteed the
value of the coin. Much of Newton's first decade in office involved
drawing up a giant web of information concerning the "clippers and
coiners" who were committing treason by defacing the coin of the
realm. Although he allegedly burned boxfuls of depositions towards
the end of his life, many survived, showing just how committed he
was to catching criminals and to seeing that they were brought to
justice. By means of this extraordinary effort, he was able to successfully prosecute a large number of counterfeiters, including the greatest of them all, William Chaloner.[21]

Thanks in part to pioneering "time and motion" studies,
Newton also reorganized the internal workings of the Mint to make
it much more efficient than before. His input was central to the success of the Great Recoinage that took place from the mid 1690s, and
as Master of the Mint he had a significant input in the reorganization
of the English and Scottish Mints that was necessary in the wake of
the Act of Union of 1707. His knowledge of chemistry and metallurgy
was clearly useful in assessing the quality of work produced by Mint
employees, particularly during the so-called "trial of the pyx." This
examination of the fineness of pieces of silver and gold, carried out
approximately every four years, was a test not only of the skill of the
workers but also of the moral probity of the Master. Newton passed
all the trials held during his lifetime, though the procedure often
brought him into conflict with the London goldsmiths who actually
tested the quality of the coin. Newton believed that his administra-
tion had had a very large effect on the quality of production of coin.

Later in his career he boasted that he was responsible for bringing the "sizing" of pieces of gold and silver to a much greater exactness than it had been before he arrived, thus saving thousands of pounds for the country.[22]

Newton also took on a number of other tasks in the early eighteenth century, including designing classical motifs for coins and celebratory medals, and supervising the work of engravers. Most importantly, he exercised a striking influence in determining monetary policy. He received weekly reports concerning the price of silver and gold on the Amsterdam and other markets during this period, and strove to ensure that the face value of silver coinage in Britain would not fall beneath the value of the bullion. Famously, he was instrumental in fixing the value of the gold guinea at 21s (£1.05), the figure still in use today, thereby making gold and not silver the standard of value recognized by the British government. Newton performed his tasks as an administrator with his customary skill and diligence, and should be seen as one of the most important government officials operating in the period from the middle of the reign of William III to the end of the reign of George I. Nevertheless, although the basic facts regarding his important work are well established, his memoranda on the internal operations of the Mint, and his writings on economic policy, await detailed analysis.

CONCLUSION: THE COHERENCE OF NEWTON'S WORK

The fact that Newton studied such a wide range of topics (though he had no interest in poetry or any other fiction) raises the issue of how it all hangs together. Since the late eighteenth century, this question has been at the heart of assessments of the man and his work, with analysts falling into two major camps. The first assumed a radical separation between Newton's work in the areas of theology and natural philosophy. In Britain, as Scott Mandelbrote shows in his chapter, this was because many orthodox Anglicans were alarmed by what they saw as anti-Trinitarian sentiments in his published work and believed – and indeed exulted in that fact – that Newton had over-reached himself in his religious writings. That said, the second group, comprising the vast majority of British writers believed that his discoveries had bolstered natural theology by strengthening belief in the existence of an intelligent designer. By the early nineteenth century, however, a number of commentators (particularly in France) were routinely explaining away all his non-scientific work as the result of senility, dilettantism and even madness. Partly as a result of fallout from debates over Darwinism, belief in the fundamental incompatibility of these two areas of his research hardened into something like common knowledge in the late nineteenth and early twentieth centuries.

Two factors altered this situation. First, in the 1960s intellectual historians such as D. P. Walker and Frances Yates showed that the so-called "occult" interests of many Renaissance thinkers had lasted well into the seventeenth century, and were commonly held by scholars who were ostensibly paragons of rationality. Newton did not escape the effects of this historiographical revolution. Indeed, historians almost immediately found that he was strongly committed to the existence of a dynamic cosmos (in which God periodically intervened) and of a foundational religion that had been spread all over the world after the Flood. These studies seemed to confirm what the economist and Newtonophile John Maynard Keynes had provocatively suggested two decades earlier, namely that Newton was a Renaissance figure rather than a hero of the Enlightenment.[23] Second, almost all of Newton's non-scientific writings became available for study. The alchemical writings had been available at King's College Cambridge since the early 1950s thanks to Keynes's generous donation of the papers to the institution. Keynes had bought them at the 1936 Sotheby Sale of Newton's non-scientific writings, and had delivered his fascinating paper on Newton's "occult" interests in 1942 (on the tercentenary of his birth).[24]

Although Keynes had the papers at his disposal, he had more important war-related issues to deal with, and his analysis of the writings was superficial. Two scholars, Karin Figala and Betty Jo Dobbs, did make a serious study of these papers and published their results in the mid 1970s. Around the same time, David Castillejo and Frank Manuel examined Newton's voluminous theological writings, which after three decades of peregrination had arrived at the Jewish National and University Library in Jerusalem in 1967 following their dispersal at the Sotheby Sale. Anxious to rebut the positivist division that made the alchemical and theological work both inferior and irrelevant to his scientific work, Manuel, Dobbs, and a number of other historians contended that these writings all sprang from the same "mind," and constituted a unified whole. They pointed to a number of points of crossover between Newton's various intellectual fields, for example, between his conception of God and his notion of Absolute Space. In some places they went even further, suggesting that the non-scientific interests underpinned his work in the exact sciences, as in the case of the relationship between his alchemical theories and his notion of universal gravitation. The repressed Other of Newton's life had returned with a vengeance.[25]

It is true, of course, that Newton's works were all written by him, and it is true that there are a number of interesting links between disparate domains of his work. However, while historians who want to know the source of given ideas are trained to spot such connections, there are three potential problems with this approach. To begin with, the presupposition of general coherence runs the risk of locating false positives, and thus of saying more about the historian's preconceptions than about Newton's work. Beyond this, *prima facie* there are far more dissimilarities than similarities between Newton's style of argument and use of evidence in, say, mathematics and in Church history. As things stand, it is impossible to see how such radical differences can be subsumed under the same general approach. The fact that Newton deployed distinct modes of proof and rhetorical strategies in these fields of enquiry is hardly surprising, since each field or discipline had its own practices and styles of argument. Indeed, it was surely a mark of his greatness that he was able to very quickly attain technical expertise in a variety of intellectual traditions that had very different requirements in terms of argument, use of evidence, and style of demonstration. It is worth adding that Newton himself recognized a strict compartmentalization in his approach to distinct disciplines, and frequently cautioned against mixing approaches and demonstrations that were appropriate in one domain with those that were appropriate in another.[26]

Finally, the inward focus of the coherentist approach has distracted historians from looking at his sources or at the contexts in which he wrote. There are a number of reasons why this attitude should have characterized Newtonian research in particular. In the first place, there is his unique status as an independent thinker of genius, which has long seduced commentators into believing that he was unbeholden in any way to ancestors or contemporaries – a man without past or present intellectual debts. Newton himself deliberately cultivated this view of his own extreme intellectual autonomy, and there are occasions in his manuscript writings where one can see that he has deliberately erased evidence that he had taken information from a particular source. Second, and in relation to the last point, it has been impossible until the recent publication of all of his writings in alchemy and theology to see exactly what Newton read, and hence to assess the degree of his engagement with the sources he consulted. Third, his secretiveness and disdain for publication was matched by his refusal to refer, even in private, to contemporary arguments. With a handful of exceptions Newton left no trace of his attitude to current issues in religion or politics, despite the fact that he was twice an MP, and indeed was a public administrator for half of his working life. More remarkably still, although he wrote millions of words on prophecy and theology, he made almost no reference to contemporary theological controversies, and had little or no interest in publicly entering them. Instead, he preferred to immerse himself in the complexities of the early Christian Church from the comfort of his private Cambridge and London closets.

The question of what links exist between different areas of Newton's research can only be tackled by engaging in a more detailed empirical study of his writings. Although there are certainly a number of conceptual and methodological overlaps between the various areas of Newton's work, the editors of this volume believe that his writings as a whole are characterized by radically variant approaches appropriate to different intellectual traditions. Nevertheless, while we cannot identify one "method" that governs all of his many intellectual activities, we would like to offer a few generalizations about the man and his attitude to his research. We believe that four research "traits" are especially worth noting. Newton was blessed with a supreme confidence in his talents and in his intellectual vocation, and he believed that, in contrast with those who worshipped the uncertain products of their own imaginations, he always followed the dictates of his reason. Moreover, in theology as well as natural philosophy, he was always on a quest for one extra piece of supporting empirical evidence for his theories, and he constantly re-examined conclusions he had reached earlier. His relentless pursuit of ever more certain knowledge is what makes the title of Richard Westfall's biography, *Never at Rest*, so appropriate. This work ethic is the third feature of his approach to his studies, and only someone for whom hard intellectual labor was a core aspect of his religious life could have devoted himself so intensively to his research. And finally, one must never forget that he was, from a very young age, an extraordinary problem-solver, as good, it would appear, as humanity has ever produced.[27]

NOTES

1 See DiSalle's chapter in this book, note 31.

2 The Julian calendar then used in England was 10 days behind the Gregorian calendar used in most of Europe, and in many countries his birth is listed as occurring on January 4, 1643.

3 It should be pointed out that Smith's rectory was less than two miles away, on a practically straight line from Woolsthorpe Manor.

4 The documentary evidence of Newton's early research in natural philosophy and chemistry can be found in Cambridge University Library (hereafter CUL) Additional Manuscripts 3996 (the so-called 'Questiones'

notebook) and 3975. Images of all of Newton's scientific and mathematical writings are available via the website of the Cambridge University Digital Library.

5 The two notebooks that detail the astonishing development of Newton's mathematical work are CUL Add. Mss. 4000 (the "Mathematical Notebook") and 4004 (the "Waste Book"); both are published in full for the first time as part of the online Newton Project. The role of Barrow as a mentor to Newton is analyzed in M. Feingold, "Newton, Leibniz and Barrow too. An attempt at a re-interpretation," *Isis* 84 (1993), 310–38.

6 The exchanges with Hooke and Flamsteed are to be found in *The Correspondence of Isaac Newton*, 7 vols., ed. H. W. Turnbull *et al.* (Cambridge: Cambridge University Press, 1960), vol. 2, pp. 336–67 (hereafter Newton, *Correspondence*). Because he had discovered early on that heated lodestones lost their power, Newton was antagonistic to claims that such forces operated over long distances, and in particular to the notion that the Sun attracted the planets by means of such a force.

7 Strictly speaking, this famous account, taken from the so called "De Moivre memorandum," is untrue since, under the influence of an inverse-square force, an object could move in a straight line or any conic section. For Halley's visit and its consequences, see I. B. Cohen, *Introduction to Newton's "Principia"* (Cambridge, MA: Harvard University Press, 1971), pp. 47–81, esp. p. 50.

8 Isaac Newton (anonymously), "An Account of the Book entituled Commercium Epistolicum Collinii & aliorum," *Philosophical Transactions of the Royal Society*, 342 (1715), 222.

9 The background to the controversy is described in A. R. Hall, *Philosophers at War: The Quarrel between Newton and Leibniz* (Cambridge: Cambridge University Press, 1980).

10 Letter from Newton to Hooke, February 5, 1676; Newton, *Correspondence*, vol. 1, p. 416.

11 As noted in the first edition of the *Companion*, Smith owes this point to Alan Shapiro.

12 Newton's greatness as a mathematician can be fully appreciated in the eight-volume edition of his papers edited by D. T. Whiteside.

13 See N. Guicciardini, *Isaac Newton on Mathematical Certainty and Method*, (Cambridge, MA: MIT Press, 2009).

14 The Newton Project and the Chymistry of Isaac Newton projects are at www.newtonproject.ox.ac.uk and http://webapp1.dlib.indiana.edu/newton/.

15 Newton's work appeared in 1728 as *The Chronology of Ancient Kingdoms Amended.*

16 Betty Jo Teeter Dobbs, *The Foundations of Newton's Alchemy, or "The Hunting of the Greene Lyon"* (Cambridge: Cambridge University Press, 1975); Karin Figala, "Newton as Alchemist," *History of Science* 15 (1977), 102–37, and Richard Westfall, *Never at Rest: A Biography of Isaac Newton* (Cambridge: Cambridge University Press, 1980). The chemical notebook is now CUL Add. Ms. 3975, while another series of experiments are recorded in CUL Add. Ms. 3973.

17 "Of Nature's Obvious Laws & Processes in Vegetation" is now Smithsonian Institution, Dibner Ms. 1031B.

18 See Newman, "Newton's 'Clavis' as Starkey's 'Key'," *Isis* 78 (1987), 564–74.

19 The best introductions to Newton's life and work at the Mint remain John Craig, *Newton at the Mint* (Cambridge: Cambridge University Press, 1946) and Westfall, *Never at Rest*, pp. 551–626, esp. pp. 556–8, 564–6 and 604–6. The Comptroller's role, sometimes held by more than one person during Newton's time at the Mint, was to pass the accounts.

20 See P. G. M. Dickson, *The Financial Revolution: A Study in the Development of Public Credit, 1680–1756* (New York: St. Martin's Press, 1967).

21 Newton's confrontation with Chaloner is examined in John Craig, "Isaac Newton and the Counterfeiters," *Notes and Records of the Royal Society* 18 (1963), 136–45, and T. Levenson, *Newton and the Counterfeiter* (London: Mariner Books, 2009).

22 See Westfall, *Never at Rest*, pp. 607–14.

23 The canonical text in this historiographical revolution was Yates's *Giordano Bruno and the Hermetic Tradition* (Chicago, IL: University of Chicago Press, 1964). See also David C. Kubrin, "Newton and the Cyclical Cosmos: Providence and the Mechanical Philosophy," *Journal of the History of Ideas* 28 (1967), 325–46, and J. E. McGuire and P. M. Rattansi, "Newton and the 'Pipes of Pan,'" *Notes and Records of the Royal Society* 21 (1996), 118–43.

24 The impact of the Sotheby Sale is examined in Sarah Dry, *The Newton Papers: The Strange and True Odyssey of Newton's Manuscripts*

(Oxford: Oxford University Press, 2014). Virtually all the mathematical and scientific papers had been donated to Cambridge University Library in 1888 by the 5th Earl of Portsmouth, after a sedate cataloging process lasting sixteen years.

25 The pioneering studies of Newton's alchemy and religion were Dobbs, *Foundations*, Figala, "Newton as Alchemist," and Westfall, *Never at Rest*, esp. pp. 281–309 and 524–31. Manuel's Fremantle lectures on Newton's religion were published as *The Religion of Isaac Newton* (Oxford: Oxford University Press, 1974).

26 For more on this issue see Rob Iliffe, "'Abstract Considerations': Disciplines and the Incoherence of Newton's Natural Philosophy," *Studies in the History and Philosophy of Science* 35 (2004), 427–54.

27 The phrase comes from a letter written by Newton to Nathaniel Hawes (Treasurer of Christ's Hospital Royal Mathematical School) on May 25, 1694; see Newton, *Correspondence*, vol. 3, p. 360. In a concise semi-autobiographical remark, Newton noted that the boys at Hawes's school should be well versed in the theoretical principles of their art because, unlike unlearned mechanics, "he that is able to reason nimbly and judiciously about figure, force and motion, is never at rest till he gets over every rub."

1   Newton's philosophical analysis of space and time

Robert DiSalle

INTRODUCTION: PHILOSOPHICAL CONTROVERSY OVER NEWTON'S IDEAS OF SPACE, TIME, AND MOTION

Newton's concepts of "absolute space," "absolute time," and "absolute motion" met with serious objections from such philosophical contemporaries as Huygens, Leibniz, and Berkeley. Among philosophers of the early twentieth century, after the advent of Special and General Relativity, the objections bordered on scorn: Newton's concepts were not only lately outmoded, but they were also epistemologically inherently defective, empirically unfounded – concepts not scientific at all, but "metaphysical," in so far as science is concerned precisely with "sensible measures" rather than obscure notions of what is "absolute." The prevailing idea was that Einstein had established not only a new theory of space and time, but a deeper philosophical viewpoint on space and time in general. From this viewpoint, space, time, and motion are essentially relative, and to call them absolute was an elementary philosophical error. As Einstein put it, General Relativity had taken from space and time "the last remnant of physical objectivity."[1]

The philosophical motivation for this viewpoint seems obvious. Space cannot be observed; all that we can observe is the relative displacement of observable things. Therefore, if we observe two bodies in relative motion, to say that one of them is "really" moving, or that it is moving "relative to absolute space," is to pass beyond the bounds of empirical science. If we wish to decide which

I would like to thank John Earman and William Demopoulos for their advice and comments. I also thank the Social Sciences and Humanities Research Council of Canada for financial support. This chapter is dedicated to my son Christopher.

bodies are moving, we have to construct a frame of reference – that is, we must designate some reference-points to be fixed, and compare the motions of other bodies to these. Einstein held that any such choice of a reference-frame is inherently arbitrary, and that a philosophically sound physics would be independent of such arbitrary choices; the "General Theory of Relativity" was supposed to be a theory in which all reference-frames are equivalent. To his philosophical followers, especially Hans Reichenbach and Moritz Schlick, Einstein was only saying what philosophers ought to have known, and a few had already suspected, on purely philosophical grounds. Contemporaries who had rejected Newton's views now seemed to have anticipated the eventual emergence of physics from its naive state.

In the 1960s and 1970s, however, many scientists and philosophers began to recognize what a few had known all along: that general relativity does not make space, time, and motion "generally relative," as Einstein had thought.[2] Instead, the theory postulates a spatio-temporal structure that is, in an obvious sense, just as "absolute" as the structures postulated by Newton. On the one hand, Einstein's field equation relates the geometry of space–time to the distribution of matter and energy. Thus, if "absolute" means "fixed and uniform," or "unaffected by material circumstances," then we can say that spacetime in general relativity is not "absolute," but "dynamical." On the other hand, spacetime in general relativity remains "absolute" in at least one philosophically decisive sense: it is not an abstraction from relations among material things, but a "physically objective" structure open to objective empirical investigation. Moreover, the theory does indeed make "absolute" distinctions among states of motion; it draws these distinctions in a way that departs dramatically from Newton's theory, but they remain physically objective distinctions that do not depend on the arbitrary choice of a reference-frame.

It became clear, then, that Newton's theory and Einstein's special and general theories all make essentially similar claims about the world: each specifies a certain "absolute" spatio-temporal structure, along with physical assumptions – primarily about the nature of force and inertia – that enable us to connect that structure with experience. In other words, conceptions of space and time are not arbitrary metaphysical hypotheses appended to otherwise empirical physics; they are assumptions implicit in the laws of physics. Defenders of Newton began to argue that "absolute" space–time structures are not so very different from other unobservable "theoretical entities" introduced into physics, such as fundamental particles and fields. Accordingly, they ought to be judged by how well they function in explanations of observed phenomena. Any reasonable metaphysical question about space, time, and motion could thus be translated into a straightforward question about physics. For example, "is rotation absolute?" becomes, "does our best-established physical theory distinguish between absolute rotation and relative rotation?" and "is there an equally good or a better physical theory that dispenses with absolute rotation, or that refers only to relative motions?"[3]

From this point of view, we can ask of Newton's conceptions of absolute time, absolute space, absolute rotation, and absolute motion, "are they required by Newtonian physics?" And the answer is straightforward: Newton's laws presuppose absolute time, but not absolute space; they enable us to distinguish a truly rotating or accelerating body from one that is merely relatively rotating or accelerating; but they do not enable us to distinguish which bodies are "at rest in absolute space," or to determine the "absolute velocity" of any thing. Therefore Newton's laws require not absolute space, but a four-dimensional structure known as "Newtonian space–time." A straight line of this structure represents uniform motion in a straight line, and therefore its physical counterpart is the motion of a body not subject to forces.[4] Einstein's theories postulate different space–time structures, based on different physical assumptions. Thus the theories should not be judged on purely philosophical grounds; it is, rather, a simple question of which theory is best supported by the empirical evidence. Had Newton said, "Spacetime is a four-dimensional affine space," instead of "Absolute space remains similar and immovable," there would have been no philosophical grounds for objection, but only (eventually) new developments in physics demanding new spacetime structures. Generally, on this point of view, our philosophical views about space and time should depend on our beliefs about physics.

Yet this seemingly simple approach to space and time has always been under philosophical suspicion. Einstein's chief objection had been anticipated by Leibniz: only the relative motions of bodies are observable, while space and time are not. How, then, could space, time, and motion be absolute? If we could construct a theory that made no reference to absolute space, time, and motion, ought we not to prefer it just for that reason? And even if "our best" physical theory does make claims about space, time, and motion, do we not nonetheless have independent philosophical grounds to doubt their "absolute" status? For it seems absurd that any argument about observed spatial relations could prove that space itself is "absolute." Even to Newton's sympathizers, objections like these have always seemed challenging; to his opponents, they have seemed decisive. Hence whether motion is absolute or relative has appeared to be one of the perennial questions of philosophy.

As we shall see, however, this approach to the philosophical questions of space and time is based on a fundamental misunderstanding of what Newton accomplished – indeed, a misunderstanding of the role that space and time play in physics. What it assumes is that what we *mean* by space, time, and motion, and what we mean by claiming that they are "absolute," is already established on purely philosophical grounds, so that we can then ask what physics has to say about these philosophical concepts. What it overlooks is that Newton was *not* taking any such meanings for granted, but *defining* new theoretical concepts within a framework of physical laws. Independently of such a framework, it is premature to ask, "did Newton successfully prove that space, time, and motion are absolute?" The proper questions are, what were Newton's *definitions* of "absolute space," "absolute time," and "absolute motion"? And, how do those definitions function in his physical theory?

NEWTON'S PHILOSOPHICAL CONTEXT

It was natural for Newton's contemporaries to misunderstand his purpose. Leibniz, for example, had an understanding of space, time, and motion, and of what it means to be a "substance" or to be "absolute," that arose from his own peculiar metaphysics. And to say that "space," "time," and "motion," as he understood them, are "absolute," rather than essentially relative, seemed to be an obvious mistake. But Newton explicitly proposed to ignore the prevailing philosophical uses of these terms, and to introduce theoretical notions of his own.

> Although time, space, place, and motion are very familiar to everyone, it must be noted that these quantities are popularly conceived solely with reference to the objects of sense perception. And this is the source of certain preconceptions; to eliminate them it is useful to distinguish these quantities into absolute and relative, true and apparent, mathematical and common.[5]

As Howard Stein first emphasized,[6] the preconceptions that Newton had in mind were those of Descartes and his followers. Descartes had purported to prove that space is identical with extended substance. It followed that a vacuum is impossible, for wherever there is extension, there is, by definition, substance as well; it also followed that what we call motion "in space" is really motion relative to a fluid material plenum. From these foundations, Descartes developed a vortex theory of planetary motion: the rotation of the Sun creates a vortex in the interplanetary fluid, and the planets are thereby carried around in their orbits; similarly, the planets with satellites create smaller vortices of their own. Descartes would thus seem to have advanced a version of the Copernican theory, and attributed real motion to the Earth. But he equivocated on this point by his definition of "motion in the philosophical sense": while motion "in the vulgar sense" is "the action by which a body passes from one place to another," its motion "in the philosophical sense" is the body's "transference from the vicinity of those bodies contiguous to it to the vicinity of others."[7] On this definition, Descartes could claim to hold both the heliostatic and geostatic views of the planetary system: the Earth is indeed revolving around the Sun in the vortex, but "in the philosophical sense" it is at rest, since it remains contiguous to the same particles of the fluid. Hence Descartes's assertion: "I deny the movement of the earth more carefully than Copernicus, and more truthfully than Tycho."[8]

Newton saw that such a definition is completely unsuitable for any *dynamical* analysis of motion, and in particular the dynamical understanding of the solar system. It implies that the choice between Copernicus or Kepler, on the one hand, and Ptolemy or Tycho, on the other, has nothing to do with the dynamical causes and effects of motion, but can only be made on the grounds of simplicity or convenience. From a certain philosophical point of view, of course, this is the desired conclusion. But the vortex theory itself – as advanced not only by Descartes, but by Leibniz and other "relativists" as well – assumed that the planetary system really is a dynamical system: that is, a system that is subject to the laws of motion, and whose parts are related by *causal interactions*. On that assumption, the fact that planets orbit the Sun, instead of moving uniformly in a straight line, requires some kind of causal explanation. Thus, Descartes's theory, *as a causal explanation* of the planetary motions, required a distinction between inertial motion and motion under the causal influence of a force. But this requirement is completely neglected by his definition of "motion in the philosophical sense." We begin to understand Newton's Scholium by properly understanding the question it addresses: what concepts of time, space, and motion are required by a dynamical theory of motion?

Asking this question about Newton's theory does not deny its connection with his profound metaphysical convictions – not only about space and time, but about God and his relationship to the natural world. On the contrary, it illuminates the nature of those convictions and their relationship to Newton's physics. For Newton, God and physical things alike were located in space and time. But space and time also formed a framework within which things act on one another, and their causal relations became intelligible through their spatio-temporal relations – above all, through their effects on each other's state of motion. The latter principle, which was implicit in seventeenth-century physics, was for Newton the link between physics and metaphysics: if physics is to understand the real causal connections in the world, then physics must define space, time, and motion so as to make those connections intelligible.

NEWTON'S DEFINITIONS

Newton begins by defining "absolute time" as time that, "without reference to anything external, flows uniformly."[9] This means that, regardless of whether any particular mechanical or natural process flows equably – for example, regardless of whether the motion of any real clock or rotating planet really sweeps out equal angles in equal times – there is an objective fact, in "absolute time," about whether two intervals of time are truly equal. Absolute time also implies absolute simultaneity, so that each moment of time is defined everywhere, and it is an objective fact whether any two events happened at the same moment. These two principles define precisely what is presupposed about time in the subsequent arguments of the *Principia*. Newton's critics, however, have traditionally taken him to be asserting that "time is absolute," and that the meaning of such a claim is established independently of physics. Leibniz, for example, assumed that if time is absolute, it must be (what he would call) a "substance," and so each moment must be a distinguished individual. This would mean that if the beginning of the universe were shifted from one to another moment of absolute time, some real difference would be made. But no such difference could be discernible; absolute time therefore violates the "Principle of the Identity of Indiscernibles," by which there cannot be two distinct things that do not differ discernibly. Therefore, to Leibniz, time cannot be "absolute," but can only be an "order of succession."

Yet in the notion of absolute time *as defined by Newton*, no such difference is implied. In fact, Newton explicitly rejects the idea that the moments of time (or space) have any identity above and beyond their mutual order and position, asserting (in strikingly "Leibnizian" terms) that "all things are placed in time with reference to order of succession; and in space with reference to order of position."[10] The defining characteristic of absolute time is not the distinct individuality of its moments, but the *structure* of time, that is, the fact that it flows equably and that equal intervals of time are objectively defined. The critical question is not whether Newton successfully proves that "time is absolute" – for this was never his purpose – but whether his definition of absolute time is a good one. And in the context of the *Principia*, this amounts to asking, does this definition have objective physical content? That is, can we define equal intervals of elapsed time without recourse to some arbitrary standard? Is there a good physical definition of what it means for time intervals to be equal, even if no actual clock measures such intervals exactly? The answer is "yes": this is precisely the definition of time implied by Newton's laws of motion, which postulate an objective distinction between inertial motions, which cross equal distances in equal times, and motions that are accelerated by an impressed force. In short, an ideal clock that keeps absolute time is simply an inertial clock: impossible to achieve in practice, but approachable to an arbitrary degree of approximation. Thus Newton's definition of absolute time is as well founded as his laws of motion. And this is why, in spite of all the traditional philosophical objections to it, it could only be overthrown by Einstein's introduction of new fundamental physical laws.

A similar analysis can be given of Newton's definitions of absolute space and motion. For Leibniz and others, to say that "space is absolute" is to say that space is a substance, and thereby to attribute a distinct identity to each point of space. But if the locations of all things in space were shifted any distance in any direction, no real difference would be made; therefore (again by the Principle of the Identity of Indiscernibles), space cannot be absolute. Here again, however, in the definition of absolute space *given by Newton*, no such difference is implied. The defining characteristics of absolute space are that it remains "homogeneous and immovable," so that the parts of absolute space (the "absolute places") are truly at rest, and that translation from one to another absolute place is "absolute motion."[11] This means that there is a real difference between motion and rest in *the same* absolute place over time; but it does not imply any real difference between one universe, and another in which everything is shifted to a *different* absolute place; a body's state of motion depends on whether it remains in *the same* absolute place, but not on *which* absolute place it occupies. (Similarly, in Newtonian spacetime we can determine whether two velocities are the same, independently of their actual magnitude.) So Leibniz's classic arguments from the Principle of the Identity of Indiscernibles, cogent though they may be against a certain conception of space and time as "substances," are *not* arguments against the concepts Newton designated by "absolute time" and "absolute space."

Now, however, if we ask of absolute space what we asked of absolute time (is this a legitimate definition on physical grounds?) we encounter a problem. Unlike absolute time, absolute space entails a distinction that is not well defined according to Newton's laws: the distinction between rest and motion in absolute space. According to the laws of motion, a body moves uniformly in a straight line until an applied force causes it to accelerate, and the effect of the force is independent of the velocity of the body it acts upon. In other words, Newton's laws embody the principle of Galilean relativity, which Newton himself derived as Corollary 5 to the laws: "When bodies are enclosed in a given space, their motions in relation to one another are the same whether the space is at rest or whether it is moving uniformly straight forward without circular motion."[12] This means that nothing in the behavior of the solar system, for example, would enable us to determine whether it is at rest or moving inertially. Corollary 6 undermines absolute motion even further: "If bodies are moving in any way whatsoever with respect to one another and are urged by equal accelerative forces along parallel lines, they will all continue to move with respect to one another in the same way as they would if they were not acted on by those forces."[13] That is, nothing in the behavior of the solar system can even tell us whether the system is moving inertially, or being accelerated equally by some force from outside the system. Thus, though absolute space is invulnerable to the familiar criticisms from Leibniz, it is devastated by Newton's own concepts of force and inertia. Evidently this might have been otherwise: if the laws of physics measured force by velocity rather than acceleration, then dynamics could identify which bodies are truly at rest. Then we would have the physical definition of absolute space that Newtonian physics lacks. But in a Newtonian world, Newton's distinction between absolute motion and absolute rest cannot be realized.

That Newton was aware of this problem is clear from his discussion of absolute motion. He proposes to distinguish absolute from relative motion by its "properties, causes, and effects." And in the discussion of absolute translation, the properties can be simply defined: that bodies at rest are at rest relative to one another; that parts of a body partake of the motion of the whole; that whatever is contained in a given space shares the motion of that space. These properties together imply that we cannot determine the true state of rest or motion unless we refer motion to immovable space, rather than to some object or relative space that may be in motion. The latter properties, moreover, are directed against Descartes (without naming him, however). For they are not necessarily true of motion in Descartes's sense: if an apple moves, for example, the core remains at rest, as it is not moving relative to the skin that is contiguous to it. So Newton has given a more sensible analysis than Descartes of what we might mean by motion, assuming that we know which bodies are moving or resting in space. But that is precisely what we do *not* know: none of these properties enables us actually to determine empirically what a body's absolute motion is. An empirical distinction between absolute and relative motion first appears when we move from the properties of true motion to the causes and effects – causes and effects that have to do with inertia and force. And forces, as we have seen, can distinguish between acceleration and uniform motion, but not between "absolute motion" and "absolute rest."

The causes that distinguish absolute from relative motion are "the forces impressed upon bodies to generate motion."[14] Obviously, relative motion can be generated or changed without the action of any force, but true motion is only generated or changed by a force. By the same token, a body's true motion necessarily "suffers some change" from the application of a force, whereas its relative motion need not: for example, if the reference-point by which we measure its relative motion is subject to the same force. Here a "relativist" might be tempted to ask, how does Newton know all of this about true motion? To ask this is to forget that Newton is elaborating the *definition* of true motion that is implicit in the principle of inertia. The critical question is, instead, does the definition define exactly what Newton wanted to define? Corollary 5 (or Corollary 6, for that matter) shows explicitly that it does not: the effects of impressed forces on the "true motions" of bodies are completely independent of the initial velocities of those bodies; therefore the causes of "true motion" provide a definition, not of motion with respect to absolute space, but of acceleration.

The same is true of the effects that distinguish absolute from relative motion: "the forces of receding from the axis of circular motion," or centrifugal forces.[15] "For in purely relative circular motion these forces are null, while in true and absolute circular motion, they are larger or smaller in proportion to the quantity of motion." Such effects, even if we assume that they distinguish a true rotation from a relative motion, certainly cannot reveal whether a rotating body is at rest in absolute space. But what do they reveal? Newton discusses this[16] in the most controversial part of the Scholium, the "water-bucket experiment." The experiment is extremely simple: suspend a bucket of water by a rope, and turn the bucket in one direction until it is "strongly twisted"; then, turn the bucket in the contrary direction and let the rope untwist. As the bucket now rotates, the surface of the water will initially be flat, but relative to the bucket, it is rotating. By the friction of the rotating bucket, the water will gradually begin to rotate as well, eventually equaling the speed of the bucket, so that its motion relative to the bucket gradually ceases. Yet as the relative rotation of the water decreases, its "endeavor to recede from the axis of motion" – exhibited by the water's climbing the sides of the bucket – increases correspondingly. The significance of this is plain. Newton is identifying the water's rotation by its dynamical effect, which is least when the motion in Descartes's sense is greatest, and greatest when the Cartesian motion is least.

> Therefore, that endeavor does not depend on the change of position of the water with respect to surrounding bodies, and thus true circular motion cannot be determined by such changes of position. The truly circular motion of each revolving body is unique, corresponding to a unique endeavor as its proper and sufficient effect.[17]

Thus the Cartesian definition of motion ignores the very dynamical effects with which physics ought to be concerned. Newton explicitly points out, however, that his dynamical concept of motion is implicit in Descartes's own vortex theory. For in that theory,

> the individual parts of the heavens [i.e., of the fluid vortex], and the planets that are relatively at rest in the heavens to which they belong, are truly in motion. For they change their positions relative to one another (which is not the case with things that are truly at rest), and as they are carried around together with the heavens, they participate in the motions of the heavens and, being parts of revolving wholes, endeavour to recede from the axes of those wholes.[18]

The true rotation of a body, then, cannot be judged from its motion relative to contiguous bodies, but only from the magnitude of the centrifugal effects it causes.

Critics of this argument have generally not defended the Cartesian view of motion against Newton's objections. But Newton was evidently trying to do more than distinguish true rotation from rotation in Descartes's "philosophical sense." This is clear from another thought-experiment: suppose that two globes, joined by a cord, revolve around their common center of gravity; suppose, further, that there are no other bodies, contiguous or otherwise, to which we can refer their motions. Even then, "the endeavor of the balls to recede from the axis of motion could be known from the tension of the cord, and thus the quantity of circular motion could be computed."[19] In other words, the true rotation of a body is not only independent of its rotation relative to contiguous bodies; it is independent of *any* relative rotation. If Newton is correct, one could say of one body, in an otherwise empty universe, whether it is rotating or not.

This is the step that has always raised philosophical doubts: do the experiments prove that the water, or the pair of globes, is really rotating? Could such an experiment possibly demonstrate the existence of absolute space? Is rotation relative to absolute space really the cause of the observed centrifugal forces? Perhaps the centrifugal forces on the water are not caused by motion relative to the bucket, but does this mean that they are independent of *any* relative motion, as the experiment of the globes purports to show? According to Ernst Mach, writing two hundred years after Newton, if Newton saw no need to refer motion to contiguous bodies, this is because he was tacitly referring all motion to the "fixed stars." And even if we can deduce from Newton's laws how bodies would behave in the absence of the fixed stars, we cannot deduce whether, in those circumstances, Newton's laws would still hold anyway.[20]

To Einstein, under Mach's influence, Newton's argument illustrated the inherent "epistemological defect" of Newtonian physics. Consider two spheres S_1 and S_2 rotating relative to one another, and suppose that S_2 bulges at its equator; how do we explain this difference? Einstein says,

> No answer can be admitted as epistemologically satisfactory, unless the reason given is an observable fact of experience ... Newtonian mechanics does not give a satisfactory answer to this question. It pronounces as follows: The laws of mechanics apply to the space R_1, in respect to which the body S_1 is at rest, but not to the space R_2, in respect to which the body S_2 is at rest. But the privileged space R_1 ... is a merely factitious cause, and not a thing that can be observed.[21]

Einstein's view became the "received view" of absolute rotation among philosophers of science. And even philosophers who have defended absolute rotation have accepted this challenge to show that absolute motion does provide a legitimate explanation.[22] As our reading of Newton suggests, however, this critical view simply asks the wrong questions. Newton never claims to *prove* that the centrifugal forces on the water or the globes are caused by rotation relative to absolute space, or claims that any such experiment could demonstrate the existence of absolute space. What he says, instead, is that the centrifugal forces *define* absolute rotation. It makes no sense to ask, how does Newton know that S_2 is really rotating? S_2 is rotating *by definition* – more precisely, S_2 is rotating just because it satisfies the definition of absolute rotation. Thus Newton has not tried to *justify* the causal link between rotation and centrifugal effects, but simply to identify it as definitive of true rotation. Thus he has defined a theoretical quantity, absolute rotation, by exhibiting how it is detected and measured by centrifugal effects. His discussion of the water-bucket makes this explicit: from the endeavor to recede from the axis, "one can find out *and measure* the true and absolute circular motion of the water, which here is the direct opposite of its relative motion" [emphasis added].[23] And concerning the globes, he states not only that from the tension on the cord "we might compute the quantity of their circular motions," but also that changes in the tension would provide a measure of the increase or decrease in rotation. "In this way both the quantity and the direction of this circular motion could be found in any immense vacuum, where nothing external or sensible existed with which the balls could be compared."[24] Again, we might think to ask how we really know that these effects provide a measure of absolute rotation, or by what right we can infer from such effects the quantity of absolute rotation. But this is as pointless as asking, by what right do we infer the magnitude and direction of an impressed force from the magnitude and direction of an acceleration? For this is just how Newton's laws define impressed force. In both cases, we are not inferring a theoretical entity from a phenomenon, but defining a phenomenon as the measure of a theoretical quantity.[25]

Newton's argument, in sum, was never an argument from physical phenomena to metaphysical conclusions about the "absoluteness" of rotation. Instead, it was an argument of a sort that is fundamental to every empirical science: an argument that a novel theoretical concept has a well-defined empirical content. Like the definition of absolute time, and unlike the definition of absolute translation, the definition of absolute rotation does indeed have a basis in Newton's laws. And this means, again, that it is no less well founded than Newton's laws; if the universe in fact obeys those laws, we can always measure the true rotation of any body.

This interpretation of Newton's Scholium defies a long and continuing tradition, though its main point was already made by Stein in 1967.[26] But it is explicitly corroborated by Newton's other extended discussion of space, the manuscript "De gravitatione et aequipondio fluidorum."[27] For example, here Newton explicitly denies the conception of space and time as "substances" that provoked Leibniz's "indiscernibility" objection: "The parts of duration and space are only understood to be the same as they really are because of their mutual order and position; nor do they have any hint of individuality apart from that order and position which consequently cannot be altered."[28] Newton concludes that space "has its own way of being, which fits neither substances nor accidents." He even suggests, for reasons not unlike those later given by George Berkeley, that the philosophical notion of "substance" is itself "unintelligible."[29]

More important, "De gravitatione," much more explicitly than the Scholium, emphasizes that Newton's dynamical arguments concern the *definition* of true motion. His entire discussion of space and motion is contained in a "Note" to Definition 4: "Motion is change of place."[30] As Stein pointed out (1967), Newton begins immediately to justify this definition against "the Cartesians," by showing that Descartes's definition of motion is incompatible with the basic principles of mechanics. In particular, it is incompatible with the principle of inertia: if a body's true motion is defined relative to contiguous bodies, and the latter are the constantly flowing particles of the vortex, it will be impossible to define a definite path for the body. And in that case, it will be impossible to say whether that path is rectilinear or uniform. "On the contrary, there cannot be motion since there can be no motion without a certain velocity and determination."[31]

Newton also points out, however, that, alongside the "philosophical" conception of motion, Descartes makes casual or implicit use of a *physical* and *causal* conception of motion. For example, Descartes acknowledges that the revolution of a planet or comet around the Sun creates centrifugal forces in the planet, a centrifugal tendency that must be balanced by the resistance of the fluid in the vortex. And this physical motion of the vortex itself is referred, not to "the ambient bodies," but to "generic" extension. Of course Descartes says that the latter is an abstraction from extended matter that exists only in thought; the vortical motion that produces the centrifugal forces is thus mere "motion in the vulgar sense," not true motion. But Newton observes that of these two parallel concepts of motion, it is the "vulgar" one, rather than the "philosophical" one, that Descartes appeals to in giving a *physical* and *causal* account of celestial motion. Therefore he argues that, of the possible ways of defining motion, we ought to choose that one that successfully defines a physical quantity, and that can therefore play a role in causal explanation: "And since the whirling of the comet around the Sun in his philosophical sense does not cause a tendency to recede from the center, which a gyration in the vulgar sense can do, surely motion in the vulgar sense should be acknowledged, rather than the philosophical."[32]

It might seem that Descartes's theory of motion is too easy a target, especially compared to a sophisticated account of the relativity of motion like that of Leibniz.[33] But Newton's objection to Descartes's definition is not merely its inadequacy or even incoherence, but also its inconsistency with dynamical principles that Descartes himself accepted. And this same objection applies to Leibniz: he appeals to a causal account of motion that is incompatible with his professed philosophical account. On philosophical grounds, as we have seen, Leibniz denies that there is a real distinction between one state of motion and another, and asserts the general "equivalence of hypotheses" about which bodies are at rest or in motion; consequently, he asserts that the Copernican and Ptolemaic systems are equivalent. Yet he very clearly does attach a *physical* meaning to the distinction between one state of motion and another. On the one hand, Leibniz presents a strange argument for the relativity of all motion. He claims to agree with Newton on "the equivalence of hypotheses in the case of rectilinear motions." But a curved motion is really made up of infinitesimal rectilinear motions, and so he concludes that a curved path is equivalent to a straight one, because they are equivalent in the mathematical sense that both are "locally straight." So all motions, rectilinear or curved, are equivalent.[34] On the other hand, according to Leibniz's own dynamical theory, the curved path is not *physically* – therefore not *causally* – equivalent to the straight path. This is because, on that theory, a body by its own inherent force can maintain its motion in a straight path, whereas a body cannot maintain a curved motion without the constant intervention of some other body.

Indeed, the crux of his objection to Newtonian action at a distance is that it violates this principle:

> If God wanted to cause a body to move free in the aether round about a certain fixed center, without any other creature acting upon it, I say it could not be done without a miracle, since it cannot be explained by the nature of bodies. For a free body naturally recedes from a curve in the tangent.[35]

This passage establishes that Leibniz's understanding of rotation and centrifugal force was, at least in the context of physical explanation, the same as Newton's. And this is a natural consequence of Leibniz's commitment to the vortex theory, in which the harmonic circulation of the planets results from a balance between their own "centrifugal tendencies" and the pressure of the ambient fluid.[36] More generally, such remarks reveal that, despite his "general law of equivalence," Leibniz's convictions about the fundamental nature of bodies, and their causal interactions with one another, depended on the concept of a privileged state of motion.

Leibniz's view exhibits the conflict, characteristic of seventeenth-century "relativist" views of space, time, and motion, between two opposing motives. On the one hand was the desire for a "relativistic" account of motion, in reaction against traditional Aristotelian objections to the motion of the Earth. The classical argument was simply that terrestrial phenomena seem to reveal none of the expected effects of a rapid rotation or revolution; to accept the Copernican theory, one had to grasp the idea of "indistinguishable" states of motion, and to accept an "equivalence of hypotheses" about whether the Earth is at rest. Only thus could Galileo argue that the terrestrial evidence is necessarily inconclusive, and appeal to the advantages of Copernicanism as an elegant account of celestial phenomena. On the other hand, the demise of Aristotle's theory of celestial motion – the "crystalline spheres" – produced the need for a causal account of motion, which would reveal the physical connections among the Sun and the planets. And the founding principle of that account, at least for Newton and Leibniz and their contemporaries, was Descartes's principle that the planets tend to travel in straight lines, but are forced by some physical cause into circulations around the sun. Leibniz maintained the mechanistic view that any such cause must act by immediate contact, while Newton accepted the possibility of "action at a distance," but, in any case, they shared the principle that a certain state of motion is "natural," and that any deviation from that state requires a causal explanation. Therefore, a "general law of equivalence" of states of motion would vitiate the very celestial mechanics that Leibniz and other Cartesians hoped to construct. If it made no *physical* difference whether the Sun orbited the Earth, or the Earth the Sun; if it made no physical difference whether the interplanetary medium were at rest, or rotating in a vortex; then there would be little hope of explaining the celestial motions by the physical interactions among the celestial bodies.

All of this shows that Newton's definition of absolute motion, in so far as it identifies the latter by its "causes and effects," is by no means an arbitrary definition, or an idiosyncratic one derived solely from his metaphysical views. Rather, Newton's definition identifies the very conception of motion that was implicit in seventeenth-century thinking about physical causes and physical explanations. His Scholium attempts (not entirely successfully, as we have seen) to characterize this conception precisely, and especially to separate it from philosophical "preconceptions" about relativity that are irrelevant to the task of physical explanation. In other words, instead of a metaphysical hypothesis to account for dynamical effects, Newton has offered a conceptual analysis of what is presupposed about motion – by Descartes, Leibniz, and every other seventeenth-century mechanist – in ordinary reasoning from motion to its physical cause.

THE SYSTEM OF THE WORLD

The Newtonian conception of motion has an obvious yet remarkable consequence: whether the planetary system is geocentric or heliocentric can no longer be settled by adopting the simplest hypothesis, but is now a straightforward empirical question. For, assuming the laws of motion, Book 3 of Newton's *Principia* argues from the celestial motions to the physical forces that cause them. Again, any post-Cartesian physicist would infer, from the fact that a planet travels in a closed orbit rather than a straight line, that *some* force keeps it from following the tangent; Newton, drawing on the work of Galileo, Huygens, and others, reasoned mathematically from the precise characteristics of the orbit to the precise characteristics of the force. And this reasoning leads eventually from Kepler's laws of planetary motion to universal gravitation.[37]

Throughout this reasoning from motions to forces, Newton remains neutral between the geocentric and heliocentric theories. Once the forces are known, however, we can compare the masses of the celestial bodies by comparing the forces they exert on their satellites. From there, a very simple argument determines the physical center of the system. First, suppose (Hypothesis 1) that the center of the system (whatever it is) is at rest.[38] "No one doubts this, although some argue that the earth, others that the sun, is at rest in the center of the system." Then (Proposition 11) the common center of gravity of the system must be at rest. For by Corollary 4 to the laws of motion, "that center either will be at rest or move uniformly straight forward. But if that center always moves forward, the center of the universe will also move, contrary to the hypothesis." The conclusion is immediate: "Proposition 12: That the sun is engaged in continual motion but never recedes far from the common center of gravity of all the planets."[39] In other words, if the planetary system is a dynamical system, whose members interact according to the accepted dynamical laws, then no body is at rest, for, by the third law of motion, to every action of every body there is an equal and opposite reaction, and only the center of gravity of the system can remain at rest. However, the comparison of masses reveals that most of the mass of the system is contained in the sun. Therefore, "if that body toward which other bodies gravitate most had to be placed in the center . . . that privilege would have to be conceded to the sun."[40]

Newton's argument is that, given the laws of motion and the observed behavior of the planets and the sun, we can infer their causal influences on one another and their relative masses; when all of this is known, the structure and motion of the system – "the frame of the system of the world" – is determined. But, as Newton well knew, the system is determined only up to a point. By Corollary 5, no dynamical analysis of the solar system can reveal whether the system as a whole is at rest or in uniform motion. And Corollary 6 renders the analysis still less determinate. But none of this affects Newton's dynamical analysis:

> It may be alleged that the sun and planets are impelled by some other force equally and in the direction of parallel lines; but by such a force (by Cor. VI of the Laws of Motion) no change would happen in the situation of the planets to one another, nor any sensible effect follow; but our business is with the causes of sensible effects. Let us, therefore, neglect every such force as imaginary and precarious, and of no use in the phenomena of the heavens.[41]

The causal analysis of the motions within the solar system establishes a close approximation to Kepler's heliocentric system, whatever the motion of the system as a whole. And the geocentric theory is revealed to be physically impossible, precisely as it would be physically impossible for a baby to whirl a large adult around its head on a string: in both cases the smaller body must revolve further from the center of gravity.

Philosophically this argument is not very different from the Leibnizian argument for a heliocentric vortex. The latter, too, reasons from accelerated motions to their physical causes, and it infers from the nature and magnitude of the Sun that it, rather than the Earth, has the required causal efficacy to serve as the physical center of the system. Therefore, on Leibniz's physical theory as well as on

Newton's, whether Ptolemy or Copernicus was more nearly right is a physically meaningful question. It should be emphasized, moreover, that the same comparison can be made between Newton's theory and general relativity. Philosophers used to say that general relativity had finally established the equivalence of the Copernican and Ptolemaic systems, except to the extent that one might be "simpler" than the other.[42] Precisely as in Newton's theory, however, in general relativity the planetary orbits are determined by the mass of the Sun. The mass causes spacetime curvature, instead of a gravitational field in Newton's sense, but there remains an essential similarity: the mass required to account for the precise curvature of the planetary orbits is the same in both theories, and on either theory the Earth's mass is too small. So the two systems are, on physical grounds, as *inequivalent* in Einstein's theory as they are in Newton's. The decision between them is not an arbitrary choice of reference-frame, but the outcome of a dynamical analysis, based on the principle that states of motion can have genuine dynamical differences.

CONCLUSION: AN EMPIRICIST VIEW OF SPACE, TIME, AND MOTION

Newton's conceptions of space, time, and motion were long regarded as metaphysical ideas whose place in empirical science was open to dispute. Now we can finally see that they were, instead, exemplary of the way in which science gives empirical meaning to theoretical notions. A spatio-temporal concept belongs in physics just in case it is defined by physical laws that explain how it is to be applied, and how the associated quantity is to be measured; Newton called "absolute" precisely those quantities that could be so defined. By this standard, absolute space does not belong in Newtonian physics, since absolute translation in space is not a physically measurable quantity. But absolute time, absolute acceleration, and absolute rotation are well-defined concepts that are, as we saw, implicit in classical thinking about physical causes. Thus philosophical questions about these concepts could become empirical questions. In particular, the question of what is really moving in the solar system was reduced to simple empirical questions. Which bodies exhibit the dynamical effects that are definitive of true rotation? Where is the center of gravity of the system, and what body is closest to that center?

The controversy over this theory of motion can be compared to the controversy over Newton's theory of gravitation as an action at a distance. To his scientific and philosophical contemporaries, action at a distance contradicted the very concept of physical action, which was supposed to be possible only by direct contact. But for Newton, action is defined by the laws of motion, which provide empirical criteria for measuring the action of one thing on another; if the planets and the sun satisfy these criteria in their direct mutual relations, then they are acting on one another. Thus the question of action at a distance became an empirical question. We can also compare this to the controversy over non-Euclidean geometry in the nineteenth century. Many philosophers found it inconceivable that space could possibly be curved; this seemed contrary to the very concept of space.[43] According to Gauss, Riemann, and Helmholtz, however, when we make precise the empirical meaning of the claim that space is curved, we see that it is no more contradictory than the claim that space is not curved. Both claims derive their meaning from physical assumptions about the behavior of bodies and light – for example, that "light rays travel in straight lines"; just this understanding of the meaning of curvature makes it an empirically measurable quantity, and makes the question whether space is curved an empirical question. Similarly, Newton showed that the familiar assumptions about inertia and force – specifically, that "bodies not subject to forces travel uniformly in straight lines" – suffice to define acceleration and rotation as empirically measurable quantities. His critics insisted that, to be an empiricist about space and time, one had to define motion as change of relative position; Newton's philosophical insight was that empirical definitions of motion, space, and time come from the laws of empirical science.

NOTES

1 Albert Einstein, "The Foundation of the General Theory of Relativity," in Einstein *et al.*, *The Principle of Relativity*, trans. W. Perrett and G. B. Jeffery (New York: Dover Publications, 1952), p. 117. This is a translation of Einstein's "Die Grundlagen der allgemeinen Relativitätstheorie," *Annalen der Physik* (4) 49 (1916), 769–822.

2 Among the earliest expressions of this view was Hermann Weyl, *Raum–Zeit–Materie* (Berlin: Springer-Verlag, 1918); Weyl was followed by (for example) A. d'Abro, *The Evolution of Scientific Thought* (1927; Dover Publications reprint, 1950), and Karl Popper, "Three Views Concerning Human Knowledge" (1953, reprinted in Popper's *Conjectures and Refutations*, New York: Harper, 1963). This view was later brought to philosophical prominence by Howard Stein, "Newtonian Space–Time," *Texas Quarterly* 10 (1967), 174–200; this was followed by John Earman and Michael Friedman, "The Meaning and Status of Newton's Law of Inertia and the Nature of Gravitational Forces," *Philosophy of Science* 40 (1973), 329–59; Howard Stein, "Some Philosophical Prehistory of General Relativity," in J. Earman, C. Glymour, and J. Stachel (eds.), *Foundations of Space-Time Theories*, Minnesota Studies in Philosophy of Science 8 (Minneapolis: University of Minnesota Press, 1977), pp. 3–49.

3 See, for example, Roberto Torretti, *Relativity and Geometry* (Oxford: Pergamon Press, 1983); Michael Friedman, *Foundations of Space–Time Theories* (Princeton, NJ: Princeton University Press, 1983); and John Earman, *World Enough and Spacetime: Absolute versus Relational Theories of Space and Time* (Cambridge, MA: MIT Press, 1989).

4 For further explanation see Stein, "Newtonian Space–Time" and "Some Philosophical Prehistory," or Friedman, *Foundations*, ch. 1.

5 Isaac Newton, *The Principia, Mathematical Principles of Natural Philosophy: A New Translation*, trans. I. Bernard Cohen and Anne Whitman (Berkeley, CA: University of California Press, 1999), p. 408.

6 Stein, "Newtonian Space–Time."

7 René Descartes, *The Principles of Philosophy*, trans. Valentine Rodger Miller and R. P. Miller (Dordrecht: Reidel, 1983), Part 2, article 28, p. 52.

8 *Ibid.*, part 3, article 19.

9 Newton, *The Principia*, p. 408.

10 *Ibid.*, p. 410.

11 *Ibid.*, pp. 408–9.

12 *Ibid.*, p. 423.

13 *Ibid.*, p. 423.

14 *Ibid.*, p. 412.

15 *Ibid.*, p. 412.

16 *Ibid.*, p. 412.

17 *Ibid.*, p. 413.

18 *Ibid.*, p. 413.

19 *Ibid.*, p. 414.

20 Ernst Mach, *Die Mechanik in ihrer Entwickelung, historisch-kritisch dargestellt* (Leipzig: F. A. Brockhaus, 1883).

21 Einstein, "The Foundation of the General Theory of Relativity," p. 113.

22 For example, Friedman, *Foundations.*

23 Newton, *The Principia*, p. 414.

24 *Ibid.*, p. 414.

25 For further discussion, including a comparision of Newton's arguments with Einstein's arguments for special and general relativity, see Robert DiSalle, "Spacetime Theory as Physical Geometry," *Erkenntnis* 42 (1995), 317–37.

26 Stein, "Newtonian Space–Time." This paper has been frequently cited in literature on the "absolute versus relational" debate, but, I would argue, generally misinterpreted. To the extent that that debate takes the question, "are space, time and motion absolute?" to be well defined in purely philosophical terms, Stein is taken to have shown that Newton had good arguments, or better arguments than "relativists" or "relationalists" had ever acknowledged, for the "absolutist" side. (See, e.g, Friedman, *Foundations*, and Earman, *World Enough.*) Thus the essential point, that Newton's Scholium introduces *definitions* of absolute space, time, and motion – and to that extent transcends the traditional debate – has not been generally appreciated.

27 "On the Gravity and Equilibrium of Fluids" (hereafter "De gravitatione"). In A.R. Hall and M.B. Hall (eds.), *Unpublished Scientific Papers of Isaac Newton* (Cambridge: Cambridge University Press, 1962), pp. 89–156. The most important philosophical commentary on this paper is found in Stein, "Newtonian Space–Time"; see also Stein, this volume.

28 Hall and Hall, *Unpublished Scientific Papers*, p. 136.

29 *Ibid.*, pp. 139–49. See also DiSalle, "On Dynamics, Indiscernibility, and Spacetime Ontology," *British Journal for the Philosophy of Science* 45 (1994), 265–87, and Stein, this volume.

30 Hall and Hall, *Unpublished Scientific Papers*, p. 122.

31 *Ibid.*, pp. 129–31. Stein suggests that "if Huygens and Leibniz . . . had been confronted with the argument of this passage, a clarification would have been forced that could have promoted appreciably the philosophical discussion of space-time" ("Newtonian Space–Time," p. 186). It is interesting to note that essentially the same argument was advanced by Leonhard Euler in 1748, and had a very serious impact on the philosophy of space and time. Euler's general theme was the relation between science and metaphysics; he claimed that the truths of physics – in particular the laws of mechanics – are so well founded that they must serve as a guide for metaphysical researches into the nature of bodies. "For one has the right to reject in this science [metaphysics] all reasoning and all ideas, however well founded they might otherwise appear, that lead to conclusions contrary to those truths [of mechanics]" ("Reflexions sur l'espace et le temps," in Euler's *Opera Omnia*, series 3, vol. 2, pp. 377–83; p. 377). In particular, the principle that bodies continue to move in the same direction until a force is applied cannot be reconciled with the relativistic account of space: "For if space and place were nothing but the relation among co-existing bodies, what would be the same direction? . . . However bodies may move or change their mutual situation, that doesn't prevent us from maintaining a sufficiently clear idea of a fixed direction that bodies endeavour to follow in their motion, in spite of the changes that other bodies undergo. From which it is evident that identity of direction, which is an essential circumstance in the general principles of motion, is absolutely not to be explicated by the relation or the order of co-existing bodies" (*Ibid.*, p. 381). Euler's essay, in turn, profoundly influenced the development of Immanuel Kant's thought away from Leibnizian relationalism, toward a deeper understanding of the Newtonian theory of space, time, and motion, and eventually toward a complete reexamination of the roles of space and time in our understanding of the external world. See Michael Friedman, "Introduction" to *Kant and the Exact Sciences* (Cambridge, MA: Harvard University Press, 1993).

32 Hall and Hall, *Unpublished Scientific Papers*, p. 125.

33 See, especially, Julian Barbour, *Absolute or Relative Motion?* (Cambridge: Cambridge University Press, 1991).

34 Cf. "A Specimen of Dynamics," in Leibniz's *Philosophical Essays*, ed. and trans. R. Ariew and D. Garber (Indianapolis, IN: Hackett Publishing Co., 1989), pp. 136–7. This argument is evidently based on a

misunderstanding of Galilean relativity, which, again, asserts the equivalence of motions that are rectilinear *and uniform*. Even though curved lines may be considered "infinitesimally straight," their distinguishing characteristic is that one "infinitesimal straight segment" has a different *direction* from the next; the tangent to a circle at one point, for example, is not parallel to the tangent at a nearby point. Of course Leibniz was well aware of this. But this is just the distinguishing characteristic of curvilinear motion that, on Leibniz's own theory, requires a causal explanation!

35 From Leibniz's Third Letter to Samuel Clarke, in *Philosophical Essays*, p. 327.

36 Cf. Leibniz's letter to Christiaan Huygens (1690), in *Philosophical Essays*, pp. 309–12.

37 See the chapter by W. Harper, this volume.

38 This "Hypothesis" is sometimes misinterpreted as indicating Newton's belief that the center of the solar system is at absolute rest in the center of the universe. But Newton knew (cf. below and note 40) that the dynamical analysis of the solar system cannot determine whether the entire system is at rest, in uniform motion, or even uniformly accelerated. The function of Hypothesis 1 is, rather, purely *dialectical*. That is, it is taken as the common assumption of the Keplerian and Tychonic accounts of the structure of the planetary system, in order to show that *both sides are mistaken*: neither the Earth nor the Sun is in the center.

39 Newton, *The Principia*, p. 816.

40 *Ibid.*, p. 817.

41 Newton, *The System of the World*, in *Sir Isaac Newton's Mathematical Principles of Natural Philosophy and his System of the World*, ed. Florian Cajori, trans. Andrew Motte, 2 vols. (Berkeley, CA: University of California Press, 1962), vol. 2, p. 558.

42 For example, Hans Reichenbach, *The Philosophy of Space and Time*, trans. Maria Reichenbach (New York: Dover Publications, 1957); Moritz Schlick, *Space and Time in Contemporary Physics*, trans. H. Brose (New York: Oxford University Press, 1920).

43 For the history of this controversy, see Roberto Torretti, *Philosophy of Geometry from Riemann to Poincaré* (Dordrecht: Reidel, 1977).

2 Newton's concepts of force and mass, with notes on the laws of motion

I. Bernard Cohen

VARIETIES OF FORCE IN THE *PRINCIPIA*[1]

Newton's physics is based on two fundamental concepts: mass and force.[2] In the *Principia* Newton explores the properties of several types of force. The most important of these are the forces that produce accelerations or changes in the state of motion or of rest in bodies. In Definition 4 of the *Principia*, Newton separates these into three principal categories: impact or percussion, pressure, and centripetal force. In the *Principia*, Newton mentions other types of forces, including (in Book 2) the forces with which fluids resist motions through them.[3] Of a different sort is Newton's "force of inertia," which is neither an accelerative force nor a static force and is not, properly speaking in the context of dynamics, a force at all.[4]

The structure of Newton's *Principia* follows a classical pattern: definitions and axioms, followed by the statement of propositions and their demonstrations. Newton's treatise differs, however, from classical (or Greek) geometry in two respects. First, there is a constant appeal to the method of limits – Newton's "first and ultimate ratios," as set forth in Book 1, Section 1. Second, the validity of propositions is tied to evidence of experiment and critical observation.

In the demonstrations in the *Principia*, Newton generally proceeds by establishing a series of proportions from a geometric configuration. He then allows one or more of the parameters to be diminished without limit, thereby obtaining a limiting ("ultimate") value of the geometric ratio. It is in the limit that Newton's proofs are valid.

THE STRUCTURE OF THE *PRINCIPIA*

The propositions in the *Principia* are set forth in three "books." Book 1 analyzes motion in free spaces, that is, spaces devoid of fluid resistance. Book 2 then considers various conditions of fluid resistance and a variety of related topics. Finally, in Book 3, Newton applies the results of Book 1 to the physics of the heavens, to the "System of the World." Here he shows that gravity extends to the Moon and that the Earth is an oblate spheroid. He investigates the motions of the Moon, calculates planetary densities and relative masses, explains the motions of the tides, and shows that comets are like planets and thus move in conic sections, some of which are ellipses. Book 3, as Edmond Halley reported to the Royal Society, displays a demonstration of the Copernican system as amended by Kepler.[5]

As is well known, Book 3 centers on the concept of a universal gravitating force, one which is shown by Newton to act between any two particles in the universe. This force is directly proportional to the product of the masses and inversely proportional to the square of the distance between them.

In the final (second and third) editions, Newton has a concluding General Scholium which sets forth a philosophical point of view that has dominated most of physical science ever since. According to this philosophy, the goal of science is not to explore ultimate causes, as for example the cause of gravity, nor to "feign" hypotheses.[6] Rather, Newton writes, it "is enough" that "gravity really exists and acts according to the laws that we have set forth and is sufficient to explain the motions of the heavenly bodies and of our sea."

THE DEFINITIONS – NEWTON'S CONCEPT OF MASS

The *Principia* opens with a set of "Definitions," of which the first is "mass," a new concept formally introduced into physics by Newton and a fundamental concept of all physical science ever since. In the actual statement of the definition, Newton does not use the word "mass." Rather, he states what he means by the then-current expression, "quantity of matter" ("quantitas materiae"). He writes that *his* measure of quantity of matter is one that "arises from" (the Latin is "orta est") two factors jointly: density and volume. He indicates that this particular measure is what he means whenever he writes of "body" or "mass."

Newton introduced the concept of mass because his physics demanded a measure of matter that is not the result of a body happening to be at one place rather than another or being subject to some particular physical circumstance such as an external pressure. In other words, Newton's measure – to use the language of Aristotelian physics – is not an "accidental" property.

In Definition 1, Newton effectively rejects then-current measures of matter such as extension (favored by Descartes) or weight (Galileo's measure). He abandoned weight as the measure of matter because the reported experiences of Richer and Halley had shown that the weight of a body varies with its terrestrial latitude. Newton points out that, at any given place, the mass of a body "can always be known from a body's weight"; he has found "by making very accurate experiments with pendulums" that at any given place mass is proportional to weight. The report on these experiments is given in Book 3, Proposition 6.

Newton's views concerning density were strongly influenced by the pneumatic experiments of Boyle and others and by his own concept of the theory of matter. He was aware that a given quantity of air could be expanded or contracted. Under such varying conditions, the density would change, but the quantity of matter would remain fixed, depending on the volume and density jointly.

The quantity of matter in a given sample would, according to Newton, remain unaltered if it were transported from one place on Earth to another. According to Newton's concept, the quantity of matter would remain fixed even if the sample of matter were transported to the Moon or to Jupiter.

Newton's concept of mass has been criticized, notably by Ernst Mach,[7] on the grounds of circularity. If density is mass per unit volume, how can mass be defined as jointly proportional to density and volume?[8] In the *Principia*, however, Newton does not define density, nor did he ever write a gloss on his Definition 1. Apparently, however, he was thinking of density as a measure of the degree of concentration of the number of fundamental particles of which all matter is composed.[9] As such, density would not depend on mass and volume.

Newton came to his concept of mass only as the *Principia* was taking form. Mass does not occur in the several versions of "De motu," the tract that Newton wrote just before composing the *Principia*, a tract which he expanded into the *Principia*. In a list of definitions drawn up just before writing the *Principia*,[10] Newton used the noun "pondus" or "weight" as the measure of matter, but he was careful to note that he did not mean weight as commonly understood. He thus wrote that because of the "want of a suitable word," he will "represent and designate quantity of matter by weight," even though he is aware that this usage is not appropriate in all circumstances. Indeed, in an earlier statement in this same set of definitions, he wrote that by "weight" ("pondus"), "I mean the quantity or amount of matter being moved, apart from considerations of gravity, so long as there is no question of gravitating bodies."

NEWTON'S "QUANTITY OF MOTION"

The subject of Definition 2 is "quantity of motion," our momentum. Newton says that it "arises from the velocity and quantity of matter jointly." Here he uses the same verb ("oriri") as in the definition of quantity of matter.

NEWTON'S CONCEPT OF "INERTIA" – *VIS INSITA* AND "FORCE OF INERTIA"

In Definition 3, Newton declares the sense in which he will use a term then current in discussions of motion, *vis insita*.[11] This term was not an invention of Newton's; it occurs in many books with which Newton was familiar, even appearing as an entry in Rudolph

Goclenius's widely read dictionary, *Lexicon Philosophicum* (1613). According to Goclenius, *vis insita* is a "natural power," a force (*vis*) that can be either *insita* (inherent or natural) or *violenta* (violent). In Aristotelian physics this means that force is either according to a body's nature or contrary to it. The term *vis insita* also appears in Johann Magirus's *Physiologiae Peripateticae Libri Sex* (1642), which Newton studied while a Cambridge undergraduate, entering many extracts in his College Notebook. *Vis insita* occurs in both Magirus's text and his accompanying Latin version of Aristotle's *Nichomachean Ethics*. Newton would also have encountered this term in the writings of Henry More, an influential figure in Newton's intellectual development.[12]

In Definition 3, Newton declares that because he is giving a new sense to this term, he will give it another name: *vis inertiae* or "force of inertia."

The traditional or older physics held that if the motive force applied to a body were to cease acting, the body would then seek its natural place and there come to rest. Kepler, however, in his radical restructuring of the science of motion, held that a primary quality of matter is its "inertness," its inability to move by itself, by its own internal power. Accordingly, if an externally applied force producing motion were to cease, then – according to Kepler – the body would come to rest and do so wherever it happened to be.

Newton encountered this Keplerian concept of motion in a Latin edition of Descartes's correspondence, in an exchange of letters between Descartes and Mersenne concerning "natural inertia"; neither correspondent referred to Kepler by name in this context.[13] Newton made a radical transformation of this Keplerian concept. No longer would the inertia of matter merely bring a body to rest when an external force ceased to act; rather, this inertness would tend to maintain a body in whatever "state" it happened to be, whether a state of resting or of moving "uniformly straight forward."[14] The concept of a body being in a "state" of motion was taken by Newton from Descartes's *Principia*.

Two further aspects of Newton's concept of inertia should be noted. One is that generally Newton does not refer, as we do today, to "inertia" as such; rather he tends to write of a "force of inertia," a *vis inertiae*. The second is that he identified mass and inertia. The *vis insita* of a body, he writes in Definition 3, "is always proportional to the body," that is, proportional to the mass. Furthermore, it "does not differ from the inertia of the mass" save for "the manner in which it is conceived." Hence, he writes, we may give *vis insita* a new and "very significant name," force of inertia (*vis inertiae*). And, indeed, throughout the *Principia*, Newton generally uses *vis inertiae* rather than *vis insita*.

Newton explains that, because of "a body's inertia," a body is only "with difficulty" made to change its "state" of resting or moving uniformly. It is for this reason, he declares, that *vis inertiae* is a better name than *vis insita*. Although the use of *vis* or "force" in the context of inertia seems outlandish to a twenty-first-century reader, this was not the case for Newton's successors in developing the science of dynamics. For example, Jean d'Alembert, in his *Traité de dynamique* (1743), wrote: "I follow Newton in using the name 'force of inertia' for the properties which bodies have of remaining in the state in which they are."

Newton's concept of *vis inertiae* has one puzzling feature. As he makes clear, especially in Definition 4, this is not an "impressed" force, one that can produce a change in state or an acceleration. Therefore, this "force" cannot be combined by means of a force triangle with continuous or instantaneous external forces.

Newton never explained why he wrote of a *vis inertiae*, a "force of inertia," rather than a property of inertia and we have no basis for guessing what was his state of mind. Perhaps he was merely transforming *vis insita* into a *vis* of a new and different sort.

THREE VARIETIES OF IMPRESSED FORCE

In Definition 4, Newton deals with "impressed force," a term that has a long history of usage before the Principia. Newton is concerned with the "action" of forces to alter the "state" of a body, to alter a body's condition of resting or moving uniformly straight forward. According to Newton, this action occurs only while the force is being impressed, while the force is actually producing a change of state. It does not remain in the body after the action is over. Newton says explicitly that "a body perseveres in any new state solely by the force of inertia."

It is in the conclusion of Newton's discussion of Definition 4 that he declares that there are "various sources of impressed force, such as percussion, pressure, or centripetal force."

CENTRIPETAL FORCE

Newton has no need of comment on the first two of his three types of impressed force: percussion and pressure. The case is different, however, for centripetal force. The concept of centripetal force was introduced into rational mechanics and celestial dynamics in the Principia. In a memorandum, Newton said that he had invented the name in honor of Christiaan Huygens, who had used the oppositely directed *vis centrifuga*.

Centripetal force differs from percussion and pressure in one notable aspect. Percussion and pressure are the result of some kind of observable physical action. In both, there is a contact of one body with another, typically providing visual evidence of a force acting, for example, a billiard ball striking another billiard ball. These are the kinds of force on which the so-called "mechanical philosophy" was built, in particular the philosophy of nature of Descartes. These forces display the principle of matter in contact with other matter to produce or alter a motion.

Centripetal force, however, is very different. In important cases, such as orbital motion, we do not know that there is a centripetal force by seeing an action, as is the case for a pressure or a percussion; the only evidence that a centripetal force is acting is that there is a continuous change in a body's state, a continuing departure from a uniform rectilinear motion. Accordingly, in introducing centripetal force in Definition 5, Newton is in effect declaring his independence from the strait-jacket rigidity of the mechanical philosophy. It is a fact of record that Continental natural philosophers – notably Huygens and Leibniz – rejected the Newtonian science of motion because it departed from the strict condition that forces must occur only by the action of matter in contact with matter; they rejected the notion of centripetal force, as posited by Newton, because this "force" acts at a distance and is not produced by matter in contact with matter.

In Definition 5, Newton refers to three examples of centripetal force. One is gravity, by which he means terrestrial gravity, the force that causes bodies to descend downward, "toward the center of the Earth." Another is magnetic force, in which a piece of iron "seeks a lodestone." And, finally, there is the "force, whatever it may be, by which the planets are continually drawn back from rectilinear motions and compelled to revolve in curved lines." Note that it is the departure from uniform linear motion that provides evidence that there is a centripetal force acting.

Newton then turns to an important example of centripetal force taken from Descartes, a stone being whirled in a sling. The stone naturally tends to fly off on a tangent, but is restrained by the force of the hand, constantly pulling the body inward toward the center via the string. Newton calls such a force "centripetal" because "it is directed toward the hand as toward the center of an orbit." And then he boldly asserts that the case is the same for "all bodies that are made to move in orbits." They all tend to fly off "in straight lines with uniform motion" unless there is a force. We may note an anticipation of the first law in the statement that if there were no gravity, a projectile or an orbiting body would move off in a straight line "with uniform motion." It follows from this discussion that planets moving in orbits must similarly be subject to some kind of centrally directed force.

THREE MEASURES OF FORCE

The remaining definitions (Definitions 6–8) are concerned with the three measures of centripetal force. These are the absolute quantity

(Definition 6), the accelerative quantity (Definition 7), and the motive quantity (Definition 8). The most important of these is the "accelerative" quantity, defined as the velocity which is generated "in a given time." This measure is the rate at which velocity changes, our acceleration. It is this measure that Newton has in mind during the first ten sections of Book 1.

In Definition 8, Newton introduces a measure that is "proportional to the motion" (i.e., momentum) which a force "generates in a given time." This measure is, in other words, the rate at which "motion" (i.e., momentum) changes.

THE LAWS OF MOTION: NEWTON'S FIRST LAW

In the *Principia*, the definitions are followed by Newton's "Axioms or Laws of Motion." Newton's "Axiomata sive leges motus" was an obvious transformation of Descartes's "Regulae . . . sive leges naturae," which appear in the latter's *Principia*. This source of Newton's name for the "axioms" would have been obvious to most of Newton's readers, who would also have appreciated that the title of Newton's treatise, *Philosophiae Naturalis Principia Mathematica*, was a rather obvious recasting of the title of Descartes's *Philosophiae Principia*.[15]

The first law of motion, sometimes known as the law of inertia, states: "Every body perseveres in its state of being at rest or of moving uniformly straight forward [i.e., moving uniformly forward in a straight line] except insofar as it is compelled to change its state by forces impressed." In the brief paragraph which follows (consisting of three short sentences), Newton mentions three examples of inertial motion, each of which is based on an analysis of curved motion produced by the action of a form of centripetal force. In each case, the curved motion is, by Newton's analysis, compounded of a linear or tangential component of inertial motion and an inward accelerated motion produced by a centripetal force.

Thus a major purpose of the first law is to make explicit the condition under which we can infer the action of a continuously acting, centrally directed force. Newton's three examples, accordingly, invoke centripetal forces and not pressure or percussion.

The first example is the motion of projectiles. These "persevere in their [linear forward] motions" except in so far as they are retarded by air resistance and are "impelled downward by the force of gravity." Newton's second example is the circular motion of a spinner or a top. Here Newton explains that the particles that compose the spinning object tend to fly off in straight lines along tangents to their curves of motion. They do not fly off, however, but are kept in circular orbits by the cohesive forces that hold the top together. When a top is subjected to a degree of rotation beyond some structural limit, the cohesive force is no longer great enough and the particles fly off in all directions tangent to their original paths of rotation.[16] Newton's third example is the long-term orbital motion of the planets and of comets.

The "forces impressed" which Newton mentions in the statement of the law can be any of the three varieties of impressed force: pressure, percussion, or centripetal force. In other words, the law is equally valid for impulsive or instantaneous forces and continuous forces.

THE SECOND LAW OF MOTION

The second law states that a "change in motion" is proportional to "the motive force impressed" and adds that this change in motion is directed along "the straight line in which this force is impressed." Some commentators have added a word or phrase to Newton's law so as to have it read that the *rate* of "change in motion" (or the change in motion per unit time) is proportional to the force.[17] This alteration would make Newton's second law read like the one found in today's physics textbooks.

Newton, however, did not make an error here. He chose his words very carefully. In his formulation of the second law, Newton was explicitly stating a law for impulsive forces, not for continuous forces. Thus Newton's second law states quite correctly that an impulsive force – that is, a force acting instantaneously or nearly instantaneously, or acting in an infinitesimally small "particle" of time – produces a change in the "quantity of motion" or momentum.

Newton's discussion of this law, following its formal statement, leaves no doubt that this is the correct reading of Newton's intention. He says that the "effect" of the action of a force is the same "whether the force is applied at once or successively by degrees."

Consider the following example. Let an impulsive force F produce a certain change in momentum $\Delta(mV)$ and let that force be divided into three equal parts, each of which will produce a change in momentum $1/3\ mV$. Then, the successive application of these three forces will produce a corresponding total change in momentum of $3 \times 1/3 \times mV = mV$. The net change in momentum is the same whether the impacts are delivered seriatim or all at once. This makes perfect sense for impulsive forces, but has no meaning for continuous forces since the latter produce a net change of momentum that depends on both the magnitude of the force and the time during which the force acts.

This interpretation is further confirmed in Corollary 1 to the Laws. Here (see Figure 2.1), Newton considers a body struck by a blow. "Let a body in a given time," he writes, "by a force M impressed in A, be carried with uniform motion from A to B." Here is a plain case of an impulsive force generating a motion. After receiving the blow, the body then, according to Definition 4, "perseveres" in the "new state" by its "force of inertia."

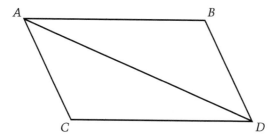

FIGURE 2.1 Newton's parallelogram rule for motions produced by impulsive forces.

In such statements as these, we can see the influence of Descartes. In explaining how refraction takes place, Descartes – in his *Dioptrique* (1637) – invokes an analogy with the motion of a tennis ball striking a body of water. At the moment of impact, at the interface between the air and the water, Descartes supposes, the ball is given a blow or is struck by an impulsive force. The ensuing motion, originating from the instantaneous action at the interface, is uniform and rectilinear, with a new magnitude and direction, as is the case in a refracted light beam.[18]

Of course, Newton knew the second law as a law for continuously acting forces. This form of the second law is implied in Definitions 7 and 8. In Book 2, Proposition 24, Newton writes that "the velocity that a given force can generate in a given time in a given quantity of matter is as the force and the time directly and the matter inversely." The factor of time shows that this is a case of the second law for continuous forces.[19]

A reason why Newton may have given priority to the impulsive form of the law rather than the continuous version is that in this case one can witness an act of impact or pressure. As we have noted, the most important class of continuous forces is in the orbital motion of planets, planetary satellites, and eventually comets. In each of these cases, the effect of the force is not associated with an observable physical act.

Another factor of importance is that Newton formed his dynamics in the context of the great advances in the science of motion made, during the decades before the *Principia*, by studies of impact – the work of such giants as Wallis, Wren, and Huygens. Descartes had set the scene in his *Principia*, which contained a series of statements about impacts which are wrong.

In the *Principia*, Newton described at length the experiments he himself had made on impact, including the distinction between elastic and non-elastic collisions. In short, the primacy given by Newton to impulsive forces would have been in keeping with the cutting edge of the science of motion in those days.

Yet it is a fact that the propositions of Book 1, beginning with the first group of propositions (Propositions 1–14), deal with varieties of centripetal force and orbital motions and not with impulsive forces. As we shall see shortly, in these opening propositions, Newton begins with a series of impulsive forces and effects a transition from a sequence of impulsive forces to a continuous force. Indeed, from Newton's point of view, the impact form of the second law led so readily into the continuous form that he did not even bother to state the continuous form as a separate entity. In other words, the distinction between the two forms of the law is more significant for us than it would have been for Newton.

THE THIRD LAW

Newton's third law has been characterized by Ernst Mach as the most original of the three laws of motion. It is the only one of the laws of motion that Newton did not allege had been known to Galileo. In fact, Newton had found the law some years before he composed the *Principia*.[20] As commonly stated, the third law declares that action is always equal and opposite to reaction. In Newton's own words, "To any action there is always an opposite and equal reaction."

This law, however, simple as it is, is easily subject to misinterpretation. For example, it is often mistakenly believed that this law provides for an equilibrium of two forces, the equal and oppositely directed action and reaction. But the law actually says that if a body A exerts a force F_a on body B, then body B will exert an equal and opposite force F_b on body A. There is no equilibrium because the forces F_a and F_b are exerted on different bodies, one on body A and the other on body B.

Newton himself apparently saw that this law might be subject to misinterpretation and so he included a second version in the statement of the third law. In "other words," he wrote, "the actions of two bodies upon each other are always equal and always opposite in direction."

In the discussion of the law, Newton says that it applies specifically to collisions. He shows the way in which this law is related to
the law of conservation of momentum, previously announced by the
mathematician John Wallis, and known to Huygens. He concludes
with the important statement that this "law is valid also for attractions, as will be proved in the next scholium."

WHY A SEPARATE LAW I AND LAW 2?

A number of critics and authors of textbooks on mechanics have criticized Newton for having a separate Law 1 and Law 2. After all, they
argue, if there is no net external force F, the second law (for continuous forces) implies that the acceleration A is zero and so there is no
change in a body's state. In the case of the impact form of the second
law, there is similarly no change in state.

There are two sets of reasons, however, why Newton had a
separate Law 1. First, in Newton's day – as during many preceding
centuries – the common belief was that all motion requires a mover,
a moving force. The very statement of this law as an axiom was a
radical step, a declaration of an important new principle of motion,
too important to be a special case of another law. Indeed, such a statement was possible only after Descartes's bold assertion that uniform
rectilinear motion can be considered a "state," thus existing without
a driving or motive external force.

Second, Newton's first two laws of motion depended heavily
on the prior statements of Descartes, Galileo, and Huygens. The
form in which Newton expressed the first law, including the choice
of language and the separate statement of Law 1 and Law 2, shows
the influence of Descartes's *Principia*, where these are part of the
"regulae quaedam sive leges naturae."

In the 1660s, some two decades before developing the mature
ideas expounded in the *Principia*, Newton had already seen how
basic was Descartes's law of inertia. He wrote out (in English) what
he called a series of "Axiomes and Propositions," of which the

first one reads: "If a quantity once move it will never rest unlesse hindered by some external caus." Another version reads as follows: "A quantity will always move on in the same streight line (not changing the determination nor celerity of its motion) unlesse some external caus divert it." He then started a new series of axioms, of which the first is labeled "Ax: 100." It reads: "Every thing doth naturally persevere in that state in which it is unlesse it bee interrupted by some externall caus, hence axiome 1st and 2nd." Note that, early on, he recognized the importance of Descartes's concept of uniform motion as a "state."[21]

An even more important reason why Newton had a separate Law 1 and Law 2 is that he was following the example set by Christiaan Huygens in his *Horologium Oscillatorium* of 1673, a work that Newton greatly admired. In the *Horologium*, Huygens axiomatized Galileo's rules for the motion of bodies such as projectiles, moving in the Earth's gravitational field. Huygens's first law (he calls these laws "Hypotheses") is that if there were no gravity and no resistance of air to motion, "any body will continue its motion with uniform velocity in a straight line."[22] Here is Newton's first law stated for a system in which the only possible forces are gravity and air resistance (and possibly some force that gets forward motions started, as in the firing of a projectile). That is, Huygens first considers a kind of inertial motion without falling. Then, in a second law, he allows such a moving body to be acted on by gravity so as to fall according to the laws of falling bodies. Although Huygens does not state his second law in the full generality found in the *Principia*, the model is structurally the same: first, an inertial motion in the absence of forces and then a new motion produced by the action of a force.

In the *Principia*, Newton added a statement about Galileo's discovery of the laws of projectile motion. According to Newton, Galileo did so by using the first two laws of motion. Thus Galileo would have been Newton's third source for a first and second law. There is no evidence, however, that Newton had ever read Galileo's *Two New Sciences* and his knowledge of Galileo's ideas must have come from secondary sources, such as the books of Kenelm Digby and John Anderson.

FROM IMPULSIVE FORCES TO CONTINUALLY ACTING FORCES

Newton's transition from the action of impulsive forces to the action of continuous forces occurs in the first proposition in the *Principia*. Here Newton's goal is to find the significance of Kepler's law of areas (which Newton does not attribute to Kepler).

Newton's proof starts out with a body (actually a mass point) moving freely with a component of linear inertial motion along a straight line. Newton shows (see Figure 2.2) that this motion is area-conserving, that is, a line drawn from the moving body to any point *P* (not on the line of motion) will sweep out equal areas in any equal times. Actually, this was a startling result. Here Newton revealed for the first time the link between the law of areas and the principle or law of inertia.

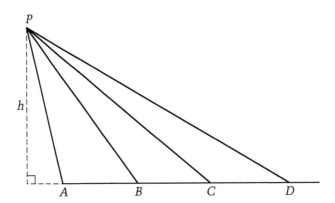

FIGURE 2.2 The area law for uniform rectilinear motion. *A* body moves with uniform motion along the straight line *ABCD* . . . Then in equal times the distances *AB*, *BC*, *CD* . . . will be equal. Therefore, a line from the moving body to any point *P* (not on the line of motion) will sweep out equal areas in any equal time intervals, since the triangles *ABP*, *BCP*, *CDP* . . . have a common altitude *h* and equal bases.

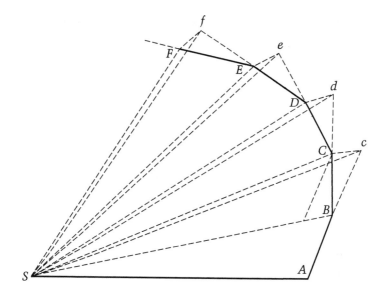

FIGURE 2.3 Newton's polygonal path (from the first edition of the *Principia*, 1687). During the first equal time-interval *T*, the body moves from *A* to *B*. At *B* it receives a thrust toward *S*. Had there not been such a thrust, the body would have moved in the second time *T* from *B* to *c*, where *Bc* = *AB*. But, as a result of the thrust, the body moves from *B* to *C*. By the parallelogram rule and simple geometry, Newton shows that the area of triangle *BSC* equals the area of triangle *BSc*. In this way Newton constructs the polygonal path *ABCDEF*...

Next, after a time interval *T*, the body is given an impulsive blow directed toward the point *P*. The body will now move on a new linear path, with a new velocity, according to the second law. By simple geometry (see Figure 2.3), Newton proves that the area swept out in time *T* by a line from the body to P will be the same along the new path as it was when the body moved from *A* to *B*. After the passage of another time *T*, the whole procedure is repeated. In this way, Newton produces a polygonal trajectory, each side corresponding to motion during a time interval *T* and each such side the base of a triangle; all such triangles have the same area.

At this point, Newton says, "Now, let the number of triangles be increased and their width decreased indefinitely," that is, without limit. Then he continues, "the ultimate perimeter ADF will (by lem. 3, corol. 4) be a curved line." In this way, "the centripetal force by which the body is continually drawn back from the tangent of this curve will act uninterruptedly." Furthermore, "any areas described, SADS and SAFS, which are always proportional to the times of description, will be proportional to those times in this case." In other words, Newton has essentially proved that a centrally directed force will always produce (or is a sufficient condition for) the law of areas. This example shows how Newton used his method of limits to make a transition from the action of a force consisting of a series of impulses to the action of a continuously acting force.

NEWTON'S SHIFT FROM A SECOND LAW FOR IMPULSIVE TO A SECOND LAW FOR CONTINUOUS FORCES – NEWTON'S CONCEPT OF TIME

In analyzing Book 1, Proposition 1 of the *Principia*, attention has been called to Newton's mode of transition from a series of impulses to a continuously acting force. This distinction between continuous and instantaneous forces was also seen in the statement of Law 2. But a careful reading of the *Principia* shows that the distinction between these forms of the second law, and the distinction between impulsive and continuous forces, did not have the same significance for Newton that it does for us.

In Newton's system of dynamics, the two concepts of force – continuous and impulsive – are linked by Newton's concept of time. That this should be so is hardly surprising since the difference between the two forms of force lies in the factor of time of action: a finite time for a continuous force and an infinitesimal time for an impulsive force. We make a distinction between them but Newton could effect an easy transition from one to the other, conceiving (as in Book 1, Propositions 1 and 4) a continuous force to be the limit of a sequence of impulses. Newton's procedure is troubling to us because there is a difference in dimensionality between the impulsive force, which we measure by $d(mV)$, and the continuous force, measured by $d(mV)/dt$. Thus if we were to write these two forms of the law as algebraic statements of proportion,

$$F = k_1 d(mV)$$
$$F = k_2 d(mV)/dt$$

it becomes at once obvious that k_1 and k_2 have different dimensionality. It is for this reason that we would write the first of these equations as

$$Fdt = k_1 d(mV).$$

This was not a problem for Newton, however, since he did not write proportions as algebraic equations and so was not concerned by the fact that if the force F has the same dimensionality in both forms of the second law, then the constants of proportionality must have different dimensionality.

Newton generally compared one value of a quantity with another rather than make computations that involve the numerical value of the constant of proportionality. Thus, in Book 3, Proposition 12, he compares the quantity of matter in the Sun to the quantity of matter in Jupiter but does not compute either quantity in terms of some fixed set of units such as pounds. In the Scholium to Book 2, Section 6, he writes of a globe encountering a resistance which is to its weight as 61,705 to 121. But he also makes some computations that, in effect, involve evaluating a constant of proportionality (although he does not use this form of expression). But he did not ever compute numerical values (with units of dimensionality) in which he had to be concerned about the difference in dimensional units that arise because of the two forms of the second law.

It is well known that in Newton's mathematics, as in his physics, time is the primary independent variable, the one on which all other quantities depend. Newton does not have an entry for time in the section of definitions in the *Principia*, merely saying in a Scholium that "time, place, space, and motion are very familiar to everyone." He then alerts the reader to "absolute, true, and mathematical time," which "without reference to anything external, flows uniformly."

It is, therefore, paradoxical that a consequence of Newton's concept of time as a uniform flow should be that it is composed of units (dt) which are essentially constant infinitesimal increments. And yet, in the *Principia*, Newton often writes of a "particle of time" ("particula temporis"). These are not finite atoms of time in the sense of tiny finite particles of matter. Rather, for Newton, time is finitely continuous and only infinitesimally discrete. Thus the "fluxional" character of the *Principia* depends in practice on a discrete kind of infinitesimal of time in which quantities do not really flow evenly or smoothly, but rather jerk, jerk along – to use a metaphor suggested by D. T. Whiteside. But this aspect of time appears only on an infinitesimal level so that to our finite eyes time appears to be flowing smoothly, as postulated by the method of first and ultimate ratios.

Thus, in Book 2, Proposition 2, Newton divides a time-interval into "equal particles" and eventually lets "the equal particles of time . . . be diminished and their number increased without limit" ("in infinitum"). On first encounter, such a passage gives rise to many problems because we would ask how a continuous flow of time could possibly be composed of discrete units, even infinitesimal ones. This post-Newtonian problem may serve as an index of the difficulties that arise in the use of infinitesimals.

In considering the consequences of Newton's concept of time, we may anachronistically (that is, by using the Leibnizian algorithm of the calculus) consider dt as Newton's constant infinitesimal unit of time. Thus dt represents the Newtonian concept of a primitive or fundamental "time," flowing uniformly at a constant rate everywhere, at all times, and under all conditions. Then it will follow at once that there are a number of equivalent forms of the second law as follows:

(1) $F \propto dV$

(2) $F \propto dV/dt = d^2s/dt^2$, where $V = ds/dt$

(3) $F \cdot dt \propto dV$

(4) $F \cdot dt^2 \propto d^2s$

where F is taken as the accelerative measure of force. The only difference between eq. (1), the impact form of the second law, and eqs. (2)–(4), the continuous form, is that there is a different dimensionality in the constant of proportion (not shown). That is, the constant dt can be absorbed in the constant of proportionality at will. In these equations, if the force is itself a variable, then F must be the average value during the time dt.

In considering these equations for a "force" F, it must be kept in mind, as mentioned previously, that Newton did not write equations of motion but rather expressed his principles as statements of proportion. Hence the constant of proportionality did not need to appear explicitly, nor did Newton need to have any regard for the dimensionality of the various forces he was studying. This was especially the case since Newton tended to compare one force with another rather than compute numerical values in some given system of units – which would have required a consideration of the physical dimensions of the computed quantities. We may thus understand how it was possible to hold simultaneously the validity of a second law symbolized by eq. (1) and a second law symbolized by eq. (3), whereas we would encounter a problem with the quantity "F" in eq. (1) and would consider an impulsive force to be $F\,dt$ rather than F.

A FINITE OR INFINITESIMAL LEVEL OF DISCOURSE?

A critical study of the *Principia* reveals that much of the discourse is pitched on an infinitesimal level. For example, in Book 1, Proposition 41, Newton introduces a ratio of a distance to a time, "the line-element IK, described in a minimally small time." These, clearly, are not a finite distance and time, as is evident from the terms "line-element" and "minimally small." In the language of the calculus, Newton is invoking an infinitesimal distance ds and an infinitesimal unit or "particle" of time dt. Thus the ratio in question is Newton's way of expressing what we would write in Leibnizian terms as ds/dt.

An admirable exposition of the infinitesimal character of Newton's dynamics has been given by D. T. Whiteside,[23] who has made a careful analysis of the proof of the area law in Book 1, Proposition 1, of the *Principia*, essentially the proof given in the prior tract "De motu." In this proof, as we have seen, the continuous curved trajectory is the limit of a polygonal path. In this process, according to Whiteside, Newton replaces the continually acting central force by the limit of "a series of component discrete impulses, each acting instantaneously but separated from its predecessor by a measurable if indefinitely small time-interval." Under these circumstances, Whiteside finds, the elements of force must be "of a second order of the infinitely small." Whiteside then notes that since dt^2 is a constant (a consequence of dt being a constant), Newton's proof of Proposition 1 would accordingly make use of the second law in a form expressed by a variant of our eq. (4),

$$F \propto d^2s$$

which would be another way of saying that the force impulse must be a second-order infinitesimal.[24]

A final example will show in a striking manner the importance of keeping in mind that much of the treatment of forces in the *Principia* is couched on an infinitesimal level. Newton's manuscripts show that in the early 1690s he was planning a new edition of the *Principia* in which he would revise his presentation of the second law. These attempts to alter the presentation of the second law are of special interest because there are no similar attempts to recast the presentation of Law 1 or Law 3.

In one set of these revisions, Newton writes of "a motion generated in a space either immobile or mobile," saying that such a motion "is proportional to the motive force impressed and occurs along the straight line in which that force is impressed." As the manuscript makes clear, Newton was thinking of a situation like Galileo's example of motion on a moving ship; Galileo compared the motion as seen by an observer on the ship with the motion as seen by an observer on the shore.

In the course of these revisions, Newton writes of the generated motion as follows:

> [it] has the same determination [i.e., direction] as the impressed force and occurs from that place in which the body, before the force was impressed upon it, was at rest either truly or at least relatively. And, therefore, if the body was moving before the impressed force, the generated motion is either added to the original motion or is subtracted from it if contrary or is added obliquely to it if oblique and is compounded with it in accordance with the direction of both.

Newton then proceeds to examine the manner in which the two oblique motions are compounded, that is, combined according to the laws of composition of velocities. In the oblique case, the resulting motion, Newton says, "is neither parallel to, nor perpendicular to, the original motion to which it is added."

In this paragraph Newton will have anticipated Corollary 1 to the laws by giving a proof of the method of composition of two motions. But there is a major difference. In Corollary 1 to the laws, two impulsive forces act either separately or simultaneously on a body at rest, whereas in this revision a single impulsive force acts by giving an oblique blow to a body in uniform motion.

This manuscript presents a problem, however, because although the original motion is explicitly said to be uniform ("uniformiter continuato"), the trajectory resulting from the action of the impulsive force or blow is not a straight line as we would have expected. Rather (see Figure 2.4), the new trajectory AB is curved, seeming to imply that the action did not simply generate a new straight-line motion, as Newton's text might have led us to expect. Rather, the effect of the force seems to be to produce an acceleration, as if the force had been continuously acting rather than having been an impulse.

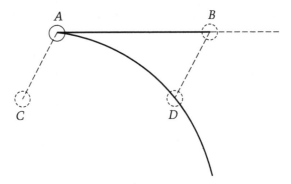

FIGURE 2.4 The trajectory of a moving body that has received a blow or has been struck by an impulsive force. There can be no doubt that the force is a thrust, an instaneous force, a force of impact, or a force of percussion, since the text reads that the imparted motion "is proportional to the force."

The trajectory AD, it should be noted, is the same parabola-like curve in three separate occurrences of the diagram. In none of these is the curve the result of a carelessly drawn free-hand diagram. AD is simply not the diagonal of a parallelogram of forces. Hence, the conclusion must be that Newton was thinking of a trajectory produced by a continuous force, even though the text indicates that the force is an impulse, an instantaneous blow.

Our bewilderment arises from our having assumed that these manuscript texts were conceived on a finite rather than an infinitesimal level. In the proposed revisions of the second law, Newton was dealing with the effects of a blow or instantaneous force, that is, an infinitesimal force-impulse acting in an infinitesimal time-unit δt. If we now divide that infinitesimal time-unit δt into sub-units or parts $(\delta t/n)$, then the limit of the initial condition of the proposed revisions of Law 2 (as $n \to \infty$) will correspond to a sequence of infinitely small quantities (which are infinitesimals of a higher order) of time. It is on such an infinitesimal level, but not on a finite level (and only on an infinitesimal level), that the two modes of action of an impulse – Newton's "simul et semel" and "gradatim et successive" – produce the effects illustrated by Newton within the framework of the stated Law 2 of the *Principia*.[25]

This analysis would accord with Newton's statement concerning the two ways in which a given force-impulse may act. Thus an impulse P may in an instant produce a change in motion (or momentum), acting – as Newton says – "altogether and at once." Alternatively, the impulse P can be considered as composed of a succession of infinitesimal force-impulses. This is the mode of action that Newton calls "by degrees and successively." The difference between the two lies in the mode of conceiving the actual production of the change in motion. In the first case, there is an instantaneous change that can occur in the direction and magnitude of the motion. In the second, there is a succession of infinitesimal blows that in the limit produce a curved motion, whose final direction and magnitude is the same as in the first case.

THE REALITIES OF FORCE – THE NEWTONIAN STYLE

Newton came to believe in the existence of forces that could produce curved or orbital motion without contact, thereby holding a drastically revised form of the then-current mechanical philosophy. In effect he now enlarged the basis of explanation from effects produced by matter and motion, adding the further concept of force. In the *Principia*, he avoided this issue as long as possible by starting out on a mathematical level in which he did not need to consider the physical aspects of his concepts. Thus the first ten sections of Book 1 explore a purely mathematical problem: the motions of bodies attracted to a mathematical point. These are mathematical bodies in so far as there are no considerations of mass, no physical dimensions, and no physical properties such as hardness. In the opening of Section 11 of Book 1, Newton states clearly that in the preceding sections he has "been setting forth the motions of bodies attracted toward an immovable center, such as, however, hardly exists in the natural world," where "attractions are always directed toward bodies." Newton, in other words, stated as clearly as possible that this opening part of Book 1 was a work of mathematics. Even though he had used the verb "to attract," he was not (in Book 1) concerned with a physical force of attraction, with an attractive force of gravity.

Some readers, especially on the Continent, did not take Newton at his word and did not read Book 1 as a work of "mathematical principles." In the early eighteenth century, Fontenelle argued that, no matter what Newton said, the word "attraction" implied a force of a kind that is unacceptable in discussions of physics, of "natural philosophy." This same charge has been repeated in our times by Alexandre Koyré.[26] The reviewer of the first *Principia* in the *Journal des Sçavans* could quite legitimately say that Newton had produced a work on "mechanics" but not "physics."

Since the primary difference between the subject of the first ten sections of Book 1 and the world of nature is that in the world of nature forces orginate in bodies, Newton – in Section 11 – introduces the mathematics of two-body systems. These, however, are not as yet "real" or physical bodies in the full sense. That is, they are not characterized by such physical properties as size, shape, degree of hardness, and so on. From a two-body system Newton next advances to a system of three mutually attracting bodies. Every reader would recognize that Newton's mathematical construct is getting more and more closely to resemble the physical universe. And indeed, in the twenty-two corollaries of Book 1, Proposition 66, Newton indicates how his study of three interacting bodies will eventually be related to the motion of the Moon. The diagram has a central body labeled T (for Terra or Earth), about which there moves in orbit a satellite or secondary planet P whose motion is being perturbed by a body marked S (Sol or Sun).

I have called this mode of studying successive mathematical constructs "the Newtonian style." Basically it consists of starting out with a simple mathematical "system," a mass point moving in orbit about a mathematical center of force toward which it is attracted. Among the properties of this "system" developed mathematically by

Newton are that Kepler's law of areas is a necessary and sufficient condition for motion in a central force field and that Kepler's law of elliptical orbits implies that the central force varies inversely as the square of the distance. Similarly, Newton shows that in a two-body system, each of the bodies will move around the common center of gravity.

Of course Newton's goal is eventually to get to the dynamics of the system of the world. But he makes it abundantly clear that in Book 1 he is primarily concerned with elaborating the properties of mathematical systems that have features resembling those found in nature. And here he makes an important distinction between mathematics and physics. In this way, Newton is free to develop the properties of mathematical forces of attraction without having to face the great problem of whether such forces can actually exist or can be considered an element of acceptable physics. This distinction is stressed by Newton in a concluding statement to Book 1, Section 11.[27]

As Newton proceeds step-by-step, he introduces into the mathematical system one-by-one such further properties as will make the system more and more closely resemble what we observe in the world of nature. Thus he considers the properties of bodies with physical shapes, for example bodies composed of a sequence of homogeneous spherical shells. Eventually, in Book 2, he will add another set of conditions found in the world of nature – various kinds of resisting mediums.

The essence of the "Newtonian style" is this sequence of adding one by one the conditions resembling those of the world of nature. The goal is to produce eventually a dynamics that will apply to the external world, to elaborate the properties of a mathematical system that will closely resemble the world of nature. This style has a number of advantages for Newton. The most important is that it permits him to explore the mathematical consequences of his assumptions one by one without having to face the impossible task of analyzing the properties of the complex physical world all at once. Furthermore, if we accept Newton's position, expressly stated in Book 1, Section 11, we can study the effects of forces of attraction without having to face the inhibiting fact that the reigning natural philosophy, the "mechanical philosophy," will not consider acceptable the concept of a force that is not the result of a material push or pull, that is not the result of some kind of contact between bodies.

Of course, it would have been obvious to every reader that Newton's goal was to display and analyze the physics of planetary motion. In the end, he would show that the celestial phenomena declare the action of an inverse-square force and he would boldly assert that this force is gravity, by which he means the force (whatever its cause) that produces weight here on Earth and that he can show must extend as far out as the Moon.

Newton himself was troubled by the idea of a universal gravitating force extending through space, and he tried again and again to find a way to account for its action. But, as he explained in the final General Scholium, he had no doubt that a force of universal gravity "really" exists. Newton did not disparage attempts to explain how gravity might act, but he believed that such considerations should not inhibit the use of the concept of universal gravity. His successors – including such giants as Euler, Clairaut, d'Alembert, Lagrange, and above all Laplace – were not inhibited by concerns about the nature of a force like universal gravity, and thus they found new principles and tremendously enlarged the subject that Newton had explored in the *Principia*.[28]

NOTES

1 All translations from the *Principia* in this chapter come from Isaac Newton, *The Principia, Mathematical Principles of Natural Philosophy: A New Translation*, trans. I. Bernard Cohen and Anne Whitman (Berkeley, CA: University of California Press, 1999), containing a "Guide to Newton's *Principia*" by I. B. Cohen.

2 On Newton's concepts of force, see Richard S. Westfall, *Force in Newton's Physics: The Science of Dynamics in the Seventeenth Century* (London: Macdonald; New York: American Elsevier, 1971); Max Jammer, *Concepts of Force* (Cambridge, MA: Harvard University Press, 1957). On Newton's

concept of force in the *Principia*, see Bruce Brackenridge, *The Key to Newton's Dynamics: The Kepler Problem and the Principia* (Berkeley, CA: University of California Press, 1995); vol. 6 of D. T. Whiteside (ed.), *The Mathematical Papers of Isaac Newton*, 8 vols. (Cambridge: Cambridge University Press, 1967–81); François de Gandt, *Force and Geometry in Newton's Principia*, trans. Curtis Wilson (Princeton, NJ: Princeton University Press, 1995); and my "Guide to Newton's *Principia*"; also my "Newton's Concept of Force and the Second Law," pp. 143–85 in Robert P. Palter (ed.), *The Annus Mirabilis of Sir Isaac Newton 1666–1966* (Cambridge, MA: MIT Press, 1970) and my *The Newtonian Revolution* (Cambridge: Cambridge University Press, 1980).

3 Here and there in the *Principia*, Newton introduces some other types of force, among them magnetic force (said in Book 3, Proposition 6, Corollary 5, to be as the inverse cube of the distance), a general force of attraction that is as the inverse cube of the distance (Book 1, Proposition 41, Corollary 3), and a hypothesized force of repulsion between particles of an "elastic fluid" (or compressible gas) inversely proportional to the distance between adjacent, proximate particles (Book 2, Proposition 23).

4 In his thinking about the forces of nature, Newton also developed the concept of "passive" and "active" forces. On this topic, see J. E. McGuire, "Force, Active Principles, and Newton's Invisible Realm," *Ambix* 15 (1968) 154–208, and "Neoplatonism, Active Principles and the Corpus Hermeticum," pp. 93–142 of Robert S. Westman and J. E. McGuire, *Hermeticism and the Scientific Revolution* (Los Angeles, CA: William Andrews Clark Memorial Library, University of California, 1977). See, further, Betty Jo Teeter Dobbs, *The Janus Faces of Genius: The Role of Alchemy in Newton's Thought* (Cambridge: Cambridge University Press, 1991).

5 Alan Cook, *Edmond Halley: Charting the Heavens and the Seas* (Oxford: Clarendon Press, 1998), p. 151.

6 This translation was first proposed by Alexandre Koyré and later confirmed by I. B. Cohen.

7 Ernst Mach, *The Science of Mechanics: A Critical and Historical Account of Its Development*, trans. Thomas J. McCormack, 6th edn, with revisions from the 9th German edn (La Salle, IL: Open Court, 1960), ch. 2, §7: "As we can only define density as the mass of unit volume, the circle is manifest."

8 But such criticism ignores Newton's own statement. Newton does *not* say that mass "is proportional to" the product of density and volume. The verb, as we have seen, is "oriri" in the form "orta est," meaning "arises from." If Newton had intended to say that a body's mass is jointly proportional to its volume and density, he would have done so. Such statements of joint proportionality are not uncommon in the *Principia*.

9 Furthermore, in Newton's day, densities were usually given as relative numerical quantities rather than as independent values. Thus John Harris, in his *Lexicon Technicum* of 1704, follows Newton in giving relative densities of substances, for example "the Density of Water to Air" or "the Density of Quick-Silver to Water." Newton himself, in Book 2, Part 3, Proposition 10, of the *Opticks* (1704), describes how density is to be determined. The "Densities of the Bodies," he writes, are to be "estimated by their Specifick Gravities." There follows a table in which one column gives "The density and specifick gravity of the Body."

10 See my *Introduction to Newton's "Principia"* (Cambridge, MA: Harvard University Press; Cambridge: Cambridge University Press, 1971), ch. 4, §3.

11 I have translated *vis insita* by "inherent force," which seems to be Newton's equivalent term in English, but others have rendered it as "innate force." See my *Introduction*, chs. 3, 5.

12 *Vis insita* also appears in the writings of Kepler, notably in the *Astronomia Nova* and in the *Epitome Astronomiae Copernicanae*, but we have no evidence that Newton had read either of these Keplerian works before composing the *Principia*. See, further, my *Introduction* and "Guide."

13 For details see my "Guide," pp. 101–2.

14 On the choice of "uniformly straight forward" rather than the traditional "uniformly in a straight line," see the new translation cited above.

15 On the identity of phrases used by Newton and Descartes, see my *Introduction*.

16 Although Newton's example is a sound one, in accord with the accepted principles of physics, it was willfully misunderstood by Clifford Truesdell, who alleged that Newton was here expressing a belief in a kind of "circular inertia."

17 For example, W. W. Rouse Ball, *An Essay on Newton's Principia* (London: Macmillan and Co., 1893), p. 77: "The rate of change of momentum [per unit of time] is always proportional to the moving force impressed." In order to indicate that he was giving a modern paraphrase

of what Newton wrote, Rouse Ball enclosed his insertion in square brackets.

18 For details see my paper in the *Annus Mirabilis* volume, cited in note 2 *supra*.

19 In other words, a speed V is proportional to the force and time and inversely proportional to the mass of the body in question. If t is the time in which a velocity V is generated in a mass m by a force F, then

$$V = (1/k) \times Ft/m$$

where k is a constant of proportionality. In this case,

$$F = km(V/t)$$

where V/t is the acceleration A. Plainly, Newton knew the second law for continuous forces. As we shall see below, Newton showed how to get from the second law as stated for impulsive forces to the continuous form of the law.

20 See the notes by Whiteside in his edition of Newton's *Mathematical Papers*, vol. 6, pp. 98–9 (n. 16), 148–9 (n. 152).

21 Quoted in full in my *Newtonian Revolution*, pp. 183–4; see John W. Herivel, *The Background to Newton's Principia: A study of Newton's Dynamical Researches in the Years 1664–84* (Oxford: Clarendon Press, 1965), pp. 141, 153.

22 Christiaan Huygens, *The Pendulum Clock*, trans. Richard J. Blackwell (Ames, IA: Iowa State University Press, 1986).

23 D. T. Whiteside, "Newtonian Dynamics," *History of Science* 5 (1966), 104–17.

24 For a different view, see the chapter by Brackenridge and Nauenberg on curvature in Newton's dynamics in the first edition of the *Companion to Newton*, p. 132 n.30.

25 In my discussions of this question with D. T. Whiteside, he has pointed out that there are two possibilities which lead to "*exactly* the same theory of central forces." One, favored by Leibniz, is that on a finite level "the orbit is built up of a series of infinitesimal discrete force-impulses." The other, Newton's favored approach, is that there is a "series of infinitesimal arcs generated by a continuous force (composed of infinitesimal discrete force-impulses)." The first is what Newton in 1687 and afterwards called "simul et semel," the latter being "gradatim et successive."

26 Alexandre Koyré, *Newtonian Studies* (Cambridge, MA: Harvard University Press; London: Chapman & Hall, 1965).

27 This concluding statement is examined in detail in George Smith's chapter in this volume.

28 At the time of the second edition of the *Principia* (1713), Newton had hopes that a physical cause of the action of gravity might be found in the study of electricity; see A. Rupert Hall and Marie Boas Hall, *Unpublished Scientific Papers of Isaac Newton* (Cambridge: Cambridge University Press, 1962), pp. 361–2 and my "Guide," pp. 280–7. Also see Henry Guerlac's studies on Newton and Francis Hauksbee's electrical experiments in his *Essays and Papers in the History of Modern Science* (Baltimore, ML: Johns Hopkins University Press, 1977). In the 1717–18 edition of the *Opticks*, Query 21, Newton expressed the thought that the cause of gravity might be an "aetherial medium" of varying density.

3 Instantaneous impulse and continuous force: the foundations of Newton's *Principia*

Bruce Pourciau

I INTRODUCTION

According to a long and established tradition of Newtonian scholarship, the *Principia*[1] has a foundation of sand and fog, with crucial parts of the early foundational sections – on the measurement of centripetal forces, on the second law of motion, on limits and ultimate ratios, on orbital motion about an immovable center, on the transition between discrete impulses and continuous force – seen as supplying more questions and confusions than clarity and rigor. This received view of the *Principia*'s foundations, as muddled, unnatural, inconsistent, and full of holes, has become entrenched, by the weight of the supporting scholarship, the gravitas of the scholars supporting it, and the passing of years.

Nevertheless, this received view is a distortion. Definitions left ambiguous or absent by Newton have led to the misinterpretation of fundamental concepts in the *Principia*, which in turn has led first to the misreading of fundamental laws, theorems, and arguments, and then to the mischaracterization of the foundations. Yet once the meanings that Newton intended have been uncovered – for a finite, continuous, or centripetal force; for the "motive force" and "change in motion" in the second law; for the second law itself; for an ultimate ratio; for the motion of a "bod[y] made to move in orbit" in Proposition 1; and for the "centripetal force" and "sagitta" in Proposition 6 – then a radically different view of Newton's foundational work emerges, one in which his handling of these basic

93

concepts is far more assured, coherent, natural, and correct than the received view would have us believe. Getting the intended meanings right profoundly alters the way we see the *Principia*.

Consider for example the *Principia*'s second law of motion: *A change in motion is proportional to the motive force impressed and takes place along the straight line in which that force is impressed.* In the received view, this law is seen as applying directly only to an instantaneous impulse (the mathematical representation of an instantaneous blow) and to a continuous force only indirectly via a (non-trivial) approximation by impulses in series. Under this interpretation, Newton's Law 2 would owe more to the impacts of Descartes than the continuous accelerations of Galileo and Huygens. But in fact the impulse-only interpretation is a *mis*interpretation, and the actual situation is just the reverse: Law 2 owes far more to Galileo and Huygens, for it is a direct descendent, indeed a natural generalization, of an explicit assumption in the *Discorsi* and Hypotheses II and III in the *Horologium oscillatorium*.

On manuscript pages penned by Newton in the early 1690s[2] and containing various revisions, some little some large, which were planned for but (mostly) never made it into the second (1713) edition, we find a passage and an accompanying figure that make the intended meaning of the *Principia*'s second law crystal clear:

> If the body *A* should, at its place *A* where a force is impressed upon it, have a motion by which, when uniformly continued, it would describe the straight line *Aa*, but by the impressed force be deflected from this line into another one *Ab* and, when it ought to be located at the place *a*, be found at the place *b*, then, because the body, free of the impressed force, would have occupied the place *a* and is thrust out from this place by that force and transferred therefrom to the place *b*, the translation of the body from the place *a* to the place *b* will, *in the meaning of this Law*, be proportional to this force and directed to the same goal towards which this force is impressed.

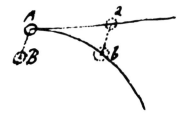

Whence, if the same body deprived of all motion and
impressed by the same force with the same direction, could
in the same time be transported from the place A to the place
B, the two straight lines AB and ab will be parallel and equal.
For the same force, by acting with the same direction and in
the same time on the same body whether at rest or carried on
with any motion whatever, will *in the meaning of this Law*
achieve an identical translation towards the same goal; and in
the present case the translation is AB where the body is at rest
before the force was impressed, and ab where it was there in a
state of motion.[3]

A commentator committed to an impulse-only interpretation
of Law 2 is forced to "explain away" Newton's figure, which very
clearly shows the smoothly curved trajectory of a body moving with
a continuous acceleration, by seeing this smooth motion as a limit of
polygonal motions, with each polygonal motion generated by a series
of instantaneous impulses. But of course this is totally unnatural, for
it turns the figure, obviously intended to be a *simple illustration* of
the *Principia*'s second law, into a *complicated application* of that law.
In a far more natural interpretation, we instead take the smoothly
curved trajectory as illustrating *one case* of the second law and infer
that the second law was intended by Newton to apply *directly* to a
continuous force. (From other evidence, Corollary 1 of the laws for
example, we know the second law was intended to apply directly to
an instantaneous impulse as well.) Newton writes "in the meaning
[*mente*] of this Law" twice, to stress that his description gives the

very meaning of Law 2 and *not* merely some application of that law. And the meaning is this:

> COMPOUND SECOND LAW. (The *Principia*'s Second Law as Newton Understood It) *A given impressed force (continuous or impulsive) acting on a given body generates in a given time the same deflection, whether the body is in motion or at rest:* $\overrightarrow{ab} = \overrightarrow{AB}$.[4]

Note that the "resting deflection" $\overrightarrow{AB}$ is the result of a thought experiment. Some impressed force (i.e., some "thrust" or "pull") acts on the moving body at A and generates in a given time the "moving deflection" $\overrightarrow{ab}$. The resting deflection $\overrightarrow{AB}$, generated in the same given time, is then the imagined result of having *this same impressed force* (this same "thrust") act on the same body *at rest at A*. It is crucial to understand that $\overrightarrow{AB}$ is *not* defined as the deflection that would have been observed had we placed the body at rest at A in its environment (a force field or resisting fluid, say) and watched what happened.

Once we come to understand the second law as Newton himself understood it, as the Compound Second Law, our view of the *Principia*'s foundations will conflict dramatically with the received view, for the problems seen in those foundations from the received view, at least those associated with the second law, will vanish. Here we provide just one example. Under the standard impulse-only interpretation, the second law appears unexpected and unnatural, as an assertion about impulses surrounded in the *Principia* by examples that involve continuous forces, examples that could be related to an impulse-only second law only via a complicated approximation by impulses in series, while under Newton's own interpretation the second law becomes completely natural, in two senses: it is precisely the law one would expect as a sequel to the first law, for it tells us we can measure an impressed force by the deflection it generates, and it is the obvious generalization, from surface gravity to any force, of Hypotheses II and III in *Horologium oscillatorium*, the magnum opus of Huygens, a work Newton read closely and greatly admired. Let us explain the first of these senses, leaving the second for later.

According to Law 1, a deflection $\overrightarrow{ab}$ from uniform straight line motion signals the presence of an impressed force. This impressed force is a specific "action," intuitively a specific "thrust" or "pull." To impress this meaning upon us, let us for the moment replace "impressed force" by "thrust." What could be more natural than to measure the direction and magnitude of this given thrust by the direction and length of the deflection $\overrightarrow{ab}$ it generates? But suppose *one and the same thrust* could generate (in a given time on a given body) one deflection $\overrightarrow{ab}$ when the body is in motion and a different deflection $\overrightarrow{AB}$ when the body is at rest. Then the deflection would be no measure of the thrust at all, since a *fixed* thrust could then have one direction and magnitude (as measured by $\overrightarrow{ab}$) when it acts on a body in motion and a different direction or magnitude (as measured by $\overrightarrow{AB}$) when it acts on the same body at rest. Of course this would violate our understanding of a fixed thrust: a fixed thrust must have a fixed direction and a fixed magnitude. Consequently, to ensure that the deflection $\overrightarrow{ab}$ can be used to measure the thrust that generates that deflection, one must assume that the deflection generated by the *given* thrust is the same (in direction and length), whether the body is in motion or at rest, that is, one must assume the Compound Second Law: $\overrightarrow{ab} = \overrightarrow{AB}$.[5] Thus the *Principia*'s second law, understood as Newton himself understood it, is the obvious and natural sequel to the first law, for the first law tells us an observed deflection signals the *presence* of a given impressed force (i.e., a given "thrust" or "pull"), while the second law tells us we can use that deflection to *measure* the given impressed force.

What follows is our attempt to get the intended meanings right, not just for the second law, but for many of the most basic concepts and assertions treated in the first four sections of the *Principia* – *Definitions*, *Axioms*, *The Method of First and Ultimate Ratios*, *To Find Centripetal Forces* – and then, in light of those meanings, to re-evaluate the clarity, coherence, and correctness of Newton's work in these foundational sections. This study will take us from Newton's definitions for ultimate ratios and finite, continuous, impulsive, and centripetal forces, through his measures of centripetal force and the second law of motion, and on into the approximation of continuous force by impulses and the meanings of and arguments for the fundamental Propositions 1 and 6.

2   FIRST THINGS

2.1   *Motions*

Across the pages of the *Principia*, bodies move: from the first proposition of Book 1, where "bodies [are] made to move in orbit," to the last proposition of Book 2, where "bodies are carried along in a vortex," to the final two propositions of Book 3, which "determine the trajectory of a comet moving in a parabola." And when a body moves, there corresponds to each time a position in space.

DEFINITION. A *motion* is a correspondence (that is, a function) $t \to P(t)$ that to each time t assigns a location $P(t)$ in space. The curve traced out or traversed by a motion is called its *trajectory*. For a centripetal motion – defined later – the trajectory is sometimes called the *orbit*.

The word "motion" (*motus*) has multiple meanings in the *Principia*. It can mean momentum, either linear momentum (as in Definition 2 for "quantity of motion" [*Principia*, p. 404]) or a kind of vector momentum (as in the "change in motion" [*Principia*, p. 416] in Newton's own interpretation of Law 2, which we take up in Section 5.1); it can mean a change in position, as in the famous scholium to the Definitions on time, space, and motion; and it can mean a correspondence between times and locations for a body moving along a curve in space, as in the titles to Sections 3 and 6 (Book 1): "The motions of bodies in eccentric conic sections" and "To find motions in given orbits." We shall be using the word "motion" in this final sense, a correspondence $t \to P(t)$ between times and positions, as recorded in the definition given above.

Intuitively, we think of a given motion $t \to P(t)$ as the record of a particular "trip" and its trajectory as the "route" of that trip.

An example might help to make this distinction more clear: the two *different motions* $t \to (\cos t, \sin t, 0)$ and $t \to (\cos t^2, \sin t^2, 0)$ both traverse the *same trajectory*, namely the unit circle, the first with constant speed, the second with increasing speed. Keeping this distinction in mind, between a motion and its trajectory, helps to clarify much of what goes on in the *Principia*, especially in Book 1. For example, when Newton supposes a "bod[y] made to move in orbit" in the fundamental Proposition 1, he is supposing a *motion*, a particular sort of motion (one that "move[s] in orbit" about "an unmoving center of forces"), but still a motion. While that given motion traverses a certain trajectory – the given "trip" traverses a certain "route" – it is the motion, and not merely its trajectory, which is given in the hypothesis of Proposition 1. Consider also Proposition 30 (Problem 22) which opens Section 6: "*If a body moves in a given parabolic trajectory, to find its position at an assigned time,*" in other words, given a particular parabola, to find the time–position correspondence, that is, to find the *motion*, which has the given parabola as its trajectory. Of course, infinitely many different motions can traverse this given parabola, but two implicitly understood constraints in this problem make the motion sought unique: the motion must be centripetal about the given focus (so by Proposition 1 its radius from that focus must sweep out areas proportional to the times) and the motion must leave the vertex of the given parabola with a given speed.

Newton carefully observes a body's motion to detect and classify any impressed force (intuitively, any "thrust" or "pull") acting on that body. Let a body moving with the motion $t \to P(t)$ come to the place P at a time t_0. This body, had its speed and direction at P been uniformly continued, would have described the line segment PL in a given brief time h, but instead suppose the body describes the arc segment (or possibly line segment) PQ in that time. Then the directed line segment $\overrightarrow{LQ}$, called here the "moving deflection," measures the deviation from uniform straight line motion during the time interval from t_0 to $t_0 + h$. When this moving deflection is nonzero, the first law of motion predicts the presence of an impressed force. How fast the moving deflection $\overrightarrow{LQ}$ tends toward zero as h tends toward zero determines what kind of impressed force – a finite force or an instantaneous impulse – acts at P, the direction that $\overrightarrow{LQ}$ tends toward determines the direction of this force at P, and, as we shall see, the second law of motion (as Newton understood it) ensures that these characterizations of the impressed force are *stable*, in the sense of being, for a given impressed force, independent of the speed and direction of the body at P and therefore dependent only on the given impressed force.

Clearly the moving deflection $\overrightarrow{LQ}$ *does* tend toward zero as the time increment $h \to 0$, which makes it, in Newton's words, an "evanescent quantity," and the reasons we have just given make it the most fundamental evanescent quantity in the *Principia*.

2.2 Evanescent quantities

The mathematical analysis in the *Principia* abounds with evanescent quantities (quantities that tend toward zero) and their ratios. Open to almost any demonstration – the argument for Proposition 10, Book 2, to pick just one – and you see them (*Principia*, p. 657):

> . . . since gravity generates the velocity $\frac{2NI}{t}$ in the same time in a falling body, the resistance will be to the gravity as $\frac{GH}{T} - \frac{HI}{t} + \frac{2MI \times NI}{t \times HI}$ to $\frac{2NI}{t}$ . . .

Here the quantities $\frac{GH}{T} - \frac{HI}{t} + \frac{2MI \times NI}{t \times HI}$ and $\frac{2NI}{t}$ are each evanescent (as the brief time intervals T and t tend toward zero), and the Newtonian code "will be . . . as" signals that their ratio tends toward a non-zero, finite limit.

In general, Newton calls a quantity $A(h)$ that depends on h eva-nescent[6] if $A(h)$ tends toward zero as h tends toward zero, that is, if in Newton's own words, $A(h)$ can be made "less than any given quantity" (*Principia*, p. 442) by choosing h sufficiently small. Given two evanescent quantities $A(h)$ and $B(h)$, Newton writes that $A(h)$ *will be as* $B(h)$ to mean the ratio $A(h)/B(h)$ tends toward a non-zero, finite limit. Intuitively, one might regard such quantities as being

"proportional in the limit." The variations seen in the *Principia* –
will be as, is as, is ultimately as – all mean the same thing. The limit
of the ratio $A(h)/B(h)$ is called the *ultimate ratio* – an unfortunate
name, because the limit of such a ratio is not in fact a ratio, but only
the quantity toward which the ratio tends. Sometimes the "$A(h)$ *will
be as* $B(h)$" limit language is used when the quantities $A(h)$ and $B(h)$
have not just magnitude, but *direction*. For example, $A(h)$ and $B(h)$
might be (essentially) directed line segments, and in such cases the
words "will be as" signal not just that $\vec{A}(h)$ and $\vec{B}(h)$ have lengths
that are "proportional in the limit" but also that $\vec{A}(h)$ and $\vec{B}(h)$ have
directions that are "parallel in the limit," the latter meaning that the
directed line segments become more and more nearly parallel (with
the same sense of direction) as $h \to 0$.

The conclusion of Proposition 6 (Book 1) – "*the centripetal
force in the middle of the arc will be as the sagitta directly and as
the time twice* [*i.e., as the square of the time*] *inversely*" (*Principia*,
p. 454) – nicely illustrates this fuller vectorial meaning of the "will be
as" language. Whatever Newton means by the "centripetal force" and
the "sagitta" (and we will uncover his intended meanings in Sections
4 and 9), these quantities, generated in a small time increment h, certainly have both direction and magnitude. Denoting the "centripetal
force" and "sagitta," respectively, by $\vec{F}(h)$ and $\vec{S}(h)$, and their magnitudes by $F(h)$ and $S(h)$, Proposition 6 asserts *two* limit statements,
both as $h \to 0$: first that

$$\frac{F(h)}{S(h)/h^2} \to k$$

where k is finite and non-zero, and second that the direction
of the sagitta $\vec{S}(h)$ tends toward the direction of the centripetal
force $\vec{F}(h)$.

Why *does* the *Principia* abound with the ratios of evanescent quantities? One answer is this: much of the analysis in the
Principia is essentially calculus (generally dressed in geometric garb),[7] and every derivative is the limit of a ratio of evanescent

quantities. For example, the derivative of tan x is $\sec^2 x$, and at $x=0$ this means that

$$\frac{\tan{(0+h)} - \tan 0}{h} = \frac{\tan h}{h} \to \sec^2 0 = 1$$

as $h \to 0$. Newton would say that tan h *is as* h or, more specifically, since here the limit happens to be 1, that the "ultimate ratio of [tan h to h] is the ratio of equality" (*Principia*, p. 436). Actually, he would and did say something more geometric and more general:

> LEMMA 7. *With the same suppositions, I say that the ultimate ratios of the arc [ACB], the chord [AB], and the tangent [AD] to one another are ratios of equality.* [*Principia*, p. 436]

For the case of a *circular* arc, the arc and tangent in Lemma 7 have lengths proportional to h and tan h; thus the lemma does indeed generalize the limit statement $\frac{\tan h}{h} \to 1$.[8]

But over and above the notion of derivative, taking the limit of a ratio of evanescent quantities lets Newton compare *how fast* the quantities tend toward zero. For instance, we can gauge how fast the evanescent quantity $1 - \cos h$ tends toward 0 (as $h \to 0$ with $h > 0$) by comparing it to the evanescent quantities h, h^2, and h^3, which tend toward 0 increasingly fast:

$$\frac{1-\cos h}{h} \to 0 \qquad \frac{1-\cos h}{h^2} \to \frac{1}{2} \qquad \frac{1-\cos h}{h^3} \to +\infty$$

These limits tell us that $1 - \cos h$ tends toward 0 faster than h, at the same rate as h^2, and slower than h^3. Newton would write that $1 - \cos h$ *will be as* h^2 (as $h \to 0$).[9] From the middle limit statement above, we have the close approximation $1 - \cos h \approx \frac{1}{2}h^2$ for all h sufficiently small; so we can also think of the Newtonian code "will

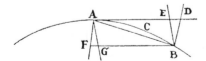

FIGURE 3.1 The figure illustrating Lemma 7 in the *Principia*.

be as" as signaling an "ultimate proportion": $1 - \cos h$ is essentially proportional to h^2 for sufficiently small h. Of course it does not matter that the limit of the ratio happens to be $\frac{1}{2}$, only that the limit is non-zero and finite.

A general concluding comment about Newton and the notion of limit: The received view from historians of mathematics paints Newton as vague and confused in his understanding and handling of limits. To provide evidence for this view, some have cherry-picked from the *Principia*'s discussion of limits in the scholium that ends Section 1, citing, for example, the following description (*Principia*, p. 442), where Newton addresses the ratios of evanescent quantities and specifically the limits of those ratios, limits which he calls "ultimate ratios" or "ultimate proportions":

> It may be objected that there is no such thing as an ultimate proportion of vanishing quantities, inasmuch as before vanishing the proportion is not ultimate, and after vanishing it does not exist at all. But by the same argument it could equally be contended that there is no ultimate velocity of a body reaching a certain place at which the motion ceases; for before the body arrives at this place, the velocity is not the ultimate velocity, and when it arrives there, there is no velocity at all. But the answer is easy: to understand the ultimate velocity as that with which a body is moving, neither before it arrives at its ultimate place and the motion ceases, nor after it has arrived there, but at the very instant when it arrives, that is, the very velocity with which the body arrives at its ultimate place and with which the motion ceases. And similarly the ultimate ratio of vanishing quantities is to be understood not as the ratio of quantities before they vanish or after they have vanished, but the ratio with which they vanish.

It would be a serious error to take this passage as Newton's definition or best understanding of the limit concept, rather than what it really is: just an intuitive description, with the aim being to provide a somewhat vague but very useful physical intuition for an "ultimate ratio." Newton's actual definition, his best understanding, comes a few lines later: "ultimate ratios . . . are not actually ratios of ultimate quantities, but limits which the ratios . . . approach so closely that their difference is less than any given quantity."

It is often said, and justifiably, that Cauchy gave us the first $\varepsilon - \delta$ arguments to establish limits. In this definition of Newton's, the δ may be hiding but the ε is certainly not, for "less than any given quantity" means "less than any given ε." According to this definition, a ratio $A(h)/B(h)$ of evanescent quantities – meaning that $A(h)$ and $B(h)$ each tend toward zero as h tends toward zero – has the quantity L as its *ultimate ratio* (what we would call its *limit*) provided we can make "their difference" $\frac{A(h)}{B(h)} - L$ "less than any given quantity," that is, less than any given ε – by, of course (and here's the hidden δ), choosing h sufficiently small.

Lest anyone think that our reading here overlays a level of understanding by Newton that is just not there, we flip back two pages, to his demonstration for Lemma 11, the last of the preliminary lemmas that fill out Section 1 (*Principia*, p. 439):

> It is evident that the distance GJ can be less than any assigned
> distance . . . But since GJ can be taken as less than any assigned
> length, it can happen that the ratio of AG to Ag differs from the
> ratio of equality by less than any assigned difference, and thus
> that the ratio of AB^2 to Ab^2 differs from the ratio of BD to bd by
> less than any assigned difference.

Here AB^2/Ab^2 and BD/bd are each ratios of evanescent quantities (where the four individual evanescent quantities tend toward zero as the quantity GJ tends toward zero, that is, as G tends toward J, where J is fixed). The demonstration argues that the difference $AB^2/Ab^2 - BD/bd$ can be made "less than any assigned difference" (there's the given arbitrary ε) by choosing the quantity GJ "less than any assigned length" (there's the δ chosen in response!). Plainly, by the time he wrote the *Principia*, Newton had a remarkably modern and sophisticated understanding of the limit notion.

Overall, Newton handles evanescent quantities, their ratios, and the limit concept adroitly and accurately, with greater rigor and precision than the generally accepted view would suggest. The *Principia* also reveals a more serious commitment to and appreciation for mathematical rigor than we see in the works of his contemporaries. For example, he banished infinitesimals ("indivisibles") from his analysis in the *Principia*, "prefer[ing] to make the proofs . . . depend on . . . the limits of . . . sums and ratios," [*Principia*, p. 441], because he found the "hypothesis of indivisibles problematical [*durior*]," [*Principia*, p. 441] yet Leibniz, who also regarded "indivisibles" as *durior* –

> Philosophically speaking, I no more believe in infinitely small quantities than in infinitely great ones . . . I consider both as fictions of the mind for succinct ways of speaking, appropriate to the calculus . . .[10]

– allowed these fictional infinitesimals to infest his dynamical studies. What could be less rigorous than manipulating nothingness, "quantities" whose self-contradictory nature proves their nonexistence?[11]

3   KINDS OF FORCE

3.1   *Finite and continuous forces*

According to Definition 4, by an "impressed force" Newton means an "action exerted on a body to change its state either of resting or of moving uniformly straight forward." Intuitively, we may think of an impressed force as a particular "thrust" or "pull." He employs the ratios of evanescent quantities to characterize basic notions in the *Principia*, including, for example, different kinds of impressed forces – finite, continuous, impulsive, and centripetal – which he defines, for

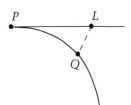

FIGURE 3.2 The moving deflection $\overrightarrow{LQ}$ measures the deviation from uniform straight line motion.

a given body moved by a force, in terms of the ratio $\overrightarrow{LQ}/h^2$, where the directed line segment $\overrightarrow{LQ}$, what we call the "moving deflection" generated in the small time h, is viewed as the observed effect of the impressed force.

DEFINITION. Consider a body in a motion $t \to P(t)$. Fix a time t_0 and set $P := P(t_0)$.[12] Had its speed and direction at P been uniformly continued, suppose the body would have described the segment PL in a time interval h, but instead, deflected from this line, suppose the body describes the arc segment (or possibly line segment) PQ in the same time h. Then the directed line segment $\overrightarrow{LQ}$ is called the *moving deflection generated in the time h*.

To see how the *Principia* defines a "finite force," for instance, consider Lemma 10, one of the preliminary mathematical lemmas from Section 1:

> LEMMA 10. *The spaces which a body describes when urged by any finite force, whether that force is determinate and immutable or is [continuously (continuo)[13]] increased or [continuously] decreased are at the very beginning of the motion in the squared ratio of the times.* [*Principia*, pp. 437–8]

Observe that the lemma assumes a "finite force," yet because the *Principia* never characterizes a "finite force" anywhere else, or in any other way, one has no choice but to take Lemma 10 as *defining* what Newton means by a "finite force." Of course, we first have to understand what this lemma asserts, before we can use it as a definition. The deflection $\overrightarrow{LQ}$ (from where the body would have been

without the force to where the body actually ends up *with* the force)
can be viewed as the "space the body is drawn through by the force."
It follows that this deflection must represent the "spaces which [the]
body describes when urged by [the] finite force" in Lemma 10, even
though the body (unless it begins from rest) never actually traverses
the directed line segment (or "space") $\overrightarrow{LQ}$. This is certainly the
natural interpretation of the "spaces which the body describes" in
Lemma 10, but the argument for Proposition 6 in the 1687 *Principia*
(a proposition which becomes Corollary 1 of a new Proposition 6 in
the second and third editions) removes any doubts, for there Newton
claims the "line-element" LQ "if the force is given, is as the square
of the time (by Lemma 10)."[14]

Now we understand what Lemma 10 asserts: the moving deflec-
tion $\overrightarrow{LQ}$ generated by the given impressed force in a given time increment h *is as* h^2 as $h \to 0$. We take this characterization as Newton's
definition of a "finite force":

DEFINITION. An impressed force which moves a body with the motion
$t \to P(t)$ is called a *finite force* if at each fixed time t_0 the deflection
$\overrightarrow{LQ}$ generated in a time increment h is as the square of that increment: LQ/h^2 tends toward a non-zero, finite limit as $h \to 0$.

We insert here a crucial observation concerning the measurement of force. In Newton's mechanics, a given impressed force (intuitively, a given "thrust" or "pull") and its observed effect are seen
as conceptually distinct.[15] We naturally think of the deflection $\overrightarrow{LQ}$
as the observed effect generated by the given force over the arc PQ,
or, equivalently, during the time increment h. (Of course, we would
think of the limit of $\overrightarrow{LQ}/h^2$ as $h \to 0$ as the observed effect generated
at P.) We certainly expect this observed effect, this deflection $\overrightarrow{LQ}$, to
depend on the given impressed force, the body, and the time incre-
ment h, but until an axiom stipulates otherwise (see Law 2, discussed
in Section 5.1), the deflection (generated by a *given* impressed force)
could conceivably also depend on the speed and/or direction that the

body has when the given force acts. In such a case, a given impressed force acting on a given body could generate in a given time one deflection $\vec{LQ}$ when the body is in *motion* and a *different* deflection $\vec{PG}$ (different in length, direction, or both) when the body is at *rest*. It would then be conceivable, for example, that $\vec{LQ}/h^2$ has a finite limit while $\vec{PG}/h^2$ grows arbitrarily large, both as $h \rightarrow 0$, meaning that one and the same impressed force (one and the same "thrust") could act on a given body as a finite force when that body is in motion and an "infinite force" when the body is at rest. (Of course, such a result would be at odds with the very meaning of an impressed force as a particular "action.") For this reason, it would have been more logically pristine to have phrased the above definition, and the other force definitions below, as characterizing only the observed effect of the force, rather than the force itself: writing, for example, "is said to *act finitely*," in place of "is called a *finite force*." But later on, with his second law of motion, Newton will rule out any dependence of the moving deflection (generated by a *given* impressed force) on the (vector) velocity of the body: by the second law, the deflection $\vec{LQ}$ generated in a given time by a given impressed force on a given body will be the same (in direction and length) whether the body is in motion or at rest, in other words, $\vec{LQ} = \vec{PG}$. The second law will therefore justify, retroactively, our decision to write these definitions as characterizing the force itself, rather than just the observed effect of the force.

Among the finite forces, those forces which make a body "move in orbit" about "an unmoving center of force" (*Principia*, p. 444) occupy center stage in Book 1. Of course these forces are "centripetal," in that they "act toward a fixed center," but they also act "continuously" or "uninterruptedly." For example, following Definition 5 for "centripetal force," Newton describes "bodies that are made to move in orbits" as "[continuously (*perpetuo*)] draw[n] . . . back toward . . . the center" (*Principia*, p. 405). Then, at the close of his argument for Proposition 1, he claims to have constructed a "centripetal force by which the body is [continuously (*perpetuo*)] drawn back from the tangent," a force which "will act uninterruptedly [*indes-inenter*]." What does it mean when Newton says that a force acts "continuously" or "uninterruptedly"?

Suppose a finite force moves a body with the motion $t \to P(t)$. At each fixed time t_0, we then know the limit of the ratio LQ/h^2 is non-zero and finite as $h \to 0$, where $\overrightarrow{LQ}$ is the moving deflection generated at t_0 in the time increment h. The obvious candidate for the "action of the force a time t_0" would be that non-zero, finite limit: $\lim_{h \to 0}(\overrightarrow{LQ}/h^2)$.[16] And then a force which "acts uninterruptedly" would have to be a force for which the value of this limit varies uninterruptedly, that is, *continuously*, as the time t_0 varies.[17]

DEFINITION. A finite force that moves a body with the motion $t \to P(t)$ is said to *act uninterruptedly* or to be a *continuous force*, provided the non-zero, finite value $\lim_{h \to 0}(LQ/h^2)$ varies continuously with the time t_0, where $\overrightarrow{LQ}$ is the moving deflection generated at t_0 in the time increment h.

3.2   Instantaneous impulse

We shall use "instantaneous impulse" or just "impulse" to mean the mathematical representation of an "instantaneous blow," where a body instantaneously alters its speed, its direction, or both. Newton uses "impulse" in just this way in the demonstration for Proposition 1, where he lets "a centripetal force act with a single but great impulse and make a body deviate from the straight line Bc and proceed in the straight line BC [*Principia*, p. 444]."

DEFINITION. Had its speed and direction at P been uniformly continued, suppose a body would have continued on to describe the line segment $\overrightarrow{PL}$ in a time h, but instead suppose the body proceeds with uniform motion to describe the line segment $\overrightarrow{PQ}$ in that same time. If $\overrightarrow{PQ}$ and $\overrightarrow{PL}$ differ in length, direction, or both, in other words if the moving deflection $\overrightarrow{LQ}$ is non-zero, then we say an *instantaneous impulse* or *impulsive force acts at P*.

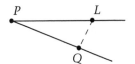

P L

Q

FIGURE 3.3 The moving deflection $\overrightarrow{LQ}$ generated in a given time by an instantaneous impulse acting on a body at P.

For an instantaneous impulse, each of the directed line segments $\overrightarrow{PL}$ and $\overrightarrow{PQ}$, and hence also the deflection $\overrightarrow{LQ} = \overrightarrow{PQ} - \overrightarrow{PL}$, increases in length at a constant rate. As a consequence, the ratio $LQ/h^2 = (LQ/h)/h \rightarrow +\infty$ as $h \rightarrow 0$, because the rate LQ/h is constant for all $h > 0$. Thus an instantaneous impulse is not a finite force, but rather an example of what might be called an "infinite force."[18]

3.3   Centripetal force

According to the *Principia*'s Definition 5, a "centripetal force is the force by which bodies are drawn from all sides, are impelled, or in any way tend, toward some point as to a center." Let us see if we can clarify what Newton has in mind here. Consider first the case of an impulse.

DEFINITION. If an impulse acts at P on a body in uniform straight line motion and generates the deflection $\overrightarrow{LQ}$ in a given time h, then the direction of that deflection is called the *direction of the impulse*. Given a fixed point S, if $\overrightarrow{LQ}$ and $\overrightarrow{PS}$ have the same direction (that is, if $\overrightarrow{LQ}$ and $\overrightarrow{PS}$ are parallel with the same sense of direction), we say the *impulse is directed toward S*.

It makes little sense to call a single impulse "centripetal," as a single impulse has a single direction, yet a *series* of impulses is another matter. In the *Principia*'s argument for Proposition 1, a fixed point S is given, and a body is made to move along the edges AB, BC, CD, DE, and EF of a polygonal trajectory, with (generally different) uniform motions on each edge, by a series of impulses, each directed toward S, acting at the points B, C, D, and E. It would be natural to call such a series of impulses (and the "polygonal impulse motion" these impulses generate) "centripetal," or to say, as Newton does, that a "centripetal force act[s] with single but great impulse[s]" at the points B, C, D, and E; but we will not follow Newton here, preferring instead, for brevity's sake,[19] to apply the term "centripetal" to *continuous* forces only.[20]

Speaking of which, consider a body moving with the motion $t \to P(t)$ under the influence of a *continuous* force. By definition then the deflection $\overrightarrow{LQ}$ generated in a given time h at any point $P := P(t_0)$ will be as h^2, which means the limit of $\overrightarrow{LQ}/h^2$ as $h \to 0$ will be finite and non-zero, and also the value of this limit will vary continuously with the time t_0. The direction of the deflection $\overrightarrow{LQ}$ represents a sort of averaging of the directions of the force acting over the little arc PQ, and the direction of $\lim_{h \to 0}(\overrightarrow{LQ}/h^2)$ should give the direction of the force *at P*. Newton would call the direction of this limit the "ultimate direction" of the deflection $\overrightarrow{LQ}$.

DEFINITION. For a body moving with the motion $t \to P(t)$ under the influence of a continuous force, the ultimate direction of the moving deflection $\overrightarrow{LQ}$, that is, the direction of $\lim_{h \to 0}(\overrightarrow{LQ}/h^2)$, is called the *direction of the force at P* $:= P(t_0)$. Given a fixed point S, if at each point P of the trajectory the direction of the force at P is the direction of $\overrightarrow{PS}$, then both the *force* and the *motion* are said to be *centripetal with center S*.

This definition squares *exactly* with Newton's characterization of a motion generated by a centripetal force: "A stone whirled in a sling," he writes (in the second, 1713, edition),

> endeavors to leave the hand that is whirling it, and by
> its endeavor stretches the sling . . . The force opposed to that
> endeavor, that is, the force by which the sling [continuously
> (*perpetuo*)] draws the stone back toward the hand and keeps it
> in orbit, I call centripetal, since it is directed toward the hand as
> toward the center of an orbit. And the same applies to all bodies
> that are made to move in orbits. They all endeavor to recede from
> the centers of their orbits, and unless some force opposed to that

endeavor is present, restraining them and keeping them in orbits and hence called by me centripetal, they will go off in straight lines with uniform motion. [*Principia*, p. 405]

Clearly the deflection $\overrightarrow{LQ}$ generated at P in a given time h represents the "drawing back" as the force acts over the arc PQ to "draw the [body] back toward . . . the center." To measure the "drawing back" *at the point P*, rather than over the arc PQ, we naturally compute the limit of $\overrightarrow{LQ}/h^2$ as $h \to 0$. Hence the direction of this limit gives the direction of the force at P.

Newton may use a longer name, the motion of a "bod[y] made to move in orbit [about] an unmoving center of forces," but a centripetal motion by any other name would be just as fundamental. *The fundamental object of study in Book 1 is the centripetal motion*: of its ninety-eight propositions, all but a handful have a centripetal motion in the hypothesis or conclusion.[21]

4   MEASURES OF FORCE

As we have already noted, the moving deflection $\overrightarrow{LQ}$ generated in a given time by a given impressed force (i.e., intuitively, a given "thrust" or "pull") acting on a given body could in principle depend on the speed or direction of the body – at least until an axiom outlaws this behavior.[22] Such a dependence would not only make the deflection $\overrightarrow{LQ}$ an unstable and hence unusable measure of a given impressed force, but would also not conform to Newton's experience with experimental facts. So, not surprisingly, he explicitly rules this dependence out: Law 2, as Newton understands it, asserts that *a given impressed force (continuous or impulsive) acting on a given body generates in a given time the same deflection, whether the body is at rest or in motion*. We take up Newton's interpretation of Law 2 in the following section.

But what does this imply about Newton's "motive quantity of centripetal force," or, more briefly, "motive force," a measure of centripetal force whose definition in the *Principia* comes *before* the statement of the laws?

> DEFINITION 8. The motive quantity of centripetal force is the measure of this force that is proportional to the motion which it generates in a given time. [*Principia*, p. 407]

In this context, "motion which it generates in a given time" means the "quantity of matter" multiplied into the "accelerative quantity of centripetal force," the latter being the "velocity which [the centripetal force] generates in a given time," by Definition 7. But at this point the *Principia*'s second law has yet to be stipulated; so in this definition the velocity generated – whatever this might mean, especially with a force oblique to the direction of motion – by a given impressed force (i.e., by a given "thrust" or "pull") acting on a given body could conceivably depend on the speed or direction the body has when the given impressed force acts, making this generated velocity no measure of the impressed centripetal force at all. Newton therefore has no choice: to be a stable measure of a given force, the motive force of a given impressed force acting on a given body must be calculated on a body *at rest.*

DEFINITION 8 (CLARIFIED). The *motive quantity of centripetal force* (or *motive force*, for brevity) is the measure of this impressed force that is proportional to the motion which it would generate in a given time on the body at rest: if a given centripetal force would make a body move from rest, describing the line $\vec{PG}$ in a given time h, then the *motive force* is the product $M \cdot \frac{\vec{PG}}{h}$, where M is the quantity of matter.

It should be no surprise that Newton would measure the strength (and direction) of a centripetal force by observing the deflection generated on a body *at rest*, as this was standard practice in the seventeenth century for scientists measuring gravity. Mersenne, Riccioli, and Huygens, for example, all used the distance fallen in the first second to measure surface gravity.[23] Newton himself recorded

> force in the middle of the arc will be as the sagitta directly
> and as the time twice [i.e., as the square of the time] inversely.
> [*Principia*, pp. 453–4]

– that the definition we have given above is correct, for making the natural assumption that the two measures of centripetal force, the centripetal force and the motive force $M \cdot (\overrightarrow{PG}/h)$, should be closely related, the claim in Proposition 6 that the measure called centripetal force is "as the time twice inversely" gives it away: the *Principia*'s implicit definition for the measure called centripetal force is the quantity $M \cdot (\overrightarrow{PG}/h^2)$. We will have more to say about Proposition 6 in Section 9.

5 LAW 2: WHAT IT MEANS

5.1 The meaning according to Newton

The meaning of the *Principia*'s second law –

> LAW 2. *A change in motion is proportional to the motive force impressed and takes place along the straight line in which that force is impressed.* [*Principia*, p. 416]

– as Newton himself understood it, has been an unsettled question since 1687. Over 320 years of confusion and controversy, and all of it, all but twenty-six years of it anyway, could have been avoided, had Newton actually done what he had planned to do: to insert into the second (1713) edition a figure and an explanatory paragraph which together make plain the meaning of Law 2.

Manuscript pages preserved in the Portsmouth Collection of the Cambridge University Library[25] and composed during the period 1692–3 record a flurry of projected revisions to Book 1 of the 1687 *Principia*, ranging from merely stylistic changes to a radical restructuring centered on the notion of curvature.[26] Apart from some isolated portions of this restructuring that Newton jammed into nooks and crannies for the second edition, most of these planned revisions never made it into the *Principia*. On four loose sheets (fol. 274r, ULC Ms. Add. 3965), we find Newton crafting eight rewordings of the second law.[27] One of these rewordings, the only one of the eight not crossed out –

> LAW 2. *All new motion by which the state of a body is changed is proportional to the motive force impressed, and occurs from the place which the body would otherwise occupy towards the goal at which the impressed force aims.*

– is accompanied by the following passage and figure (where Newton's original hand-drawn figure, on the left, has been redrawn on the right, in order to switch notation, from his *A, a, B, b* to our *P, L, G, Q*):

> NEWTON'S INTERPRETATION OF HIS SECOND LAW. If the body *P* should, at its place *P* where a force is impressed upon it, have a motion by which, when uniformly continued, it would describe the straight line *PL*, but by the impressed force be deflected from this line into another one *PQ* and, when it ought to be located at the place *L*, be found at the place *Q*, then, because the body, free of the impressed force, would have occupied the place *L* and is thrust out from this place by that force and transferred therefrom to the place *Q*, the translation of the body from the place *L* to the place *Q* will, in the meaning of this Law, be proportional to this force and directed to the same goal towards which this force is impressed.

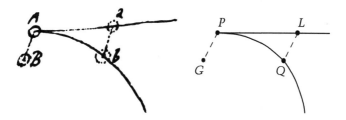

FIGURE 3.4 Newton's original figure (on the left) and a redrawn version (on the right), illustrating the meaning of the second law, for the continuous force case, in his notation ($\vec{ab} = \vec{AB}$) and ours ($\vec{LQ} = \vec{PG}$).

> Whence, if the same body deprived of all motion and impressed
> by the same force with the same direction, could in the same
> time be transported from the place P to the place G, the two
> straight lines PG and LQ will be parallel and equal. For the same
> force, by acting with the same direction and in the same time
> on the same body whether at rest or carried on with any motion
> whatever, will in the meaning of this Law achieve an identical
> translation towards the same goal; and in the present case the
> translation is PG where the body is at rest before the force was
> impressed, and LQ where it was there in a state of motion.[28]

Those firmly rooted in the standard interpretation of Law 2,
where the force can only be an instantaneous impulse, will look
at this smoothly curved trajectory and see a figure both unnatural and unexpected, an anomaly which must be "explained away."
(Unfortunately, any such "explanation" will necessarily be quite
complicated, involving an approximation by impulses in series followed by a limit process, even though Newton obviously drew this
figure as a *simple illustration* of the law, not a complex application.[29])
But the rest of us can look at this curved trajectory and see something
entirely different, something both natural and simple: an illustration
for *one case* (the continuous force case) of the second law.

In Newton's hand-drawn figure, the force deflects the body from
the line PL into what is very clearly a *smooth curve PQ*. This tells us the
law is intended to apply *directly* to a *continuous* force. We know, from
Corollary 1 of the laws (the parallelogram law), that the law is intended
to apply directly to an instantaneous impulse as well, in which case
the body would be deflected into a *straight line PQ*. Newton's wording, "deflected from this line into another one PQ," accommodates
both these cases, since "another *one*," meaning "another *line*," allows
a straight line or a curved line. Thus the force in the second law may
be either continuous or impulsive.

When we turn from the figure to the passage, we see *the meaning of the second law finally made plain*. Observe that Newton twice
writes the phrase "in the meaning [*mente*] of this Law," to stress that

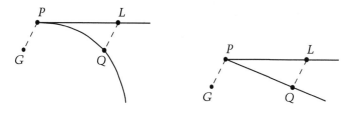

FIGURE 3.5 Illustrating the Compound Second Law ($\vec{LQ} = \vec{PG}$) for a continuous force and an instantaneous impulse.

he is recording here the actual *meaning* of Law 2, and not merely some implication or application of that law. Let us distill that meaning down to its essence. Suppose a body in motion arriving at P would have gone on to describe the line PL in a given time h, had its speed and direction at P been uniformly continued, but instead suppose an impressed force (continuous or instantaneous) makes the body describe the arc (or line) segment PQ in that same time. (According to Definition 4, as we have noted, an "impressed force" is an "action exerted on a body," that is, intuitively, a particular "thrust" or "pull.") We say the impressed force has generated, in the given time h, the *moving deflection* $\vec{LQ}$. Suppose this *same* impressed force – that is, the same "thrust" or "pull" – had it acted on the same body *resting* at P, would have made the body describe the line segment PG in the same time h, generating the *resting deflection* $\vec{PG}$. Here then is the meaning of the second law, according to Newton himself:

COMPOUND SECOND LAW. (The Second Law as Newton Understood It). *A given impressed force (continuous or impulsive) acting on a given body generates in a given time the same deflection, whether the body is in motion or at rest: if $\vec{LQ}$ is the deflection generated by a given impressed force acting on a given body in motion and if $\vec{PG}$ is the deflection that would have been generated had that given impressed force acted on the given body at rest, then*

$$\vec{LQ} = \vec{PG}$$

In other words, when a given impressed force acts on a given body, the inertial motion of the body compounds independently with the deflection that would have been generated if the impressed force acting on the moving body had acted on the given body at rest:

$$\vec{PQ} = \vec{PL} + \vec{PG}$$

Calling this axiom the second law of motion or Law 2, which, after all, is what it is, would have risked confusion either with the equation $\mathbf{f} = m\mathbf{a}$, which has become generally known as "Newton's second law," or with other interpretations (not Newton's own) for the statement of Law 2 in the *Principia*. Instead, we call this axiom the Compound Second Law, for two reasons: it applies directly to both continuous[30] and impulsive impressed forces and it asserts that the effect that the given impressed force would have had on the given body at rest, namely the resting deflection $\vec{PG}$, compounds independently with the inertial motion $\vec{PL}$.[31]

To prevent a common misreading of Newton's passage, which we have rephrased in the Compound Second Law, we should stress that Newton is *not* referring to a *fixed environment* (a magnetic field or resisting fluid, say) that might, quite reasonably, generate different impressed forces (different "thrusts" or "pulls"), depending on the speed or direction of the body. Instead, he is referring to a *fixed impressed force* (a fixed "thrust" or "pull") that might, quite *unreasonably*, generate different deflections, depending on the speed or direction of the body. The point of Law 2, as Newton makes clear in the above passage, is to rule out any such unruly and unreasonable behavior by a given impressed force.

To put this in a different way, the deflection $\vec{PG}$ in Newton's passage and the Compound Second Law is *not* the deflection $\vec{PG}^E$ (which we might call the "environmental resting deflection") that would be observed had we placed the given body at rest at P and watched the environment (a force field or a resisting fluid) act on that resting body. Instead, the deflection $\vec{PG}$ is the result of a thought experiment: we take the impressed force (the "thrust" or "pull") which acts on the given body in motion at P and generates the deflection $\overrightarrow{LQ}$, and we imagine that *same impressed force* (that same "thrust" or "pull") acting on the given body *at rest* at P and generating the deflection $\overrightarrow{PG}$. Newton's axiom, the Compound Second Law, stipulates that this thought experiment results in an equality: $\overrightarrow{LQ} = \overrightarrow{PG}$. As we shall see below in Section 5.3.1, *it is this axiom that makes it legitimate to use the (direction and length of the) moving deflection to measure the (direction and magnitude of the) impressed force that generates that deflection.*

5.2   Squaring the meaning with the statement

Now let us see whether we can square Newton's *understanding* of his second law, as given by his 1692–3 passage and the Compound Second Law, an understanding expressed in terms of the deflections $\overrightarrow{LQ}$ and $\overrightarrow{PG}$, with the *Principia's* statement of the second law, expressed in terms of "change in motion" and "motive force." In Section 4 we have already addressed the ambiguity in Definition 8, the *Principia's* definition for the "motive quantity of centripetal force" –

> DEFINITION 8. The *motive quantity of centripetal force* is the measure of this force that is proportional to the motion which it generates in a given time. [*Principia*, p. 407]

– and we argued for the following interpretation:

DEFINITION 8 (CLARIFIED). The *motive quantity of centripetal force* (or, more briefly, the *motive force*) is the motion which that centripetal force would generate in a given time from rest. In other words, if under the influence of a centripetal force a body with quantity of matter M would move from rest at P, describing the line segment PG in a given time h, then the motive quantity of this centripetal force is the quantity $M(PG/h)$ generated in the given time h and taking place along the line PG, that is, the quantity $M(\overrightarrow{PG}/h)$.

Oddly, the *Principia* offers no definition at all for the remaining ingredient of Law 2, the "change in motion" – as distinct from the change in "*quantity* of motion," which, by Definition 2, would be the change in *linear* momentum $\Delta Mv = M\Delta v$, where Δv denotes the change in *speed* – but we do not need one: if, as Newton assures us, the equality[32] "change in motion = motive force" reduces to the underlying equality $\overrightarrow{LQ} = \overrightarrow{PG}$ and if the motive force is $M(\overrightarrow{PG}/h)$, then of course the change in motion must be $M(\overrightarrow{LQ}/h)$.[33]

DEFINITION. Suppose a body having quantity of matter M and having any motion at P which, when uniformly continued for a given time h, would describe the line segment PL, is deflected during this given time from this line into an arc (or line) segment PQ. Then the *change in motion* is the quantity $M(LQ/h)$ generated in the given time h and taking place along the line LQ, that is, the quantity $M(\overrightarrow{LQ}/h)$.

Newton's "motive force" and "change in motion" are quantities that "take place along [a] straight line" (*Principia*, p. 417), that is, quantities that have a direction. Writing, as we do, the motive force and change in motion as $M(\overrightarrow{PG}/h)$ and $M(\overrightarrow{LQ}/h)$, respectively, captures this directional aspect perfectly, albeit in an anachronistic notation.

We have now squared the language of Law 2 as stated in the *Principia* with its meaning as given by Newton himself in the passage from 1692–3:

COMPOUND SECOND LAW. (Newton's Second Law as Newton Understood It). *By the action of any impressed force, continuous or impulsive, a change in motion equals the motive force impressed and takes place in the direction of that motive force:*

$$M\frac{\overrightarrow{LQ}}{h} = M\frac{\overrightarrow{PG}}{h}$$

Equivalently, a given impressed force acting on a given body generates in a given time the same deflection, whether the body is in motion or at rest: if $\overrightarrow{LQ}$ is the deflection generated by a given *impressed force acting on a given body in motion and if $\overrightarrow{PG}$ is the deflection that would have been generated had that given impressed force acted on that given body at rest, then*

$$\overrightarrow{LQ} = \overrightarrow{PG}$$

In other words, when a given impressed force acts on a given body, the inertial motion of the body compounds independently with the deflection that would have been generated if the given impressed force had acted on the given body at rest:

$$\overrightarrow{PQ} = \overrightarrow{PL} + \overrightarrow{PG}$$

A more precise Definition 8 for "motive force," together with an addition to the eight existing definitions, namely the definition above for the "change in motion," might well have prevented more than three centuries of confusion over the meaning of the *Principia*'s second law.

5.3   Comments on the Compound Second Law

5.3.1   The natural sequel to the first law

Physics and history – simple inferences from each tell the same story: that Newton's own interpretation of Law 2, the Compound Second Law, is exactly the axiom one would naturally expect as a sequel to Law 1. Turning to the physics first, let us consider how we might measure the direction and magnitude of a given impressed force. According to Law 1, any observed deviation from uniform straight line motion or rest signals the existence of an "impressed force." In Newton's mechanics, the word "force" may refer, depending on the context, to an *origin* or *mechanism* (gravity or magnetism, say), to an *action* (intuitively, a specific "thrust" or "pull") produced by that mechanism in the presence of a given body, or to the *observed effect* (a moving or resting deflection, for example) generated by that action on a given body. The "impressed force" of Law 1 and Law 2 refers to an *action*, a specific "thrust" or "pull." As such, a given "impressed force" has a given magnitude and direction.[34] What could be more natural for Newton than to measure the magnitude and direction of a given impressed force by the length and direction of the observed deviation which signals (by Law 1) the existence of that impressed force?

Consider a body in motion at P that would have gone on to describe the line segment PL, had its speed and direction at P been uniformly continued for a given time h. Suppose a given impressed force (that is, a specific "thrust" or "pull") acts at P, deflecting the body from this inertial motion and making it describe instead the arc segment (or line segment, in case the impressed force is an instantaneous impulse) PQ in the time h. The moving deflection $\overrightarrow{LQ}$, recording the observed deviation from uniform straight line motion, is (by Law 1) the observed sign of the given impressed force. Of course, Newton would like to measure (the magnitude and direction of) the given impressed force (which represents a specific "thrust" or "pull") by (the length and direction of) the deflection $\overrightarrow{LQ}$.

Now what would make such a measurement impossible? Consider the following unreasonable yet certainly conceivable behavior: our given impressed force has generated the deflection $\overrightarrow{LQ}$ when it acts on the given body in motion at P, but suppose that *same* impressed force (that same "thrust") could generate a *different* deflection $\overrightarrow{PG}$ when it acts on the same body *at rest* at P. In such a case, if we were trying to use the deflection to measure the given impressed force, we would have to conclude that one and the same impressed force (one and the same "thrust") could have one direction and magnitude (as measured by the deflection $\overrightarrow{LQ}$) when it acts on the given body in motion, but a different direction or magnitude (as measured by the deflection $\overrightarrow{PG}$) when it acts on the same body at rest. It would even be conceivable that a given impressed force (a given "thrust") could act finitely (meaning the ratio $\overrightarrow{LQ}/h^2$ has a finite limit as $h \to 0$) on a body in motion and act infinitely (meaning the ratio $\overrightarrow{PG}/h^2$ grows without bound as $h \to 0$) on that same body at rest.

Of course, such unreasonable behavior would violate what is inviolate: a given impressed force (a given "thrust") must have a given direction and a given magnitude. It is a simple matter to rule out such unruly behavior with an axiom: $\vec{LQ} = \vec{PG}$, that is, *a given impressed force acting on a given body generates in a given time the same deflection, whether the body is in motion or at rest.* But this axiom is just Law 2 as Newton understood it, the Compound Second Law. In other words, given an observed deflection from uniform straight line motion or rest, Law 1 guarantees the *existence* of an impressed force, while Law 2 (interpreted as the Compound Second Law) guarantees the *measurement* of that impressed force via that observed deflection.

From the physics point of view then, the Compound Second Law is the natural sequel to Law 1. To see that this is true from the historical point of view as well, consider Huygens's 1673 *magnum opus, Horologium oscillatorium sive de motu pendulorum ad horologia aptato demonstrationes geometricae (The Pendulum Clock or Geometrical Demonstrations Concerning the Motion of Pendulums as Applied to Clocks)*, a work much admired by and very familiar to Newton, as his own well-thumbed copy attests. Part II of the *Horologium oscillatorium*, devoted to bodies falling in (uniform) gravity at the Earth's surface, opens with three hypotheses:[35]

HYPOTHESIS I. *If there were no gravity, and if the air did not impede the motion of bodies, then any body will continue its given motion with uniform velocity in a straight line.*

HYPOTHESIS II. *By the action of gravity, whatever its sources, it happens that bodies are moved by a motion composed both of a uniform motion in one direction or another and of a motion downward due to gravity.*

HYPOTHESIS III. *These two motions can be considered separately, with neither being impeded by the other.*[36]

Newton would have been quite familiar with both the form and the fruitfulness of these hypotheses for Huygens's study of gravitational dynamics, but restricted as they are to uniform gravity at the surface of the Earth, these hypotheses have a narrow focus unsuited to Newton's more celestial ambitions: to deduce "the motions of the planets, the comets, the moon, and the sea" (*Principia*, p. 382).

What could be more natural than for Newton to generalize these three hypotheses in order to fashion axioms more suited to his studies in the *Principia*? Concentrating on Hypotheses II and III together, note first that "a motion downward due to gravity" in the second hypothesis means the motion that would have been generated if the force due to gravity which acts on the body in motion had acted instead on the body *at rest* and "considered separately" in the third hypothesis means the two motions "compound independently." We then make two obvious revisions: replace "gravity" by "any impressed force" and erase the restriction "downward" on the direction of the force. With these simple changes, we obtain:

THE NATURAL GENERALIZATION OF HUYGENS'S HYPOTHESES II AND III. *By the action of any given impressed force, whatever its sources, a body is moved by a motion independently compounded of the motion [speed and direction] of the body uniformly continued and of the motion that would have been generated if the given impressed force had acted on the given body at rest.*

This natural generalization of Huygens's second two hypotheses is precisely Newton's second law as Newton himself understood it, that is, the Compound Second Law. No surprise then that Newton drew essentially the same figure to illustrate his Compound Second Law around 1692 that Huygens drew to illustrate his second and third hypotheses in 1673, the only difference being that Huygens's figure (on the left) shows the effect of varying the initial speed and directon of the body:

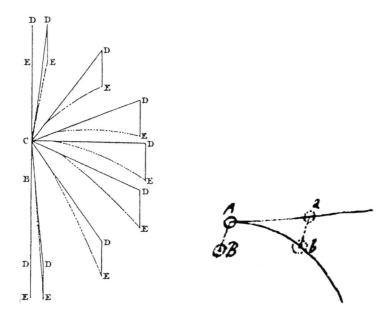

FIGURE 3.6 The figure that Huygens drew (on the left) to illustrate his second and third hypotheses in the *Horologium oscillatorium* and the figure that Newton drew (on the right) to illustrate his second law.

Newton also drew essentially the same figure to illustrate the application of his first two laws to the special case of an impressed force in the direction of motion that Huygens drew to illustrate the application of his three hypotheses to the special case of gravity in the direction of motion.[37] We have redrawn the figure of Huygens and reproduced the hand-drawn figure of Newton:[38]

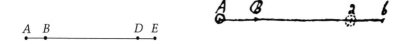

FIGURE 3.7 The redrawn figure that Huygens drew (on the left) to illustrate the application of his three hypotheses to gravity acting in the direction of motion and the reproduced figure that Newton drew (on the right) to illustrate the application of his first two laws to a force in the direction of motion.

These (essentially) identical figures record identical equalities between the moving and resting deflections ($\vec{DE} = \vec{AB}$ on the left, $\vec{ab} = \vec{AB}$ on the right) and hence provide more evidence that Newton's second law in the *Principia* (as Newton understood that law, i.e., as the Compound Second Law) is the natural generalization of Huygens's second and third hypotheses in the *Horologium oscillatorium*.

5.3.2   *Where is f = ma?*

With the meaning of the *Principia*'s second law (as Newton understood it) now clear, we may wonder about the conceptual distance between *that* second law, the Compound Second Law, and what today we call the second law, the equality $\mathbf{f} = m\mathbf{a}$. According to the Compound Second Law, a given impressed force (continuous in this case) acting on a given body will generate in a given time h the same deflection, whether that body is in motion or at rest: $\vec{LQ} = \vec{PG}$. This equality between the moving and resting deflections implies an equality between what we call the moving and resting accelerations: $\vec{A} = \vec{A}_0$, where $\vec{A} := \lim_{h \to 0} 2(\vec{LQ}/h^2)$ and $\vec{A}_0 := \lim_{h \to 0} 2(\vec{PG}/h^2)$. (These limits are finite, because a continuous force is, in particular, a finite force.) If M stands for Newton's "quantity of matter" and $\vec{F}$ for $M\vec{A}_0$, then $\vec{A}_0 = \vec{A}$ turns into $\vec{F} = M\vec{A}$. We see an obvious outward similarity between this Newtonian equation $\vec{F} = M\vec{A}$ and the classical equation $\mathbf{f} = m\mathbf{a}$,[39] a similarity heightened by the fact that the Newtonian and modern vector accelerations, $\vec{A}$ and $\mathbf{a}$, though defined and calculated differently, end up being equal (as a simple Taylor series argument confirms).[40]

The *Principia*'s second law, which asserts the equality $\vec{LQ} = \vec{PG}$ between the moving and resting deflections, would not seem to justify the modern practice of calling the equation $\mathbf{f} = m\mathbf{a}$ "Newton's second law." Yet, as we have just seen, the equation $\vec{LQ} = \vec{PG}$ does have a "limiting form," $\vec{F} = M\vec{A}$, which *could* be seen as justifying this practice, provided we can point to a result in the *Principia* which, either explicitly or implicitly, contains this limiting form.

Consider Proposition 6:

PROPOSITION 6. *If in a nonresisting space a body revolves in any orbit about an immobile center and describes any just-nascent arc in a minimally small time, and if the sagitta of the arc is understood to be drawn so as to bisect the chord and, when produced, to pass through the center of forces, the centripetal force in the middle of the arc will be as the sagitta directly and as the time twice [i.e., as the square of the time] inversely.* [*Principia*, pp. 453–4]

No one thinks of this fundamental proposition as the *Principia's* version of the equation **f** = m**a**, but it is: in general, Newton's "will be as" construction signals a limit statement (see Section 2.2); in particular, to say "*the centripetal force in the middle of the arc will be as the sagitta directly and as the time twice [i.e., as the square of the time] inversely*" is to say

$$F(h) = k(h) \cdot \frac{S(h)}{h^2}$$

where the quantity $k(h)$ tends toward a non-zero, finite limit as $h \to 0$ (which in this case turns out to be the "quantity of matter" M). Here $F(h)$ and $S(h)$ stand, respectively, for (twice the magnitude of) the centripetal force $(M(\overrightarrow{PG}/h))$ and (twice the magnitude of) the sagitta (whatever *that* is – see Section 9). As we shall see later, when we take up Proposition 6 in earnest, taking the limit in this equation as $h \to 0$, and noting that $\vec{F}(h)$ and $\vec{S}(h)$ have the same direction in the limit, yields

$$\vec{F} = M\vec{A}$$

In this sense it is Proposition 6, rather than Law 2, which justifies calling the classical equation **f** = m**a** Newton's second law. For more on Proposition 6 seen as a Newtonian version of the vector equation **f** = m**a**, see other Pourciau references.[41]

"at rest," and a line in the *Principia*'s demonstration confirms that expectation: the impulse N, for example, which makes the body describe the side $\overrightarrow{PG}$, is said to "act along the line" $\overrightarrow{PG}$, and only in the case where the impulse N acts at P on the body *at rest* would the line the body describes be the same as the line the impulse "acts along."[43] Of course, the same applies to the impulse M, which makes the body describe the side $\overrightarrow{PL}$.

Its meaning now clear, we can prove Corollary 1, in just a few lines, from Law 2 (the Compound Second Law) and Law 1: let the impulse M act first, on the body *resting* at P', and let the impulse N act second, when the body comes to P (in a brief time h'). The Compound Second Law applies to the motion generated by the impulse N: the body first describes the handle $\overrightarrow{P'P}$ in the time h' and then, after N acts at P, the diagonal $\overrightarrow{PQ}$ in the time h, both uniformly (by Law 1). In the limit, as h' tends toward zero, the body will just describe the diagonal $\overrightarrow{PQ}$. But then, by our definition, this limiting motion is the motion generated by the impulses M and N "acting jointly" on the body at P.

Thus, with Law 2 given Newton's own interpretation, Corollary 1 justifies its name, as a simple consequence of the laws.[44]

6.2   "The increment . . . of the velocity . . . is proportional to the . . . force"

At several places in the *Principia*, Newton calls on Law 2 to conclude that an increment in speed is proportional to the generating force in the direction of motion. For example, in the infamous "falling body passage," inserted to illustrate the first two laws and found at the beginning of the scholium that follows the laws of motion, we read that "impresse[d] equal forces upon that body generate equal veloci-ties" (*Principia*, p. 424). Also the demonstrations of Proposition 3 and 8, Book 2, claim, respectively, that "the absolute forces . . . [are] (by the second law of motion) as the increments of the velocities" and "the increment . . . of the velocity (by the second law of motion) is proportional to the generating force" (*Principia*, pp. 635, 650). We shall show that such assertions do in fact follow directly from the second law (understood as the Compound Second Law), when we

P G   L Q   FIGURE 3.9 The Compound Second Law applied to
•——•   •——•   the motion of a body that describes a line under the
                      influence of a force that remains parallel to that
                      line: $\vec{LQ} = \vec{PG}$.

apply that law to the special case of an impressed force parallel to the
direction of motion.

Let a body traversing a line be moved by an impressed force
that remains parallel to that line. Suppose this body, had its speed
and direction at P been uniformly continued, would have gone on to
describe the segment $\vec{PL}$ in a given time h, but instead suppose this
body, acted on by the impressed force, describes the segment $\vec{PQ}$ in
that same time. Suppose further that this given impressed force, had
it acted on the given body at rest at P, would have made the body
describe the segment $\vec{PG}$ in the given time h. Then the moving deflection equals the resting deflection by Law 2 (as Newton understood it),
that is, by the Compound Second Law: $\vec{LQ} = \vec{PG}$.

For the straight line motion considered here, the arrow sum

$$\vec{PQ} = \vec{PL} + \vec{LQ} = \vec{PL} + \vec{PG}$$

becomes a *scalar* sum $PQ = PL \pm PG$ (or difference, when the direction
of force opposes the direction of motion, as with resistance forces),
and dividing by the time increment h, we have

$$\frac{PQ}{h} = \frac{PL}{h} \pm \frac{PG}{h}$$

In other words, the average speed over the segment PQ equals the
speed at P plus or minus PG/h, which makes PG/h the increment
(or decrement) in speed generated by the impressed force that acts
at P. Given that PG/h is obviously proportional to the motive force
$M(\vec{PG}/h)$ we arrive at the following important corollary of the
Compound Second Law, a corollary which applies to bodies in straight
line motion moved by a force parallel to the direction of motion:

COROLLARY OF THE COMPOUND SECOND LAW. *Let a body traversing a
line be moved by an impressed force that remains parallel to that
line. Then at any given time, the increment (or decrement) in speed*

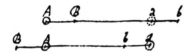

FIGURE 3.10 Newton's hand-drawn figures illustrating the Compound Second Law for motion along a line moved by a force in (above) and opposite to (below) the direction of motion.

generated (in a brief time increment) by the impressed force is proportional to the motive force (generated in that time increment).

To illustrate both the increment and decrement cases of this corollary, Newton drew the two figures shown in Figure 3.10, as we noted earlier, on the *verso* side (the side *not* printed by Whiteside in *The Mathematical Papers*, vol. VI, pp. 539–42) of the folio (ULC Ms. Add. 3965, fol. 274) where Newton recorded his statement of the Compound Second Law.[45]

Now, more generally, let a body, under the influence of a centripetal force, describe *any* trajectory. Citing Corollary 2 of the laws,[46] on the composition and resolution of forces, resolve the impressed force at P into its tangential and normal components. Under the influence of the tangential component only, the body would move along the tangent line at P, and the corollary above would apply to tell us the increment in speed is proportional to motive force of that tangential component. On the other hand, as Newton points out (in his argument for Proposition 40, Book 1), the normal component, "acting along the line . . . perpendicular to the path [PQ] of the body, will in no way change the [speed] of the body in that path but will only draw the body back . . . from the tangent of the orbit . . ." (*Principia*, p. 528). From this it follows that the increment in speed generated by the impressed force at P will be proportional to the motive quantity of the *tangential* component of that force. This yields a second, more general, corollary of the Compound Second Law:

COROLLARY OF THE COMPOUND SECOND LAW. *Let a body be moved by a centripetal force. At any given time, the increment (or decrement) in speed along the trajectory generated (in a brief time increment) by the force is proportional to the motive quantity of the tangential component of that force (generated in that time increment).*

In one common misinterpretation of the *Principia*'s Law 2, the law is taken to apply only to a force parallel to the direction of motion, and the *corollary* of Law 2, a law we have just stated, is then taken to *be* Law 2. Under such a misreading, a force *not* parallel to the direction of motion would require a "just resolution" before the second law could be applied to the *tangential* component of the force: "When gravity or any centripetal force," argues MacLaurin, "acts upon a body moving with a direction oblique to the right line drawn from it to the centre, the change of its motion is not proportional to the whole centripetal force . . . but to that part only, which, after a just resolution of the force, is found to act in the direction of the motion."[47] This misinterpretation of Law 2 would have Newton meaning "change in [quantity] of motion" (which, by the *Principia*'s Definition 2, would be the quantity of matter times the change in speed), but writing "change in motion" instead, in his statement of Law 2. Yet, as we noted earlier, between 1685, when the second law first appears in a revision of the tract "De motu corporum in gyrum," and 1726, when the second law makes its final appearance, in the third edition of the *Principia*, Newton had (at least) *fourteen* opportunities to revise his statement of the law,[48] and not once did he insert "quantity of" into "change in motion." As it beggars belief that Newton, an exquisitely careful writer, would miss fourteen chances to clarify his statement of Law 2 with such a simple insertion, one can only conclude that he meant exactly what he wrote, writing "a change in motion" to mean something *other* than the "change in quantity of motion," to mean in fact the quantity $M(LQ/h)$ acting along the direction from L to Q, which we have written as $M(\overrightarrow{LQ}/h)$, the lefthand side of the Compound Second Law.

6.3 The "falling body passage"

A long scholium follows the corollaries to the laws of motion. For the third edition of the *Principia*, Newton inserted into this scholium a now infamous passage, a passage intended to show how the first two laws alone predict, in a supposedly simple way, what Galileo had found: "that the descent of heavy bodies is in the squared ratio of the time and that the motion of projectiles occurs in a parabola . . ." (*Principia*, p. 424), neglecting the resistance of the air. Why infamous? Why supposedly simple? Because no commentator has been able to deduce the parabola from the assumption of uniform gravity and the first two laws alone, by any argument at all, much less any simple argument, and much less by the brief argument described in the passage. The "falling body passage," writes Pierson, "has exercised . . . historians of science . . . at considerable, controversial, and inconclusive length."[49] But all this inconclusive debate, often seen as stemming from Newton's "confusion," stems instead from a different sort of confusion: misinterpretations of the second law.

Following Newton's argument in the passage, let us now see how the parabolic trajectory arises in a wholly elementary way from uniform gravity and the first two laws of motion alone, *provided the second law is understood as Newton himself understood it.* (See also Pourciau, "Newton's Interpretation of Newton's Second Law," pp. 196–7.) Below we record the "falling body passage" (or most of it), split into three parts, with a commentary following each part (and with our P, L, G, Q replacing Newton's A, B, C, D):

> When a body falls, uniform gravity, by acting equally in individual equal particles of time, impresses equal forces upon that body and generates equal velocities; and in the total time it impresses a total force and generates a total velocity proportional to the time. [*Principia*, p. 424]

Explanation: In its fall, let the body, beginning from rest at P, describe the line segment $\overrightarrow{PG}$ in a given total time t. Divide this total time t into n equal very small subintervals of length h. By the corollary of the Compound Second Law on straight line motion (in the preceding section), gravity, during each subinterval of time, generates an increment in (average) speed proportional to the motive force generated during that same subinterval. But with gravity assumed uniform, the motive forces, and hence the increments in speed, generated in the different subintervals, are all the same, say Δv. Letting $v(t)$ stand for the speed generated in the total time t, this yields

$$v(t) \approx \Delta v + \Delta v + \cdots + \Delta v = n\Delta v = \frac{t}{h}\Delta v = \frac{\Delta v}{h}t$$

where we have only an approximation to $v(t)$, because each Δv, an increment in average speed, is not exactly the increment in instantaneous speed. As $n \to \infty$, the ratio $\Delta v/h$ will tend toward a finite limit,[50] which we shall call g, and the approximation above becomes exact, yielding a "total velocity proportional to the time":

$$v(t) = gt$$

> And the spaces described in proportional times are as the velocities and the times jointly, that is, in the squared ratio of the times.

Explanation: Newton puts this more explicitly in his demonstration of Proposition 10 (Book 2), where we have replaced his *NI* with our *PG*: "In a body falling and describing in its fall the space *PG*, [uniform] gravity generates . . ., as Galileo proved, . . . the velocity $2PG/t$" (*Principia*, p. 657). Thus

$$PG = \frac{1}{2}v(t) \cdot t = \frac{1}{2}gt^2$$

This is Galileo's "law of fall," derived from uniform gravity and the Compound Second Law.

> And when a body is projected along any straight line, its motion arising from the projection is compounded with the motion arising from gravity. For example, let body P by the motion of projection alone describe the straight line PL in a given time, and by the motion of falling alone describe the vertical distance PG in the same time; then complete the parallelogram PLQG, and by the compounded motion the body will be found in place Q at the end of the time; and the curved line . . . which the body will describe will be a parabola which the straight line PL touches at P and whose ordinate LQ is as PL².

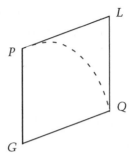

FIGURE 3.11 The figure, redrawn with our notation, used in the *Principia* to illustrate the motion of a body projected along the line $\overrightarrow{PL}$ and acted on by uniform gravity. By the Compound Second Law, the motion $\overrightarrow{PL}$ compounds independently with the motion $\overrightarrow{PG}$ that uniform gravity would have generated had it acted on the given body at rest.

Explanation: By the Compound Second Law (which is the second law as Newton understood it), the motion $\overrightarrow{PL}$ that would have been generated in the total time t by the projection alone compounds independently with the motion $\overrightarrow{PG}$ that would have been generated in the time t if the uniform gravity that acts on the body in motion had acted instead on the body *at rest*. Since, as we have just seen, $\overrightarrow{PG} = \frac{1}{2}\vec{g}t^2$ (where $\vec{g}$ has the length g and the direction of $\overrightarrow{PG}$), the body will arrive in the time t at the place Q, where

$$\overrightarrow{PQ} = \overrightarrow{PL} + \overrightarrow{PG} = \overrightarrow{PL} + \frac{1}{2}\vec{g}\,t^2$$

But $PL = v(0)t$, where $v(0)$ is the speed with which the body is projected, and it follows that Q will trace out a parabola.[51]

Observe that this simple derivation of the parabolic trajectory called on the Compound Second Law *twice*, once when we invoked the corollary of the Compound Second Law for straight line motion and then again when we compounded the law of fall with the inertial motion.

6.4   Law 2 uncited

The major treatises on mechanics in the eighteenth century – by Varignon, Hermann, Euler, MacLaurin, d'Alembert, Euler (again),

Lagrange, and Laplace – all bow deeply to Newton, citing the *Principia* generally and various of its laws, propositions, corollaries, and conclusions in particular. Yet there is one assertion in the *Principia* that these works never mention: the second law of motion. The major mechanical treatises of the eighteenth century neither state nor even cite the second law *as it appears in the Principia*. What we now call Newton's second law, the equation $\mathbf{f} = m\mathbf{a}$, certainly does appear, at least in its component form, in the works for example of Euler and Lagrange, but the second law as given in the *Principia* –

> LAW 2. *A change in motion is proportional to the motive force impressed and takes place along the straight line in which that force is impressed.*

– is completely ignored. This despite the fact that Newton clearly regarded his second law as a fundamental axiom of mechanics.

Now how can this possibly be? How can a law which Newton sees as absolutely basic, be seen as completely irrelevant by those who followed him? The answer lies in a misinterpretation. Looking at the second law as recorded in the *Principia*, Newton saw a fundamental axiom of his mechanics – *the inertial motion of the body compounds independently with the deflection that would have been generated had the impressed force that acts on the moving body been applied to the same body at rest* – while the scientists who came after him, misled by the ambiguous account of the law in the *Principia*, saw something else entirely, some law apparently irrelevant to their mechanics.

Nonetheless, even as they *ignored* the *Principia*'s second law (as they understood it) these scientists, all of them, from Varignon to Laplace, in fact *assumed* the *Principia*'s second law (as Newton understood it) as a fundamental axiom in their mechanics, some implicitly and some explicitly, but always unaware that they should have been citing Law 2 of the *Principia*.[52]

To give just one example, *Theoria motus corporum solidorum seu rigidorum* (*Theory of Motion for Bodies Solid or Rigid*), published in 1765, Euler's second major treatise on mechanics, implicitly assumes the *Principia*'s second law (the Compound Second Law) as a basic axiom of mechanics. To see how this comes about, consider the following definition which, in Euler's own words, supplies the fundamental "ground of measuring" forces that act on bodies in motion:[53]

> **EXPLANATION 2**
>
> 144. For the forces, then, by which bodies already in motion are acted upon, we set up this ground of measuring, so that we shall judge these equal to those which would have executed the same effect on the same bodies at rest in the same time. This ground, however, does not require proving, because it rests upon a definition and thus it was open to us to establish it. For if for any motion the small space $[\overrightarrow{s\sigma}]$ should be equal to small space $[\overrightarrow{S\Sigma}]$, through which the same small body at rest is brought forward in that same little time by force p, we also call those forces equal to this . . .[54]

In this passage, Euler uses the word "force" to mean a specific "action exerted on a given body," what Newton calls an "impressed force," and by the "effect" of such a force (generated in a given time), acting on a moving or resting body, Euler means the deflection, either the deflection $\overrightarrow{s\sigma}$ of the body in motion or the deflection $\overrightarrow{S\Sigma}$ of the body at rest. The passage, which Euler calls "Explanation 2," is really a *definition* of what it means for two forces, acting on bodies in motion, to be equal:

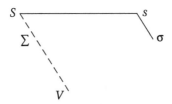

FIGURE 3.12 From Euler's *Theoria motus corporum solidorum seu rigidorum*, published in 1765, a figure drawn to illustrate what he calls the basic "ground of measuring" forces: $\overrightarrow{s\sigma} = \overrightarrow{S\Sigma}$. The point Σ has been inserted to represent Euler's meaning more clearly.

EULER'S DEFINITION. Two forces are said to be equal if they would have "executed the same effect," that is, if they would have generated in the same time the same deflection, on the same body at rest.

But it is not hard to see that this definition makes sense only if one assumes the *Principia*'s Law 2 (the Compound Second Law), that is, only if one assumes that a given impressed force (a given "thrust" or "pull") acting on a given body will always generate in the same time the same deflection (the same "effect"), whether the body is in motion or at rest. For if, in violation of Law 2, it would be possible for a given impressed force acting on a given body to generate in the same time different deflections, depending on whether that body was in motion or at rest, then two such impressed forces could be equal, according to Euler's definition above, because they would generate in the same time the same deflection on the given body at *rest*, yet these equal impressed forces could possibly generate in the same time *different* deflections on the given body in *motion*! And of course, no one, least of all Euler, would ever want to say that two impressed forces, acting on the same body in motion, could be equal, if they could generate in the same time different deflections.

Thus Euler's definition, for the equality between forces, is legitimate only if one assumes the Compound Second Law. In other words, to ensure the validity of his fundamental "ground of measuring" forces, Euler should have cited Neutonus, *Principia*, Lex II.

7 THE TRANSITION FROM INSTANTANEOUS IMPULSES TO CONTINUOUS FORCE

7.1 *Formulating the transition*

Between September 1664 and January 1665, Newton recorded his earliest known work on orbital motion on twelve folios of the "Waste Book," a commonplace book which had belonged to Newton's stepfather, the Rev. Barnabas Smith. An extended list of "Axiomes and Propositions" begins on folio 10v and contains, on folio 11, the following assertion of an equivalence,[55] there labeled "Axiome 18" and here called

NEWTON'S EQUIVALENCE ASSUMPTION (THE YOUNGER).

18. If a body move progressively in some crooked line [about a center of motion] . . ., [then this] crooked line may bee conceived to consist of an infinite number of streight lines. Or else in any point of the croked line the motion may bee conceived to be on in the tangent.

This youthfully vague and aphoristic axiom would appear to assert the equivalence between two mathematical models for motion in orbit about a fixed center. We now ask: How would Newton have stated this axiom twenty years or so later, in the time of "De motu corporum in gyrum" and the *Principia*? Once we have a more mature version of this axiom, NEWTON'S EQUIVALENCE ASSUMPTION (THE ELDER), if you will, it will be easier for us to recognize any explicit application or implicit assumption of this axiom in Newton's later work on orbital motion.

In the *Principia*, a motion that "in any point . . . may bee conceived to be on in the tangent" would surely be described as a motion "[continuously (*perpetuo*)] draw[n] . . . back [from the tangent] toward the . . . center of an orbit," which is Newton's definition for the motion of "bodies that are made to move in orbits" (*Principia*, p. 405). We have already made this definition more mathematically precise in Section 3.3, taking the moving deflection $\overrightarrow{LQ}$ as the obvious measure of the "drawing back" generated at a place P in a time increment h:

DEFINITION. For a body moving with the motion $t \to P(t)$ under the influence of a *continuous* force, the ultimate direction of the moving deflection $\overrightarrow{LQ}$, that is, the direction of $\lim_{h\to 0}(\overrightarrow{LQ}/h^2)$, is called the *direction of the force at* $P := P(t_0)$. Given a fixed point S, if at each point P of the trajectory the direction of the force at P is the direction of $\overrightarrow{PS}$, the radius at P, then both the *force* and the *motion* are said to be *centripetal with center S*.

Thus what we have been calling a "centripetal motion" is a precisely defined version of what the *Principia* calls the motion of a "body made to move in orbit," which in turn is a more mature version of the motion described in the "Waste Book" as "conceived to be on in the tangent" at each point.

Now we need a more mature version of the other motion in Newton's Equivalence Assumption (The Younger), the motion that "consist[s] of an infinite number of streight lines." But this is easy. The *Principia*'s argument for Proposition 1 describes, and illustrates with a lovely figure, the explicit construction of a motion generated by a series of instantaneous impulses all directed toward a fixed center, a motion therefore consisting of a *finite* number of (uniform) straight line motions. Clearly a (smooth) *limit* of such a "polygonal impulse motion," as the time between impulses shrinks toward zero or, equivalently, as the number of impulses grows arbitrarily large, would then be the mature version we seek.

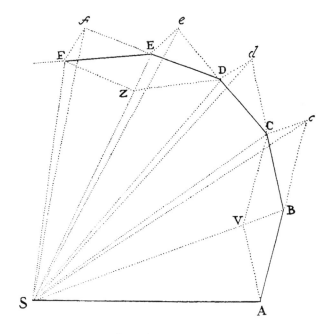

FIGURE 3.13 Newton's figure for Proposition 1 and its demonstration in the *Principia*, showing the polygonal trajectory described by a body acted on by a series of instantaneous impulses, all directed toward S, impulses that generate the moving deflections $\overrightarrow{cC}, \overrightarrow{dD}, \overrightarrow{eE}, \ldots$

Newton's figure displays a simple geometry: each "edge extension" $Bc, Cd, \ldots$ has the length of the edge it extends, and each "edge deflection" $cC, dD, \ldots$ is parallel to the previous radius $SB, SC, \ldots$ As a consequence, the triangles $SAB, SBC, \ldots$ all have equal area.[56] With a series of impulses directed toward S and applied at the vertices B, C, D, E, Newton then defines a *motion* which traverses the polygonal path $ABCDEF$: this motion traverses each edge in the same time and traverses each edge with constant speed (constant speeds that differ, generally, from edge to edge).

DEFINITION. With n denoting the number of edges or impulses, any motion $t \to P_n(t)$ constructed as above will be called a *polygonal impulse motion about the center S*.

For future reference, observe that any *single* polygonal impulse motion, by the geometry of its trajectory and the motion defined on that trajectory, satisfies the

AREA PROPERTY. *The areas described by the radius are proportional to the times.*

as well as the

FIXED PLANE PROPERTY. *The areas described by the radius lie a fixed plane.*[57]

If, as n grows arbitrarily large, a sequence of polygonal impulse motions converges to a (smooth[58]) limit motion, then that limit motion would be the obvious candidate for Newton's mature version of a motion that "consist[s] of an infinite number of streight lines." Having now found elder versions of the two motions in Newton's Equivalence Assumption (The Younger), we can record the elder version of the equivalence:

NEWTON'S EQUIVALENCE ASSUMPTION (THE ELDER).

(a) *Every (smooth) limit of polygonal impulse motions about S is a centripetal motion about S, and*
(b) *every centripetal motion about S is a limit of polygonal impulse motions about S.*

Because a centripetal motion is, in particular, a motion generated by a continuous force, and a polygonal impulse motion is a motion generated by a series of impulses, *this Equivalence Assumption represents, in mathematical form, the transition from instantaneous impulses to continuous force assumed in Newton's mature dynamics.*[59]

7.2 Demonstrating the transition

As we shall soon see, the *Principia*'s argument for Proposition 1, and hence also much of Newton's work on orbital motion in Book 1, depends crucially on part (b) in particular, which suggests that the second half of the Equivalence Assumption, befitting its fundamental role, deserves its own title:

NEWTON'S IMPULSE ASSUMPTION. *Every centripetal motion about S is a limit of polygonal impulse motions about S.*

After his youthful assertion of this assumption in "Axiome 18" of the "Waste Book," Newton never again explicitly asserts the Impulse Assumption. He never even alludes to it, and yet this assumption operates in the background of Newton's work, not just on Proposition 1, but on orbital motions generally, as an unstated, even unrecognized, axiom, implicitly assumed in the way he conceives centripetal force and centripetal motion, rather than as a proposition to be tested. From *our* standpoint, though, the Impulse Assumption is a *mathematical assertion*, a claim to be investigated.[60] It is either true or false (at least once we specify reasonable smoothness conditions on the motions). If the Impulse Assumption turns out to be false, then the *Principia*'s demonstration for Proposition 1 collapses, taking with it the support for many of Newton's subsequent theorems on orbital motion. On the other hand, if the Impulse Assumption turns out to be true, at least under reasonable smoothness assumptions, Newton's intuition is vindicated.

Let us then think about how one might establish Newton's Impulse Assumption, that *every centripetal motion about S is a limit of polygonal impulse motions about S*. Because whatever argument we give must apply to *every* centripetal motion, simple logic demands that we begin with an *arbitrarily* given centripetal motion $t \to P(t)$ about a center S. Somehow we must then construct a sequence of polygonal impulse motions $t \to P_n(t)$ generated by impulses directed toward S (see Section 3.3), a sequence that converges to the given centripetal motion in the sense that for each fixed time t, the location $P_n(t)$ converges toward the location $P(t)$ as $n \to \infty$. (Note that the required convergence is a convergence of *motions*, that is, time–position correspondences, not just *trajectories* – roughly speaking a convergence of *trips*, not just *routes*.) But to construct such a sequence of polygonal impulse motions which converges to the given centripetal motion, it would be necessary (but of course not at all sufficient) to have the vertices of each polygonal impulse motion lie on the trajectory of the given centripetal motion. Yet the vertices of any particular polygonal impulse motion lie in a fixed plane (together with the center S), so we cannot place its vertices on the trajectory of the given centripetal motion unless we already know that every such centripetal motion also lies in a fixed plane (together with the center S) or, equivalently, that every such centripetal motion satisfies the Fixed Plane Property:[61] *The areas described by the radius lie in a fixed plane.*

As a result, *a proof of the Impulse Assumption's validity cannot begin until one of two things happens: either we* establish *the Fixed Plane Property for centripetal motions (necessarily via some non-polygonal argument) or we* assume *it.* We take the second option here, putting off a further discussion of planarity issues until Section 8.1.

The demonstration that the Impulse Assumption is valid, given below in outline only with the Fixed Plane Property for centripetal motions assumed, employs Newton's polygonal impulse motion construction from the argument for Proposition 1, but adapts that construction to make sure (1) that the vertices lie on the trajectory of the arbitrarily given centripetal motion and (2) that the *motion* defined on the polygonal path approximates the given centripetal motion. From the mathematical point of view, the rigor of the argument depends on being able to estimate the small but accumulating errors in the approximation of the given centripetal motion by a polygonal impulse motion. Chosen appropriately, a particular polygonal impulse motion can approximate the given centripetal motion well at first, but the approximation achieved by any particular polygonal impulse motion will necessarily become less and less accurate as the polygonal motion traverses the edges of its trajectory. Consider, for example, Figure 3.14 below, which shows the trajectory of the given centripetal motion and the trajectory of a constructed polygonal impulse motion. In order to force the polygonal impulse motion to approximate the centripetal motion, at least in the first subinterval of time, we naturally choose the polygonal motion so it traverses the first edge *AB* with a constant speed that makes it arrive at *B* when the given centripetal motion arrives at *B*. But we cannot then demand that the polygonal impulse motion arrives at the later

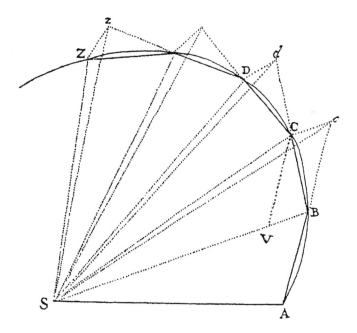

FIGURE 3.14 The argument for the validity of the Impulse Assumption: Newton's original figure for Proposition 1, adapted to illustrate his polygonal impulse strategy applied to a given arbitrary centripetal motion.

vertices $C, D, \ldots$ when the centripetal motion arrives at these points, since every polygonal impulse motion, by definition, traverses each edge in the same time, namely the time it takes to traverse the initial edge AB. Thus our constructed polygonal impulse motion will approximate the given centripetal motion quite well on the edge AB but then less and less well on subsequent edges. As we choose B closer and closer to A, and the number n of edges grows ever larger, we need to know that the error in the approximation of the given motion, even along the last edges where the error is greatest, will tend toward zero. In other words, we need to know that for *every* fixed time t, the location $P_n(t)$ of the n-edged polygonal impulse motion at time t tends toward the location $P(t)$ of the given centripetal motion at time t. (For a rigorous demonstration of this convergence, which turns the Impulse Assumption into a theorem, read Pourciau, "The Importance of Being Equivalent," pp. 308–12.)

No one would expect Newton to have supplied the error estimates required to validate the Impulse Assumption that he takes for granted in the *Principia*'s argument for Proposition 1, and yet he certainly could have improved the cogency of that argument with a simple revision: begin the demonstration with an arbitrary given centripetal motion; either explicitly assume the Fixed Plane Property for centripetal motions (as we do now, below, and as Newton himself did – see Section 8.1 – in the earliest ancestors of Proposition 1) or supply some (necessarily non-polygonal) argument for the Fixed Plane Property;[62] and then describe the construction of polygonal impulse motions that approximate and converge to that given centripetal motion. The Area Property for the given centripetal motion then follows from this convergence and the Area Property for the polygonal impulse motions. We record just such a revision in Section 8.3.

Establishing the Validity of the Impulse Assumption, in outline only, with the Fixed Plane Property assumed: Let $t \to P(t)$ be an arbitrarily given centripetal motion about a center S. Assume the areas described by the radius lie in a fixed plane. Suppose this centripetal motion starts at a place A and traverses the smooth trajectory shown in Figure 3.14. We first construct a polygonal path, with vertices on the trajectory of the given centripetal motion. (After that we will define a motion that traverses this polygonal path). Choose a point B near A on the smooth trajectory. Produce the segment AB to the point c where $Bc = AB$. From c draw the line parallel to the radius SB meeting the smooth trajectory (because, by assumption, S and the smooth trajectory lie together in a fixed plane) in a point C. Produce the segment BC to the point d where $Cd = BC$. From d draw the line parallel to the radius SC meeting the smooth trajectory (again because S and the smooth trajectory lie together in a fixed plane) in a point D. Continue in this way to construct the n vertices of the polygonal path $ABCD...Z$. (The closer we choose B to A, the larger the number n of vertices.) By elementary geometry, the triangles SAB, SBC, SCD, ... all have the same area.

Next we define a motion $t \to P_n(t)$ that traverses the constructed polygonal path: have this motion traverse each edge with constant speed and traverse each edge in the same amount of time h, where h is the time it takes the given centripetal motion to traverse the arc AB. (The constant speed on each edge will generally vary from edge to edge.) We may view this polygonal motion as being generated by a series of instantaneous impulses directed toward S, because the moving deflections $\overrightarrow{cC}$, $\overrightarrow{dD}$, ... generated in the given time h at the vertices B, C, ... have the same directions, respectively, as the radii $\overrightarrow{BS}$, $\overrightarrow{CS}$, ... This constructed polygonal impulse motion also approximates the given centripetal motion $t \to P(t)$ closely at first and then less and less well as time passes.

As we choose the point B closer and closer to A, the number n of vertices increases, yielding a sequence of polygonal impulse motions $t \to P_n(t)$. One can prove that this sequence does in fact converge to the given centripetal motion $t \to P(t)$ as n grows arbitrarily large, in the required sense: that for each fixed time t the location $P_n(t)$ converges to the location $P(t)$. With the Fixed Plane Property assumed, this establishes the Impulse Assumption, that every centripetal motion is a limit of polygonal impulse motions. (To see this convergence, as well as the full Equivalence Assumption, proved rigorously, read Pourciau, "The Importance of Being Equivalent," pp. 308–12.)[63]

Given this demonstration, recorded only in outline here and with the Fixed Plane Property assumed, a restricted version of Newton's Impulse Assumption becomes a theorem:

NEWTON'S WEAK IMPULSE THEOREM. *With the Fixed Plane Property for centripetal motions supposed, every centripetal motion about S is a limit of polygonal impulse motions about S.*

As a consequence of arguments – a rigorous modern proof in note 73 below and a less rigorous but more Newtonian demonstration in Pourciau, "The Importance of Being Equivalent" (pp. 306–8) – that every centripetal motion satisfies the Fixed Plane Property, Newton's Impulse Assumption is actually valid in its general form:

NEWTON'S STRONG IMPULSE THEOREM. *Every centripetal motion about S is a limit of polygonal impulse motions about S.*

Thus Newton's implicit assumption, apparent in his argument for Proposition 1 and elsewhere, *that every motion generated by a centripetal force acting uninterruptedly may be expressed as the limit of motions generated by instantaneous impulses,* has been vindicated.

Ever since the publication of the *Principia,* commentators have been troubled by Newton's unsupported transition from instantaneous impulses to a continuous force. With impulses and continuous forces in mind, Westfall charges that Newton's dynamics are "bedeviled by dimensionally incompatible definitions of force."[64] In his 1974 analysis of the argument for Theorem 1 in "De motu corporum in gyrum," an earlier version of Proposition 1 in the *Principia,* Whiteside criticizes Newton for "ignor[ing] whether significant error is introduced in the total action by supposing at each stage that a continuous force instantaneously directed toward the centre . . . is adequately approximated by an equivalent impulse of force . . . Whether Newton himself ever appreciated these underlying subtleties and the validity of neglecting them is not clear. . ."[65] How, asks Michel Blay, "does Newton respond to . . . Huygens's challenge, to construct a continuous action on the basis of . . . impulses and impacts?" Not well, according to Blay, for Newton never "account[s] for the exact relation between 'the force acting at once with a great impulse' and the centripetal force acting 'uninterrupted.'"[66] I. B. Cohen expresses similar worries: "In Newton's system of dynamics, the two concepts of force – continuous and impulsive – are linked by Newton's concept of time. . . . We make a distinction between them but Newton could effect an easy transition from one to the other, conceiving . . . a continuous force to be the limit of a sequence of impulses. Newton's procedure is troubling to us . . ."[67] Indeed, "it has been argued," writes Cohen, "that the limit of a series of impulsive blows cannot be a continually acting force."[68]

With these Newton scholars, we may fairly criticize Newton for *assuming* – with no justification supplied, indeed, with no recognition of an assumption being made – that every motion generated by a centripetal force acting uninterruptedly may be expressed as the limit of motions generated by impulses. But at least we now know, given the demonstration above, that he was right: "the limit of a series of impulsive blows [*can*] be a [continuously] acting force."

8 PROPOSITION I

As we stressed earlier, common sense tells us to agree on meaning before we ask about truth. Hence in any study of the *Principia*'s fundamental Proposition 1 –

> PROPOSITION I. *Areas which bodies made to move in orbits describe by radii drawn to an unmoving center of forces lie in unmoving planes and are proportional to the times.*
> [*Principia*, p. 444]

– we must clarify the *meaning* of its statement, before we investigate the *truth* of its statement or the cogency of its demonstration. As its conclusion –

(a) FIXED PLANE PROPERTY. *The areas described by the radius lie in a fixed plane, and*
(b) AREA PROPERTY. *The areas described by the radius are proportional to the times*

– needs no clarification,[69] understanding the meaning of Proposition 1 reduces to understanding its hypothesis: *the motion of a "bod [y] made to move in orbit" about "an unmoving center of forces."* In the *Principia* these motions go by various names: a motion "made to move in orbit" (Proposition 1), a motion "urged by a centripetal force" (Proposition 2), an "orbital motion" (scholium preceding Proposition 4), a motion "revolv[ing] in any orbit" (Proposition 6), a motion "attracted toward an immovable center" (Introduction to Section 11). But here, because such motions are under the sole influence of a centripetal force, we have just called them *centripetal motions*.

Oddly, these motions, *the fundamental object of study in Book 1*, receive only a vague description in the *Principia*. An explicit definition – a *mathematical* definition, since Proposition 1 is a mathematical theorem[70] – must be inferred. Fortunately, we have already made the inference. Let us review here the mathematical definition we found in Section 3.3 to be implicit in the *Principia*'s description of a centripetal motion. According to a passage following Definition 5 of centripetal force, a motion $t \to P(t)$ is the motion of a "bod[y] made to move in orbit," (that is, a centripetal motion) about a center S, provided the body is "[continuously (*perpetuo*)] draw[n] . . . back toward" that center. Of course, at any given point $P := P(t_0)$ the obvious measure of this "drawing back" (generated in a brief time h) is the moving deflection $\overrightarrow{LQ}$ generated in that time, and the measure of this "drawing back" *at the point P* would have to be the limit of $\overrightarrow{LQ}/h^2$ as $h \to 0$. The direction of this limit (the "ultimate direction")

must therefore define the direction of the "drawing back" at P.
For a "bod[y] made to move in orbit" about a center S, this direction,
at every time t_0, points toward S. Implicit then in Newton's description is this fundamental mathematical definition:

DEFINITION. Let S be a fixed point. Given the motion $t \to P(t)$ of a body
moved by a continuous force, if at each fixed point P the ultimate
direction of the deflection $\overrightarrow{LQ}$ (that is, the direction of the limit
$lim_{h \to 0}(\overrightarrow{LQ}/h^2)$) is the direction of $\overrightarrow{PS}$, the radius at P, then the motion
is said to be a *centripetal motion about S*.

    With the meaning of its hypothesis, an arbitrarily given centrip-
etal motion, now clear, the meaning of Proposition 1 becomes clear,
and it becomes legitimate to debate questions of truth: *Does Newton
provide a convincing argument for Proposition 1?* Not convincing in
a modern mathematical sense, of course, but as convincing, say, as
the more rigorous arguments in the *Principia?*

    We begin with the logic of his argument. If $p(x)$ stands for a
mathematical statement whose truth depends on x, then Proposition 1
has a common logical form: "For every x in the set A, $p(x)$ is true,"
where here A is the set of all centripetal motions. Any (direct) proof
of such a proposition must begin with an *arbitrarily given* element
of the set A, so that all subsequent conclusions apply to *every* element of A. In the case of Proposition 1, the *Principia's* demonstration
should therefore begin with an arbitrarily given centripetal motion.
But it does not. Instead, Newton constructs a polygonal motion generated by a sequence of n impulses directed toward a fixed point S,
observes that any such "polygonal impulse motion" satisfies both
the Fixed Plane Property and Area Property, and then, letting $n \to \infty$,
claims that his sequence of polygonal impulse motions converges to a
centripetal limit motion which also satisfies the Fixed Plane Property
and Area Property.

    It may be plausible to assume, as Newton apparently does, that
every centripetal motion can be expressed as a limit of polygonal

impulse motions, but without a mathematical proof that would validate this assumption, the *Principia*'s argument for Proposition 1 has an obvious logical defect: at most the argument establishes that every centripetal motion *which happens to be a limit of polygonal impulse motions* satisfies the Fixed Plane Property and Area Property. Without evidence to the contrary, it could well be that some centripetal motions *cannot* be expressed as a limit of polygonal impulse motions, and Newton's argument would tell us nothing about such centripetal motions.

Now as it turns out, Newton was right, as he always seems to be, for we have validated (Section 7 in outline, with the Fixed Plane Property assumed, and in full in Pourciau, "The Importance of Being Equivalent," pp. 308–12) Newton's Impulse Assumption: *that every centripetal motion is the limit of polygonal impulse motions*. But the fact is that Newton *assumes* it, with no comment on it, much less any argument for it. This omission produces a gap in the *Principia*'s argument for Proposition 1. Retaining Newton's strategy, based on the construction of a sequence of polygonal impulse motions, can we close this gap in the *Principia*'s argument for Proposition 1? And is the gap a crack or a crevasse? As we delve further into the demonstration for Proposition 1, let us examine the arguments given for the fixed plane and area properties separately.

8.1   Fixed Plane Property

Appearing in the 1684 tract "De motu corporum in gyrum" as Theorem 1, the earliest ancestor of the *Principia*'s Proposition 1 *implicitly assumes* the planarity of the areas described:[71]

> *Gyrantia omnia radijs ad centrum ductis areas temporibus proportionales describere.*

In the initial revision of "De motu corporum in gyrum," composed in the winter or early spring of 1684–5 and deposited as part of the Lucasian lectures, Theorem 1, now called "Proposition 1, Theorem 1," remains unchanged, but in the early summer of 1685,

Newton composed a revision of this theorem for "De motu Corporum Liber primus"[72] –

> *Areas quas corpora in gyros ad immobile centrum virium*
> *ductis describunt, et in planis immobilibus consistere et esse*
> *temporibus proportionales.*

– a revision whose text passed almost unchanged into the 1687 *Principia*. Notice that the Fixed Plane Property, which had been an *implicit assumption*, has now become an *explicit conclusion*. But Newton would have been better off rewinding this revision process, keeping the Fixed Plane Property as an *assumption* in the *Principia's* Proposition 1:

PROPOSITION I (AMENDED). *The areas which a body made to move in orbit describe by a radius drawn to an unmoving center of force, supposing those areas to lie in an unmoving plane, are proportional to the times.*

Why? Because moving the Fixed Plane Property from assumption to conclusion leads to a non-trivial mathematical error in the *Principia*: *Newton's strategy for demonstrating Proposition 1, based on an approximation by polygonal impulse motions, does not, in fact cannot possibly, establish the Fixed Plane Property for centripetal motions.*

To see that this is so, let us start by repairing the initial logic of the demonstration, beginning the argument the way it should have begun, with an arbitrarily given centripetal motion about a center S, and think about how we might express this centripetal motion as a limit of polygonal impulse motions about S. (We are repeating what we have already seen in Section 7, but it bears repeating.) Each individual polygonal impulse motion, using impulses directed toward S, would have to be constructed to approximate the given centripetal motion (with the approximation improving as the number of impulses increases), and in any such approximation the vertices of the constructed polygonal impulse motion would have to lie on the trajectory of the centripetal motion. Now the vertices of any single polygonal impulse motion, by the way these motions are defined by Newton, will lie in a fixed plane. But we do not yet know – for this is half of what we are trying to establish – that the trajectory of a centripetal motion must also lie in a fixed plane. It follows that we *cannot* place the vertices of a polygonal impulse motion on the trajectory of our given centripetal motion. This circularity – that we cannot approximate a given centripetal motion with a sequence of polygonal impulse motions unless we already know the planarity of the centripetal motion, a planarity our demonstration seeks to prove – is *a fatal flaw for the polygonal impulse strategy in any argument for the Fixed Plane Property of centripetal motions.*

Planarity is the problem. Before we can construct a sequence of polygonal impulse motions approximating the given centripetal motion, we have to know that the centripetal motion and the center S lie together in a fixed plane. But we have just seen that this Fixed Plane Property cannot be established by Newton's polygonal impulse approximation. It follows that the Fixed Plane Property must be assumed in the hypothesis of the proposition or else demonstrated *first, before* polygonal impulse approximation can be used to prove the Area Property, and this demonstration would have to apply some mathematical technique *other* than polygonal approximation.

Knowing that polygonal approximation cannot work, and given the other mathematical tools available to him, could Newton have given a convincing argument for the Fixed Plane Property? The answer is *probably not.* Calling on vector functions, cross-products, and vector derivatives, the modern proof is simple,[73] but restricted to Newtonian mathematics a convincing argument would be hard to construct. Why? Because any proof of the Fixed Plane Property for centripetal motions must, either explicitly or implicitly, measure the inclination of the local plane of motion at each location P – this is the plane that contains the radius SP and the tangent line PL to the orbit at P – and then demonstrate that this inclination never varies as P traverses the orbit. As the inclination of such a local plane of motion is determined by a vector perpendicular to that plane, any argument for the Fixed Plane Property must show a vector perpendicular to the local plane of motion at P will remain parallel to itself as P moves with the given centripetal motion along the orbit. With his mathematical tools nicely adapted to analyze motion in a *plane*, but not the direction of moving vectors in space, it is therefore difficult to see how Newton could have put together a persuasive argument for the Fixed Plane Property, as persuasive, say, as the more rigorous demonstrations in the *Principia*.

Difficulties with the Fixed Plane Property are not Newton's alone. Indeed, no treatise on orbital motion in the eighteenth century, nor any book on mechanics from the nineteenth century (in a personal sample), gives a convincing demonstration of the Fixed Plane Property. The planarity of a centripetal motion is implicitly or explicitly assumed, said to be obvious, or "deduced" from an unconvincing argument. As late as 1914, we find Lamb's *Dynamics* taking the middle option, that the planarity is obvious: "The particle will obviously remain in the plane containing the centre of force and the tangent to the orbit at any given instant."[74] Of course, it does indeed seem "obvious" that the orbit of a centripetal motion must lie in a fixed plane that contains the center, for anything else would violate both our physical and mathematical intuition. But such intuitions do not constitute a rigorous mathematical argument, even assuming just a *Principian* level of rigor. A reasonably persuasive demonstration of the Fixed Plane Property for centripetal motions, one written in Newtonian style, but probably not one that Newton could have given, can be found in Pourciau, "Newton's Argument for Proposition 1," pp. 306–8.

It is interesting to note that in the extensive literature critical of Newton's argument for Proposition 1, what commentators have worried about – the convergence of motions generated by impulses to a motion generated by a continuous force (indeed, necessarily to an *arbitrary* centripetal motion) – *can* be justified (see Section 7 and below); what commentators have *not* worried about – the Fixed Plane

Property – *cannot* be justified, at least not by the *Principia*'s strategy of polygonal approximation.

8.2   Area Property

> But here it is too blithely said that the aggregate of the infinity
> of discrete infinitesimal impulses of force acting "instantly"
> towards *S* at "every" point of the arc . . . becomes a force acting
> "without break" over the arc "ever" towards the centre *S*.

So writes D. T. Whiteside[75] regarding the lines that conclude Newton's argument for Proposition 1, perhaps the most notorious lines in the entire *Principia*:

> Now let the number of triangles be increased and their width
> decreased indefinitely, and their ultimate perimeter . . . will . . .
> be a curved line; and thus the centripetal force by which the body
> is [continuously (*perpetuo*): see note 16] drawn back from the
> tangent of this curve will act uninterruptedly. . . [*Principia*, p. 445]

Why notorious? Because, at the crux of the demonstration for this most fundamental proposition, these lines assert a crucial convergence – the convergence of a sequence of motions generated by instantaneous impulses to a (centripetal) motion generated by a continuous force – but they assert this convergence baldly, with little justification. The *Principia*'s analysis of orbital motion in Book 1 depends crucially on Proposition 1 – as it provides a fixed plane for making the analysis and a geometrical clock for recording the time – and yet the argument for Proposition 1 seems to hang by the slimmest of threads: an unsupported and suspect claim that a body moved in a polygonal path by a series of impulses, as the time between impulses tends toward zero, can have a limit motion that moves *exactly* like a body moved in a smooth curve by a continuous force. Actually the thread is even slimmer: Yes, the argument for Proposition 1 assumes that the constructed polygonal motions generated by impulses have as their limit a (centripetal) motion generated by a continuous force, and over the years the extensive critical commentary has worried about this assumption. But to concentrate solely on this assumption is to miss the *real* worry, for Newton implicitly assumes (and the validity of his argument requires) much more: *that every "body made to move in orbit" (that is, every centripetal motion) can be expressed as such a limit of polygonal impulse motions.*

Of course, we have seen this assumption before, in Section 7, where it was called Newton's Impulse Assumption and where, *supposing the Fixed Plane Property for centripetal motions,* we provided the outline of a proof which turned a weaker version of that assumption into a theorem:

NEWTON'S WEAK IMPULSE THEOREM. *With the Fixed Plane Property for centripetal motions supposed, every centripetal motion about S is a limit of polygonal impulse motions about S.*

By replacing Newton's implicit assumption with an explicit demonstration (at least in outline) of this theorem, we can dramatically increase the cogency of the *Principia*'s argument for the Area Property in Proposition 1. See the repaired demonstration below. *Note, though, that any attempt to apply the Weak Impulse Theorem in an argument for the* other *half of Proposition 1, the Fixed Plane Property, would be guilty of assuming what we are trying to prove, and any attempt to apply the Strong Impulse Theorem (that every centripetal motion about S is a limit of polygonal impulse motions about S) for the same purpose would also be circular, since the polygonal approximation used to establish the Strong Impulse Theorem requires the Fixed Plane Property.*

8.3   A repaired demonstration

We now offer a revised and more convincing version of the *Principia*'s demonstration of the Area Property in Proposition 1, with the Fixed Plane Property assumed. This demonstration, cast in the style of the *Principia* (or, rather, in the style of the English translation by Cohen and Whitman), follows the outlined argument provided for the Weak

Impulse Theorem in Section 7: given an arbitrary centripetal motion, we adapt Newton's construction of polygonal impulse motions in a manner that forces the sequence of polygonal impulse motions to converge to the given centripetal motion.

By the way, in the construction below of the sequence of polygonal impulse motions, note the explanation, courtesy of the Compound Second Law (the second law as Newton understood it), of the point V in Newton's figure drawn to illustrate his argument for Proposition 1: $\overrightarrow{BV}$ is the resting deflection of the impulse required at B to make the polygonal impulse motion approximate (at least initially) the given centripetal motion. (Figure 3.14 shows Newton's original figure, revised to include the trajectory of an arbitrarily given centripetal motion.)

PROPOSITION I (AMENDED). *Areas which bodies made to move in orbits describe by radii drawn to an unmoving center of forces, supposing those areas to lie in an unmoving plane, are proportional to the times.*

A revised and partially repaired demonstration of Proposition 1, with the Fixed Plane Property assumed. Let a body be made to move in orbit about an immovable center S. This given motion, for brevity, may be called a *centripetal motion.* Suppose the total time to be divided into equal small parts. In the first part of time, if this body describes the arc AB, then in this same part of time let a second body (identical to the first) by its inherent force uniformly describe the straight line AB. In the second part of the time, if nothing hindered it, this second body would (by law 1) go straight on to c describing line Bc equal to AB, so that – when radii AS, BS, and cS were drawn to the center – the equal areas ASB and BSc would be described. (Refer to Figure 3.14.)

The line cC drawn parallel to BS will meet the given curved trajectory, in some point C, because the triangle SAB and hence the line cC lie in the unmoving plane of the given centripetal motion. Let V complete the parallelogram $BcCV$. When the second body comes to B, let an impulse act, an impulse which in the second part of time would move this body, were it deprived of all motion, from B to V. This impulse will make the moving body deviate from the straight line Bc and proceed in the straight line BC, arriving at C (by Law 2 [the Compound Second Law]) when the second part of time has been completed. Because SB and cC are parallel, triangle SBC will be equal to triangle SBc and thus also to triangle SAB. By a similar argument, if impulses act toward S successively at $C, D, E, \ldots$, making the body in each of the individual small and equal parts of time describe the individual straight lines $CD, DE, \ldots$, then triangle SCD will be equal to triangle SBC, SDE to SCD, and so on.

Hence in equal times equal areas are described by a radius drawn from the second body to S. As the individual parts of the time decrease toward zero, the number of vertices will increase beyond all bounds, the final vertex will tend toward the final position of the first body in the given centripetal motion, and the resulting constructed sequence of polygonal impulse motions of the second body will approximate the given centripetal motion of the first body more and more nearly. The ultimate motion (the limit motion) of the second body will therefore move as one with the given centripetal motion of the first body. As each polygonal impulse motion, by a radius drawn to S, describes areas proportional to the times, so will the ultimate motion of these polygonal motions, and therefore so will the given centripetal motion. QED

9 PROPOSITION 6

In May of 1694, when David Gregory arrived in Cambridge for a visit, Newton showed him manuscript pages from his most recent project: a radical restructuring, based on the mathematical notion of curvature, of the 1687 *Principia*'s first book.[76] For whatever reason, this restructuring, planned for the second edition, never made it into the *Principia*. Instead, bits and pieces of this scheme were shoehorned into the existing first edition structure, surfacing in the second edition as new corollaries or, under the heading *Idem aliter*, as alternate solutions.

In the case of Proposition 6, both the original first edition Proposition 6 and an alternate measure of centripetal force expressed in terms of curvature appear as corollaries (Corollary 1 and Corollary 3, respectively) of a new Proposition 6:

> PROPOSITION 6 [1713 AND 1726 PRINCIPIA]. *If in a nonresisting space a body revolves in any orbit about an immobile center and describes any just-nascent arc in a minimally small time, and if the sagitta of the arc is understood to be drawn so as to bisect the chord and, when produced, to pass through the center of forces, the centripetal force in the middle of the arc will be as the sagitta directly and as the time twice [i.e., as the square of the time] inversely. [Principia, pp. 453–4]*

Propositions 7 through 13 record and articulate the *Principia's* solutions to specific instances of the so-called *Direct Problem: given a centripetal motion, to deduce the law of force from the location of the center and the shape of the orbit.* To arrive at these solutions, Newton applies a method for computing the centripetal force (which is his measure of the given impressed force) from the motion of the body. It is Proposition 6 which supplies this method.

To understand Proposition 6, we must understand its four ingredients: the motion of a body that "revolves in any orbit about an immobile center," the "centripetal force," the "sagitta of the arc," and "will be as."

Fortunately, from our work on centripetal force and its measures, in Sections 3.3 and 4, two of these ingredients are already understood: the motion of a body that "revolves in any orbit about an immobile center" is just a centripetal motion $t \rightarrow P(t)$, and the "centripetal force" is the quantity $M \cdot (\overrightarrow{PG}/h^2)$, where $\overrightarrow{PG}$ is the segment the body would have described in the time h, had the impressed force that acts on the moving body at P, "in the middle of the arc," acted on the body *at rest* at P. And from our work on evanescent quantities, in Section 2.2, we remember what the "will be as" language is telling us: first, that the ratio

$$\frac{M(PG/h^2)}{PX/h^2},$$

tends toward a non-zero finite constant as $h \to 0$, where PX stands for the length of the "sagitta" $\overrightarrow{PX}$, whatever *that* is, and second, that the direction of $\overrightarrow{PX}$ tends toward the direction of $\overrightarrow{PG}$. Only this "sagitta" $\overrightarrow{PX}$ remains then to be clarified.

But to get this right requires some care, for the little "sagitta" (literally "arrow") has caused not so little problems for commentators. In his "Guide to the *Principia*," Cohen tells us the "sagitta" of an arc was used rather loosely by Newton and his contemporaries to refer to a line segment or "arrow" $\overrightarrow{PX}$ drawn from some point P of the arc to some point X of the chord of that arc, where either P is the middle of the arc or X is the middle of the chord (or both).[77]

In Proposition 6, where the arc would be a small arc qQ of a given centripetal motion $t \to P(t)$ about some center S, Newton describes his particular sagitta this way: drawn from the "middle of the arc," it "bisects the chord and, when produced, [passes] through the center of forces" (*Principia*, p. 454). But taking this description *literally*, which would have Newton requiring his sagitta to satisfy the following three conditions – (1) P is the middle of the arc qQ, (2) X bisects the chord qQ, (3) the sagitta $\overrightarrow{PX}$, when produced, passes through the center S – would be a mistake, for clearly Newton *cannot* mean that the sagitta should satisfy all three of these conditions, at least

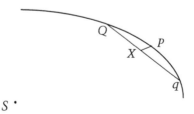

FIGURE 3.15 Uncovering the meaning of Newton's "sagitta" in Proposition 6.

not all three *exactly*, since the unique sagitta determined by any two of the conditions would not in general satisfy the third. Rather he must mean that his sagitta satisfies two of these conditions *exactly* and the third *approximately* (and with that third condition holding exactly only *in the limit* as q and Q tend toward P). But which two must hold exactly and which one only approximately? Doubling this ambiguity, note that condition (1), that P is the middle of the arc, is open to multiple interpretations: "middle" with respect to what measure? Arc length? Time? Some other measure? Depending on which of the three conditions on the sagitta is supposed to hold only approximately and depending on the interpretation of "middle," at least *six* different sagittas could be the particular sagitta that Newton has in mind. Which is it?

Such ambiguities, arising from the *statement* of a theorem, often find their resolution in the *argument* for that theorem. In the case of Proposition 6, Newton's argument calls on Corollary 4 of Proposition 1, a corollary which refers to "those sagittas of arcs described *in equal times* which [when produced] *converge to the center of forces* and *bisect the chords*" (*Principia*, p. 446, emphasis added). Because the demonstration cites this corollary, the sagitta of Proposition 6 must be the sagitta of this corollary. Thus Newton's sagitta $\overrightarrow{PX}$, when produced, will *not* pass through the center S, except in the limit, for it "converges to" that center. Now, of the three conditions above on the sagitta, we know that it is condition (3) which holds only approximately. Moreover, the point P, the "middle of the arc" qQ by condition (1), is the middle with respect to *time*, not arc length nor any other measure, for the "arcs [qP and PQ] are described in equal times."

We have thus identified which of the six sagittas is Newton's:

DEFINITION. Given any motion $t \to P(t)$, with $P := P(t_0)$, $q := P(t_0 - h)$, and $Q := P(t_0 + h)$, the arrow $\overrightarrow{PX}$, where X bisects the chord qQ, is called the *sagitta of the arc* qQ.

This sagitta $\overrightarrow{PX}$ satisfies conditions (1) and (2) above exactly and condition (3) – assuming a *centripetal* motion – only approximately (but exactly in the limit): the point P is the middle of the arc qQ with respect to *time*, X bisects the chord qQ, yet $\overrightarrow{PX}$, when produced, will *not* in general pass through the center S, although it will "*converge to the center of forces*" S as $h \to 0$. Indeed, the proof of Proposition 6 below confirms in particular that the limit of $\overrightarrow{PX}/h^2$ as $h \to 0$ has the same direction as $\overrightarrow{PS}$.

With Newton's "sagitta of the arc" pinned down, and already knowing what he means by the other three ingredients of Proposition 6 – the motion of a body that "revolves in any orbit about an immobile center," the "centripetal force," and the "will be as" language in the conclusion – we now know exactly what Proposition 6 asserts. Recall that a body with "quantity of matter" M moves in a centripetal motion $t \to P(t)$ about some center S provided at each fixed place $P := P(t_0)$ the moving deflection $\overrightarrow{LQ}$ (generated in a small time h) points toward S in the limit as $h \to 0$, in the sense that the direction of $\lim_{h\to 0}(\overrightarrow{LQ}/h^2)$ is the direction of $\overrightarrow{PS}$. Consider the impressed force that generates the deflection $\overrightarrow{LQ}$ when it acts on the moving body at P, and imagine that same impressed force would generate the deflection $\overrightarrow{PG}$ had it acted on the same body *resting* at P. Then recall that the measure of this impressed force that Newton calls the *centripetal force* is the quantity $M(\overrightarrow{PG}/h^2)$.

PROPOSITION 6 (CLARIFIED). *If a body with quantity of matter M "revolves in any orbit about an immobile center," then the "centripetal force in the middle of the arc . . . will be as the sagitta directly and as the time twice inversely." In other words, at any given point P of a centripetal motion $t \to P(t)$,*

$$M \frac{\overrightarrow{PG}}{h^2} \text{ will be as } \frac{\overrightarrow{PX}}{h^2}$$

as $h \to 0$; that is, the ratio

$$\frac{M \cdot PG/h^2}{PX/h^2}$$

tends toward a non-zero finite constant as $h \to 0$, and the sagitta $\overrightarrow{PX}$ ultimately has the direction of $\overrightarrow{PG}$.

Only now, with its meaning resolved, does it make sense to consider the *truth* of Proposition 6.

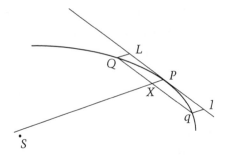

FIGURE 3.16 Newton's "sagitta" $\overrightarrow{PX}$, from the center P (with respect to time) of the arc qQ to the center X (with respect to length) of the chord qQ, turns out to be the average of the moving deflection $\overrightarrow{LQ}$ and the "backwards" moving deflection $\overrightarrow{lq}$. Newton may well have this property in mind when he writes that the deflection $\overrightarrow{LQ}$ "is equal to the sagitta of an arc that is twice the length of arc QP, with P being in the middle" (*Principia*, p. 454).

Proof. Let a body with quantity of matter M revolve in an arbitrary centripetal motion $t \to P(t)$ about the center S. Fix a time t_0 and let $\overrightarrow{PX}$ be the sagitta of the arc qQ: $P := P(t_0)$, $q := P(t_0 - h)$, $Q := P(t_0 + h)$, and X bisects the chord qQ. Let $\overrightarrow{LQ}$ be the moving deflection generated by the force acting along the arc PQ. Provided we take $\overrightarrow{Pl}$ to be $- \overrightarrow{PL}$, we may consider $\overrightarrow{lq}$ as the moving deflection generated by the force acting along the arc Pq for the same body, with time flowing (and the body therefore moving) in the opposite direction.[78]

If the time increment h is very small, then the impressed force is nearly constant (in direction and magnitude) during the time interval from $t_0 - h$ to $t_0 + h$. If the impressed force *were* exactly constant, then the Compound Second Law (Newton's second law as he understood it) would apply exactly: $\overrightarrow{LQ} = \overrightarrow{PG}$ and $\overrightarrow{lq} = \overrightarrow{PG}$, where $\overrightarrow{PG}$ is the deflection that would be generated had the same impressed force that generated $\overrightarrow{LQ}$ and $\overrightarrow{lq}$ been applied to the body at rest at P. We would then have

$$\overrightarrow{PX} = \frac{1}{2}(\overrightarrow{PQ} + \overrightarrow{Pq})$$
$$= \frac{1}{2}(\overrightarrow{PL} + \overrightarrow{LQ} + \overrightarrow{Pl} + \overrightarrow{lq})$$
$$= \frac{1}{2}(\overrightarrow{LQ} + \overrightarrow{lq})$$
$$= \frac{1}{2}(\overrightarrow{PG} + \overrightarrow{PG}) = \overrightarrow{PG}$$

But of course the impressed force over the time interval $t_0 \pm h$ is not exactly constant no matter how small we take h, so instead of the equality $\overrightarrow{PX} = \overrightarrow{PG}$, we have the approximation $\overrightarrow{PX} \approx \overrightarrow{PG}$, where the error in the approximation is so small (tending to zero faster than h^2) that we have equality in the limit:

$$\lim_{h \to 0} \frac{\overline{PX}}{h^2} = \lim_{h \to 0} \frac{\overline{PG}}{h^2} \qquad (*)$$

From this equality, we infer that the limiting direction of the sagitta $\overrightarrow{PX}$ is the (fixed) direction of $\overrightarrow{PG}$, and we infer as well the limit

$$\frac{M \cdot PG/h^2}{PX/h^2} \to M \qquad (**)$$

In other words, the "centripetal force $[M \cdot \overrightarrow{PG}/h^2]$ in the middle of the arc ... will be as the sagitta $[\overrightarrow{PX}]$ directly and as the time twice $[h^2]$ inversely." QED

Notice, in particular, that the "ultimate direction" of the sagitta $\overrightarrow{PX}$, that is, the direction of $\lim_{h \to 0}(\overrightarrow{PX}/h^2)$, is the direction of the resting deflection $\overrightarrow{PG}$, which is the direction of the radius $\overrightarrow{PS}$; so that condition (3) above – that the sagitta $\overrightarrow{PX}$, when produced, passes through the center S – does in fact hold *in the limit as $h \to 0$*, as promised.

Before we leave this fundamental proposition, let us verify a claim we made earlier, in Section 5.3.2, that Proposition 6 asserts the *Principia's* version of $\mathbf{f} = m\mathbf{a}$. The limit statement $(**)$ in the argument above can be written horizontally, as

$$M \cdot \frac{PG}{h^2} = M_h \cdot \frac{PX}{h^2}$$

where $M_h \to M$ as $h \to 0$. Multiplying both sides by 2, taking the limit, and noting from $(*)$ that the sagitta $\overrightarrow{PX}$ ultimately has the direction of the resting deflection $\overrightarrow{PG}$, we obtain[79] $\overrightarrow{F} = M\overrightarrow{A}$.

10   CONCLUSION

The history of commentary on the *Principia*'s early foundational sections is a history of questions and confusions: What, exactly, and *mathematically*, does Newton mean by a centripetal force? By the "motive quantity of centripetal force"? This "motive force" is defined as (being proportional to) the "motion which it generates in a given time"; so it must be the "quantity of matter" times a change in velocity or speed. But what sort of change in velocity does Newton have in mind? Is it measured on a body in motion or at rest? Is it directional? A scalar? And how does the "motive force" differ from the "change in motion" in the statement of the second law? What, exactly, does the second law assert? Is it more a definition than a law? Does it apply only to an impulse? If so, how can it be used to solve even the most basic dynamical problems – such as finding the parabolic motion of a projected body subject to uniform gravity? Would any application of the second law to a continuous force have to involve an approximation by instantaneous impulses in series? Can a continuous (centripetal) force really *be* the limit of such impulses? What would this even mean? Is this Newton's best understanding of limits, of an ultimate ratio: that the "ultimate ratio of vanishing quantities is . . . the ratio with which they vanish"? What would that say about his understanding of the limit processes which underlie the fundamental concepts and arguments of the *Principia*? The argument for Proposition 1 depends on approximating the motion of a body "made to move in orbit" by a sequence of polygonal motions generated by impulses, an approximation baldly asserted in the demonstration. How would such an approximation work, exactly? And *does* it work? But these last two questions make no sense until we answer a prior question: What does Newton mean by the motion of a "body made to move in orbit"? And what about the fundamental Proposition 6, cipher-like because of its mysterious ingredients: "a body revol[ving] in any orbit," the "saggita of the arc," a measure of force called "centripetal force," and the assertion that one quantity "will be as" another?

Yet all this confusion, though Newton's fault, is not Newton's confusion. The *Principia*'s often ambiguous and sometimes missing definitions for fundamental concepts have led commentators to mistaken interpretations for these definitions, interpretations that do not capture Newton's intended meanings, and these interpretations in turn have led to misreadings – of laws, propositions, and demonstrations – and ultimately to a distorted view of the *Principia*'s early sections, a view that makes these foundations, and Newton's understanding, appear muddled, incoherent, and unnatural. But, as the present study documents, once we get the meanings right, once, that is, we uncover the precise definitions that represent Newton's intended meanings, then the distortions of the received view fall away, and we see the *Principia*'s foundations as they really are: natural, coherent, and (almost completely) correct. Indeed, in the long stretch of definitions, laws, lemmas, propositions, corollaries, and demonstrations leading to Proposition 6,[80] Newton makes just *one* serious (meaning fundamental and irreparable) error: assuming that his polygonal approximation argument for Proposition 1 establishes the Fixed Plane Property for centripetal motions.[81] Other flaws are sins of imprecision and omission only, not conception. This is remarkable, revealing a mastery of the fundamental notions in "rational mechanics" – "the science," as Newton puts it, "expressed in exact propositions and demonstrations, of the motions that result from any forces whatever and of the forces that are required for any motions whatever" (*Principia*, p. 382) – dramatically at odds with the picture drawn in the received view.

11 EDITORS' NOTE

The distinction Pourciau draws between "The *motive quantity of centripetal force*" in his "Definition 8 (Clarified)" and "The *centripetal quantity of centripetal force*," in his immediately subsequent Definition has no textual basis in the *Principia* or in earlier writings, including the 1685 version of Newton's "System of the World," where the technical distinction between accelerative and motive force is first introduced: "And the motive force by which one globe is drawn toward the other one, and which people commonly designate in terrestrial bodies by the word weight, is as the product of the quantities of matter in the two globes divided by the square of the distance between their centers" [ULC Add. 3990, Article 26]. By replacing Newton's Definition 8 with his "Definition 8 (Clarified)," Pourciau devises a means for reading Newton's second law of motion, as it is stated in all editions of the *Principia*, to conform with Newton's explication of "the meaning of the Law" in the manuscript from the early 1690s that is the centerpiece of this chapter. This is the virtue of Pourciau's "Definition 8 (Clarified)" and the distinction he draws with his Definition of "the centripetal quantity of centripetal force."

Whether Newton's word-for-word statement of the second law in the *Principia* can be legitimately interpreted as Pourciau is proposing or not, the various other claims he makes about the relation between the citations of the second law in the *Principia* and the interpretation of it that Newton offered in the early 1690s are independent of this question. Perhaps Newton did intend the phrase "in a given time" in his statement of Definition 8 to open the way to reading his second law as applying to both discrete and continuous forces. If this was his intention, it did not succeed, for (as Pourciau notes) no major physicists in the eighteenth century seem to have seen this possible reading in so far as they do not credit Newton with what we now regard as his second law. The alternative, as noted in the Introduction to this volume, is to take the second law as stated at face value, and deny that Newton anywhere in any edition of the *Principia* makes clear how it can be reconciled with the many places in which it is cited as applying to continuous, uninterrupted forces, as measured by the product of the mass and an incremental distance divided by a time increment squared (i.e., in Pourciau's notation, by $M \cdot (PG/h^2)$. This alternative is the position the late I. B. Cohen adopted in his chapter, but who then (as Pourciau stresses above) had to face the problem of explaining how Newton understood the second law as applying to continuous, uninterrupted forces in so many places in the *Principia*, starting with Lemma 10 and Proposition 6. Difficulty in resolving the conflict between these two positions on any textual basis is a reason why both chapters have been included in this volume.

NOTES

1 Isaac Newton. *The Principia, Mathematical Principles of Natural Philosophy: A New Translation*, trans. I. Bernard Cohen and Anne Whitman, assisted by Julia Budenz, preceded by "A Guide to Newton's Principia" by I. B. Cohen (Berkeley, CA: University of California Press, 1999). Hereafter referred to as *Principia*.

2 Isaac Newton, *The Mathematical Papers of Isaac Newton, Volume VI*, edited and with extensive commentaries by D. T. Whiteside (Cambridge: Cambridge University Press, 1967–1981), pp. 538–609.

3 Newton, *Mathematical Papers Volume VI*, pp. 538–43, emphasis added.

4 The anachronistic overhead arrow notation does not distort Newton's meaning. Indeed, it is used merely to record that a particular line segment has a direction, not just a length. Such directed line segments are found all through the *Principia*. We write $\vec{ab} = \vec{AB}$ to mean that the directed line segments are, as Newton puts it, "parallel and equal," that is, parallel, with the same sense of direction, and equal length.

5 Indeed Euler called this assumption the basic "ground of measuring" forces in his *Theoria motus corporum solidorum seu rigidorum* (Theory of Motion for Bodies Solid or Rigid), published in 1765, and he took it as a fundamental axiom of his mechanics (not realizing that the axiom was the *Principia*'s second law). (Leonhard Euler, *Theoria motus corporum solidorum seu rigidorum: ex primus nostrae cognitionis principiis stabilita et ad omnes motus, qui in huis modi corpora cadere possunt, accommodata*, vol. 3 of Leonhardi Euleri, *Opera Omnia, Series II: Opera Mechanica et Astronomica* [Berlin: Birkhäuser, 1948; originally published by Orell Füssli 1765], p. 69.)

6 Cohen and Whitman, in *Principia*, render "evanescentium" as "vanishing," but "evanescent" would be more accurate, since these quantities do not generally ever "vanish," but they do "evanesce" (as in "fade from sight"): they do not actually *become* zero, but they do *tend toward* zero.

7 The question is often asked, Is there evidence that Newton derived his propositions initially by the methods of (algebraic) calculus, before recasting his arguments geometrically for inclusion in the *Principia*? The short answer is no. For the long answer, see D. T. Whiteside, "The Mathematical Principles Underlying Newton's *Principia Mathematica*," *Journal for the History of Astronomy* 1 (1970), 116–38 and Niccolò Guicciardini, *Isaac Newton on Mathematical Certainty and Method* (Cambridge, MA: MIT Press, 2009), pp. 252–4. Both Whiteside (in "The Prehistory of the Principia from 1664 to 1686," *Notes and Records of the Royal Society of London* 45 [1991], 11–61) and Guicciardini, because the issues involved are complex, regard the question as "ill-formed and therefore meaningless."

8 Recall that tan h = sin h/cos h and cos h → 1 as h → 0, which tells us the limit (tan h)/h → 1 is essentially equivalent to the limit (sin h)/h → 1, often called the "The Basic Trigonometric Limit" in calculus because it yields the derivative of the sine function and hence the derivatives for the rest of the trigonometric functions. Thus Lemma 7 can be seen as a geometric version of this basic trigonometric limit. Indeed, apart from Lemma 10, which characterizes a finite force, *every* lemma in Section 1 (Book 1), a collection of eleven preliminary mathematical lemmas, can be seen as a natural geometric replacement for an elementary and fundamental definition, property, or theorem of calculus. See Bruce Pourciau, "The Preliminary Mathematical Lemmas of Newton's *Principia*," *Archive for History of Exact Sciences* 52 (1998), 279–95.

9 The quantity 1 − cos h would have been called by Newton the "versed sine" of the (circular) arc of length h. In the figure below (*Principia*, p. 306), originally found in Charles Hutton's *A Course in Mathematics*, published in 1798–1801, the circular arc AB has sine BF, cosine CF, tangent AH, and versed sine AF (=1 − CF).

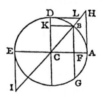

Newton can be found (in Proposition 6, for example) using the versed sine – or, more precisely, the "sagitta," a generalized version of the versed sine for noncircular arcs (*Principia*, p. 307) – to gauge the moving deflection, generated by the centripetal force, from the tangent back toward the force center. Starting from B in Hutton's figure, produce a line parallel to AE until it meets the tangent AH in, say, R. Then $\overrightarrow{RB}$ can be seen as (almost) measuring the "deflection from the tangent," and of course $\overrightarrow{RB} = \overrightarrow{AF}$, the versed sine. Just as the versed sine $1 - \cos h$ of the circular arc h is as h^2 as $h \to 0$, so we shall see later that the deflection from the tangent (the moving deflection) generated in a time h by a finite force is as the square h^2 of that time.

10 Niccolò Guicciardini, *Reading the Principia: The Debate on Newton's Mathematical Methods for Natural Philosophy from 1687 to 1736* (Cambridge: Cambridge University Press, 1999), p. 159; Gottfried W. Leibniz, *Die philosophischen Schriften von G.W. Leibniz*, 7 vols. (Berlin: Weidmannische Buchhandlung, 1875–1890; reprinted Hildesheim: Olms, 1978), vol. 2, p. 305.

11 Some might argue that the work of Abraham Robinson (*Non-Standard Analysis* [Amsterdam: North-Holland, 1966]) finally justified Leibniz's analysis with infinitesimals, by rigorously establishing their mathematical existence and properties. But Robinson could only establish their existence by finding them in a very different place. In his theory, non-standard analysis, infinitesimals still do not exist in the standard real line, the real line of Cauchy and Weierstrass; they exist only in the so-called "hyperreal line," a set characterized by some quite complicated axioms. In any case, at the time of the *Principia*, "infinitesimals" could not be justified, but limits could.

12 We shall be using the "colon-equal symbol" := to mean equals *by definition*.

13 See note 16 below.

14 Newton actually refers, not to LQ, but to RQ, where R, on the tangent to the orbit at P, makes RQ parallel to the radius SP. But LQ or RQ, it does not matter, for these "line-elements" are virtually the same: their difference tends toward zero *faster* than the square of the time h, so that LQ/h^2 and RQ/h^2 have the same limit as $h \to 0$.

15 In the case of d'Alembert, for example, who strove to retain only directly observable measures in his mechanics, this distinction between force and the deflection it generates did not exist. To him, the observed deflection *was* the force. "Forces inherent to bodies in motion," he argued, are "obscure and metaphysical beings, capable of nothing but spreading darkness over a science clear by itself" (Jean d'Alembert, *Traité de Dynamique* [New York: Johnson Reprint Corporation, 1968; reprint of the second edition, Paris: David, 1758], p. xvii). See also C. Truesdell, *Essays in the History of Mechanics* (New York: Springer-Verlag, 1968), p. 113.

16 Or the limit of $2\overrightarrow{LQ}/h^2$, which gives the modern vector acceleration: using modern notation and Taylor series, with $\mathbf{r}$, $\mathbf{v}$, and $\mathbf{a}$ standing for the motion, the vector velocity, and the vector acceleration, respectively, we have $\overrightarrow{SL} = \mathbf{r}(t_0) + \mathbf{v}(t_0)h$ and $\overrightarrow{SQ} = \mathbf{r}(t_0 + h) = \mathbf{r}(t_0) + \mathbf{v}(t_0)h + \frac{1}{2}\mathbf{a}(t_0)h^2 + \cdots$, where S is the origin, so that $\overrightarrow{LQ} = \frac{1}{2}\mathbf{a}(t_0)h^2 + \cdots$ and $2(\overrightarrow{LQ}/h^2) = \mathbf{a}(t_0) + \cdots \to \mathbf{a}(t_0)$.

Today we define and compute the vector acceleration $\mathbf{a}(t) = \mathbf{v}'(t)$ by taking the derivative of the vector velocity, but through the end of the eighteenth century scientists still used (twice) the moving or resting deflection over the square of the time to compute the acceleration and hence the force. For example, in *Mécanique analytique* (first published in 1788, with a second expanded edition in two volumes, the first appearing in 1811, the second in 1815) Lagrange writes that

> the value of the applied force on a body at any instant of time can always be determined by comparing . . . the distance [namely the resting deflection $\overrightarrow{PG}$] the body traverses with the square [h^2] of the duration of that instant. It is not even necessary that the body actually traverses this distance. It is sufficient that it can be imagined to be traversed by a composite motion [namely the moving deflection $\overrightarrow{LQ}$, which is the composite motion $\overrightarrow{PQ} - \overrightarrow{PL}$] since the effect is the same in one case [$\overrightarrow{PG}$] as in the other [$\overrightarrow{LQ}$] according to the principles of motion discussed above. [J. L. Lagrange, *Analytical Mechanics*, trans. and ed. Auguste Boissonnade and Victor N. Vagliente, from *Mécanique analytique*, novelle édition of 1811 (Dordrecht: Kluwer Academic, 1997), p. 171]

Note, by the way, that Lagrange assumes the Compound Second Law, that $\overrightarrow{LQ} = \overrightarrow{PG}$, without realizing that he should have cited Law 2 of the *Principia*.

17 Cohen and Whitman, in the *Principia*, render *perpetuo* (meaning "without interruption") as "continually," rather than "continuously," even though in modern English "continually" can describe an action which is interrupted at short intervals. In his "Guide to the *Principia*," Cohen offers two justifications for what he calls this "seemingly incorrect use of . . . 'continually'" (p. 42): first, to avoid any conflict with the technical use of "continuous" in mathematics, and, second, to join with Newton himself, who generally used "continually" when writing in English. But rendering perpetuo as "continuously" actually meshes perfectly with the technical meaning in mathematics. Indeed, given

any motion $t \rightarrow P(t)$, a simple Taylor series argument tells us the limit of $2(\overrightarrow{LQ}/h^2)$ as $h \rightarrow 0$, the limit defining the "action" of a finite force, equals the modern vector acceleration of the motion (see note 16 above), which means the action varies uninterruptedly (or continuously) if and only if the vector acceleration varies continuously in the mathematical sense. Turning to Cohen's second justification, it is true that Newton, writing in English on orbital motion, uses "continually" where, in equivalent Latin passages in other documents, he uses *perpetuo* (see, for example, John Herivel, *The Background to Newton's Principia: A Study of Newton's Dynamical Researches in the Years 1664–84* [Oxford: Clarendon Press, 1965], p. 248 or Isaac Newton, *The Preliminary Manuscripts for Isaac Newton's 1687 Principia, 1684–1685* [Cambridge: Cambridge University Press, 1989; facsimiles of the original autographs, now in Cambridge University Library, with an introduction by D. T. Whiteside], p. 242), but in Newton's time "continual" did *not*, as it does today, admit interruptions: for example, Elisha Coles, *An English Dictionary, explaining the difficult terms that are used in divinity, husbandry, physick, philosophy, law, navigation, mathematicks, and other arts and science* (London: printed for Peter Parker, 1684), defines "continual" as "without interruption," with no secondary meanings.

A reader taking "continually" in the modern sense of a possibly interrupted action would necessarily misinterpret Newton's intent, which is that the action takes place *perpetuo*, that is, *without interruption*. Either "uninterruptedly" or "continuously," because they do not permit interruptions, would offer a less misleading and more accurate translation for *perpetuo*. Thus, for example, motions "in orbit about an immobile center," which are described in the Cohen and Whitman translation as being "continually [*perpetuo*] drawn back from the tangent" would more accurately be described as being "*continuously* drawn back from the tangent."

18 Thus an instantaneous impulse or impulsive force is not a force at all, at least not in the modern sense of the word.

19 The brevity derives from being able to write just "centripetal force," rather than "continuous centripetal force" or "centripetal force acting uninterruptedly" whenever we refer, as we generally do, to the continuous force case.

20 The point here is the continuity of the *force* (or, equivalently, the acceleration), not the continuity of the *motion*. A "polygonal impulse

motion" generated by a series of impulses will be nonsmooth or "jerky," but still continuous.

21 Centripetal motions may be fundamental in the mathematical propositions of Book 1, but as Newton observes in the opening to Section 11, such motions "hardly exist in the natural world" (*Principia*, p. 561). George Smith points out (this volume) that Newton addresses the complexity of real orbital motion in a sequence of successive approximations, with each approximation an idealized motion and systematic deviations from it providing evidence for the next stage in the sequence. Centripetal motions are just the first stage in this sequence of idealized motions. For a study of this "Newtonian style" in the *Principia*'s Book 2, see George Smith, "The Newtonian style in Book II of the Principia," in Jed Z. Buchwald and I. Bernard Cohen (eds.), *Isaac Newton's Natural Philosophy* (Cambridge, MA: The MIT Press, 2001), pp. 249–313.

22 We do *not* refer here to a *given environment* (a given magnetic field or resisting fluid, for example) that might well generate different impressed forces (different "thrusts") on a given body, depending on the speed or direction of the body. There would be no need to outlaw such reasonable behavior. We refer instead to the following *unreasonable* behavior: a *given impressed force* (a given "thrust") that might generate different deflections, depending on the speed or direction of the body.

23 Read Alexandre Koyré, "An Experiment in Measurement," *Proceedings of the American Philosophical Society* 97(1953), 222–37; reprinted in Koyré, *Metaphysics and Measurement* (London: Chapman and Hall, 1968), 89–117. Also see Joella G. Yoder, *Unrolling Time: Christiaan Huygens and the Mathematization of Nature* (Cambridge: Cambridge University Press, 1988), chs. 2–4.

24 Of course, Newton himself is not confused: "they no less corrupt mathematics and philosophy who confuse true quantities with their relations and common measures" (*Principia*, p. 414).

25 Isaac Newton, *The Mathematical Papers of Isaac Newton*, Volumes I–VIII, edited and with extensive commentaries by D. T. Whiteside (Cambridge: Cambridge University Press, 1967–81), vol. VI, pp. 538–609.

26 Regarding the latter, read J. Bruce Brackenridge, "The Critical Role of Curvature in Newton's Developing Dynamics," in P. M. Harman and Alan E. Shapiro (eds.), *The Investigation of Difficult Things: Essays on Newton and the History of Exact Sciences* (Cambridge: Cambridge

University Press, 1992), pp. 231–60; J. Bruce Brackenridge and Michael Nauenberg, "Curvature in Newton's Dynamics," in I. Bernard Cohen and George E. Smith (eds.), *The Cambridge Companion to Newton* (Cambridge: Cambridge University Press, 2002), pp. 85–137, also available online: http://philpapers.org/rec/BRACIN-3; and Bruce Pourciau, "Radical Principia," *Archive for History of Exact Sciences* 44 (1992), 331–63.

27 Newton, *Mathematical Papers*, vol. VI, pp. 539–43; I. Bernard Cohen, "Newton's Second Law and the Concept of Force in the *Principia*," in Robert Palter (ed.), *The Annus Mirabilis of Sir Isaac Newton 1666–1966* (Cambridge, MA: MIT Press, 1970), pp. 143–85, a revised version of an article originally published in *Texas Quarterly* 10:3 (1967), 160–9.

28 See Newton, *Mathematical Papers*, vol. VI, pp. 540–3. Parts of this description of the second law can be found in ULC Add. 3965.19: 731v/731r, but "the lower half of [this] manuscript," comments Whiteside, "is badly charred and a considerable section of it is completely burnt away: the ensuing gaps in the text are here restored (within square brackets [in the Latin only]) on the pattern of Newton's preliminary drafts on Add. 3965.12: 274r/274v."

29 For example, Cohen's commitment to an impulse-only interpretation of Law 2 forces him into a convoluted explanation, as he tries to understand Newton's smoothly curved hand-drawn figure:

> The parabola-like orbit is thus an infinitesimal orbital segment, produced by a first-order infinitesimal force-impulse which itself proves to be compounded of an infinite number of second-order infinitesimal force-impulses, each of which we may consider to be acting instantaneously in a time-interval which is not the whole interval dt but rather dt/n as $n \to \infty$, itself infinitesimally small. [Cohen, "Newton's Second law," p. 181]

See also the chapter by Cohen, this volume.

30 The Compound Second Law does apply to continuous impressed forces, but strictly speaking it applies in its exact form only when the continuous force has a fixed direction during the time increment h. For if an impressed force, acting on a resting body at P, would move that body along the segment $\overrightarrow{PG}$ in a time increment h, then that impressed force must have a fixed direction, namely the direction of $\overrightarrow{PG}$, at least for the time increment h. Hence the hypothesis of the Compound Second Law – that the same impressed force (meaning the same in direction and

magnitude) that acts on the moving body is imagined to act on the same body at rest – could not conceivably hold unless the force that acts on the moving body has a fixed direction during the time increment h. In particular, this means that the Compound Second Law does not apply (at least not in its exact form) to the centripetal forces of Book 1, because a centripetal force, with force center S, acting on a moving body at P, cannot have a fixed direction over any time increment (unless the body at P was moving along the line PS when the force acted), since the direction of the force must change continuously in order to remain aimed at S. Nevertheless, the Compound Second Law does apply to the centripetal forces in Book 1, as well as the resistance forces in Book 2, as an approximation over very small time increments h during which the direction of these forces is nearly fixed.

31　We have used the vector addition of directed line segments to represent this independent compounding in our statement of the law above.

32　The statement of the second law in the *Principia* asserts a *proportionality*, not an equality: "A change in motion is proportional to the motive force impressed . . ." But since, as Newton himself makes clear, the underlying meaning of the second law is an equality (between the moving and resting deflections), we lose little by taking the proportionality constant to be one and the proportionality to be an equality.

33　In a standard interpretation of the second law, the "change in motion" is taken to be the "change in [the quantity of] motion, that is, by the *Principia*'s Definition 2, the change in linear momentum $\Delta Mv = M\Delta v$, where Δv stands for the change in speed. But Newton's own words, giving the meaning of the second law above, tell us he has something more directional in mind. Indeed, as a very careful wordsmith, Newton would surely have written "quantity of motion," rather than "motion," if that is what he meant. Between the first appearance of Law 2, in the tract "De motu sphaericorum Corporum in fluidis," probably composed during December of 1684, and its final appearance, in the third (1726) edition of the *Principia*, Newton had at least fourteen documented opportunities to revise his statement of the law, by say inserting "quantity of" before "motion." Yet in every statement of the law, "motion" remains just "motion." Note that the change in motion $M(\overrightarrow{LQ}/h)$ can be seen as the "Newtonian directional momentum generated by the force," since the quantity $\overrightarrow{LQ}/h$, the "deflection per unit time," is Newton's directional version of the change in speed.

34 For simplicity, we assume that this impressed force is either an instantaneous impulse or a continuous force with fixed direction and magnitude (at least over some small time increment).

35 *Christiaan Huygens' The Pendulum Clock or Geometrical Demonstrations Concerning the Motion of Pendula as Applied to Clocks,* translation and notes by Richard Blackwell, based on the original 1673 edition (Ames, IA: Iowa State University Press), 1986, p. 33.

36 This explicit assumption, that the downward motion due to gravity *compounds independently* with the uniform straight line motion of the body, can be traced back (in forceless language) to Galileo: in the *Discorsi* (1638), at the beginning of the Fourth Day, Sagredo comments on an underlying assumption in the argument for the parabolic motion of a projectile: "It cannot be denied that the reasoning is novel, ingenious, and conclusive," he says, "being argued *ex suppositione*; that is, by assuming that the transverse motion is kept always equable, and that the natural downward <motion> likewise maintains its tenor of always accelerating according to the squared ratio of the times; also that such motions, or their speeds, in mixing together do not alter, disturb, or impede one another." (Galileo Galilei, *Two New Sciences, Including Centers of Gravity and Force of Percussion,* translated, with introduction and notes, by Stillman Drake, from the original 1638 edition [Madison, WI: University of Wisconsin Press, 1974], p. 222; angle brackets mark the translator's insertion.)

37 Huygens, *The Pendulum Clock,* p. 35.

38 Newton's figure can be found on the *verso* side of the folio (ULC Ms. Add. 3965, fol. 274) that contains Newton's statement of the Compound Second Law on the *recto* side. Whiteside (*Mathematical Papers,* pp. 539–42) prints only folio 274r. Newton also draws a similar figure to illustrate the case of a force directed opposite to the direction of motion (see Figure 3.10). Thanks to G. E. Smith for bringing these figures to my attention. Cohen, having in mind an impulse-only interpretation, reproduces both these straight line figures in "Newton's Second Law," p. 166.

39 Of course, the outward similarity also hides serious differences. In classical Newtonian dynamics, f represents the vector sum of the "individual forces" that act on the body and the mass m is defined by comparing the accelerations generated on the given body and a standard body. On the other hand, $\vec{F}$ represents the measure of a single impressed

force and Newton's "quantity of matter" M is defined in the *Principia* as "a measure of matter that arises from its density and volume jointly," (p. 403) with "density" taken as intuitively understood or determined by specific gravity measurements. For more on the "quantity of matter," see Cohen's discussion in *Principia*, pp. 86–95.

40 See note 16.

41 Bruce Pourciau, "Is Newton's Second Law Really Newton's?" *American Journal of Physics* 79:10 (2011), 1015–22.

42 Others may be found in Bruce Pourciau, "Newton's interpretation of Newton's second law," *Archive for History of Exact Sciences* 60 (2006), 157–207.

43 Suppose the impulse N acts at P on the given body *in motion*, and suppose the body would have described the segment $\overrightarrow{PL}$ had its motion (speed and direction) at P been uniformly continued for the time increment h. Then, by the Compound Second Law, although the impulse "acts along" $\overrightarrow{PG}$, the body will describe, not $\overrightarrow{PG}$, but the segment $\overrightarrow{PQ}$, where $\overrightarrow{LQ} = \overrightarrow{PG}$.

44 Not just Corollary 1 of the laws, but Corollaries 3, 4, 5, and 6 as well, become what they were intended to be – simple and natural consequences of the laws – provided we understand Law 2 as Newton understood it. See Pourciau, "Newton's Interpretation of Newton's Second Law," pp. 190–5. Corollary 2 is another matter. See note 46.

45 Cohen reproduces these figures in "Newton's Second Law," p. 166. See note 38.

46 Corollary 2, the so-called "parallelogram law of forces" – on the "composition of a direct force . . . out of any oblique forces, and conversely the resolution of any direct force . . . into any oblique forces" (*Principia*, p. 418) – is not in fact a "corollary" of the laws, at least not in the modern sense of being a logical consequence. (See Ernst Mach, *The Science of Mechanics: A Critical and Historical Account of Its Development*, trans. Thomas J. McCormack, 6th edition [La Salle, IL: Open Court, 1960], pp. 55–7; Pourciau, "The *Principia*'s Second Law"; and especially Michael Spivak, *Physics for Mathematicians: Mechanics I* [Lombard, IL: Publish or Perish, 2010], pp. 278–82.) It is, though, a "corollary" in the late-seventeenth-century sense, when the primary meaning was "an addition beyond what was proposed" (Joseph Moxon, *Mathematicks Made Easy* [London: Moxon, 1679]. p. 37).

47 Colin MacLaurin, *An Account of Sir Isaac Newton's Philosophical Discoveries*, facsimile of the first edition originally published in 1748 (Westport, CT: Johnson Reprint Corporation, 1968), pp. 115–16.

48 The fourteen are: in the first revision and second recasting of the tract "De motu corporum in gyrum" (*Mathematical Papers*, vol. VI, pp. 92ff); in the so-called "Locke manuscript" (Herivel, *Background to Newton's Principia*, pp. 246–56); in the first (1687) edition of the *Principia*; in eight different rewordings of the second law as part of Newton's plans in the early 1690s for a radical revision of the first edition (Cohen, "Newton's Second Law," pp. 160–77); in the second (1713) edition; and in the third (1726) edition.

49 Stuart Pierson, "'corpore cadente. . .': Historians Discuss Newton's Second Law," *Perspectives on Science* 1 (1993), 627–58, esp. pp. 654–5.

50 The increment Δv is itself a moving deflection over h, so $\Delta v/h$ is a moving deflection over h^2, a ratio which, by Newton's characterization of a finite force (in Section 3.1), tends toward a finite limit.

51 Any motion of the form $\mathbf{r}(t) = \mathbf{a}t + \mathbf{b}t^2$, for fixed vectors $\mathbf{a}$ and $\mathbf{b}$, will traverse a parabola, as long as $\mathbf{a}$ and $\mathbf{b}$ are not collinear. To see this, let $\mathbf{i}$ and $\mathbf{j}$ be perpendicular vectors, with $\mathbf{i}$ in the plane determined by $\mathbf{a}$ and $\mathbf{b}$ and $\mathbf{j}$ parallel to $\mathbf{b}$. Using the dot product, set $x := \mathbf{r} \cdot \mathbf{i} = (\mathbf{a} \cdot \mathbf{i})t$ and $y := \mathbf{r} \cdot \mathbf{j} = (\mathbf{a} \cdot \mathbf{j})t + (\mathbf{b} \cdot \mathbf{j})t^2$, solve for t in the expression for x and substitute into the expression for y to find constants A and B (with B not zero because $\mathbf{a}$ and $\mathbf{b}$ are not collinear) such that $y = Ax + Bx^2$. This is the equation of a parabola.

52 See Pourciau, "The *Principia*'s Second Law (as Newton Understood It)".

53 Leonhard Euler, *Theoria*, volume 3 of Leonhardi Euleri, *Opera Omnia, Series II: Opera Mechanica et Astronomica*, originally published by Orell Füssli in 1765 (Berlin: Birkhäuser, 1948), p. 69.

54 My thanks to Mary Ann Rossi, who kindly and expertly translated portions of Euler's *Theoria*, including this crucial passage.

55 Herivel, *The Background to Newton's Principia*, p. 145.

56 Triangles *SAB* and *SBc* have equal bases and altitudes, as do triangles *SBc* and *SBC*. Thus triangles *SAB* and *SBC* have equal area. And so forth.

57 Saying the areas described by the radius lie in a fixed plane (Newton's phrasing in Proposition 1) is equivalent to saying the trajectory and the center lie together in a fixed plane.

58 A motion is said to be *smooth* if its vector acceleration varies continuously or, in equivalent Newtonian terms, if the limit of $2\overrightarrow{LQ}/h^2$ as $h \to 0$ varies continuously with the place P where the moving deflection $\overrightarrow{LQ}$ is generated.

59 This might be a good place to recall the discussion of limits in Section 2.2. Newton understood very well that the limit of a sequence of quantities is not in general the "final form" of that sequence. Instead, the limit, by definition, is that unique quantity the sequence gets arbitrarily close to. This is what he means when he points out that "ultimate ratios [of evanescent quantities] . . . are not actually ratios of ultimate quantities, but limits which the ratios . . . approach so closely that their difference is less than any given quantity." Of course, what one might call the "final form" of the sequence of ratios would be the ratio of the ultimate quantities, namely the meaningless expression 0/0. To say, for example, in a comment on the transition from instantaneous impulses to continuous force, that a limit of polygonal impulse motions is a motion generated by an "infinity of discrete infinitesimal impulses" or that its trajectory is a "polygon with infinitely many infinitesimal sides" is to trade in meaningless "final form" descriptions which can lead our intuitive understanding astray. Rather the limit is merely whatever motion the sequence of polygonal motions becomes arbitrarily close to. See also Bruce Pourciau, "The Importance of Being Equivalent: Newton's Two Models of One-body Motion," *Archive for History of Exact Sciences* 58 (2004), 283–321; esp. 313 and 317–19.

60 Our position (see Section 3.3) has been that the motion given in the hypothesis of Proposition 1, the motion of a "bod[y] made to move in orbit," which we have called a *centripetal motion* for short, is *defined* by Newton to be a motion satisfying the

DRAWBACK PROPERTY. The motion is "continuously drawn back" [*perpetuo retrahuntur*] from rectilinear motion toward a fixed center. More precisely, the limit of $\overrightarrow{LQ}/h^2$ as $h \to 0$, which represents the "drawing back" at a given place P, varies continuously with P and always points toward a fixed point S.

From this standpoint, the assertion of the Impulse Assumption – that *every centripetal motion about S is a limit of polygonal impulse motions about S* – is a mathematical claim that requires proof. The evidence for this position – that the motion of a "bod[y] made to move in orbit" is *defined* in the *Principia* by the Drawback Property – would appear overwhelming: in the passage directly following the *Principia*'s Definition 5 for "centripetal force," Newton writes that "planets are [continuously (*perpetuo*)] drawn back from rectilinear motions" and then, of a "stone whirled in a sling [that] endeavors to leave the hand," that

> the force opposed to that endeavor, that is, the force by which the sling [continuously (*perpetuo*)] draws the stone back toward the hand and keeps it in orbit, I call centripetal, since it is directed toward the hand as toward the center of an orbit. *And the same applies to all bodies that are made to move in orbits.* [*Principia*, p. 405, emphasis added]

We have quoted just two, but in this short passage Newton goes on to use the Drawback Property to characterize the motion of a "bod[y] made to move in orbit" a total of *five* times. Indeed, throughout the *Principia*, whenever Newton wishes to describe the motion of a body in orbit, he does so with the Drawback Property. To give just one example from Book 3, Proposition 1 begins: *"the forces by which the circumjovial planets are [continuously (*perpetuo*)] drawn away from rectilinear motions . . ."* (*Principia*, p. 802). The message is clear: the Drawback Property is the *defining* property for the motion of a "bod[y] made to move in orbit." Nevertheless, Michael Nauenberg ("Kepler's Area Law in the *Principia*: Filling in Some Details in Newton's Proof of Proposition 1," *Historia Mathematica* 30 [2003], 441–56) has taken a different position: that the motion of a "bod[y] made to move in orbit" in Proposition 1 is *defined*, not by the Drawback Property, but by the

> LIMIT IMPULSE PROPERTY. *The motion is the (smooth) limit of polygonal impulse motions.*

From this different standpoint, Nauenberg's take on Newton's argument for Proposition 1 is, of course, also different. But the evidence for his position is slim indeed, for the Limit Impulse Property appears *just once*, in the argument for Proposition 1, and then never again in the entire *Principia*. In particular, Definition 5 and its following passage, where Newton would appear to be *defining* motions generated by centripetal forces (the motions of "bodies made to move in orbit"), contain multiple

references to the Drawback Property, but not one reference to the Limit
Impulse Property. See Pourciau, "The Importance of Being Equivalent,"
pp. 300–3.

61 This is why, as we shall stress later, when we discuss Proposition 1
below, Newton's polygonal impulse construction does not establish,
and cannot be used to establish, the Fixed Plane Property for centripetal
motions.

62 It is unlikely, given the mathematical tools available to him, that
Newton could have given a truly convincing argument for the Fixed
Plane Property. See Section 8.1.

63 In Pourciau, "The Importance of Being Equivalent," centripetal motions
are called "tangent deflected motions."

64 Richard S. Westfall, *Force in Newton's Physics: The Science of Dynamics
in the Seventeenth Century* (New York: American Elsevier, 1971), p. 437.

65 *Mathematical Papers*, vol. VI, pp. 35–7, n. 19.

66 Michel Blay, "Force, Continuity, and the Mathematization of Motion at
the End of the Seventeenth Century," in Jed Z. Buchwald and I. Bernard
Cohen (eds.), *Isaac Newton's Natural Philosophy* (Cambridge, MA: MIT
Press, 2001), pp. 225–48, at pp. 225–6 and 231.

67 Cohen, this volume, pp. 78–9.

68 I. Bernard Cohen, "A Guide to Newton's Principia," in *Isaac Newton,
The Principia, Mathematical Principles of Natural Philosophy: A
New Translation* (Berkeley, CA: University of California Press, 1999),
pp. 1–370; at p. 71, n. 73.

69 Just to clarify anyway, observe the Fixed Plane Property certainly implies
that the trajectory of the motion lies in a fixed plane, but it tells us
more: that the trajectory and the given center lie *together* in this
fixed plane. This may seem a trivial distinction, but, for example, this
distinction makes a crucial difference in Proposition 2 –

> PROPOSITION 2. *Every body that moves in some curved line
> described in a plane and, by a radius drawn to a point, either
> unmoving or moving uniformly forward with a rectilinear
> motion, describes areas around that point proportional to
> the times, is urged by a centripetal force tending toward that
> same point.*

– which is actually *false* as stated: a constant speed motion along the
arctic circle lies in a fixed plane and the areas described, by a radius

drawn to the center of the *Earth*, are proportional to the times, yet the centripetal force maintaining this motion points toward the center of the circular trajectory rather than the center of the Earth. Newton could easily have mended the statement of Proposition 2 by inverting the phrasing of Proposition 1, stressing that not just the curve, but the areas described by a radius from the given point, lie in a fixed plane. For more on Proposition 2, read Bruce Pourciau, "Proposition II (Book I) of Newton's *Principia*," *Archive for History of Exact Sciences* 63 (2009), 129–67.

70 The propositions of Book 1 are *mathematical* propositions: "I use interchangeably and indiscriminately," stresses Newton,

> words signifying attraction, impulse, or any propensity toward a center, considering these forces not from a physical but only from a mathematical point of view. Therefore, let the reader beware of thinking that by words of this kind I am anywhere defining a species or mode of action or a physical cause or reason, or that I am attributing forces in a true and physical sense to centers (which are mathematical points) if I happen to say that centers attract or that centers have forces. [*Principia*, p. 408]

And later, in his preface to Book 3: "In the preceding books I have presented principles of philosophy [physics] that are not, however, philosophical but strictly mathematical – that is, those on which the study of philosophy can be based" (*Principia*, p. 793).

71 *Mathematical Papers*, vol. VI, pp. 34–5.

72 *Ibid.*, p. 195.

73 Using vector notation: A motion $t \to \mathbf{r}(t)$, with vector velocity $\mathbf{v}(t)$ and vector acceleration $\mathbf{a}(t)$, is said to be *centripetal* if $\mathbf{a}(t)$ remains parallel to $\mathbf{r}(t)$, or, equivalently, if the cross-product $\mathbf{a}(t) \times \mathbf{r}(t)$ remains the zero vector. For a centripetal motion, the vector $\mathbf{h}(t) := \mathbf{r}(t) \times \mathbf{v}(t)$ is a constant vector $\mathbf{h}$, because its vector derivative vanishes at every t: $\mathbf{h}'(t) = \mathbf{v}(t) \times \mathbf{v}(t) + \mathbf{r}(t) \times \mathbf{a}(t) = \mathbf{0} + \mathbf{0} = \mathbf{0}$. The plane which is perpendicular to $\mathbf{h}$ and contains the origin is therefore a fixed plane. But (because the factors of a cross-product are perpendicular to that cross-product) this fixed plane contains the vector $\mathbf{r}(t)$ for all t and hence also the areas described by that vector.

74 Horace Lamb, *Dynamics*, second edition (Cambridge: Cambridge University Press, 1923, reprinted 1960), p. 219. (First edition 1914.)

75 Whiteside, "The Prehistory of the *Principia*," p. 30.

76 See *Mathematical Papers*, vol. VI, pp. 568–99; Brackenridge, "The Critical Role of Curvature," and Pourciau, "Radical *Principia*."

77 Cohen, "A Guide to Newton's *Principia*," p. 307.

78 Note that the segments $\overrightarrow{lq}$, $\overrightarrow{PX}$, and $\overrightarrow{LQ}$ may look parallel in Figure 3.16, but they are only *nearly* so and exactly so only in the limit (after dividing by h^2 of course) as $h \to 0$. The same goes for the chord qQ and the tangent segment lL.

79 A simple Taylor series argument shows that $2\overrightarrow{PX}/h^2$ tends toward the vector acceleration at P:

$$
\begin{aligned}
2\overrightarrow{PX} &= \overrightarrow{PQ} + \overrightarrow{Pq} \\
&= [\mathbf{r}(t_0 + h) - \mathbf{r}(t_0)] + [\mathbf{r}(t_0 - h) - \mathbf{r}(t_0)] \\
&= [h\mathbf{v}(t_0) + \tfrac{1}{2}h^2\mathbf{a}(t_0) + \cdots] + [-h\mathbf{v}(t_0) + \tfrac{1}{2}h^2\mathbf{a}(t_0) - \cdots] \\
&= h^2\mathbf{a}(t_0) + \cdots
\end{aligned}
$$

and it follows that

$$
2\frac{\overrightarrow{PX}}{h^2} = \mathbf{a}(t_0) + \cdots \to \mathbf{a}(t_0)
$$

80 And even all the way to the solution of the so-called Inverse Kepler Problem – a body attracted toward an immovable center by a centripetal force inversely proportional to the square of the distance from the center must move on a conic having a focus in that center – given by Corollary 1 to Propositions 11, 12, and 13. See Bruce Pourciau, "From Centripetal Forces to Conic Orbits: A Path Through the Early Sections of Newton's *Principia*," *Studies in History and Philosophy of Science, Part A*, 38 (2007), 56–83.

81 An error easily forgiven, since persuasive arguments for the Fixed Plane Property for centripetal motions did not appear until the early twentieth century.

4 The methodology of the *Principia*

George E. Smith

In the Preface to the first edition (1687) Newton informs the reader straight off that he intends the *Principia* to illustrate a new way of doing what we now call empirical science:

> And therefore our present work sets forth mathematical
> principles of natural philosophy. For the whole difficulty
> of philosophy seems to be to find the forces of nature from
> the phenomena of motions and then to demonstrate the other
> phenomena from these forces. It is to these ends that the general
> propositions in Books 1 and 2 are directed, while in Book 3
> our explanation of the system of the universe illustrates these
> propositions . . . If only we could derive the other phenomena of
> nature from mechanical principles by the same kind of reasoning!
> For many things lead me to have a suspicion that all phenomena
> may depend on certain forces by which the particles of bodies, by
> causes yet unknown, either are impelled toward one another
> and cohere in regular figures, or are repelled from one another and
> recede. Since these forces are unknown, philosophers have
> hitherto made trial of nature in vain. But I hope that the
> principles set down here will shed some light on either this
> mode of philosophizing or some truer one.[1]

Surprisingly, however, the main body of the first edition contains only two further comments about methodology: (1) a cryptic remark at the end of the opening discussion of space and time, announcing that the purpose of the work is to explain "how to determine the

I thank Kenneth G. Wilson, Eric Schliesser, and I. Bernard Cohen for several useful comments on an earlier draft of this chapter.

true motions from their causes, effects, and apparent differences, and, conversely, how to determine from motions, whether true or apparent, their causes and effects";[2] and (2) a scholium buried at the end of Book 1, Section 11 in which Newton proposes that his distinctive approach will make it possible to *argue more securely* in natural philosophy.

In the second edition (1713), clearly in response to complaints about his methodology, Newton introduces separate sections for the Phenomena and Rules for Natural Philosophy[3] involved in his derivation of universal gravity (adding a fourth rule in the third edition, 1726), and he adds at the end the General Scholium containing his most famous – and troubling – methodological pronouncement:

> I have not as yet been able to deduce from phenomena the reason for these properties of gravity, and I do not feign hypotheses. For whatever is not deduced from the phenomena must be called a hypothesis; and hypotheses, whether metaphysical or physical, or based on occult qualities, or mechanical, have no place in experimental philosophy. In this experimental philosophy, propositions are deduced from the phenomena and are made general by induction.[4]

In a later (anonymous) work, Newton softened his renunciation of hypotheses by adding, "unless as conjectures or questions proposed to be examined by experiments."[5]

With or without this qualification, the thrust of the pronouncement remains mostly negative: Newton's new *experimental philosophy* does not proceed hypothetico-deductively, even under the supposedly safe constraint imposed by the then-prevailing *mechanical philosophy* that all hypothesized action arises strictly through contact of matter with matter. How, then, does theory construction proceed on Newton's approach? Vague talk of "deductions from phenomena" provided no more adequate an answer to this question then than it does now.

Newton leaves the task of extracting the answer from the *Principia* largely to the reader. Three centuries of disagreement give reason to think that the answer is far more complex than the hypothetico-deductive alternative, which Christiaan Huygens, the foremost figure in science at the time, managed to lay out in a single paragraph in his January 1690 Preface to his *Treatise on Light*, published thirty months after the *Principia*:

> One finds in this subject a kind of demonstration which does not carry with it so high a degree of certainty as that employed in geometry; and which differs distinctly from the method employed by geometers in that they prove their propositions by well-established and incontrovertible principles, while here principles are tested by the inferences which are derivable from them. The nature of the subject permits of no other treatment. It is possible, however, in this way to establish a probability which is little short of certainty. This is the case when the consequences of the assumed principles are in perfect accord with the observed phenomena, and especially when these verifications are numerous; but above all when one employs the hypothesis to predict new phenomena and finds his expectations realized.[6]

Huygens's *Discourse on the Cause of Gravity*, which contains his critical evaluation of the *Principia*, was published in combination with his *Treatise on Light*, making this paragraph prefatory to both.

The nearest Newton ever comes to such a capsule summary of his approach is the one methodological pronouncement from the first edition from which I have yet to quote, the Scholium at the end of Book 1, Section 11:

> By these propositions we are directed to the analogy between centripetal forces and the central bodies toward which those forces tend. For it is reasonable that forces directed toward bodies depend on the nature and the quantity of matter of such bodies, as happens in the case of magnetic bodies. And whenever cases of this sort occur, the attractions of the bodies must be reckoned by assigning proper forces to their individual particles and then taking the sums of these forces.

I use the word "attraction" here in a general sense for any endeavor whatever of bodies to approach one another, whether that endeavor occurs as a result of the action of the bodies either drawn toward one another or acting on one another by means of spirits emitted or whether it arises from the action of ether or of air or of any medium whatsoever – whether corporeal or incorporeal – in any way impelling toward one another the bodies floating therein. I use the word "impulse" in the same general sense, considering in this treatise not the species of forces and their physical qualities but their quantities and mathematical proportions, as I have explained in the definitions.

Mathematics requires an investigation of those quantities of forces and their proportions that follow from any conditions that may be supposed. Then, coming down to physics, these proportions must be compared with the phenomena, so that it may be found out which conditions of forces apply to each kind of attracting bodies. And then, finally, it will be possible to argue more securely concerning the physical species, physical causes, and physical proportions of these forces. Let us see, therefore, what the forces are by which spherical bodies, consisting of particles that attract in the way already set forth, must act upon one another, and what sorts of motions result from such forces.[7]

The goal in what follows is to describe the methodology of the *Principia* in the light of this too often neglected Scholium.[8]

First, however, the Scholium (which remained word-for-word the same in all three editions) should be put into context. Section 11 treats bodies moving under centripetal forces directed not toward a point in space, as in the preceding sections, but toward other moving bodies – so-called "two-body" and "three-body" problems. By far the largest portion of Section 11 presents Newton's limited, qualitative results for three-body effects on the motions of the planets and the Moon, results that he called "imperfect" in the Preface. The Scholium thus occurs just after it should have become clear to readers that the true orbital motions are so intractably complex as to preclude hope of exact agreement between theory and observation. To concede that theory can at best only approximate the real world, however, appears to concede that multiple conflicting theories can claim equal support from the available evidence at any time. Seventeenth-century readers would have been quick to note this, for equipollence of astronomical theories had been a celebrated concern for over a century,[9] and such leading figures as Descartes and Marin Mersenne had frequently called pointed attention to the limitations of experimental evidence.[10] Newton would have accordingly expected his readers to see his remark about *arguing more securely* as making a startling claim in the face of a concession that the real world is intractably complex.

Proposition 69, to which the Scholium is attached, lays the groundwork for Newton's law of gravity by asserting that in the relevant inverse-square case the forces directed toward the various bodies must be proportional to the masses of those bodies. Sections 12 and 13 examine the characteristics of forces directed toward bodies when these forces are composed out of forces directed toward the individual particles of matter making up the bodies. In other words, they lay the groundwork for Newton's claim that his law of gravity holds *universally* between individual particles of matter. Now, the mechanical philosophy did not bar "attractive" forces among macroscopic bodies, for intervening unseen matter could be hypothesized to effect these forces in the manner Descartes had proposed in the case of magnets, and also gravity.[11] As Newton well realized, however, no hypothetical contact mechanism seems even imaginable to effect "attractive" forces among particles of matter generally. The Scholium thus occurs at the point where adherents to the mechanical philosophy would start viewing Newton's reasoning as "absurd" (to use the word Huygens chose privately).[12] The Scholium attempts to carry the reader past this worry, but not by facing the demand for a contact mechanism head-on. Instead, Newton warns that he is employing mathematically formulated theory in physics in a new way, with forces treated abstractly, independently of mechanism. What we need to do first, then, is to understand how Newton is using mathematical theory and talk of forces in the *Principia*, and how he is departing from his predecessors. Then we can turn, in the last two sections of the chapter, to the questions of how Newton prefers to argue for theoretical claims and whether this way of arguing is more secure.

MATHEMATICAL THEORY IN NEWTON'S *PRINCIPIA*

The two most prominent books presenting mathematical theories of motion before the *Principia* were Galileo's *Two New Sciences* (1638)[13] and Huygens's *Horologium Oscillatorium* (1673).[14] Newton almost certainly never saw the former, but he knew the latter well, and it together with Galileo's *Dialogues on the Two Chief World Systems* (1632)[15] and various secondary sources[16] made him familiar with Galileo's results. Outwardly, the *Principia* appears to take the same mathematical approach as these two earlier books, proceeding from axioms to a series of rigorously demonstrated propositions. In fact, however, the approach to mathematical theory in Books 1 and 2 of the *Principia* differs from that taken by Galileo and Huygens in two important respects.

The first difference is subtle. Almost without exception, the demonstrated propositions of Books 1 and 2 of the *Principia* are of an "if-then" logical form, as illustrated by Propositions 1 and 2, restated in modern form: *if the forces acting on a moving body are all directed toward a single point in space, then a radius from that point to the body sweeps out equal areas in equal times, and conversely.*[17] So far as strict logic is concerned, the same can be said of the demonstrated propositions of Galileo and Huygens, as illustrated by the latter's celebrated isochronism theorem: *if a body descends along a path described by a cycloid, then the time of descent is the same regardless of the point along the path from which its descent begins.*[18] From the point of view of empirical science, however, this and the other demonstrated propositions of Galileo and Huygens are better described as having a "when-then" form, in which the antecedent describes an experimental situation and the consequent, a prediction of what will occur whenever that situation is realized. A primary aim of Galileo's and Huygens's mathematical theories is to derive observable consequences from their axioms that can provide evidence supporting these axioms, taken as hypotheses, or that can facilitate practical applications, such as the design of pendulum clocks.[19]

What lies behind this "when-then" form is the kind of quantities employed in the theories laid out by Galileo and Huygens. With the notable exception of the latter's theorems on centrifugal force, appended without proofs at the end of *Horologium Oscillatorium*, their axioms and demonstrated propositions make no reference to forces. Surprising as it may be, even the rate of acceleration in vertical fall – for us, g, and for them the distance of fall in the first second – enters nowhere into Galileo's propositions. This quantity does enter into the very last propositions of *Horologium Oscillatorium*, enabling Huygens to carry out a theory-mediated measurement of it to very high accuracy by means of pendulums; nonetheless, it plays no role in the development of his theory. The quantities central to the mathematical theories of motion under uniform gravity laid out by Galileo and Huygens were all open to measurement without having to presuppose any propositions of the theories themselves.

Unlike Galileo and Huygens, Newton takes his "axioms or laws of motion" to hold true from the outset of Books 1 and 2 of the *Principia*. His demonstrated "if-then" propositions amount to *inference-tickets*[20] linking motions to forces, forces to motions, and macrophysical forces to microphysical forces composing them. As Newton indicates in the quotation given earlier from the Preface to the first edition, the aim of the mathematical theories of Books 1 and 2 is first to establish means for inferring conclusions about forces from phenomena of motion and then to demonstrate further phenomena from these conclusions about forces. In Newton's hands *force* is a flagrantly theoretical quantity. The principal problem Newton's mathematical theories address is to find ways to characterize forces.

The second critical difference between Newton's mathematical theories and those of Galileo and Huygens concerns their respective scopes. Galileo offered a mathematical theory of uniformly accelerated motion, and Huygens extended this theory to curvilinear trajectories and uniform circular motion. Newton, by contrast, does not offer a theory of motion under inverse-square centripetal forces, much less under gravity, alone. Rather, Book 1 offers a *generic* theory of centripetal forces and motion under them. Inverse-square forces receive extra attention, but the theory also covers centripetal forces that vary linearly with distance to the force-center, that vary as the inverse-cube, and finally that vary as any function whatever of distance to the center. Similarly, while Book 2 emphasizes resistance forces that vary as the square of the velocity, it ultimately derives "if-then" propositions that allow resistance forces to vary as the sum of any powers of velocity whatever, including non-integer powers.[21] Book 2 thus strives to offer a generic theory of resistance forces, where these are characterized as arising from the velocity of a moving body in a fluid medium. The generic scope of these two theories is not simply a case of Newton displaying his mathematical prowess, as is sometimes suggested. The theories need to be generic in order to allow him to establish strong conclusions about forces from phenomena of motions, conclusions that exclude potential competing claims.

The propositions from Books 1 and 2 that become most important to the overall *Principia* are of two types. The first type consists of propositions that link parameters in rules characterizing forces to parameters of motion. The historically most significant example of this type is Newton's "precession theorem" for nearly circular orbits under centripetal forces.[22] It establishes a strict relationship between the apsidal angle θ – the angle at the force-center between, for example, the aphelion and the perihelion – to the square root of the index n, namely $n = (\pi/\theta)2$, where the centripetal force varies as $r^{(n-3)}$. This relationship not only confirms that the exponent of r is exactly -2 when the apsidal angle is 180 degrees and exactly $+1$ when the angle is 90 degrees, but also yields a value of n and hence of the exponent for any other apsidal angle, or in other words for any rate at which the overall orbit precesses. This proposition and others of its type thus enable *theory-mediated measurements* of parameters characterizing forces to be made from parameters characterizing motions.[23] The propositions laid out earlier relating centripetal forces to Kepler's area rule, and their corollaries, provide another example of this type in which areal velocity yields a theory-mediated measure of the direction of the forces acting on a body.

As alluded to above, in his theory of motion under uniform gravity Huygens had derived propositions expressing the laws of the cycloidal and small-arc circular pendulums; and these results had enabled him to obtain from the periods and lengths of such pendulums a theory-mediated measure of the strength of surface gravity to four significant figures. This was a spectacular advance over prior attempts to measure the distance of vertical fall in the first second directly. Also, Huygens's theory of centrifugal force in uniform circular motion had allowed him to characterize the strength of these forces in terms of such motions, and from this to derive the law of the conical pendulum; and this result had enabled him to obtain a still further theory-mediated measure of the strength of surface gravity, in precise agreement with his other measures.[24] So, regardless of whether Newton first learned about propositions enabling theory-mediated measurements from Huygens, he at the very least had seen the utility of such propositions in *Horologium Oscillatorium*. Huygens, however, seems never to have seen any special evidential significance in his precise, stable measures of gravity. In Newton's hands, by contrast, theory-mediated measures became central to a new approach to marshaling evidence.

It is difficult to exaggerate the importance of measurement to the methodology of the *Principia*[25] or, for that matter, the sophistication with which Newton thought through philosophical issues concerning measurement. The importance is clear even in the definitions of key quantities with which the *Principia* opens, which are at least as much about measures of these quantities as they are about terminology. As the discussion of astronomical measures of *time* in the Scholium immediately following these definitions makes clear, Newton recognized that measures invariably involve theoretical assumptions, and hence remain provisional, even if not theory-mediated in the more restricted sense invoked above. He also seems to have appreciated that, because measurements in physics involve physical procedures and assumptions, a distinctive feature of this science is that it cannot help but include within itself its own empirically revisable theory of measurement. This insight may explain why Newton was so quick to view success in measurement as a form of evidence in its own right; here success includes (1) stability of values as a measure is repeated in varying circumstances – as illustrated by the stability of Huygens's measure of surface gravity by cycloidal pendulums of different lengths – and (2) convergence of values when the same quantity is determined through different measures involving different assumptions – as illustrated by the convergence of Huygens's cycloidal and conical pendulum measures. (Being open to increasingly greater precision appears to be a still further dimension of success in measurement for Newton.) Achieving success of this sort in determining values for forces is almost certainly what Newton had in mind with the cryptic remark at the end of the Scholium on space and time about the book explaining "how to determine the true motions from their causes, effects, and apparent differences."

The second type of proposition important to the *Principia* consists of combinations that draw clear contrasts between different conditions of force in terms of different conditions of motion. An historically significant example is the contrast between the simple form of Kepler's 3/2 power rule and the form requiring a specific small correction for each individual orbiting body; the latter holds if the orbiting and central bodies are interacting with one another in accord with the third law of motion, while the former holds if the orbiting body does not exert a force causing motion of the central body. Another historically significant example is the contrast between inverse-square celestial gravity acting to hold bodies in their orbits – a form of gravity that Huygens thought Newton had established – and inverse-square *universal* gravity between all the particles of matter in the universe: only under the latter does gravity vary linearly with distance from the center beneath the surface of a (uniformly dense) spherical Earth; and only under the latter does a particular relationship hold between the non-sphericity of a (uniformly dense) Earth and the variation of surface gravity with latitude. Combinations of propositions of this type thus provide contrasts that open the way to crossroads experiments – *experimenta crucis* – enabling phenomena of motion to pick out which among alternative kinds of conditions hold true of forces.

As these examples and the examples for the first type suggest, Newton prefers "if-and-only-if" results with both types. When he is unable to establish a strict converse, he typically looks for a result that falls as little short of it as he can find, as illustrated by the qualitative theorems on the "three-body" problem in Section 11.

Once these two types are identified, an examination of the overall development of the mathematical theories of Books 1 and 2 makes clear that the propositions Newton was most pursuing in these books are of these two types. His preoccupation with these explains why he included the propositions he did and not others that he could easily have added. Propositions that do not fall into these types generally serve to enable ones that do. By contrast, an examination of the overall development of the mathematical theories of Galileo and Huygens indicates that the propositions they were most pursuing are ones that make a highly distinctive empirical prediction, that provide an answer to some practical question, or that explain some known phenomenon. In other words, the mathematical theories of motion of Galileo and Huygens are primarily aimed at predicting and explaining phenomena. The mathematical theories of motion developed in Books 1 and 2 of the *Principia* do not have this aim. Rather, their aim is to provide a basis for specifying experiments and observations by means of which the empirical world can provide answers to questions – this in contrast to conjecturing answers and then testing the implications of these conjectures. Newton is using mathematical theory in an effort to turn otherwise recalcitrant questions into empirically tractable questions. This is what he is describing when he says:

> Mathematics requires an investigation of those quantities of forces and their proportions that follow from any conditions that may be supposed. Then, coming down to physics, these proportions must be compared with the phenomena, so that it may be found out which conditions of forces apply to each kind of attracting bodies.

This initial picture of Newton's approach is too simple in one crucial respect: if only because of imprecision of measurement, the empirical world rarely yields straightforward univocal answers to questions. That Newton was acutely aware of this is clear from his supplementing key "if-then" propositions with corollaries noting that the consequent still holds *quam proxime* (i.e., very nearly) when the antecedent holds only *quam proxime*. Nothing adds to the complexity of Newton's methodology more than his approach to inexactitude. We will return to this subject after considering the way in which he talks of force.

NEWTONIAN FORCES: MATHEMATICAL AND PHYSICAL

The theories developed in the *Principia*, unlike the theory of uniformly accelerated motion developed by Galileo and extended by Huygens, are first and foremost about forces. Book 1 develops a general theory of centripetal forces and motions under them, and the first two-thirds of Book 2, a general theory of resistance forces and motions under them; the last third of Book 2 then develops a theory of the contribution the inertia of fluid media makes to resistance forces, and Book 3, a theory of gravitational forces and their effects. Newton was not the first to employ talk of forces in theories of motion. As the warning in the Scholium at the end of Section 11 about how he uses "attraction" and "impulse" indicates, he saw his way of employing such terms as novel, threatening confusion he needed to obviate. Definition 8 at the beginning of the *Principia* includes essentially the same warning about these terms, and "force" as well, adding, "this concept is purely mathematical, for I am not now considering the physical causes and sites of forces."[26] The warnings themselves are clear enough: Newton wants to be taken as talking of forces in the abstract, as quantities unto themselves, totally without regard to the physical mechanisms producing them. Not so clear are the ramifications of talking in this way.

The prior work that comes closest to treating forces in the manner of Newton is Huygens's theory of centrifugal force arising from uniform circular motion.[27] Like Descartes, Huygens uses the contrapositive of the principle of inertia to infer that something must be impeding any body that is not moving uniformly in a straight line. He further concludes that the magnitude of the force acting on the impediment is proportional to the extent of departure from what we now call inertial motion, obtaining for uniform circular motion the familiar v^2/r result. What Huygens means by "centrifugal force," however, is the force exerted on the impediment – for example, the tension in the string retaining the object in a circle. Huygens's centrifugal force is thus a form of static force, expressly analogous to the force a heavy object exerts on a string from which it is dangling. Talk of static forces was widespread in accounts of mechanical devices during the seventeenth century. Huygens was reaching beyond such talk only in inferring the magnitude of the force from the motion.

As Newton's discussion of his laws of motion makes clear, he too intended his treatment of forces to be continuous with the traditional treatment of static forces. Unlike Huygens, however, he singles out the unbalanced force that acts on the moving body, making it depart from inertial motion. Where Descartes and Huygens used the contrapositive of the principle of inertia to infer the existence of an impediment in contact with the non-inertially moving body, Newton uses it to infer the existence of an unbalanced force, *independently of all consideration of what is effecting that force.* His second law of motion then enables the magnitude and direction of any such force to be inferred from the extent and direction of the departure from inertial motion. Unbalanced force as a quantity can thus be fully characterized in abstraction from whatever might be producing it. This is what Newton means when he speaks in Definition 8 of considering "forces not from a physical but only from a mathematical point of view."

Newton had reason to expect that this way of talking of forces would confuse many of his readers. In his writing on light and colors in the early 1670s he had adopted essentially the same strategy in talking of rays of light as purely mathematically characterizable, independently of the underlying physics of light and the process or mechanism of its transmission. His warnings notwithstanding, many readers had insisted on equating his rays of light with paths defined by hypothetical particles comprising light; they had then argued, to his consternation, that his claims about refraction had not been established because he had not established that light consists of such particles.[28] His warnings about considering forces "from a mathematical point of view" were scarcely any better heeded.

From the mathematical point of view any unbalanced force acting on a body is a quantity with magnitude and direction. The general theory of centripetal forces developed in Book 1 considers forces from this point of view, with the direction specified toward a center and the magnitude taken to vary as a function of distance from that center. The same is true of the general theory of resistance forces developed in the first two-thirds of Book 2, but with the direction specified opposite to the direction of motion and the magnitude varying as a function of velocity. An unbalanced force that is thus fully characterized by its direction and magnitude can be resolved into correspondingly fully characterized components in any way one wishes, without regard to the particular physical components that happen to be giving rise to it. This absence of constraint in resolving forces into components is important in several places in Books 1 and 2, perhaps most strikingly in Proposition 3 of the former:

> Every body that, by a radius drawn to the center of a second body moving in any way whatever, describes about that center areas that are proportional to the times is urged by a force compounded of the centripetal force tending toward that second body and of the whole accelerative force by which that second body is urged.[29]

In principle – indeed, in practice – this situation can occur without there being any form of physical interaction, or physical forces, between the two bodies.

Still, as Newton's remark about "arguing more securely concerning the physical species, physical causes, and physical proportions of these forces" indicates, it does make sense according to his way of talking about forces to ask what physical forces a net unbalanced force results from. The theory of gravitational forces of Book 3 and the theory of the constituent of resistance forces arising from the inertia of the fluid at the end of Book 2 both treat forces from a physical point of view. Judging from the development of these two theories, Newton requires five conditions to be met for a component of a mathematically characterized force to be considered a physical force: (1) its direction must be determined by some material body other than the one it is acting on;[30] (2) all respects in which its magnitude can vary must be given by a general law that is independent of the first two laws of motion, such as the law of gravity, $F \propto Mm/r^2$; (3) some of the physical quantities entering into this law must pertain to the other body that determines the direction of the force; (4) this law must hold for some forces that are indisputably real, such as terrestrial gravity in the case of the law of gravity; and (5) if the force acts on a macroscopic body, then it must be composed of forces acting on microphysical parts of that body – this primarily to safeguard against inexactitude in the force law introduced by inferring it from macroscopic phenomena.

Notably absent from this list is anything about the mechanism or process effecting the force. Adherents to the "mechanical philosophy," such as Descartes and Huygens, and undoubtedly Galileo as well, would have required not just a mechanism effecting the force, but specifically a contact mechanism. Otherwise the putative force might be beyond explanation and hence occult. This is where Newton's new "experimental philosophy" departed most radically from the prevailing "mechanical philosophy."

The law characterizing a force from a physical point of view gives its "physical proportions" and assigns it to a "physical species." Two forces are of the same physical species only if they are characterized by the same law. Thus the inverse-square forces retaining the planets and their statellites in their orbits are the same in kind as terrestrial gravity, while (for Newton) the constituent of resistance forces arising from the inertia of the fluid is different in kind from that arising from its viscosity in so far as the former varies as velocity squared, and the latter does not. A theory of any physical species of force is required to give (1) necessary and sufficient conditions for a force to be present, (2) a law or laws dictating the relative magnitude and direction of this force in terms of determinable physical quantities, and (3) where relevant, an account of how it is composed out of microstructural forces.

Microstructural forces have a more fundamental status in the overall taxonomy of forces. In the *Principia* Newton identifies three species of microstructural force, gravity, pressure, and, percussion, where the theory of the latter had already been put forward by Huygens, Christopher Wren, and John Wallis.[31] The remark in the Preface to the first edition – "all phenomena may depend on certain forces by which the particles of bodies, by causes yet unknown, either are impelled toward one another and cohere in regular figures, or are repelled from one another and recede" – points to a program of pursuing theories of further species of microstructural force. This program is described in more detail in the unpublished portion of this Preface and an unpublished Conclusion, as illustrated by this passage from the former:

I therefore propose the inquiry whether or not there be many forces of this kind, never yet perceived, by which the particles of bodies agitate one another and coalesce into various structures. For if Nature be simple and pretty conformable to herself, causes will operate in the same kind of way in all phenomena, so that the motions of smaller bodies depend upon certain smaller forces just as the motions of larger bodies are ruled by the greater force of gravity. It remains therefore that we inquire by means of fitting experiments whether there are forces of this kind in nature, then what are their properties, quantities, and effects. For if all natural motions of great or small bodies can be explained through such forces, nothing more will remain than to inquire the causes of gravity, magnetic attraction, and the other forces.[32]

To his contemporaries, what seemed most confusing about Newton's way of talking about forces was his willingness to put forward a theory of gravitational "attraction" without regard to the causal mechanism effecting it. They generally concluded that he had to be committed to action at a distance as a causal mechanism in its own right. The outspoken opposition to the *Principia* in many quarters stemmed primarily from the inexplicability of action at a distance. Present-day readers, viewing the *Principia* in the light of 300 years of success in physics, are not likely to find the way Newton talks of forces from a physical point of view confusing. What most tends to confuse them is the distinction between considering forces from a physical point of view and considering them purely from a mathematical point of view. A symptom of this confusion is the tendency to read Book 1 as if its subject is gravitational forces, wondering why Newton bothered to include in it so many seemingly irrelevant propositions.

ARGUING FROM PHENOMENA OF MOTION
TO LAWS OF FORCE

In the Scholium at the end of Section 11 Newton says, rather vaguely, that the transition from mathematically to physically characterized forces is to be carried out by *comparing* the mathematically characterized proportions with phenomena. As other methodological remarks in the *Principia* make clear, the specific approach he prefers is to use the "if-then" propositions of his mathematical theory to "deduce" the physical laws characterizing forces from phenomena[33] – most notably, to deduce the law of gravity from the phenomena of orbital motion specified by two of Kepler's rules,[34] along with Thomas Streete's conclusion that the planetary aphelia are stationary.[35] Serious difficulties stand in the way of any such deduction, however. Much of the complexity of Newton's methodology comes from his approach to these difficulties.

One difficulty, noted earlier, is that limits of precision in observation entail that statements of phenomena hold at most *quam proxime*. This limitation was evident at the time in the case of Kepler's rules. Ishmaël Boulliau had replaced Kepler's area rule with a geometric construction, yet had achieved the same level of accuracy relative to Tycho Brahe's data as Kepler – roughly the level of accuracy that Tycho had claimed for observations at Uraniborg; and Vincent Wing had done almost as well using an oscillating equant instead of the area rule.[36] Jeremiah Horrocks and Streete were the only orbital astronomers to claim that the lengths of the semi-major axes of the planetary orbits could be inferred more accurately from the periods using Kepler's 3/2 power rule than by classical methods that were known to be sensitive to observational imprecision.[37] Even in the case of the ellipse, which virtually all orbital astronomers were using, the question whether it is merely a good approximation or the true exact trajectory remained open.[38] In short, Kepler's rules were at best established only *quam proxime*, and any "deduction" from them would have to concede that other ways of stating the phenomena could not be eliminated on grounds of accuracy alone.

From Newton's point of view, however, imprecision was not the worst difficulty. In the brief "De motu" tracts that preceded the *Principia* he had concluded that there are inverse-square centripetal acceleration fields (to use the modern term) around the Sun, Jupiter, Saturn, and the Earth, with the strength of each given by the invariant value $[a^3 / P^2]$ for bodies orbiting them, where a is the mean distance for any orbit and P is the period.[39] Presumably, the acceleration fields around Jupiter, Saturn, and the Earth extend to the Sun, putting it into motion. By a generalization of the principle of inertia to a system of interacting bodies – a generalization that is equivalent to the third law of motion of the *Principia* – the interactions among the bodies cannot alter the motion of the center of gravity of the system. From this Newton reached a momentous conclusion:

> By reason of the deviation of the Sun from the center of gravity, the centripetal force does not always tend to that immobile center, and hence the planets neither move exactly in ellipses nor revolve twice in the same orbit. There are as many orbits of a planet as it has revolutions, as in the motion of the Moon . . . But to consider simultaneously all these causes of motion and to define these motions by exact laws admitting of easy calculation exceeds, if I am not mistaken, the force of any human mind.[40]

In other words, before he began writing the *Principia* itself (and, if I am right, before he had even discovered the law of gravity[41]), Newton had concluded that Kepler's rules can at best be true only *quam proxime* of the planets and their satellites, not because of imprecision of observation, but because the true motions are immensely more complicated than Kepler's or any other such rules could hope to capture.

Newton was not the first to conclude that real motions are exceedingly complex. Galileo had concluded that the multiplicity of factors affecting motion in resisting media preclude "fixed laws and exact description";[42] and, in a letter to Mersenne, Descartes too had denied the possibility of a science of air resistance.[43] Newton was most likely unaware of these remarks of Galileo and Descartes on resistance, but he definitely did know that Descartes, in his *Principia* (1644), had denied that the planetary orbits are mathematically exact, remarking that as "in all other natural things, they are only approximately so, and also they are continuously changed by the passing of the ages."[44] The response of Galileo, Huygens, and Descartes to the complexities of real-world motions and limits in precision of measurement was to employ the hypothetico-deductive approach to marshaling evidence, deducing testable conclusions from conjectured hypotheses and then exposing these conclusions to falsification. From the beginning of his work in optics in the 1660s, Newton had always distrusted the hypothetico-deductive approach, arguing that too many disparate hypotheses can be compatible with the same observations.[45] Inexactitude, whether from imprecision in observation or from the complexity of the real world, exacerbates this shortcoming. In saying that the approach illustrated by the *Principia* puts one in position to argue more securely about features of underlying physics, Newton was claiming to have a response to inexactitude that surmounts limitations of the hypothetico-deductive approach of his predecessors.

Because Newton never describes his approach in detail, we have to infer what it involves from the evidential reasoning in the *Principia*. A key clue is provided by what I. Bernard Cohen has called the "Newtonian style"[46] – proceeding from idealized simple cases to progressively more complicated ones, though still idealized. Thus, in the case of inverse-square centripetal forces, Book 1 first considers so-called "one-body" problems, for which Kepler's three rules hold exactly. Next are one-body problems in which inverse-cube centripetal forces are superposed on the inverse-square; Kepler's rules still hold exactly, but for orbits that rotate, that is, whose lines of apsides precess. Next are "two-body" problems subject to the third law of motion. The results for these show that two of Kepler's rules continue to hold, but the 3/2 power rule requires a correction. Last are problems involving three or more interacting bodies. For these Newton succeeds in obtaining only limited, qualitative results, yet still sufficient to show that none of Kepler's three rules holds. A distinctive feature of this sequence is the extent to which it focuses on systematic deviations from Kepler's simple rules that can serve as evidence for two-body and three-body interaction. Newton is putting himself in a position to address the complexity of real orbital motion in a sequence of successive approximations, with each approximation an idealized motion and systematic deviations from it providing evidence for the next stage in the sequence.

Here too Huygens had foreshadowed the Newtonian style, though again only up to a point. The initial theory of pendulum motion in *Horologium Oscillatorium* is for pendulums with idealized "point-mass" bobs.[47] Huygens then turns to the question of physical bobs with a distinctive shape and real bulk, solving the celebrated problem of the center of oscillation that Mersenne had put forward as a challenge decades earlier. The small-arc circular pendulum measurement of gravity presented near the end of the book incorporates a small correction to the length of the pendulum, corresponding to the distance between the center of gravity of the bob and its center of oscillation. This correction, however, holds only for the circular pendulum, not for the cycloidal pendulum that was the crowning achievement of Huygens's initial theory. For the correction depends not only on the shape of the bob, but also on the length of the string, and this length varies along the cycloidal path. (Indeed, it is this variation that makes the cycloid the isochronous path for a point-mass bob.) Huygens had tried to find the corrected path required for strict isochronism with a physically real bob, only to despair when the problem proved intractably complex. In the manner typical of pre-Newtonian science, the small residual discrepancies between idealized theory and the real world were dismissed as being of no practical importance. This is one more example of the way in which the complexity of the real world ended up being viewed as an impediment, limiting the quality of empirical evidence, and not as a resource for progressively higher-quality evidence that it became with Newtonian successive approximations.

Newton's "deductions" of the various parts of the law of gravity from phenomena of orbital motion reveal two restrictions, beyond mathematical tractability, that he at least prefers to impose on the successive approximations.[48] First, in every case in which he deduces some feature of celestial gravitational forces, he has taken the trouble in Book 1 to prove that the consequent of the "if-then" proposition licensing the deduction still holds *quam proxime* so long as the antecedent holds *quam proxime*. For instance, two corollaries of Proposition 3 show that the force on the orbital body is at least very nearly centripetal so long as the areas swept out in equal times remain very nearly equal. This, by the way, explains why Newton himself never deduced the inverse-square variation from the Keplerian ellipse even though he had proved in Book 1 that an exact Keplerian ellipse entails an exact inverse-square variation: an orbital motion can approximate a Keplerian ellipse without the exponent of *r* in the rule governing the centripetal force variation being even approximately minus 2.[49] Restricting the deductions to ones that hold *quam proxime* so long as the phenomenon describes the true motions *quam proxime* provides a guarantee: under the assumption that the laws of motion hold, the deduced feature of the physical forces holds at least *quam proxime* of the specific motions that license the statement of the phenomenon. In other words, thanks to this restriction, unless his laws of motion are seriously wrong, Newton's law of gravity is definitely true at least *quam proxime* of celestial motions over the century of observations from Tycho to the *Principia*.

Second, in every case in which Newton deduces some feature of celestial gravitational forces, mathematical results established in Book 1 allow him to identify specific conditions under which the phenomenon from which the deduction is made would hold not merely *quam proxime*, but exactly. For instance, the orbiting body would sweep out equal areas in equal times exactly if the only forces acting on it were centripetal, and its line of apsides would be stationary if the only forces acting on it were inverse-square centripetal forces. The choice of the subjunctive here is not mine, but Newton's: in Proposition 13 of Book 3, for example, he remarks, "if the Sun were at rest and the remaining planets did not act upon one another, their orbits would be elliptical, having the Sun at their common focus, and they would describe areas proportional to the times."[50] By imposing this restriction on the phenomena from which force laws are deduced, Newton is assuring that these phenomena are not just arbitrary approximations to the true motions; at least according to the theory of the "deduced" physical force, the true motions would be in exact accord with the phenomena were it not for specific complicating factors.

Let me here restrict the term "idealization" to approximations that would hold exactly in certain specifiable circumstances. If, as I have proposed, Newton is addressing the complexity of real orbital motion in a sequence of successive approximations, then he had profound reasons for preferring that each successive approximation be an idealization in this sense. For any deviation of the actual motions from a given approximation will then be physically meaningful, and not just a reflection of the particular mathematical scheme employed in achieving the approximation, as in curve fitting. Of course, omniscience is required to know whether any approximation really is an idealization in the requisite sense, and (as Book 2 attests) Newton was far from omniscient. The most he could demand is that the theory being "deduced" from the approximations entails that they be idealizations of this sort. At least from the point of view of the theory, then, any observed systematic pattern in the deviations from a given approximation would have the promise of being physically informative, and hence a promise of becoming telling evidence.

In sum, judging from details of Newton's "deductions" from phenomena, his approach to the complexities of real-world motions is to try to address them in a sequence of progressively more complex idealizations, with systematic deviations from the idealizations at any stage providing the "phenomena" serving as evidence for the refinement achieved in the next. Such systematic deviations are appropriately called "second-order phenomena" in so far as they are not observable in their own right, but presuppose the theory. Thus, for example, no one can observe the famous 43 arc-seconds per century discrepancy in the motion of the perihelion of Mercury that emerged in the second half of the nineteenth century and then became evidence for Einstein's theory of general relativity: they are the residual left over after subtracting the 531 arc-seconds per century produced by the other planets according to *Newtonian* theory from the 574 arc-seconds derived from observation once allowance is made for the 5600 arc-seconds associated with the precession of the equinoxes.

Attempting to proceed in *successive* approximations in this way involves restrictions on how second-order phenomena are to be marshaled as evidence. In the case of orbital motions, any systematic discrepancy from the idealized theoretical motions has to be identified with a specific physical force – if not a gravitational force, then one governed by some other generic force law. This restriction precludes inventing *ad hoc* forces to save the law of gravity. It thereby makes success in carrying out a program of successive approximations far from guaranteed.

A second, less familiar example shows this in a different way. In Propositions 19 and 20 of Book 3 Newton first calculates a 17 mile difference between the radii to the poles and to the equator of the Earth, and then a specific variation of surface gravity with latitude. These calculations presuppose *universal* gravity. Indeed, as Huygens was quick to notice (and Maupertuis and Clairaut forty years later), this is the sole result in the *Principia* amenable at the time to empirical assessment that differentiates *universal* gravity from macroscopic inverse-square celestial gravity. Newton's calculations also presuppose that the density of the Earth is perfectly uniform. Hence, his results are not straightforwardly testable predictions, for they apply only to an idealized Earth. In all three editions Newton pointed out that any deviation from the calculated results is a sign that the Earth's density increases from the surface to the core. In the first edition he went so far as to propose that a linear increase in density be assumed for the next idealized approximation.[51] This was not an *ad hoc* way of protecting the law of universal gravity from refutation because, as Huygens's efforts in his *Discourse on the Cause of Gravity* showed, different assumptions about gravity yield very different relationships between the Earth's oblateness on the one hand, and the variation of surface gravity with latitude on the other.[52] Therefore, a variation in density inferred from, say, an observed oblateness differing from Newton's 17 miles was not guaranteed to yield a corresponding improvement between the observed variation in surface gravity and Newton's calculated variation. (From Clairaut forward the field of physical geodesy has been inferring the internal density distribution of the Earth from features of its shape and gravitational field, always presupposing the law of universal gravity; the discrepancies between observation and current theory have grown continually smaller.[53])

Needless to say, Newton's theory of gravity provides an explanation of Kepler's rules and of each of the subsequent idealized orbital motions in the sequence of successive approximations. That is, the theory explains why these idealizations hold at least *quam proxime* and why they have claim to being preferred descriptions of the actual motions even though they are not exact and observation is not precise. Providing such explanations, however, is not the distinctive feature of the theory. As Leibniz showed in print within months after the *Principia* first appeared, a theory of a very different sort, one that meets the demands of the mechanical philosophy, can explain Kepler's rules too.[54] The distinctive feature of Newtonian theory is the spotlight it shines on discrepancies between theory and observation. In his "System of the World" in Book 3 Newton no sooner spells out the conditions under which, for example, Keplerian motion would hold exactly than he turns to the principal real-world respects in which it does not, such as the gravitational effect of Jupiter on the motion of Saturn and on the precession of the aphelia of the inner planets. In adopting his approach of successive approximations, with its focus on theory-dependent second-order phenomena, Newton was turning theory into an indispensable instrument for ongoing research. Exact science as illustrated by the *Principia* is thus not exact science in the sense of Newton's predecessors, an account of how the world would be if it were more rational. It is exact science in the sense that every systematic deviation from current theory automatically has the status of a pressing unsolved problem.

Even with the above restrictions, the "deduction" of the law of gravity, or any other force law, from phenomena of motion that hold only *quam proxime* shows at most that it holds *quam proxime*. When the restrictions are met, however, as they by and large are in the case of the law of gravity,[55] Newton views the derivation as authorizing the force law to be *taken*, provisionally, as exact. Specifically, his fourth Rule for Natural Philosophy says:

> In experimental philosophy, propositions gathered from phenomena by induction should be considered either exactly or very nearly true notwithstanding any contrary hypotheses, until yet other phenomena make such propositions either more exact or liable to exceptions.

This rule should be followed so that arguments based on induction may not be nullified by hypotheses.[56]

Taking the force law to be exact when the evidence for it shows at most that it holds *quam proxime* amounts to an evidential strategy for purposes of ongoing research. This strategy is transparently appropriate when the goal is to use systematic deviations from current theory as evidence in a process of successive approximations.

ARGUING *MORE SECURELY*

The preceding section has offered a detailed description of how Newton prefers to *argue* from phenomena to physically characterized forces. Nothing has yet been said, however, about why this way of arguing might have claim to yielding conclusions that are *more secure*.

One respect in which it offers more security is easy to see. The "if-then" propositions used in deducing the law, as well as their approximative counterparts ("if-*quam-proxime*-then-*quam-proxime*"), are rigorously derived from the laws of motion. The phenomena – that is, the propositions expressing Newton's phenomena – are inductive generalizations from specific observations, and hence they hold at least *quam proxime* of these observations. But then, unless the laws of motion are fundamentally mistaken, the force law too is guaranteed to hold at least *quam proxime* of these observations.

By way of contrast, the fact that a consequence deduced from a hypothesized force law holds *quam proxime* of specific observations need not provide any such guarantee. A conjectural hypothesis can reach far beyond the observations providing evidence for it not merely in its generality, but in its content. In practice Newton's first Rule for Natural Philosophy – *no more causes . . . should be admitted than are both true and sufficient to explain their phenomena* – has the effect of confining the content of theory to no more than the data clearly demand. Calling for the force law to be deduced from phenomena is a way of meeting this Rule.

Put another way, Newton's demand for a deduction from phenomena is an attempt to confine risk in theorizing as much as possible to "inductive generalization." What Newton means by "made general by induction" and "propositions gathered from phenomena by induction" amounts to more than merely projecting an open-ended generalization from some of its instances. The Phenomena he lists at the beginning of Book 3 involve first projection from discrete observations to orbital rules that fill in the gaps among these observations, and then projection of these rules into the indefinite past and future. His second Rule for Natural Philosophy – *same effect, same cause* – authorizes inferences that Charles Saunders Peirce would have labeled *abductive* in contrast to inductive. Even his third Rule, which at first glance seems most akin to induction, authorizes inferences of much greater sweep than is customary in simple induction: it specifies conditions under which conclusions based on observations and experiments within our reach may be extended to the far reaches of the universe and to microphysical reaches far beyond our capacity to observe. The care Newton put into this third Rule,[57] which he formulated in the early 1690s when he was in close contact with John Locke, indicates that he was acutely aware of the risk in "propositions gathered from phenomena by induction." So too does his insistence on the provisional status of these propositions in the subsequently added fourth Rule.

Newton's further demand that the theory entail specific conditions under which the phenomena in question hold exactly provides some support for projecting these phenomena inductively beyond the available observations. Specifically, as noted earlier, such a "re-deduction" gives reason to take the phenomena as lawlike, and not just one among many possible curve-fits. The deduced force law itself, however, can hold *quam proxime* of these observations and still turn out not to be suitable for inductive generalization; the most that can be said is that its deduction and the subsequent re-deduction of the phenomena make it an exceptionally promising candidate for inductive generalization.

Over the long term, pursuit of refinements in a sequence of successive approximations can provide a further source of security. Any current approximation to, for example, orbital motions is an idealization predicated on the force law. Hence observed deviations from it continually, so to speak, put the law to test. Recalcitrant deviations point to deficiencies in the law. If, however, second-order phenomena emerge and the presence of further forces complicating the motions is successfully established from them, then new evidence accrues to the law. Such new evidence does more than just support the original inductive generalization. The process of successive approximations leads to increasingly small residual deviations from current theory, which in turn tighten the range over which the force law holds *quam proxime*. More important, because the process of successive approximations presupposes the force law, continuing success in it leads to progressively deeper *entrenchment* of the law, to use Nelson Goodman's term.[58] This, of course, is precisely what happened in the case of Newton's law of gravity, with continuing improvement over the last three centuries in the agreement between theory and observation not only for orbital motion within celestial mechanics, but also for the Earth's shape and gravity field within physical geodesy. Indeed, the process of successive approximations issuing from Newton's *Principia* in these fields has yielded evidence of a quality beyond anything his predecessors ever dreamed of.

Evidence from long-term success in pursuit of successive approximations, however, can in principle be achieved by a hypothetico-deductive approach as well. The most that can be said for Newton's approach in this regard is that its confining the risk to the extent it does to inductive generalization may enhance its prospects for achieving such success.

What form does the risk take with Newton's approach? His inductively generalized law of *universal* gravity is presupposed as holding exactly in evidential reasoning at each stage after the first in the process of successive approximations. The main risk is a discovery that would falsify this law in a way that nullifies all or part of the evidential reasoning that has been predicated on it. Suppose, for example, that a discovery entails that various second-order phenomena that had been crucial as evidence were not phenomena at all, but mere artifacts of a supposed law that just so happens to hold *quam proxime* under parochial circumstances. Then, to the extent the evidence for this discovery is predicated on advances based on these second-order phenomena, the discovery itself would, in a sense, be self-nullifying. The conclusion would have to be that the pursuit of successive approximations had been proceeding down a garden path, and the area of science in question would have to be restarted from some earlier point.

Newton's attempt to initiate successive approximations in the case of resistance forces was shown to be going down just such a garden path by Jean d'Alembert twenty-five years after the third edition of the *Principia* appeared.[59] Surprising as it may seem to many readers, however, this has yet to happen in the case of his theory of gravity. The large conceptual gap between Newtonian and Einsteinian gravitation notwithstanding, the theory of gravity in general relativity has not nullified the evidential reasoning predicated on Newton's theory. In particular, it has not nullified the evidential reasoning from which the phenomenon of the residual 43 arc-seconds per century precession of the perihelion of Mercury emerged; if it had, this phenomenon could not be used directly as evidence supporting it. The reason why evidential reasoning predicated on Newtonian gravity was not nullified is because general relativity entails that Newton's law holds in the weak-field limit, and virtually none of this reasoning, viewed in retrospect, required anything more of Newton's law than that it hold to very high approximation in weak gravitational fields.[60]

The risk of a garden path with Newton's approach, therefore, does not as such derive from the possibility that the force law deduced from phenomena at the outset is not exact. This law itself can be open to refinement as part of the process of successive approximations without undercutting the process and having to restart from some earlier point. The relativistic refinements to Newton's first two laws of motion show that the same can be said about the axioms presupposed in the deduction of the force law. Rather, the risk comes from the huge inductive leap, from a celestial force law that holds at least *quam proxime* over a narrow body of data to the law of universal gravity – a leap authorized by Newton's first three Rules governing inductive reasoning. More specifically, the risk comes from two "taxonomic" presuppositions entering into this leap. Newton's vision of a fundamental taxonomy based on physical forces – or, more accurately, interactions[61] – is largely beside the point so far as gravity alone is concerned. Nevertheless, his inductive generalization does presuppose (1) that there is a distinct species – or natural kind, to use our current term – of elementary motion and a distinct species of static force which are characterized at least to a first approximation by his deduced law of gravity. The risk lies in the possibility that subsequent research will conclude either that there are no such distinct species or that they are species of limited range, even artifacts of the data from which he was working. Further, his inductive generalization presupposes (2) that certain specific motions – primarily planetary motions – are pure enough examples of motions of a specific elementary species to typify this species as a whole.

The risks from both of these presuppositions are evident in the garden path formed by Newton's efforts on resistance forces. In the first edition of the *Principia* he thought that phenomena of pendulum decay would allow him to demarcate the different species of resistance force and their respective variation with velocity.

Recognizing the failure of this,[62] in the second and third editions he assumed that vertical fall of ordinary-size objects is dominated by resistance forces arising purely from the inertia of the fluid – at least to a sufficient extent to allow a law to be established for this kind of resistance force. His announced plan was for the other kinds to be addressed using discrepancies between observations and this law.[63] The garden path arose because both of these taxonomic presuppositions were wrong. First, there are no distinct species of resistance force, but only one species governed by interaction between inertial and viscous effects in the fluid, interaction that is so complicated that we still have no law for resistance of the sort Newton was pursuing, but only empirically determined relationships for bodies of various shapes.[64] Second, as d'Alembert showed, resistance in an idealized inviscid fluid of the sort Newton had assumed in deriving his law for purely inertial resistance is exactly zero, regardless of shape and velocity. Newton's supposed "law" for the purely inertial effects of the fluid turns out to amount to nothing more than a very rough approximation to the total resistance on spheres for a limited combination of diameters, velocities, and fluid densities and viscosities – a mere curve-fit over a restricted domain.[65]

Newton's taxonomic presuppositions are best regarded as working hypotheses underpinning his inductive generalizations. As with all such working hypotheses, some immediate protection is afforded by demanding that the evidence developed out of the data be of high quality, without lots of loose ends. Newton's "deduction" of the law of gravity met this demand to a much greater extent than did his evidential reasoning on resistance.[66] Still, the "deduction" was based primarily on the motion of only five planets over an astronomically brief period of time. The danger of being misled by such limited data is always high.

I know of nowhere that Newton acknowledges the risk that such taxonomic working hypotheses introduce into inductive generalization. He does acknowledge the risk of inductive generalization in the most famous methodological passage in the *Opticks*, in the discussion of the methods of "analysis and synthesis" in the next to last paragraph of the final Query, which was added in 1706:

> This Analysis consists in making Experiments and Observations, and in drawing general Conclusions from them by Induction, and admitting of no Objections against the Conclusions, but such as are taken from Experiments, or other certain Truths. For Hypotheses are not to be regarded in experimental Philosophy. And although the arguing from Experiments and Observations by Induction be no Demonstration of general Conclusions; yet it is the best way of arguing which the Nature of the Thing admits of, and may be looked upon as so much the stronger, by how much the Induction is more general. And if no Exception occur from Phenomena, the Conclusion may be pronounced generally. But if at any time afterwards any Exception shall occur from Experiments, it may then begin to be pronounced with such Exceptions as occur. By this way of Analysis we may proceed from Compounds to Ingredients and from Motions to the Forces producing them; and in general, from Effects to their Causes, and from particular Causes to more general ones, till the Argument end in the most general.[67]

Perhaps Newton saw success in achieving unrestricted generality as the ultimate safeguard against the risk introduced by the unavoidable taxonomic hypotheses entering into induction.

This brings us to the last distinctive aspect of the approach to theory construction illustrated by the *Principia* – that is, illustrated in the case of gravity, though not in the case of resistance. After establishing the law of universal gravity and the conditions for Keplerian motion, Book 3 goes on to "applications" of the law in unresolved problems at some remove from the phenomena from which it was "deduced": (1) the non-spherical shape of the Earth and the variation of surface gravity with latitude; (2) the area-rule violation in the orbit of the Moon, the motion of its nodes, and its fluctuating inclination; (3) the tides; (4) the precession of the equinoxes; and

(5) the trajectories of comets. The idea seems to be to protect against risks arising in the inductive leap by immediately pushing the theory for all it is worth, employing it as a tool of research on problems that *prima facie* have nothing to do with the original evidence for it. It goes without saying that, regardless of how far afield such "applications" may be, they still provide no *guarantee* against a garden path. Nevertheless, they do represent a concerted effort to expose limitations in the taxonomic presuppositions set out above. As already noted, the shape of the Earth and the variation of surface gravity directly involve the generalization from celestial to universal gravity, as does the precession of the equinoxes indirectly. The vagaries in the lunar orbit address the most glaring known counterexample to Keplerian motion and hence worries about generalizing beyond planetary motion. Both the tides and the precession of the equinoxes involve the generalization from simple centripetal forces to interactive gravity, as does a gravitational treatment of vagaries in the motions of Jupiter and Saturn. And finally the comets involve the extension of the law of gravity to bodies that appear to consist of matter very different from that of the planets and their satellites and that pass through the intermediate distances from the Sun between the orbits of the planets.[68] The fact that all of these address evidential worries in the original inductive generalization indicates that the process of comparison with phenomena, and hence the argument for securing universal gravity, extends across all of Book 3.[69]

The efforts occupying the rest of Book 3 were extraordinarily innovative. In this respect they are akin to predictions of novel phenomena of the sort Huygens singled out as the strongest form of evidence for empirical theories. None of them, however, is a truly straightforward prediction of the sort classically called for in hypothetico-deductive evidence. In every case some further, contestable assumptions were needed beyond Newton's theory, if only the assumption that no other forces are at work besides gravity. Still, Newton's inductive generalization to *universal* gravity clearly introduced a large conjectural element in his theory; and the applications of it beyond Keplerian motion put this element to the test, ultimately supplying the most compelling evidence for it. The key prediction put to the test in these applications was not so much that every two particles of matter interact gravitationally, but rather one that is more abstract: *every discrepancy between Newtonian theory and observation will prove to be physically significant and hence can be taken to be telling us something further about the physical world.* Contrast this with deviations from a curve-fit, which usually reflect nothing more than the particular mathematical framework that happened to have been used. Lacking omniscience, the only way we have of deciding whether a discrepancy is physically significant is from the point of view of ongoing theory. The issue of physical significance from this point of view turns most crucially on whether the taxonomic working hypotheses underlying Newton's inductive step to universal gravity remain intact as theory advances. Does the discrepancy give reason to conclude that a taxonomy of interactions is not fundamental or that gravitational interactions do not comprise a distinct kind within that taxonomy?

In part because of the further contestable assumptions, every one of the efforts occupying the rest of Book 3, as well as Newton's brief suggestions about the motions of Jupiter and Saturn, initiated its own historical sequence of successive approximations subsequent to the *Principia*. Moreover, even at the time the third edition appeared, almost forty years after the first, serious loose ends remained in the treatment of every one of these topics in the *Principia*. These loose ends may help to explain why so many capable scientists who came of age after the *Principia* were initially so cautious in accepting Newton's theory. A decade or so after Newton died, Clairaut, Euler, and d'Alembert began their efforts to tie up these loose ends, followed by Lagrange and Laplace over the last forty years of the eighteenth century.[70] In a very real sense, then, Newton's argument for universal gravity was not completed until a century after the publication of the first edition of the *Principia*. With its completion, the new approach to theory construction that the book was intended to illustrate – that is, the new type of generic mathematical theory, the contrast between mathematical and physical points of view, the roles of "deduced" theory and idealizations in ongoing research, and the insistence on pushing theory far beyond its original basis – became a permanent part of the science of physics.

NOTES

1 Isaac Newton, *The Principia, Mathematical Principles of Natural Philosophy: A New Translation*, trans. I. Bernard Cohen and Anne Whitman (Berkeley, CA: University of California Press, 1999), pp. 382f.

2 *Ibid.*, p. 415; see Robert DiSalle's chapter in this volume for a discussion of Newton's views on relative versus absolute motion.

3 In Latin, *Regulae Philosophandi*; see William Harper's chapter in this volume for a discussion of Newton's use of these Rules in his "deduction" of universal gravitation.

4 Newton, *Principia*, p. 943.

5 Isaac Newton, "An Account of the Book Entituled *Commercium Epistolicum*," reprinted in A. Rupert Hall, *Philosophers at War: The Quarrel between Newton and Leibniz* (Cambridge: Cambridge University Press, 1980), p. 312. Newton made much the same concession to hypotheses in 1672 in one of his exchanges with Pardies on his light and colors experiments; see I. Bernard Cohen and Robert E. Schefield (eds.), *Isaac Newton's Papers and Letters on Natural Philosophy*, revised edition (Cambridge, MA: Harvard University Press, 1978), p. 106; see note 45 below.

6 Christiaan Huygens, *Traité de la Lumière*, in *Oeuvres complètes de Christiaan Huygens*, vol. 19 (The Hague: Martinus Nijhoff, 1937), p. 454; the English translation is from Michael R. Matthews, *Scientific Background to Modern Philosophy* (Indianapolis, IN: Hackett, 1989), p. 126. The hypothesis which Huygens had most in mind was the longitudinal wave theory of light.

7 Newton, *Principia*, pp. 588f.

8 A few Newton scholars have emphasized this Scholium, most notably I. Bernard Cohen in his *The Newtonian Revolution* (Cambridge: Cambridge University Press, 1980), Clifford Truesdell in "Reactions of Late Baroque Mechanics to Success, Conjecture, Error, and Failure in

Newton's *Principia*," reprinted in his *Essays in the History of Mechanics* (New York: Springer-Verlag, 1968), and E. W. Strong in "Newton's 'Mathematical Way'," *Journal of the History of Ideas* 12 (1951), 90–110.

9 See N. Jardine, *The Birth of History and Philosophy of Science: Kepler's A Defence of Tycho against Ursus* (Cambridge: Cambridge University Press, 1984).

10 See Alexandre Koyré, "An Experiment in Measurement," in his *Metaphysics and Measurement* (Cambridge, MA: Harvard University Press, 1968).

11 René Descartes, *Principles of Philosophy*, trans. Valentine Rodger Miller and Reese P. Miller (Dordrecht: D. Reidel, 1983); gravity and magnetism are discussed in Part 4, the former in Propositions 20 through 27 and the latter in Propositions 133 through 183.

12 In a letter of 1690 from Huygens to Leibniz; see *Oeuvres complètes de Christiaan Huygens*, vol. 9 (1901), p. 538.

13 Galileo Galilei, *Dialogues Concerning Two New Sciences*, trans. Henry Crew and Alfonso de Salvio (Buffalo: Prometheus Books, 1991).

14 Christiaan Huygens, *The Pendulum Clock; or, Geometrical Demonstration concerning the Motion of Pendula as Applied to Clocks*, trans. Richard J. Blackwell (Ames, IA: Iowa State University Press, 1986).

15 Galileo Galilei, *Dialogue concerning the Two Chief World Systems*, 2nd edn, trans. Stillman Drake (Berkeley, CA: University of California Press, 1967). Newton read the English translation by Thomas Salusbury, published in 1661.

16 For example, Robert Anderson's *The Genuine Use and Effects of the Gun*; Kenelm Digby's "The Nature of Bodies" in his *Two Treatises*; and Walter Charleton's *Physiologia: Epicuro-Gassendo-Carltoniai, or A Fabrick of Science Natural, Upon the Hypothesis of Atoms*. Newton either owned copies or copied out portions of each of these. I thank I. B. Cohen for this point.

17 See Newton, *Principia*, pp. 444 and 446.

18 See Huygens, *The Pendulum Clock*, Proposition 25, p. 69.

19 In his *Horologium Oscillatorium* Huygens expressly calls the three opening principles (the first of which is the principle of inertia) "hypotheses" (p. 33). Apparently following Huygens, Newton too called the forerunners of his laws of motion "hypotheses" in his tract, "De motu corporum in gyrum," the seed from which the *Principia* grew;

the change to "laws" appears first as a correction to "hypotheses" in the revised version of this tract. See D. T. Whiteside (ed.), *The Preliminary Manuscripts for Isaac Newton's 1687 Principia: 1684–1686* (Cambridge: Cambridge University Press, 1989), pp. 3 and 13.

20 The term is Arthur Prior's.

21 See Newton, *Principia*, Book 2, Proposition 30 and 31, pp. 708–12.

22 Newton, *Principia*, Book 1, Proposition 45, pp. 539–45. This proposition is discussed in See Ram Valluri, Curtis Wilson, and William Harper, "Newton's Apsidal Precession Theorem and Eccentric Orbits," *Journal for the History of Astronomy* 28 (1997), 13–27.

23 Newton's use of such measurements has been discussed in several places by William Harper; see his chapter in this volume.

24 Huygens presents his simple pendulum measurement in Part 4 of his *Horologium Oscillatorium*, Proposition 26 (*The Pendulum Clock*, pp. 170–2), and he describes a conical pendulum measurement in Part v (pp. 173–5). See chapters 2–4 of Joella Yoder's *Unrolling Time: Christiaan Huygens and the Mathematization of Nature* (Cambridge: Cambridge University Press, 1988) for a discussion of the original measurements Huygens carried out in 1659.

25 E. W. Strong makes clear the indispensability of measurement to Newton's "mathematical way" in his "Newton's 'Mathematical Way'," cited in note 8 above. Unfortunately, the passage from the English translation of Newton's *System of the World* from which Strong develops his essay appears to be spurious, added by the translator; Strong's argument, however, requires no recourse to this passage.

26 Newton, *Principia*, p. 407.

27 Huygens lists 13 propositions on centrifugal force, a term he coined, at the end of his *Horologium Oscillatorium* (*The Pendulum Clock*, pp. 176–8). A full manuscript including proofs was published in 1703, in the edition of his posthumous papers prepared by de Volder and Fullenius. See *Oeuvres complètes de Christiaan Huygens*, vol. 16 (1929), pp. 255–301.

28 This complaint was voiced most outspokenly by Robert Hooke; see p. 111 of *Isaac Newton's Papers and Letters on Natural Philosophy*, cited in note 5 above. Newton's mathematical treatment of rays of light is discussed in Alan Shapiro's chapter in this volume.

29 Newton, *Principia*, p. 448.

30 This requirement is met in the case of resistance forces because the velocity which determines their direction is the velocity of the resisted body *relative* to the fluid medium.

31 Papers summarizing the "laws of motion" by Wallis and Wren appeared in *Philosophical Transactions of the Royal Society* in the spring of 1669 (pp. 864–8), followed shortly after (pp. 925–8) by a summary of the theorems of Huygens, who had in effect refereed the papers by Wallis and Wren. Huygens's beautiful proofs of his account of impact did not appear in print until his posthumous papers were published in 1703; see *Oeuvres complètes de Christiaan Huygens*, vol. 16, pp. 29–91.

32 A. Rupert Hall and Marie Boas Hall (eds.), *Unpublished Scientific Papers of Isaac Newton* (Cambridge: Cambridge University Press, 1962), p. 307.

33 The word "phenomena" for Newton does not refer to individual observations, but to inductively generalized summaries of observations, such as Kepler's area rule.

34 The word "rules" best describes Kepler's famous orbital claims at the time Newton was writing the *Principia*. They came to be called "laws" only after the *Principia* was published – first apparently in Leibniz's *Illustrio Tentaminis de Motuum Coelestium Causis* of 1689 (a translation of which can be found in Domenico Bertolini Meli's *Equivalence and Priority: Newton versus Leibniz* [Oxford: Oxford University Press, 1993], pp. 126–42).

35 Streete's *Astronomia Carolina*, from which Newton first learned his orbital astronomy, was published in 1661. Streete's claim that the orbits are stationary was challenged in Vincent Wing's *Examen Astronomiae Carolinae* of 1665, and then defended anew in Streete's *Examen Examinatum* of 1667.

36 See Curtis Wilson, "Predictive Astronomy in the Century after Kepler," in René Taton and Curtis Wilson (eds.), *Planetary Astronomy from the Renaissance to the Rise of Astrophysics, Part A: Tycho Brahe to Newton* (Cambridge: Cambridge University Press, 1989), pp. 172–85.

37 *Ibid.*, pp. 168 and 179.

38 Thus we find Robert Hooke, in the correspondence of 1679–80 with Newton that initiated his key discoveries on orbital motion, asking Newton to calculate the curve described by a body under inverse-square forces, and remarking, "this curve truly calculated will show the error of those many lame shifts made use of by astronomers to approach the true

motions of the planets with their tables." (*The Correspondence of Isaac Newton*, vol. 2, ed. H. W. Turnbull [Cambridge: Cambridge University Press, 1960], p. 309.)

39 Newton, "De motu corporum in gyrum," in D. T. Whiteside (ed.), *The Mathematical Papers of Isaac Newton*, vol. 6 (Cambridge: Cambridge University Press, 1974), pp. 30–74.

40 *Ibid.*, pp. 74–80. An English translation of the augmented version of "De motu" can be found in *Unpublished Scientific Papers of Isaac Newton*, cited in note 32 above, pp. 239–92. The English translation given here is from Curtis Wilson, "The Newtonian Achievement in Astronomy," in Taton and Wilson (eds.), *Planetary Astronomy*, p. 253.

41 See William Harper and George E. Smith, "Newton's New Way of Inquiry," in Jarrett Leplin (ed.), *The Creation of Ideas in Physics: Studies for a Methodology of Theory Construction* (Norwell: Kluwer, 1995), pp. 133–9.

42 Galileo, *Two New Sciences*, cited in note 13 above, p. 252.

43 René Descartes, *The Philosophical Writings of Descartes*, vol. 3, trans. John Cottingham, Robert Stoothoff, Dugald Murdoch, and Anthony Kenny (Cambridge: Cambridge University Press, 1991), pp. 9ff.

44 Descartes, *Principles*, cited in note 11 above, p. 98.

45 Thus, Newton remarked in a response to objections to his early publications in optics, For the best and safest method of philosophizing seems to be, first to inquire diligently into the properties of things, and establishing those properties by experiments and then to proceed more slowly to hypotheses for the explanation of them. For hypotheses should be subservient only in explaining the properties of things, but not assumed in determining them; unless so far as they may furnish experiments. For if the possibility of hypotheses is to be the test of the truth and reality of things, I see not how certainty can be obtained in any science; since numerous hypotheses may be devised, which shall seem to overcome new difficulties. (Cohen, *Isaac Newton's Papers and Letters on Natural Philosophy*, cited in note 5 above, p. 106.) Newton's attitude toward hypotheses in his work in optics is discussed in detail in Alan Shapiro's chapter in this volume.

46 Cohen, *The Newtonian Revolution*, cited in note 8 above, ch. 3; see his chapter in this volume as well.

47 The term "point-mass" is Euler's, not Newton's or Huygens's.

48 Newton's "deduction" of universal gravity from phenomena is examined in detail in William Harper's chapter in this volume.

49 For details, see my "From the Phenomenon of the Ellipse to an Inverse-Square Force: Why Not?," in David Malament (ed.), *Reading Natural Philosophy: Essays in the History of Science and Mathematics to Honor Howard Stein on his 70th Birthday* (La Salle, IL: Open Court, 2002).

50 Newton, *Principia*, pp. 817ff.

51 Newton, *Principia*, textual note bb, p. 827.

52 See Huygens, *Discours de la Cause de la Pesanteur*, in *Oeuvres complètes de Christiaan Huygens*, vol. 21 (1944), pp. 462–71, and pp. 476ff.

53 For a discussion of the current state of these discrepancies, see Kurt Lambeck, *Geophysical Geodesy: The Slow Deformations of the Earth* (Oxford: Oxford University Press, 1988).

54 See Leibniz, *Tentamen*, cited in note 34 above.

55 The one notable exception is the tacit assumption that the third law of motion holds between the Sun and the individual planets. This assumption has been pointed out by Howard Stein in his "'From the Phenomena of Motions to the Forces of Nature': Hypothesis or Deduction?" (*PSA* 2 [1990], 209–22); Dana Densmore in her *Newton's Principia: The Central Argument* (Santa Fe: Green Lion Press, 1995), p. 353; and before them by Roger Cotes, the editor of the second edition of the *Principia*, in correspondence with Newton (see *The Correspondence of Isaac Newton*, vol. 5, ed. A. Rupert Hall and Laura Tilling [Cambridge: Cambridge University Press, 1975], pp. 391ff). William Harper's chapter in this volume discusses this and the other details of Newton's "deduction" of universal gravity from phenomena.

56 Newton, *Principia*, p. 796.

57 The history of Newton's third Rule for Natural Philosophy is discussed in I. Bernard Cohen's *Introduction to Newton's "Principia"* (Cambridge, MA: Harvard University Press, 1978), pp. 23–6.

58 Nelson Goodman, *Fact, Fiction, and Forecast*, 3rd edn (Indianapolis: Bobbs-Merrill, 1973).

59 Jean d' Alembert, *Essai d'une nouvelle théorie de la résistance des fluides* (Paris: David, 1752).

60 Newton, by the way, took the trouble in Book 1, Section 10 to show that Galileo's and Huygens's results similarly hold in the limit in the case of *universal* gravity, namely the limit of the linear variation of gravity

up to the surface of a uniformly dense Earth as the radius of this surface approaches infinity. This result authenticates Newton's use of Huygens's precise theory-mediated measurement of surface gravity in his crucial argument in Book 3, Proposition 4 that the Moon is held in orbit by terrestrial gravity.

61 See the chapter by Howard Stein in this volume for a discussion of the centrality of interactions in Newton's metaphysics.

62 See George E. Smith, "Fluid Resistance: Why Did Newton Change His Mind?" in Richard Dalitz and Michael Nauenberg (eds.), *Foundations of Newtonian Scholarship* (Singapore: World Scientific, 2000), pp. 105–36.

63 Newton, *Principia*, p. 749.

64 See L. D. Landau and E. M. Lifshitz, *Fluid Mechanics*, vol. 6 in Course in Theoretical Physics (Oxford: Pergamon, 1959), pp. 31–6, 168–79.

65 See George E. Smith, "The Newtonian Style in Book 2 of the *Principia*," in J. Z. Buchwald and I. B. Cohen (eds.), *Isaac Newton's Natural Philosophy* (Cambridge, MA: MIT Press, 2001), pp. 249–98, esp. p. 278, Fig. 9.7.

66 *Ibid.*, pp. 276–87.

67 Isaac Newton, *Opticks: or, A Treatise of the Reflections, Refractions, Inflections and Colours of Light* (New York: Dover, 1952), p. 404. The quotation continues: "This is the Method of Analysis: And the Synthesis consists in assuming the Causes discover'd, and establish'd as Principles, and by them explaining the Phenomena proceeding from them, and proving the Explanations." This passage was undoubtedly a direct response to Huygens's description of the hypothetico-deductive method quoted at the beginning of this chapter.

68 Extending gravity to comets was more important than first meets the eye. Hooke had expressed a general principle of celestial attraction in his *Attempt to Prove the Motion of the Earth* of 1674, but had denied that it extends to comets in his *Cometa* of 1678. See Curtis Wilson, "The Newtonian Achievement in Astronomy," p. 239.

69 Newton indicates as much in a letter to Leibniz in 1693 when he defends the *Principia* by remarking, "all phenomena of the heavens and the sea follow precisely, so far as I am aware, from nothing but gravity acting in accordance with the laws described by me." (*The Correspondence of Isaac Newton*, vol. 3, ed. H. W. Turnbull [Cambridge: Cambridge University Press, 1961], pp. 284 ff.)

70 See Curtis Wilson's chapter in this volume for a discussion of the development of celestial mechanics during the eighteenth century. This development culminates in the five volumes of Laplace's *Mécanique Céleste*, the first four of which appeared from 1798 to 1805, and the fifth in 1825. (All but the fifth volume are available in English in the translation of 1829–39 by Nathaniel Bowditch [Bronx, NY: Chelsea Publishing Company, 1966].)

5   Newton's argument for universal gravitation

William Harper

The aspect of Newton's *Principia* that has provoked the most controversy within the philosophy of science, other than his invocation of absolute space, time, and motion, has been his claim to have "deduced" the law of universal gravity from phenomena of orbital motion. In particular, a tradition that began with Pierre Duhem[1] and continued with Karl Popper[2] and then Imre Lakatos[3] has argued that this claim is at best misleading (Duhem) and at worst a subterfuge (Lakatos). Among other reasons they have advanced against any such deduction is the objection that no deduction from consistent premises can yield a conclusion that entails one or more of these premises is false; yet one consequence of the law of universal gravity is that all the orbital phenomena from which Newton proceeds in his supposed deduction are, strictly, false. Duhem, Popper, and Lakatos insist, to the contrary, that only a hypothetico-deductive construal of Newton's evidence for universal gravity makes sense, Newton's outspoken objections to hypothetico-deductive evidence notwithstanding. More recently, Clark Glymour[4] has offered a "bootstrapping" construal of Newton's evidence, proposing that it captures the logical force of the reasoning for universal gravitation in the *Principia* better than a straightforward hypothetico-deductive construal can. Glymour too, however, sees no way around concluding that some of what Newton seems to think he is doing cannot be correct.

One issue this raises is understanding the reasoning Newton offers in arriving at the law of universal gravity and describes as a "deduction" from phenomena. Another is the extent to which such reasoning is cogent and illuminates scientific method. The simplest way to respond to these questions is to proceed step-by-step through Newton's reasoning. I will argue that his argument from phenomena

to universal gravitation, which opens his system of the world in
Book 3, illustrates a general methodology in which phenomena con-
strain theory to approximations established by measuring parameters.
This methodology, which continues to guide research in gravitational
physics, has not been as well appreciated by philosophers of science
as it ought to be. Nevertheless, it becomes clear and easy to defend
once attention is paid to the details of the argument in Propositions 1
to 8 of Book 3 in the third edition.

INFERENCES FROM PHENOMENA

Jupiter's moons

> PROPOSITION I. *The forces by which the circumjovial planets [or*
> *satellites of Jupiter] are continually drawn away from rectilinear*
> *motions and are maintained in their respective orbits are*
> *directed to the center of Jupiter and are inversely as the squares*
> *of the distances of their places from that center.*[5]
>
> *The first part of the proposition is evident from phen. 1 and*
> *from prop. 2 or prop. 3 of book 1, and the second part from phen.*
> *1 and from corol. 6 to prop. 4 of book 1.*
>
> *The same is to be understood for the planets that are*
> *Saturn's companions [or satellites] by phen. 2.*

The cited phenomenon (Phenomenon 1) consists of two parts. The first
part is that the moons of Jupiter, by radii drawn to the center of Jupiter,
describe areas proportional to the times. This is what we call Kepler's
"law" of areas for these moons with respect to that center.[6] The second
part is that the periodic times of the orbits of these moons – the fixed
stars being at rest[7] – are as the 3/2 power of their distances from the
center of Jupiter. This is Kepler's harmonic law for these orbits.

Newton demonstrates that the law of areas carries the information that the force maintaining a body in an orbit which satisfies it is
directed toward the center with respect to which it sweeps out equal
areas in equal times. He also demonstrates that the harmonic law for
a system of orbits carries the information that the accelerative forces

maintaining bodies in those orbits are inversely as the squares of the distances from the center about which those orbits are described.

The law of areas as a criterion for centripetal force

Propositions 1 and 2 of Book 1, together, yield a biconditional equivalence between the centripetal direction of the force maintaining a body in an orbit about an inertial center and the motion of that orbit being in a plane and satisfying Kepler's law of areas. According to Corollary 1 of Proposition 2, the rate at which areas are described is increasing only if the force is angled off-center toward the direction of motion, while a decreasing rate obtains only if the force is angled off-center in the opposite direction. These dependencies make the constancy of the rate at which areas are being swept out by radii to a center *measure* the centripetal direction of the force maintaining a body in an orbit about that center, provided the center can be treated as inertial.

Treating Jupiter's center as inertial ignores the substantial centripetal acceleration toward the Sun as the Jupiter system orbits it. To the extent that the Sun's actions on Jupiter and its moons approximate equal and parallel accelerations, the Jupiter system can be treated as unperturbed by the forces accelerating it toward the Sun.[8] To the extent that this approximation holds and the center of Jupiter approximates the center of mass of the Jupiter system, the center of Jupiter can be treated as inertial.[9]

Having the area rule hold, very nearly, for the orbits of these moons with respect to the center of Jupiter carries information that these approximations are not appreciably inaccurate.[10] In his discussion of Phenomenon 1, Newton pointed out that the orbits of Jupiter's moons so closely approximate uniform motion on circles concentric to Jupiter that no appreciable differences from such motions were detected in observations by astronomers. That good observations detected no appreciable departures from uniform motion on concentric circular orbits for Jupiter's moons indicates that no appreciable errors result from treating Jupiter's center as inertial for purposes of using the area rule as a criterion for the centripetal direction of the forces maintaining those moons in their orbits.

Newton's proofs of the theorems underwriting the area rule as a criterion for centers toward which orbital forces are directed make no assumptions about any power law for these forces. Given that the centripetal direction of the forces maintaining these moons in their orbits is inferred from the law of areas, Newton can appeal to his theorems about orbital motion under centripetal forces to argue that the harmonic law phenomenon, for the system of those orbits, carries the information that the accelerative forces are inversely as the squares of their distances from that center. This illustrates that Newton's inferences are not merely hypothetico-deductive.[11]

The harmonic rule as a criterion for inverse-square forces
Corollary 6 of Proposition 4 of Book 1 states that the harmonic law for a system of circular orbits is equivalent to having the accelerative centripetal forces maintaining bodies in those orbits be inversely as the squares of the distances from the center. Corollary 7 is equivalent to the following universal systematic dependency

$$t \propto R^s \quad \text{iff} \quad f \propto R^{1-2s}$$

where f is the accelerative force maintaining a body in uniform motion in a circular orbit with period t and radius R. Corollary 6 follows when s equals $3/2$. For each of a whole range of alternative power law proportions of periods to orbital radii, Corollary 7 establishes the equivalent power law proportion to radii for the centripetal forces that would maintain bodies in those orbits. To have the periods be as some power $s > 3/2$ would be to have the centripetal forces fall off faster than the -2 power of the radii, while to have the periods be as some power $s < 3/2$ would be to have the centripetal forces fall off less fast than the -2 power of the radii. These systematic dependencies make the harmonic law phenomenon $(s = 3/2)$ for a system of orbits *measure* the inverse-square (-2) power law for the centripetal forces maintaining bodies in those orbits. This constitutes a very strong sense in which the harmonic law carries the information that the forces maintaining bodies in those orbits satisfy the inverse-square power law.

As evidence for the harmonic law Newton offers a table citing periods agreed upon by astronomers and four distance estimates from astronomers for each of the four moons of Jupiter known at the time. The fit of the harmonic law to these data is quite good. He also offers more precise data from observations taken by Pound in 1718–20. The fit of the harmonic rule to these considerably more precise data[12] is very much better than the already good fit of the harmonic law to the earlier data.

Primary planets

PROPOSITION 2. *The forces by which the primary planets are continually drawn away from rectilinear motions and are maintained in their respective orbits are directed to the sun and are inversely as the squares of their distances from its center.*

The first part of the proposition is evident from phen. 5 and from prop. 2 of book 1, and the latter part from phen. 4 and from prop. 4 of the same book. But this second part of the proposition is proved with the greatest exactness from the fact that the aphelia are at rest. For the slightest departure from the ratio of the square would (by book 2, prop. 45, corol. 1) necessarily result in a noticeable motion of the apsides in a single revolution and an immense such motion in many revolutions.

The area rule for the planets

PHENOMENON 5. *The primary planets, by radii drawn to the earth, describe areas in no way proportional to the times but, by radii drawn to the Sun, traverse areas proportional to the times.*

That Newton considers radii drawn to the Earth as well as radii drawn to the Sun illustrates that he does not assume the Copernican system as a phenomenon to argue from. He points out that with respect to the Sun as center the angular motion is almost uniform and the departures from uniform motion – "a little more swiftly in their perihelia and more slowly in their aphelia" – are such that the description of areas is uniform.[13]

The harmonic rule for the planets

Newton provides a separate phenomenon stating that the orbits of the primary planets encircle the Sun. This phenomenon does not include the Earth as one of these planets.

> PHENOMENON 3. *The orbits of the five primary planets – Mercury, Venus, Mars, Jupiter, and Saturn – encircle the Sun.*

Tycho Brahe's geo-heliocentric system in which the other planets orbit the Sun, while the Sun together with those planets orbits the Earth, is compatible with this phenomenon. To every Copernican system a corresponding Tychonic system is defined by taking the center of the Earth rather than the center of the Sun as a reference frame.[14]

Newton's statement of the harmonic law is neutral between such Sun-centered and Earth-centered systems.

> PHENOMENON 4. *The periodic times of the five primary planets and of either the sun around the earth or the earth around the sun – the fixed stars being at rest – are as the 3/2 power of their mean distances from the sun.*

Newton cites periods agreed upon by astronomers and estimates of mean distances from Kepler and the French astronomer Boulliau which exhibit the excellent fit of the harmonic law to available data. This fit is nicely illustrated by plotting log periods against log distances, as in Figure 5.1.

That a straight line of some slope s fits the result of plotting $\log t$ against $\log R$ is to have the periods be as some power s of the distances. To have the harmonic law hold is to have the slope s of this line be $3/2 = 1.5$.

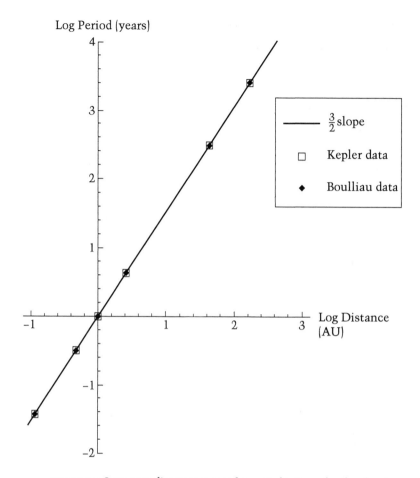

FIGURE 5.1 Log mean distances versus log periodic times for the planets.

The mean distances cited in Newton's table are the semi-major axes of elliptical orbits, not radii of concentric circular orbits. Unlike Jupiter's moons, the orbits of the primary planets were known to have non-negligible eccentricities. Newton's proofs of Proposition 4, Book 1 and of its Corollaries 6 and 7 are for concentric circular orbits. These results, however, extend to elliptical orbits with forces toward a focus.[15]

Given that the orbit of each planet fits the area rule with respect to the Sun, that the mean distances are the semi-major axes of those orbits construed as ellipses with the Sun at their common focus, and that the periods are as some power s of the mean distances, then to have the harmonic law hold, that is, to have $s = 3/2$, carries the information that the forces maintaining them in their respective con-focal elliptical orbits agree with those of a single inverse-square centripetal acceleration field directed toward the Sun.[16] This makes the harmonic law ratios for the planets into agreeing measurements of the strength of this single Sun-centered inverse-square acceleration field.[17]

Aphelia at rest

Newton claims that the inverse-square variation with distance from the Sun of the forces maintaining the planets in their orbits is proved "with the greatest exactness" from the fact that the aphelia are at rest.[18] He cites Corollary 1 of Proposition 45, Book 1, according to which

> Precession is p degrees per revolution   if and only if   The centripetal force f is as the $(360/360 + p)^2 - 3$ power of distance

If a planet in going from aphelion (the furthest point from the Sun) to return to it again makes an angular motion against the fixed stars of $360 + p$ degrees, then the aphelion is precessing forward with p degrees per revolution. According to this corollary, zero precession is equivalent to having the centripetal force be as the -2 power of distance; forward precession is equivalent to having the centripetal force fall off faster than the inverse-square; and backward precession is equivalent to having the centripetal force fall off slower than the inverse-square.

Newton's Proposition 45, Book 1 and its corollaries are proved for orbits that are very nearly circular. The results, however, can be extended to orbits of arbitrarily great eccentricity. Indeed, orbital eccentricity increases the sensitivity of absence of unaccounted for precession as a null experiment measuring inverse-square variation of a centripetal force.[19]

UNIFICATION AND THE MOON

The Moon

> PROPOSITION 3. The force by which the moon is maintained in its
> orbit is directed toward the earth and is inversely as the square of
> the distances of its places from the center of the earth.

Newton claims that the first part (the centripetal direction) is evident
from Phenomenon 6 (and Proposition 2 or 3 of Book 1).

> PHENOMENON 6. The moon, by a radius drawn to the center of the
> earth, describes areas proportional to the times.
>
> This is evident from a comparison of the apparent motion
> of the moon with its apparent diameter. Actually, the motion of
> the moon is somewhat perturbed by the force of the sun, but
> in these phenomena I pay no attention to minute errors that are
> negligible.

The comparisons of apparent diameter and apparent motion
mentioned by Newton are in good rough agreement with the law
of areas.[20]

The observed motion of the apogee makes the argument for
inverse-square variation more problematic than the corresponding argument for the planets. This apsidal motion is, Newton tells
us, only about 3 degrees and 3 minutes forward in each revolution.
According to Corollary 1, Proposition 45, Book 1, this is equivalent
to a centripetal force varying inversely as the $2\frac{4}{243}$ power. As he also
points out, this is $59\frac{3}{4}$ times closer to the square than to the cube.

Newton claims that this motion of the lunar apogee is to be
ignored because it arises from the action of the Sun. He appeals to
Corollary 2 of Proposition 45, Book 1 to suggest that the action of the
Sun to draw the Moon away from the Earth is roughly as $1/178.725$
of the centripetal force of the Moon.[21] Newton, however, does not
provide an account of how the lunar precession is due to the action of
the Sun on the Moon's motion.[22]

Gravitation toward the Earth

> PROPOSITION 4. The moon gravitates toward the earth and by the
> force of gravity is always drawn back from rectilinear motion and
> kept in its orbit.

The Moon-test

In the Moon-test, Newton cites six estimates by astronomers
and assumes a mean Earth–Moon distance of 60 terrestrial semidiameters. He cites a lunar period established by astronomers and
a circumference for the Earth according to measurements by the
French, which, together with the assumption of 60 Earth radii as
the lunar distance, give 15.009 Paris feet as distance the Moon would
fall in one minute if it were deprived of all its motion and let fall by
the force by which it is maintained in its orbit.

Newton's assumption of 60 terrestrial semidiameters as the
lunar distance, together with inverse-square variation, makes
the one-minute fall corresponding to the strength of this force at the
lunar distance exactly equal to the one-second fall corresponding
to the increased strength this force would have at the surface of
the Earth.

Huygens had used his experimentally established length of a
seconds pendulum to measure the one-second fall produced on terrestrial bodies by the Earth's gravity. His determination of the length
of a seconds pendulum was so stable over repetitions that his measured value for the one-second fall at Paris of 15.096 Paris feet could
be trusted to about ±0.01 Paris feet.[23]

Newton's assumption of 60 Earth radii as the lunar distance,
together with his appeal to a correction factor to offset a supposed
1/178.725 reduction due to the action of the Sun, leads to an extraordinarily close agreement with Huygens's measurement.[24] If we do not
apply that correction and use all six (59, 60, 60, $60\frac{1}{3}$, $60\frac{2}{5}$, $60\frac{1}{2}$) of
Newton's cited lunar distance estimates together with his cited cir-
cumference of the Earth (123,249,600 Paris feet) and lunar period

(39,343 minutes), we arrive at 15.041 ± 0.429 Paris feet as the measured value of the one-second fall at the surface of the Earth corresponding to the centripetal acceleration of the lunar orbit. That Huygens's value is well within these error bounds shows that the positive outcome of the Moon-test did not depend either upon the selection of 60 as the lunar distance[25] or upon Newton's assumed correction factor.

Rules 1 and 2

Newton makes an explicit appeal to his first two rules for reasoning in natural philosophy to infer that the force maintaining the Moon in its orbit is terrestrial gravity.

> And therefore that force by which the moon is kept in its orbit, in descending from the moon's orbit to the surface of the earth, comes out equal to the force of gravity here on earth, and so (by rule 1 and rule 2) is that very force which we generally call gravity.

The basic argument for Proposition 4 is the equality established in the Moon-test together with this appeal to Rules 1 and 2.

> RULE 1. No more causes of natural things should be admitted than are both true and sufficient to explain their phenomena.

> RULE 2. Therefore, the causes assigned to natural effects of the same kind must be, so far as possible, the same.

The statement of Rule 2 suggests that it is intended as a consequence or implication of Rule 1. We can read these two rules, together, as telling us to opt for common causes whenever we can find them. This seems to be exactly their role in the application we are considering.

We have two phenomena: the centripetal acceleration of the Moon and the length of a seconds pendulum at Paris. Each measures a force producing accelerations at the surface of the Earth. These accelerations are equal and equally directed toward the center of the Earth. Identifying the forces makes these phenomena count as agreeing measures of the very same inverse-square force. This makes them count as effects of a single common cause.

The identification of the centripetal force maintaining the Moon in its orbit with terrestrial gravity transforms the notion of terrestrial gravity by making it now count as varying inversely with the square of distance from the center of the Earth. This was acclaimed as an unexpected, and highly regarded, new discovery about gravity by such critics of universal gravitation as Huygens and Leibniz.[26]

Inverse-square centripetal acceleration field

Newton's Scholium[27] to Proposition 4 opens with a thought experiment which appeals to induction to extend Kepler's harmonic relation $(t \propto R^{3/2})$ to a hypothetical system of several moons revolving around the Earth. He explicitly calls this harmonic relation a "law" and backs up the inverse-square assumption in the Moon-test by appeal to the corresponding inverse-square $(f \propto R^{-2})$ relation among the centripetal forces that would maintain moons in orbits satisfying it.

Howard Stein[28] has argued that the scholium version of the Moon-test –

> Therefore, since both forces – vis., those of heavy bodies and those of the moons – are directed toward the center of the earth and are similar to one another and equal, they will (by rule 1 and rule 2) have the same cause. And therefore that force by which the moon is kept in its orbit is the very one that we generally call gravity.

– should be interpreted in light of Newton's discussion (Definitions 5–8) of centripetal force and its three measures: absolute, accelerative, and motive. The motive measure of a centripetal force on a body is its mass times its centripetal acceleration – this is the measure of force familiar to students of Newtonian physics today. The accelerative measure is the acceleration produced and is referred to distances from the center. Stein[29] argues that Newton's discussion makes it clear that he intends this measure to be appropriate to a centripetal acceleration field – a centripetal force field that would produce equal centripetal accelerations on unsupported bodies at equal distances from the center. The harmonic law ratio for a system of orbits about a common center requires that the orbits exhibit centripetal accelerations corresponding to a single inverse-square centripetal acceleration field. The absolute measure of such a centripetal acceleration field is its strength. The ratio of the absolute measures of two such centripetal acceleration fields is the common ratio of the accelerations they would produce at any equal distances from their respective centers.

This suggests that, in the above passage from the Scholium Moon-test, the several forces – those of heavy bodies and those of the moons – are the motive forces exerted on those heavy bodies and moons. Their common cause is a single inverse-square centripetal acceleration field surrounding the Earth – the Earth's gravity. On this interpretation, all these motive forces directed toward the center of the Earth are the weights toward it of those moons and other bodies.

Empirical success

This application of Rules 1 and 2 is backed by an ideal of empirical success exhibited in Newton's inferences from phenomena. According to this ideal, *a theory succeeds empirically by having its causal parameters receive convergent accurate measurements from the phenomena it purports to explain.* On the identification Newton argues for, we have a single inverse-square acceleration field the strength of which is given agreeing measurements by the length of a seconds pendulum at the surface of the Earth and by the centripetal acceleration exhibited by the orbit of the Moon.

Each of these counts as a phenomenon. The length of a seconds pendulum established by Huygens is a generalization that is backed up by a large and open-ended body of precise data. The centripetal acceleration exhibited by the orbital motion of the Moon is also a generalization backed up by a large and open-ended body of data. In this case the data are far less precise than those backing up Huygens's measurements. Even though they are less precise, their agreement in measured value of the strength of the common acceleration field makes the lunar data count as additional empirical support backing up Huygens's measurement of the acceleration of gravity at the surface of the Earth.[30] It also makes Huygens's very precise data back up estimates of the centripetal acceleration of the lunar orbit.

Empiricists, who limit empirical success to prediction alone, would see the appeal to simplicity in Rules 1 and 2 as something extraneous to empirical success. According to such a view, these rules endorse a general commitment to simplicity imposed as an additional, pragmatic, requirement beyond empirical success. No merely pragmatic commitment to simplicity can do justice to the way in which identifying the force that maintains the Moon in its orbit with terrestrial gravity is empirically backed up by agreeing measurements. This gives reason to consider the richer notion of empirical success that informs Newton's methodology.

GENERALIZATION BY INDUCTION

Rule 4

> PROPOSITION I. The circumjovial planets [or moons of Jupiter]
> gravitate toward Jupiter, the circumsaturnian planets [or satellites
> of Saturn] gravitate toward Saturn, and the circumsolar
> [or primary] planets gravitate toward the sun, and by the force
> of their gravity they are always drawn back from rectilinear
> motions and kept in curvilinear orbits.

This generalization is a unification – all these orbital phenomena are effects of gravitation of satellites toward primaries. On it, we can understand each of these phenomena as an agreeing measurement of such general features of gravitation toward primaries as centripetal direction and inverse-square accelerative measure.

Newton further generalizes centripetal forces of gravity (the first part of Corollary 1) that are inversely as the squares of distances from their centers (Corollary 2) to all planets universally. For planets without satellites there are no centripetal accelerations of bodies toward them to measure gravitation toward them.

The following Scholium is offered in support of this generalization to all planets.

> SCHOLIUM. Hitherto we have called "centripetal" that force by which celestial bodies are kept in their orbits. It is now established that this force is gravity, and therefore we shall call it gravity from now on. For the cause of the centripetal force by which the moon is kept in its orbit ought to be extended to all planets, by rules 1, 2, and 4.

This appeal to Rules 1 and 2 is backed up by appeal to an additional rule.

> RULE 4. In experimental philosophy, propositions gathered from phenomena by induction should be considered either exactly or very nearly true notwithstanding any contrary hypotheses, until yet other phenomena make such propositions either more exact or liable to exceptions.

This rule instructs us to consider propositions gathered from phenomena by induction as "either exactly or very nearly true"[31] and to maintain this in the face of any contrary hypotheses. We want to clarify what are to count as propositions gathered from phenomena by induction and how they differ from what are to count as mere hypotheses.

We have seen that the classic inferences from phenomena which open the argument for universal gravitation are measurements of the centripetal direction and the inverse-square accelerative quantity of gravitation maintaining moons and planets in their orbits. To extend attribution of centripetally directed inverse-square gravitational acceleration to planets without moons is to treat such orbital phenomena as measurements of these quantifiable features of gravitation for planets universally.

What would it take for an alternative proposal to succeed in undermining this generalization of gravity to planets without moons? The arguments we have been examining suggest that Newton's Rule 4 would have us treat such an alternative proposal as a mere "contrary hypothesis" unless it is sufficiently backed up by measurements from phenomena to count as a rival to be taken seriously.

Weight proportional to mass

> PROPOSITION 6. All bodies gravitate toward each of the planets, and at any given distance from the center of any one planet the weight of any body whatever toward that planet is proportional to the quantity of matter which the body contains.

The centripetal forces that have been identified as gravitation toward planets are acceleration fields. The ratio of weight to inertial mass is the same for all bodies at any equal distances.[32] In arguing for this proposition Newton backs up his earlier arguments by providing explicit measurements of the equality of these ratios of weight to mass.

Gravitation toward the Earth

Newton begins with gravitation toward the Earth. He describes pendulum experiments which measure the equality of the ratio of weight to inertial mass for pairs of samples of nine varied materials. The equality of the periods of such pairs of pendulums counts as a phenomenon which measures the equality of these ratios for laboratory-sized bodies near the surface of the Earth to a precision of 0.001.

A second phenomenon is the outcome of the Moon-test. The agreement between the acceleration of gravity at the surface of the Earth and the inverse-square-adjusted centripetal acceleration exhibited by the lunar orbit measures the further agreement between, on the one hand, the ratio of the Moon's weight toward the Earth to its mass and, on the other, the common ratio to their masses of the inverse-square-adjusted weights toward the Earth that terrestrial bodies would have at the lunar distance. The lunar distance data Newton cites measure the equality of these ratios to < 0.03.

Rule 3

> COROLLARY 2 (PROPOSITION 6, BOOK 3). All bodies universally that are on or near the earth are heavy [or gravitate] toward the earth, and the weights of all bodies that are equally distant from the center of the earth are as the quantities of matter in them. This is a quality of all bodies on which experiments can be performed and therefore by rule 3 is to be affirmed of all bodies universally.
>
> RULE 3. Those qualities of bodies that cannot be intended and remitted [that is, qualities that cannot be increased and diminished] and that belong to all bodies on which experiments can be made should be taken as qualities of all bodies universally.

Those qualities of bodies that cannot be intended or remitted are those that count as constant parameter values. This rule, therefore, endorses counting such parameter values found to be constant on all bodies within the reach of experiments as constant for all bodies universally. In Corollary 2, the quality of bodies which is generalized is weight toward the Earth. To have gravitation toward the Earth count as an inverse-square acceleration field is to have the ratio between inverse-square-adjusted weight toward the Earth and inertial mass be a constant value for all bodies.

The equal periods of pairs of pendulums in Newton's experiments is a phenomenon established with sufficient precision to measure to 0.001 the equalities of ratios of weight to mass for terrestrial bodies.[33] Similarly, the outcome of the Moon-test counts as a rougher measurement bound (< 0.03) in agreement with the more precise measurement bound (< 0.001) that would result from extending the outcome of Newton's pendulum experiments to the equality of ratios to masses of the inverse-square-adjusted weights bodies would have at the lunar distance. These phenomena count as agreeing measurements bounding toward zero a parameter Δ_e representing differences between ratios of inverse-square-adjusted weight toward the Earth to mass for bodies.[34]

Rule 3 tells us to conclude that the ratio of mass to gravitation toward the Earth is equal for all bodies at any distance from the center of the Earth if that equality holds for all the bodies in reach of our experiments. The agreement exhibited by Newton among measurements of this equality by phenomena is an example of what he would take as sufficient to count the proposition that it holds for all bodies within reach of our experiments as gathered from phenomena by induction. This makes his Rule 4 tell us to put the burden of proof on a skeptic to provide evidence for bodies within reach of our experiments that would exhibit phenomena making this equality liable to exceptions.

The argument for Proposition 6 continued

Newton follows up his argument for the Earth with an appeal to the harmonic law for Jupiter's moons as a phenomenon which measures, at the distance of each moon, the equality of the ratio of mass to inverse-square-adjusted weight toward Jupiter for bodies at that distance. Rule 3 would extend this equality to bodies at any distances. The data Newton cites from other astronomers measure the equality of these ratios to fair precision ($\Delta_j < 0.03$), while Pound's more precise data do considerably better ($\Delta_j < 0.0007$). Similarly, the data Newton cites for the harmonic law for the primary planets measure bounds ($\Delta_s < 0.004$) on the equality of ratios between inverse-square-adjusted weight toward the Sun and mass for bodies at the mean distances of the planets.

For equality of ratios of mass to weight toward the Sun at equal distances Newton also appeals to three additional phenomena – absence of polarization toward or away from the Sun of orbits of respectively Jupiter's moons, Saturn's moons and the Earth's moon. If the ratio of mass to weight toward the Sun for a moon were greater or less than the corresponding ratio for the planet, then the orbit of that moon would be shifted toward or away from the Sun. Absence of such orbital polarization counts as a phenomenon measuring the equality of ratios of mass to weight toward the Sun at equal distances. The data on Jupiter's moons cited in Newton's table establish this phenomenon with sufficient precision to measure the equality of these ratios to a precision of $\Delta_s < 0.034$, while his data from Pound are precise enough to reach $\Delta_s < 0.004$.[35]

All these phenomena count as agreeing measurements bounding toward zero a single general parameter Δ representing differences between bodies of the ratios of their inertial masses to their inverse-square-adjusted weights toward planets.[36]

Parts of planets

Newton concludes his argument for Proposition 6 by explicitly extending the argument to equal ratios between mass and weight toward other planets to individual parts of planets. Here, instead of direct measurements by phenomena, we have a thought experiment which makes salient that it would be very improbable to have parts differing in ratios of weight to inertial mass so exactly proportioned that whole planets had equal ratios. This is made especially implausible by the additional fact that the Moon-test establishes agreement between outer parts of the Earth (ordinary terrestrial bodies) and the whole of the Moon.

GRAVITATION IS A UNIVERSAL FORCE OF INTERACTION

Applying the third law of motion

> PROPOSITION 7. Gravity exists in all bodies universally and is proportional to the quantity of matter in each.

Gravitation toward planets

> We have already proved that all planets are heavy [or gravitate] toward one another and also that the gravity toward any one planet, taken by itself, is inversely as the square of the distance

of places from the center of the planet. And it follows (by book 1, prop. 69 and its corollaries) that the gravity toward all the planets is proportional to the matter in them.

In Proposition 69, Book 1, Newton considers a system of bodies A, B, C, D, etc. He argues that under the assumption that body A attracts all the others (including body B) with inverse-square accelerative forces and the assumption that body B, similarly, attracts all the others (including A), then the absolute force of A (the strength of the acceleration field toward A) will be to the absolute force of B as the mass of A is to the mass of B.

Newton's proof begins by pointing out that the supposition that each body attracts all the rest with inverse-square accelerative forces requires the ratios of accelerations produced by such forces at equal distances to be independent of distance. The distance of A from B equals the distance of B from A. Therefore,

$$acc_A(B)/acc_B(A) = absF_A/absF_B \qquad (\text{i.1})$$

The ratio of the magnitude of B's acceleration toward A to the magnitude of A's acceleration toward B equals the ratio of the strength of the attractive force toward A to the strength of the attractive force toward B.

The key step in Newton's proof is an application of his third law of motion to the motive force attracting B toward A and the motive force attracting A toward B.

LAW 3. To any action there is always an opposite and equal reaction; in other words, the actions of two bodies one upon the other are always equal and always opposite in direction.

To have the motive forces of A on B, $f_A(B) = m(A)acc_B(A)$, and of B on A, $f_B(A) = m(B)acc_A(B)$, count as equal action and reaction makes

$$m(A)/m(B) = acc_A(B)/acc_B(A) \qquad (\text{i.2})$$

where $m(B)$ and $m(A)$ are the masses of B and A. Combining i.2 with i.1 yields Newton's conclusion,

$$m(A)/m(B) = \mathrm{abs}F_A/\mathrm{abs}F_B \qquad (\mathrm{i.3})$$

In the assumption of the argument for Proposition 7, gravitation of any planets A and B toward one another is treated as an *interaction*, so that the equal and opposite reaction to the weight of B toward A is the weight of A toward B. This makes the argument of Proposition 69 apply, so the strengths of the centripetal attractions toward each are proportional to their masses.

Gravitation toward parts of planets

Further, since all the parts of any planet A are heavy [or gravitate] toward any planet B, and since the gravity [weight toward B] of each part is to the gravity [weight toward B] of the whole as the matter of the part is to the matter of the whole, and since to every action (by the third law of motion) there is an equal reaction, it follows that planet B will gravitate toward all the parts of planet A, and its gravity toward any one part will be to its gravity toward the whole of the planet as the matter of that part to the matter of the whole. Q.E.D.

For any planets A and B, each part a of planet A is itself a body being accelerated toward planet B. Newton's supposition follows from Proposition 6. We have

$$f_B(a)/f_B(A) = m(a)/m(A) \qquad (\mathrm{ii.1})$$

where $f_B(a)$ and $f_B(A)$ are the weights of part a and planet A toward planet B.

As in the proof of Proposition 69, the third law of motion is applied to yield the conclusion. The weight, $f_a(B)$, of planet B toward part a is taken to be the equal and opposite reaction to the weight, $f_B(a)$, of part a to planet B, just as the weights $f_A(B)$ and $f_B(A)$ of the whole planets toward one another are taken to be equal action and reaction. This yields

$$f_a(B)/f_A(B) = f_B(a)/f_B(A). \qquad \text{(ii.2)}$$

Combining ii.2 with ii.1 gives Newton's conclusion,

$$f_a(B)/f_A(B) = m(a)/m(A). \qquad \text{(ii.3)}$$

The weight of planet B toward part a is to its weight toward the whole planet A as the mass of the part is to the mass of the whole planet.[37]

The extension of the argument to include, in addition to gravitation toward planets,[38] gravitation toward parts of planets would count, in Newton's day, as an extension to include gravitation toward all bodies within reach of experiments. This would make Rule 3 endorse extending to all bodies universal gravitation toward them proportional to their masses.

Inverse-square gravitation toward particles

> COROLLARY 2 (PROPOSITION 7, BOOK 3). The gravitation toward each of the individual equal particles of a body is inversely as the square of the distance of places from those particles. This is evident by book 1, prop. 74, corol. 3.

> COROLLARY 3 (PROPOSITION 74, BOOK 1). If a corpuscle placed outside a homogeneous sphere is attracted by a force proportional to the square of the distance of the corpuscle from the center of the sphere, and the sphere consists of attracting particles, the force of each particle will decrease in the squared ratio of the distance from the particle.

The inference in this corollary is from inverse-square variation of the total force on a corpuscle outside a sphere toward its center to the inverse-square variation of the component attractions toward particles. Just as is the case with Newton's classic inferences from phenomena, this inference is backed up by systematic dependencies. Any difference from the inverse-square law for attraction toward the particles would produce a corresponding difference from the inverse-square for the law of attraction toward the center resulting from summing the attractions toward the particles.[39] These dependencies make phenomena measuring inverse-square variation of attraction toward the whole count as measurements of inverse-square variation of the law of attraction toward the particles.

Resolving the two chief world systems problem

In Proposition 8, Newton appeals to theorems on attraction toward spheres to extend his conclusions to gravitation toward bodies approximating globes made up of spherically homogeneous shells. Attraction between such bodies is directly as the product of their masses and inversely as the square of the distance between their centers.

Proposition 7 is applied to use harmonic law ratios to measure the masses of the Sun and planets with moons (Corollary 2, Proposition 8). The resulting convergent agreeing measurements of the masses of these bodies count as a significant realization of Newton's ideal of empirical success – a realization that is especially important because it adds support to his appeal to Law 3 in the argument for Proposition 7.[40]

These measurements lead to his surprising center-of-mass resolution of the two chief world systems problem.

> PROPOSITION 12 (BOOK 3). The sun is in continual motion but never recedes far from the common center of gravity of all the planets.

Both the Copernican and the Brahean systems are wrong; however, the Sun-centered system closely approximates true motions while the Earth-centered system is wildly inaccurate.

In this center of mass frame the separate centripetal acceleration fields toward solar system bodies are combined into a single system where each body undergoes an acceleration toward each of the others proportional to its mass and inversely proportional to the square of the distance between them.

General Relativity

Newton transformed the two chief world systems problem into a physically meaningful question that could be answered by analysis of relative accelerations and the information they carry about the distribution of mass. General Relativity incorporates the basic dependencies between acceleration fields and spherical mass distributions that inform Newton's account, even though it reinterprets gravitational free fall as motion along a shortest-distance path – "geodesic motion" – in a curved space–time.[41] Therefore, contrary to Reichenbach,[42] General Relativity does not undercut the objectivity of Newton's solution to the two chief world systems problem.[43]

Contrary to Kuhn,[44] the revolutionary change to General Relativity is in accordance with the evaluative procedures of Newton's methodology. The development and applications of perturbation theory, from Newton through Laplace at the turn of the nineteenth century and on through Simon Newcomb at the turn of the twentieth, led to increasingly accurate successive corrections of Keplerian planetary orbits. At each stage, departures from motion in accord with the model developed counted as higher-order phenomena carrying information about further interactions. These successive corrections led to increasingly precise specifications of solar system phenomena backed up by increasingly precise measurements of the masses of the interacting solar system bodies. The extra 43 arc-seconds per century of Mercury's perihelion precession was a departure from the Newtonian theory that resisted attempts to account for it by such interactions. The successful account of this extra precession, together with the Newtonian limit which allowed it to recover the empirical successes of Newtonian perturbation theory (including the account of the other 531 arc-seconds per century of Mercury's perihelion precession[45]), made General Relativity do better than Newton's theory on Newton's own ideal of empirical success. Since its initial development General Relativity has continued to improve upon what Newton's methodology counts as its clear advantage over Newtonian gravitation theory.[46]

NOTES

1 P. Duhem, *The Aim and Structure of Physical Theory*, trans. P. P. Wiener (Princeton, NJ: Princeton University Press, 1991), pp. 190–5.

2 K. Popper, "The Aim of Science," in *Objective Knowledge: An Evolutionary Approach* (Oxford: Oxford University Press, 1972).

3 I. Lakatos, "Newton's Effect on Scientific Standards," in J. Worrall and G. Currie (eds.), *The Methodology of Scientific Research Programmes* (Cambridge: Cambridge University Press, 1978), pp. 193–222.

4 C. Glymour, *Theory and Evidence* (Princeton, NJ: Princeton University Press, 1980), pp. 203–26.

5 The cited passages are from *The Principia, Mathematical Principles of Natural Philosophy: A New Translation*, trans. I. Bernard Cohen and Anne Whitman, preceded by "A Guide to Newton's *Principia*" by I. B. Cohen (Berkeley, CA: University of California Press, 1999).

6 Curtis Wilson suggests that Leibniz in his "Tentamen de motuum coelestium causis" of 1689 (after reading the first edition of Newton's *Principia*) was the first author to call Kepler's rules "laws." C. Wilson, "From Kepler to Newton: Telling the Tale," in Richard H. Dalitz and Michael Nauenberg (eds.), *The Foundations of Newtonian Scholarship* (Singapore: World Scientific, 2000), pp. 223–42, at pp. 225–6.

7 Newton's clause – the fixed stars being at rest – tells us that the periods are calculated with respect to those stars. This treats a reference frame at the center of Jupiter with fixed directions with respect to the stars as non-rotating. Such non-rotating frames are also used to calculate areas in the areal law.

8 *Corollary* 6 (laws of motion). If bodies are moving in any way whatsoever with respect to one another and are urged by equal accelerative forces along parallel lines, they will all continue to move with respect to one another as they would if they were not acted upon by those forces.

9 *Corollary* 4 (laws of motion). The common center of gravity of two or more bodies does not change its state whether of motion or of rest as a result of the actions of the bodies upon one another; and therefore the common center of gravity of all bodies acting upon one another (excluding external actions and impediments) either is at rest or moves uniformly straight forward.

10 Newton explicitly gives corollaries (Corollaries 2 and 3 of Proposition 3, Book 1) to cover such approximations. These extensions show that the

areal rule can be a quite general criterion for finding centers toward which forces maintaining bodies in orbits are directed.

11 Clark Glymour (*Theory and Evidence*) used these inferences as examples of good scientific practice that could not be accounted for by hypothetico-deductive (H-D) methodology. The systematic dependencies backing up Newton's inferences make such inferences avoid the counterexamples put forward to challenge bootstrap confirmation, Glymour's proposed alternative to H-D confirmation. See W. L. Harper, "Measurement and Approximation: Newton's Inferences from Phenomena versus Glymour's Bootstrap Confirmation," in G. Weingartner, G. Schurz, and G. Dorn (eds.), *The Role of Pragmatics in Contemporary Philosophy* (Vienna: Hölder-Picher-Tempsky, 1998).

12 The mean error of Pound's observed estimates from today's values is only +0.135 of Jupiter's diameter, while the average mean error for the other four astronomers cited by Newton is −1.098.

13 Newton also suggests that the area rule for Jupiter is "especially provable by the eclipses of its satellites." Each eclipse gives a heliocentric longitude (see D. Densmore, *Newton's Principia: The Central Argument* [Santa Fe, CA: Green Lion Press, 1995], pp. 275–7). This allows triangulation of its heliocentric distance from observations of its angular position with respect to the Earth. The shortness of the time intervals between them compared to Jupiter's period allows sequences of such eclipses to afford sequences of triangles approximating areas swept out. The area law for Jupiter can be tested by checking that the areas of those triangles are proportional to the intervals of time.

14 In his *Dialogue concerning the Two Chief World Systems*, Galileo had appealed to the phases of Mercury and Venus and the absence of phases of Mars, Jupiter, and Saturn in concluding that the orbits of the first two encompass the Sun, but not the Earth, while the orbits of the last three encompass both. While ruling out Ptolemaic systems, this still left open the question of a Copernican versus a Tychonic system (or intermediates between them). See G. Galileo, *Dialogue concerning the Two Chief World Systems*, trans. S. Drake (Berkeley, CA: University of California Press, 1967), pp. 322ff.

15 See W. L. Harper, "The First Six Propositions in Newton's Argument for Universal Gravitation," *St. John's Review* 45, no. 2 (1999), 74–93, at 84–7.

16 Newton's orbital data can be fit as well or better by a higher-order curve that would not have the periods be any constant power s of the

mean distances. On such a hypothesis, the application of Corollary 7 of Proposition 4 would be undercut. The orbits would, therefore, not carry information about any simple power law relating the accelerative forces to distances from the sun.

Similarly, the orbital data are not precise enough directly to rule out an ellipse with the Sun slightly displaced toward the center from the focus so that the force is not directed exactly at that focus. As George Smith points out, Newton knew that any such orbit would be incompatible with an inverse-square power law. G. E. Smith, "From the Phenomenon of the Ellipse to an Inverse-Square Force: Why Not?" in David Malament (ed.), *Reading Natural Philosophy: Essays in the History and Philosophy of Science and Mathematics to Honor Howard Stein on his 70th Birthday* (La Salle, IL: Open Court, 2002).

These alternative hypotheses illustrate the fact that Newton's inferences from phenomena are not logically forced by the data, even together with mathematical theorems derived from the laws of motion.

17 Boulliau uses the same mean distances as Kepler for the Earth and Mars. For the ten distinct estimates cited by Newton, the ratio of sd^+ to the mean value of the harmonic law ratios $[R^3/t^2]$ is 0.007.

18 In his *System of the World*, an earlier version of Book 3 composed "in a popular method that it might be read by many" (Introduction to Book 3), Newton points out:

> But now, after innumerable revolutions, hardly any such motion has been perceived in the orbits of the circumsolar planets. Some astronomers affirm there is no such motion; others reckon it no greater than what may easily arise from causes hereafter to be assigned, which is of no moment to the present question. [F. Cajori (ed. and trans.), *Newton's Principia, Motte's Translation Revised* (Los Angeles, CA: University of California Press, 1934), p. 561]

Any precession that can be accounted for by perturbation due to forces toward other bodies can be ignored in using stable apsides to measure inverse-square variation of the centripetal force toward the Sun maintaining planets in their orbits.

19 See S. R. Valluri, C. Wilson, and W. L. Harper, "Newton's Apsidal Precession Theorem and Eccentric Orbits," *Journal of the History of Astronomy* 27 (1997), 13–27.

20 See Densmore, Newton's *Principia*, p. 282.

21 Using 1/178.725 in Corollary 2, Proposition 45 yields fairly close to what Newton cites as the lunar precession per revolution.

   In Proposition 26, Book 3, however, Newton shows that the average, over a lunar orbit, of the Moon–Earth radial component of the force of the Sun to perturb the Moon is a reduction of 1/357.45 of the basic inverse-square centripetal force on the Moon. The result of using 1/357.45 in Corollary 2, Proposition 45 shows that the radial component alone of the Sun's force on the Moon would account for only about half of the lunar precession. See G. E. Smith, "The Motion of the Lunar Apsis," in *The Principia*, ed. and trans. Cohen and Whitman, pp. 257–64.

22 It was not until 1749 that a solution showing how the lunar precession could be accounted for by the Sun's perturbation of the lunar orbit was achieved. See R. Taton and C. Wilson, *The General History of Astronomy*, vol. 2B (Cambridge: Cambridge University Press, 1995), pp. 35–46.

23 Huygens's one-second fall of 15.096 Paris feet corresponds to 980.7 cm/s^2 for the acceleration of gravity at Paris. The modern value for q at Paris is 980.87 cm/s^2.

24 When the correction is applied we get 15.0935 Paris feet.

25 Newton's main text for Proposition 4 concludes with an appeal to the two-body correction which can defend using 60 in the Moon-test when the measured distance is somewhat greater.

26 See H. Stein, "'From the Phenomena of Motions to the Forces of Nature': Hypothesis or Deduction?," *PSA 1990* 2 (1991), 209–22; also Taton and Wilson, *General History*, vol. 2B, pp. 7, 12.

27 This Scholium was added in the third (1726) edition; see *Isaac Newton's Philosophiae Naturalis Principia Mathematica, the Third Edition with Variant Readings*, ed. A. Koyré, I. B. Cohen, and Anne Whitman (Cambridge, MA: Harvard University Press; Cambridge: Cambridge University Press, 1972), p. 569.

28 Stein, "'From the Phenomena of Motions'," pp. 211–13.

29 Stein, "'From the Phenomena of Motions'," p. 213, and H. Stein, "On the Notion of Field in Newton, Maxwell, and Beyond," in R. H. Stuewer (ed.), *Historical and Philosophical Perspectives on Science* (Minneapolis, MN: University of Minnesota Press, 1970) pp. 264–87.

30 The lunar data will provide more epistemic resistance to conjectures that would make the acceleration of gravity at the surface of the Earth

differ from Huygens's measure by enough to go outside the error bounds set by the Moon-test estimate than would have been provided by Huygens's data alone. Agreeing measurements by several phenomena contributes to increase the resiliency – resistance to large changes – of estimates of parameter values.

31 The provision for approximations fits with construing such propositions as established up to tolerances provided by measurements. This makes Rule 4 very much in line with the methodology guiding testing programs in relativistic gravitation today (Harper, "Measurement and Approximation," pp. 284–5; W. L. Harper, "Isaac Newton on Empirical Success and Scientific Method," in J. Earman and J. D. Norton [eds.], *The Cosmos of Science* [Pittsburgh, PA: University of Pittsburgh Press, 1997], pp. 55–86).

32 Where f_1/m_1 and f_2/m_2 are ratios of weights toward the center of a planet to inertial masses of attracted bodies while a_1 and a_2 are their respective gravitational accelerations toward it, it follows from $f = ma$ that $a_1 = a_2$ if and only if $f_1/m_1 = f_2/m_2$.

33 These experiments extend to this, much greater, precision the many long-established, rougher but agreeing, observations that bodies fall at equal rates "at least on making an adjustment for the inequality of the retardation that arises from the very slight resistance of the air."

34 For any body x, let $Q_e(X) = (W_e(X)[d_e(X)]^2)/m(X)$, where $W_e(X)$ is the weight of x toward the Earth, $d_e(X)$ is the distance of x from the center of the Earth, and $m(x)$ is the inertial mass of x. For bodies x and y, $\Delta_e(X, Y) = Q_e(X) - Q_e(y)$ is the difference in the ratios of their inverse-square-adjusted weights toward the Earth to their inertial masses.

35 Newton does not provide the details of his calculation and the result he cites is incorrect. The 0.034 results from applying a modern calculation to the tolerances for distance estimates exhibited by the data cited by Newton from other astronomers and the 0.004 from applying it to tolerances estimated from comparing Pound's data with current estimates of orbital distances for Jupiter's moons. See W. L. Harper, S. R. Valluri, and R. Mann, "Jupiter's Moons and the Equivalence Principle," in *Proceedings of the Ninth Marcel Grossmann Meeting on General Relativity*, for discussion and references.

36 Bounds limiting this universal parameter toward zero are what count today as bounds limiting violations of the weak equivalence principle – the identification of passive gravitational with inertial mass. The

phenomena cited by Newton together with additional phenomena
of far greater precision count today as agreeing measurements
supporting this identification. (See Harper, "Isaac Newton on
Empirical Success," and "Measurement and Approximation," for
discussion and references.)

37   This extends the identification of gravitational and inertial mass to
include *active* as well as *passive* gravitational mass (see note 36).

38   The classic use of "planet" to refer to heavenly wanderers would
include the Sun, the Moon, and primary planets and their satellites.
The argument for Proposition 6 includes gravitation toward the Earth,
which suggests that Newton extends the classic use to count the
Earth, also, as a planet.

His thought experiment with terrestrial bodies raised to the Moon
illustrates that a body can count as part of a planet just by falling on it.

39   S. Chandrasekhar (*Newton's Principia for the Common Reader*
[Oxford: Clarendon Press, 1995], formula 9, p. 289) provides an integral
formulating the dependencies Newton provides in Lemma 29 and
Propositions 79–81, Book 1.

According to Proposition 74, Book 1, inverse-square attraction
toward the center of a uniform sphere on corpuscles outside, right down
to the surface, results from summing the inverse-square attractions
on the corpuscle toward the particles making up the sphere. This
proposition follows from Chandrasekhar's integral when the law of
attraction toward particles is the –2 power of distance.

A power law differing even slightly from the inverse-square, e.g., a
–2.01 power law, for the particles will approach the same power law for
attractions to the whole at great distances but will yield attractions to
the whole corresponding to differing non-uniform relations to distance
for locations close to the surface of the sphere. The inverse-square case,
and the simple harmonic oscillator case where attraction is directly as
the distance, are special in that the law of attraction toward particles
yields the same law of attraction toward the whole all the way down to
the surface of the sphere. These are the two cases Newton singles out for
detailed treatment.

40   Howard Stein, in "'From The Phenomena of Motions'," pointed out
that Newton's application of Law 3 in his argument for Proposition 7
is not an inference from the phenomena cited in the argument for

Propositions 1–7. This significant objection was anticipated by Cotes and responded to by Newton in letters to Cotes. For a discussion of how issues raised by this challenge illuminate Newton's methodology, see W. L. Harper, "Howard Stein on Isaac Newton: Beyond Hypotheses?" in David Malament (ed.), *Reading Natural Philosophy: Essays in the History and Philosophy of Science and Mathematics to Honor Howard Stein on his 70th Birthday* (La Salle, IL: Open Court, 2002).

41 See DiSalle, this volume, for discussion and further references.

42 According to Hans Reichenbach (*The Philosophy of Space and Time* [New York: Dover, 1958], p. 217):

> The relativity theory of dynamics is not a purely academic matter, for it upsets the Copernican world view. It is meaningless to speak of a difference in truth claims of the theories of Copernicus and Ptolemy; the two conceptions are equivalent descriptions. What had been considered the greatest discovery of western science compared to antiquity, is now denied its claim to truth.

43 The mass of the Sun with respect to the masses of the planets is large enough to support geodesics approximating orbits of the planets about it, while the mass of the Earth (measured by the motion of the Moon) is far too small. These mass differences, together with the difficulties imposed on construing the irregularities of Brahean orbits as geodesics in a curved space–time generated by the Earth as a spherically symmetric mass distribution, make General Relativity agree with Newton in counting Earth-centered systems as wildly inaccurate. See DiSalle, this volume.

44 T. S. Kuhn, *The Structure of Scientific Revolutions*, 2nd edn (Chicago, IL: University of Chicago Press, 1970), p. 94:

> Like the choice between competing political institutions, that between competing paradigms proves to be a choice between incompatible modes of community life. Because it has that character, the choice is not and cannot be determined by the evaluative procedures characteristic of normal science, for these depend in part upon a given paradigm, and that paradigm is at issue. When paradigms enter, as they must, into a debate about paradigm choice, their role is necessarily circular. Each group uses its own paradigm to argue in that paradigm's defense.

45 This 531 arc-seconds per century does not include the general precession of 5025.6 arc-seconds resulting from the precession of the equinoxes (see C. M. Will, *Theory and Experiment in Gravitational Physics* [Cambridge: Cambridge University Press, 1993], p. 4). The contrast between the approximately 531+43 arc-seconds per century that needs to be dynamically accounted for and the general precession, which results merely from rotating coordinates, illustrates that General Relativity continues to distinguish between true and merely relative motion.

As Smith points out ("From the Phenomenon of the Ellipse"), General Relativity's solution to the Mercury perihelion problem requires that it be able to recover also the precession accounted for by Newtonian perturbations.

46 In addition to the famous three basic tests there are now a great many post-Newtonian corrections required by the more precise data made available by such new observations as radar ranging to planets and laser ranging to the Moon. These provide not just predictions but also measurements of parameters, such as those of the PPN testing framework, which support General Relativity. See Will, *Theory and Experiment*, and Harper, "Isaac Newton on Empirical Success," for discussion and references.

6　Newton and celestial mechanics

Curtis Wilson

Newton's achievements in celestial mechanics tend in popular accounts to be underestimated in some respects, exaggerated in others. This chapter seeks to correct a number of misconceptions arising from inattention to the detailed history.

KEPLER'S FIRST TWO LAWS, SO-CALLED, AND NEWTON

The claim that the planets move in elliptical orbits, with the *radii vectores* from Sun to planet sweeping out equal areas in equal times, first appeared in Kepler's *Astronomia Nova* of 1609. Since the late eighteenth century the two parts of this claim have been referred to as Kepler's first two planetary "laws," understood as empirical laws. According to the popular account, Newton relied on these "laws" as thus established.

Writing to Halley on June 20, 1686, Newton stated: "Kepler knew ye Orb to be not circular but oval & guest it to be elliptical."[1] Whether Newton ever saw the *Astronomia Nova* is unknown.

The *Astronomia Nova* is an innovative work. It establishes important empirical results, such as the passage of the planet's orbital plane through the Sun's center and the orbit's oval shape. Was the orbit's ellipticity also a straightforwardly empirical result, say by means of triangulations of Mars, as sometimes asserted?[2] Kepler carried out many such triangulations, but they were subject to sizeable observational error, of which he was acutely aware.[3]

At the end of Chapter 58 we at last find him asserting that "no figure is left for the planetary orbit but a perfect ellipse." This chapter attempts to refute another oval orbit, the *via buccosa* or puffy-cheeked path. Kepler's whole effort, he tells us, has been to find a hypothesis yielding not only distances in agreement with observation, but also correct "equations" – "equation" here meaning the difference between the mean and the true heliocentric motions, measured from aphelion. To derive the true position at any time, Kepler used his area rule, in which area swept out is proportional to time. He had already found that this rule, when applied to a particular ellipse – the ellipse with the Sun at one focus – yielded the true positions with no more than expected observational error; but he was unable to explain why the planet should move in this ellipse. He turned to another hypothesis which he called the "libration," and which, so he supposed, implied a different orbit.

In the "libration," the planet oscillates sinusoidally along the radius vector. The cause of this oscillation, Kepler proposed, was a quasi-magnetic attraction and repulsion from the Sun. (In Kepler's preinertial physics, separate causes had to be assumed for the planet's forward motion about the Sun, and for its motion toward and away from the Sun.) The libration gave the Sun–planet distances correctly, agreeing with the triangulations to within the range of observational error. In another respect it was indeterminate: the radius vector started at the Sun's center, but where did the other end go? Kepler at first imagined he knew where it went, and his initial placement yielded the puffy-cheeked orbit (we omit details). Then he discovered that a different placement, just as plausible, would yield the Sun-focused ellipse. Thus the libration hypothesis could be combined with this ellipse to give both correct equations and correct distances.

But in his diagram he found the alternative *radii vectores* in the ellipse and puffy-cheeked orbit to be separated by observationally detectable angles, +5'.5 at 45° of anomaly and −4' at 135° of anomaly. Since the ellipse gave correct equations, Kepler concluded that the puffy-cheeked orbit could not do so. Hence, "no figure is left for the planetary orbit but a perfect ellipse."

The conclusion is unwarranted. Motion on the puffy-cheeked orbit in accordance with the area rule, when calculated by integration throughout the orbit, differs at maximum from motion in the ellipse by about 1', a difference not observationally significant in Tycho's data.[4] (Of course, with the mathematics available to him Kepler would have been hard put to carry out an equivalent of the modern integration.)

If the ellipticity of the orbits was not empirically established by Kepler, then neither was the so-called second law: determination of areas presupposes orbital shape. For Kepler the area rule was the expression of a dynamical hypothesis, the idea of a motive virtue issuing from and rotating with the Sun so as to push the planets round, its strength varying inversely with distance from the Sun. Kepler's dynamics was Aristotelian, making speed proportional to force. His conception implied that the *component* of orbital speed at right angles to the radius vector varied inversely with distance.[5] The area rule, he belatedly realized, was a consequence.

Given his two rules, Kepler in his *Tabulae Rudolphinae* (1627) derived tables for calculating planetary and lunar positions. These proved more accurate than all earlier tables, and so confirmed the two rules *in combination*.

Newton was aware of the principal features of Kepler's causal account of planetary motion: he had read (probably in 1685 or 1686) the critique of it given by Ishmaël Boulliau (1605–94) in his *Astronomia Philolaica* (Paris, 1645). This astronomical treatise was the first after Kepler's *Rudolphine Tables* to take elliptical orbits as a basis for calculating planetary tables. But Boulliau entirely rejected Kepler's hypothetical physical causes, devoting the bulk of his Chapter 12 to refuting them.[6] He preferred to believe that each planet is moved by its "proper form."[7] To Boulliau, Kepler's assumption of a *virtus movens* issuing from the Sun was mere conjecture.

Also, to Kepler's assumption of an inverse proportionality of the *virtus movens* to solar distance Boulliau objected that corporeal virtues issuing from a point source should vary inversely with the square of the distance from the source. Newton picked up on this assertion in a long postscript to his letter to Halley of 20 June 1686: "Bullialdus [Boulliau] wrote that all force respecting ye Sun as its center & depending on matter must be reciprocally in a duplicate ratio of ye distance from ye center."[8] Newton was here seeking to rebut Robert Hooke's claim to have furnished him originally with the idea of an inverse-square variation for gravity.

From Boulliau's critique Newton learned that Kepler's dynamics violated the principle of inertia, and that Kepler, in seeking to explain the planet's alternate approach to and recession from the Sun, had invoked a hypothetical magnetism in the Sun and planet – a hypothesis that Boulliau dismissed as merely conjectural. Newton, corresponding with Flamsteed in 1681, had argued that the Sun, being hot, could not be a magnet.[9]

In the inertial mechanics of Newton, equable description of area becomes equivalent to a centripetal force, a single cause for a single effect, namely the departure of the orbiting body from its instantaneous rectilinear path. His derivation of the ellipticity of the planetary orbits in Proposition 13, Book 3 of the *Principia* rested on the laws of motion announced at the beginning of the *Principia*, and on the inverse-square law of universal gravitation argued for in the first seven propositions of Book 3.[10] In contrast with Kepler's attempted derivation, it contained no bare conjectures.

Universal gravitation did not become the guiding idea in Newton's thinking on planetary motion till much later than was long supposed: not before 1685. How had Newton viewed the Keplerian rules in the years before the *Principia*?

In the mid 1660s Newton made notes on Thomas Streete's *Astronomia Carolina* (1661). In 1669 or 1670 he perused Vincent Wing's *Astronomia Britannica* (1669), and wrote notes on its endpapers.[11] Both authors took the orbits of the planets to be elliptical, without offering justification for the assumption. Neither mentioned or used Kepler's area rule. Instead, each proposed a different calculative procedure for passing from mean anomaly (angle from aphelion that would be traversed at the planet's mean rate) to true anomaly (the planet's actual angle from aphelion). The area rule did not admit of such a direct procedure, except by approximation. Both

Wing's and Streete's procedures were corrections to a faulty procedure proposed in Boulliau's *Astronomia Philolaica* (we omit details[12]), and produced results differing by only small amounts from those derived by the area rule. Streete's procedure gives a maximum error for Mars of 1'51". In Wing's procedure the corresponding error is 20".

Newton's reaction to these hypothetical devices, as his notes on Wing's *Astronomia Britannica* attest, was to doubt both the ellipticity of the orbits and the accuracy of the calculative procedures. Both orbital shape and motion, he proposed, should be controlled empirically, and he showed in a construction how this could be done.[13]

Both Streete and Wing assumed that the planets are moved by a solar vortex. Newton in the 1660s, while rejecting the Cartesian identification of matter and extension (on which for Descartes the necessity of vortices rested), accepted planetary vortices. In his speculations about planetary motion during the 1670s, he again assumed such vortices. A document datable to 1681 shows him still doing so.[14] The supposition of vortices with their hydrodynamical complexities could hardly fail to give rise to doubts about the mathematical accuracy of the elliptical orbits accepted by his contemporaries.

KEPLER'S THIRD OR HARMONIC LAW, AND NEWTON

Streete differed sharply from Wing in asserting the strict accuracy of Kepler's third law – the law according to which the planetary periods are as the three-halves power of their mean solar distances. In a departure from Kepler's *Rudolphine Tables*, he used the law to derive the mean solar distances from the periods. The solar distances could be determined observationally only by imprecise triangulations, whereas the periods were precisely determinable from comparisons of ancient and modern observations. Hindsight tells us that, for the planets from Mercury to Mars (but not for Jupiter or Saturn), the new rule improved the accuracy of the solar distances by three orders of magnitude.

Streete took this procedure from the as yet unpublished *Venus in Sole Visa* of Jeremiah Horrocks (1618? – January 3, 1641). Horrocks had found empirical support for it in his observations of Mars and Venus.[15]

Newton, on reading about this rule in Streete's *Astronomia Carolina*, made a note of it. A few years later, perusing Wing's *Astronomia Britannica*, he found that Wing's values for the mean solar distances disagreed with this "regula Kepleriana." They would better agree with observations, he wrote in the endpapers of his copy, if they were reduced to the rule.

Newton's interest had a theoretical dimension. Probably in 1666 he had derived a formula for "the endeavor from the center of a body revolving in a circle," thus quantifying the Cartesian concept; in a not yet published work Huygens had given the name "centrifugal force" to the pull on a string that retains the body in the circle, counteracting this endeavor.[16] According to the formula, when bodies are moving in different circles, their endeavors from the centers of those circles are as the radii divided by the squares of the periodic times. Since by the "regula Kepleriana" the squares of the periods of the planets are as the cubes of their mean solar distances, their endeavors from the Sun will be reciprocally as the squares of their solar distances. Newton also compared the Moon's endeavor to recede from the Earth with gravity at the Earth's surface, and found the latter to be "4000 and more times greater" than the former – not $(60)^2 = 3,600$ times, as an inverse-square relation would imply.

David Gregory on a visit to Newton in 1694 was shown a manuscript with these calculations, and wrote afterwards that here "all the foundations of his [Newton's] philosophy are laid: namely the gravity of the Moon to the Earth, and of the planets to the Sun."[17] From Henry Pemberton, writing in 1728,[18] and William Whiston, writing in 1749,[19] we have similar accounts. According to Whiston, the failed lunar calculation led Newton to suspect that the force on the Moon was due partly to gravity and partly to "Cartesius's Vortices."

These tales give us a Newton about to embark on the enterprise of the *Principia* in the 1660s, but delaying for twenty years on account of a computation's failing to match expectation. As Florian

Cajori has pointed out, the computation could easily have been corrected. Newton had used an inaccurate value for the length of a degree of terrestrial latitude. Better values were readily available; Newton came to know of them by 1672.[20]

During these years Newton employed aethereal hypotheses to account for optical, electrical, chemical, and other phenomena. In the *Hypothesis Explaining y*e *Properties of Light* which he transmitted to the Royal Society in December 1675,[21] he assumed an elastic aethereal medium – not "one uniforme matter," but rather compounded of various "aethereall Spirits." These aethereal Spirits could be condensable, so that "the whole frame of Nature may be nothing but various Contextures of some certain aethereall Spirits or vapours condens'd as it were by precipitation." Terrestrial gravitation could be due to a certain aethereal Spirit which is condensed in the body of the Earth; in descending from above, it would "beare downe with it the bodyes it pervades with a force proportionall to the superficies of all their parts it acts upon." This aethereal matter, transformed alchemically within the Earth, would then slowly ascend to constitute the Earth's atmosphere for a time, before vanishing again into the aethereal spaces."And as the Earth, so perhaps may the Sun imbibe this Spirit copiously to conserve his shineing, & keep the Planets from receding further from him." This downward flux, Newton supposed, was separate from the aethereal vortex carrying the planets about the Sun; the two fluxes passed through one another without mixing. He considered that the downward flux of aether into the central body would lead to an inverse-square law.[22]

The dynamics that Newton here relied on was the Cartesian dynamics of an endeavor from the center – plausible for a stone twirled in a sling or a planet carried about in a vortex. What if the planet moves inertially in a straight line, and is simultaneously attracted to a center? Robert Hooke proposed the latter conception to Newton in a letter of November 24, 1679.[23]

The import of facts changes with the changing ideas in the light of which they are viewed. Evidence for an inverse-square law of force may be taken, in a universe of vortices, as evidence for a certain kind of aethereal flux; but it hardly suggests an opening into an exact, quantitative theory of planetary motion: unknown aethereal pressures within and between vortices may be operative. In a universe empty of aethereal matter, on the other hand, such evidence suggests a force somehow acting across the space from Sun to planet, as the predominant determinant of the planet's motion.

Newton in a tract "De motu" that he sent to Edmond Halley in November 1684 proceeded along the lines of this latter conception. Centripetal force, he showed, implied equable description of areas. Also, given a conic-section orbit about the Sun in a focus, the force is inverse-square. Further, assuming inverse-square law implies conic-section orbit, he showed how to find the conic section corresponding to any particular initial conditions of position and velocity. "Therefore," he astonishingly claimed, "the major planets gyrate in ellipses having their foci in the center of the Sun; and by radii drawn to the Sun, describe areas proportional to the times, just as Kepler supposed."[24]

What led Newton to pursue Hooke's conception we do not know. Perhaps Comet Halley, appearing in 1682 in its retrograde orbit across the sky, at last convinced him that vortices could not exist.[25]

At least as interesting is Newton's lack of conviction after November 1684 as to the exact truth of Hooke's conception or its sufficiency to account for the phenomena. As he wrote Flamsteed on January 12, 1685, "Now I am upon this subject I would gladly know yᵉ bottom of it before I publish my papers."[26]

Newton had sought Flamsteed's help in December. From Flamsteed's letter of December 27, he learned that the maximum elongations of Jupiter's four satellites "are as exactly in sesqui-alte proportion to theire periods as it is possible for our sences to determine."[27] This was good news: "Your information about yᵉ Satellits of Jupiter gives me very much satisfaction."[28] Flamsteed's determinations, made with the screw micrometer, were precise to one-thousandth of the semi-diameter of Jupiter's disk.

Whether the mean solar distances of the primary planets agreed with Kepler's harmonic rule was still a question. "The orbit of Saturn," Newton wrote Flamsteed on December 30, "is defined by Kepler too little for ye sesquialterate proportion." He went on to explain how he thought the motion of Saturn might be perturbed by Jupiter. The idea astonished Flamsteed, but, responding on 5 January, he acknowledged that his determinations had not yet been strict enough to exclude "such exorbitation as you suggest of Saturn."[29] Newton replied:

> Your information about ye error of Keplers tables for Jupiter & Saturn has eased me of several scruples. I was apt to suspect there might be some cause or other unknown to me, wch might disturb ye sesquialtera proportion . . . It would ad to my satisfaction if you would be pleased to let me know the long diameters of ye orbits of Jupiter & Saturn assigned by your self & Mr Halley . . . that I may see how the sesquiplicate proportion fills ye heavens together wth another small proportion wch must be allowed for.[30]

The "small proportion wch must be allowed for" is presumably the modification of Kepler's harmonic rule introduced in Propositions 57–60, Book 1 of the *Principia*.

Evidently Newton was now embarked on a program of substantiating a dynamical conception whose full reach was in doubt. He had yet to satisfy himself that the force between the planets and the Sun was solely gravitational, that terrestrial gravity like the solar and Jovial attractions was directly proportional to mass, that the gravitational attraction of a body arose from the gravitational attractions of all its least particles, etc.

The argument for universal gravitation is the crowning achievement of the *Principia*. The book abounds in mathematical triumphs as well. True, not all its demonstrations are valid; it does not achieve everything it attempts to achieve; it leaves unanswered questions that the idea of universal gravitation can raise. These judgments of a pioneering work should not surprise. Both by what it achieved and by what it failed to achieve, it set the agenda for the celestial mechanics of the next two centuries.

How Newton and his successors responded to this agenda will be our concern in the following sections.

NEWTON ON THE MOON'S MOTION

In Proposition 22, Book 3 of the *Principia* (all editions), with the aid of Corollaries of Book 1 Proposition 66, Newton showed qualitatively how the known inequalities of the Moon arise from the varying difference between the accelerations that the Sun causes in the Moon and the Earth. These include the inequalities called "the Variation" and the "annual equation," the oscillations in the Moon's orbital eccentricity and apsidal line postulated in the lunar theory of Jeremiah Horrocks, the inequalities in the lunar latitudes detected by Tycho, and the general forward advance of the lunar apse.

Horrocks's lunar theory had first been published by Flamsteed in 1672, and then republished with Flamsteed's revised constants in 1681. It combined the Moon's unperturbed elliptical orbit with the second inequality due to the Sun (the "evection" as Boulliau called it) to obtain an ellipse with oscillating eccentricity and apse. The Horrocksian theory was the first lunar theory to admit in a direct way of a Newtonian analysis in terms of forces.

The *Principia* includes certain quantitative derivations with regard to the Moon's motions. Such are the derivations of the motions of the Moon's nodes (Propositions 30–33, Book 3) and of the changes in the Moon's orbital inclination (Propositions 34, 35, Book 3); these are valid and the results correct. Newton derives the Variation in Propositions 26, 28, and 29, Book 3, with an accurate result (it assumes without proof that the Sun has the effect of transforming an idealized circular lunar orbit into one that can be approximated by an ellipse with the Earth at the center).

In the first edition Scholium to Proposition 35, Book 3 of the *Principia*, Newton speaks of computing the motion of the Moon's apogee, and finding its annual mean motion to be 40°. "The computations, however, as being too complicated and impeded by approximations, and insufficiently accurate, it is better to omit." The manuscript in which these computations were made was discovered in the late nineteenth century, and has been published by Whiteside.[31] It shows Newton taking account of both the radial and transverse components of the Sun's perturbing force; the analysis is in many respects brilliant. It includes, however, an illegitimate step, and the final result, as Whiteside judges, is fudged. In later editions Newton omitted all reference to this computation.

In Corollary 2 of Proposition 45, Book 1 (all editions), Newton calculated the effect of the *radial* component of the solar perturbation in producing motion of the Moon's apse, but without identifying the calculation as having to do with the Moon. The calculated apsidal advance per revolution was 1°31' 28". In the third edition Newton added the remark: "The apse of the Moon is about twice as swift." To eighteenth-century readers, this appeared to be the sum total of what Newton had supplied in the way of a quantitative derivation of the Moon's apsidal motion. "Neither," wrote John Machin in 1729, "is there any method that I have ever yet met with upon the commonly received principles, which is perfectly sufficient to explain the motion of the Moon's apogee."[32]

On September 1, 1694 Newton visited Flamsteed at Greenwich. Flamsteed showed him about 150 observed places of the Moon, along with the corresponding places derived from his (Flamsteed's) lunar theory. The errors averaged to about 8 arc-minutes, but went as high as 20 arc-minutes. Now, a primary purpose of Flamsteed's appointment as "the King's Astronomer" (in 1675), and of the establishment of the Greenwich Observatory, was to obtain star positions and a lunar theory accurate enough to enable navigators to determine the longitude at sea. For determining the angular distance in longitude from a given meridian to within 1°, the lunar theory had to be accurate to 2 arc-minutes. Newton, seeing that Flamsteed's theory was insufficiently accurate, undertook to develop a more accurate theory.

From Flamsteed Newton received a total of about 250 lunar observations, the most extensive and accurate database a lunar theorist had yet had to base a theory upon. Newton's new theory was published in 1702, first in Latin, then in English, as *A New and most Accurate Theory of the Moon's Motion; Whereby all her Irregularities may be solved, and her Place truly calculated to Two Minutes.*

The elements of the new theory are presented without explanation of their derivation. The core of the theory is (like Flamsteed's theory) Horrocksian but with revised numerical parameters. A few specifically Newtonian features are added: special annual equations in the mean motions of the lunar apsides and node, with coefficients of 20' and 9'30" respectively, and four new small terms whose origin is unexplained, although in the second edition of the *Principia* Newton asserted that they were derived from the theory of gravity.

Newton's theory is not as accurate as claimed in the title of the English version. But, when comparison is made with an historically accurate modern ephemeris, he is found to have determined the Moon's mean motion for the period 1680–1700 with greater accuracy than any of his contemporaries. And, when the small error in the mean motion is removed, the corrected theory proves to have a standard deviation of 1.9 arc-minutes; 95% of its values thus fall within 3.8 arc-minutes of the correct values. The errors in Flamsteed's theory of 1681 were about twice as large.[33] Not till 1753 would a lunar theory accurate to within 2 arc-minutes be devised.

ABERRATION, NUTATION, PRECESSION

In 1725 Samuel Molyneux and James Bradley undertook to replicate observations of the meridian transits of Gamma Draconis that Robert Hooke had made in 1669 – observations ostensibly confirming annual parallax in this star, and thus proving the Copernican hypothesis. Hooke's observations, they found, were mistaken: Gamma Draconis was moving in an annual cycle, but not the one that annual parallax implied. Later Bradley verified that other stars moved in such annual cycles. The pattern of motion could be explained by assuming that light has a finite velocity, and that the Earth is moving about the Sun, so that the direction of the light with respect to the moving Earth had a component in the direction of the Earth's motion. Thus all the stars move annually in ellipses, with a long axis of about 40"; the ellipses reduce to a straight line for stars on the ecliptic, and to circles for stars near the ecliptic North Pole. Bradley announced the discovery of this effect, which he named *the aberration of light*, to the Royal Society early in 1729.

Thereafter he discovered that, besides aberration, further stellar motions were occurring; and he was able to account for them as a kind of wobble in the precessional motion of the Earth's axis – a nutation – with a period of eighteen years, the period of revolution of the Moon's nodes. He announced this discovery to the Royal Society in January 1748, after verifying the hypothesis over a complete cycle.

For the attainment of an astronomy accurate to arc-seconds, these discoveries were crucial. Previously, aberration and nutation, unrecognized, had played havoc with attempts to found observational astronomy on a secure basis. As the astronomer Nicolas-Louis de Lacaille (1713–62) put it, "Many obscurities thus arose . . . it finally seemed that hardly anything certain could be deduced from the heavens. Fortunately, to meet such evil, at length came Bradley."[34]

The nutation, which Newton had not predicted, required an explanation in terms of inverse-square gravitation, and in mid 1748 Jean le Rond d'Alembert (1717–83) set about deriving it. Nutation is a refinement of the precession of the equinoxes, and d'Alembert soon found that Newton's explanation of the precession (Proposition 66, Corollary 22, Book 1, and Proposition 39, Book 3 with the preceding lemmas) was deeply flawed.[35] Newton's basic error arose from his lack of an appropriate dynamics for the rotational motions of solid bodies, and his attempt to treat problems involving such motions in terms of linear momentum rather than angular momentum. D'Alembert now furnished the elements of the appropriate dynamics, and Leonhard Euler systematized it.

THE MOTION OF THE LUNAR APSE DERIVED
FROM THE INVERSE-SQUARE LAW

The first to apply Leibnizian-style mathematics, that is to say differential equations, to the problem of the Moon's motions was Leonhard Euler. He published lunar tables in 1745, then revised them for his *Opuscula Varii Argumenti* of 1746. In the preface to the tables in the *Opuscula*, he stated that they were derived from Newton's theory of attraction, but gave no details.

In the spring of 1746 Alexis-Claude Clairaut (1713–65) and d'Alembert separately set out to derive differential equations for the three-body problem, and to apply them to the Moon's motions. By the summer of 1747 Clairaut knew that a first-order solution to his equations yielded reasonable values for the major perturbational terms, but only about half the observed motion of the Moon's apse. Meanwhile, Euler's essay on the perturbations of Jupiter and Saturn, submitted in the Paris Academy's prize contest for 1748, arrived, and Clairaut, as a member of the prize commission, read it in September 1747. Therein Euler expressed doubt as to the accuracy of the inverse-square law of gravitation, and, in support of his doubt, stated that Newton's law led to but half the observed motion of the lunar apse.

Addressing the Paris Academy in November 1747, Clairaut proposed that Newton's law be altered by the addition of a small, inverse fourth power term, whereby the full motion of the lunar apse would become deducible. This proposal unleashed a storm of controversy.[36] Clairaut retracted his proposal in May 1749. In outline, the reversal came about as follows.[37]

From his differential equations, Clairaut had obtained by a double integration the result

$$\frac{f^2}{Mr} = 1 - g \sin v - q \cos v + \sin v \int \Omega \, dv \cos v - \cos v \int \Omega \, dv \sin v, \quad (1)$$

where f, g, and q are constants of integration, M is the sum of the masses of the Earth and the Moon, v is the true anomaly, and Ω is a function of r and the perturbing forces. To solve this equation for r, it was necessary to substitute an approximate value of r into Ω on the right-hand side. It was known empirically that the Moon's apse moves, and Clairaut proposed using the formula $k/r = 1 - e \cos mv$, which represents a precessing ellipse. Here k, e, m are presumptive constants, determinable in terms of other constants in the equation. The resultant motion, Clairaut hoped, could be largely accounted for – small oscillations excepted – as motion on a precessing ellipse.

In the initial outcome, this hope appeared to be satisfied. Clairaut's modified equation took the form

$$\frac{k}{r} = 1 - e \cos mv + \beta \cos \frac{2v}{n} + \gamma \cos\left(\frac{2}{n} - m\right)v + \delta \cos\left(\frac{2}{n} + m\right)v, \quad (2)$$

where n is the Moon's mean sidereal motion divided by its mean synodic motion, and β, γ, δ evaluated in terms of the other constants in the theory were found to be 0.007090988, −0.00949705, 0.00018361, hence small relative to e (known empirically to be about 0.05).

From the beginning, Clairaut had supposed that a second-order approximation was eventually to be carried out, to refine the coefficients of the several terms of the theory preparatory to constructing tables. In this second approximation, formula (2), with β, γ, δ retained as symbols, would be substituted back into Ω in (1), and the latter equation would again be solved for r. Before the spring of 1749, Clairaut had not supposed that this refinement could lead to other than minor improvements in the coefficients; certainly it could not result in a doubled value for m! The calculation proved him wrong. The contributions coming to m from the term with coefficient γ were especially sizeable. This term was proportional to the *transverse* perturbing force, whereas the initially computed contribution to m had been proportional to the *radial* perturbing force. Clairaut's final result for the apsidal motion per month was 3°2′6″, just 2′ shy of the empirical value he accepted.

Euler, learning of Clairaut's turnabout, tried to find the error in his own derivation. At last on April 10, 1751 he was able to tell

Clairaut of his success.[38] Euler's unstinting praise for Clairaut's achievement overflows into another letter of June 29, 1751:

> the more I consider this happy discovery, the more important it seems to me, and in my opinion it is the greatest discovery in the Theory of Astronomy . . . For it is very certain that it is only since this discovery that one can regard the law of attraction reciprocally proportional to the squares of the distances as solidly established; and on this depends the entire theory of astronomy.[39]

THE "GREAT INEQUALITY" OF JUPITER AND SATURN

The values for the mean motions of Jupiter and Saturn given in the *Rudolphine Tables* were early recognized to require correction. Jupiter was moving faster than Kepler's numbers implied, and Saturn slower. Flamsteed labored for nearly five decades to correct the theories of these planets, at first by simply refining their Keplerian elements. In the 1690s he asked Newton for help. Newton proposed taking as the focus of Saturn's orbit the center of gravity of Jupiter and the Sun, and introducing Horrocksian-style oscillations into Saturn's eccentricity and line of apsides (see Proposition 13, Book 3 of the *Principia*); his suggestions were not numerically specific. Flamsteed, left to his own devices, sought an oscillation in the motion of each of the two planets, such as might bring their theories into line with observations, but eventually gave up in despair.[40]

Edmond Halley (1656–1742), in planetary tables published posthumously in 1749, introduced a secular acceleration of Jupiter's mean motion of +3°49'.4 in 2,000 years, and a secular deceleration of Saturn's mean motion of −9°16'.1 in 2,000 years. This proposal was widely accepted by astronomers.

In a paper completed in 1774, Pierre-Simon Laplace (1749–1827) demonstrated that, to the first order with respect to the masses, and to the second order with respect to the eccentricities and inclinations, mutual planetary perturbations could not produce secular variations of the mean motions. Joseph Louis Lagrange (1736–1813) in 1776 extended this result to all powers of the eccentricities and inclinations. In 1784 he showed that secular acceleration of the mean motions arising indirectly from secular accelerations in other orbital elements would be negligible for Jupiter and Saturn. Thus the anomalous motions of these planets remained unexplained. Laplace thought they might be due to perturbation by comets. Up to late 1785, they posed for Laplace the chief obstacle to asserting the stability of the solar system – its freedom from runaway variables.

At last, on November 23, 1785, Laplace announced to the Paris Academy that he had succeeded in resolving the anomalies. He had found that a periodic inequality of the third order with respect to the orbital eccentricities and inclinations of Jupiter and Saturn was large, with a coefficient of 49' for Saturn and 20' for Jupiter, and a period of some 900 years. A few shorter-term inequalities resulted from the combination of this long-term inequality with known inequalities, and all the inequalities taken together yielded a theory agreeing with both ancient and modern observations. Laplace's completed theory of Jupiter and Saturn appeared in 1786.

Inequalities of the third order in the eccentricities and inclinations had not been computed earlier because of the labor involved; only zeroth-order and first-order perturbations had been computed systematically. Laplace in attacking the higher-order inequalities proceeded by a species of sharpshooting, which left uncertain whether all terms to a given order of smallness had been accounted for. But his methods were empirically successful.

By December 1787 Laplace had an explanation for the one remaining major anomaly in the solar system, the secular acceleration of the Moon originally discovered by Halley in the 1690s. The secular decrease in the Earth's orbital eccentricity, Laplace showed, would lead to a secular diminution of the radial component of the Sun's perturbing force; consequently the Moon's mean motion would accelerate. (As we shall see later, this explanation was only partially correct.) To Laplace, it now appeared that Newton's law of gravitation was sufficient to account for all the motions in the solar system, and that the system was stable, like well-designed clockwork. This idea inspired his *Exposition du système du monde* (1796) and his *Traité de mécanique céleste* (first four volumes, 1798–1805).

ACCURATE LUNAR PREDICTION

The first three analytic theories of the Moon to be published, those of Clairaut (1752), Euler (1753), and d'Alembert (1754), proved accurate only to 4 or 5 arc-minutes, hence insufficiently accurate to meet the needs of navigation. But in 1753 Tobias Mayer (1723–62) published lunar tables which, compared with 139 lunar longitudes observed by Bradley from 1743 to 1745, deviated on average by only 27″, and at maximum by only 1′37″. In subsequent years Mayer refined his tables; his final version of them, submitted by his widow to the British Board of Admiralty in 1762, became the basis for the British *Nautical Almanac*. How did Mayer achieve such accuracy?

He had carried out an analytic derivation of the lunar inequalities from Newton's law in his *Theoria Lunae juxta Systema Newtonianum*, completed in 1754 but published only in 1767. In this he deduced forty-six perturbational corrections to the mean motion. They could be reduced, he then showed, to thirteen steps of progressive correction. In his preface he stated:

> the theory has this inconvenience, that many of the inequalities cannot be deduced from it accurately, unless one should pursue the calculation – in which I have now exhausted nearly all my patience – much further. My aim is rather to show that at least no argument against the goodness of my tables can be drawn from the theory. This is most evidently gathered from the fact that the inequalities found in the tables, which have been corrected by comparison with many observations, never differ from those that the theory alone supplies by more than $\frac{1'}{2}$.

How did Mayer carry out his "comparison with many observations"? In all likelihood by applying a statistical procedure he had learned from Euler. Multiple equations of condition, derived from observation, were used in evaluating differential corrections to the elements of a theory; the equations were solved by neglecting small terms. (The invention of the more reliable method of least squares was still a half-century away.) The predictive accuracy of Mayer's tables rested on the empirical refinement of coefficients.

Revisions of Mayer's tables were carried out by Charles Mason in 1778 and by Johann Tobias Bürg a little later, in each case on the basis of large numbers of observations. "[Their tables] correspond with the observations made on the Moon," Laplace remarked, "with a degree of accuracy that it will be difficult to surpass."[41] In a few respects Laplace's lunar theory (published in 1802) improved on the empirically grounded tables; in other respects Laplace could aim only to match the accuracy of these tables. In 1811 Johann Karl Burckhardt (1773–1825) completed new lunar tables, based on Laplace's theory together with 4000 observations; they would serve as the basis for the French and British lunar ephemerides until 1861.

Not till 1862 did the national ephemerides come to be based on a lunar theory in which the inequalities (a very few excepted) were deduced from the Newtonian theory without resort to statistical correction. This was the lunar theory of Peter Andreas Hansen (1795–1874), elaborated by a method derived from the Lagrange–Poisson theory of variation of orbital constants. Hansen's theory was the first perfectly rigorous deduction of the lunar inequalities from Newton's theory. It would remain the basis of the national ephemerides until 1922.

Hansen's theory was numerical rather than literal: it did not give for each coefficient an algebraic formula that could be re-derived and so independently checked for accuracy. A literal theory, at least as accurate as Hansen's, was achieved by Charles Eugène Delaunay in the 1860s. The series giving the coefficients, however, converged all too slowly. The problem of slow convergence was at length overcome in a new and innovative theory whose foundations were laid by G. W. Hill in the 1870s. In 1888 E. W. Brown commenced the process of developing Hill's foundational ideas into a complete lunar theory.

The resulting tables, demonstrably more accurate than all their pre-decessors, became the basis of the British and American ephemerides in 1923.

Nevertheless, small, long-term changes in the Moon's mean motion remained puzzling.

COMETARY ORBITS, UNPERTURBED AND PERTURBED

On June 20, 1686 Newton reported to Halley that "the third [book] wants ye Theory of Comets."[42] He had been hard put to discover a way of fitting an orbit to cometary observations. Sometime before April 1687 when he sent the completed manuscript of Book 3 to Halley, he hit on a graphical method of fitting a parabolic trajectory to three observations. The longitude of the perihelion and node and the orbital inclination determined in this way are very nearly correct even if the orbit is elliptical rather than parabolic.

Edmond Halley used a partially arithmetized version of Newton's procedure to determine the parabolic orbital elements of some twenty-four comets, as presented in his *Synopsis Astronomiae Cometicae* (1705). The elements of the retrograde comets appearing in 1531, 1607, and 1682 were nearly identical, and Halley declared himself convinced that these three comets were one and the same. The two intervals between the three apparitions differed by nearly a year, but Halley believed the difference could be caused by perturbation due to Jupiter. In an expanded version of the *Synopsis* published posthumously with his *Tabulae Astronomicae* of 1749, Halley predicted that the comet would reappear toward the end of 1758 or the beginning of 1759.

For astronomers of the 1750s, Halley's prediction presented two challenges: to locate the returning comet as soon as possible and determine its parabolic elements; and to predict from Newton's theory and the previous apparitions the time of the new perihelion passage. The second task was undertaken by Clairaut, assisted by Lalande and Mme. Lepaute.

For his calculation Clairaut used the differential equations he had derived for the three-body problem. The new application was far more labor-intensive than the earlier application to the Moon. In the Moon's case, the integrands were approximated by trigonometric series and so rendered integrable. The goodness of the approximation depended on the rapidity of convergence of the series, which in turn depended on the orbit being nearly circular. The orbit of Halley's comet is very elongated. Trigonometric series could not be used, and Clairaut and his colleagues had to resort to numerical integration. This was the first large-scale numerical integration ever performed.[43]

In November 1758, Clairaut, in order not to be forestalled by the comet, announced preliminary results, predicting a perihelion passage in mid April 1759, give or take a month. The comet was first detected by Johann George Palitzsch on December 25, and then independently by Charles Messier on January 21. In March it disappeared into the rays of the Sun, then reappeared on March 31. Calculation showed that the perihelion had occurred on March 13, a month earlier than Clairaut had predicted. This was the first proof that comets may indeed return, and move in accordance with the Newtonian law.

THE PROBLEM OF THE EARTH'S FIGURE
AND THE PROBLEM OF THE TIDES

Newton addressed both these problems in his *Principia*; in both cases his attack on them proved inadequate, and further advances were made only after the introduction of new and more powerful mathematical techniques.

In Proposition 19, Book 3 Newton showed that for a homogeneous spherical Earth subject to inverse-square gravity and rotating diurnally, the downward acceleration at the Equator would be 288/289 of that at the Pole. Supposing the Earth to have been initially fluid, and assuming as its equilibrium shape an infinitesimally flattened ellipsoid of revolution, he claimed that all linear columns from center to surface would weigh the same, and inferred a flattening of 1/229.

Could the assumptions be justified, and could Newton's conclusions be extended to cases (like Jupiter's) where the flattening was greater? Newton asserted without demonstration that, if the density increased toward the center, the flattening would be greater.

In analytical studies using partial differentiation and culminating in his *Théorie de la terre* of 1743, Clairaut showed that a homogeneous, rotating ellipsoid of revolution with infinitesimal flattening could be a figure of equilibrium. He showed further that for an Earth consisting of individually homogeneous ellipsoidal strata with infinitesimal flattening but with densities increasing toward the center, the Earth would be less flattened than in the homogeneous case, with a flattening between 1/576 and 1/230. He supplied a new necessary condition for a rotating figure to be in equilibrium: the work to take a unit mass round any closed path within the body must add to zero.

The discussion was taken up again by Adrien-Marie Legendre (1752–1833) and Laplace in the 1780s. Legendre introduced the Legendre polynomials for expressing the attraction, potential, and meridian curve of equilibium figures of revolution. Laplace then generalized these results to "spheroids," understood as any figures given by a single equation in r, θ, and φ.

A reconciliation of these mathematical results with practical geodetical measurements was effected only after F. W. Bessel's introduction of a sophisticated statistical understanding of the geodesist's task.

Newton's account of the tides appears in Propositions 24, 36, and 37, Book 3. Newton assumed that the waters would be raised in places directly underneath the Sun or the Moon, and also on the opposite side of the Earth, and would be depressed in places 90° distant. He supposed the height of the tide would be as the force raising it. He in effect assumed that the instantaneous figure of the waters raised by the Sun or the Moon would be a prolate ellipsoid with longer axis directed toward the attracting body. The height of the tide at any given place and time would be the sum of the *radii vectores* in the two ellipsoids at that place, minus the radius vector for the undisturbed sea. But the highest tide, Newton knew, did not occur at the syzygies, when the two ellipsoids combined to give a maximum height, but rather some forty-three hours later. He attributed this delay to the inertia of the waters.

Newton's theory leads to a number of predictions that are contradicted by observation. Thus it implies that two consecutive high tides at the time of the syzygies should differ greatly in height, especially when the difference in declination of the Sun and Moon is greatest; whereas these tides are known to be of nearly equal height. Laplace, stimulated by this and other anomalies, devised an analytical account of the tides based on the solution of partial differential equations; modern tidal theory has its starting point in his account. He showed that inertial maintenance of motion is negligible in the tides, and that the differences in linear speed of the waters at different latitudes owing to diurnal rotation play a significant role.

LIMITATIONS OF NEWTON'S THEORY OF GRAVITATION

In 1787, as we have seen, Laplace claimed to show that the Moon's secular acceleration arose from a secular decrease in the radial component of the Sun's perturbing force. The tangential component, he assumed, contributed nothing to the effect. In 1853 J. C. Adams showed that, in fact, the tangential component diminished the overall effect, reducing it to 6″ per century. Delaunay confirmed Adams's calculation in 1859.

In 1865 Delaunay suggested that the tidal protuberances raised by the Moon, being carried eastward of the Moon by the Earth's diurnal rotation, would be attracted backward by the Moon; friction between the tidal water and the solid Earth could then slow the Earth's rotation, making the Moon appear to accelerate. To the Moon's action on the tidal bulge must correspond a contrary force on the Moon, speeding it up so that it rises into a higher orbit with a reduced mean angular motion in longitude. This effect appeared to be confirmed in 1920 by J. K. Fotheringham in studies of ancient eclipses.[44] He found 10″.8 for the secular acceleration of the Moon, and $1''.5$ for the secular acceleration of the Sun. The latter effect presumably arises solely from the retardation in the Earth's diurnal rotation. Because the Moon's mean motion is 13.4 times the Sun's, the acceleration of the Moon due to the same cause should be $13.4 \times 1''.5 = 20''T^2$. With the $6''T^2$ found by Adams added, the total result is $26''T^2$, exceeding the observed secular acceleration by about $15''$. The difference is attributable to the second half of the action–reaction pair in the interaction between the Moon and the terrestrial tides.

The Earth–Moon system is thus evolving in time, and so, it appears, are other satellite–planet pairs in the solar system. In our Moon's case, the effects of tidal friction appear to undergo irregular variations in rate. We have consequently to allow that the Moon's places are, to a small extent, subject to temporal changes in tidal friction.

Non-gravitational forces are now accorded a role in cometary motion. The second periodic comet to be discovered was Comet Encke, first located in 1818. It had a period of 3.3 years, but when Encke computed the perturbations he found a non-gravitational decrease of about 2.5 hours per period, which he attributed to aethereal resistance. Those who in the 1830s computed the perturbations of Halley's Comet to predict its perihelial passage in 1835 found its period to be increasing – a change not attributable to aethereal resistance. Current opinion assigns these non-gravitational accelerations to outgassing in the comet's near approach to the Sun; the comet is rotating, and the thrust it receives from the outgassing is a little delayed, so as to have a component accelerating or decelerating the comet's orbital motion.[45]

In 1859 U. J. J. Le Verrier discovered that some 38 arc-seconds per century of the precession of Mercury's perihelion could not be accounted for on the basis of Newton's inverse-square law.[46] (The total observed apsidal precession is about $5,596''$ per century, of which over $5,000''$ is due to the precession of the equinoxes, and over $500''$ to planetary perturbation.) In 1882 Simon Newcomb revised Le Verrier's value for the discrepancy upward to 43 arc-seconds per century. Asaph Hall in 1894 proposed accounting for the discrepancy by taking the exponent in the gravitational law to be −2.00000016.[47] In 1903, however, Ernest W. Brown showed this suggestion to be untenable: he had by this time developed the Hill–Brown lunar theory far enough to rule out an exponent differing from −2 by 0.00000016.[48] In 1915 Einstein showed that the anomalous apsidal precession could be derived from his Theory of General Relativity.[49]

Thus Newton's law of gravitation is not strictly correct. The basis of the national ephemerides remained essentially Newtonian till 1984, when a post-Newtonian basis, incorporating relativistic terms, was adopted. The measurement of time, derived from atomic clocks on a rotating Earth, also requires correction for relativistic effects.[50]

NOTES

1 *The Correspondence of Isaac Newton*, vol. 2, ed. H. W. Turnbull (Cambridge: Cambridge University Press, 1960), p. 436.

2 Some authors making this claim are referenced in my "Newton and Some Philosophers on Kepler's Laws," *Journal for the History of Ideas* 35 (1974), 231–58.

3 Curtis Wilson, "Kepler's Derivation of the Elliptical Path," *Isis* 59 (1968), 5–25. But see also A. E. L. Davis, "Grading the Eggs (Kepler's Sizing Procedure for the Planetary Orbits)," *Centaurus* 35 (1992), 121–42.

4 D. T. Whiteside, "Keplerian Eggs, Laid and Unlaid, 1600–1605," *Journal for the History of Astronomy* 5 (1974), 1–21, esp. 12–14.

5 See A. E. L. Davis, "Kepler's 'Distance Law' – Myth not Reality," *Centaurus* 35 (1992), 103–20.

6 Ishmaël Boulliau, *Astronomia Philolaica* (Paris, 1645), pp. 21–4.

7 On Boulliau's planetary theory, see Curtis Wilson, "From Kepler's Laws, So-called, to Universal Gravitation: Empirical Factors," *Archive for History of Exact Sciences* 6 (1970), 106–21.

8 *The Correspondence of Isaac Newton*, vol. 2, p. 438.

9 *Ibid.*, p. 360.

10 As to whether Newton in fact provided an adequate sketch of a derivation of the elliptical orbit from the inverse-square law in Corollary 1 of Proposition 13, Book 1, see Bruce Pourciau, "On Newton's Proof that Inverse-Square Orbits Must Be Conics," *Annals of Science* 48 (1991), 159–72.

11 See Derek T. Whiteside, "Newton's Early Thoughts on Planetary Motion: A Fresh Look," *British Journal for the History of Science* 2 (1964), 117–29.

12 For a detailed account see René Taton and Curtis Wilson (eds.), *Planetary Astronomy from the Renaissance to the Rise of Astrophysics, Tycho Brahe to Newton*, vol. 2, part A of *The General History of Astronomy* (Cambridge: Cambridge University Press, 1989), pp. 172–85.

13 D. T. Whiteside, "Newton's Early Thoughts," pp. 125–6.

14 See James Alan Ruffner, "The Background and Early Development of Newton's Theory of Comets" (Ph.D. thesis, University Microfilms, 1966), pp. 308ff.

15 See my "Horrocks, Harmonies, and the Exactitude of Kepler's Third Law," in Erna Hilfstein, Pawel Czartoryski, and Frank D. Grade (eds.), *Science and History: Studies in Honor of Edward Rosen*, Studia Copernicana 16 (Warsaw: Ossolineum, 1978), pp. 235–59, esp. 248–55.

16 See John Herivel, *The Background to Newton's Principia: A Study of Newton's Dynamical Researches in the Years 1664–84* (Oxford: Clarendon Press, 1965), pp. 192–8; and Richard S. Westfall, *Force in Newton's Physics* (New York: American Elsevier, 1971), pp. 350–60.

17 See *The Correspondence of Isaac Newton*, vol. 3, ed. W. H. Turnbull (Cambridge: Cambridge University Press, 1961), p. 331.

18 H. Pemberton, *A View of Sir Isaac Newton's Philosophy* (Dublin, 1728), Preface.

19 W. Whiston, *Memoirs of the Life of Mr. William Whiston by himself* (London, 1749), vol. 1, pp. 35–6.

20 Florian Cajori, "Newton's Twenty Years' Delay in Announcing the Law of Gravitation," in *Sir Isaac Newton, 1727–1927: A Bicentenary Evaluation of His Work* (Baltimore: Williams and Wilkins, 1928), pp. 127–88, esp. 168–70.

21 *The Correspondence of Isaac Newton*, vol. 1, ed. W. H. Turnbull (Cambridge: Cambridge University Press, 1959), pp. 362ff.

22 *Ibid.*, vol. 2, pp. 446–7.

23 *Ibid.*, vol. 2, pp. 297–8.

24 A. Rupert Hall and Marie Boas Hall (eds.), *Unpublished Scientific Papers of Isaac Newton* (Cambridge: Cambridge University Press, 1962), p. 253.

25 Private communication from Nicholas Kollerstrom.

26 *The Correspondence of Isaac Newton*, vol. 2, p. 413.

27 *Ibid.*, p. 404.

28 *Ibid.*, p. 407.

29 *Ibid.*, p. 408.

30 *Ibid.*, p. 413.

31 D. T. Whiteside (ed.), *The Mathematical Papers of Isaac Newton*, vol. 6 (Cambridge: Cambridge University Press, 1974), pp. 508–37.

32 John Machin, *The Laws of the Moon's Motion According to Gravity* (London, 1729), p. 31.

33 Nicholas Kollerstrom, *Newton's 1702 "Theory of the Moon's Motion"* (based on a doctoral thesis at the University of London; University College, London, 1997), p. 155.

34 Lacaille, *Astronomiae Fundamenta* (Paris, 1757), p. 2.

35 See d'Alembert, *Recherches sur la précession des équinoxes, et sur la nutation de l'Axe de la terre, dans le système Newtonien* (Paris: David, 1749), pp. x–xxiii; Curtis Wilson, "D'Alembert versus Euler on the Precession of the Equinoxes and the Mechanics of Rigid Bodies," *Archive for History of Exact Sciences* 37 (1987), 238–42; G. J. Dobson, "Newton's Problems with Rigid Body Dynamics in the Light of his Treatment of the Precession of the Equinoxes," *Archive for History of Exact Sciences* 53 (1998), 125–45.

36 See Craig B. Waff, "Universal Gravitation and the Motion of the Moon's Apogee: The Establishment and Reception of Newton's Inverse-Square Law, 1687–1749" (Ph.D. thesis, Johns Hopkins University, 1975), ch. 4.

37 *Ibid.*, ch. 5.

38 G. Bigourdan, "Lettres inédites d'Euler à Clairaut," *Comptes rendus du Congrès des sociétés savantes de Paris et des Départments tenu à Lille en 1928* (Paris: Imprimerie Nationale, 1930), p. 36.

39 *Ibid.*, pp. 38–9.

40 Francis Baily, *An Account of the Revd. John Flamsteed* (London, 1835), p. 327.

41 Laplace, *Celestial Mechanics*, vol. 3 (Boston, 1832; Chelsea Publishing Company reprint, 1966), p. 357.

42 *The Correspondence of Isaac Newton*, vol. 2, p. 437.

43 For a detailed account, see my "Clairaut's Calculation of the Eighteenth-Century Return of Halley's Comet," *Journal for the History of Astronomy* 24 (1993), 1–15.

44 John K. Fotheringham, "A Solution of Ancient Eclipses of the Sun," *Monthly Notices of the Royal Astronomical Society* 81 (1920), 104–26.

45 B. G. Marsden, Z. Sekanina, and D. K. Yeomans, "Comets and Nongravitational Forces," *Astronomical Journal* 78 (1973), 211–23.

46 U. J. J. Le Verrier, "Théorie du mouvement de Mercure," *Annales de l'Observatoire Impériale de Paris* 5 (1859), esp. 98–106.

47 A. Hall, "A Suggestion in the Theory of Mercury," *Astronomical Journal* 14 (1894), 49–51.

48 E. W. Brown, "On the Degree of Accuracy in the New Lunar Theory," *Monthly Notices of the Royal Astronomical Society* 64 (1903), 524–34, esp. 532.

49 A. Einstein, "Erklärung der Perihelbewegung des Merkur aus der allgemeinen Relativitätstheorie," *Königlich Preussische Akademie der Wissenschaften* [Berlin]: *Sitzungsberichte* (1915), 831–9.

50 See P. Kenneth Seidelmann (ed.), *Explanatory Supplement to the Astronomical Almanac* (Mill Valley, CA: University Science Books, 1992), pp. 41, 70, 96, 615.

7   Newton's optics and atomism

Alan E. Shapiro

After his first optical publications in 1672 Newton was identified by his contemporaries and later generations as a supporter of the corpuscular or emission theory of light, in which light is assumed to consist of corpuscles, or atoms, emitted from a luminous source such as the Sun. While it is true that Newton believed in a corpuscular theory, utilized it in developing many of his optical experiments and theories, and argued vigorously against the wave theory of light, he never believed that it was a demonstrated scientific truth and considered it to be only a probable hypothesis. This distinction explains why, for example, he never set forth a synthetic account of the emission theory and eschewed it in his public accounts of his scientific theories. In order to understand Newton's advocacy and use of atomism in his optics it is necessary to understand his views on hypotheses and certainty in science.

HYPOTHESES IN NEWTON'S SCIENCE

From the beginning of his scientific career Newton was concerned with establishing a new, more certain science to replace contemporary science, which he felt was rife with "conjectures and probabilities."[1] He believed that he could establish a more certain science both by developing mathematical theories and by basing his theories on experimentally discovered properties. To establish a more certain science, Newton insisted that one must "not mingle conjectures with certainties."[2] To avoid compromising rigorously demonstrated principles by hypotheses, he developed the techniques of clearly labeling hypotheses as such and setting them apart, as with his "An hypothesis explaining the properties of light discoursed of in my severall Papers" in 1675, or with the queries appended to the *Opticks* in 1704 and in subsequent editions.

As part of his campaign to reform science, Newton continually railed against hypotheses, that is, conjectural causal explanations. His condemnations of hypotheses – the most famous being his "hypotheses non fingo" (I do not feign hypotheses) in the *Principia* (1687) – are always aimed at preserving the certainty of scientific principles rather than objecting to the use of hypotheses in themselves. Newton held that hypotheses without any experimental support whatever, such as Cartesian vortices, had no place in science, but those based on some experimental evidence, though insufficient to establish them as demonstrated principles, could be used to understand properties already discovered and to suggest new experiments. The corpuscular theory of light fell into the second category.

Newton believed that by formulating his theories phenomenologically, in terms of experimentally observed properties, or principles deduced from them, without any causal explanations (hypotheses) of those properties, he could develop a more certain science. While he considered causal explanations to be desirable, they never play an essential or necessary role in his science. As we shall see, however, in his private work Newton did use hypotheses to develop theories and predict new properties. When he used hypothetical causes such as light corpuscles and the aether in this way, he then purged them (or, at least, attempted to do so) from his public work and reformulated his theories in terms of experimentally discovered "properties" such as unequal refrangibility and periodicity. Newton appears never to have questioned the possibility of constructing an hypothesis-free science. To have denied such a possibility would have been tantamount to denying his conception of science.

By examining the role of atomism in Newton's theory of color and refraction and the colors of thin films, we will see how his attitude on the proper use of hypotheses in science played a fundamental role in the development and formulation of those theories. In investigating the colors of thin films, he introduced another hypothesis – a vibrating aether – in order to account for the periodicity of light. The hypothesis of a vibrating aether suffered a very different fate from that of light corpuscles, for the former – as "fits" devoid of the aether – was eventually raised to a demonstrated principle, while the latter always remained an hypothesis. We will examine the different fate of these two hypotheses. Although Newton's methodology can be considered to be very conservative, I shall argue that his refusal to accept the corpuscular theory as true was justified by the course of his own research program. Finally, we will consider Newton's theory of colored bodies, where he used an atomic theory of matter, but did not consider that to be an hypothesis.

THEORY OF LIGHT AND COLOR

Given this philosophical background, we should not expect Newton's use of the corpuscular theory of light to be readily evident in his published scientific works; rather we have to turn to his unpublished papers and his speculative writings. Optics was one of the subjects to which Newton devoted himself in his early years of discovery, 1664–6. In his commonplace book "Questiones quaedam philosophicae" (Certain Philosophical Questions) from this period Newton recorded, under the entry "Of Colours," his thoughts on optical subjects such as the nature of color and the cause of reflection and refraction. In all of his speculations he consistently worked with a corpuscular theory, though he seemed to be trying out a whole range of ideas for the physical interactions between bodies and light corpuscles, or, as he then called them, "globuli."[3] He considered the reflection of the light corpuscles variously to occur from the aether within the pores of bodies, from loose particles within the pores, and from the particles of the body. He also could not decide whether the color of light rays was due to their speed alone or their speed and mass (momentum), and he carried out a calculation of the change of momentum of light corpuscles of different size after colliding with particles of different size.

In the midst of these notes Newton made one of his most fundamental discoveries, namely, that rays of different color are refracted different amounts.[4] While his notes show that he made an attempt to explain this discovery in terms of the mechanical parameters of the particles, he soon largely abandoned such speculations to carry out a further series of experiments and develop a theory of the nature of sunlight and color. Newton worked out the essential elements of his theory by 1666. He formulated it in substantial detail in his *Optical Lectures* delivered at Cambridge University between 1670 and 1672, but he did not publish the theory until February 1672, when his "New theory about light and colors" appeared in *Philosophical Transactions*. In order to see what role, if any, atomism or the corpuscular theory of light played in the development and formulation of that theory, I will briefly sketch its key elements.

Newton established his theory with a series of experiments with prisms that by the early eighteenth century became a model of an experimental science.[5] All of his optical investigations, which were gathered together in the *Opticks*, were founded on an extensive series of interlocking experiments, usually variants on a small number of fundamental experimental arrangements. His experiments play a variety of roles in his researches, for example determining the precise nature of the phenomenon and its causes, confirmation of them, and elimination of alternatives. Sometimes, as in the *Optical Lectures*, the large number of experiments with slight variations to establish various points may seem tedious, but Newton attempted to leave no room for objections.

The essential point of his theory of light and color is that sunlight or white light is a mixture of rays differing in degree of refrangibility and color. He found that, at the same angle of incidence, rays of different color are refracted different amounts and that there is a constant correspondence between color and degree of refrangibility; that is, the red rays are always least refracted, the violet most, and the intermediate colors intermediate amounts (Figure 7.1). Rays of each color apart obey Snell's law of refraction, but with a different index of refraction for each.

The color of a ray, he found, is immutable and cannot be changed by reflection, refraction, transmission, or any other means. In order

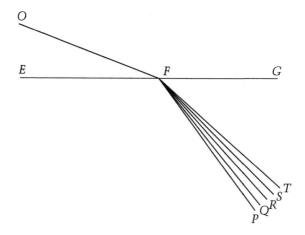

FIGURE 7.1 Refraction at the surface *EG* decomposes a ray of sunlight *OF* into rays of different degrees of refrangibility and color.

to develop his new theory further, he introduced his new concepts of simple and compound colors. Though these two sorts of color appear identical to the eye, simple or primary colors consist of rays of a single degree of refrangibility and compound ones are a mixture of rays of different refrangibility. They can always be distinguished by refraction, which separates or decomposes the rays of different refrangibility that make up compound colors while leaving simple colors unchanged.

The colors of the spectrum – red, yellow, green, blue, and violet – together with their intermediate gradations, are primary colors. "But," Newton announced, "the most surprising and wonderful composition was that of Whiteness . . . 'Tis ever compounded." This was the most revolutionary part of the theory, for sunlight had universally been considered to be simple, homogeneous, and pure, whereas colors were assumed to be some modification of sunlight. "Colours are not *Qualifications of Light*," Newton concluded, "derived from Refractions, or Reflections of natural Bodies (as 'tis generally believed,) but *Original* and *connate properties*."[6] Whenever colors appear, they are only separated from sunlight; they are never created. The theory of color was the foundation for all of Newton's subsequent optical research.

The fundamental idea underlying Newton's theory, that light rays always preserve their identity – color and degree of refrangibility – whether they are isolated or mixed together, or whatever processes they undergo, certainly seems to be most naturally understood in terms of light rays as atoms. Indeed, the three early and eminent critics of Newton's theory – Robert Hooke, Ignace Gaston Pardies, and Christiaan Huygens – perceived that Newton supported an atomic theory of light and were concerned that his color theory was incompatible with a wave theory. In replying to Hooke's accusation, Newton did not deny that he believed in the emission theory, but insisted that it played no part in his theory of color. He replied that,

> Had I intended any such Hypothesis I should somewhere have explained it. But I knew that the Properties wch I declared of light were in some measure capable of being explicated not onely by that, but by many other Mechanicall Hypotheses. And therefore I chose to decline them all, & speake of light in generall termes, considering it abstractedly as something or other propagated every way in streight lines from luminous bodies, without determining what that thing is.[7]

Newton's remarks illustrate many of the features of his optical science that I sketched in the introduction: its phenomenological formulation, which considers light "abstractedly" and describes properties and avoids hypotheses, and his clear declaration that the emission theory of light is an hypothesis.

To reassure his opponents that his theory does not depend on light corpuscles he then explained how the wave theory could be accommodated to it. If wave theorists considered sunlight to consist of a mixture of waves of various wavelengths ("depths or bignesses") each of which is refracted differently and excites a different color, then their theories would be compatible with his color theory without any need to adopt light corpuscles. After offering this pioneering suggestion, he then set out what would throughout his life be his principal objection to the wave theory, the violation of rectilinear propagation: "namely that the waves or vibrations of any fluid can like the rays of Light be propagated in streight lines, without a continuall & very extravagant spreading & bending every way into ye quiescent Medium where they are terminated by it. I am mistaken if there be not both *Experiment & Demonstration* to the contrary."[8] Of course, light rays conceived of as atoms would naturally move in a straight line when they were in a uniform medium.

It cannot be doubted that Newton fruitfully utilized the emission theory in devising his color theory or that it was easier to imagine his theory within a corpuscular theory where the light corpuscles retained their identity throughout, but there is insufficient evidence to conclude that it was an essential element in his thinking.[9]

EXPLAINING REFLECTION, REFRACTION,
AND DISPERSION

Newton most systematically utilized the emission theory of light in his quest to explain refraction and chromatic dispersion (the amount that the rays of different color are separated by refraction, angle *PFT* in Figure 7.1). His aim was to derive quantitative measures of these effects for different substances by a strict mechanical approach, assuming that light corpuscles are deflected at the interface of different media.

The law of reflection had been known since antiquity and had been relatively easy to explain in a corpuscular theory by a simple collision model in analogy to the reflection of a ball from a hard surface. In his earliest notes Newton used collisions between the corpuscles of light and bodies to explain both reflection and refraction. However, he soon recognized that when matter was assumed to have an atomic structure, this model broke down. On an atomic scale the surface of a reflecting body is not smooth like a mirror but very rough, with corpuscles separated by pores. Reflection could not occur from the corpuscles of the body because this would require the fortuitous arrangement of all the corpuscles, whatever the angle of incidence, such that the rays were reflected from the body at an angle equal to their angle of incidence. This required reflection to occur from the aether or, later in the *Opticks*, "some power of the Body which is evenly diffused all over its Surface," namely, a force.[10] These solutions were hypothetical, though the experimental and observational evidence that he marshaled in the *Opticks* against reflection actually occurring from the corpuscles of bodies was overwhelming.

Newton moved beyond such qualitative physical models in an essay "Of Refractions," probably written between 1666 and 1668, and calculated a table for the index of refraction of the extreme rays (red and violet) in various media passing into air from water, glass, and "christall." From an entry in the table, "The proportions of y^e *motions* of the Extreamely Heterogeneous Rays," it is clear that he is considering the motion of corpuscles.[11] It is possible to reconstruct his table on this assumption, especially since he utilized the same model in his *Optical Lectures*, though he there suppressed any mention of corpuscles or motions.[12] Newton assumes (Figure 7.2) that when a light ray *IX* in air enters glass at the boundary *AB* at grazing incidence (i.e., parallel to the refracting surface), rays of each color receive the same increase of velocity perpendicular to the refracting surface. If *XC, XD, XE* represent the parallel component of the motion of the violet, green, and red rays in air, which is unchanged after refraction, then *XP, XR,* and *XT* represent the refractions of these rays. Each has had the identical quantity of velocity perpendicular to the surface, *CP, DR, ET,* added to its parallel component of velocity. The refractions at any other medium may be readily determined by this model once the mean refraction *Xρ* is known. This model assumes that the projections parallel to the surface of all spectra are of equal length and that the same colors always occupy equal portions of it, that is, that chromatic dispersion is a property of light and not of the refracting media.

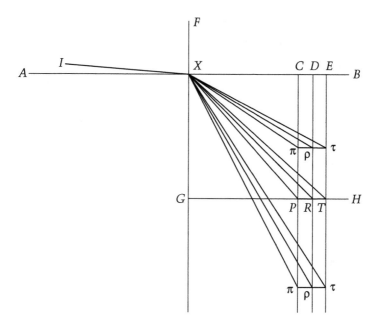

FIGURE 7.2 Newton's dispersion model from his *Optical Lectures*.

In his *Optical Lectures* Newton left the origin of this dispersion law totally mysterious, while conceding that "I have not yet derived the certainty of this proposition from experiments . . . meanwhile being content to assume it gratuitously."[13] For much of the *Optical Lectures* he pursued the implications of this law and derived numerous spurious properties of colored light, all with little or no concern with reality. Meanwhile, he had deduced another dispersion law on different grounds.[14] Newton was unable to choose between them on the limited number of measurements that he made. Had he examined a greater range of substances, he would have found that neither is true.[15] Newton abandoned his plans to publish the *Optical Lectures* for a number of reasons, but it is hard to believe that he did not recognize that his dispersion law was an hypothesis that went nowhere. Nevertheless, throughout his career he continued his quest to find a mathematico-mechanical explanation of refraction and dispersion, since the promised payoff was so high – namely, a mathematical foundation for a theory of color – and the models so tractable by the new science. He would return to it in the *Principia*.

Newton's dispersion model was inspired by Descartes's derivation of the law of refraction (Snell's law) in the *Dioptrique* (1637). The derivation was based on an analogy to a ball that has its velocity altered on crossing the boundary of two refracting media. In a mechanics that was based solely on contact action, it was difficult for Descartes to explain how the speed of the projectile was changed, especially when its speed increased in passing into an optically denser medium. In his "An hypothesis explaining the properties of light discoursed of in my severall Papers," which he sent to the Royal Society in December 1675, Newton explained how an aether could serve as the cause of refraction. He assumed that the aether permeates all space and is rarer in denser substances that have narrow pores, such as glass and water, than in free space such as air. When a light corpuscle moves through a region of aether of varying density, as near the boundary of two bodies, it is pressed by the denser aether towards the rarer, "& receivs a continuall impulse or ply from that side to recede towards the rarer, & so is accelerated if it move that way, or retarded if the contrary." If it is further assumed that the change of motion occurs perpendicular to the refracting surface, then Snell's law will follow.[16]

When Newton had developed the concept of force in the *Principia*, he concluded Book 1 with Section 14 on the analogy between the motion of corpuscles and light. By replacing the action of the aether in his earlier model of refraction by an intense short-range force between the corpuscles of the refracting body and light, he offered a powerful approach to optics and, more generally, to physics. In Figure 7.3 the force is assumed to act in the very small region between the refracting surfaces *Aa*, *Bb* and perpendicular to them. The motion of the particles in this field behaves exactly like that of a projectile "falling" in the Earth's gravitational field. Newton demonstrated that its path *HI* in the region of the force field is a parabola ("from what Galileo demonstrated"), and that the angles

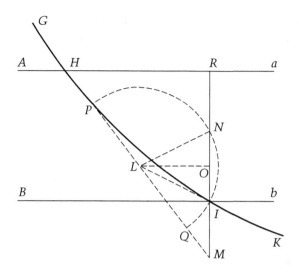

FIGURE 7.3 Newton's derivation of Snell's law of refraction in the
Principia, Book 1, Proposition 94.

of incidence *QMI* and refraction *MIK* obey Snell's law.[17] The derivation yielded an expression for the index of refraction *n* in terms of
mechanical parameters. If we let $f(\rho)$ be the force per unit mass, where
i and *r* are the angles of incidence and refraction, and ρ the distance
from the refracting surface, then Newton's result in analytic form is:

$$n = \frac{\sin i}{\sin r} = \sqrt{1 - \frac{2\varphi}{v^2}},$$

where *v* is the incident velocity and $\varphi = \int_{o}^{R} f(\rho)d\rho$.

By at least 1675 in the "Hypothesis" Newton had recognized
that if the change of motion of the light corpuscles occurs perpendicular to the refracting surface, then Snell's law will always follow.
Thus, the aim of this demonstration was not to derive Snell's law, but
rather to show that corpuscular optics could be brought into the realm
of the new mechanics and to explore its physical implications and,
in particular, to explain the cause of the different colors and refrangibility of light rays. The most natural explanation of the cause of
the different refrangibility of rays of different color according to this

model is that the velocity of the corpuscles varies. Four years after the publication of the *Principia*, Newton realized that this could be tested by observing the color of the eclipses of Jupiter's moons. When a satellite disappears behind the planet, the slowest color should be seen last, and when it reemerges, the fastest color should be seen first. In August 1691 Newton asked John Flamsteed if he had ever observed any color changes in eclipses of Jupiter's moons; the following February Flamsteed replied that he had not.[18] This was a serious blow to explaining refraction and dispersion by short-range forces, for it eliminated velocity as a cause of color and refraction. The model could be applied only with some radical assumptions that conflicted with the principles of terrestrial mechanics. Choosing mass instead of velocity would contradict the motion of projectiles, which is independent of their mass. Allowing the force to vary with the nature of the corpuscle and refracting substance would make the force a selective one like a chemical reaction, which was decidedly unlike any force in the new mechanics.[19] Newton's elegant demonstration based on his concept of short-range forces had to be restricted to monochromatic rays since color could not be explained with his new mechanics.

The model was not, however, without a notable success. In 1691 Newton used it to calculate the refraction of light rays entering the atmosphere and prepared a table of atmospheric refraction that was vastly superior to anything that then existed.[20] In a Scholium to this section of the *Principia* Newton also suggested that short-range forces acting on light corpuscles could explain diffraction. A few years later, as we shall see, he tried to carry out this program of applying short-range forces to diffraction before he hit a dead end. Newton concluded this Scholium by reminding his readers that he was proposing only an analogy and not arguing that light actually consists of corpuscles:

> [B]ecause of the analogy that exists between the propagation
> of rays of light and the motion of bodies, I have decided to
> subjoin the following propositions for optical uses [namely,

on geometrical optics], meanwhile not arguing at all about the nature of the rays (that is, whether they are bodies or not), but only determining the trajectories of bodies, which are very similar to the trajectories of rays.[21]

The two theorems that Newton added determined the surfaces, Cartesian ovals, that refracted light from a point to a point. Newton had in fact solved this problem more than fifteen years earlier in his *Optical Lectures* without the corpuscular theory of light.[22]

Newton attempted to provide a mechanical account of the actions of light corpuscles throughout his career, because it promised to unify optics as part of the mathematical science of mechanics and offered enough promising results to continue pursuing it. However, he did not limit himself to mechanical models in his speculations on the nature of light and always left his options open. For example, when he was writing the *Opticks* in the early 1690s, he briefly toyed with the idea that the force between light corpuscles and bodies might be selective like a chemical force: "If ye rays of light be bodies they are refracted by attraction [of] the parts of refracting bodies by some such principle as the parts of acids & alcalies rush towards one another & coalesce."[23] All these options remained hypothetical, since none of them had more than occasional experimental support.

AETHEREAL VIBRATIONS AND THE COLORS OF THIN FILMS

In his investigation of the colors of thin films, which he began while he was still developing his theory of color, Newton imaginatively expanded his corpuscular hypothesis to incorporate the aether and its interactions with light corpuscles in order to explain the periodicity of light. The essential feature of his aether is its vibrations, which reflect light corpuscles at condensations and transmit them at rarefactions. He was able to develop this qualitative, mechanical model into a relatively sophisticated mathematical one that agreed with his observations to a high degree of precision. Just as with the corpuscular model in his theory of color, Newton suppressed the vibrations in his formal accounts of his research on the colors of thin films. It was only in his speculative "Hypothesis" in 1675 that he chose to expound this model fully. Yet his aethereal vibrations differed in two significant ways from the light corpuscles that he used in his theory of color and refraction: (i) the vibrations were essential to the development of his explanation of the colors of thin films, and not just an heuristic; and (ii) he eventually elevated the vibrations – recast as "fits" in the *Opticks* – from an hypothesis to a confirmed scientific result, namely, the periodicity of light, whereas light corpuscles always remained hypothetical.

Newton learned about the colors of thin films from Hooke's account in the *Micrographia* (1665) of the colors seen in sheets of mica. Hooke had conjectured that the appearance of the colors was periodic, though he was unable to measure the thickness of such thin films in order to demonstrate this. Newton's key breakthrough was his insight that if he put a lens (which is really just a segment of a circle) on a flat plane, then by a principle from Euclidean geometry about tangents to circles he could readily determine the distance between them simply by measuring the circle's diameter. If (Figure 7.4) a convex lens *ABC* is placed on a glass plate *FBG* and illuminated and viewed from above, a set of concentric colored circles – now known as "Newton's rings" – produced by the thin film of air *ABCGBF* will be seen through the upper surface of the lens. The circles will form an alternating sequence of bright and dark colored rings, and their common center, the point of contact *B*, will be surrounded by a dark spot. If the diameter of any of these colored circles be denoted by *D*, the thickness of the air film producing that circle by *d*, and the radius of the lens by *R*, then $d = D^2/8R$ by Euclid's *Elements*, Book 3, Prop. 36.

Newton apparently had this insight while reading the *Micrographia* and quickly carried out a rough and ready test in 1666 and entered it in his essay "On Colours." To establish that the circles do appear at integral multiples of some definite thickness, he

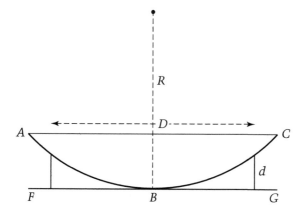

FIGURE 7.4 Newton's method for determining the thickness d of a thin film of air formed between a spherical lens and a plane.

simply had to measure the diameter of successive circles and see if their squares increased as the integers. For the first six circles he found that the thickness of the air between the lens and the plate increased by integral multiples of the thickness at the first ring, that is, as 1, 2, 3, 4, 5, 6. He then calculated that "y^e thickness of y^e aire for one circle was $\frac{1}{64000}$ inch, or 0,000015625. [wch is y^e space of a pulse of y^e vibrating medium.]."[24] His results, though quantitatively wide of the mark, as he later noted, were enough to demonstrate to his satisfaction that the appearance of the colors was a periodic phenomenon, and he succeeded in determining a measure of the periodicity. His method for determining the thickness of the film was in principle valid, and it later allowed him to develop a mathematical theory of the appearance of periodic colors. Moreover, from his remark in square brackets we can see that from the beginning of his research he was already utilizing vibrations in the aether as the physical cause of the rings.

Since one of Newton's immediate aims was to show that the colors of thin films are compatible with his recent discovery of the compound nature of sunlight, he would quite naturally have assumed that those colors in the incident sunlight that were not reflected by the film were transmitted. By examining the transmitted rings, he readily confirmed that the transmitted and reflected rings were complementary. And by examining the rings produced by rays of a single color, it was possible for him to understand their formation in white light when the colors are not separately visible because of their overlapping and mixing. Namely, he was able to see that at the same place some rays are reflected whereas the others are transmitted, and that rays of the same color are at some places reflected and at others transmitted. At this stage Newton had not fully elaborated these points, especially the second, which requires assigning a particular thickness or vibration length to each color.

Satisfied with this fundamental result and convinced that his method worked, Newton set it aside until he had fully worked out his theory of color. In about 1671 he undertook a serious investigation of the colors of thin films, and his record of this investigation, "Of ye coloured circles twixt two contiguous glasses," survives.[25] Newton's primary aim was to examine and describe Newton's rings quantitatively through a series of mathematical propositions and supporting measurements and observations; but he apparently also hoped to confirm his belief in the corpuscular constitution of light and its interactions with the aether. In the following year he wrote up his results for submission to the Royal Society, but because of the controversies over his theory of color he withheld it. When Newton once again felt sufficiently comfortable in revealing his works to the public, in 1675, he revised the "Observations" from 1672 and submitted it with a new companion piece, "An hypothesis explaining the properties of light," to the Royal Society.[26] The 1675 version of the "Observations," which also contains his theory of colored bodies, was later minimally revised to become the greater part of Book 2 of the Opticks. In the progression from the preliminary investigation in "Of Colours" through the "Observations" the variety of experiments carried out expanded significantly.

Before turning to Newton's model of corpuscles and aethereal vibrations, I will sketch his description of the conditions for the appearance of the rings and their periodicity. Although Newton did not write his results as an equation, they are equivalent to the following

$$d = \frac{D^2}{8R} = \frac{mI}{2}$$

where the first two terms of the equation express the Euclidean theorem cited above for the thickness of the film of air, and I is an interval such that for m odd the ring is a bright one and for m even a dark one. The interval I is the length of an aethereal vibration and, later, in the *Opticks* that of a fit.[27] However, in neither version of the "Observations" nor in the two parts of the *Opticks* does Newton introduce this physical interpretation, though it is apparent from "Of Colours" and "Of ye coloured circles" that he actually arrived at these results by working with the vibrations. He treats the interval solely as an experimentally determined property of the film – "the interval of the glasses, or thickness of the interjacent air, by which each colour was produced" – and not of light.[28] Although Newton did not calculate the value of the interval I in "Of ye coloured circles," in the "Observations" he adopted 1/80,000 of an inch – "to use a round number" – for the middle of white light (i.e., for a yellow).[29]

Only one other result from his investigation need concern us, his determination of the variation of the diameters of the rings when water was placed between the lenses. From his measurements he found that the diameters of the circles, and thus the thickness of the film, decrease in proportion to the index of refraction. Thus the earlier equation becomes

$$d = \frac{D^2}{8R} = \frac{mI}{2n}$$

where n is the index of refraction of the film. Newton was probably led to accept this as a general rule valid for any medium, because he was able to deduce it from his model of light particles and aethereal vibrations. In "Of y^e coloured circles" he had stated this law in

Proposition 4 in terms both of the index of refraction (the "subtilty" of the medium) and "yᵉ motions of yᵉ rays in that medium."[30] Like all the other propositions in "Of yᵉ coloured circles," no derivation was presented, but it is readily inferred. If the particles move faster in water in proportion to the increase of index of refraction (as the emission theory required), then they would more quickly reach the lower surface of the film and encounter the first aethereal condensation. The vibration length would then be shorter in the inverse proportion.

From his first effort at explaining the colors of thin films in "Of colours" Newton tried to derive their properties from the corpuscular theory. He set forth a law for the increase of the diameter of the colored circles as they are observed more obliquely to the surface as a proportion expressed in terms of the motion (momentum) and velocity of the incident light corpuscles. This passage is still not fully understood, but the proportion certainly does not agree with the phenomenon and Newton deleted it with a large ×.[31]

Newton later made one more attempt in "Of yᵉ coloured circles" to describe the variation of the circles in terms of the motion of the light corpuscles. The paper opens with six propositions to be confirmed in the subsequent observations. The properties of the circles are mathematically described, and many of them are interpreted in terms of the "motion," "force," and "percussion" of the corpuscles or rays, though no derivations are presented. The following two are typical:

> PROPOSITION 2. That they [i.e., the colored circles] swell by yᵉ obliquity of the eye: soe yᵗ the diameter of yᵉ same circle is as yᵉ [co]secants of yᵉ rays obliquity in yᵉ interjected filme of aire, or reciprocally as yᵉ sines of its obliquity; that is, reciprocally as yᵗ part of the motion of yᵉ ray in yᵉ said filme of aire wch is perpendicular to it, or reciprocally as yᵉ force it strikes yᵉ refracting surface wᵗʰall.

> PROPOSITION 3. And hence yᵉ spaces wᶜʰ yᵉ rays passe through twixt yᵉ circles in one position to the said spaces in another position are

as ye squares of ye said [co]secants or reciprocally as y^e [s]quares of ye sines, motion, or percussion.[32]

Both of these propositions were subsequently contradicted by the observations that follow in the manuscript. At this point Newton undoubtedly recognized that the phenomenon was simply not amenable to a description using corpuscles. In all his later quantitative work on the colors of thin films he worked only with the vibrations set up by the corpuscles. However, in his physical thinking the encounter of the corpuscles with the compressions and rarefactions of the vibrations played a fundamental role, as we saw in his deduction of the variation of the diameters of the rings with index of refraction.

Newton submitted "An hypothesis explaining the properties of light discoursed of in my severall Papers" to the Royal Society, because he hoped that revealing the hypotheses or physical models that underlay his phenomenological theories would make them more intelligible. He insisted, however, "that no man may confound this with my other discourses, or measure the certainty of one by the other."[33] The "Hypothesis," which Newton did not allow to be published, is his most openly speculative work and – unlike the thirty-one queries which roam over the scientific landscape – reveals how he used his speculations to explore a single scientific theory. It shows clearly how he was able to control and mathematize speculative mechanical models and arrive at experimentally confirmed laws.

The first two hypotheses assert that the aether exists and is capable of vibrating. This aether is almost without resistance, for it resists the motion of light particles only initially, at their emission from a luminous source, and at the boundaries of different bodies, where its density changes. When light particles are emitted, they are accelerated "by a Principle of motion . . . till the resistance of the Aethereal Medium equal the force of that principle." Henceforth the aether offers as little resistance as a vacuum. This is contrary to the principles of Galilean mechanics, and Newton knew it: "God who gave Animals self motion beyond our understanding is without doubt able to implant other principles of motion in bodies wch we may understand as little. Some would readily grant this may be a Spiritual one; yet a mechanical one might be showne, did not I think it better to passe it by."[34] Although the problem of the aether's resistance would vanish when Newton replaced the contact action of the aether with forces, this shows how he was able to elide physical difficulties in order to pursue the mathematical representation of a phenomenon. Newton emphasizes that he considers the particles to be light and not the vibrations, "I suppose Light is neither this Aether not its vibrating motion," which is simply an effect of light.[35]

The aether has a stiff surface that is responsible for the reflective power of bodies. The constant bombardment of light particles excites vibrations in the surface that are propagated throughout the aether. If a light corpuscle strikes the surface when it is compressed, it will be reflected because the surface is too stiff and dense to let the corpuscle pass; but if a corpuscle happens to strike the surface when it is expanded, it will pass through. This is the physical mechanism that Newton uses to introduce periodicity to a corpuscular theory of light. That he had failed in quantifying the relationship between the corpuscles and the magnitude of the excited vibrations did not hinder him from using it as the basis for describing the periodic colors of thin films. The corpuscles still play a fundamental, if less prominent, role in that one has to keep track of the location of both the corpuscles and the vibrations to determine the observed phenomenon.

The periodicity of Newton's rings is now readily explained (Figure 7.5). At the center A, where the glasses touch, the corpuscles will be transmitted because the aether in the two glasses is continuous, and a central dark spot will be seen. At a certain thickness BC ($= I/2$) away from the center the corpuscle will encounter the condensed part of the first overtaking vibration and be reflected, and a bright ring will be seen; at double that thickness DE, it will encounter the rarefied part of that wave and be transmitted, and a dark ring will be seen; at triple the thickness FG it will encounter the condensed part of the second wave and be reflected; and so on in arithmetic

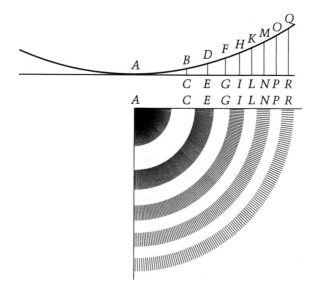

FIGURE 7.5 One quadrant of Newton's rings produced with light of a
single color.

progression, in agreement with observation. To extend this model
to white light, Newton only had to introduce the idea that the rays
or particles of different color vary in "magnitude, strength or vig-
our" and so excite vibrations of different size.[36] The red vibrations
are assumed to be larger than the violet ones and thus to form larger
circles, as is observed.

In the *Opticks* Newton transformed the aethereal vibrations
into the "fits of easy reflection and transmission," and raised them
to an established principle. The fits were now held to be a property
of light, and not of the aether. Merely purging the vibrations of their
hypothetical elements was insufficient ground for Newton to raise
them to a demonstrated truth. More evidence for the periodicity of
light was required. Newton found this in the new phenomenon
of the colors of thick plates, which he set forth in Book 2, Part 4 of
the *Opticks*. He was able to explain them with the same vibration
lengths *I* and mathematical-physical theory as for thin plates, and he

was able to predict the size of colored rings of thick plates with the same precision as those of thin films.[37] The existence of light corpuscles never achieved this level of generality or confirmation.

THE ATOMIC STRUCTURE OF MATTER
AND COLORED BODIES

If Newton always considered the existence of light corpuscles to be an hypothesis, he assumed the existence of corpuscles of matter in his explanation of the colors of natural bodies – the colors of all the things we see around us, like grass, cloth, and clouds. He was as certain of the existence of atoms as he was of the existence of God. Although the theory of colored bodies is an extension of his explanation of the colors of thin films and an integral part of his optical theory, it is as much a theory about the structure and properties of matter.

The essence of Newton's theory is the idea that the colors of bodies are produced in the same way as they are in thin films. He developed this theory in the early 1670s simultaneously with his account of the colors of thin films, and it forms the third part of the "Observations" of 1672 and 1675 and of Book 2 of the *Opticks*. In the more than thirty years between the time it was first developed and published in the *Opticks*, he abandoned the aether and developed the concepts of force and fits, but the theory of colored bodies scarcely changed.

Newton opens his theory by arguing that colored transparent and opaque bodies consist of transparent corpuscles and pores. The existence of aether in the pores is hypothetical, but he does not question the existence of corpuscles. His reasoning is straightforward: since reflection occurs only where there is a difference in optical density, for reflection to occur from the corpuscles composing bodies, the bodies must have pores that are of a different optical density from the corpuscles. Opacity is attributed to multiple reflections caused by the internal parts of the body. Newton's evidence for these claims comes almost entirely from macroscopic bodies, and it is then extended to the imperceptible corpuscles. For example, he argues that the "least parts" of bodies are transparent from observations that show that, when made sufficiently thin, bodies become transparent; and he argues that opacity arises from a multitude of internal reflections by observing that transparent substances like glass become opaque when they are shattered into tiny pieces. This can be a tricky mode of argument.[38]

The central proposition of Newton's theory establishes that: "The transparent parts of bodies, according to their several sizes, must reflect rays of one colour, and transmit those of another, on the same grounds, that thin plates or bubbles do reflect or transmit those rays: and this I take to be the ground of all their colours."[39] Newton demonstrates this by what would become his second Rule of Reasoning in the *Principia*, namely, that "the causes assigned to natural effects of the same kind must be, so far as possible, the same."[40] He presents evidence showing that the colors of natural bodies and thin plates are of the same kind, and therefore have the same cause. With this demonstrated, Newton estimated the size of the corpuscles composing various bodies from their color. He assumed that the corpuscles are of the same optical density as water or glass, "as by many circumstances is obvious to collect." In his account of the colors of thin films, Newton had prepared a table of the thicknesses of films of air, water, and glass that produce the various colors of each ring or order. For example, he deduced that the green of vegetation corresponds to the green in the third colored ring, and from his table he found that the corpuscles of vegetable matter are $17\frac{1}{2} \times 10^{-6}$ or about $1/60,000$ inch in diameter, assuming that they had the same density as glass.[41] The corpuscles of black and colorless transparent bodies must be less than any of those producing colors, just as the central spot in Newton's rings is colorless and reflects no light.

While it is not possible to see light corpuscles, Newton anticipated actually seeing the corpuscles of bodies. He explained that he deduced the sizes of the corpuscles "because it is not impossible, but that microscopes may at length be improved to the discovery of the corpuscles of bodies, on which their colours depend." If their magnification could be increased five or six hundred times, we might be able to see the largest corpuscles, and if "three or four thousand times, perhaps they might be discovered but those, which produce blackness."[42]

A closer examination of the corpuscles responsible for the color of bodies reveals some characteristic features of Newton's theory of matter. Despite their apparent smallness, the corpuscles are none the less macroscopic, compound bodies. If we consider a thin sheet of colorless glass that is of this green color, or even one so thin (approximately 1/160,000 inch) that it exhibits a yellow of the first order, it must contain within that thickness a number of the corpuscles that make it glass. A segment of that glass as wide as it is thick is a small, albeit very small, piece of glass with all the properties of glass. Green glass (or grass) will be composed of corpuscles of the same size as these fragments, each of which is composed of the corpuscles that compose colorless glass. Thus, the corpuscles' composing bodies already have a structure and are themselves composed of parts; they are not atoms.

"And hence we may understand," Newton wrote in the *Opticks*, "that Bodies are much more rare and porous than is commonly believed."[43] If we recall his explanation of the colors of thin films and the model expounded in the "Hypothesis," a thin film or plate consists primarily of aether with some interspersed solid parts. The only function he assigns to the parts, besides defining the pores, is to stop and absorb any light particles that collide with them. The vibrations of the aether cause rays of some colors to be reflected while allowing others to be transmitted. Since colored bodies are composed of corpuscles the thickness of which is the same as a thin film of that color, then those corpuscles must likewise primarily consist of aether and some parts. Consequently, for Newton matter actually consists mostly of aether or empty space.[44]

To explain how apparently solid matter could consist mostly of pores, Newton finally revealed his ideas on the hierarchical structure of matter in the Latin translation of the *Opticks*, though he had held this idea from almost the beginning of his scientific career. He had probably first encountered it in his reading of Boyle, and it was not an uncommon view in seventeenth-century (al)chemical works. If we imagine a body to consist of parts and pores and that the pores occupy as much space as the parts; and then imagine each of those parts to be similarly composed of much smaller pores and parts that occupy equal space; and then imagine this process to proceed until solid particles or atoms are reached, bodies would consist mostly of pores (Figure 7.6). A body, for example, with four such compositions would have fifteen times more pores than solid parts, and with ten compositions above one thousand times more pores than parts. It is important to recognize that Newton offered this particular structure only as a possibility, for "there are other ways of conceiving how Bodies may be exceeding porous. But what is really their inward Frame is not yet known to us."[45]

That Newton did not consider the existence of atoms to be an hypothesis becomes apparent from a preface that he drafted for the *Opticks* in 1703 but did not publish. He considered the possibility

FIGURE 7.6 A compound corpuscle of matter illustrating Newton's hierarchical conception of the structure of matter. A light ray *T* is transmitted through a corpuscle if it does not hit one of its parts.

of deducing all phenomena from just four "general suppositions" or "principles." These principles were not hypotheses, but derived by induction, for "there is no other way of doing any thing with certainty then by drawing conclusions from experiments & phaenomena untill you come at general Principles." The first three principles are the existence of God, the impenetrability of matter, and the law of gravitational attraction. In describing the fourth principle, he announced that he intended to derive the theory of the colors of natural bodies from his hierarchical, corpuscular theory of matter:

> A fourth Principle is that all sensible bodies are aggregated of particles laid together wth many interstices or pores between them . . . As by the third Principle we gave an account heretofore of ye motions of the Planets & of ye flux & reflux of ye sea, so by this Principle we shall in ye following treatise give an acc^t of ye permanent colours of natural bodies, nothing further being requisite for ye production of those colours then that ye coloured bodies abound with pellucid particles of a certain size & density. This is to be understood of the largest particles or particles of ye last composition. For as bodies are composed of these larger particles with larger pores between them so it is to be conceived that these larger particles are composed of smaller particles with smaller pores between them.[46]

The corpuscular theory of matter was thus for Newton not an hypothesis but a demonstrated principle established with as much certainty as the existence of God or the theory of gravitation. He cites two principal sorts of evidence in its support: various substances penetrate the pores of bodies, like water into vegetable and animal matter, and quicksilver into metals; and transparency, which shows that light passes through the pores of a great variety of bodies (which, to be sure, assumes an emission theory of light). The theory of colored bodies was not only founded on the corpuscularity of matter; it was a theory of matter attributing specific properties and arrangements to the corpuscles that cause the transparency or opacity and colors of bodies. For Newton to have considered corpuscularity to be an hypothesis or a working assumption would have been to violate one of his most fundamental methodological principles.

ATOMISM AND HYPOTHESES

When Newton was completing the *Opticks* in the early 1690s, he undertook an investigation of diffraction and wrote it up as the last book of the *Opticks*. He took his usual phenomenological approach and described his observations and experiments while eschewing physical hypotheses. His unpublished papers show that as in his other investigations he fully used the corpuscular theory of light and – as this was carried out post-*Principia* – short-range forces. He assumed that diffraction occurred when light corpuscles pass very close to an edge of a body and are deflected by the short-range forces of the corpuscles of the body. He was able to develop this model mathematically and carried out measurements and calculations with it. He even derived some laws governing diffraction. After completing the manuscript, however, he carried out an experiment that showed conclusively that this model with forces and corpuscles could not possibly be correct. Newton removed this book from the manuscript of the *Opticks* with the intention of carrying out more experiments and revising it. It turned out that he was near the end of his scientific career and never carried out any more optical experiments. Shortly before he published the *Opticks* in 1704, he simply revised the book and eliminated the results that depended on the corpuscle-force model.[47]

If Newton had hoped that his investigation of diffraction would finally vindicate the corpuscular nature of light, this episode would have disabused him of that hope. The corpuscular theory of light would remain an hypothesis. This was by no means the first time that his efforts to establish that theory were stymied. His dispersion models could not be experimentally confirmed; his attempt to deduce the properties of the colors of thin films from the motion of the light corpuscles failed; the derivation of refraction in *Principia* was elegant, but it encountered serious problems when eclipse tests failed to confirm the velocity interpretation. Newton had some successes, especially with his qualitative models, such as in his interpretation of his theory of color, and the cause of Newton's rings, and the calculation of atmospheric refraction. This is not a sterling record, and we can understand Newton's conviction that the corpuscular theory of light was an hypothesis. It certainly was fruitful, guiding him through a series of major investigations by suggesting experiments and new laws, but it had not been confirmed in any generality, as had the periodicity of light. Newton was not acting out of methodological fussiness in distinguishing certainties from conjectures, but rather exercising sound scientific judgment.

Because he judged the corpuscular theory of light to be an hypothesis, most of Newton's published writings on it are in the queries of the *Opticks*. Here Newton discusses such topics as the corpuscular theory and the cause of colors, fits, diffraction, and double refraction, and also devotes substantial attention to refuting rival wave or continuum theories of light, not to mention sensation, heat, and especially chemistry. In an anonymous review in 1715 Newton clearly described the hypothetical nature of the queries and explained why he set them apart from the rest of the *Opticks*. In the *Principia* and *Opticks*, he wrote, "Mr. Newton" adopted the "experimental philosophy," in which "Hypotheses have no place, unless as Conjectures or Questions proposed to be examined by Experiments. For this Reason Mr. Newton in his Optiques distinguished those things which were made certain by Experiments from those things which remained uncertain, and which he therefore proposed in the End of his Optiques in the Form of Queries."[48] In the eighteenth century the queries were widely interpreted as representing Newton's declared views on the topics discussed rather than as speculations. Our study of *Newton's* use of the corpuscular hypothesis in his optical investigations, that is, his actual scientific practice, shows how mistaken this view was.[49]

NOTES

1 Alan E. Shapiro (ed.), *The Optical Papers of Isaac Newton, Volume 1: The Optical Lectures, 1670–1672* (Cambridge: Cambridge University Press, 1984), p. 89.

2 Newton, "New Theory about Light and Color," in *The Correspondence of Isaac Newton,* ed. H. W. Turnbull, vol. 1 (Cambridge: Cambridge University Press, 1959), p. 100 (hereafter Newton, *Correspondence*).

3 J. E. McGuire and Martin Tamny (eds.), *Certain Philosophical Questions: Newton's Trinity Notebook* (Cambridge: Cambridge University Press, 1983), p. 432.

4 Newton did not think that light rays are colored; rather he held that they have a power or disposition to cause the perception of color: see the definition following Book 1, Part 2, Proposition 2, *Opticks: or, A Treatise of the Reflections, Refractions, Inflections and Colours of Light. Based on the Fourth Edition London, 1730* (New York: Dover Publications, 1952), pp. 124–5. None the less, to avoid cumbersome circumlocutions it is easier to refer to red rays, blue rays, and so on.

5 For the historical development of Newton's theory of color see Richard S. Westfall, "The Development of Newton's Theory of Color," *Isis* 53 (1962), 339–58; and A. Rupert Hall, *All Was Light: An Introduction to Newton's Opticks* (Oxford: Clarendon Press, 1993).

6 Newton, "New Theory," *Correspondence,* pp. 97, 98.

7 Newton to Oldenburg for Hooke, June 11, 1672, Newton, *Correspondence,* p. 174.

8 *Ibid.,* p. 175. Newton developed this objection in the *Principia,* Book 2, Propositions 41–2, and in the *Opticks,* Query 28.

9 See John Hendry, "Newton's Theory of Colour," *Centaurus* 23 (1980), 230–51.

10 *Opticks,* Book 2, Part 3, Proposition 8, p. 266.

11 See Newton, *Correspondence,* p. 103, n. 6, italics added; and D. T. Whiteside (ed.), *The Mathematical Papers of Isaac Newton,* 6 vols. (Cambridge: Cambridge University Press, 1967–81), vol. 1, pp. 559–74.

12 Newton, *Optical Lectures,* pp. 199–203; see also Zev Bechler, "Newton's Search for a Mechanistic Model of Colour Dispersion: A Suggested Interpretation," *Archive for History of Exact Sciences* 11 (1973), 1–37, esp. 3–6.

13 Newton, *Optical Papers,* p. 201.

14 What I have called his linear dispersion law, which is based on the musical division of the spectrum; Shapiro, "Newton's 'Achromatic' Dispersion Law: Theoretical Background and Experimental Evidence," *Archive for History of Exact Sciences* 21 (1979), 91–128. Newton adopted this law in the *Opticks*, Book 1, Part 2, Proposition 3, Expt. 7.

15 In the eighteenth century it was discovered that there is no law relating dispersion to mean refraction, and that dispersion is a property of matter and not, as Newton had assumed, of light.

16 Newton, *Correspondence*, p. 371.

17 Newton, *The Principia, Mathematical Principles of Natural Philosophy: A New Translation*, trans. I. Bernard Cohen and Anne Whitman (Berkeley, CA: University of California Press, 1999), Book 1, Part 1, Proposition 94, p. 622.

18 This episode is recounted in Alan E. Shapiro, *Fits, Passions, and Paroxysms: Physics, Method, and Chemistry and Newton's Theories of Colored Bodies and Fits of Easy Reflection* (Cambridge: Cambridge University Press, 1993), pp. 144–7. See also Bechler, "Newton's Search," p. 22; and Jean Eisenstaedt, "L'optique balistique newtonienne à l'épreuve des satellites de Jupiter," *Archive for History of Exact Sciences* 50 (1996), 117–56.

19 In fact, Newton did consider the possibility that the optical force behaved like a chemical force; see note 23 below.

20 See D. T. Whiteside (ed.), *Mathematical Papers of Isaac Newton*, vol. 6 (1974), pp. 422–5, 431–4; D. T. Whiteside, "Kepler, Newton and Flamsteed on Refraction through a 'regular aire': The Mathematical and the Practical," *Centaurus* 24 (1980), 288–315; and Bechler, "Newton's Search," pp. 23–6.

21 Newton, *Principia*, Book 1, Part 1, Proposition 96, Scholium, p. 626.

22 Newton, *Optical Papers*, pp. 417–19.

23 Shapiro, *Fits, Passions, and Paroxysms*, p. 142, n. 16.

24 McGuire and Tamny (eds.), *Certain Philosophical Questions*, pp. 476–8. The square brackets here are Newton's way of setting off his speculative or interpretive comments. For a comprehensive account of Newton's investigations of the colors of thin films and the theory of fits see Shapiro, *Fits, Passions, and Paroxysms*, chs. 2 and 4; and for a philosophical discussion, which historically is somewhat dated, Norwood Russell Hanson, "Waves, Particles, and Newton's 'Fits'," *Journal of the History of Ideas* 21 (1960), 370–91.

25 Richard S. Westfall, "Isaac Newton's Coloured Circles twixt Two Contiguous Glasses," *Archive for History of Exact Sciences* 2 (1965), 183–96.

26 Since Newton left what I call the "Observations" untitled, it has received various names. In I. Bernard Cohen (ed.), *Isaac Newton's Papers and Letters on Natural Philosophy and Related Documents* (Cambridge, MA: Harvard University Press, 1958) it was called "Newton's Second Paper on Color and Light"; and in Newton's *Correspondence*, "Discourse of Observations."

27 The thickness of air at which the first bright ring is produced is one half the physical vibration, or pulse length, that I call the interval I. All other rings, bright and dark, appear at integral multiples of this thickness. Newton's law for the appearance of rings is the same as that derived according to the modern wave theory except for a factor of 2, because his interval I turns out to be one half of the wavelength λ in the wave theory of light.

28 Observation 5, in Thomas Birch (ed.), *The History of the Royal Society of London, for Improving of Natural Knowledge, From Its First Rise*, 4 vols. (London, 1756–7; reprinted Brussels: Culture et Civilisation, 1968), vol. 3, p. 274; which is reprinted in Cohen, *Newton's Papers and Letters*.

29 Observation 6, Birch, *History*, vol. 3, p. 275. In the *Opticks* Newton redetermined this value and found it to be a whopping 11% smaller or 1/89,000, which is very close to the modern value; see Shapiro, *Fits, Passions, and Paroxysms*, pp. 167–9.

30 Westfall, "Newton's Coloured Circles," p. 191.

31 *Ibid.*, pp. 187–9.

32 *Ibid.*, p. 191.

33 Newton, *Correspondence*, p. 364.

34 *Ibid.*, p. 370.

35 *Ibid.*, p. 370.

36 *Ibid.*, p. 376.

37 See Shapiro, *Fits, Passions, and Paroxysms*, ch. 4.

38 For a discussion of Newton's theory of colored bodies and its mode of demonstration, see *Ibid.*, ch. 3.

39 Birch, *History*, vol. 3, p. 299.

40 Newton, *Principia*, p. 795.

41 Birch, *History*, vol. 3, p. 301.

42 *Ibid.*, p. 303.

43 Newton, *Opticks*, Book 2, Part 3, Proposition 8, p. 267. This passage was not in the "Observations."

44 In the *Opticks* the aether is replaced by empty space and the vibrations by fits, but Newton's conviction that bodies contain little ponderable matter did not change. On Newton's theory of matter and atomism, see McGuire, "Body and Void and Newton's *De mundi systemate*: Some New Sources," *Archive for History of Exact Sciences* 3 (1966), 206–48.

45 Newton, *Opticks*, Book 2, Part 3, Proposition 8, p. 269. This particular example of continual halving is merely an example. In his unpublished papers Newton has calculations with other divisions, such as seven parts of matter and six parts of pores; see Newton's draft of an addition to the *Principia*, Book 3, Proposition 6, in A. Rupert Hall and Marie Boas Hall (eds.), *The Unpublished Scientific Papers of Isaac Newton: A Selection from the Portsmouth Collection in the University Library, Cambridge* (Cambridge: Cambridge University Press, 1962), pp. 314, 317.

46 J. E. McGuire, "Newton's 'Principles of Philosophy': An Intended Preface for the 1704 *Opticks* and a Related Draft Fragment," *British Journal for the History of Science* 5 (1970), 178–86, at 183, 184.

47 For Newton's investigation of diffraction see Alan E. Shapiro, "Newton's Experiments on Diffraction and the Delayed Publication of the *Opticks*," in Jed Z. Buchwald and I. Bernard Cohen (eds.), *Isaac Newton's Natural Philosophy* (Cambridge, MA: MIT Press, 2001).

48 [Newton], "An Account of the Book Entituled *Commercium epistolicum*," *Philosophical Transactions* 29 (1714/15), 173–224, on 222.

49 On the reception of the queries in the eighteenth century see I. Bernard Cohen, *Franklin and Newton: An Inquiry into Speculative Newtonian Experimental Science and Franklin's Work in Electricity as an Example Thereof*, Memoirs of the American Philosophical Society 43 (Philadelphia: American Philosophical Society, 1956); Arnold Thackray, *Atoms and Powers: An Essay on Newtonian Matter-Theory and the Development of Chemistry* (Cambridge, MA: Harvard University Press, 1970); and Casper Hakfoort, *Optics in the Age of Euler: Conceptions of the Nature of Light, 1700–1795*, trans. Enid Perlin-West (Cambridge: Cambridge University Press, 1995).

8 Newton's metaphysics

Howard Stein

When one speaks of Newton's "metaphysics," it should be noted that the word itself was rarely used by Newton; further, that in point of general philosophical usage, that word has not had in our own time a fixed and well-established acceptation. For the purposes of the present study, a rather broad view will be adopted – suggested on the one hand by Newton's most influential near predecessor, the previous author of a book called *Principia Philosophiae*,[1] Descartes, according to whom metaphysics treats of the *principles of* [all] *knowledge*, and serves as *the root* of the "tree of philosophy" (whose "trunk" is physics, and whose "branches" are what we should call the "applied sciences");[2] and on the other by the author of the article "Metaphysics" in the eleventh edition of the *Encyclopaedia Britannica*, Thomas Case, who summarizes the concern of this discipline in the two questions: "1. What is the world of things we know? 2. How do we know it?"[3] Thus metaphysics will here be understood to be the discussion of the most general features, *both* of the constitution of the world, *and* of the principles of human inquiry into the nature of the world.

It will be useful for our discussion to put Newton's position in comparison with that of Descartes; for the work of the latter was both enormously influential in general – in the seventeenth century, and also, so far as metaphysics (in contrast to natural philosophy) is concerned, right down to the present day – and of great moment for Newton in particular.

On the methodological side, Descartes's program for a reformation of knowledge – for the establishment of a science that should be both secure in its theoretical attainments and of unexampled power in its aid to the control of the natural conditions of human life[4] – was based upon the demand that every item of knowledge be either *immediately clear and certain beyond a doubt*, or be *connected to*

321

such clear and certain foundations by clear and certain links. Both the guarantee of the truth of what the mind perceives clearly and with no possible doubt,[5] and the identification of the fundamental principles so perceived, come, according to Descartes, from metaphysics or "first philosophy"; therefore this science is indeed "first" in the order of investigation: as already remarked, metaphysics is the "root" of that tree of which physics – natural philosophy – is the "trunk."

It is important to emphasize that this radical position does *not* mean, as it has sometimes been taken to, that Descartes thinks all of physics can be *deduced* from principles known through "pure reason." In his program for the investigation of the natural world, *experiment* plays a central role. But to characterize that role, something must be said about the deliverances of Cartesian metaphysics on what one might call its "ontological" side. The chief points that are relevant here are these:

Descartes, like Aristotle and the scholastic tradition, takes "substance" to be the primary category of "being" in the world: the "things that are" are "substances." A central *innovation* by Descartes is his principle that there are two fundamentally distinct sorts of substance, each distinguished by its characteristic essential "attribute": "thinking things" (*res cogitantes*) or minds, and "extended things" (*res extensae*) or bodies. Bodies form the subject of natural philosophy. Since it is of the essence of these simply *to be extended*, the notion of empty space – extension void of body – is just contradictory; so the world is a plenum: body is everywhere. The only distinctions or diversities that are conceivable among bodies *as* extended things are diverse *motions*. Therefore, the processes of nature consist solely in the motions of bodies and the changes of those motions; and the foundations of physics consist in the principles that govern those motions and changes of motions. The task of natural philosophy, therefore, is to account for all natural phenomena by describing the motions and changes of motion in which they consist, and exhibiting those processes of motion and change of motion as consequences of such fundamental principles.

Now, at the very base of this conception lies a serious difficulty: namely, how to characterize "motion" *at all*, when it has been declared that there is nothing more to body than its attribute of *extension*. In his earliest treatise on physics, *The World*, Descartes takes for granted what one may call the "naive" conception of motion: it is "that by which bodies pass from one place to another and successively occupy all the spaces between"; and what *place* is, is a question not even raised. If, however, bodies are essentially just "what is extended," there is no real distinction between "bodies" and "spaces"; so one is baffled what to make of the notion of *the same body* successively occupying *different spaces*. It is in fact clear that in *The World* Descartes is taking it for granted that we possess – presumably as clear and innate ideas – two distinct notions of *identity* (over time) for "the extended": (1) identity of place, and (2) identity of body. On the other hand, since Descartes himself does not explicitly signalize this twofold notion of identity – which, as we shall see presently, Descartes drastically revises in his decisive work, the *Principles of Philosophy* – it seems impossible to acquit him of a *lack* of "clarity and distinctness" on this point.

The World was not published during Descartes's lifetime. In a letter to Mersenne of July 22, 1633, Descartes says that the treatise is nearly finished. In late November, he wrote again. This time he says that he had intended to give Mersenne a copy of the completed work as a New Year's present. But he has just learned that Galileo's *World System*[6] has been condemned in Rome; and the only reason he can think of for such a condemnation is the fact of its having "tried to establish that the earth moves" – on which issue, he continues: "I must admit that if the view is false, so too are the entire foundations of my philosophy, for it can be demonstrated from them quite clearly. And it is so closely interwoven in every part of my treatise that I could not remove it without rendering the whole work defective." Consequently, Descartes set the work aside, and – after a considerable lapse of time – proceeded to revise its foundations so far as the nature of motion is concerned.

The *Principles of Philosophy*, published in 1644, is repeatedly referred to by Descartes in his correspondence as a new version of "my *World*." In it he presents, in place of what has above been called the "naive" conception of motion, a new and sophisticated one. Motion "in the ordinary sense of the term" is still "the action by which a body travels from one place to another";[7] but *place* is now said to be an ambiguous, or relative, notion[8] and, "rightly taken," to be defined by *the surface of the surrounding body.*[9] Accordingly, "motion in the strict sense of the term" is defined as "the transfer of one piece of matter, or one body, from the vicinity of the other bodies which are in immediate contact with it, and which are regarded as being at rest, to the vicinity of other bodies." (This "sophisticated" – and semi-relativist[10] – conception raises new problems of its own, as Newton's critique will make plain.)

In any case, having posited the realm of "extended things" and its character as a plenum, Descartes appeals to the testimony of the senses (itself warranted as reliable on such an issue by God's necessarily non-deceptive character) to establish both that this realm *actually exists,*[11] and that *it is in continual and very diversified motion.*

The principles that govern such motion are on the other hand *not*, according to Descartes, to be ascertained by means of, or with any help from, empirical observation: these principles or rules he claims to infer directly from God's immutability – from the *constancy of his action* in preserving the world from moment to moment, which implies (a) the conservation of all states which are not necessarily altered through the postulated fact of motion, and (b) the conservation of the total "quantity of motion" itself (of all bodies together – not, of course, of each individually), from moment to moment. The actual rules stated by Descartes need not concern us (although it should be remarked that they – and the arguments he gives for them – are really bizarre); what is important is that these principles of motion constitute, in Descartes's system, the analogue of what the physicists of our own time call the "fundamental forces" of nature. Thus Descartes's position is (1) that a sound physics presupposes a (certain, indubitable) knowledge of the fundamental forces; (2) that such knowledge – prior to the rest of physics – is indeed possible; and (3) that this knowledge is possible through, and *only* through, unaided thought. In *this* sense, Descartes demands, and claims to have achieved, a "purely rational" physics – more accurately, a purely rational *foundation* for physics. In his *Rules for the Direction of the Mind*, this demand is expressed, in connection with the particular example of a problem in optics, as the stipulation that for a satisfactory solution of the problem it must be traced back to a knowledge of *what a natural power in general is* – "this last being the most absolute term in [the] whole series" (of conditions upon which the solution depends).[12]

The role of experiment in Cartesian method can now be briefly characterized as follows: by experiment we learn the existence of features of our natural environment, which pose *problems* for science. The *solution* of such problems, the very task of physics, consists in the tracing back of these observed natural phenomena to their *fundamental causes* – that is, the demonstration that the phenomena do (or would) result from the fundamental principles of physics, themselves derived as we have seen from first philosophy, when we have correctly attributed the phenomena we observe to underlying structures of Cartesian matter-in-motion: that is, when we have constructed (to use a later terminology) the appropriate *mechanical model* for each phenomenon. How *this* is to be done is certainly the most vexing problem in the interpretation of Descartes's scientific method; but what is most important in respect of Descartes's historical influence on later seventeenth-century investigators is the fact that the early attempts of Descartes to proceed *systematically and with certainty* from observed phenomena to their causes (i.e., to mechanical models that represent the *true* nature of the processes underlying the observed phenomena) were abandoned – perhaps even in some degree by Descartes himself – in favor of a far more tentative procedure of seeking for *likely* models, that might "save" or "satisfy" the phenomena, and whose correctness could be rendered at least *highly probable* by their success in doing so.[13] In short, the method of investigation of nature that eventually came to complement Cartesian metaphysics – a method that grew out of the *failure* of his more stringent original prescription – was that of attempting to *invent mechanical hypotheses* that would explain, with the help of "rational" deduction from the fundamental principles of motion, whatever was discovered by experiment.

One other feature of the intellectual environment in which Newton developed should be mentioned: namely, that many adherents to some variety of the "new philosophy" came to reject Descartes's identification of matter with whatever is extended, in favor of the classical view of *atomism*: that (a) there is void space as well as occupied space – the world is not a plenum; and (b) the ultimate parts of matter are "corpuscles" or "atoms": *rigid* and *indivisible* bodies.[14] Within this "revisionist" conception – also known as the "corpuscular philosophy" – it was still maintained as a fundamental tenet that all the processes of nature consist in the motions of bodies, and that all natural *changes* of motion are occasioned by direct actions of one body *pushing* on another.[15] The features common to this position and Descartes's constituted the framework of the celebrated "mechanical philosophy." It is *from* the mechanical philosophy that the metaphysics, as well as the natural philosophy, of Newton *departed*: that philosophy was Newton's point of departure; and he indeed departed from it, in profound ways.

Taking Descartes as the first point of comparison, a radical difference between his view of metaphysics and Newton's lies in the fact that for Newton metaphysics is *not* the "root" or foundation of natural philosophy – the "beginning of wisdom." His position may rather be said to agree with that of Aristotle – a conception symbolized by the fact that the followers of Aristotle placed his treatises on first philosophy "after the physical ones."[16] Aristotle, distinguishing between what is "first and better known to nature" and what is "first and better known to us," regards the most basic principles – "prior," *in nature*, to those of the special sciences – as *to be known* only *after* the special sciences themselves have been established. An indication that Newton thought similarly is to be seen in the fact that his chief published discussions of the metaphysics of nature, and of his views concerning God in relation to nature, occur *at the end* of his two great treatises: in the General Scholium to the *Mathematical Principles of Natural Philosophy*, and at the end of the long concluding Query 31 in Book 3 of the *Opticks*. In his discussion of theological matters in the General Scholium, Newton says of God: "We know him only by his most wise and excellent contrivances of things, and final causes"; and concludes that discussion with the words: "And thus much concerning God; to discourse of whom *from the appearances of things*, does certainly belong to Natural Philosophy" (emphasis added). In Query 31 of the *Opticks*, after a long review of the most diverse phenomena (chiefly of chemistry), he says: "*All these things being consider'd*, it seems probable to me, that God in the Beginning form'd Matter in solid, massy, hard, impenetrable, moveable Particles, [etc.]" (again, emphases added here). In both places the views put forward are thus expressed as, in point of knowledge, *a posteriori*; and in the latter place, the view is explicitly described as *probable* (this is a lower degree of confidence than Newton attaches to his principal results in physics).[17] Further, it is not only man's knowledge of God, among doctrines one would call metaphysical, that Newton describes as deriving from experience rather than from pure reason. In the preface to the first edition of the *Principia*, and in the third of the "Rules of Philosophizing" at the beginning of Book 3 of that work,[18] Newton expresses the opinion that (a) *geometry* is founded in experience (in, as he says, "mechanical practice"), and (b) so is *everything* we know about *bodies* (in particular, their "extension, hardness, impenetrability, mobility, and *vis inertiae*"). This is a matter to which we shall return later; for the present, let it suffice to note that these statements leave little scope, in Newton's view of knowledge, whether in "first philosophy" or in natural philosophy, for the *a priori* or purely rational.[19]

Let us now turn to the content of Newton's metaphysical doctrine: what, according to him, is the basic constitution of the world – what are its constituents, and how are they interconnected?

The question does not have an entirely straightforward answer. In order to see why – and in order to arrive at as clear as possible a picture of his mature doctrine – it will be useful to pay some attention to the apparent development of Newton's view over time.

It is clear from Newton's early notebooks[20] that he moved rapidly, in his student years, towards adherence to the general views in natural philosophy represented by Galileo and – in part – Descartes, in opposition to the scholastic ("peripatetic") teachings; and also that he quickly became critical of some of the basic tenets of Descartes. For example, in a very early manuscript Newton discusses with evident skepticism various scholastic views about projectile motion;[21] argues against Aristotle's rejection of a vacuum;[22] and notes without comment Descartes's definition of motion in the strict sense of the term: "Cartes defines motion . . . to be the Transplantation of one part of matter or one body from the vicinity of those bodys which immediately touch it and seem to rest, to the vicinity of others."[23] Not long afterwards, in what is clearly an attempt (somewhat awkward) to sketch a systematic theory of motion, Newton states his own definition: "When a Quantity is translated/passeth from one parte of Extension to another it is saide to move"[24] – a definition not very remarkable, but which clearly deviates from the conception advocated by Descartes in his *Principles*. The result was a position that fell within the framework of the corpuscular philosophy. It is important to note, in particular, that in the manuscript last cited Newton offers a general characterization of force, as follows: "Force is the pressure or crouding of one body upon another."[25]

We come now to a crucial document, and what the present commentator regards as a crucial turn in the character and depth of Newton's thought on fundamental issues. The document – first published in 1962, in the original Latin followed by an (unfortunately defective) English translation[26] – is of a curious kind. It is an incomplete and untitled draft of what was evidently intended to be a treatment of hydrostatics, and begins with the statement: "De gravitatione et aequipondio fluidorum et solidorum in fluidis scientiam duplici methodo tradere convenit"; that is: "It is fitting to treat the science of the gravitation [i.e., the "weighing down"] and equilibrium of fluids and of solids in fluids by a twofold method."[27] The opening phrase, "De gravitatione et aequipondio fluidorum," is the title by which the piece has come to be known.

What makes the fragment both odd and extraordinarily interesting is the fact that, after a brief introduction and four definitions, there occurs a digression into questions of metaphysics, taking up about two-thirds of the entire length of the manuscript; then the technical presentation resumes, with another fifteen definitions followed by two propositions (with five corollaries) – and breaks off. Thus in spite of the title under which it is known, and its evident original intent, the entire interest of the piece is as an essay in metaphysics – of a kind that is unique among Newton's writings.

The first four definitions are introduced and stated as follows:

DEFINITIONS. The terms quantity, duration, and space are too well known to be susceptible of definition by other words.

Def: 1. A place is a part of space that a thing fills adequately.
Def: 2. A body is that which fills a place.
Def: 3. Rest is remaining in the same place.
Def: 4. Motion is change of place.

Newton explains that in saying that a body *fills* (Latin: *implet*) a space, he means to imply "so fully occupies it as utterly to exclude other things of the same kind (other bodies) as if it were an impenetrable thing." Why, one may ask, "as if"? Does not a body's exclusion of other bodies mean that it *is* an "impenetrable thing"? The answer to this emerges later: Newton believes that *minds*, as well as bodies, have their definite places in space; and he believes that bodies and minds can occupy the same – or overlapping – places; so bodies are not absolutely impenetrable, but are so only to one another.

After a few further preliminary clarifications, Newton calls attention to the fact that in these definitions he has departed fundamentally from the doctrines of the Cartesians: both in *distinguishing* between space and bodies, and in that he has "determined motion with respect to the parts of that space, not with respect to the positions of the contiguous bodies." It is this remark that leads to the metaphysical digression, in which Newton is concerned, first, to refute the theory of space and motion of Descartes's *Principles of Philosophy*; then to present his own conception of the nature of space (and, with less elaboration, of time); finally – and with greatest originality – to present his conception of the nature of *body* – how it is related to, and how distinguished from, space.

The refutation of Descartes on place and motion has two main parts. In the first, Newton argues that Descartes himself, in the development of his physics in Parts 2 and 3 of his *Principles*, proceeds in a way that is inconsistent with his own theory of motion, and thus "seems to acknowledge" its inadequacy. Since we are not here primarily concerned with Descartes, one example may suffice – the one that is most directly connected with Newton's evidence for the view he himself favors. According to Descartes, the Earth – and, indeed, each of the planets – is, "if we are speaking properly and according to the truth of the matter" (Newton paraphrases the second phrase as "according to the philosophical sense"), *not moved*, but rather *at rest*; since each of these bodies, according to Descartes's theory of the planetary system, is carried around the sun by a material vortex: each planet, then, is at rest *relative to the bodies that immediately surround it*, and is therefore at rest in the "proper" sense of the word.[28] This is the basis of Descartes's claim that his view in the *Principles* is immune to the charge of attributing motion to the Earth. But, Newton points out, in his *dynamical theory* of the planetary system Descartes attributes to the planets *a tendency to recede from the Sun* on account of *their motion around it*. So in developing the principles *of his philosophy* Descartes makes use of a conception of motion that is *not* the one he puts forward as "proper and according to the truth of the matter"; or, again to use Newton's paraphrase, "according to the philosophical sense."[29]

In the second main part of his argument against the Cartesian theory of place and motion, Newton shows that the basic principles of the physics of motion generally agreed upon in his time cannot even be *formulated* within the conceptual framework provided by that Cartesian theory. (Thus we may say that whereas in the first part Newton had shown Descartes to be in contradiction with himself, in the second part he shows that the contradiction is not merely with some *special* features of *Cartesian* physics: rather, it is with the general principles – to which Descartes himself was a contributor – that underlie all of what for him is "modern" physics.) Again it will suffice here to consider one central point. Newton says it follows from Descartes's position "that a moving body has no determinate velocity and no definite line in which it moves. And," he adds, "what is much more, that the velocity of a body moving without resistance cannot be said to be uniform, nor the line straight in which its motion is accomplished." In other words, what is still called the "first law of motion" *does not make sense* in Cartesian terms. The reason is straightforward. In Descartes's terms, "according to the truth of the matter," a body's motion should be described in relation to bodies in immediate contact with it that "are regarded as at rest"; these define the body's "place" (at a given time). But over time, bodies that were once relatively at rest will in general no longer be so – they will disperse. Therefore, over time, these (former) "places" will no longer exist; so that it will be impossible to speak of the *distance a body has traveled* (the distance between its present and its former place) – and equally impossible to speak of the *path* it has followed (the ordered array of places through which it has passed).[30]

It is important to note that this argument of Newton's does not claim to rest on principles that are epistemologically *a priori*. When he claims that Descartes's concept of motion is *not the one needed for physics*, he is speaking of the *existing* physics of his time – and, indeed, of features of that physics that are *accepted* by the Cartesians as well as by himself. This physics had had some considerable success; therefore it was reasonable to make use of its principles, and to frame basic conceptions so as to be consistent with them. Objections should be considered out of order, unless (a) they are drawn from demonstrable inadequacies in the application of the accepted theory to phenomena, or (b) the objector has an alternative to offer that is at least as good as that theory, and better in respect of the points he objects to.[31]

Newton summarizes his results so far in the following words:

> It follows indubitably that Cartesian motion is not motion, for it has no velocity, no direction, and hence there is no space or distance traversed by it. So it is necessary that the determination of places, and hence of local motion, be referred to some immobile being, such as extension alone, or space in so far as it is seen to be truly distinct from body. And this the Cartesian Philosopher may the more willingly acknowledge, if only he notices that Descartes himself had an idea of extension as distinct from bodies, which he wished to distinguish from corporeal extension by calling it "generic." Art. 10, 12, & 18, part 2 Princip. And that the whirlings of the vortices, from which he deduced the force of the aether in receding from the centers (and therefore his whole mechanical Philosophy), are tacitly referred to this generic extension.

He turns, then, to the question of what, in his own view, the nature is of the "immobile being" – *space* or *extension* itself, distinguished from body – to which places and motions are to be referred. He raises three possibilities, arising out of the philosophical tradition, as to how he might "now be expected" to define extension: either as itself a kind of *substance*; or as a kind of *accident* (note: this was the standard philosophical term for an *attribute*: anything that can be "predicated" of a substance); or, third, as "*simply nothing*." The third alternative looks odd, but is undoubtedly meant to refer to the anti-establishment ancient tradition of atomism, in which the fundamental ontological contrast of atoms and the void was also expressed as that of "being" and "non-being." Newton repudiates all three answers, and offers instead something rather new: he says that extension "has a certain mode of existence of its own, which agrees neither with substances nor accidents." It is not substance for two reasons: (1) "because it subsists, not absolutely of itself, but as, so to speak, an emanative effect of God, and a certain affection of every being"; (2) because it is not something that *acts*.[32] The first point we must presently examine more closely. The second is of capital importance for Newton's view: he says that although philosophers do not traditionally define substance as "a being that can *act* upon something," they in fact all tacitly hold such a definition – "as for instance is plain from this, that they would easily concede extension to be a substance like a body if only it could move and could exercise the actions of a body; and on the other hand, they would by no means concede a body to be a substance if it neither could move nor arouse any sensation or perception in any mind whatever." To be noted well, then: (a) the definitive criterion of substantiality is the ability to act; (2) one of the characteristics that belongs to the essential nature of *bodies*, to their character as substances, is their ability to arouse perceptions in a mind. As to the question whether space is an "accident" – something that can exist only as "inhering in some subject" – Newton denies this emphatically: we can, he says, clearly conceive of empty space, and thus of "extension existing as it were without any subject"; "we believe it to exist wherever we imagine there to be no bodies; nor are we to believe that, if God were to annihilate some body, its extension [that is: the *place* of that body] would perish with it." This leads Newton to his repudiation of the third putative answer as well: so far is extension from being "nothing," that "it is more 'something' than is an accident, and rather approaches to the nature of substance" – namely, in that it needs no "subject" to "support" its existence. Further: "Of nothing, no Idea is given, nor has it any properties, but of extension we have an Idea the clearest of all, namely by abstracting the affections and properties of body so that there remains only the uniform and unlimited stretching out of space in length breadth and depth."[33]

But what does Newton mean by the statement quoted under (1) in the preceding paragraph, that space or extension "subsists . . . as, so to speak, an emanative effect of God, and a certain affection of every being"? There are a number of problems to be considered here: What are we to understand by an "emanative effect"? What *reason* can there be for Newton's statement that space is "an emanative effect of God"? And if space subsists as "a certain *affection*" – that is, a kind of "qualification" or "mode" – of every thing ("every being"), then how can it be said *not* to be an "accident," but more like substance than accident? Of these questions, the first is very much clarified by what Newton goes on to say, in six numbered articles in which he proposes "to show not only that [space] is something, but what it is."

The fourth of these articles begins as follows:

Space is an affection of a being just as a being. No being exists
or can exist that does not have relation in some way to space.
God is everywhere, created minds are somewhere, and a body
in the space that it fills; and whatever is neither everywhere
nor anywhere is not. And hence it follows that space is an
emanative effect of the first-existing being, for if I posit any being
whatever I posit space. And the like may be affirmed of Duration:
namely both are affections or attributes of a being in accordance
with which the quantity of the existence of any individual is
denominated, as to amplitude of presence and perseverance in
its being. So the quantity of the existence of God, according to
duration has been eternal, and according to the space in which
he is present, infinite; and the quantity of the existence of a
created thing, according to duration has been just so much as the
duration since its first existence, and according to the amplitude
of its presence, as much as the space in which it is.[34]

This paragraph sheds great light on the statement that extension is an emanative effect of God. In the first place, although Newton's theology is deeply involved in that statement, *and* in this paragraph, the latter actually makes it quite explicit that

Newton does *not* derive his "Idea" of space – its ontological status included – *from* his theology (as has often been claimed); for he tells us that if *anything* is posited, space is posited. He infers – quite simply – that space (in some sense) "results from" *the existence of anything*. Now, in Newton's theology – which in some respects was heterodox, but certainly not on this point – the "first-existing being" was God, whom he regards as the creator of the universe; so space (in some sense) "results from" the existence of God. However, what follows from Newton's "metaphysics of space" is precisely the weaker statement he makes in this paragraph: that space is (some kind of) effect of the existence of anything; and therefore, of the first-existing thing.

But what kind of effect? What is here meant by an "emanative effect"? Here some historical consideration of the word is helpful. In the philosophical tradition of the neo-Platonic school, there was a quite elaborate doctrine of "emanations" from the godhead; and Newton was closely acquainted with members of the group at Cambridge University known as the Cambridge Platonists – most closely with Henry More. However, the neo-Platonist doctrine, in its ancient version, was concerned with the origin of the universe; whereas – as we shall presently see – Newton in the piece we are discussing sharply distinguishes between space, as an emanative effect of God, and both bodies and minds, as God's "creations." As for the Cambridge doctrines, it is instructive that the *Oxford English Dictionary*, under "emanation," I.1, quotes the following from Henry More's philosophical *Poems*: "Man's soul's not by Creation . . . Wherefore let't be by emanation." On the one hand, this supports the view that "emanation," whatever it is, is to be *distinguished* from creation; on the other hand, it is clearly *not* in agreement with Newton's view – expressed in the very paragraph we are discussing – that human "souls" (or "minds") are *created*; indeed, that *all* minds save that of God are so[35] (for Newton writes, clearly intending a complete survey of all the kinds of "being" [or "beings"]: "God is everywhere, *created minds* are somewhere, and a body is in the space it fills"). So the grounds for thinking that Newton's theory of emanation is neo-Platonic, or "Cambridge Platonic," are very weak. On the other hand, the OED in the same entry, I.1.c, gives the definition (noted as obsolete): "Logical development from premises; inference" – with an illustrative quotation from the *Logic* of T. Spencer (1628); and gives in II.3.b the related definition (*not* designated obsolete): "A necessary consequence or result" – with two illustrative quotations, the first from Richard Steele in *The Tatler* (1710), the other the following phrase, from John Stuart Mill's *Utilitarianism* (1861): "A direct emanation from the first principles of morals."

But this sense of the word – simply *a necessary consequence*, with no connotation of "causal efficacy" or "action" – *exactly* fits the rest of what Newton says; indeed, this meaning might have been inferred directly from Newton's words: "[S]pace is an emanative effect of the first-existing being, for *if I posit any being whatever I posit space*": the second clause tells us precisely what the first clause *means*.

For our second question – what reason Newton thought there was that justified this view of space as an "emanative effect" of whatever exists – it is to be noted that he describes the proposition as *inferred from* a preceding one: that "no being exists or can exist that does not have relation in some way to space"; and this in turn he founds upon an enumeration of all the kinds of "beings" he takes actually to exist, and their several relations to space. In the light of this, and of the fact that there is no suggestion – here or indeed anywhere the present writer knows of in Newton's writings – of an *a priori* epistemological ground for any item of knowledge, it appears reasonable to conclude that the reason in question is an empirical one: our experience affords no grounds for a conception of real existents – beings capable of acting – that do not have an appropriate relation to space.

It might well be asked how *experience* could be said to ground Newton's assertion that "God is everywhere." But first – although the claim that God is everywhere *present in space* was a controversial one, and even somewhat dangerous to advocate – Newton thought the doctrine of the *ubiquity* or *omnipresence* of God amply founded in the tradition of revealed truth; and second, he clearly thought experience shows that *minds* can act only *where they are*;[36] so the doctrine of God's omnipotence (likewise founded in revelation) itself entails his omnipresence. As to the possible outright heretical implications of the doctrine, Newton guards himself in the following passage (the second paragraph of the same fourth article as quoted above), which is of interest in its own right for its further elaboration of Newton's view both of space and of time ("duration"):

> Moreover lest anyone imagine from this that God is extended and made of divisible parts like a body: it should be known that spaces themselves are not actually divisible, and furthermore that each being has its own proper mode of presence in spaces. Thus, the relation to space of duration is far different from that of body. For we do not ascribe different durations to the different parts of space, but say that they all endure together. A moment of the duration of Rome and of London is the same, as is one of the Earth and of [any] star in the entire heavens. And just as we understand any one moment of duration to be thus diffused through all spaces, in its own way, without any conception of its parts: so it is no more contradictory that a Mind can likewise, in its own way, be diffused through space without any conception of parts.

But this in turn calls for commentary. What does Newton intend by the statement that "spaces themselves are not actually divisible"? He certainly does *not* mean that, for instance, a line-segment is not, in the ordinary sense, "divisible into two equal parts." That space has parts is implied by Newton's definition of *place*, quoted earlier; and the first numbered article in the series enumerating the properties of extension begins with the assertion: "Space can be distinguished everywhere into parts whose common boundaries we are accustomed to call surfaces; and these surfaces can be distinguished everywhere into parts, whose common boundaries we call lines; and these lines in turn can be distinguished everywhere into parts that we call points." Newton means, rather, that this "distinguishing into parts" is not an "*actual*" division: the parts of space are not "divisible," or *separable* from one another, as the parts of a(n ordinary) body[37] are. So we must say: *spaces* have *parts*, but are not "actually divisible"; God, furthermore, who is present everywhere in space, *not only* is indivisible, but *does not have parts at all*: this is what the analogy of "durations" emphasizes: moments of duration, too, are present throughout space, but do not have spatial – or any – parts; just as, again, on Newton's conception of ("absolute") space, *points of space* are present throughout time, but do not have temporal – or any – parts.

Finally (in this series of questions), as to the sense in which space can be said to subsist "as a certain affection" of every being, and yet not to be an "accident," but "more like substance than accident," Newton has already given a part of the answer explicitly: space is not an accident because *we can conceive it to exist without any subject*. But, says the objector, can we – on Newton's view – conceive space without *any* subject of which it is an "affection"? Can we conceive space without God? We face again the question of the relation of Newton's conception of space to his theology, on which a view contrary to the one that has perhaps most often been held has already been stated above. But there is in fact explicit testimony from Newton himself. Later in the piece under discussion, in reverting to his objections to the Cartesian identification of body with extension, Newton says the following (emphases added here):

> If we say with Descartes that extension is body, do we not
> manifestly offer a path to Atheism, both because extension is
> not a creature but has existed eternally, *and because we have an*
> *absolute Idea of it without any relationship to God*, and therefore
> *we are able to conceive of it as existent while feigning the non-*
> *existence of God?*[38]

That, surely, is decisive! Space, the existence of space, or extension, *follows from* that of anything whatsoever; but extension does not require a subject in which it "inheres," as a property; and it can be conceived as existent without presupposing any *particular* thing,

God included. On the other hand, it is an "affection of every being." We can perhaps understand this better with the help of another article in Newton's enumeration of the fundamental characteristics of space – the third article:

> The parts of space are immobile . . . For just as the parts of duration are individuated by their order, so that (for example) if yesterday could change places with today and become the later, it would lose its individuality and be no longer yesterday but today: So the parts of space are individuated by their positions, so that if any two could interchange their positions, they would at the same time interchange their individualities, and each be converted numerically into the other. The parts of duration and of space are understood to be the same as they truly are solely by their order and mutual positions; nor have they any other principle of individuation beyond that order and those positions – which therefore cannot change.

This can be taken, in rather modern terms, as saying that space is a *structure*, or "relational system," which can be conceived of independently of anything else; its constituents are individuated just by *their relations to one another, as elements of this relational system.* But the system, or its constitutive elements, none the less can *and must* "affect," in the appropriate way, all things that exist: all existing things have spatial and temporal relations to one another by virtue of their having, each one of them, the appropriate kind of relation to the parts of space and of duration (again: *God is everywhere, created minds are somewhere, and a body is in the place it fills* – but, for the last two, we must add: *at each moment of its own duration*).

Having presented his view of the ontological status of space, Newton turns to the corresponding question about *bodies*. Before describing his answer, a comment about a rather curious historical connection seems in order – both for its intrinsic interest, and because it bears upon the question whether the views of this manuscript fragment can be taken to be those held by Newton in his mature years (opinion being divided as to the date of the fragment itself).[39]

In Locke's *Essay Concerning Human Understanding* (Book 4, ch. 10, § 18) the following remark appears (but not in the first edition – 1690; it was introduced only in the second edition – 1694): "possibly, if we would emancipate ourselves from vulgar Notions . . . we might be able to aim at some dim and seeming conception how Matter might at first be made, and begin to exist by the power of [the] eternal first being"; but he immediately adds that to discuss this "would perhaps lead us too far from the Notions, on which the Philosophy now in the World is built," and so excuses himself from saying more about it. In his commentary on Locke's *Essay*, his *New Essays on Human Understanding* (in dialogue form), Leibniz's representative, Theophilus, responding to Philalethes, who presents the thoughts expressed by Locke, says of this: "You have given me real pleasure, sir, by recounting something of a profound thought of your able author, which his overscrupulous caution has stopped him from offering in its entirety. It would be a great pity if he suppressed it and, having brought us to a certain point with our mouths watering, left us standing there. I assure you, sir, that I believe there is something fine and important hidden under this rather enigmatic passage."[40] The second French edition of the *Essay* (1729 – after the deaths of all three concerned: Locke, who died in 1704; Leibniz, 1716; Newton, 1727) contained a note to this passage by the translator, Pierre Coste: "Here Mr. Locke excites our curiosity, without being inclined to satisfy it. Many persons, imagining that he must have communicated to me this mode of explaining the creation of matter" – Coste had served as Locke's amanuensis for several years, and had translated the work under Locke's supervision – "requested, when my translation first appeared, that I would inform them what it was; but I was obliged to confess that Mr. Locke had not made even me a partner in the secret. At length, long after his [Locke's] death, Sir Isaac Newton, to whom I was accidentally speaking of this part of Mr. Locke's book, discovered to me the whole mystery. He told me, smiling, that he himself had suggested to Mr. Locke this way of explaining the creation of matter; and that the thought had struck him one day, when this question chanced to come up in a conversation between himself, Mr. Locke, and the late Earl of Pembroke. He thus described to them his hypothesis:" – and there follows a brief statement of the same account of the creation of matter that appears in the present chapter.[41] It is clear, then, that the account we are about to consider, whenever it may have been written down, was in its general lines communicated by Newton to Locke at some time in the early 1690s. It is clear, also, that this account was considered by Locke to be a very radical philosophical departure – and that Leibniz thought that it must indeed be so, and was very eager to learn what it was.[42]

As all this has intimated, Newton's analysis of the fundamental nature of bodies takes the form of a discussion of *how bodies might have been created*. In one respect, this is of secondary importance; for one can reasonably see it as merely a vivid way of focusing attention on what bodies "fundamentally are" – to "create a body somewhere," God has to bring it to pass that *whatever* bodies "fundamentally *are*," by hypothesis not there before, *comes to be* there (for Newton is not going to tell us "how" God does this in the sense of analyzing his *power* to bring such-and-such to pass: this power he takes for granted, since he takes God to be omnipotent; he is going to tell us "how" a body is created, rather, in the sense of *exactly what has to be brought about* to achieve such a creation). To put the point another way: what "God creates" is simply "the fundamental constitution of corporeal nature"; we might leave God out of the story, and take it to be a description, or analysis, *of* the fundamental constitution of corporeal nature.

In another respect, however, there is something very important that this strategy of Newton implies – something that can be seen from the words with which this part of his discussion is introduced:

> Extension having been described, for the other part the nature
> of bodies remains to be explained. Of this, however, since it
> exists not necessarily but by the divine will, the explanation
> will be more uncertain, because it is not at all given to us to
> know the limits of the divine power – namely, whether matter

could have been created in one way only, or whether there are several ways by which other beings similar to bodies might have been produced. And although it hardly seems credible that God could create beings like bodies, that should perform all their actions and exhibit all their phaenomena, and yet in essential and metaphysical constitution should not be bodies: since nevertheless I do not have a clear and distinct perception of this matter, I should not dare to affirm the contrary, and accordingly I will not say positively what the nature of bodies is, but rather shall describe a certain kind of beings, in every way similar to bodies, whose creation we cannot fail to acknowledge to be within the power of God – and which thus we cannot certainly declare not to be bodies.

So Newton distinguishes between the epistemological status of his theory of space – which he has presented as something he regards as exceptionally clear in conception (or "Idea"), and as entirely convincing in its doctrine – and that of his theory of body, which is fundamentally *conjectural*, because bodies, unlike space, are *effects of God's will*;[43] and it is not given to us to know all the ways in which the exercise of that will might accomplish given observable effects. This, again, is a proposition that can be paraphrased non-theologically: "Our conception of the fundamental constitution of nature – that is, of the *substantial world* of *things capable of acting* – is a conception of how every phenomenon we observe *could be* effected; but since we have no epistemologically *a priori* knowledge of this, the possibility always remains that those phenomena *are* effected in some (perhaps even very) *different* way."

Newton's creation story starts by supposing that a corporeal world already exists; what, Newton asks, would God have to do to create a new body – or, rather, what *might* he do that would create a new entity *indistinguishable from the bodies we know*?

First, he says, "let us feign empty spaces scattered through the world, some one of which, defined by certain limits, by the divine power becomes impervious to bodies": bodies simply cannot enter this region, but are, let us say, constrained to bounce back from its boundary. Such a "region of impenetrability" will be like a body, except that (so far as we have gone) it will be immobile. Second, then, we may "feign that impenetrability not conserved always in the same part of space, but able to be transferred hither and thither according to certain laws, yet so that the quantity and shape of that impenetrable space are not changed."[44]

This is not the last step, but it is worth pausing over. First, one may ask whether, according to Newton, it is in some way a "conceptual necessity" that bodies be impenetrable. The answer to this question – at least, at the stage of the composition of the third of the "Rules of Philosophizing" in Book 3 of the *Principia*[45] – is unequivocally negative; for in the discussion of that Rule, Newton says: "That all bodies are impenetrable, we gather, not from reason, but from sensation." Second, we should note that in conferring mobility upon the new (quasi-)bodies – that is, in making the property of impenetrability "able to be transferred hither and thither" – it is essential that this "transfer" be regulated by suitable *laws*. Of these, all Newton specifies is that the transfer *preserve the size and shape* of the regions of impenetrability; this, in effect, gives to the new (quasi-)*particles* the distinguishing property of (rigid) *atoms*. It is, however, clear that the motion of these new things is to be governed by the "first law of motion": namely, that, in the absence of encounters with bodies (or with other "quasi-bodies"), a quasi-particle is propagated through space with uniform speed in a straight line (understood to include the case of *rest* – that is, no "transfer" at all); and that when encounters do occur, they are to be governed by the ordinary laws of impact (which, in turn, implies that each quasi-particle is characterized by a parameter corresponding – in "ordinary" particles – to their *mass*).

So far, we have a constitution for (quasi-)corporeal nature that looks very much like just what is needed for bodies, according to the corpuscular philosophy: rigid and indivisible ultimate particles, interacting only by impact – "*by impulse*, and nothing else," as Locke says: "It being impossible to conceive, that Body should operate on what it does not touch . . . or when it does touch, operate any other way than by Motion."[46] Yet Locke *also* tells us the following:

> Another *Idea* we have of Body, is the power of *communication of Motion by impulse*; and of our Souls, the power of *exciting of Motion by Thought*. These *Ideas*, the one of Body, the other of our Minds, every days experience clearly furnishes us with: But if here again we enquire how this is done, we *are equally in the dark*. For in the communication of Motion by impulse, wherein as much Motion is lost to one Body, as is got to the other, which is the ordinariest case, we can have no other conception, but of the passing of Motion out of one Body into another; which, I think, is as obscure and unconceivable, as how our Minds move or stop our Bodies by Thought; which every moment we find they do . . . I think, we have as many, and as clear *Ideas* belonging to Spirit, as we have belonging to Body, the Substance of each being equally unknown to us; and the *Idea* of Thinking in Spirit, as clear as of Extension in Body; and the communication of Motion by Thought, which we attribute to Spirit, is as evident, as that by impulse, which we ascribe to Body. Constant Experience makes us sensible of both of these, though our narrow Understandings can comprehend neither. For when the Mind would look beyond those original *Ideas* we have from Sensation or Reflection, and penetrate into their Causes, and manner of production, we find still it discovers nothing but its own short-sightedness.[47]

In other words, according to Locke, the only way in which we can conceive bodies to act, is a way in which we *cannot* conceive bodies to act: it is a way that is *"obscure and unconceivable,"* and is beyond the capacity of "our narrow Understandings [to] comprehend."

Locke is here wrestling with a fundamental incoherence in the philosophical foundations of the corpuscular philosophy; the fact that he appears to contradict himself – that he *does* contradict himself! – is testimony to the basic honesty of his mind, and to his penetrating insight. For although he accepts the corpuscular philosophy as the most plausible hypothesis about nature, and accepts the widespread view that it represents the only basis on which we can *hope* to understand natural processes, he also sees (sometimes, at least) that the underpinnings of that philosophy are *not* "clear and distinct principles" such as the Cartesians thought they had, but principles whose *own* grounds are *obscure*. Partly for this reason, Locke draws very pessimistic conclusions concerning the possible advance of science; indeed, he thinks that a truly *systematic* knowledge of nature is beyond human capacity.[48]

Newton sees the very same impossibility of a "transparent" system of fundamental principles; but he faces it squarely, and it does not create for him a desperate predicament: the *fundamental* constitution of nature is simply not (directly) open to us; but we can nevertheless form perfectly clear conceptions of *what structures may underlie phenomena*; not *why* they do – nor even for certain *that* they do – but what structures *would suffice* as a basis for the constitution of the world we know, at the stage of knowledge we have reached. And what allows us to do this is a clear understanding of the *lawful relationships* that we have so far managed to discover among phenomena. Thus, first of all, we have "of extension an Idea the clearest of all." How did we obtain it? From experience – and, of course, *thought* (in particular, thought of the kind we call "mathematical") *based* upon experience: "geometry is founded in mechanical practice"; and "it is the glory of geometry that from [a] few principles, *brought from* without, it is able to produce so many things."[49] And in the second place, we have a perfectly clear conception of those attributes of bodies that the mechanical, corpuscular, philosophy has conceived as fundamental, including the laws governing the interactions of those bodies: the laws of impact. *That means*, in Newton's view, that we have a sufficiently clear conception of *what bodies are* if the mechanical philosophy is true.

To appreciate the clarifying power of this analysis, it is helpful to describe another perplexity in which Locke finds himself.

In agreement with *both* the Aristotelian tradition *and* the Cartesian philosophy, Locke calls all "real existents" *substances*; and he asks what goes to make up our "*Ideas* of Substances."[50] His general answer is exemplified by one of his favorite examples: "the greatest part of the *Ideas*, that make up our complex *Idea* of *Gold*, are Yellowness, great Weight, Ductility, Fusibility, and Solubility in *Aqua Regia, etc.* all united together in an unknown *Substratum*."[51] This "unknown substratum," the "idea" of which makes a part of *all* our ideas of particular substances according to Locke, he calls, simply, "substance" (or "substance in general"). At the same time, however, Locke tells us that we have of substance no idea at all:

> I confess, there is [an] *Idea*, which would be of general use for
> Mankind to have . . . and that is the *Idea of Substance*, which
> we neither have, nor can have, by *Sensation* or *Reflection* . . .
> We have no such *clear Idea* at all, and therefore signify nothing
> by the word *Substance*, but only an uncertain supposition of
> we know not what . . . which we take to be the *substratum*, or
> support, of those *Ideas* we do know.[52]

There has been much discussion of the precise nature of Locke's dilemma here – that of holding both that we *require* a certain "idea," and that we do not *have* it. If we "do not have" the *idea*, how can it be an idea at all – how can we know what it *is* that we need but do not have? The following is a passage that helps to clarify the issue: "[I]n Substances, besides the several distinct simple *Ideas* that make them up, the confused one of Substance, or of an unknown Support and Cause of their Union, is always a part."[53] What this suggests we "need" is an *answer* to the twofold question: "(1) *In what* do the qualities we attribute to a substance *exist together*? (2) What is the *cause* of their existing thus together?"

Newton's analysis may be said to separate these two questions. To the first, his answer is that the qualities that fundamentally constitute a body can be coherently and clearly conceived to *exist in*, or to have as their "logical subject" or the metaphysical "support" of their "being," simply *extension*: regions or "parts" of space. In the language of later natural philosophy, the distribution of bodies through space can be described as a kind of *field* on space: the "field of impenetrability," characterized, at each point of space, by the simple indication "filled" or "not filled."[54] Newton's own comment upon this part of the question (in his summing-up, later in the piece) is illuminating, both of his own view and for the possible light it sheds on the perplexity Locke felt – since Newton (quite independently of Locke's thoughts on the matter) names a perplexity that his account *removes*:

> [F]or the existence of these beings [– that is, the beings whose creation by God he has imagined –] it is unnecessary to feign some unintelligible substance to be given in which as in a subject a substantial form should inhere: extension and an act of the divine will suffice. Extension takes the place of the substantial subject in which the form of the body is conserved by the divine will; and that effect of the divine will is the form or formal reason of the body, denominating as a body every region of space in which it is produced.

Newton goes on to assimilate the "unintelligible substance," the need for which he claims he has obviated, to the "materia prima" posited by the scholastics:[55] the notion of a totally "formless" ultimate "support" of all forms or attributes; and says the following (Articles (3) and (4) of his summary):

> (3) Between extension and the form imposed upon it there is almost the same Analogy that the Aristotelians posit between the *materia prima* and substantial forms, namely when they say that the same matter is capable of assuming all forms, and borrows the denomination of numerical body from its form. For thus I suppose that any form may be transferred through any space, and everywhere denominate the same body.

> (4) They differ, however, in that extension . . . has more reality than *materia prima*, and also in that it is intelligible, as likewise

is the form that I have assigned to bodies. For if there is any
difficulty in this conception, it is not in the form that God
imparts to space, but in the way in which he imparts it. But that
is not to be taken for a difficulty, since the same [point] occurs
with respect to the way we move our limbs, and nevertheless
we do believe that we can move them. If that way were known
to us, by parity of reason we should also know how God can
move bodies, and expel them from a certain space terminated
in a given figure, and prevent the expelled bodies or any others
from entering into it again – that is, cause that space to be
impenetrable and to assume the form of a body.

Here, then, we have Newton's answer (in effect) to the second
part of the above-posed twofold Lockean question: what *causes* the
coexistence of the basic qualities of his "new" or "quasi-"bodies, as
well as *the laws of propagation and interaction*, which form a part of
the essential character of these entities, is just "God's action" itself;
or, in our neutral paraphrase, this coexistence and these laws just *are*,
on this view, *the fundamental constitution of corporeal nature*. This
may indeed be wrong – it is possible that the phenomena we know
are produced in a different way; but *if* it is right, it is *enough*: the
demand for a further "explanation" of this constitutional fact stems
from the Cartesian illusion that we must in principle have a "clear
and distinct" apprehension of the necessity of the basic constitution
of nature – precisely the illusion that Locke on the one hand shares
when he speaks of "impulse" as *the only way we can conceive bodies
to act*, and that he on the other hand *explodes* when he asks: "Have
we indeed a clear conception of this mode of transfer of motion?"

But there still remains a step to be taken in the creation of the
"new" bodies. Why so? If the "beings" so far described have all
the fundamental properties posited by the corpuscular philosophy,
why is that not sufficient? The reason is this: we must ask, *would*
these beings have *all* the attributes required for us to take them
for bodies of the sort we know? In particular, how could we detect
the existence of these beings *at all*? So far, we have assumed that

"*ordinary*" bodies *already* exist (including our own bodies!). Then we could detect the "new" bodies by the interaction of ordinary bodies with them: for instance, we should perceive that ordinary bodies bounce off the new ones, and so detect their presence; *light* might be reflected from them, so that we could *see* them; etc. But the metaphysical hypothesis Newton intends to suggest is that what we have been calling "new" or "quasi-"bodies are in fact just the bodies we know. And for *this*, he says, it is necessary to suppose that these beings are endowed, further, with the power to *interact with minds*: "[t]hat they be able to excite various perceptions in the senses and the fancy in created minds, and in turn to be moved by the latter" – most especially, that they are able, when they form part of what he calls our "sensorium" (the crucial region of our brain), to induce specific forms of *awareness* as a consequence of specific motions on their part; and, correspondingly, that our acts of will cause suitable motions in those that initiate activity in what we now call our motor neurons.

This is another rather original idea. Descartes placed the "essence" of bodies in extension alone; to this, Locke objects that impenetrability, which he calls "solidity," is equally essential to bodies;[56] and in an important summary passage, he suggests as the "primary and original" *ideas* we have of *anything* the following: "*Extension, Solidity, Mobility*, or Power of being moved; which by our Senses we receive from Body: *Perceptivity*, or the Power of perception, or thinking; *Motivity*, or the Power of moving: which by reflection we receive from our Minds."[57] But Newton points out (again, quite without any acquaintance with Locke's discussion) that just as "mobility" is correlative with "motivity," so must *perceptibility* be correlative with perceptivity; that, indeed, contrary to what the grammatical formation of the words might suggest, "perceptivity" is a *susceptibility* to being *affected*: a process in which it is *bodies* that "act on" *minds*. That such a power is essential to bodies is something he argues for rather strongly:

> But should anyone object that bodies not united to minds cannot directly arouse perceptions in minds, and that hence . . . this

power is not essential to them: it should be noted that there is no
question here of an actual union, but only of a faculty in bodies
by which they are capable of a union through the forces of nature.
From the fact that the parts of the brain, especially the finer ones
to which the mind is united, are in a continual flux,
new ones succeeding to those which fly away, it is manifest that
that faculty is in all bodies. And, whether you consider divine action
or corporeal nature, to remove this is no less [a violation of the
nature with which God has endowed bodies] than to remove that
other faculty by which bodies are enabled to transfer mutual actions
amongst one another[58] – that is, to reduce body to empty space.

Towards the end of this lengthy digression,[59] Newton makes
the claim that "the usefulness of the described Idea of bodies
shines forth most in that it clearly involves and best confirms and
explicates the chief truths of Metaphysics." What he goes on to
contend is that the conception of body in question provides a powerful argument against atheism. But the end of this passage has an
importance beyond, and quite independent of, its theological claims.
Having argued that the chief, or even the only, support of atheism is
the "prejudice" or "notion" of bodies "as if having in themselves a
complete absolute and independent reality," he adds:

> Thus the prejudice just mentioned ought to be laid aside, and
> substantial reality rather ascribed to these kinds of Attributes
> which are real and intelligible in themselves and do not require a
> subject in which they inhere . . . And this we can manage without
> difficulty if (besides the Idea of body expounded above) we reflect
> that we can conceive of space existing without any subject,
> when we think of a vacuum . . . In the same way, if we should
> have an Idea of that Attribute or power by which God, through
> the sole action of his will, can create beings: we should perhaps
> conceive that Attribute as it were subsisting of itself, without any
> substantial subject, and involving his other attributes. But while
> we cannot form an Idea of this Attribute, nor even of our own

power by which we move our bodies, it would be rash to say what is the substantial foundation of minds.

The boldness of this would be hard to exaggerate. In his rejection of the notion of "substance" as having reference to what he calls an "unintelligible" support or subject of attributes, in favor of a notion of "substantiality" *of the attributes themselves* (the criterion of substantiality being, as indicated by him earlier, the role played in *actions*), Newton goes so far as to suggest that even God might be conceived entirely in terms of his attributes, if only we could form clear "Ideas" of these. It is well known that Newton's theologico-religious convictions (which he kept carefully concealed from all but a few very trusted contemporaries)[60] were unorthodox; in particular, that he rejected the doctrine of the Trinity. Well, of course the view of substantial reality described here would make not so much false, as entirely unintelligible, the proposition that God is "three persons, but one substance"!

However, as has been remarked, the reach of Newton's suggestion is by no means only theological; it bears explicitly upon the so-called "mind–body problem" – or, perhaps better put as Newton put it: upon the problem of understanding "the substantial foundation of minds." Just as in the theological case, the suggestion sets aside the distinction of "kinds of substance": mind–body dualism or monism, in favor of the program: *to seek to understand mental attributes and their relation to corporeal ones.* When these relations are sufficiently understood, Newton implies, we may expect to know all that there is to know about the "substantial foundation of minds"; *before* they are sufficiently understood,[61] "it would be rash to say what is the substantial foundation of minds."

It remains now to discuss what consequences for Newton's metaphysics resulted from his greatest discovery in natural philosophy: that of the law of universal gravitation.

The short answer is that this discovery led Newton to a quite new conception of the nature of what Descartes had called "a natural power in general"; that is, to a new conception of how it *may be fruitful* – not, as for Descartes, how *it is necessary* – to conceive of the "actions" that characterize nature, with a view to the deeper understanding of natural phenomena. In the Preface to the *Principia*, Newton formulates this conception in the following way: having first remarked that, whereas the Ancients cultivated mechanics as the science of *machines* – that is, as the "art" of *moving weights* – his design in the present work concerns "not arts but philosophy," and his subject is "not manual but natural powers," he goes on:

> And therefore we offer this work as mathematical principles of philosophy. For all the difficulty of philosophy seems to consist in this, from the phaenomena of motions to investigate the forces of Nature, and then from these forces to demonstrate the other phaenomena . . . In the third book we give an example of this in the explication of the System of the World. For by the propositions mathematically demonstrated in the first books, we there derive from the celestial phaenomena, the forces of Gravity with which bodies tend to the Sun and the several Planets. Then from these forces by other propositions, which are also mathematical, we deduce the motions of the Planets, the Comets, the Moon, and the Sea. I wish we could derive the rest of the phaenomena of Nature by the same kind of reasoning from mechanical principles. For I am induced by many reasons to suspect that they may all depend upon certain forces by which the particles of bodies, by some causes hitherto unknown, are either mutually impelled towards each other and cohere in regular figures, or are repelled and recede from each other; which forces being unknown, Philosophers have hitherto attempted the search of Nature in vain. But I hope the principles here laid down will afford some light either to that, or some truer, method of Philosophy.[62]

This is the new program for natural philosophy: deriving the phenomena of nature from "mechanical principles," not in the sense previously understood by the mechanical philosophy, but in the sense of *principles governing forces of attraction and repulsion* – themselves to be discovered by reasoning from the phenomena, as in Book 3 of the *Principia* itself. It is important to note that the program is put forward as *tentative* and *open to revision*. But what bearing does this change have on Newton's metaphysics?

For the answer to this, we must consider Newton's exposition of the general framework of his system of mechanical principles, both in the *Principia* and near the end of that thirty-first Query of the *Opticks* to which brief reference has already been made.

At the opening of the *Principia* we find first a section of "Definitions," and then one of "Axioms, or Laws of Motion." Among the eight definitions, six treat of concepts associated with the general notion of *force*. Definition 3 tells us that the "innate force of matter" is "a power of resisting, by which every body, as much as in it lies, endeavours to persevere in its present state, whether it be of rest, or of moving uniformly forward in a right line." The paragraph of discussion following this definition introduces the alternative expression *vis inertiae* – "force of inactivity" – for this same power; makes the important remark that this force is quantitatively measurable by "the [mass of the] body whose force it is"; and explains further that whenever a force is "impressed" upon one body, *A*, by another body, *B*, so as to tend to change the condition of *A*, the force of inactivity is *exercised* in a twofold way: (a) in the degree to which *A* "withstands" the force impressed – i.e., in the *smallness* of the change of velocity that results; and (b) in that *A*, "by not easily giving way," reciprocally "endeavours to change the state" of *B*. Definition 4 is of a term already used in the passage just described: it says that an "impressed force" is an action exerted upon a body, tending to change its state of rest or motion. One might assume from this that "intrinsic force" and "impressed force" are, for Newton, correlative contrary terms; but as we shall see, this would be not quite correct. The paragraph of explanation following this definition remarks first that impressed force "consists in the action only; and remains no longer in the body, when the action is over." Thus, whereas the "force of inactivity" is a *permanent* attribute of a body – not always *exercised*, but always *present* – impressed force is by its nature *episodic*. The explanation ends with the remark, "Impressed forces are of different origins; as from percussion, from pressure, from centripetal force." The phraseology here – a force said to be "from" another (kind of) force as its "origin" – is rather odd. But the point is this: the "intrinsic force of matter" is, in Newton's terminology, one of the "natural powers" or forces of nature. The various "origins" of impressed forces, too, are natural powers: permanent features of material nature, not transient episodes. An *impressed* force is the *action* upon a body of one of these natural powers.

Of the three kinds of "origin" instanced by Newton, two – percussion and pressure – are recognizably the ones assumed by the mechanical philosophy. It is the third – "centripetal force" – that is the characteristic novelty of the *Principia*; and Definitions 5–8 are devoted to aspects of this notion.

Definition 5 tells us simply that a centripetal force is one directed towards a point as center. In the paragraph of discussion, Newton cites three characteristic examples – "Gravity by which bodies tend to the centre of the Earth; Magnetism, by which iron tends to the loadstone; and that force, whatever it is, by which the Planets are perpetually drawn aside from the rectilinear motions, which otherwise they wou'd pursue, and made to revolve in curvilinear orbits." These, it is clear, rightly count as "forces of nature"; and the main business of the *Principia* will be to establish that the first and third of them are the same, and to establish the fundamental law that characterizes this force. Unfortunately, with an uncharacteristic lapse in clarity, Newton adds a fourth example: that of the force by which a sling holds a stone in its orbit about the hand. In what sense this example obscures the concept Newton has chiefly in view, we shall soon see.

The remaining three definitions concern three "quantities," or "measures," of a centripetal force, which Newton calls the *absolute*, the *accelerative*, and the *motive* quantities; and it is in his characterization of these three measures – above all, in the second paragraph of discussion following Definition 8, which paragraph is devoted to a fuller explication of all three measures – that Newton gives us the deepest information about his conception of a centripetal force itself as a natural power. Of the three definitions taken by themselves, the first two are, in different ways, a little puzzling. Definition 6 says that the absolute quantity of a centripetal force is the measure of that force "proportional to the efficacy of the cause that propagates it from the centre, through the spaces round about"; and Newton adds by way of example that "the magnetic force is greater in one load-stone and less in another, according to their sizes and strength." This makes clear the general idea of what it is that the absolute quantity is supposed to measure; however, it fails to tell us *how* this is to be measured: the phrase "proportional to the efficacy of the cause" presupposes that we know how to express the efficacy of the cause in a quantitative way.[63] But in spite of this, when the issue arises concretely, in the case of the force of gravity, the appropriate quantitative measure is entirely clear. With Definition 7, on the other hand, the quantity is explicitly named – the "accelerative quantity" of a centripetal force is its measure, "proportional to the velocity which it generates in a given time": in other words, the accelerative quantity is in effect just what we call the *acceleration* produced by the force; what is puzzling is Newton's remark in explanation of this notion: "Thus the force of the same load-stone is greater at less distance, and less at greater: also the force of gravity is greater in valleys, less on tops of exceeding high mountains; and yet less (as shall be hereafter shown) at greater distances from the body of the Earth; but at equal distances, it is the same everywhere . . ." The puzzle is, why choose *acceleration* as the measure that varies in this sort of fashion with distance? But here, the puzzle vanishes upon a little reflection. In the case of a magnet, acceleration is indeed *not* an appropriate choice for the measure Newton really has in mind; for it is by no means true (nor does Newton say it is) of the acceleration produced by a magnet that "at equal distances, it is the same everywhere." But that *is* true of gravitational force. This is the centrifugal force Newton is chiefly concerned with in the *Principia*, and he has formulated his *general* definition in a way that strictly fits only this *special* case. Finally, Definition 8 presents us with the quantity that we normally associate with the word "force" in Newtonian mechanics: it defines the motive quantity of a centripetal force as its measure, "proportional to the motion which it generates in a given time." Since (1) according to Newton's Definition 2 the "quantity of motion" is jointly proportional to the mass and the velocity of a body, and since (2) the quantity generated "in a given time" means, in more modern language, *the rate, per unit time*, with which it is generated, the definition says that the motive quantity measures the force by the *rate of change of momentum* produced thereby; in other words, it measures the force impressed upon a body by the product of the mass of the body and the resulting acceleration.

Newton considers these interrelated notions important enough to devote a few paragraphs to their further clarification. Of these the most important part, for our concerns, is the following:

> These quantities of Forces, we may for brevity's sake call by
> the names of Motive, Accelerative, and Absolute forces; and for
> distinction sake consider them, with respect to the Bodies that
> tend to the centre; to the Places of those bodies; and to the Centre
> of force towards which they tend: That is to say, I refer
> the Motive force to the Body, as an endeavour and propensity
> of the whole towards a centre, arising from the propensities of
> the several parts taken together; the Accelerative force to the
> Place of the body, as a certain power or energy[64] diffused from
> the centre to all places around to move the bodies that are in
> them; and the Absolute force to the Centre, as indued with
> some cause, without which those motive forces would not be
> propagated through the spaces round about; whether that cause is
> some central body, (such as is the Load-stone, in the centre of the
> force of Magnetism, or the Earth in the centre of gravitating force)

or any thing else that does not yet appear. For I here design to give a Mathematical notion of those forces, without considering their Physical causes and seats.

This passage describes the conception of what in a later terminology is called a *field of force*, distributed about – and everywhere tending towards – a center.[65] The "absolute quantity" of this force (this field) is meant to characterize the strength of the field *as a whole* – the "efficacy of the cause" by which it is produced, or "propagated through the spaces round about"; again, in later terms, it is the "source-strength" at the center of the field. The "accelerative quantity" is *meant* to characterize the intensity of the field *at any given place* (and in the special case of gravitation, the "acceleration due to gravity" at the place in question successfully does so).[66] Finally, the "motive quantity" characterizes the action of the field upon an actual *body*: it measures, in other words, the force *impressed upon* a body by the field – the impressed force that has the given (field of) centripetal force as its "origin." In the case of gravity, the motive quantity of the force on a body is simply the *weight* of that body.[67]

When this array of concepts is juxtaposed with the passage quoted earlier from the preface to the *Principia*, in which the program is laid out of trying to account for the phenomena of nature as the effect of *forces of attraction and repulsion*, what emerges is the view that the natural powers – that of the *vis inertiae* of matter excepted – may all take the form of fields of force associated with the particles of matter; and, indeed, "central" fields (tending *either* toward *or away from* a center).[68]

One further essential point remains to be made – this derived from the laws of motion: namely, that the forces of nature constituted by the central fields are forces of *interaction*, governed by the third law of motion: that is, they produce *equal and opposite* motive forces between *pairs* of bodies. In Newton's argument in Book 3 culminating in the law of universal gravitation, this conception of a force of nature as an interaction subject to the third law plays a most crucial role.[69] Newton's awareness that there is in this a novel and important idea is clearly shown in a passage in the first version of Book 3, written (he tells us) "in a popular method,"[70] not published during his lifetime, but published both in Latin and in an English translation in 1728. The passage in question is striking in its iteration, which contrasts with Newton's usual conciseness of exposition (all emphases are added here, chiefly to highlight the main point – the one exception is explained in note 71):

> Since the action of the centripetal force upon a body attracted
> is, at equal distances, proportional to the matter in this body, it
> accords with reason that it should be proportional also to
> the matter in the body attracting. For action is mutual, and
> (by the third Law of Motion) makes bodies by a mutual tendency
> approach one another, and hence must be conformable with itself
> in each body. *One body may be considered as attracting, another*
> *as attracted; but this distinction is more mathematical than*
> *natural. The attraction really is of each body towards the other,*
> and is thus of the same kind in each.
>
> *And hence it is that the attractive force is found in each.*
> The Sun attracts Jupiter and the other Planets, Jupiter attracts the
> Satellites; and by parity of reason, the Satellites act among
> themselves reciprocally and upon Jupiter, and all the Planets
> mutually among themselves. *And though the mutual actions*
> *of two Planets may be distinguished from one another, and*
> *considered as two actions, by which each attracts the other: yet in*
> *so far as these [actions] are intermediate, they are not two, but a*
> *single operation between two terms.* By the contraction of a single
> interceding cord two bodies may be drawn each to the other. The
> cause of the action is twofold, indisputably [that cause is]
> the disposition of each body; the action is likewise twofold in
> so far as it is upon two bodies; but *as between two bodies it is sole*
> *and single. It is not one operation by which the Sun for instance*
> *attracts Jupiter, and another operation by which Jupiter attracts*

the Sun, but it is one operation by which the Sun and Jupiter mutually endeavor to approach one another. By the action by which the Sun attracts Jupiter, Jupiter and the Sun endeavor to come nearer together (by the third Law of Motion) and, by the action by which Jupiter attracts the Sun, Jupiter and the Sun likewise endeavor to come nearer together: *but the Sun is not attracted towards Jupiter by a double action, nor Jupiter by a double action towards the Sun, but it is one intermediate action by which both approach nearer together.* Iron draws the loadstone as much as the loadstone draws the iron; for all iron in the neighborhood of the loadstone also draws other iron. *But the action between the loadstone and the iron is single, and is considered as single by the Philosophers* . . . Conceive a single operation arising from the conspiring nature of both to be exerted in this way between two Planets; and this will be disposed in the same way *towards* both: hence being manifestly proportional to the matter in one of them, it will be proportional to the matter in the other.[71]

To repeat, then: the almost obsessive iteration in this passage seems clear evidence of Newton's intention to bring emphatically forward a new notion of the *unity* of interaction as the form of a force of nature. In terms of the fields already referred to, this means that exactly those bodies that are susceptible to the action of a given interaction-field are also the *sources* of the field; and that the measures of susceptibility and of source-strength (the "absolute quantity" of the body's force) are the same.

If all this is brought into relation to the metaphysical analysis in "De gravitatione et aequipondio fluidorum," it implies that in creating a body, God (or in the "constitution" of a body, *nature*) must impose, not only the field of impenetrability and the laws of motion appropriate thereto, but other fields as well, with their laws, characterizing forces of interaction of the kind that have been described – which fields, according to the Preface to the *Principia*, it becomes the presumed task of natural philosophy to discover.

And this is precisely the picture presented by Newton near the end of Query 31 of the *Opticks*. He there makes the explicit distinction, among natural powers or forces of nature, between the *vis inertiae*, as a "passive principle," and the other forces, which are "active principles"; but in both cases, he makes clear, what characterizes or identifies a particular such force is a *law* of nature (of the appropriate kind). Here are the principal relevant statements; they are preceded by a lengthy survey of physical and chemical phenomena, all tending to show that our understanding of nature depends upon the determination of forces of attraction and repulsion among particles:

> And thus Nature will be very conformable to herself and very
> simple, performing all the great Motions of the heavenly Bodies
> by the Attraction of Gravity which intercedes those Bodies,
> and almost all the small ones of their Particles by some other
> attractive and repelling Powers which intercede the Particles.
> The *Vis inertiae* is a passive Principle by which Bodies persist in
> their Motion or Rest, receive Motion in proportion to the Force
> impressing it, and resist as much as they are resisted.[72]

We see, then, that Newton regards as *the law or principle* characterizing the intrinsic force of matter as a natural power, not what *we* call the "law of inertia," but the *conjunction of all three laws of motion*. This is quite in accord with what he has said in his discussion of Definition 3 of the *Principia*, where he describes the twofold manifestation or "exercise" of the force of inertia: in reducing the acceleration of the body acted upon by an impressed force (Law 2), and in the reciprocal "endeavor to change the state" of the body responsible for that impressed force (Law 3).

After some further discussion, which culminates in the statement: "All these things being consider'd, it seems to me probable that God in the Beginning form'd Matter in solid, massy, hard, impenetrable, moveable Particles, [etc.],"[73] mentioned earlier – a statement that in itself can be regarded as a pretty close counterpart of the creation story of "De gravitatione et aequipondio fluidorum," but with its deeper ontological analysis omitted – Newton goes on:

> It seems to me farther, that these Particles have not only a *Vis inertiae*, accompanied with such passive Laws of Motion as naturally result from that Force, but also that they are moved by certain active Principles, such as is that of Gravity, and that which causes Fermentation, and the Cohesion of Bodies. These Principles I consider, not as occult Qualities, supposed to result from the specifick Forms of Things, but as general Laws of Nature, by which the Things themselves are form'd; their Truth appearing to us by Phaenomena, though their Causes be not yet discover'd. For these are manifest Qualities, and their Causes only are occult.[74]

We have, then, once again, the explicit distinction of the one passive principle and the several active principles; the explicit identification of such a principle with a "general Law of Nature"; and further, the indication that these principles, forces, or laws, are taken not to *result from* something like Aristotelian "substantial forms," which are "occult Qualities," but to *replace* them: it is *by* these "general Laws of Nature" that "*the Things themselves are form'd*" – just as, in "De gravitatione et aequipondio fluidorum," the *clear* attributes of impenetrability and laws of transference of the fields of impenetrability through the parts of space *replaced* the obscure notions of substance and substantial forms. The contrast is further drawn – and the *tentative* character of Newton's philosophic program further emphasized – in these words:

> [O]ccult Qualities put a stop to the Improvement of natural Philosophy, and therefore of late Years have been rejected. To tell us that every Species of Things is endow'd with an occult specifick Quality by which it acts and produces manifest Effects, is to tell us nothing: But to derive two or three general Principles of Motion from Phaenomena, and afterwards to tell us how the

Properties and Actions of all corporeal Things follow from those manifest Principles, would be a very great step in Philosophy, though the Causes of those Principles were not yet discover'd: And therefore I scruple not to propose the Principles of Motion above-mentioned, they being of very general Extent, and leave their Causes to be found out.[75]

Combining what Newton says here with the words previously quoted from the Preface to the *Principia*, one sees that – apart from the obvious openness to the future of a *program of investigation for physics* – the *metaphysics* that Newton presents is open and tentative in two respects: First, the words just cited imply that, although we are asked to consider the active principles as *candidates* to replace the old substantial forms as fundamental constitutional elements of nature, we are *not* to suppose, dogmatically, that whatever principles we have managed to discover are *necessarily* "the" fundamental ones: it will be a question for the future whether (yet deeper) *causes* of these principles may remain to be found out. In particular, this explains why Newton never claimed – and strongly denied holding – that gravity is "essential" to bodies. In the *Principia*, in the General Scholium to that work (added in the second edition, 1713), he says in a very celebrated passage:

Hitherto we have explain'd the phaenomena of the heavens and of our sea, by the power of Gravity, but have not yet assign'd the cause of this power. This is certain, that it must proceed from a cause that penetrates to the very centers of the Sun and Planets, without suffering the least diminution of its force . . . But hitherto I have not been able to discover the cause of those properties of gravity from phaenomena, and I feign no hypotheses. For whatever is not deduc'd from the phaenomena, is to be called an hypothesis; and hypotheses, whether metaphysical or physical, whether of occult qualities or mechanical, have no place in experimental philosophy.[76]

And in the *Opticks* (in Query 21, added in its second edition, in 1717), Newton does actually sketch an hypothesis as to a possible "mechanical" cause of gravity by the action of a highly elastic aethereal medium (NB: a *possible* cause: one to be *considered*, not *adopted*; hence, although an hypothesis, not "feigned").

The second respect in which the metaphysics is left open to revision is more far-reaching (and commensurately vaguer). It is related to Newton's statement in "De gravitatione et aequipondio fluidorum" that we cannot know with certainty the ultimate constitution of things: namely, the general "probable" metaphysical conclusions Newton has reached on the basis of a comprehensive consideration of what has been discovered from phenomena are in the nature of the case open to possible *re*-consideration when *more* things have been learned; hence the form in which Newton expresses his hopes for the success of his program in the Preface to the *Principia*: "I hope the principles here laid down will afford some light either to that, or some truer, method of Philosophy."

In conclusion, it is worth considering briefly what the *actual* success has been of Newton's metaphysics, in the perspective of the natural philosophy of the present time. Of course, in our own physics, *all* the foundations of Newtonian physics have been radically modified: space and time, since the work of Einstein, are not conceived as Newton conceived them; finitely extended rigid and impenetrable ultimate particles have been replaced by far more exotic beings; fields that are *not* rigidly associated with particle sources, as Newton's were, but that are capable of existing to some degree independently, and that have their own internal structure and interaction among their parts (as in the propagation of *waves*), have come to have an "ontological" standing no less fundamental than "fundamental particles" themselves; and – especially since the advent of quantum mechanics – we have even had to abandon the notion of particles as having, at each instant of time, definite locations in space, and as interacting through Newtonian "impressed motive forces." On the other hand, in the developments that have led to the present state of physics, the conceptions introduced by Newton have played an indispensable role. And what are arguably his two most characteristic – and in his own time most sharply controverted – basic conceptions remain, *although* radically modified, as basic characteristics of the structure envisaged by our own science. The first of these is the structure of space-time. It was once thought that the development of the general theory of relativity had decided the issue of "absolute" versus "relative" space and motion against Newton and in favor of his strongest contemporary critic in this matter, Leibniz; but more careful consideration has shown that in spite of the very far-reaching changes wrought by Einstein – in spite of the fact that absolute space and absolute time have been abandoned, and the geometric structure of space-time has proved to be *interdependent with* the distribution of matter (or, rather, of "energy-momentum") – it remains necessary to regard space-time and its geometry as having a status as "real" as that of matter: the program of "reducing" the properties of space-time to properties and interrelations of "bodies" has not succeeded. So on this *general* score – although certainly *not* in *detail* – Newton was, in the eyes of our own science, "right" to take space and time as fundamental entities.[77]

The other characteristic notion of Newton's that has proved quite remarkably durable is that of a natural power, or force of nature. This statement may seem as surprising as the claim that Newton was "right" in a general sense about space and time: for (a) as has been already remarked, Newtonian "motive force" has disappeared from quantum mechanics, and (b) it *is* "motive force" – the "force" of Newton's second law, $f = ma$ – that is usually taken as the characteristic notion of "Newtonian mechanics." But as we have seen, as important as this concept is in Newton's *Principia*, it does not express his most basic notion; for instance, whereas an impressed force is not a natural power, the "force of inertia" – which is something entirely different from the force that is equal to ma – is one. Newton's basic notion of a force of nature is, however, so far from being antiquated that it is substantially the same – although again, as in the case of space and time, with profound modifications in detail – as the notion used when physicists today speak of the "four fundamental forces." Of these, the gravitational force is the first to have been discovered; it was, of course, a great discovery of Newton's – and, on the analysis here offered, provided the grounds on which Newton's general conception was based. Two of the four fundamental forces – the weak and the strong nuclear force – obviously could not have been foreseen in Newton's time. Of the remaining one – the electromagnetic force, whose classical definitive form was discovered by Maxwell in the 1860s – we find some traces in Newton's work. References to the loadstone have been quoted above. In the long closing query of the *Opticks*, from which material occurring near the end has been cited as illuminating Newton's general concept of a force of nature, there is also the following incidental speculation about electrical force, in the midst of a more general consideration (itself showing again exactly the *tentative* view of the "fundamental" that has been suggested as characteristic of Newton):

> What I call Attraction may be perform'd by impulse, or by some
> other means unknown to me. I use that Word here to signify
> only in general any Force by which Bodies tend towards one
> another, whatsoever be the Cause. For we must learn from the
> Phaenomena of Nature what Bodies attract one another, and what
> are the Laws and Properties of the Attraction, before we enquire
> the Cause by which the Attraction is perform'd. The Attractions
> of Gravity, Magnetism, and Electricity, reach to very sensible
> distances, and so have been observed by vulgar Eyes, and there
> may be others which reach to so small distances as hitherto
> escape Observation; and perhaps electrical Attraction may reach
> to such small distances, even without being excited by Friction.[78]

When we remember that electrical attractions, in Newton's time, constituted a rather isolated phenomenon, observed only when certain bodies were suitably rubbed – and when we recall that the "attractions [and repulsions as well] extending to small distances *within* bodies" that Newton had in mind were the ones that should eventually account for cohesion and for chemical processes – this glimmering of a suspicion that electricity might not be merely a special effect of rubbing, but might exist and be responsible for forces at short range as a general fact of nature surely deserves to be considered a remarkable one. In our own science, it is the electromagnetic force that is in fact seen to be responsible (but only in the light of quantum mechanics, not of Newtonian mechanics) for the physical and chemical properties of ordinary bodies.

"To derive *two or three* general Principles of Motion from Phaenomena, and afterwards to tell us how the Properties and Actions of all corporeal Things follow from those manifest Principles, would be a very great step in Philosophy, though the Causes of those Principles were not yet discover'd." Such is the great step in philosophy that Newton's metaphysics was conceived to facilitate: "I hope the principles here laid down will afford some light either to that, or some truer, method of philosophy." It seems fair to say that that hope has been amply realized.

EDITORS' NOTE

In note 71 of this chapter, Professor Stein calls attention to the section numbers in Cajori's version of the English translation of *A Treatise of the System of the World* and their absence in both the English and Latin editions of 1728. The history of these section numbers is complicated. The manuscript from which the Latin edition was printed, entitled "De motu corporum liber secundus," is in the hand of Humphrey Newton (Isaac's amanuensis at the time), with modifications in Isaac's hand. This manuscript contains eighty section-headings in the margins, with the first twenty-eight numbered in Roman numerals, precisely in the manner of Descartes's published *Principia*; the remaining fifty-two sections, however, are not numbered. In every edition of the English translation before Cajori's, and in all Latin editions save one, the section-headings are placed in the margin without numbers.

The exception is Samuel Horsley's Latin edition in his *Isaaci Newtoni Opera Quae Exstant Omnia* of 1779–85. Horsley, who had gained access to the "De motu corporum liber secundus" manuscripts, kept the eighty section-headings in the margins, but placed Arabic numerals at the beginning of the text of seventy-eight of the sections, electing to omit a number in the case of the seventy-fifth section-heading (introducing Table II) and the eightieth (introducing the lemmata near the end). In his German translation, attached to his 1872 translation of Newton's *Principia*, Jakob Phillipp Wolfers put numbered section-headings in the text rather than the margins, and he dropped the seventy-fifth and eightieth section-headings entirely. Cajori, who acknowledged his use of this German translation, followed Wolfers save for putting the numbers in brackets, presumably to signify their absence in the English translation that he was modifying.

NOTES

1 "The previous author" of a book with that title: for the title Newton used – *Philosophiae Naturalis Principia Mathematica* – is clearly a deliberate allusion to Descartes's work.

2 René Descartes, *Principles of Philosophy*, trans. Valentine Rodger Miller and Reese P. Miller (Dordrecht: D. Reidel, 1983), p. xxiv (in the "Letter from the Author to the Translator of this Book [into French], which can serve here as a Preface").

3 *Encyclopaedia Britannica*, 11th edn, vol. 18, p. 253.

4 Descartes hoped that his goals for a new science would be achieved *entirely* in his *own lifetime*, and indeed by his own efforts – aided only by the work of artisans and trained technicians he needed to construct equipment for experiments and to help in carrying out the experiments. The most ambitious of these goals was the establishment, on sound principles, of a science of medicine that should succeed in prolonging human life to a term measured in centuries.

5 The guarantee, that is, of what we should call the "objective validity" of those principles that carry complete "subjective" conviction. (Descartes's terminology, following that of the medieval philosophers, is the reverse: for him, "subjective" means what characterizes the proper

subject of knowledge – the "real things"; whereas "objective" means characteristic of the "object of the mind," *as* mental object, whatever it may be in reality – or indeed whether or not it exists in reality.) The guarantee of truth is obtained by the famous argument of Descartes's *Meditations*, a crucial turn in which is the (alleged) demonstration (a) of the existence of God as a "perfect being," and (b) of the consequence that, since a perfect being cannot be a deceiver, everything we perceive as true beyond the possibility of doubt must be true in reality.

6 That is, the *Dialogue concerning the Two Chief World Systems*.

7 *Principles of Philosophy*, Part 2, §24.

8 *Ibid.*, §13.

9 *Ibid.*, §15. In the *Rules for the Direction of the Mind*, in stark contrast, "place" is offered as an example of those "simple natures" which are self-evident in themselves, and cannot be defined or "explained" in terms of something even more evident; and Descartes adds: "And when told that 'place' is the surface of the surrounding body, would anyone conceive of the matter in the same way? For the surface of the 'surrounding body' can change, even though I do not move or change my place; conversely, it may move along with me, so that, although it still surrounds me, I am no longer in the same place." (Quoted from *The Philosophical Writings of Descartes*, ed. John Cottingham, Robert Stoothoff, and Dugald Murdoch, vol. 1 [Cambridge: Cambridge University Press, 1985], p. 45.) So here Descartes has ridiculed, as a bizarre doctrine of the scholastic philosophy he is attacking, the very notion he puts forward in his Principles as the scientifically "correct" one. (We shall later see that Newton makes mincemeat of this way of conceiving place and motion.)

10 "*Semi-*"relativist, because some bodies are singled out – or *partially* singled out – as the ones to which motion *in the strict sense* should be referred; but only partially singled out because of the arbitrariness implied by "and which are regarded as being at rest."

11 Both in his *Meditations on First Philosophy* and in his *Principles of Philosophy*, what Descartes claims to establish by thought without the aid of sensation is the *essential attribute* of material things, in the sense of "what they would be if they *did* exist"; then sensory experience is called upon to show that such things *do* exist.

12 Quoted from the fourth paragraph in the discussion of *Rule Eight*; edition of Cottingham *et al.*, p. 29.

13 In the *Rules for the Direction of the Mind*, Descartes deprecates in the
strongest terms any reliance upon hypotheses ("conjectures") and any
"merely probable cognition"; and at least as late as 1637, in replying to
an objection of Fermat to the argumentation of Descartes's *Dioptrics*
(which was published in that year in the same volume as his *Discourse
on the Method of Rightly Conducting One's Reason and Seeking the
Truth in the Sciences*), he says "I consider almost as false whatever is
only a matter of probability" (letter of 5 October 1637, to Mersenne).
At the end of his *Principles of Philosophy* (1644), he says, in contrast
to that: "With regard to the things which cannot be perceived by the
senses, it is enough to explain their possible nature, even though their
actual nature may be different" (Part 4, §204) – certainly an endorsement
of the value of "hypotheses," even of ones that may in the end not be
true. He goes on, however (in the next two articles), to claim (a) that
his explanations "appear to be at least morally certain"; and (b) that his
explanations possess "more than moral certainty"; indeed that "perhaps
even these results of mine will be allowed into the class of *absolute
certainties*" (emphasis added).

14 It is of course possible to maintain proposition (a) while rejecting (b);
but hardly the reverse: for if space is *full* of *rigid, indivisible* bodies, the
possibilities for motion are extremely restricted – the kinds of motion
we encounter in the world would be quite impossible on such an
assumption. It should be added that one important philosopher, slightly
younger than Newton, who came to reject Descartes's metaphysical
characterization of matter, nevertheless *also* rejected *both* (a) and (b):
namely, Leibniz, in whose view empty space was not a *contradictory*
notion, but who claimed to derive the proposition that the world is a
plenum from his metaphysical principle of "sufficient reason."

15 A characteristic expression of this view, late in the century, by a
philosopher who was certainly *not* a Cartesian, is to be found in Locke;
cf. his *Essay Concerning Human Understanding*, Book 2, ch. viii, §11,
which reads as follows in the first edition (1690): "The next thing to
be consider'd, is how *Bodies operate* one upon another, and that is
manifestly *by impulse*, and nothing else. It being impossible to conceive,
that Body should operate on what it does not touch, (which is all one as
to imagine it can operate where it is not) or when it does touch, operate
any other way than by Motion." Quoted from John Locke, *An Essay
Concerning Human Understanding*, ed. Peter H. Nidditch (Oxford:

Clarendon Press, 1979), p. 135 (*via* the apparatus at the foot of the page – the passage having been drastically revised in the fourth edition).

16 This, as is well known, is the origin of the very word "metaphysics" (which is quite foreign to Aristotle himself): the collection of Aristotle's treatises on first philosophy was labeled – as if by a call-number -τὰ μετὰ τὰ Φυσικά: "the [writings] after the physical [ones]."

17 The point needs to be emphasized, because there is a tradition that sees the basic conceptions of Newton's natural philosophy, most especially his conceptions of space and time, as derivative from, or grounded in, his theology. Thus, J. E. McGuire claims "that the basic concepts of Newton's natural philosophy can be ultimately clarified only in terms of the theological framework which guided so much of his thought" (see his "Force, Active Principles, and Newton's Invisible Realm," *Ambix* 15 [1968], 154). McGuire goes on to remark that the thesis is not original with him, and gives the following citations:

> See the fundamental studies of H. Metzger, *Attraction universelle et religion naturelle chez quelques commentateurs anglais de Newton*, Paris, 1938, and A. Koyré, *From the Closed World to the Infinite Universe*, Harper edition, 1958. Also see H. Guerlac, "Newton et Epicure," *Conf[é]rences du palais de la découverte*, no. 91, Paris, 1963; an excellent study by David Kubrin, "Newton and the Cyclical Cosmos: Providence and the Mechanical Philosophy," J.H.I, 1967, XXVIII, 325–46; J. E. McGuire and P. M. Rattansi, "Newton and the Pipes of Pan," *Notes and Records of the Royal Society of London*, 1966, 21, 108–43; J. E. McGuire, "Body and Void and Newton's *De Mundi Systemate*: some new sources," *Archive for History of Exact Sciences*, 1966, 3, 206–48; an important lengthy study by A. Koyré and I. B. Cohen, "Newton and the Leibniz–Clarke correspondence," *Archive[s] Internationales d'histoire des Sciences*, 1962, 15, 63–126; and A. R. and M. B. Hall, *Unpublished Scientific Papers of Isaac Newton*, Cambridge, 1962, part 3.

The evidence cited in the text above, preceding and immediately following the place to which this note is attached, does not show that this opinion is wrong, so far as concerns either the psychological connections of Newton's thought or the logical or conceptual connections among his principles; but it does at least strongly suggest that the opinion is at variance with what Newton himself thought about these connections, and therefore at variance with at least the epistemological side of Newton's own metaphysics. To discuss the controversy implied with any pretence to thoroughness is beyond the scope of a chapter like the present one; but further evidence will be given, tending to show that on the objective or ontological side, too, Newton's doctrine about space and time, in the light of his explicit statements, did not teach that space and time *per se*, or their attributes, depend upon the nature of God.

On the degree of confidence attached by Newton to his main results in physics, in both his optical work and that on the solar system and the theory of gravity, cf. Shapiro's and Smith's chapters in this volume.

18 This rule, with the statement referred to in the text above, first appeared in the second edition of the *Principia*, 1713.

19 To avoid a possible wrong inference, it should be added that besides knowledge of God "from the appearances of things," which "belongs to Natural Philosophy," Newton holds that there is knowledge of God through *revelation*. This, too, of course, would be through *experience*; and what is more important so far as concerns Newton's own efforts in the domain of "revealed" theology (efforts that occupied no small part of his whole intellectual career), the deliverances of revelation are, for Newton, accessible *only through historical documents* (Newton does not subscribe to any claim of immediate religious authority – nor does he claim access to revelation through personal inspiration), and therefore demand a very arduous historical-critical investigation of such documents. In any event, there is nowhere in Newton a suggestion that our knowledge of anything pertaining to *natural philosophy* can be derived from revealed truths. (He does *relate* some aspects of his views about space, for example, to passages in ancient writings, both pagan and Judeo-Christian; but this is far from ascribing evidentiary or conceptually binding force to such relations.)

20 See the specimens given in John Herivel, *The Background to Newton's Principia: A Study of Newton's Dynamical Researches in the Years 1664–84* (Oxford: Clarendon Press, 1965).

21 Herivel, *Background to Newton's Principia*, p. 123.

22 *Ibid.*, p. 124.

23 *Ibid.*, p. 125.

24 *Ibid.*, p. 136.

25 *Ibid.*, p. 138.

26 See A. Rupert Hall and Marie Boas Hall (eds.), *Unpublished Scientific Papers of Isaac Newton* (Cambridge: Cambridge University Press, 1962), pp. 89–121 (Latin), pp. 121–56 (English). In the present text, translations from this work are my own.

27 Mistranslation begins with this first sentence, which the Halls render as: "It is proper to treat the science of gravity and of the equilibrium of fluid and solid bodies in fluids by two methods." This version has been used as the basis of a claim that the manuscript actually represents an abortive draft of an introduction to Newton's *Principia*, "[s]ince the two studies mentioned – of gravitation and of the equilibrium of fluids and of solid bodies in fluids – bear a strong resemblance to Books I and II of the published *Principia*," and since the two methods Newton describes also have a correspondence to the *Principia*. (See Betty Jo Teeter Dobbs, *The Janus Faces of Genius: The Role of Alchemy in Newton's Thought* [Cambridge: Cambridge University Press, 1991], p. 141.) But Newton's phrase has nothing to do with a "science of gravity": he is speaking of the *weight* of fluids and of solids in fluids, which is the exact subject of the classic treatise "On Floating Bodies" of Archimedes; and, on the other hand, Book 2 of the *Principia* is concerned with the *motions*, not the *equilibrium*, of fluids and of solids in fluids – an entirely *new* subject at the time of its publication.

28 For these statements, see Descartes, *Principles of Philosophy*, Part 3, §27.

29 It is important to bear in mind that for Newton – and for *all* seventeenth-century thinkers – the word "philosophy" was used for all *systematic knowledge* or *systematic inquiry*. Thus, when Newton speaks of "philosophical" usage, he means *exact*, or *systematic*, or *technical* usage; and so does Descartes. So Newton's criticism is that *in Descartes's technical discussion of motion, he does not use that conception of motion which he had put forward as technically correct;* and so he has implicitly acknowledged that the conception he calls "proper" is in fact unsuitable for technical purposes.

30 On the particular issue of the "straightness" of the path, an important argument of Galileo's is relevant, and may be clarifying. Galileo considered an object dropped from high up on the mast of a ship that is sailing, in a smooth sea, with uniform speed. To an observer on shipboard, the object will appear to fall vertically downward – that is, in a straight line – alongside the mast, with a speed that increases

proportionally to the time of fall. To an observer on the shore – who of course also sees the object as falling directly alongside the mast, but who also sees the mast itself as moving uniformly forward – the object will appear to traverse a parabolic arc. Therefore – even setting aside the issue of the *dispersal* of surrounding bodies – whether, in general, a path is straight or not will depend upon *which* bodies one chooses to "regard as at rest."

31 The force of Newton's argument is great. In a famous polemic that came to a head late in the lives of both men, Leibniz took up the cudgels against Newton on behalf of a "relational" view of space and motion – not, indeed, that of Descartes, but one that was still open to Newton's criticism that on that view neither straightness of a path of motion nor constancy of speed is a concept that makes sense. Yet Leibniz – in the same polemic – in arguing against Newton's theory of gravitation, says that for one body to move in a curved line about the other without something that pushes on the first "could not be done without a miracle; since it cannot be explained by the nature of bodies" (because a body of itself tends to move uniformly in a straight line) (Leibniz's third letter, in his correspondence with Samuel Clarke of 1715–16, §17; in, for example, H. G. Alexander [ed.], *The Leibniz–Clarke Correspondence* [Manchester: Manchester University Press, 1956], p. 30). It is unfortunate that Clarke – Newton's representative in this discussion – did not point out to Leibniz the incoherence that Newton had long ago noted in a position that simultaneously maintains that principle about the motion of bodies and regards motion as having a meaning only as "relative," among bodies. This might have led to a clarification by Leibniz of his own relational theory. For further discussion of the issues involved, in which Newton's own position – although much stronger than it was once thought to be among philosophers – is by no means the last word (so far as the foundations of "Newtonian mechanics" itself are concerned), see Howard Stein, "Newtonian Space-Time," *Texas Quarterly* 10 (1967), 174–200; also (with correction of an important typesetting error in a quotation) in Robert Palter (ed.), *The Annus Mirabilis of Sir Isaac Newton 1666–1966* (Cambridge, MA: MIT Press, 1970), pp. 258–84. For further discussion of the views of Leibniz, and also those of Huygens, on the relativity of motion, see also Howard Stein, "Some Philosophical Prehistory of General Relativity," in John Earman, Clark Glymour, and John Stachel (eds.), *Foundations of Space-Time Theories*, Minnesota

Studies in the Philosophy of Science 8 (Minneapolis, MN: University of Minnesota Press, 1977), pp. 3–49 (§§1 and 2, with relevant Notes, and Appendix). Cf. also DiSalle's chapter in the present volume.

32 Newton's words here – quite scholastic in cast – are: "it does not stand under the kind of characteristic affections that denominate substance, namely actions, such as are thoughts in a mind and motions in a body."

33 The use of the word "idea" – unusual for Newton – is striking; and so is its capitalization (here, and in similar contexts later in the piece). One is reminded of Locke's *Essay Concerning Human Understanding*, in which the word is also uniformly capitalized (and italicized as well). There can be no question of influence, in either direction: whatever the date of this fragmentary piece of Newton's, it certainly antedates Locke's *Essay*; and, as certainly, Locke had never seen it when he wrote the *Essay*.

34 Some words are necessary here concerning the translation, since this passage is one of those in which the published version is badly at fault. There, the first sentence reads: "Space is a disposition of being *qua* being." Newton's Latin is: "Spatium est entis quatenus ens affectio." Now, the word *affectio* is standard in philosophical Latin, and is regularly translated by its English cognate, "affection"; "disposition" has a rather different connotation. But this is a minor point. The major one is how to translate – and how to understand – the phrase *entis quatenus ens*. Latin "ens" and English "being" are precisely synonymous; and "entis" is the genitive of "ens"; so "an affection of being as being" – or "of being *qua* being" – that is, "of being as such" – is linguistically warranted. Further, the phrase is borrowed directly from the Aristotelian tradition, in which "being *qua* being" is the standard definition of the subject-matter of first philosophy or metaphysics. So far, therefore, the Halls' rendering seems justified. However, one must also note two things: first, that the Latin word "ens" like the English word "being" is susceptible of a concrete meaning (as when we call *ourselves* "human beings") as well as an abstract one; second, that in Latin there are no articles, definite or indefinite; and therefore the reading given in the text above is, on purely linguistic grounds, equally eligible. Two considerations may be thought to favor the Halls: first, the point just made about the formula in the Aristotelian tradition; second, the fact that the phrase "being *qua* being," understood to mean "being *in the highest sense*," had the special connotation of "*[the] divine Being*" (cf. God's answer to Moses, Exodus 3.14, in response to the question

what Moses shall tell the people is the name of the one who has sent him: "I AM THAT I AM"); this would seem to agree with Newton's former statement that space is an emanative effect of God. However, these considerations are clearly overborne by what follows – in particular, by Newton's statement, "*If I posit any being whatever, I posit space.*" The word "being" – *ens* – in *this* assertion can only be taken in its concrete sense. And since this statement is given to ground the clause immediately preceding it, there too "being" must be used in the concrete sense; indeed, in any case, only the concrete sense – "the first-existing *thing* – or *entity*" – fits that clause at all. (The translation of that phrase by the Halls – "the first existence of being," rather than "the first-existent being" – not only makes its sense obscure, but is incompatible with the grammar of the Latin. To discuss this in detail here would take us too far into purely linguistic matters.)

35 Newton, of course, under the rubric "all minds," would have included the minds of *angels*.

36 On this point it is instructive to compare what Locke says about the relation of mind ("spirit" or "soul") to place and motion: "[F]inding that Spirits, as well as Bodies, cannot operate, but where they are; and that Spirits do operate at several times in several places, I cannot but attribute change of place to all finite Spirits . . . Every one finds in himself, that his Soul can think, will, and operate on his Body, in the place where that is; but cannot operate on a Body, or in a place, an hundred Miles distant from it. No Body can imagine, that his Soul can think, or move a Body at *Oxford*, whilst he is at *London*; and cannot but know, [sic] that being united to his Body, it constantly changes place all the whole Journey, between *Oxford* and *London*, as the Coach, or Horse does, that carries him [etc.]."

37 The qualification, "ordinary," is needed to distinguish the case from the special one of an *atom*, which on Newton's (and the traditional) conception is precisely an *indivisible* body.

38 Another case of mistranslation in the published version: the latter reads, not "and therefore we are able [etc.]," but (emphasis added): "and so in some circumstances it would be possible for us to conceive of extension while imagining the non-existence of God." This suggests that only on Descartes's conception would we be able – "in some circumstances" – to conceive extension while "imagining the non-existence of God." But this is not what Newton says: (1) There is nothing in the Latin

that corresponds to the phrase "in some circumstances." (2) The verb is possumus: indicative – "we are able"; not the subjunctive possimus: "we should be able." Newton asserts unqualifiedly that we are able to conceive of space without any reference to God ("we have an absolute Idea of it without any relationship to God"); his point against Descartes is that on the identification of extension with body the same thing would hold of body: (a) it would be uncreated; (b) we could conceive of it "as existent" while "feigning" the non-existence of God. (This criticism would of course be rejected by Descartes; the point here is merely to be clear about what Newton's doctrine is.)

39 The Halls, in first publishing "De gravitatione et aequipondio fluidorum," expressed uncertainty about its date, but described the handwriting as characteristic of Newton's youth, and – although they noted the important fact that it has affinities with the General Scholium to Newton's *Principia* (introduced in the second edition of that work, thus in 1713, when Newton was seventy years old) – they characterized its general style as labored, and some of its thought as immature (see *Unpublished Scientific Papers*, pp. 89–90); on these grounds, they leaned toward an early date. The present writer, in a paper presented at a conference in 1969 and published in 1970, while not contesting the early date assigned, suggested two reasons for caution about it: first, a disagreement with the Halls' assessment of the thought; second, the testimony of Coste about to be discussed in the text of the chapter (see Howard Stein, "On the Notion of Field in Newton, Maxwell, and Beyond," in Roger H. Stuewer (ed.), *Historical and Philosophical Perspectives of Science*, Minnesota Studies in the Philosophy of Science 5 [Minneapolis: University of Minnesota Press, 1970], p. 274, n. 11). More recently, Dobbs, who gives a survey of opinions on the question (Dobbs, *The Janus Faces of Genius*, pp. 139–40), has argued for a date close to that of the *Principia* – namely, late in 1684 or early in 1685; but it must be noted that an important part of her case rests upon the mistakes noted earlier (note 27 above). It seems fair to say that uncertainty remains about the date of "De gravitatione," and evidence based upon handwriting may after all be decisive.

40 Gottfried Wilhelm Leibniz, *New Essays on Human Understanding*, trans. Peter Remnant and Jonathan Bennett (Cambridge: Cambridge University Press, 1981), p. 442.

41 Coste's account is quoted in A. C. Fraser's edition of Locke's *Essay*; see Locke, *An Essay Concerning Human Understanding*, ed. Alexander Campbell Fraser (reprinted New York: Dover Publications, 1959), vol. 2, pp. 321–2.

42 In their edition of Leibniz's *New Essays*, Remnant and Bennett cite a letter from Leibniz to Locke's friend Lady Masham in 1704, containing "an urgent request that she ask Locke to elucidate"; but it arrived after Locke's death. (See Leibniz, *New Essays*, ed. Remnant and Bennett, p. xxxix, near the end of the volume.)

43 Latin, *arbitrarius*: "depending on the will."

44 Newton's repeated use of the expression "let us feign" – Latin, fingamus: the same verb that occurs in Newton's famous declaration, in the General Scholium to the *Principia*, "Hypotheses non fingo": "I do not feign hypotheses" – is reminiscent of language used by Descartes in his own "creation fable," both in *The World* and in his *Principles of Philosophy*. For the former, see René Descartes, *Le Monde, ou Traité de la lumière*, parallel edition (French and English), trans. Michael Sean Mahoney (New York: Abaris Books, 1979), pp. 50 (French), 51 (English); the phrase in French is "Or puisque nous prenons la liberté de *feindre* cette matière à nostre fantaisie . . ." (emphasis added) – "Now since we are taking the liberty of feigning this matter to our fancy . . ."; "la liberté de feindre" is rendered by Mahoney as "the liberty of imagining." As to the *Principles*, the verb fingere occurs in Part 4, §2: "Fingamus itaque Terram hanc [etc.]" – "Let us therefore feign this earth [etc.]." (Again, in the translation by Miller and Miller cited earlier, the verb is translated "Let us imagine.") The phrase "fingamus itaque," in this last place, is exactly the same as that used by Newton in the opening sentence of his creation story: "Fingamus itaque spatia vacua . . ." – "Let us therefore feign empty spaces . . ." In view of the fact that this whole metaphysical discussion has the character of an anti-Cartesian polemic, the parody of Descartes is most probably intentional.

45 See note 18 above.

46 Cf. note 15 above.

47 Locke, *Essay Concerning Human Understanding*, Book 2, ch. xxiii, §28; Nidditch edition, pp. 311–12.

48 These pessimistic views about the possibility of systematic science were strikingly ameliorated by Locke's reflections on what Newton

had achieved, but he did not allow his changed assessment to have
any effect on the later editions of the *Essay*. The point is discussed in
Howard Stein, "On Locke, 'the Great Huygenius, and the incomparable
Mr. Newton'," in Phillip Bricker and R. I. G. Hughes (eds.), *Philosophical
Perspectives on Newtonian Science* (Cambridge, MA: MIT Press, 1990),
pp. 17–47; see esp. pp. 30–3.

49 Both quotations are from the Author's Preface to the first edition of the
Principia. They are quoted in an order the reverse to that in which they
occur there; and the emphasis (in the second passage) is added here.

50 The subject of Book 2, ch. xxiii of the *Essay Concerning Human
Understanding*.

51 *Ibid.*, §37; Nidditch edn, p. 317.

52 *Ibid.*, Book 1, ch. iv, §18; Nidditch edn, p. 95.

53 *Ibid.*, Book 3, ch. vi, §21; Nidditch edn, p. 450.

54 This characterization of Newton's theory of bodies as a theory of *fields
of impenetrability* was first given in Stein, "On the Notion of Field in
Newton, Maxwell, and Beyond" (cited in note 39 above); there follow
immediately in the same volume some critical comments by Gerd
Buchdahl and by Mary Hesse, with responses by the author defending
his view.

55 Whether Aristotle himself believed in such a thing is a debatable
question.

56 See *Essay Concerning Human Understanding*, Book 2, ch. iv.

57 *Ibid.*, ch. xxi, §73; Nidditch edn, pp. 286–7.

58 Newton's wording is a little odd, in its reference to "removing" the power
in question; he has in mind Descartes's famous thought-experiment
with a lump of wax, of which he attempts to strip away, in thought,
whatever properties can be removed from the wax without destroying
its "essential" character as bodily substance. Descartes concluded that
only extension cannot be removed; Newton argues that to remove
impenetrability, and the laws of transfer of motion, from his mobile
impenetrable regions would be to reduce them to empty space; and he
adds, here, that to remove the power to produce perceptions in minds
would be an equally serious derogation from their substantial nature.

59 (But before the passage quoted immediately above.)

60 (Locke was prominent among these.)

61 (A condition in which it would seem we remain to this day.)

62 This and subsequent passages are quoted from the (unemended!) translation of Andrew Motte: Isaac Newton, *The Mathematical Principles of Natural Philosophy*, trans. Andrew Motte (1729) (reprinted in two volumes, London: Dawsons of Pall Mall, 1968). See "The Author's Preface" (prefatory material is on unnumbered pages).

63 More precisely, for the expression "proportional to the efficacy of the cause" to have a well-defined meaning, one would have to have the conception of the *ratio* of the efficacy of one cause to that of another.

64 The Latin phrase here rendered as "a certain power or energy" is *efficaciam quandam*: that is, simply, "a certain efficacy."

65 Again, cf. Stein, "On the Notion of Field in Newton, Maxwell, and Beyond," cited in note 39 above.

66 For other fields, quite different measures of the field intensity are appropriate: e.g., for magnetism, the "force per unit pole"; for electricity, the "force per unit charge." (For a fuller discussion of the role of the concept of field in Newton's investigation, see Stein, "On the Notion of Field in Newton, Maxwell, and Beyond," cited in note 39 above.)

67 One sees, then, how far the example of the sling is from illustrating the intended pattern: here, there is indeed an impressed motive force toward the hand as a center; but no good sense can be made of the conception of "a certain efficacy diffused from the center *to all the places around*," with a definite magnitude or measure *at each point* (whether or not there is an actual body there to be acted upon).

68 In the *Opticks*, on the basis of a wide survey of phenomena – both optical and *chemical* phenomena figuring largely among them – Newton concludes that there must be some forces that are *attractive at certain distances, repulsive at others*. See Isaac Newton, *Opticks* ("based on the fourth edition, London, 1730"; New York: Dover Publications, 1952), pp. 395ff.

69 That Newton's special use of the third law, crucial to his argument, involves a risky assumption, was briefly mentioned in Stein, "On the Notion of Field in Newton, Maxwell, and Beyond" (cited in note 39 above), p. 269; the point is discussed more fully in Howard Stein, "'From the Phenomena of Motions to the Forces of Nature': Hypothesis or Deduction?" *PSA* 1990 2 (1991), 209–22, and also in Dana Densmore, *Newton's Principia: The Central Argument* (Santa Fe: Green Lion Press, 1995), p. 353.

70 See *Principia*, introductory paragraph to Book 3.

71 Translated by the present author from Newton, *De Mundi Systemate Liber* (London, 1728), pp. 24–6. Matter in square brackets has been added to help to show in clear English the sense of the Latin. Besides the emphases added to highlight the main point, the word "towards" in the last sentence has been italicized; this has been done to indicate a contrast Newton is making, perhaps somewhat subtly, by the way he manages his prepositions: that between how the "operation" arises *from* the bodies, on the one hand, and how it "behaves *towards* them" on the other (if it arises from them in the same way, it will affect them in the same way).

   The author has had the advantage of consulting both the excellent English translation of 1728 (anonymous, but presumably by Andrew Motte, whose translation of the *Principia* was published the following year) *A Treatise of the System of the World* (London, 1728), and a draft of a forthcoming translation by I. B. Cohen and Anne Whitman. The old translation was reissued with revisions in the volume: *Sir Isaac Newton's Mathematical Principles of Natural Philosophy and his System of the World*. Translated into English by Andrew Motte in 1729. The translations revised . . . by Florian Cajori. (2nd printing; Berkeley, CA: University of California Press, 1946). In that edition the sections (distinguished in the original Latin publication and in the 1728 English version by marginal section-headings) are numbered (these numbers do not appear in the 1728 English or in the 1728 or 1731 Latin editions); the paragraphs quoted are, with a small elision, §§20–21 there (pp. 568–9). Unfortunately, the revisions made in that publication introduce a serious error into the text of §21; the author is therefore particularly grateful to Benjamin Weiss, Curator of Rare Books at the Burndy Library of the Dibner Institute for the History of Science and Technology at the Massachusetts Institute of Technology, for making available photostatic copies of the 1728 English and Latin versions of those sections (and of the 1731 Latin edition as well); and to George Smith for obtaining those copies, as well as a copy of the Cohen and Whitman draft mentioned above. (See editors' note, p. 366.)

72 *Opticks* (Dover edn), p. 397.

73 *Ibid.*, p. 400.

74 *Ibid.*, p. 401.

75 *Ibid.*, pp. 401–2.

76 *Principia* (edition cited in note 62 above), vol. 2, p. 392. (One emendation has been made of the Motte translation: "I feign no hypotheses" for "I frame no hypotheses." It was pointed out by Alexandre Koyré – cited in I. Bernard Cohen, *Introduction to Newton's "Principia"* [Cambridge, MA: Harvard University Press, 1978], p. 241, n. 9 – that this is the English version of his Latin phrase "hypotheses non fingo" used by Newton himself in the *Opticks*, in Query 28; see Dover edn, p. 369.)

77 Cf., for fuller discussion of these matters, Stein, "Newtonian Space-Time" and "Some Philosophical Prehistory of General Relativity" (sections 1–3), both cited in note 31 above.

78 *Opticks* (Dover edn), p. 376.

gravity and levity, earth, water, air and fire, minerals, the faculties of memory, imagination, fantasy and invention, the soul and God, and much more. The attention of the historian of mathematics will be captured by Newton's annotations on infinity and indivisibles that open the "Questiones" with entries on first matter, atoms, the vacuum, quantity, and motion. Some of Newton's sources here are Walter Charleton's *Physiologia* (1654), Henry More's *Immortality of the Soul* (1659), and John Wallis's *De angulo contactus* (1656) and *Mathesis universalis* (1657). The young Newton was addressing the vexed question of the composition of the mathematical continuum, and the related questions concerning the composition of matter and the representation of continuously varying motion. An impact between hard atoms seemed to cause a discontinuous change of velocity. On the other hand, the speed of a body in free-fall might be conceived of as increasing continuously. These issues remained important in Newton's more mature mathematization of motion. Newton was soon to concentrate his mind on mathematical methods in which these ancient dilemmas acquired a new form, and perhaps became more tractable.

EARLY MATHEMATICAL STUDIES IN THE "WASTE BOOK" AND THE "COLLEGE NOTEBOOK" (1665)

The young Newton had very few mathematical books on his desk (see Table 9.1). His early annotations are edited in volume 1 of the

Table 9.1 *Mathematical books annotated by Newton in the 1660s*

René Descartes, *Geometria*, Amsterdam, 1659–61
François Viète, *Opera mathematica*, Leiden, 1646
Frans van Schooten, *Exercitationum mathematicarum libri*, Leiden, 1656–7
William Oughtred, *Clavis mathematicae*, 3rd edn, Oxford, 1652
John Wallis, *Operum mathematicorum Pars Altera*, Oxford, 1656
John Wallis *Commercium epistolicum*, Oxford, 1658

Mathematical Papers of Isaac Newton: some of the most interesting are to be found in the "Waste Book" and the "College Notebook."[2] The new art of algebra, in which symbols for constant and variable magnitudes were manipulated, attracted his attention. Newton was introduced to this new method by Viète and Oughtred's works.[3]

The seminal text in Newton's mathematical formation was Descartes's *Géométrie*.[4] Descartes had proposed – or so he claimed in the opening sentence of the work – a novel method for the solution of all the problems of geometry. According to tradition, geometrical problems could be solved by the intersection of plane curves: in Euclid's *Elements*, for instance, via the intersection of a circle and a straight line. More advanced problems, such as the angle trisection or the duplication of the cube, could be solved by the intersection of conics (namely the circle, the parabola, the ellipse and the hyperbola). There were certain problems (such as the section of an angle into an arbitrary number of equal parts or the "squaring" of the circle) that could only be solved by using more complex curves (as the quadratrix or the spiral). In the *Géométrie* Descartes had explained how "equations" (what we would call polynomial equations in two unknowns) could be used in the process of geometrical problem solving. The curves employed in geometrical problem solving could be conceived of as loci of points (in the plane) the coordinates of which satisfy a relation expressed by an equation.[5] In the early seventeenth-century geometry and algebra were still considered two separate disciplines, the former dealing with continuous magnitudes, and the latter with discrete ones. Descartes, therefore, had to overcome conceptual obstacles that should not be underestimated. Most notably, in order to apply algebra to geometry, one had to learn how to interpret all four algebraic operations in geometric terms.

By 1665 Newton had already mastered Descartes's method. The representation and study of plane curves via (polynomial) equations was no mystery to him. While Descartes had used oblique (and sometimes orthogonal) coordinates, Newton experimented with polar (and bipolar) coordinates as well.[6] It is in this context that he began studying the properties of cubic curves (the graphs of third-degree polynomial equations in two unknowns).[7] Newton was particularly interested in a method for determining the subnormal to a curve that Descartes had developed in the *Géométrie* and applied in the *Dioptrique* to devise non-spherical lenses.[8]

Somewhat simplifying, one might say that Newton became a mathematician by studying Descartes's *Géométrie*. This short essay, which in its Latin edition was accompanied by a lengthy commentary by Frans van Schooten and other Dutch mathematicians, provided a systematic method for tackling geometrical problems. It also contained a treatment of algebraic equations: one could learn how to reduce them to a canonical form, how to determine the interval in which their roots were to be found, and how to construct the roots geometrically via the intersection of curves. The young Newton brought these results to perfection. In this context he conceived a rule concerning the number of imaginary roots of an algebraic equation, a rule inspired by Descartes's rule of signs.[9]

There were, however, open problems in the *Géométrie*. Descartes's method for drawing normals was clumsy, whereas the algorithm by Jan Hudde featured in an appendix to the Latin edition proved much more promising. Most disappointingly, Descartes had confined himself to the algebraic treatment of what he called "geometrical" curves (those we would identify as "algebraic" curves) and had quite explicitly excluded "mechanical" curves ("transcendental" curves in modern terms) as lacking "exactness."[10] The most perceptive mathematicians of Newton's generation understood that the next step in mathematical development was to devise a method for tackling the curves that Descartes had excluded from his treatment. At the middle of the century, a mechanical curve – the cycloid – attracted the attention of French, Italian and English mathematicians (including such worthies as Torricelli, Roberval, Pascal, and Wallis). Mechanical curves were interesting as objects of study for a whole series of reasons. They naturally emerged as solutions of problems concerning technology (for example, the cycloid was used by Huygens in his study of horology) and natural philosophy (for example, in his correspondence with Mersenne, Descartes identified the logarithmic spiral as the solution of a problem on motion). Mechanical curves also occurred as solutions of problems concerning the area of curvilinear surfaces and the arc-length of curves. It was often the case that the arc-length of a geometrical curve or the area bounded by it could be expressed by a mechanical curve. Most notably, it was known that the area bounded by an hyperbola is expressed by the logarithmic curve. The calculation of logarithms, a very important issue in seventeenth-century mathematics, table making, navigation, surveying, and astronomy, was thus related to the mathematical treatment of a curve that had been excluded from Descartes's canon. Thus, mechanical curves, which are not expressible via polynomial equations in two Cartesian coordinates, emerged as a promising topic for young ambitious mathematicians – and Isaac Newton certainly wasn't lacking in ambition. But how could one deal with mechanical curves?

EARLY DISCOVERIES IN ORGANIC GEOMETRY: *HOW TO DRAW TANGENTS TO MECHANICALL LINES* (1665)[11]

A promising intake came not from the symbolism of algebra but from a research field located at the intersection between pure geometry and mixed mathematics, the so-called "geometria organica," which studied the tracing of curves by instruments. This was an important topic, since in order to determine the point of intersection of curves in the construction of geometrical solutions, it was convenient to think of the curves as generated by a continuous motion driven by some instrument (an οργανου), such as the compass and a straightedge in Euclid's *Elements*. It is the continuity of the motion generating the curves by means of a tracing mechanism that guarantees that a point of intersection can be located exactly, under the assumption that the mechanism is handled in an idealized situation in which any imprecision can be avoided.[12] Descartes had devised several mechanisms for generating curves. In *De organica conicarum sectionum in plano descriptione tractatus* (1646) van Schooten had presented several mechanisms for generating conic sections. This research field was connected with practical applications, for instance, lens grinding and sundial design. In the late 1660s Newton was able to devise a mechanism for generating conics that he later extended to higher-order curves.[13]

In 1665 in manuscripts entitled "How to Draw Tangents to Mechanicall Lines," Newton deployed organic descriptions in order to determine tangents to mechanical curves, that is, plane curves such as the spiral, the cycloid, the quadratrix, and the logarithmic curve that were not acceptable according to the criteria stated by Descartes in the *Géométrie*.[14] Indeed, Descartes had stated that "mechanical" curves (what nowadays we would call "transcendental" curves) could not be accepted in geometry: he developed a complex argument according to which they were not "exact." Descartes accepted only curves that could be expressed by algebraic equations, and he provided a method for finding the normal (and, therefore, the tangent) to a point on one of these curves. Newton was able to determine the tangent to mechanical curves by applying a kinematical technique known to Gilles Personne de Roberval. Such a method for determining tangents "without calculation" pleased Newton. By 1665, the young master in algebraic analyses was already experimenting with non-algebraic approaches to geometrical problems.

EARLY DISCOVERIES IN THE METHOD OF SERIES AND FLUXIONS: THE *OCTOBER TRACT ON FLUXIONS* (1666)

It was by reading van Heuraet and Hudde's annotations to the *Géométrie*, and Wallis's *Arithmetica infinitorum* (1656), and possibly by exchanging ideas and books with Isaac Barrow – who in 1663 had been appointed Lucasian Professor of Mathematics in Cambridge – that Newton began mastering a research field that he named "new analysis." In early modern Europe, "analysis" was a term that had a complex semantic stratification, as it was used in medicine, chemistry, philosophy, and mathematics. To mathematicians, "analysis" meant the "art of mathematical discovery," as outlined in Pappos's *Mathematical Collections*, a fourth-century CE work whose Latin edition had appeared in 1588. What was "new" in the analysis Newton was interested in was the use of the infinite and infinitesimal. Descartes's method of problem solving was confined to the use of finite magnitudes (such as finite segments) expressed by "finite equations" (i.e., polynomial equations with a finite number of terms). Wallis, instead, had conceived curvilinear surfaces as composed of an infinite number of infinitesimal components, and had calculated their areas by means of sums (or products) with an infinite number of terms (or factors).

Newton's "new analysis," the method of series and fluxions, is certainly the most celebrated among Newton's discoveries. In this section, this fundamental turning point in the history of mathematics will be very briefly sketched. Our treatment of the subject, of course, will hardly do justice to the fascinating and enthralling complexity of this intellectual adventure. For brevity's sake, we shall subdivide the discovery process into three steps.

In the first step Newton generalized the results contained in Wallis's *Arithmetica infinitorum* and made his first mathematical discovery: the binomial theorem (winter 1664–5). How to raise a binomial to a positive integer exponent was something already known.[15] Newton was instead interested in calculating binomials raised to a negative integer or even a fractional exponent.[16] What Newton did was the following: he identified a general form for the coefficients that occur when a binomial is raised to a positive integer exponent;[17] he tabulated the coefficients, and then, by an act of faith in the universality of these forms, he extrapolated and interpolated the tables, thus finding coefficients for negative and fractional exponents. Thus Newton discovered the binomial theorem.[18] He tested its validity by verifying that it led to correct results for known cases (achievable by methods such as long division and root extraction). Newton seems to have been aware that the binomial theorem lacked a conclusive demonstration: he found it by a heuristic method and he convinced himself of its validity by successful applications. Its rigorous proof remained beyond the power of the best mathematical minds until the nineteenth century.

The second step consisted in the development of a notation and algorithm for calculating tangents to plane curves. Probably following Barrow, Newton conceived curves as generated by the motion of a point. He later called "fluents" such magnitudes generated by continuous motion, and named "fluxions" their instantaneous rate of flow. Newton claimed that during an infinitesimal "moment" of time, the fluxion can be considered as constant. The infinitesimal increment of a fluent quantity (for example, a point moving along a straight line with a variable speed) will be equal to its instantaneous speed (or fluxion) multiplied by a moment of time. Such infinitesimal increments were called by Newton "moments" of the fluent quantity. Last, Newton calculated the slope of a plane curve by the ratio of the moment of the ordinate to the moment of the abscissa.[19] It was via the above conception and method that the notion of infinitesimal magnitude entered into Newton's mathematical practice. The algorithm that Newton devised for the calculation of the slope of a plane curve is basically the one still used in schools, with the crucial difference that today we think in terms of functions rather than curves, and justify the calculation of the derivative through limiting procedures, rather than through infinitesimals. It must be added that such an algorithm had already been sketched in Barrow's lectures, and it is fair to say that it is highly probable that Newton had drawn inspiration from them.[20]

The third step in Newton's discovery of the method of series and fluxions is the so-called "fundamental theorem of the calculus." This is somewhat of a misnomer, as today we understand it as an inverse relation between operators acting on functions. In Newton's day, however, it was understood as a relation between curves. Torricelli, James Gregory, van Heuraet, and Barrow had proved theorems concerning curves that showed that the operation for calculating the slope is the inverse of the operation for calculating the area subtended to a curve. Indeed, when a kinematical conception of magnitudes is accepted – that is, if one conceives of curves as traced by the motion of a point – such a relation is somewhat intuitively given as follows. It was customary, for example after Galileo and his followers, to represent the varying speed of a falling body as a graph whose ordinate is the speed and abscissa is the time. It was also understood that the area of the surface bounded by that graph is proportional to the space traveled by the body.[21] Newton's proof of the "fundamental theorem" that he penned in 1665 was probably influenced by Barrow's lectures.[22]

What was new about Newton's (and Leibniz's) approach to the fundamental theorem was the fact that they immediately seized the opportunity to use it in order to facilitate the calculation of areas of curvilinear surfaces and the arc-lengths of curves. Once an algorithm for calculating tangents is given, one can construct what Newton called "tables of curves" (namely, integral tables) by applying the algorithm to increasingly difficult curves. Newton tabulated equations of curves and of the slopes of their tangents as early as 1665–6.[23] It was in this context that he developed techniques for what we would call integration by variable substitution.

The range of problems that Newton's new art of discovery – the new analysis that he was soon to term the "method of series and fluxions" – could broach successfully is really impressive. Newton could calculate the area and arc-length of curves important for astronomy such as the ellipse, or even of mechanical curves such as the cycloid by expanding, via the binomial theorem, their equation as a power series and then integrating it term by term. He was able to express trigonometric magnitudes and logarithms in terms of power series. He could calculate tangents and radii of curvature to all known curves. He could systematize what we call the integration of irrational functions by the use of (integral) tables. The generality of this new method brought mathematics up to a level that only a handful of mathematicians in Europe could dream of, most notably the Scotsman James Gregory, who was developing similar results.

Newton systematized his notes into a short treatise that is known as the *1666 Tract on Fluxions*.[24] By the end of the 1660s, the Lucasian Professor, Isaac Barrow, realized that his younger fellow in Trinity deserved to be known outside the walls of the University.

PUBLICATION PROPOSALS: *DE ANALYSI* (1669) AND *DE METHODIS* (1671)

Whereas we are uncertain about the nature of Barrow's relationships with Newton in the early years of Barrow's tenure of the Lucasian Chair, it is certain that in 1669 the two were in deep contact on matters related to optics and mathematics.[25] When Barrow decided to quit the Chair in 1669, it was not chance that he was succeeded by Newton. The importance of this event for Newton's intellectual life cannot be overestimated, as now with a modicum of teaching duties, he could devote himself to research in a relatively safe environment. Before passing the Chair to Newton, Barrow took an equally important decision. He asked his young colleague to write about his new analysis in order to communicate this discovery to other mathematicians.

Thus, through Barrow's intermediation, a short manuscript tract entitled *De analysi per aequationes numero terminorum infinitas* (*On the analysis by means of equations with an infinite number of terms*) was dispatched in July 1669 to London.[26] The addressee was John Collins, an amateur mathematician who made a living – if only a modest one – out of his entrepreneurial activities in the field of mathematical book publishing. This sector was in crisis because of the depression in the print business caused by the Great Fire, but Collins managed to supervise the printing of several books, mostly related to algebra. In this discipline there was great need to update what was available on the English market.

Newton devoted *De analysi* to his techniques for calculating arc-lengths and curvilinear areas via infinite series. Newton was convinced that infinite power series, which he called "infinite equations," were the means for solving some of the most advanced open problems high up on the agenda of the mathematicians of his age. When he summarized its contents for Leibniz in 1676 he stated that the "limits of analysis are enlarged" by the use of "infinite equations" in such a way that "by their help analysis reaches . . . to all problems."[27] Yet, in *De analysi* Newton avoided including his most powerful method for obtaining series expansions, the binomial theorem. Instead, he relied on the safer methods of long division and root extraction. "De analysi" included power series expansions for the natural logarithm function and trigonometric functions (such as the sine, cosine, and arctangent), the quadrature of the cycloid, and the quadrature (and rectification) of the quadratrix. It ended with a proof of the fundamental theorem of the calculus and, most interestingly, with an attempt to determine the interval of convergence for power series.[28]

When Collins received Newton's tract he was thrilled, although it is debatable whether he really understood what he had in his hands. For Newton, getting in touch with Collins meant having free access to a network of mathematical correspondents, both British and Continental, and to the bustling world of printers and booksellers active in the capital. Newton could not have been offered the option to print his method of series in a more conspicuous and attractive way, although nothing came out if it. The extant correspondence between Newton and Collins reveals much of Newton's changing approach to publishing mathematics in the period from 1669 – the year in which he was elected Lucasian Professor in succession to Barrow – to the late 1670s. Collins had several proposals for Newton: for example, to issue *De analysi* together with some of Barrow's works he was expecting to publish. While waiting for Newton's permission, Collins made copies of *De analysi*, a short tract that would not have been so expensive to print, and we have good reasons to think that he circulated information about this youthful work by correspondence with British and Continental mathematicians. Reading the epistolary exchange between Newton and Collins leads the historian to follow a zigzag path: at first, Newton seems close to accepting

Collins's invitations to print *De analysi*, or even to dispatch him a more extensive treatise in which he had systematized his discoveries; but then – within a matter of weeks – we find him withdrawing his promise, much to Collins's frustration.

The new treatise was the so-called *De methodis serierum et fluxionum* (*On the methods of series and fluxions*) he had completed in 1671.[29] While *De analysi* would have been suitable for print publication, *De methodis*, a much longer treatise, would have changed the history of mathematics if it had been printed in the 1670s. In the opening lines Newton brought to perfection his method of series expansion,[30] and employed it for what we would call the integration of first order differential equations. In the second part of the treatise Newton reworked some of the results of the "1666 Tract on fluxions." He introduced a notation for fluents and fluxions (but not the familiar dotted one yet), presented his improved Hudde algorithm, which he applied to the calculation of maxima and minima, tangents and radii of curvature (a fluxional measure for the radius of curvature of a plane curve was provided). The treatise included two long tables of curves (two integral tables, to use Leibnizian terminology) that allowed Newton to solve very advanced problems related to the rectification and quadrature of curves. This was a masterpiece that was only published in an English translation more than sixty years (1736) after its composition, a delay caused primarily by Newton's idiosyncratic attitude towards publication (an attitude that was fueled by the polemics surrounding the validity of the *experimentum crucis* in the years 1672–6).[31]

Newton had achieved results that would have made him famous all over Europe as the most creative mathematician alive. Yet in letters sent to Collins he stated his increasing reluctance to print them. By the mid 1670s, Newton was quite adamant in not allowing his mathematical jewels to escape from his hands. To the few lucky ones who had corresponded with him on mathematical subjects and who had had access to his manuscripts he ordered silence and secrecy. What was the origin of Newton's anxieties over printing his mathematical discoveries?

NEWTON'S PHILOSOPHICAL AGENDA: *LUCASIAN*
LECTURES ON OPTICS (1670–1672)

To answer the above question it is necessary to broaden one's historical perspective a little in order to take into consideration the philosophical agenda that Newton set himself in the 1670s. We can learn
about it by looking briefly at his dealings with the Royal Society and
by reading some passionate annotations that he jotted down when
comparing the methods of the ancient mathematicians to those of the
moderns, as epitomized by Descartes.

Newton became a member of the Royal Society in 1672 after
having presented his reflection telescope to the society. This innovation fitted in well with the desiderata of the newly established
institution: which assigned great importance to microscopy, and the
improvement of telescopic observations. As is well known, in 1672
Newton was to submit his famous paper on the *experimentum crucis*,
in which he claimed to have proved a new theory concerning light
and colors. For most of the Royal Society's members, Newton's confidence in having "proved" a new physical theory could only sound provocatively arrogant: no such statements were expected. The theory
had already received a thorough treatment in the Lucasian lectures on
optics that Newton deposited in 1672 and dated retrospectively from
1670. In the third lecture, he stated that by the use of "geometry" the
science of colors, and natural philosophy in general, could achieve
the "highest evidence."[32] He also expressed his annoyance towards
those natural philosophers who were confining themselves to "conjectures and probabilities." Newton might have had in mind Robert
Hooke who in the *Micrographia* (1665) had warned readers to consider any discourse concerning the "causes of things" contained in
the book simply a "small conjecture," a "doubtful problem," and an
"uncertain guess."[33] Newton's discourse against probabilism offered a
view of natural philosophy at odds with what an influential member
of the Royal Society such as Boyle was promoting. It is a discourse
that intertwined with Newton's well-known rejection of what is now

known as hypothetico-deductive method, a method that was cham-
pioned by Descartes.

Hooke was expressing values deeply felt in the Royal Society. One
should bear in mind that, just after the restoration of the Stuarts, many
natural philosophers belonging to the Royal Society wished to make
it clear that no "unquestionable" or "dogmatic conclusions" should
be feared from them. Politically opinionated philosophers or dogmatic
theologians were not admitted in the society, which instead promoted
an innocuous mitigated skepticism. That is why any discourse aimed
at reaching certainty was looked upon with suspicion, while skepticism and probabilism were approved of in some of the most influential
Royal Society manifestos, such as Hooke's masterpiece on microscopy
and Glanvill's *Scepsis scientifica* (1665). In his *Lucasian Lectures on
Optics* and his 1672 paper, Newton broke with this code of behavior
by stating that the theory of colors he was proposing – a topic that he
knew was regarded as "belonging to physics"[34] – was not "an hypothesis but [of the] most rigid consequence."[35]

Newton's claim that he was reaching "the highest evidence"
in the theory of colors was targeted by Hooke in the heated debate
that poisoned Newton's life in the years following the publication of
the "New Theory about Light and Colors" (1672). The effect of the
dispute concerning the *experimentum crucis* on Newton's reluctance
to print his mathematical results cannot be overestimated. Newton's
great paper of 1672 was fiercely attacked, and this frustrating experience was to lead him – possibly out of spite – to avoid publishing his
results in other fields of enquiry. In a letter concerning the project of
printing his lectures on optics (dated May 25, 1672), Newton wrote to
Collins: "I have now determined otherwise of them; finding already
by that little use I have made of the Presse, that I shall not enjoy my
former serene liberty till I have done with it."[36]

Newton claimed that his natural philosophy was certain
because it was mathematical. However, in order to profile himself as
the philosopher who via the use of mathematics could transcend the
kind of probabilism defended in texts such as Hooke's *Micrographia*,

Newton had to avoid becoming embroiled in a further polemic concerning the certainty of mathematical methods. Newton was keenly aware that his method of series and fluxions was open to debate, because of the guesswork surrounding his theory of series (for example, when the coefficients of all the terms of the series are determined by discerning a pattern in the first terms) and the use of rather problematic concepts – such as that of "infinitesimal" or "moment" – in the method of fluxions. He knew that mathematicians who had published on the new analysis – such as Wallis, whose methods really stood at the root of his use of infinite series – had to withstand the criticisms of the defenders of the rigor and certainty of ancient geometry. Such debate would have been lethal for Newton, a philosopher who had claimed to be able to bring evidence into natural philosophy via the use of geometry: for if mathematics is to endow philosophy with evidence, it must be practiced according to criteria that guarantee the certainty of its methods. Newton showed annoyance with the qualitative models of the mechanical philosophy: Descartes, and in general the followers of the corpuscular philosophy, had attempted to explain natural phenomena in terms of impacts of invisible, hypothetical, corpuscles. Newton instead wished to "deduce" the laws of nature (most eminently, the laws of optics and the law of gravitation) from the phenomena. This deduction led to a much greater certainty compared to the "elegant perhaps and charming" romances (as Cotes would say in his preface to the second edition of the *Principia* (1713)) of the corpuscularists, and was the province of the mathematician.

The mathematics that Newton was using in his optical work was not particularly advanced, except in a few cases, such as the study of atmospheric refraction (1685–95).[37] Yet mathematics played a fundamental role in Newton's optical work, especially in the study of interference phenomena, and in the deduction of the properties of matter that exact measurements concerning these phenomena allowed. It is true that Newton's optical work is largely independent from the methods of series and fluxions. Still, what I wish to suggest is that Newton felt compelled to defend an image of himself as the natural philosopher who, because of mathematics, could go beyond the hypothetical discourse "blazoned about everywhere."[38] Newton cherished the idea that he was able to define a level of discourse where natural philosophy could be practiced "with highest evidence" and hypotheses avoided: for all his life he stood by this position. For Newton, printing *De analysi* or *De methodis* would have meant tying his name as an author to conjectural and heuristic mathematical methods, something which might have led to a deflation of the high status assigned to mathematics in his philosophical agenda.

There is another aspect of Newton's philosophy that we should consider in order to appreciate the reasons behind his reluctance to grant Collins permission to print the method of series and fluxions. In the 1670s Newton began to develop a profound distaste for Cartesianism, mechanical philosophy, and "modern philosophers" in general. Descartes epitomized the *hubris* of the moderns. The mechanical philosophy was the invention of a presumptuous Frenchman, who instead of looking with reverence to the distant past had dared to rebuild philosophy from scratch starting from an act of denial, a hyperbolic doubt cast on all past knowledge. Descartes the mathematician, at least the one revealed in the *Géométrie*, was as aggressive and innovative as the philosopher of the *Discours*. In the *Géométrie* one could read that the ancient geometers had not possessed any systematic method for solving geometrical problems: the length of their books and the disorderly presentation of their results were positive proof that they were just gathering together those propositions "on which they had happened by accident."[39]

Descartes's disparaging attitude towards the Ancients, in philosophy and mathematics, was anathema for Newton, who looked at the distant past with reverence and admiration. Of course, one should bear in mind that reverently referring to an antediluvian Hebrew sage such as Noah is something that served quite a different function for Newton from the citing of a Greek Alexandrian mathematician such as Euclid. Yet a certain resonance between Newton's philosophical and mathematical classicism can be discerned, and actually proved by textual evidence. Among Newton's contemporaries, Huygens was the one to win his admiration. In the *Horologium oscillatorium* (1673) the Dutch polymath showed him how one could carry out cutting-edge research in pure and mixed mathematics by means that were purely geometrical, without the help of any equations, infinite series, or infinitesimals. The cycloid, a daunting transcendental curve for mid-seventeenth-century mathematicians, was tamed with elegance in the *Horologium*, and put to good use in the study of pendulum motion. This example exerted a lasting impression on Newton's mind: the lesson was that one could use geometry rather than algebra, in imitation of the Ancients.

As we shall see in the next sections, Newton embarked on a research program aimed at refuting Descartes's claims about the superiority of modern algebra over ancient geometry. Newton concluded that algebra, as well as the method of series and fluxions, were just heuristic tools: they were useful in the art of discovery, but lacked the certainty and elegance of geometry. As Newton was to tell David Gregory in 1694, "algebra is fit enough to find out, but entirely unfit to consign to writing and commit to posterity."[40] Algebra should not be printed. But Newton was a great algebraist, and indeed was proud of his results in the field of algebra and calculus. From the mid 1670s to the early 1690s, he resolved this tension between his mathematical practices and methodological agendas by using the register of print publication for demonstrative geometry, and that of scribal publication (i.e., manuscript circulation and correspondence) for heuristic algebra. Indeed, in 1676 he wrote two well thought-out letters for Leibniz on his mathematical methods (including the binomial theorem).[41] What is more, in the 1680s and 1690s he allowed some of this correspondence on algebra and calculus to be printed in Wallis's works (see p. 412). Newton was thus able to circulate some of his symbolical results without having to commit them to "posterity" in the way he would have through printed books.

Studying the publishing strategies of Newton the mathematician is a challenging task. It might be too much to say that the above-mentioned philosophical factors *caused* Newton to reject Collins's publication proposals in the 1670s. Rather, one might say that it was a number of philosophical ideas, and political and religious concerns that propelled Newton's polemical reading of Descartes and the "modern philosophers"; that these concerns together with Newton's tense dealings with the Royal Society – like force vectors – pointed his mind away from the prospect of committing to print his symbolical, rather Cartesian, modern and uncertain mathematical discoveries. We should avoid describing Newton's thought and behavior as governed by causal laws. Newton's approach to publication was far from coherent, and the historical record does not afford us any simplistic description. Yet his dealings with Collins and Wallis reveal something of his authorial strategies, of the way in which he wished to profile himself vis-à-vis his contemporaries, of the role he attributed to himself as a rediscoverer of ancient exemplars and the defender of an anti-Baconian way of envisaging the relationship between mathematics and natural philosophy. Ultimately, we must accept that the late publication of Newton's early mathematical writings is also the result of contingencies such as the depression in printing caused by the Great Fire of London (1666), Collins's death (1683), and the publication conventions in England under the Restoration, an age in which scribal publication flourished.

It is often believed that after the creative outburst of the *anni mirabiles* of his youth Newton abandoned mathematics for other interests like alchemy, theology, and natural philosophy. However, the extant manuscripts distributed across the eight magnificent volumes edited by Whiteside, disprove such a view. Newton continued to be productive as a mathematician until the mid 1690s, when his move from Cambridge to London as Master of the Mint brought a real change to his lifestyle. In the following sections, I shall attempt to provide a survey of Newton's mature mathematical work.

CARTESIAN ALGEBRA: *ARITHMETICA UNIVERSALIS* (1673–1684)

Sometime between the autumn of 1683 and early winter of 1684, Newton, according to the statutes of the Lucasian Chair, deposited a set of lectures that were printed much later with the title *Arithmetica Universalis* (1707).[42] The lectures bear dates ranging from 1673 to 1683, but these were added in retrospect and it is highly unlikely that they were ever delivered to Cambridge students. In the *Lucasian Lectures on Algebra* Newton drew on results he had obtained in the 1660s and observations he had recorded in 1670 while working on the project of publishing a treatise by Gerard Kinckhuysen.[43] From several points of view, Newton's professed anti-Cartesianism notwithstanding, these lectures can be described as a fulfillment of Descartes's program, since algebra is here extensively presented as the tool to be used in the resolution of geometrical problems.

Several lectures were devoted to a systematic treatment of the roots of algebraic equations. Descartes's "rule of signs" already gave an upper bound for the number of positive roots of an equation by examining changes of sign. Newton added a new rule for determining the number of "impossible" or imaginary roots. The rules for expressing the coefficients of equations as symmetric functions of the roots were well known. Newton used these functions to find formulas for sums of powers of the roots. He also expressed rules for finding bounds between which the roots of an equation must lie.[44]

This is an impressive list that reveal Newton's prowess as an algebraist. The *Lucasian Lectures on Algebra*, however, contain some critical comments on the use of algebra that are worth considering. When, in 1707, the lectures appeared under the title of *Arithmetica Universalis*, readers were somewhat puzzled. On the one hand, Newton's lectures can be seen as a fulfillment of the program outlined by Descartes in the *Géométrie* because of the extraordinary results on the theory of equations listed above. On the other hand, the lectures contain criticisms directed at Cartesian "construction" or "synthesis."[45] In the last section Newton argues that the demarcation between acceptable and unacceptable means of construction (or synthesis), as well as the characterization of the relative simplicity of such means proposed by Descartes, are far too dependent upon algebraic criteria.

One should bear in mind the canon that Descartes had adopted in his *Géométrie*. As Henk Bos has explained, Descartes's method of problem solving was divided, according to the Pappusian canon, into an analytical part (resolution) and a synthetic one (construction).[46]

The analytical part is algebraic: it consists in reducing the problem to a polynomial equation. If the equation is in one unknown, the problem is determinate. The equation's real roots would correspond to the solutions of the problem. Methods for the calculation of the roots of algebraic equations up to the fourth degree had already been developed in the sixteenth century. But even when formulas were available, they did not provide indications about how one could achieve what was sought for the solution of a geometric problem: namely, a geometrical construction (or synthesis). Algebra could do only half of the business required by early-modern mathematicians; a geometrical construction was needed.

Descartes accepted the traditional idea that such constructions had to be performed through the intersection of curves. One had to choose two curves such that their intersections determine segments whose lengths geometrically represent the real roots of the equation.

The synthetic part of the process of problem solving, known as the "construction of the equation," opened up a series of questions. Which curves were admissible in the solution of problems? Which curves, among the admissible ones, were to be preferred in terms of simplicity? In asking himself these questions Descartes was continuing – albeit on a different plane of abstraction and generality – a long debate concerning the role and classification of curves in the solution of problems. Descartes prescribed that in the "construction of the equation" one had to use "geometric" (i.e., algebraic) curves of the lowest possible degree, whereas Euclid – it might be recalled – accepted in the geometrical constructions of the *Elements* only the use of the circle and the straight line.

In the final part of his lectures on algebra, devoted to the construction of third-degree algebraic equations (i.e., to the geometric construction of segments representing the real roots of third-degree algebraic equations), Newton fiercely disagreed with Descartes. The message that Newton wished to deliver was that in geometrical constructions algebraic criteria are misleading. Descartes had admitted all geometric (algebraic) curves as means of construction. Most of these, however, were, hopelessly complex according to Newton. On the other hand, Newton claimed that simple means of construction could be found in some "mechanical" (transcendental) curves, such as the cycloid. He maintained that it would be wrong to think that a curve can be accepted or rejected on the basis of its defining equation: "[I]t is not the equation but its description which produces a geometrical curve," he argued.[47] A circle is a simple and admissible geometrical curve not because it is expressible by means of an equation, but because its description can be carried out by means of a compass, one of the most fundamental constructions postulated in geometry. Further, expressing of a hierarchy of simplicity in terms of the degree of algebraic equations is something foreign to geometry. The circle and ellipse are of the same degree, but the former is simpler: "It is not the simplicity of its equation, but the ease of its description, which primarily indicates that a curve is to be admitted into the construction of problems . . . On the simplicity, indeed, of a construction the algebraic representation has no bearing. Here the descriptions of curves alone come into the reckoning."[48] When practicing geometry, Newton insisted, curves must be seen as being traced by motion, hence their defining equation is irrelevant.

Newton's passionate insistence on the idea that curves must be primarily seen as traced by motion rather than as loci of equations, has deep roots in his conception of the relationship between geometry and mechanical practice, a conception whose importance in Newton's mathematized natural philosophy can hardly be overestimated. In the 1690s, in writings devoted to projective geometry, Newton reconsidered this issue. Here we read that the "species" of a curve is not revealed by its equation but by the "reason for its genesis."[49] The geometer who has learned about the mechanical genesis of curves has an epistemological advantage over the algebraist: he knows the nature of curves because he masters their construction. Newton seems to suggest that we know what we can construct, not what we can calculate. Furthermore, Descartes's algebraic distinction between geometrical (algebraic) and mechanical (transcendental) curves, and his rejection of the latter, would have imposed unacceptable limitations on the geometrized natural philosophy that Newton was promoting. The non-algebraic integrability of ovals that Newton proved in Lemma 28, Book 1, of the *Principia* implies that the Kepler equation cannot be solved by the means admitted in the *Géométrie*.[50] Mechanical (transcendental) curves are basic elements of the geometrical structure of natural philosophy. In Newton's opinion, Descartes's rejection of these curves as lacking exactness (because they are not loci of polynomial equations in Cartesian coordinates) depends upon an unwarranted privilege given to algebra. Newton declared in the preface to the *Principia* that as these curves belong to Nature regardless of the complexity of their algebraic expression, their tracing is perfectly "executed by the most perfect mechanics of all." Indeed, as Newton wrote in the 1690s contra Descartes, "any plane figures executed by God, nature or any technician you will are measured by geometry in the hypothesis that they are exactly constructed."[51]

Newton's fiery invectives against the Cartesian algebraic method, which abound in the final section of the *Lucasian Lectures on Algebra*, are not at all paradoxical, as is often claimed. They are rather the expression of some of his most deeply felt philosophical convictions. Newton made it clear that in the section on the "construction of equations" he was talking about the synthetic, constructive phase of the problem-solving process. The analytical stage, discussed in the section devoted to the reduction of geometrical questions to equations, can be carried on in algebraic terms.[52] Indeed, in the Lucasian lectures algebra is proposed as one of the admissible analytical tools. In the synthetic, constructive stage, however, algebra must not play any role. Descartes had claimed that in the synthesis or construction of a problem, only intersections between geometrical (algebraic) curves could be used. For Newton, what was relevant in geometrical construction was not the equation of the curves, but the fact that an elegant and simple tracing mechanism was deployed.

IN SEARCH OF A GEOMETRICAL ANALYSIS:
SOLUTIO PROBLEMATIS VETERUM DE LOCO SOLIDO
(LATE 1670S)

Newton distanced himself from Descartes's analysis as well. "Analysis," we should bear in mind, meant a method of discovery. Newton considered his method of series and fluxions a kind of new analysis, a new method of discovery that could be used but was unworthy of publication. In writings penned in the late 1670s and early 1690s, Newton searched for a geometric analysis, a geometric method of discovery alternative to the symbolic, algebraic one.

One of the reasons why Newton distanced himself from algebra as a tool of discovery was the fact that geometry is aesthetically more pleasing. The Ancients' geometrical method – Newton often affirmed – is "more elegant by far than the Cartesian one." The enthusiastic acknowledgement of the elegance and conciseness of geometry compared to the "tediousness" of the "algebraic calculus" is a topos that recurs frequently in Newton's mathematical manuscripts.[53] The importance in Newton's mindset of such aesthetic evaluations can hardly be overestimated.

Moreover, according to Newton, algebraic analysis does not reveal how the geometrical synthesis can be performed. After the geometrical analysis of a problem it is often possible to reach a construction (a synthesis) by simply reversing the steps of the analysis, but after an algebraic analysis one is left with an additional and artificial problem: Descartes's problem of the construction of the roots of the equation. Newton concluded that such constructions were largely a Cartesian contrivance extraneous to the ancient geometrical tradition.[54]

Newton's search for a geometric analysis led him to read the compilation by Pappos entitled *Mathematicae collectiones*, published in Urbino in 1588. Newton's attention was particularly focused on a branch of the lost Euclidean corpus: the books on *Porisms*. In the early 1690s, Newton gave voice to his hopes and idiosyncrasies as follows:

> Whence it happens that a resolution which proceeds by means of appropriate porisms is more suited to composing demonstrations than is common algebra. Through algebra you easily arrive at equations, but always to pass therefrom to the elegant constructions and demonstrations which usually result by means of the method of porisms is not so easy, nor is one's ingenuity and power of invention so greatly exercised and refined in this analysis.[55]

"Porisms" are elliptically referred to in the seventh book of the *Collectiones*, where Pappos tells his readers that the Ancients possessed a method of discovery, a "method of analysis," that allowed them to reach their extraordinary results. This method had been illustrated in several works, of which Euclid's three books on porisms were the most advanced. Early modern mathematicians were tantalized and tried to reconstruct this method from Pappos, who provided some lemmas as an introduction to the reading of Euclid's work. For Pappos's fourth-century CE readers everything was quite clear, since they had Euclid's work, but for early modern mathematicians the situation was really frustrating, since that work was lost (as it still is). Newton came to the conclusion that porisms consisted in the kind of results that nowadays we would classify as pertaining to projective geometry.[56] Particularly notable, in this respect, is a small treatise entitled *Solutio Problematis Veterum de Loco Solido* that he penned in the late 1670s.[57]

A problem on which Newton had much to say was the so-called Pappos problem of 3 or 4 lines. This problem was central to the *Géométrie*, where its algebraic solution was presented as a paradigm for the superiority of Descartes's method over that of the Ancients. Indeed, according to Descartes, neither Euclid nor Apollonius had been able to thoroughly tackle the generalization of the Pappos problem to n lines. Newton was of a different opinion. In the late 1670s, commenting upon Descartes's solution, he stated with vehemence:

> To be sure, their [the Ancients'] method is more elegant by far than the Cartesian one. For he [Descartes] achieved the result [the solution of the Pappos problem] by an algebraic calculus which, when transposed into words (following the practice of the Ancients in their writings), would prove to be so tedious and entangled as to provoke nausea, nor might it be understood. But they accomplished it by certain simple proportions, judging that nothing written in a different style was worthy to be read, and in consequence they were concealing the analysis by which they found their constructions.[58]

With the benefit of hindsight, we might consider this Newtonian statement a misunderstanding of the role and strength of Cartesian algebra. Of course, when algebraic symbols are translated into connected prose, they often lead to rather opaque mathematical demonstrations. It might be claimed that the introduction of symbolism at the beginning of the seventeenth century was proposed by its defenders as a vehicle for freeing mathematical demonstrations from cumbersome verbal formulations. Further, only algebra could enable generalizations unthinkable in geometry: in the case at hand, a streamlined generalization of the Pappos problem from 4 to n lines.

Descartes solved the problem via algebra. He proved that for 3 or 4 lines the locus was expressed by a second-degree algebraic equation in x and y, and hence concluded that it was a conic section. To the contrary, Newton approached the problem in geometric terms. In the 1670s he developed many interesting ideas on projective geometry, reaching a result equivalent to Steiner's theorem. Indeed, Newton's geometric solution of the Pappos problem for 3 and 4 lines is grounded on an understanding of the projective definition of conics.

The solution of the Pappos problem could be achieved without algebra, in purely geometric terms. For Newton this meant a victory over the impudence of Descartes, who had dared to challenge the Ancients. In Section 5, Book 1, of his *Principia*, Newton presented his geometrical solution of the Pappos problem as having been achieved "as the ancients required." This result was understood by Newton as a victory over Descartes, a vindication of the Ancients against the Moderns. It is easy to see, however, that – *pace* Newton – his projective solution is quite modern (it is a child of the seventeenth century), and further that it cannot be generalized to n lines, whereas Cartesian algebra offers precisely this great advantage.

Nevertheless, one should not underestimate the values that informed Newton's opposition to Cartesian algebra. That is, in order to avoid a Whiggish approach, we should avoid judging Newton's mathematical practices and methods as dead-ends in the development of mathematics. The invectives against the use of algebraic symbols that characterize Newton's critique of Descartes's analytic geometry, and that later also informed his critique of the Leibnizian calculus, must be viewed as part of a larger philosophical project that he had in mind. Reading Newton's defense of geometry as a backward move, and identifying algebraization as a progressive element in seventeenth-century mathematics, means failing to grasp the values that underlie the confrontation between mathematicians such as Huygens, Barrow, and Newton on the one side and Descartes, Wallis, and Leibniz on the other. First, Huygens, Barrow, and Newton defended visualization over algorithmic efficiency. Second, they defended geometry over algebra as better anchored to physical reality. Finally, aesthetic criteria, such as conciseness and elegance, played a role in their choice to opt for the geometrical methods of the Ancients.

MATHEMATIZING MOTION: THE *PRINCIPIA* (1684–87)

The positions concerning mathematical methods that Newton defended in the 1670s and early 1680s, as well as the strategies of mathematical publication that characterized his correspondence in that period, may well have contributed to shape the mathematical style of his *Principia*. As is well known, in this masterpiece geometry is given pride of place. Newton's alleged triumph over Cartesian algebra, his geometrical solving of the Pappos problem – hardly a problem related to the mathematization of the System of the World – is presented in two long sections (4 and 5, Book 1) devoted to the geometry of conics. In the first section of Book 1, it is stated that infinitesimal magnitudes should be avoided. Newton opted for geometrical limit procedures, the so-called "method of the first and last ratios of vanishing quantities" that he had developed around 1680 in a treatise entitled *Geometria curvilinea*.[59] In the *Principia* Newton has much to say to his readers on his methodological preference for geometry. Yet, the *Principia* is a panoply of mathematical methods. Newton, like all great scientists, was an opportunist who deployed the methods best suited to his purposes, not only geometrical ones but also rather advanced symbolical methods of integration and power series expansion.[60]

It is thanks to a vast array of methods that Newton was able to raise the mathematization of natural philosophy to levels of generality and complexity that elicited admiration even from his harshest critics. One should bear in mind that before the *Principia* mathematicians knew how to deal with rather elementary cases such as projectile (vertical and parabolic) and pendular (circular and cycloidal) motion in a constant gravitational field, and that merely basic steps had been taken in the study of resisted motion. In the *Principia* Newton dealt with topics of unthinkable difficulty for his age, such as the three-body problem, the attraction of extended bodies, motion in resisting media, the speed of sound, the precession of equinoxes, the shape of equilibrium of a rotating fluid mass, tidal motion, the irregularities in the Moon's motion, and planetary perturbations.[61] His treatment of these subjects, however, stood in need of new mechanical concepts and mathematical improvements that were only to be provided in the eighteenth century. Indeed, the *Principia* became a repertoire of open problems that polarized the attention of mathematicians for more than a century, even those who were skeptical about gravitation.

The *Principia* would often puzzle the most competent mathematical readers. In some cases, Newton does not provide all the details necessary to grasp his demonstrations. Most notably, he often proves how to reduce a problem to a quadrature, and then proceeds to state that "granting the quadrature of curvilinear figures" certain results follow. No detail, however, is given about the quadrature techniques (integrations) just alluded to in the text. We know that at least in some cases, Newton was able to send his acolytes details about rather advanced quadratures necessary to achieve some of the results of the *Principia*. This occurred for Cor. 3. Prop. 41, Book 1, where he identifies some of the spiral trajectories traversed by a body in an inverse-cube force field; and for Cor. 2, Prop. 91, Book 1, where he determines the attraction exerted by a homogeneous ellipsoid of revolution on a point mass located on the prolongation of its axis of revolution.[62]

The richness of the mathematical methods of the *Principia*, Newton's pronouncements in favor of geometry, the contiguity of his geometrical limit procedures with techniques typical of the infinitesimal calculus, his employment of Taylor series, and his elliptical reference to quadrature techniques the details of which do not appear in the printed text, have given rise to the vexed question concerning Newton's use of calculus in the *Principia*: a question that played a prominent role in the controversy between Newtonians and Leibnizians. Did Newton use his calculus in the *Principia*? This is a question that cannot be broached here. It is a difficult question both because different readers of Newton's masterpiece have taken the term "calculus" to mean different things, and because the application of calculus techniques to the science of motion was far from being an established practice in Newton's times.[63] The contributions to the analytical treatment of mechanics made in the *Principia*, their magnitude notwithstanding, were soon to be superseded by the analytical dynamics promoted by Continental mathematicians such as Pierre Varignon, Johann Bernoulli, and Leonhard Euler.

LATER YEARS: *DE QUADRATURA, GEOMETRIAE LIBRI,*
ENUMERATIO LINEARUM TERTII ORDINIS, OF
QUADRATURE BY ORDINATES, THE BRACHISTOCHRONE
PROBLEM, AND *COMMERCIUM EPISTOLICUM*

In the 1690s Newton worked on a lengthy treatise entitled *Geometriae libri*, achieving results that would nowadays be expressed in terms of the theory of birational correspondences of second degree.[64] He also penned his masterpiece on the theory of integration, *De quadratura curvarum*, where he introduced his dotted notation for first order and higher-order fluxions and further systematized his quadrature techniques.[65] In a draft of this work, which unfortunately was never published, Newton proved that a fluent can be expanded into a Taylor power series, the terms of which are higher-order fluxions of the given fluent multiplied by the appropriate coefficients.[66] He also systematized his results on the classification of cubic curves that he had achieved in the 1670s,[67] reaching an (incomplete) enumeration of 72 species.[68] Perhaps the most striking result was the statement that all cubic curves can be subdivided into five projective classes: that is, that the five diverging parabolas[69] can generate all other cubic curves by central projection.[70] Newton also wrote a short treatise entitled *Of Quadrature by Ordinates* in the context of his studies on interpolation.[71] The Newton–Cotes formula originates from this research. Newton's work on interpolation dates from 1676 and, as we have seen, was partly published in Lemma 5, Book 3, of the *Principia*.

The above texts were Newton's last creative mathematical works. In 1696 a momentous change occurred in his life. He moved to London as Warden of the Mint, becoming a well-paid public servant. Newton had to face new challenges, as he grew involved in the political and theological debates raging in the aftermath of the Glorious Revolution. Challenges were also coming from mathematicians, since both in England and on the Continent the progress of mathematics was eroding Newton's advantage over his contemporaries. David Gregory had already threatened Newton's superiority in 1685 with the publication of his uncle James's results on infinite series. This event prompted Newton to compile a defense, the *Matheseos universalis specimina* and *De computo serierum*,[72] texts that most probably were not meant for publication but rather for private circulation. John Craig, Ehrenfried Walther von Tschirnhaus, and David Gregory were also working on quadratures, albeit still on a lower level than the one the author of *De quadratura* could achieve.

The greatest challenge came from Leibniz, who began printing his differential (1684) and integral (1686) calculi in the *Acta Eruditorum*. He promoted the new method in France, Switzerland, and Italy. A small group of aggressively innovative mathematicians began treading in his footsteps and a steady flow of papers spread knowledge about the Leibnizian calculus, which indeed started influencing even British mathematicians. Leibniz was able to establish a form of cooperation and competition with these younger mathematicians that differed from the reverent submission of Newton's acolytes towards their master. Leibniz and his followers also brought about considerable innovations in publication practices – not only were Continentals now publishing their results in newly founded journals, but more emphasis was being laid on methods than results.

In 1685 and 1693 Wallis was able to obtain permission from Newton to print extracts from the two letters to Leibniz he had penned in 1676, together with a brief presentation (1693) of the method of series and fluxions (see Table 9.2). Wallis was inflamed by nationalism. He would often complain about the machinations of the Continentals, whom he accused of stealing English discoveries. He warned Newton that his method of fluxions was circulating on the Continent "by the name of Leibniz's calculus differentialis."[73]

In 1697 Johann Bernoulli circulated the brachistochrone problem as a challenge "to the sharpest mathematicians in the whole world." Newton's solution soon appeared anonymously in the *Philosophical Transactions*. He had probably achieved this solution through a fluxional equation similar to the (unpublished) one he had employed in the *Principia* for the solid of least resistance problem.[74]

Table 9.2 *The early publication of Newton's mathematical works*

1685	Wallis, *Algebra*	paraphrased translation of letters to Leibniz (1676)
1693	Wallis, *Opera*, vol. 2	paraphrase of letters to Leibniz (1676) and additions on fluxional notation and quadratures
1697	*Philosophical Transactions*	Anonymous solution of Johann Bernoulli's two challenge problem (one is the brachistochrone)
1699	Wallis, *Opera*, vol. 3	letters to Leibniz (1676) *verbatim*
1702	David Gregory, *Astronomiae Physicae & Geometricae Elementa*	*Theoria Lunae* (in appendix). English version as a pamphlet (1702) and in English transl. of Gregory (1715)
1704	*Opticks*	*De quadratura* and *Enumeratio linearum tertii ordinis*
1706	*Optice*	*De quadratura* and *Enumeratio linearum tertii ordinis*
1707	*Arithmetica universalis*	*Lucasian lectures on algebra* (1684) edited by William Whiston. English trans., 1720, second Latin edn, 1722
1710	Harris, *Lexicon Technicum*, vol. 2	English translation of *De quadratura* and *Enumeratio linearum tertii ordinis*
1711	*Analysis per quantitatum series, fluxiones, ac differentias*	*De analysi, Methodus differentialis, De quadratura, Enumeratio linearum tertii ordinis*, some correspondence, edited by William Jones
1713	*Commercium epistolicum*	*De analysi*, mathematical correspondence (2nd edn, 1722)
1715	*Philosophical Transactions*	Anonymous *Account of the Commercium Epistolicum*
1716	*Philosophical Transactions*	Anonymous solution of Leibniz's challenge problem (on orthogonal trajectories)
1723	*Principia* (Amsterdam)	William Jones's edition of Newton's mathematical tracts (1711) printed in *Appendix*

Newton's paper contained a geometrical construction of the curve required (a cycloid) but no fluxional analysis.[75] In 1699, Fatio de Duillier, one of Newton's *protégés*, in a work devoted to the brachistochrone, *Lineae brevissimi descensus investigatio geometrica duplex*, accused Leibniz of having plagiarized Newton's method of fluxions. This episode was dealt with diplomatically, and the case was soon brought to rest.

Many in Newton's entourage, particularly those who had enjoyed privileged access to his mathematical manuscripts by visiting him in his private quarters, were convinced that – via correspondence with Collins, Oldenburg and Newton himself – Leibniz had gained information on the calculus, which he had then printed as his own discovery after changing the notation. After studying Leibniz's manuscripts, twentieth-century historians were able to disprove this accusation. It is an established fact that by 1675 Leibniz had come up with the calculus notation and algorithm that is still in use today.

The situation degenerated when, in 1708, in the journal of the Royal Society a mathematician of minor stature, John Keill, claimed that Leibniz was a plagiarist. The latter demanded that the Royal Society protect him from the "empty and unjust braying" of such an "upstart." Consequently, a committee of the Royal Society, secretly led by its president, Isaac Newton, produced a detailed report, the *Commercium epistolicum* (1713). The committee maintained that Newton had been the "first inventor" and that "Leibniz's Differential Method was one and the same with the Method of Fluxions, excepting the Name and Mode of Notation." It was also strongly suggested that Keill's offending statements were justified.

The ensuing controversy between Newton and Leibniz involved a number of Continental and British mathematicians, theologians and pamphleteers, thus causing a complex splintering of the European mathematical community. It would be simplistic to describe the controversy as a fight between two well defined opposing groups divided by the Channel. On the Continent, philo-Newtonian outposts were especially prominent in the Low Countries and in France, where Varignon, for instance, enjoyed cordial relationships with both Newton and Leibniz. In Basel, one of the main defenders of Leibniz, Johann Bernoulli, was far from confining his role to that of a follower of the German mathematician; rather, he played on the controversy to aggrandize himself. In a paper published anonymously in 1716, after recognizing Leibniz's claim to the invention of the differential calculus, Bernoulli claimed the discovery of the much more difficult integral calculus for himself.[76]

The controversy offered the two rivals a chance to make their views on mathematical method explicit. The two of them proved to have different views as to what the fundamental contribution made by the discovery of the calculus actually was. Leibniz was much more interested in defending the importance of notation and algorithm compared to Newton, who rather praised geometry. For Leibniz what was at stake in the dispute was the invention of an efficient algorithm. He also stressed the idea that the power of the algebraic method consisted in the fact that one could free the mind from the "burden of imagination" and manipulate symbols without worrying about their meaning. Newton despised those who practiced algebra like Leibniz, dismissing them as "bunglers in mathematics."[77] He instead praised mathematical procedures in which concepts "visible to the eye" are organized in the mind of the mathematician without his losing a firm grasp of the meaning of symbols. For Newton, mathematical concepts had to represent existing phenomena of which we have a clear intuition, such as motion and velocity. Leibniz rather conceived the rules of the calculus as symbolic manipulations well-grounded on metaphysical principles, such as that of continuity. One might say that Leibniz was a logician who gave pride of place to the basic notation and rules of the calculus, and who praised the generality of symbolical methods, whereas Newton was a geometer who sought conceptually profound solutions to advanced problems. The two mathematicians approached the dispute from very different angles.

The political arena, in which Leibniz and Newton each took on a leading role, also fueled the dispute, and this in part explains why the abstractions of mathematics could ignite so much fury. Newton had been a member of the Convention Parliament in 1689: he belonged to the entourage of Lord Halifax, and was very close to sectors of the Church of England that had promoted the Glorious Revolution. Contemporaneously, Leibniz had become a counselor of the Emperor and of the Czar, and was in the service of the Duke of Hanover. It was in part thanks to Leibniz's diplomatic efforts that his patron acceded to the throne of Great Britain and Ireland in 1714 as George I. The prospect of having Leibniz – a towering diplomat and metaphysician who actively pursued an ecumenical policy of reconciliation between the Christian Churches – as Royal Historian in London must have been a daunting one for Newton's party, which favored anti-Catholicism and a Protestant interpretation of Anglicanism. The priority dispute served the purpose of discrediting Leibniz at the Royal Court well.[78]

It might be contended that the anxieties and passions surrounding Newton's thought on mathematical method that we have reviewed in this chapter were determined by the fact that mathematics played such a prominent role in his broad-ranging philosophical agenda – one polemically oriented against the theological heresies of the mechanism promoted by the Cartesians and by Hobbes, the probabilism in vogue at the Royal Society, and the irenicism defended by the diplomatic endeavors of Leibniz. The greatest mathematician since Archimedes's time, like the Syracusan geometer and mechanic himself, used mathematics for belligerent purposes.

NOTES

1 Ms. Add. 3996, fols. 88r–135r edited in *Certain Philosophical Questions: Newton's Trinity Notebook*, ed. James E. McGuire and Martin Tamny (Cambridge: Cambridge University Press), 1983.

2 Ms. Add. 4004 and Ms. Add. 4000 (Cambridge University Library), respectively.

3 D. T. Whiteside (ed.) *The Mathematical Papers of Isaac Newton*, 8 vols. (Cambridge: Cambridge University Press), 1967–81, vol. 1, pp. 25–88 (hereafter cited as MP, 1: 25–88).

4 Newton worked with the second Latin edition (1659–1661), but may also have come across the smaller first Latin edition (1649). See MP, 1: 21.

5 To avoid anachronism, Descartes did not have "Cartesian axes," but he used what we identify as "Cartesian coordinates." For example, given an ellipse, he defined y as the abscissa measured from the vertex, and x as the corresponding ordinate, so that the ellipse's equation was $x^2 = ry - (r/q)y^2$, r and q constants. *The Geometry of René Descartes with a Facsimile of the First Edition*, ed. and trans. D. E. Smith and M. L. Latham (New York: Dover, 1954), pp. 95–6.

6 MP, 1: 155–212.

7 For Newton's early (1667–8) studies on cubics, see MP, 2: 10–89. He reconsidered this topic in the late 1670s (MP, 4: 346–401) and then in the mid 1690s (MP, 7: 410–653).

8 MP, 1: 213–33. The subnormal is defined as the segment of the x-axis lying between the x-coordinate of the point at which a normal is drawn to a curve and the intercept of the normal with the x-axis.

9 MP, 1: 520–7.

10 Henk Bos, *Redefining Geometrical Exactness: Descartes' Transformation of the Early Modern Concept of Construction* (New York: Springer, 2001).

11 In this subsection I draw freely from my *Isaac Newton on Mathematical Certainty and Method* (Cambridge, MA: MIT Press), pp. 6–7.

12 As Newton stated in the Preface to the *Principia*, the errors are not due to the imperfections of geometry and mechanics but rather to the "artificer" who applies them.

13 He obtained this method probably inspired by de Witt and van Schooten. See MP, 2: 106–56, esp. pp. 134–51, and MP, 4: 298–303. See also Newton to Collins (August 20, 1672) in *Correspondence*, vol. 2, pp. 230–1 and MP, 2: 156–9.

14 MP, 1: 369–82.

15 For example: $(1 + x)^2 = 1 + 2x + 1x^2$.

16 The reason for this is that Newton sought to calculate the area of the surface bounded by an hyperbola and the area of the circle segment. Indeed, the equation of the hyperbola can be written via a binomial raised to a negative exponent $(y = (a + x)^{-1})$, and the equation of the circle can be written via a binomial raised to a fractional exponent $(y = (R^2 - x^2)^{1/2})$.

17 For example, the coefficients (1, 2, 1) for $(1 + x)^2 = 1 + 2x + 1x^2$.

18 For Newton's discovery of the binomial theorem, see MP, 1: 89–142.

19 In familiar Leibnizian terms this ratio is expressed as dy/dx.

20 For Newton's early discovery (1665) of the algorithm of the fluxional
    calculus, see MP, 1: 382–9.

21 In Leibnizian notation: $s = \int v dt = \int \frac{ds}{dt} dt = \int ds$, where s is the space, v the
    speed, and t the time.

22 MP, 1: 298–305, 313–15.

23 MP, 1: 305–13, 316–17, 342–3, 348–63.

24 Ms. Add. 3958.3, fols. 48v–63v in MP, 1: 400–48.

25 In this section I am drawing from my "'Specious algebra is fit enough
    to find out, but entirely unfit to consign to writing and commit to
    posterity': Newton's publication strategies as a mathematical author,"
    Sartoniana 25 (2012) 161–78.

26 MP, 2: 206–47.

27 *The Correspondence of Isaac Newton*, ed. H. W. Turnbull *et al.*, 7 vols.
    (Cambridge: Cambridge University Press, 1959–77), vol. 2, p. 29.

28 The reader will excuse me for some anachronistic terminology in this
    paragraph.

29 MP, 3: 32–328.

30 Newton included a method (MP, 3: 50 *passim*), which was later
    improved and systematized by Victor-Alexandre Puiseux, for developing
    an algebraic equation in two variables, $f(x, y) = 0$, into a fractional power
    series.

31 *The Method of Fluxions and Infinite Series*, translated and annotated by
    John Colson (London: H. Woodfall for J. Nourse, 1736).

32 *The Optical Papers of Isaac Newton*, ed. A. Shapiro, 3 vols. (Cambridge:
    Cambridge University Press, 1984–), vol. 1, pp. 86, 88, and 436, 438.

33 Hooke, *Micrographia*, Preface.

34 *Optical Papers*, vol. 1, pp. 87 and 439.

35 *Correspondence*, vol. 1, pp. 96–7. This passage was censored by Henry
    Oldenburg, the secretary of the Royal Society.

36 *Correspondence*, vol. 1, p. 161.

37 MP, 7: 422–34.

38 *Optical Papers*, vol. 1, pp. 89 and 439.

39 *The Geometry of René Descartes with a Facsimile of the First Edition*,
    ed. and trans. D. E. Smith and M. L. Latham (New York: Dover, 1954),
    p. 17.

40 *Correspondence*, vol. 3, p. 385.

41 *Correspondence*, vol. 2, pp. 20–31 and pp. 110–29.

42 The manuscript deposited by Newton (probably written in 1683–4) bears no title: it is here referred to as *Lucasian Lectures on Algebra*. See MP, 5: 54–491.

43 The notes on Kinckhuysen's *Algebra* are edited in MP, 2: 277–447.

44 Jacqueline Stedall, *From Cardano's Great Art to Lagrange's Reflections: Filling a Gap in the History of Algebra* (European Mathematical Society: Heritage of European Mathematics, 2011).

45 MP, 5: 420–91.

46 Henk Bos, *Redefining Geometrical Exactness: Descartes' Transformation of the Early Modern Concept of Construction* (New York: Springer, 2001), pp. 287–9.

47 MP, 5: 424.

48 MP, 5: 425, 427.

49 MP, 7: 291.

50 The Kepler equation is $m = x - \varepsilon \sin x$, where m is the mean anomaly, ε is the eccentricity and x is the eccentric anomaly.

51 MP, 7: 287, 289.

52 MP, 5: 128–337.

53 See, for example, MP, 4: 277.

54 See, for example, MP, 7: 251.

55 MP, 7: 261.

56 Newton's studies on projective geometry are included in MP, 4: 230–5.

57 MP, 4: 282–321.

58 MP, 4: 277.

59 MP, 4: 420–519.

60 The attention of the historian of mathematics will be captured by several mathematical methods employed in the *Principia*. What follows is only a partial list. In Book 1: (i) a foundation for the determination of curvilinear areas, tangents and curvatures in terms of limits that was considered until Cauchy the most rigorous presentation of concepts and procedures essential for the calculus (Section 1); (ii) the application of limit procedures to the treatment of central force motion (Sections 2 and 3); (iii) the study of projective transformations in the plane (Section 5); (iv) a demonstration of the non-algebraic integrability of ovals and the application of the Newton-Raphson method to the Kepler equation (Section 6); (v) the reduction of the problem of central force motion to quadratures (Sections 7 and 8); (vi) the study of precessing orbits in terms

of power series expansions (Sections 9); (vii) a qualitative study of the three-body problem (Section 11); (viii) multiple integrations applied to the study of the attraction of extended bodies (Sections 12 and 13); (ix) the binomial theorem (Section 14). In Book 2: (i) Taylor series expansions (Section 3); (ii) a solution of the problem of the solid of least resistance (Section 7). In Book 3: (i) interpolation techniques equivalent to the Newton–Cotes formula (Lemma 5); (ii) an application of Lambert's theorem to the study of comets.

61 With respect to this last topic, he obtained a geometric method that, when translated into symbols, paved the way for the method of variations of constants. MP, 6: 508–37.

62 See Guicciardini, *Isaac Newton on Mathematical Certainty and Method*, pp. 267–90.

63 *Ibid.*, pp. 252–4.

64 MP, 7: 200–401.

65 MP, 7: 24–182.

66 MP, 7: 96–9.

67 MP, 4: 346–401.

68 MP, 7: 579–671.

69 Equation $y^2 = ax^3 + bx^2 + cx + d$.

70 MP, 7: 411–35, 634–5.

71 MP, 7: 690–702.

72 MP, 4: 526–89, 590–653.

73 *Correspondence*, vol. 4, p. 100.

74 MP, 6: 456–80. The "brachistochrone" is the curve connecting two given points along which a body slides, without friction and under the action of constant gravity, in the least possible time.

75 Newton's fluxional analysis of the brachistochrone problem is found in MP, 8: 86–91.

76 Johann Bernoulli, "Epistola pro eminente Mathematico, Dn. Johanne Bernoullio, contra quendam ex Anglia antogonistam [sic] scripta," *Acta Eruditorum*, Julii 1716, 296–315.

77 Walter George Hiscock, *David Gregory, Isaac Newton and Their Circle* (Oxford: Oxford University Press, 1937), p. 42.

78 See Bertoloni Meli's chapter in this volume.

10 Newton, active powers, and the mechanical philosophy

Alan Gabbey

Among the notable eighteenth-century expositions of Newton's achievements were Henry Pemberton's *A View of Sir Isaac Newton's Philosophy* (1728), Willem Jacob's Gravesande's *Mathematical Elements of Natural Philosophy confirm'd by experiments: or, an introduction to Sir Isaac Newton's Philosophy* (6th edn, 1747), and Colin Maclaurin's posthumous *An Account of Sir Isaac Newton's Philosophical Discoveries* (1748). To the modern eye, there is something puzzling about these titles. We note the terms "philosophy," "natural philosophy," and "philosophical," and we wonder what they mean in this setting. Take Maclaurin's *Account*, the best of the genre, and written by one of the leading Newtonians of the day. Newton made great scientific discoveries, and we can learn what most of them are from reading *An Account*, but what *philosophical* discoveries did he make? Maclaurin describes Newton's work in mechanics, rational and celestial, and in physics, theoretical and experimental (though not optics). But Newton the *philosopher*? To answer these questions requires a preliminary disentanglement of the disciplinary classifications that clustered around the business of "philosophy" in the seventeenth and eighteenth centuries.

In Newton's day the predominant framework of university instruction in philosophy was that of the Peripatetic or scholastic tradition, adapted to local religious and cultural requirements (Protestant in Germany, Holland, and Britain; Catholic in France, Spain, and Italy). In that tradition, *Philosophy* divides into *speculative* and *practical* philosophy. Speculative philosophy divides in turn into three principal *sciences* (*scientiae*): *metaphysics* or *first philosophy*, *natural philosophy*, and *mathematics*; to which are added the *middle sciences* (*scientiae mediae*), which include

421

theoretical mechanics, optics, and astronomy. Loosely speaking, science (*scientia*) is knowledge of virtually anything, or a *habitus*, an intellectual disposition enjoyed by the possessor of scientific knowledge. Properly speaking, science results from demonstration with respect to "the why" of something, and is knowledge (*cognitio*) of things through their proximate causes.[1] Mathematics is the science of number, extension, and measure, in abstraction from material things. Natural philosophy, also called physics (*physica*) or sometimes physiology (*physiologia*), is the science of the causes of change and stasis in the natural world; the middle or mixed sciences combine mathematics and physics. In its widest acceptation, *metaphysics* is the science of being *qua* being, in abstraction from particular beings, but for some, metaphysics is the science of beings that are other than physical, that is, God, angels, and separated souls or minds, though some argued that to treat of God, angels, and souls is not the business of metaphysics,[2] and others that it is not the business of physics.[3] For yet others, metaphysics is the universal science of concepts that apply transcendentally to beings in general. *Practical* philosophy divides into *active* or *moral* philosophy (ethics, home economics, and politics), and the *mechanical arts* (*artes mechanicae*), which are concerned with the production of artificial objects for human use. Some writers included logic as a branch of philosophy, though it was more commonly seen as an art or instrument of reason.[4] Another important classification of philosophy was that of the Stoics, or more generally of the Hellenistic philosophers, who divided philosophy into physics, ethics, and logic. This taxonomy shaped Locke's "Division of the Sciences" at the end of Book 4 of the *Essay concerning Human Understanding* (1690),[5] and is reflected in Newton's proposal, which dates from the early 1690s, for university reform, "Of Educating Youth in the Universities." The philosophy professor is to begin with "things introductory to natural philosophy" (space, time, laws of motion, circular motion, mechanical powers, laws of gravity, hydrostatics, projectiles), and then move to natural philosophy in the wider sense (cosmology, meteors, minerals, vegetables, animals, anatomy). "Also to examin in Logicks & Ethicks."[6]

Viewing them within a disciplinary perspective (as distinct from the revolutionary changes in their theoretical content), mathematics and natural philosophy retained the same core identity throughout the seventeenth and eighteenth centuries. Mathematics maintained its special autonomy. Natural philosophy continued to be defined in eighteenth-century dictionaries and encyclopedias as the science of natural bodies, and its topical range underwent no substantial change from the late sixteenth to well into the eighteenth century. When Newton began the study of natural philosophy in his second year at Trinity College, Cambridge, in June 1661, the textbook was Johannes Magirus's *Physiologia Peripatetica*. Magirus dealt with the full sweep of topics proper to *physiologia*: the principles of natural things, place, vacuum, motion, time; the planets, fixed stars, eclipses; the elements, primary, secondary and occult qualities, mixed bodies; meteors, comets, tides, winds; metals, minerals, plants, spirits, man, zoophytes; the soul, the senses, dreams, the intellect, the will. This was the broad agenda for natural philosophy throughout Newton's lifetime, unimpaired in his case by a possible inclination toward the Stoic classification of philosophy.[7] He wrote on many of these topics, though not in equal measure. In particular, he wrote and experimented in great measure on alchemical questions. As a speculative inquiry into the manifold reactions between metals, acids and alkalis, minerals and other substances, alchemy was part of natural philosophy. As an art (*ars*), wielding crucible and furnace for the prize of transmutation in accordance with the precepts of speculative theory, alchemy was distinguished from natural philosophy by Peripatetic encyclopedists. As for metaphysics, there were varying senses of the term in Newton's day, as we have seen, and its career in Britain, from Locke through Newton and Berkeley to Hume, was markedly at variance with its career across the English Channel, from Descartes, Spinoza, and Leibniz through Wolff to Kant.

Evidently, Newton was a natural philosopher and mathematician in the traditional senses. But he was also a metaphysician in one or other of the senses mentioned above, and to be one he did not have to have published a metaphysical discourse in the *Acta Eruditorum* or a treatise on first philosophy. In the unpublished manuscript "De gravitatione" (mid 1680s), metaphysics deals with God and his management of his Creation, doctrines of substance, the nature of mind and body and their interaction and union.[8] In the *Principia* (1687), written shortly after "De gravitatione," we find what seems a shift in perspective that is all the more significant because it appears in a public setting. The "General Scholium," which first appeared in the second edition, contains the famous passage on God, Lord over all. He is eternal, infinite, absolutely perfect, omnipotent and omniscient, and substantially omnipresent. His substance is unknown to us; we know God only through his attributes and the excellency of the natural order, and through the final causes of things. He is the God of providence: "no variation in things arises from blind metaphysical necessity, which especially is always and everywhere the same." Newton rounds off the passage with the remark: "And thus much concerning God, to reason about whom, at least from phenomena, is a concern of Natural Philosophy."[9] The study of God *qua* Author of Nature (of souls too, by implication), or rather the study of Christ's vice-regency in the world, in keeping with Newton's Arianism,[10] has become part of natural philosophy, as allowed by Locke's division of the sciences. On this view, metaphysics would be restricted to such topics as freedom and necessity, causality, and (presumably) being *qua* being. Again, the evidence of some manuscript drafts (c. 1705) relating to Query 23 of the Latin *Optice* (1706), which became Query 31 of the second English edition (1717–18), is that "metaphysical" describes non-empirical inquiries into the occult non-inertial powers, and associated laws of motion hitherto undiscovered, that might activate the interacting realms of the spiritual and the corporeal.[11] Yet part of Query 28 in the printed *Opticks* (3rd and 4th English editions, 1721, 1730) reads as though the metaphysician inquires into the divine ground of physical process, a view in keeping with that in "De gravitatione." The ancient atomists rejected a universal fluid medium for the propagation of light,

> tacitly attributing Gravity to some other Cause than dense
> Matter. Later Philosophers banish the Consideration of such
> a Cause out of natural Philosophy, feigning Hypotheses for
> explaining all things mechanically, and referring other Causes to
> Metaphysicks: Whereas the main Business of natural Philosophy
> is to argue from Phaenomena without feigning Hypotheses, and
> to deduce Causes from Effects, till we come to the very first
> Cause, which certainly is not mechanical.[12]

Taken together, these representative passages suggest ambiguities in Newton's position on the identity of metaphysics, or reveal tensions arising from an awareness of creeping unsettlement on these taxonomic matters among his philosophical peers. Perhaps the issue can be stated in another way: how much of the study of God, *qua* Author of Nature, is to belong to natural philosophy, how much to metaphysics?

Leaving the general question of how Newton understood the discipline of metaphysics, there are metaphysical aspects of his natural philosophy that are crucial to an adequate understanding of two specific issues on which I want to concentrate. These are (1) Newton's engagement with the mechanical philosophy, and (2) his account of the causal interventions of mind and soul in the physical world. As it happens, a convenient bridge to these issues is provided by Maclaurin's *Account*, of which Book 1 is a survey of previous philosophical systems designed to silhouette the superiority of Newton's system. Maclaurin's closeness to the Newtonian legacy wins him a measure of ostensible authenticity which I shall exploit for my purposes in this chapter.

Maclaurin sees natural philosophy as "the firmest bulwark against Atheism," securing natural religion equally "against the idle sophistry of *Epicureans*, and the dangerous refinements of *modern metaphysicians*."[13] He attacks those philosophers, ancient and modern, whose transgressions have compromised the firmness of that bulwark. In every case, and on nearly every issue, the paragon of all virtues philosophical, whether natural, metaphysical or mathematical, is Sir Isaac Newton.[14] Newton unmasks the monstrous Lucretian system, reborn in the extravagant system of Descartes, who banished final causes, referring all explanations to "mechanism and metaphysical or material necessity." It was Newton's delight, "as I have heard him observe," notes Maclaurin, that his philosophy called attention to final causes. Among Descartes's errors was a principle of conservation of motion, based on an "extraordinary" inference from the constancy of God's action. Yet nothing is more at odds with experience, because perfectly elastic bodies do not exist, the only circumstance that would make the principle plausible. Some motion is always lost when bodies collide, so the universe *per se* cannot be a mechanical perpetual motion. The conservation principle is the cornerstone of the mechanist's universe, whether in the Cartesian, Leibnizian, or Spinozan form. In Spinozism, "un Cartésianisme outré" (Maclaurin expediently quoting Leibniz), substance exists necessarily, all happens with absolute necessity, there are no final causes, there is no vacuum, the account of good and evil is a perversion, and the same quantity of motion, or at any rate the same proportion of motion to rest, is conserved in the universe. The absurdities of Spinozism illustrate the nonsense to which Cartesianism leads, and for those coming fresh to the Spinozan system, in trusting innocence, they reveal its source, "which is no other than the *Cartesian* fable; of which almost every article has been disproved by Sir *Isaac Newton* or others."

A philosopher who "ridiculed the metaphysics of the *English*, as narrow, and founded on unadequate notions,"[15] was responsible for "a far-fetched uncommon stretch of metaphysics" according to which there cannot be atoms or a vacuum, because a principle of the identity of indiscernibles stipulates that not even God can choose between two identical states of affairs. Leibniz's claim that "the material system is a machine absolutely perfect," a consequence of "an excessive fondness for necessity and mechanism," is refuted by Newton's observation that "the fabrick of the universe, and course of nature, could not continue for ever in its present state, but would require, in process of time, to be re-established or renewed by the same hand that formed it." Descartes's beast-machine doctrine is as nothing compared with Leibniz's preestablished harmony, or with his pretense "that the soul does not act on the body, nor the body on the soul; that both proceed by necessary laws, the soul in its perceptions and volitions, and the body in its motions, without affecting each other; but that each is to be considered as a separate independent machine."

In short, almost everybody is found wanting. Witness the absurd schemes of Plato, Aristotle, Epicurus, the Sceptics, the alleged clear ideas of Descartes, the fictitious metaphysics of Leibniz, the crazy notions of Spinoza. The obsession with mechanism has led some to exclude from the universe everything but matter and motion (presumably Hobbes); others (meaning Berkeley) admit only perceptions and what perceives; others (presumably the Occasionalists) "impair the beauty of nature" by denying intermediate causal links between God and the world. "Many who suffered themselves to be pleased with *Des Cartes's* fables, were put to a stand by *Spinoza's* impieties. Many went along with Mr. *Leibnitz's* scheme of absolute necessity, but demurred at his *monads* and *pre-established harmony*. And some, willing to give up the reality of matter, could not think of giving up their own and other minds." Such a medley of philosophies has induced skepticism in certain quarters about the ability of philosophy to furnish any knowledge at all (presumably Locke and Hume).

> But it has appeared sufficiently, from the discoveries of those who have consulted nature and not their own imaginations, and particularly from what we learn from Sir *Isaac Newton*, that the fault has lain in the philosophers themselves, and not in philosophy. A compleat system indeed was not to be expected from one man, or one age, or perhaps from the greatest number of ages; could we have expected it from the abilities of any one man, we surely should have had it from Sir *Isaac Newton*: but

he saw too far into nature to attempt it. How far he has carried
this work, and what are the most important of his discoveries, we
now proceed to consider.

Allowing for Maclaurin's hagiographical intemperance, we are
intrigued that he sends the knight of Woolsthorpe to battle against
Descartes, Spinoza, Leibniz, and, though he is shy about naming them, Locke, Berkeley, and Hume. The author of the *Principia*
and the *Opticks* seems not to belong in the same intellectual
arena as the opposing triumvirates of what some still call
"Rationalism" and "Empiricism." But that is not how Maclaurin saw
the situation. Looking at it through his eyes, without kneeling with
him at the Newtonian altar, we discover a Newton who is not a dab-
bler in metaphysical matters, but a mathematician and natural philosopher whose theorizing is inseparable from metaphysical concerns
he shared with his contemporaries and predecessors.[16]

For those working within "the new philosophy," the most
striking limitation of Peripatetic natural philosophy was its inability
to provide what they took to be properly explanatory schemes for
dealing with natural phenomena. The Peripatetics had constructed
impressive arrays of divisions and subdivisions for *describing* the
bewildering variety of principles, qualities, relations, motions, and
quantities revealed by natural bodies, but for the protagonists of the
new philosophy these classificatory proliferations were absurdly
complex and, more to the point, were useless for *explaining* natural phenomena. They welcomed the possibility of explaining nature
by recourse to three or four fundamental attributes and modes of
body.[17] The undergraduate Newton would have quickly spotted the
explanatory ineffectiveness of the Peripatetic system, and would have
appreciated the contrasting attractions of the new ways of philosophizing that he found in the writings of Galileo, Charleton, Hobbes,
Boyle, Hooke, More, Glanvill, Digby, and Descartes, when he began
to study them on his own (they were not in the curriculum!) a couple
of years after entering Trinity College.

However, Newton also quickly understood that the new physics promised more than it could ever deliver, seducing many into
believing that its explanatory simplicities would be able to cope
with the endlessly complex real worlds of (al)chemist, metallurgist,
experimental philosopher, pharmacist, physiologist, or physician.
The mechanical philosophy, of whatever stripe, was by no means an
unqualified success in explaining all natural phenomena. There is
much truth in Stahl's observation (1723) that "mechanical philosophy, though it vaunts itself as capable of explaining everything most
clearly, has applied itself rather presumptuously to the consideration
of chemico-physical matters . . . it scratches the shell and surface of
things and leaves the kernel untouched."[18] Or rather, it purported to
reveal the reality of the kernel though it was incapable of reaching
it through experimental inquisition. No one understood that better
than Isaac Newton.

Newton's engagement with the mechanical philosophy is
therefore an intractable issue. There are two immediate difficulties. The first concerns the term "mechanical." In the early modern
period it enjoyed a wide range of meanings, the shared central sense
being "concerned in some way with manual activity," that is, with
artisanal operations, practical skills, the construction and working
of machines, physical conditions and objects and the interactions
between them, chemical manipulations, and experiments. By extension, since Antiquity, "mechanical" had connoted the theory of
machines and more generally mechanics *qua* the science of bodies in
motion and rest.[19] But proper usages of "mechanical" in the "artisanal
sense" and in the "theoretical sense" did not depend on or assume any
perceived necessary relation between them. Writing in 1594, Henry
Percy extolled "the doctrine of generation and corruption," which
"unfoldeth to our understandings the method generall of all attomy-
call combinations possible in homogeneall substances, together with
the wayes possible of generating of the same substance," a part of
philosophy that "the practisse of Alkemy doeth mutche further, and it
selfe [is] incredibely inlarged, being a meere mecanicall broiling trade

without this phylosophicall project."[20] Clearly, this mechanical trade is far removed from anything in Pseudo-Aristotle's *Mechanica* or Book 8 of Pappus' *Collectiones*. When in 1667 Thomas Sprat asked whether it would not be better for children to learn through seeing and touching sensible things – "In a word, Whether a Mechanical Education would not excel the Methodical?"[21] – he was not referring to the theory of machines or to the laws of motion. Nor was Henry Power when in 1664 he looked to the day when the microscope would reveal magnetic effluvia, the atoms of light and of fluids, and air particles. "And though these hopes be vastly hyperbolical," he conceded, "yet who can tel how far Mechanical Industry may prevail; for the process of Art is indefinite, and who can set a *non-ultra* to her endeavours?"[22] Robert Boyle understood "mechanical" in both the artisanal and theoretical senses, and had a sharper insight into their relations than most of his contemporaries.[23] Shortly before the publication of Newton's *Principia* his friend Fatio de Duillier informed the Abbé Nicaise that: "They are publishing a Latin work by Monsieur Newton in which he deals with the general mechanics of the world. This work concerns mainly the system of astronomy, but it is filled with a large number of very interesting things about rather another subject and which concerns at the same time physics and mathematics."[24] The phrase "the general mechanics of the world" might be thought to refer to mechanics in the theoretical sense. But even here the substantive "the mechanics" refers to "the general workings or mechanism of the world," not to a body of mechanical laws that apply to that mechanism, though of course Fatio de Duillier knew that the *Principia* contained those as well. Newton himself wrote in the *Opticks* that one of the tasks of natural philosophy is "to unfold the Mechanism of the World" (quoted below); these are virtually the same terms used by Fatio de Duillier to describe the *Principia*.

The second difficulty is how to characterize "the mechanical philosophy." A theory of explanation of phenomena in the non-qualitative terms of the configurations and motions of atoms or corpuscles, or other homogeneous matter individuated into bodies? A theory characterized by the notion that the universe and every system within it is a machine? Or characterized by the ideal of mathematizing the world picture? Or by the belief in necessary laws of nature and of motion? A theory in which the spiritual and the immaterial have been banished from the domain of investigation? Each of these is distinct from the others, yet each of them is a candidate for inclusion under the umbrella of "the mechanical philosophy."[25] Robert Boyle seems to have been the first to coin the term, in 1661. Pairing the philosophies of Gassendi and Descartes, Boyle noted their shared wish to explain phenomena intelligibly "by little bodies diversely figured and diversely moved." Searching for a suitable name for this species of natural philosophy, Boyle suggests "the corpuscular philosophy," though sometimes he calls it the "the Phoenician philosophy," because of the believed origin of corpuscularianism. But because "it is evident and efficacious in the domain of mechanical engines, sometimes I call it also the mechanical hypothesis or philosophy."[26] Boyle's sense of the mechanical philosophy centered on its intelligible ontological content and on its marked advantages over the tautologous explanations of Peripatetic natural philosophy.

These considerations must be borne in mind when we ask to what extent Newton can be described as a proponent of "the mechanical philosophy." If there is a coherent answer to the question, it will not be easy to come by. In the first place, Newton used "mechanical" (English and Latin) in both the theoretical and artisanal senses. There are several occurrences of "mechanical" ("mechanics") in the *Principia*, the *Opticks*, and certain manuscript drafts, where it is clear that Newton has in mind either the theory of machines or rational mechanics, a division within mechanics in the theoretical sense that creates problems of its own.[27] However, his use of the artisanal sense creates problems too. In the important alchemical draft manuscript "Of natures obvious laws & processes in vegetation" (*c.* 1672), natural processes are either "mechanicall" or "vegetable," corresponding to the distinction between "common" and "vegetable" chemistry (alchemy). Mechanical processes are sensible interactions between chemical bodies, whereas vegetation is the result of an enlivening, universal aether working in a "subtile secret & noble way" in all animal, vegetable, and alchemical activity. So Newton can write:

> All these changes thus wrought in the generation of things so far as to sense may appear to be nothing but mechanism, or several dissevering & associating the parts of the matter acted upon, & that because several changes to sense may be wrought by such ways without any interceding act of vegetation . . . Nay all the operations in vulgar chemistry (many of which to sense are as strange transmutations as those of nature) are but mechanical coalitions or separations of particles, as may appear in that they return into their former natures if reconjoined or (when unequally volatile) dissevered, & that without any vegetation.[28]

Here Newton is talking about "mechanism" in the artisanal sense, not about some version of "the mechanical philosophy." Elsewhere in this manuscript, and indeed as a general rule, when Newton describes a process as "mechanical" (English or Latin), we cannot assume without further ado that he is using the term in the theoretical sense. To ignore the distinction is to risk misinterpretation. Earlier in the same manuscript Newton declares that "Natures actions are either vegetable or purely mechanicall (grav. flux. meteors. vulg. Chymistry)."[29] For Dobbs this is explicit evidence that at the time of the composition of "Of natures obvious laws" Newton "still thought . . . that his gravity was mechanical in its operation."[30] That would be so if all the bracketed examples were of the "purely mechanicall," but the operations of "vulgar chemistry" are not at all the same sort of thing as gravity (the "gravitating flux") or meteorological phenomena, and in such a disorganized draft it is just as likely that the bracketed examples refer *respectively* to the vegetable and the purely mechanical. That is (taking meteorological phenomena to be in a doubtful category), gravity is a vegetable action, and common chemistry is purely mechanical, in the artisanal sense.

Newton's employment of the term "mechanical" in the artisanal sense tells us nothing about his involvement with "the mechanical philosophy." His employment of the term (or the cognate substantive) in the theoretical sense points to the ideal of mathematizing the world picture, as is evident from the early studies on motion, the Definitions, Laws of Motion, Corollaries and their applications in the *Principia*, and the Preface to the first edition. But for Newton the mathematical way went hand-in-hand with a denial of mechanistic necessity, a denial of a purely corporeal world and an insistence on the existence of non-corporeal active powers at work in nature under God's stewardship, and a deep antipathy to the dogmatic assurance of the Cartesians and others who claimed that in a mechanical universe the causes of phenomena are already known, or are readily accessible to human inquiry.

One wonders if Newton ever was a mechanical philosopher of "the canonical" sort. The editors of the student manuscript "Questiones quaedam philosophicae" (1664–5) rightly note that there is nothing in the text that shows unqualified support for either Boyle's program or the action-by-contact condition characteristic of Descartes's mechanical philosophy.[31] Often Newton's tone is hypothetical rather than declarative. For example, he begins the section "Of Gravity & Levity" with the words: "The matter causing gravity must pass through all the pores of a body. It must ascend again, (1) for either the bowels of the Earth must have had large cavities and inanities to contain it, (2) or else the matter must swell the Earth."[32] It would be a mistake to infer from these "must"s that Newton is affirming gravity to be corporeal in nature. Rather, he means that *if* gravity is corporeal, then "the matter causing gravity must pass through all the pores of a body," but we cannot tell from the text what Newton's own views on gravity were at that time. After all, these were *quaestiones*, not *postulata*. Still, the "Questiones" does show "a unity of outlook," as the editors conclude, that of Newton as an atomist, a commitment that remained with him throughout his life.

Newton's alchemical papers of the 1660s were not expressed or conceived in mechanist terms. His first attempts to interrelate his alchemical thinking and mechanist doctrines date from 1672–5. In "An Hypothesis explaining the Properties of Light discoursed of in my severall Papers" (read to the Royal Society in 1675), Newton sought to explain these properties in terms of "an aethereall Medium much of the same constitution with air, but far rarer, subtiler & more strongly Elastic." This aether was denser outside bodies than within their pores, and its pressure deflected light corpuscles in varying directions. But it had to explain a wide range of phenomena, such as surface tension, the cohesion of solids, animal motion, the phenomena of static electricity and magnetism, and "the gravitating principle," and so was non-homogeneous, being "compounded partly of the maine flegmatic body of aether partly of other various aethereall Spirits."

Newton's aether hypothesis, of neo-Platonic origin, was a revision of the doctrine of the Universal Spirit from which embodied specific forms are born. "Perhaps the whole frame of Nature may be nothing but aether condensed by a fermental principle," wrote Newton in the initial version of his 1675 paper. For his Royal Society audience he expanded this idea in terms less redolent of the alchemical origin of the aether hypothesis: "Perhaps the whole frame of Nature may be nothing but various Contextures of some certain aethereall Spirits or vapours condens'd as it were by praecipitation . . . and after condensation wrought into various formes, at first by the immediate hand of the Creator, and ever since by the power of Nature." So forms change into forms through unending cycles, "for nature is a perpetual circulatory worker, generating fluids out of solids, and solids out of fluids, fixed things out of volatile, & volatile out of fixed, subtile out of gross, & gross out of subtile."[33]

The transformability of matter was one of Newton's abiding beliefs, as was the corresponding unity of matter implied by the notion of nature as a "perpetual circulatory worker." Both doctrines therefore fall under the umbrella of the mechanical philosophy, as indicated earlier, so they form a link between Newton's alchemy and his inclinations toward mechanism. Furthermore, despite its neo-Platonic origins, Newton's aether, here and in his later writings, is material, so when employed to explain natural phenomena, its role was indistinguishable from that of analogous material media in other mechanical philosophies.

Yet because of the materiality of this aether, Newton had a serious problem. Do the aether's actions themselves have material causes, or are they the effects of a non-material active source? Are the ultimate sources of alchemical and mechanical activity material or non-material? In "Of Natures obvious laws & processes in vegetation" the principles of (al)chemical activity are material. On the other hand, in "An Hypothesis" Newton invokes non-material "secret principles of (un)sociableness" that account for (im)miscibility between certain fluids.[34] The vitalizing magnetic principles in "the star regulus of antimony" (the crystalline star formation that appears when antimony is prepared from antimony ore – stibnite – using a non-metallic reducing agent under controlled conditions), called "magnesia" by Newton, are also non-material. In short, Newton can never quite say if the natural changes he analyzes are the effects of purely material causation or of vital causation acting through the matter undergoing change.

In the decade following "An Hypothesis" and "Of Nature's obvious laws," Newton became temporarily disenchanted with aether hypotheses. In addition to the difficulties just mentioned, he surmised that an aether ought to retard the heliocentric motions of the planets, but no retardation had ever been observed. So the general concept of forces seemed to offer a way of explaining natural phenomena, and coupled with this idea was a developed account of chemical and physical composition. All Newton's aethers, from whatever stage in his thinking, were particulate, so it was a relatively comfortable transformation from the concept of an aethereal medium to that of conglomerations of particles under the influence of attractive and repulsive inter-particulate forces acting across the pores or other spaces separating the particles. The best-known application of this idea is Newton's account of bodies in terms of hierarchies of increasingly complex aggregations of particles held together by short-range attractive forces, as detailed in his "De natura acidorum" ("On the nature of acids," 1692, published in 1710).[35] The idea of hierarchical composition appears in Query 31 of the second English edition (1717) of the *Opticks*, where, in addition, longer-range repulsive forces (at the micro-level) explain the emission, reflection, and refraction of light, and where too the aether stages a comeback (as it did in the General Scholium of the *Principia*) in the tentative hope that it might after all account for gravity and optical phenomena.

In later life Newton did take a view on the ultimate causes of corporeal activity that seemed like a decision between material or non-material, or, more accurately, seemed to reveal the ultimate ground of every cause, of whatever corporeal kind. In Query 31 of the *Opticks* (1717–18) we read:

> The *Vis inertiae* is a passive principle by which bodies persist in their motion or rest, receive motion in proportion to the force impressing it, and resist as much as they are resisted. By this principle alone there could never have been any motion in the world. Some other principle was necessary for putting bodies into motion; and now they are in motion, some other principle is necessary for conserving the motion. For from the various composition of two motions, 'tis very certain that there is not always the same quantity of motion in the world. For if two globes joined by a slender rod, revolve about their common centre of gravity with an uniform motion, while that centre moves on uniformly in a right line drawn in the plane of their circular motion; the sum of the motions of the two globes, as often as the globes are in the right line described by their common centre of gravity, will be bigger than the sum of their motions, when they are in a line perpendicular to that right line. By this instance it appears that motion may be got or lost. But by reason of the tenacity of fluids, and attrition of their parts, and the weakness of elasticity in solids, motion is much more apt to be lost than

got, and is always upon the decay. For bodies which are either absolutely hard, or so soft as to be void of elasticity, will not rebound from one another. Impenetrability makes them only stop. If two equal bodies meet directly *in vacuo*, they will by the laws of motion stop where they meet, and lose all their motion, and remain in rest, unless they be elastic, and receive new motion from their spring . . . Seeing therefore the variety of motion which we find in the world is always decreasing, there is a necessity of conserving and recruiting it by active principles, such as are the cause of gravity, by which planets and comets keep their motions in their orbs, and bodies acquire great motion in falling; and the cause of fermentation, by which the heart and blood of animals are kept in perpetual motion and heat; the inward parts of the earth are constantly warm'd, and in some places grow very hot; bodies burn and shine, mountains take fire, the caverns of the earth are blown up, and the sun continues violently hot and lucid, and warms all things by his light. For we meet with very little motion in the world, besides what is owing to these active principles. And if it were not for these principles the bodies of the earth, planets, comets, sun and all things in them, would grow cold and freeze, and become inactive masses; and all putrefaction, generation, vegetation and life would cease, and the planets and comets would not remain in their orbs.[36]

This is a far cry from the materialist universe of metaphysical necessity that Maclaurin ridiculed in the writings of Descartes and Spinoza. However, the magnificence of Newton's vision in this fine passage should not deflect us from asking a few troubling questions. Do these active principles act according to mathematical law? If not, what becomes of the mathematical architecture that informs the *Principia Mathematica*? If they do, has metaphysical necessity not just returned by the back door?

Newton was a dualist and, on the question of human volition, a libertarian. He was in no doubt whatever about the mind's freedom to create new motion in the corporeal world, though he confesses his ignorance as to how this causal transaction takes place. We learn from Query 28 of the second English edition (1717/18) of the *Opticks* that this is one of the great problems that the natural philosopher should aim to unravel:

> the main Business of natural Philosophy is to argue from Phaenomena without feigning Hypotheses . . . and not only to unfold the Mechanism of the World, but chiefly to resolve these and such like questions . . . How do the Motions of the Body follow from the Will, and whence is the Instinct in Animals?[37]

There is abundant textual evidence of Newton's belief in the motive powers of the will. For example, in a draft variant (c. 1705) of Query 23 of the 1706 Latin edition of the *Opticks*, that is, of Query 31 of the later English editions, Newton stipulates that:

> the first thing to be done in Philosophy is to find out all the general laws of motion (so far as they can be discovered) on wch the frame of nature depends . . . in this search metaphysical arguments are very slippery . . . We find in o^r selves a power of moving our bodies by o^r thoughts (but the laws of this power we do not know) & see ye same power in other living creatures but how this is done & by what laws we do not know. And by this instance & that of gravity it appears that there are other laws of motion (unknown to us) than those wch arise from *Vis inertiae* (unknown to us) wch is enough to justify & encourage o^r search after them. We cannot say that all nature is not alive.[38]

In the second edition (1713) of *Principia Mathematica*, the final paragraph of the General Scholium of Book 3 reads:

> And now we might add something concerning a certain most subtle spirit which pervades and lies hid in all gross bodies; by the force and action of which spirit the particles of bodies attract one another . . . and electric bodies operate to greater distances . . .

and light is emitted, reflected . . . and heats bodies; and all sensation is excited, and the members of animal bodies move in accordance with the will, namely, by the vibrations of this spirit, mutually propagated along the solid filaments of the nerves, from the outward organs of sense to the brain, and from the brain into the muscles. But these are things that cannot be explained in few words, nor are we furnished with that sufficiency of experiments which is required to an accurate determination and demonstration of the laws by which this electric and elastic spirit operates.[39]

A few years later, in Query 24 of the second (and subsequent) English edition (1717/18) of the *Opticks*, Newton returned to his aethereal vibrations, asking a question that was to inspire the association-ist David Hartley's "doctrine of vibrations": "Is not animal motion perform'd by the vibrations of this medium [aether], excited in the brain by the power of the will, and propagated from thence through the solid, perlucid, and uniform capillamenta of the nerves and the muscles, for contracting and dilating them?"[40]

The general reading public would have got enough hints from the General Scholium and the editions of the *Opticks*. For readers of *Philosophical Transactions*, there was Newton's 1715 anonymous review of the *Commercium Epistolicum*, which he rounds off with an explicit recognition of the opposing views he and Leibniz took on the question of volitions and their physical effects:

> It must be allowed that these two Gentlemen differ very much in Philosophy. The one proceeds upon the Evidence arising from Experiments and Phaenomena, and stops where such Evidence is wanting; the other is taken up with Hypotheses, and propounds them, not to be examined by Experiments, but to be believed without Examination . . . The one doth not affirm that animal Motion in man is purely mechanical: the other teaches that it is purely mechanical, the Soul or Mind (according to the Hypothesis of an *Harmonia Praestabilita*) never acting upon the body so as to alter or influence its Motions.[41]

Those in the know would have had the full picture. Newton explained to Antonio Conti, ultimately for Leibniz's edification, that Leibniz

> colludes in the significations of words, calling those things
> miracles wch create no wonder & those things occult qualities
> whos causes are occult tho the qualities themselves be manifest, &
> those things the souls of men wch do not animate their bodies,
> His Harmonia praestabilita is miraculous & contradicts the daily
> experience of all mankind, every man finding in himse[l]f a power
> of seeing with his eyes & moving his body by his will.[42]

As we have seen from the draft for Query 23 of the 1706 Latin *Opticks*, and as we would have expected from these anti-Leibnizian sallies, the will in Newton's universe is not shackled by the impositions of any universal conservation principle. That too carried a Newtonian seal of approval. Query 31 of the *Opticks* shows that a principle of the universal conservation of something equivalent to *vis viva* or "energy" was wholly foreign to Newtonian natural philosophy:

> The *Vis inertiae* is a passive principle by which bodies persist in
> their motion or rest, receive motion in proportion to the force
> impressing it, and resist as much as they are resisted. By this
> principle alone there could never have been any motion in the
> world. Some other principle was necessary for putting bodies
> into motion; and now they are in motion, some other principle
> is necessary for conserving the motion. For from the various
> composition of two motions, 'tis very certain that there is not
> always the same quantity of motion in the world . . . by reason
> of the tenacity of fluids, and attrition of their parts, and the
> weakness of elasticity in solids, motion is much more apt to
> be lost than got, and is always upon the decay . . . Seeing therefore
> the variety of motion which we find in the world is always
> decreasing, there is a necessity of conserving and recruiting it by
> active principles . . . And if it were not for these principles the

bodies of the earth, planets, comets, sun and all things in them
would grow cold and freeze, and become inactive masses; and all
putrefaction, generation, vegetation and life would cease, and the
planets and comets would not remain in their orbs.[43]

In creating the world, evidently, God opted not to follow Leibnizian
recipes. It is not surprising that Maclaurin denounced the conservation principles of Descartes, Leibniz, and (as he misreads him)
Spinoza.

I conclude with a couple of issues on which we find Newton and
Descartes in intriguing counterpoise. The first concerns the roles of
the divine and human will. For Descartes, the only idea we have of the
way God can move bodies is our consciousness of the power of our own
minds to move our bodies.[44] Newton takes a similar line in his discussion of the nature of body in "De gravitatione," but reaches an anti-
Cartesian conclusion. He does not know what the real nature of body
is, so he substitutes an entity which it is within God's power to create,
and which will be indistinguishable from body as known empirically:

> Since each man is conscious that he can move his body at
> will, and believes further that all men enjoy the same power of
> similarly moving their bodies by thought alone; the free power
> of moving bodies at will can by no means be denied to God,
> whose faculty of thought is infinitely greater and more swift. And
> by like argument it must be agreed that God, by the sole action
> of thinking and willing, can prevent a body from penetrating any
> space defined by certain limits.

> If he should exercise this power, and cause some space
> projecting above the Earth, like a mountain or any other body,
> to be impervious to bodies and thus stop or reflect light and
> all impinging things, it seems impossible that we should not
> consider this space to be truly body from the evidence of our
> senses (which constitute the sole judges in this matter); for it will
> be tangible on account of its impenetrability, and visible, opaque

and coloured on account of the reflection of light, and it will
resonate when struck because the adjacent air will be moved by
the blow.[45]

One lesson to be drawn from this speculation is "that the analogy between the Divine faculties and our own is greater than has
formerly been perceived by Philosophers. That we were created in
God's image holy writ testifies." Some might prefer the supposition
that God entrusts the task of "solidifying" space to "the soul of the
world," but Newton does not see why he should not do it directly,
without any intermediary, thereby creating bodies empirically on all
fours with Cartesian *res extensae*. Furthermore, this account of body
is useful in that "it clearly involves the chief truths of metaphysics,
and thoroughly confirms and explains them. For we cannot postulate
bodies of this kind without at the same time supposing that God
exists, and has created bodies in empty space out of nothing, and that
they are beings distinct from created minds, but nevertheless able to
unite with minds."[46]

Cartesian *res extensa* fails this test. It leads to atheism,
because extension is uncreated and can be conceived together
with the imagined non-existence of God. It makes the mind–body
distinction unintelligible, unless we say that mind is unextended
and therefore exists nowhere, which is to say it does not exist at
all, or at least that its union with body is completely unintelligible, if not impossible.[47] Furthermore, the Cartesian real distinction
between body and mind implies that God does not contain extension *eminenter* and so cannot create it, so God and extension are
two quite independent substances. On the other hand, if extension is contained in God *eminenter*, "the idea of extension will be
eminently contained within the idea of thinking, and hence the
distinction between these ideas will not be so great but that both
may fit the same created substance, that is, that bodies may think
or thinking things be extended."[48] This could be an allusion to
Spinoza's doctrine of Thought and Extension as the two (known)

attributes of infinite substance.[49] If it is, it is also a misunderstanding of Spinoza, who does not claim that "bodies may think." That is the well-known speculation of Locke, but that seems not to be the allusion Newton has in mind here.[50]

The second issue takes the form of a puzzling incongruity in Newton's natural philosophy that matches an incoherence at the heart of Descartes's doctrine of mind–body causal relations. Descartes claims that the freely acting mind can increase or diminish motions in the body to which it is united, from which it follows that each time I kick a ball or stop something in motion, I violate Descartes's principle of conservation of motion.[51] Descartes was aware of the difficulty, which it seems he tried to side-step by separating the jurisdiction of human volitional activity in the corporeal world from that of the divinely maintained conservation principle and the laws of nature, but this leads to difficulties in explaining how the conservation law can be applied with assurance in given cases.[52] Newton did not have a principle of conservation that might have conflicted with the consequences of the mind's actions on body, but he did share with Leibniz the principle of conservation of momentum (as I call it for the sake of convenience) in the form of the third law, which states that action and reaction are equal and opposite. However, it is unclear if and how the third law applies to corporeal actions caused by human will. If I move my finger, causing directly at least one part of my physiology to begin a new motion, on what does that part *react*, as it must do, according to the third law? Does my mind suffer in reply a reaction quantitatively equal to the action received by the part I will into motion? If so, why am I never aware of any such reaction each time I decide to move my body? The problem seems to have been recognized, though confusedly, by two Newtonians, the idiosyncratic Roger Boscovich, and the less idiosyncratic Colin Maclaurin. In the Appendix to his *A Theory of Natural Philosophy* (1763) Boscovich writes that motion

> can never be produced by the mind in a point of matter, without producing an equal motion in some other point in the opposite

direction. Whence it comes about that neither the necessary nor the free motions of matter produced by our minds can disturb the equality of action and reaction, the conservation of the same state of the centre of gravity, & the conservation of the same quantity of motion in the Universe, reckoned in the same direction.[53]

Far from resolving the difficulty, Boscovich has deftly multiplied it by two. Maclaurin offers a similar and equally unavailing resolution in his *Account*. He insists the third law is so general that

Even in the motions produced by voluntary and intelligent agents, we find the same law take place; for tho' the principle of motion, in them, be above mechanism, yet the instruments which they are obliged to employ in their actions are so far subject to it as this law requires. When a person throws a stone, for example, in the air, he at the same time reacts upon the earth with an equal force; by which means the centre of gravity of the earth and stone perseveres in the same state as before.[54]

For one Newtonian experimentalist in the domain of moral subjects, the consequence seems to have been taken as read, without any apparent puzzlement. At one point in the *Dialogues concerning Natural Religion* (1779), Hume has Philo argue for the causal fit between the parts of an organism and its environment, explaining that "thought has no influence upon matter, except where that matter is so conjoined with it, as to have an equal reciprocal influence upon it. No animal can move immediately any thing but the members of its own body; and indeed, the equality of action and re-action seems to be an universal law of nature."[55] Hume's causal match in the ecological economy of organisms might be important in the context of the emergence of Lamarckian or Darwinian evolution theory, but it does nothing to clarify how matter interacts with mind according to Newton's third law.

Newton did nothing to clarify the issue either. According to the hypothesis in "De gravitatione" that bodies are the effects of God willing that regions of space be endowed with impenetrability, a corpuscle created in this way would lack no empirically known property of body.

> It would have shape, be tangible and mobile, and be capable
> of reflecting and being reflected, and constitute a part of the
> structure of things no less than any other sort of corpuscle, and I
> do not see that it would not equally operate upon our minds and
> in turn be operated upon, because it is nothing other than the
> product of the divine mind realized in a definite quantity of space.
> For it is certain that God can stimulate our perception by his own
> will, and thence apply such power to the effects of his will.[56]

I sense Berkeley waiting in the wings. But apart from that, Newton evidently takes mind–body interactions to be unproblematic. There is no evidence that he was aware of the mismatch between his third law and his inviolable belief in the power of the human mind to intervene in the mechanism of the world. This parallel between Descartes and Newton points to the incompatibility between the doctrine of human freedom of action and the doctrine of the inviolate rule of physical law.

The *Principia* and the *Opticks* were formative influences on eighteenth-century discussions of mind–body interaction and their physiological background, providing much of the methodological and conceptual backcloth. The impact of these great works, the absence of a conservation principle in Newton's natural philosophy, the work of Locke, and the anti-Leibnizian ethos of the Newtonian Age in England – all of these help to explain why eighteenth-century British physiologists, psychologists, and theorists of mind discussed the mind's action on the body without feeling the need to address – perhaps in some cases without being aware of – the purely mechanical or dynamical considerations that had energized Leibniz's critique of Cartesian mind–body causality. There were good reasons not to pay much attention to Leibniz anyway, not only because of the *vis viva* controversy and the priority dispute over the calculus, but also because any general conservation law, whether Cartesian or Leibnizian, could be discounted on the authoritative Newtonian ground that "motion is much more apt to be lost than got, and is always upon the decay." In those circumstances, it is not surprising that mind–body interrelations could be analyzed without anyone having to confront their physiology of action with a principle of universal conservation of motion or force (however quantified).

So, rather unexpectedly, it turns out that Isaac Newton merits a recognized place in the twin histories of psychology and philosophy of mind.

NOTES

1 Rudolphus Goclenius, *Lexicon Philosophicum* (Frankfurt, 1613); reprinted in same volume with Goclenius, *Lexicon Philosophicum Graecum* of 1615 (Hildesheim: Olds, 1964), p. 1010. See Goclenius, *Lexicon Philosophicum*, pp. 623–5, 1012; Adriaan Heereboord, *Meletemata Philosophica* (Leiden, 1659), "Collegium logicum, Positionum logicarum disputatio quarta, de Qualitate," p. 6; Bartholomew Keckermann, *Operum Omnium quae Extant tomus primus* (Geneva, 1614), cols. 871–5, Lib. 1, Cap. 6 "(De explicatione qualitatum), Exemplum primae speciei qualitatis nempe *Habitus*." See also Charles Lohr, "Metaphysics and Natural Philosophy as Sciences: The Catholic and Protestant View in the Sixteenth and Seventeenth Centuries," in Constance Blackwell and Sachiko Kusukawa (eds.), *Philosophy in the Sixteenth and Seventeenth Centuries: Conversations with Aristotle* (Aldershot: Ashgate Publishing, 1999), pp. 280–95.

2 For example, Etienne Chauvin, in his *Lexicon Philosophicum*, 2nd edn (Leeuwarden, 1713; first edn, *Lexicon Rationale*, 1692). Chauvin's article on *metaphysics* gives a useful summary of differing conceptions of metaphysics in vogue in the early eighteenth century.

3 Magirus claimed that spirits, including God, being instances of pure act and immaterial form, do not have a "nature" in that they are not subjects of motion or rest, and cannot therefore be the subject of inquiries in physics. Furthermore, "since God is above nature [*supra naturam*], he cannot be part of the subject of physics." Johannes Magirus,

Physiologiae Peripateticae libri sex, cum commentariis (Cambridge, 1642), p. 8. The atomist Johann Sperling excluded the doctrine of angels from physics, and Alsted argued that divine action is neither physical nor metaphysical *motus*, but *motus hyperphysicus*. Johann Sperling, *Institutiones Physicae* (Frankfurt and Wittenberg, 1664), p. 25. Johann-Heinrich Alsted, *Theologia Naturalis Exhibens Augustissimam Naturae Scholam* (Hanover, 1623), pp. 150–1.

4 For Toletus's division into *speculative, practical,* and *factive* philosophy, see William J. Wallace, "Traditional Natural Philosophy," in Charles B. Schmitt, Quentin Skinner, Eckhard Kessler, and Jill Kraye (eds.), *The Cambridge History of Renaissance Philosophy* (Cambridge: Cambridge University Press, 1988), pp. 209–13. For the disciplinary divisions and subdivisions common in Germany, see Joseph S. Freedman, *Deutsche Schulphilosophie im Reformationszeitalter (1500–1650): ein Handbuch für den Hochschulunterricht. Arbeiten zur Klassifikation 4* (Münster: Münsteraner Arbeitskreis für Semiotik E. V, 1985), pp. 65–105. On the three-way division of moral philosophy, see Jill Kraye, "Moral Philosophy," in Schmitt *et al.* (eds.), *Cambridge History of Renaissance Philosophy*, pp. 303–6.

5 Locke divides the sciences into Natural Philosophy ("the Knowledge of Things . . . whereby I mean not only Matter, and Body, but Spirits also"), Ethics, and the Doctrine of Signs (Logic). On Newton and Locke, see G.A.J. Rogers, "The System of Locke and Newton," in Zev Bechler (ed.), *Contemporary Newtonian Research* (Dordrecht: Reidel, 1982), pp. 215–38.

6 Cambridge University Library (CUL), Ms. Add. 4005, fols. 14–15. A. Rupert Hall and Marie Boas Hall (eds.), *Unpublished Scientific Papers of Isaac Newton: A Selection from the Portsmouth Papers in the University Library, Cambridge* (Cambridge: Cambridge University Press, 1962), p. 370. Note also (pp. 372–3): "All students who will be admitted to Lectures in naturall Philosophy to learn first Geometry & Mechanicks. By mechanicks I mean here the demonstrative doctrine of forces & motions including Hydrostaticks. For without a judgment in these things a man can have none in Philosophy."

7 On Newton's involvement with Stoic natural philosophy, see B. J. T. Dobbs, "Newton and Stoicism," *The Southern Journal of Philosophy* 23 (1985, Supplement), 109–23.

8 Hall and Hall (eds.), *Unpublished Scientific Papers*, pp. 105, 108–9
   (Latin), 139, 141–3 (translation). On Newton's status as a metaphysician
   (or "philosopher" in the modern sense), I stand corrected by Robert
   Palter, "Saving Newton's Text: Documents, Readers, and the Ways
   of the World," *Studies in History and Philosophy of Science* 18 (1987),
   434–5.

9 *Isaac Newton's Philosophiae Naturalis Principia Mathematica, the
   Third Edition with Variant Readings*, ed. A. Koyré and I. B. Cohen with
   the assistance of Anne Whitman (Cambridge, MA: Harvard University
   Press; Cambridge: Cambridge University Press, 1972), vol. 2, pp. 763–4
   (my translation). In an interleaf belonging to Newton's own interleaved
   and annotated copy of the second edition of the *Principia* (1713), *caeca*
   (blind) is omitted. More strikingly, in an interleaf belonging to Newton's
   interleaved copy, and in the second edition itself, *experimentalem*
   replaces *naturalem*: "to discourse of God, at least from the phenomena,
   belongs to experimental philosophy."

10 B. J. T. Dobbs, *The Janus Faces of Genius: The Role of Alchemy in
   Newton's Thought* (Cambridge: Cambridge University Press, 1991),
   pp. 81–8.

11 See J.E. McGuire "Force, Active Principles, and Newton's Invisible
   Realm," *Ambix* 15 (1968), 154–208, at 170–1.

12 *Opticks*, p. 369.

13 Colin Maclaurin, *An Account of Sir Isaac Newton's Philosophical
   Discoveries, in Four Books* (London, Printed for the Author's Children,
   1748; Johnson Reprint, 1968), pp. xix–xx. In *An Enquiry concerning
   Human Understanding*, published by fellow-Scotsman David Hume the
   same year as *An Account*, "our modern metaphysicians" are criticized
   for their doctrine of God's direct management of creation without
   subordinate powers or secondary causes, just as Newton is praised for
   having recourse, though laudably in hypothetical terms, "to an etherial
   fluid to explain his universal attraction." David Hume, *Enquiries
   concerning Human Understanding and concerning the Principles of
   Morals*, ed. L. A. Selby-Bigge, 3rd edn, rev. P. H. Nidditch (Oxford: Oxford
   University Press, 1975), p. 73, n. 1. Hume's "modern metaphysicians"
   seem to be the occasionalists, or possibly Berkeley.

14 To avoid a clutter of references and footnotes, I list here the range of
   pages in Book 1 of Maclaurin's *Account* where the reader can find the

material that follows: pp. 4–5, 14–15, 29–30, 65–6, 76–7, 78, 79, 82–4, 86, 89–90, 94–6.

15 For the only comprehensive commentary on the Leibniz–Clarke correspondence, see Ezio Vailati, *Leibniz and Clarke: A Study of Their Correspondence* (Oxford: Oxford University Press, 1997).

16 There is strong support for this claim, grounded on other considerations, in James E. Force, "The God of Abraham and Isaac (Newton)," in James E. Force and Richard H. Popkin (eds.), *The Books of Nature and Scripture* (Dordrecht: Kluwer, 1994), pp. 179–200, esp. p. 180.

17 Steven Nadler, "Doctrines of Explanation in Late Scholasticism and in the Mechanical Philosophy," in Daniel Garber and Michael Ayers (eds.), *The Cambridge History of Seventeenth-Century Philosophy* (Cambridge: Cambridge University Press, 1998), pp. 513–52.

18 G. E. Stahl, *Fundamenta Chymiae Dogmaticae & Experimentalis* (Nuremberg, 1723), Preface, quoted in J. R. Partington, *A History of Chemistry* (London: Macmillan, 1961–70), vol. 2, p. 665. Georg Ernst Stahl (1660–1734) was the principal architect of the phlogiston theory.

19 For more on this background and on the tricky problem of Newton's conception of the discipline of "mechanics," see my "Newton's *Mathematical Principles of Natural Philosophy*: A Treatise on 'Mechanics'?" in P. M. Harman and Alan E. Shapiro (eds.), *The Investigation of Difficult Things* (Cambridge: Cambridge University Press, 1992), pp. 305–22.

20 "Advices to his Son," Petworth House Ms., HMC 24/2, fols. 30–1. I am indebted to Stephen Clucas for this quotation and reference.

21 Thomas Sprat, *The History of the Royal Society* (London, 1667), p. 329.

22 Henry Power, *Experimental Philosophy* (London, 1664), "The Preface to the Ingenious Reader." Newton too hoped for a time when improved microscopes would show all of the ultimate corpuscles on which the colors of bodies depend, "but those which produce blackness." *Opticks* (1730), Book 2, Part 3, Proposition 7, p. 261. The passage first appeared in the "Discourse of Observations," which Newton enclosed with "An Hypothesis explaining the Properties of Light discoursed of in my severall Papers" in his letter to Oldenburg of 7 December 1675: *The Correspondence of Isaac Newton*, vol. 1, ed. H. W. Turnbull (Cambridge: Cambridge University Press, 1959), p. 391.

23 See for example *The Origin of Forms and Qualities* (1666): Robert Boyle, *Selected Philosophical Papers* (Manchester: Manchester University Press and New York: Barnes and Noble, 1979), pp. 74–9. Also my "Newton's *Mathematical Principles of Natural Philosophy*," pp. 313–15.

24 Fatio de Duillier to Abbé Nicaise, 5/15 June 1687. Bibliothèque Nationale, Fds fr. nouv. acq. 4218, fols. 26r–27v: fol. 27r.

25 For a full-scale study of the problem of "the mechanical philosophy," see Sophie Roux, "La philosophie mécanique (1630–1690)," Thèse de Doctorat, préparée sous la direction d'E. Coumet, Centre A. Koyré, EHESS, 2 vols. (Paris: EHESS, 1996), vol. 1, pp. 30–2.

26 *Some Specimens of an Attempt to make Chemical Experiments useful to Illustrate the Notions of the Corpuscular Philosophy* (1661), Preface, in *The Works of the Honourable Robert Boyle*, ed. Thomas Birch, 5 vols. (London, 1744. Facsimile reprint, Hildesheim: Olms, 1966), vol. 1, p. 355. On the question of the origins and nature of the mechanical philosophy, and of its relations to mechanics, see the important preliminary discussion ("Introduction générale") in Roux, "La philosophie mécanique," vol. 1, pp. 3–39.

27 See my "Newton's *Mathematical Principles of Natural Philosophy*," pp. 316–22.

28 Smithsonian Institution Libraries, Dibner Mss. 1031 B, fol. 5v. Quoted from the transcription in Dobbs, *The Janus Faces of Genius*, Appendix *a*, p. 268. To improve readability of this extended quotation without altering the meaning, I have ignored deletions, incorporated the interlineations, inserted a few commas, and modernized the spelling.

29 Smithsonian Institution Libraries, Dibner Mss. 1031 B, fol. 5r. Quoted from the transcription in Dobbs, *The Janus Faces of Genius*, Appendix *a*, p. 267.

30 Dobbs, *The Janus Faces of Genius*, p. 99.

31 J. E. McGuire and Martin Tamny (eds.), *Certain Philosophical Questions: Newton's Trinity Notebook* (Cambridge: Cambridge University Press, 1983), pp. 323–4.

32 *Ibid.*, pp. 362, 363.

33 "An Hypothesis Explaining the Properties of Light" (1675), in I. Bernard Cohen and Robert E. Schofield (eds.), *Isaac Newton's Papers and Letters on Natural Philosophy and Related Documents* (Cambridge: Cambridge University Press, 1958), pp. 178–235, at pp. 179–81. See also Betty Jo

Teeter Dobbs, *The Foundations of Newton's Alchemy, or "The Hunting of the Greene Lyon"* (Cambridge: Cambridge University Press, 1975), pp. 175–93, 205–6; *The Janus Faces of Genius*, pp. 102–04.

34 Dobbs, *The Janus Faces of Genius*, pp. 267, 268, 269. Richard S. Westfall, *Never at Rest: A Biography of Isaac Newton* (Cambridge: Cambridge University Press, 1980), pp. 307–8.

35 "De natura acidorum" (1692), in Cohen and Schofield (eds.), *Papers and Letters*, pp. 256–58.

36 Isaac Newton, *Opticks: or, A Treatise of the Reflections, Refractions, Inflections and Colours of Light*. Foreword by Albert Einstein, introduction by Edmund Whittaker, preface by I. Bernard Cohen, analytical table of contents prepared by Duane H. D. Roller (New York: Dover, 1952 [1st English edn 1704, 1st Latin edn 1706]), pp. 397–400.

37 *Ibid.*, pp. 369–70.

38 CUL, Add. Ms. 3970, fol. 620r. Transcribed in J. E. McGuire, "Force, Active Principles, and Newton's Invisible Realm," p. 171.

39 *Principia*, ed. Koyré and Cohen, vol. 2, pp. 764–5. Translation by Motte and Cajori.

40 *Opticks*, pp. 353–4. For Hartley's doctrine of vibrations, see David Hartley, *Observations on Man, His Frame, His Duty, And His Expectations (1749)*, facsimile reproduction, introduction by Theodore L. Huguelet, 2 vols. in 1 (Gainesville, FL: Scholars' Facsimiles & Reprints, 1966).

41 "An Account of the Book entituled Commercium Epistolicum Collinii & aliorum, De Analysi promota; published by order of the Royal-Society, in relation to the Dispute between Mr. Leibnitz and Dr. Keill, about the Right of Invention of the Method of Fluxions, by some call'd the Differential Method," *Philosophical Transactions* 29 (342) (1715), 224. Also in A. R. Hall, *Philosophers at War: The Quarrel between Newton and Leibniz* (Cambridge: Cambridge University Press, 1980), Appendix.

42 Newton to Conti [for Leibniz], February 26, 1716. *Correspondence*, vol. 6, p. 285. It is perhaps significant that in one of the drafts of this letter there is a different order of words in the last couple of lines: "For all men find by experience that they can move their bodies by their will, & that they see heare & feel by means of their bodies." A. Koyré and I. B. Cohen, "Newton & the Leibniz–Clarke Correspondence with Notes on

Newton, Conti, & Des Maizeaux," *Archives Internationales d'Histoire des Sciences* 15 (1962), 63–126, at 73–4.

43 *Opticks*, pp. 397–400.

44 See for example Descartes to Henry More, April 15, 1649. René Descartes, *Oeuvres de Descartes*, ed. Charles Adam and Paul Tannery, Nouvelle présentation, en co-édition avec le Centre National de la Recherche Scientifique, ed. P. Costabel, J. Beaude, and B. Rochot, 11 vols. (Paris: Vrin, 1964–74), vol. 5, p. 347.

45 Hall and Hall (eds.), *Unpublished Scientific Papers*, pp. 105–6 (Latin), 138–9 (translation); pp. 105, 108–9 (Latin), 139, 141, 142, 143 (translation).

46 *Ibid.*, p. 109 (Latin), 142 (translation, slightly modified).

47 This is basically the same criticism of Descartes's account of spiritual substance that the Cambridge Platonist Henry More made in his *Divine Dialogues* (1668) and *Enchiridion Metaphysicum* (1671). If spirits are not extended, then neither is God, which means he is nowhere, though he exists. More ridiculed the Cartesians on this issue by calling them the "Nullibists," the "Nowhere-men." See my "Philosophia Cartesiana Triumphata: Henry More (1646–1671)," in Thomas M. Lennon, John M. Nicholas, and John W. Davis (eds.), *Problems of Cartesianism*, McGill–Queen's Studies in the History of Ideas 1 (Kingston and Montreal: McGill–Queen's University Press, 1982), pp. 171–250, at pp. 238–9.

48 Hall and Hall (eds.), *Unpublished Scientific Papers*, p. 109 (Latin), 143 (translation, modified and corrected).

49 As far as I can tell, nowhere does Newton mention Spinoza's name or refer to any of his works. No work of Spinoza's is listed as having been in Newton's library (John Harrison, *The Library of Isaac Newton* [Cambridge: Cambridge University Press, 1978]), but I find it hard to believe that he never read Spinoza or did not hear about his ideas from others. At any rate, it is utterly impossible to believe that he (would have) found Spinoza to his liking.

50 Hall and Hall (eds.), *Unpublished Scientific Papers*, pp. 105, 108–9 (Latin), 139, 141, 142, 143 (translation).

51 "That God is the primary cause of motion and conserves always the same quantity of motion in the universe." *Principia Philosophiae*, Part 2, Article 36, in *Oeuvres de Descartes*, ed. Adam and Tannery, vol. 8(i), p. 61.

52 The separation of human and divine spheres of volitional activity has been argued in Daniel Garber, "Mind, Body and the Laws of Nature in Descartes and Leibniz," *Midwest Studies in Philosophy* 8 (1983), 105–33; Garber, "Descartes and Occasionalism," in Steven Nadler (ed.), *Causation in Early Modern Philosophy: Cartesianism, Occasionalism, and Preestablished Harmony* (University Park: Pennsylvania State University Press, 1993), pp. 9–26; and in Peter McLaughlin, "Descartes on Mind–Body Interaction and the Conservation of Motion," *The Philosophical Review* 102 (1993), 155–82. Garber and McLaughlin see this separation as a reason for preserving the coherence of Descartes's position; I see it as a reason to conclude that it is ultimately incoherent. Cf. my "The Mechanical Philosophy and Its Problems: Mechanical Explanations, Impenetrability, and Perpetual Motion," in J. C. Pitt (ed.), *Change and Progress in Modern Science* (Dordrecht: Reidel, 1985), pp. 9–84, at pp. 19–28.

53 Roger Boscovich, *A Theory of Natural Philosophy* (Cambridge, MA: MIT Press, 1966), p. 190.

54 Maclaurin, *An Account*, pp. 144–6.

55 David Hume, *Dialogues concerning Natural Religion*, ed. Norman Kemp Smith (London: T. Nelson, 1947), p. 186.

56 Hall and Hall (eds.), *Unpublished Scientific Papers*, p. 106 (Latin), p. 139 (translation, slightly modified).

11 A preliminary reassessment of Newton's alchemy

William R. Newman

INTRODUCTION: PROBLEMS WITH THE RECEIVED VIEW OF NEWTON'S ALCHEMY

Despite their relative obscurity, Isaac Newton's alchemical manuscripts have long engendered strong claims. In the mid nineteenth century, Newton's biographer David Brewster marveled at the fact that "a mind of such power, and so nobly occupied with the abstractions of geometry" could concern itself with the alchemical charlatanry "of a fool and a knave."[1] More recent historians, on the other hand, have seen Newton's alchemy alternatively as the wellspring of his theory of universal gravitation, as occupying a central place in his attempt to return to an uncorrupted, primitive Christianity, or as an attempt to derive "positive knowledge" of chemistry from the obscurity of alchemical writings. This chapter will take a different approach. After describing the *status quaestionis* of Newton's chymistry found in the existing scholarship and discussing its problems, I will pass to a brief outline of recent discoveries that shed a quite different light on Newton's alchemical project. As we shall see, the decades that Newton spent studying alchemical texts and performing alchemical experiments were neither a quixotic and fruitless dream nor a romantic rebellion against the natural philosophy of his day, nor for that matter an attempt to form an alternative religion. Like Robert Boyle, G. W. Leibniz, and many other natural philosophers of the seventeenth century, Newton tried both to integrate chymical findings

The author would like to thank Roger Ariew, Domenico Bertoloni Meli, Jed Buchwald, John Henry, and Gideon Manning, all of whom read and offered valuable comments upon the present chapter.

into his natural philosophy as a whole and to learn the secrets of chrysopoeia. Although his long engagement with alchemy did not lead Newton to his fundamental discovery of universal gravitation, it had highly significant impacts on other aspects of his science, particularly in the realms of optics and in the study of the Earth's internal processes.

Already in 1946, John Maynard Keynes used the alchemical papers to make his famous declaration that "Newton was not the first of the age of reason" but "the last of the magicians."[2] More specific, if less evocative, is the position of B. J. T. Dobbs and Richard Westfall, who at various times both argued that Newton's alchemy contributed in a major way to his mature theory of gravitation, and more broadly to his conviction that immaterial forces in general could operate at a distance. The ultimate source for this view may well have been a brief remark made by J. E. McGuire in a 1968 study devoted mainly to Newtonian forces and active principles in the period after the publication of the *Principia*.[3] Far more significant for the subsequent historiography, however, was Westfall's 1971 book *Force in Newton's Physics*, in which he explicitly linked gravitational force to alchemy and what he called "the hermetic tradition," a locution that clearly betrays the influence of Frances Yates's 1964 *Giordano Bruno and the Hermetic Tradition*.[4] Westfall developed this idea further in an article of 1972. There he argued that Newton's concept of force at a distance "derived initially from the world of terrestrial phenomena, especially chemical reactions." In fact, Westfall even went so far as to claim that Newton's concept of gravitational attraction emerged only after "he applied his chemical idea of attraction to the cosmos."[5] Dobbs explicitly adopted Westfall's position in her 1975 *Foundations of Newton's Alchemy* and even suggested that Newton's concept of immaterial attraction might first have emerged during the composition of his "Clavis," a treatise that Dobbs thought to have been composed by Newton early in his career.[6] As it turns out, however, the "Clavis" was not by Newton at all – rather it was a fragment of a letter written by the New England alchemist George Starkey in

1651 to his friend Robert Boyle.[7] More importantly, there is no direct evidence for the claim that Newton's alchemical research contributed to his view of gravitation as an immaterial force in any of the documents submitted by Dobbs or Westfall for scrutiny. In fact, on the very few occasions where Newton does describe the causes of gravity in an explicitly alchemical context, he explains the falling of bodies by *mechanical means*, not as a result of force at a distance. This is particularly the case in Newton's important early manuscript "Of Natures obvious laws & processes in vegetation" (Smithsonian Institution, Dibner Ms. 1031B), a work that has only recently received a full edition on the online *Chymistry of Isaac Newton* site.[8] In this acephalous text, which gets its name from the incipit rather than from an actual title, Newton postulates a material ether that forces bodies downward and is also responsible for chymical properties such as cohesion. As he argues, "minerall dissolutions & fermentations" occur continually within the Earth, and like the dissolutions of metals in mineral acids that take place in a laboratory, they often generate "air," or as we would say, gases. This air rises up until "it straggle into ye ethereall regions," but eventually is forced back down along with the subtler ethereal matter. At this point in "Of Natures obvious laws," Newton makes it clear that the resulting circulation provides an explanation of gravity (fol. 3v):

> This constantly crouding for room y^e Æther will bee comprest
> thereby & so forced continually to descend into ye earth
> from whence the air cam & there tis gradually condensed &
> interwoven wth bodies it meets there ^& promotes their actions
> being a tender ferme<n>t. But in its descent it endeavours to
> beare along w^t bodys it passeth through, that is makes them
> heavy & this action is promoted by the tenacious elastick
> constitu<ti>on whereby it takes ye greater hold on things in its
> way; & by its vast swiftness.

The mechanical operation of the ether given here is quite similar to explanations of gravity that Newton provides in his

"Trinity College Notebook" *Certain Philosophical Questions* and
in the 1675 *Hypothesis of Light*. The earliest version of the theory
as found in Newton's student notebook argues that bodies receive
their gravity from a fine, descending matter (Newton does not use the
term "aether" here) that passes through their pores and forces them
downwards. This subtle, particulate matter then enters the globe of
the Earth and evidently combines with other matter so that when it
re-ascends, it is "in a grosser consistence" than before.[9] As a result of
its increased particle size, the rising stream of matter can no longer
penetrate the fine pores of bodies; hence the falling bodies will push
it out of the way rather than being significantly impeded by it. As
Martin Tamny and J. E. McGuire have noted, the theory probably
owes a significant debt to Kenelm Digby's *Two Treatises on Body
and the Soul*.[10]

It is true that in later works, such as his unfinished draft preface
to the *Principia* written in 1686 or 1687 and in Query 23 of the 1706
Latin *Optice*, Newton does import chymical powers into the realm
of immaterial forces. In the draft *Principia* preface, for example, he
speaks of "certain forces by which the particles of bodies" are made
to attract or repel one another generally.[11] Chymical phenomena form
a large part of the ensuing discussion, but then so do surface tension,
capillary action, emission of light, transparency and opacity, and magnetism, alongside gravity. Newton's explicit desire here is to suggest
a research program whereby interparticular forces in general would
be subjected to the mathematical treatment given to "the planets,
comets, the moon and the sea" in the *Principia*. There is no hint to
support the claim of Dobbs and Westfall that Newton first adopted
immaterial forces in the realm of chymistry and then transferred
them to gravity. The same may be said of his arguments in Query 23
of the 1706 *Optice:* Newton speaks there of fermentation in the same
breath as gravity, since both require the help of "active principles"
in order to be maintained or increased.[12] The ultimate origin of this
"fermentative force" may well be the Flemish chymist Joan Baptista
Van Helmont or his expositor George Starkey, who may also have

contributed to Newton's discussion of short-range attractions and repulsions of particles engaging in what we would now call chemical reactions.[13] But the presence of either fermentation or attraction and repulsion at the micro-level does not help the Dobbs–Westfall hypothesis since both are quite distinct from gravitational attraction: these chymical phenomena appear in Newton's text as parallel examples rather than as sources.

Finally, it should be obvious that Newton had more immediate sources to draw upon for the idea of immaterial forces acting on matter than alchemical literature, a point that John Henry made in an important article published over a quarter of a century ago.[14] In particular, Newton was the beneficiary of several centuries of research on the immaterial attraction exercised by magnets, beginning in the thirteenth century and proceeding through the works of many seventeenth-century figures ranging from William Gilbert to Johannes Kepler.[15] In short, when one considers the evidence for and against the idea that Newton derived his theory of universal gravitation from alchemy, the inescapable conclusion is that this claim has acquired the unenviable status of a canard.

A second received view lies in the more subtle claim made by Dobbs in her 1991 *Janus Faces of Genius* that Newton's alchemy was primarily the expression of his heterodox religious quest, and that he thought of the philosophical mercury of the alchemists as a spirit that mediated between the physical and transcendent realms in a way analogous to the mediation of Jesus between God and man. As Dobbs herself put it in one of many similar passages of *Janus Faces*:

> Newton's God acted in time and with time, and since He was transcendent, He required for His interaction with the created world at least one intermediary agent to put His will into effect. Just such an agent was the alchemical spirit, charged with animating and shaping the passive matter of the universe.[16]

In reality, Dobbs was not the first person to argue that Newton's alchemy was part and parcel of his unorthodox religiosity. In a 1967 article published in *Chymia*, Mary Churchill was already making similar declarations. Like Dobbs, Churchill used the idea of the analytical psychologist Carl Jung that the "religious element in alchemy quite outweighs its technical aspect," to bolster a claim that Newton saw the alchemists as upholders of a "pristine religion" closely related to his heterodox anti-Trinitarianism.[17] It is worth quoting Churchill *in extenso* in order to gain an appreciation of the full scope of her vision, later adopted by Dobbs:

> Before Protestantism could speak openly, the alchemists must have seemed to him the early protestants against Romanism. He believed that alchemy in its symbolic search for rebirth and man's perfection held the true soteriological secret, which had been lost in the gross practices of the church. And so he collected and cherished throughout his life alchemical documents not solely for scientific reasons, but because he felt kinship with the often outlawed adepts. Their secret creed supported him in his own unorthodox beliefs in a primitive Christianity.[18]

Now in a certain restricted and highly qualified sense one can agree that Newton's interest in alchemy had a religious origin, since Newton's science as a *whole* was undoubtedly linked to his deep Christian convictions. But when we pass from Newton's transcribing and anthologizing of other alchemists' writings to his own compositions, there is little indeed to support Dobbs's and Churchill's view or even to mark out alchemy as the pinnacle of a theocentric science. To the contrary, Newton's two chymical laboratory notebooks, Cambridge University Library Additional Mss. 3975 and 3973, are resolute in their avoidance of these topics. The word "God" in English or Latin is found only once in these manuscripts, despite the fact that they comprise 452 manuscript pages between them, and despite the fact that those pages are replete with alchemical experiments and *Decknamen*. As for the one case where the word "God" does appear, it occurs in CUL Add. Ms. 3975 (fols. 110r–110v), where Newton has lifted an admonition verbatim from George Starkey's 1658 *Pyrotechny Asserted*:

> O foolish operators! that by yo[r] devised heats would ~~draw~~
> introduce ferments (y[e] true parents of all forms) & yet know not
> by any of yo[r] heats to imitate the Sun in Bermuda in producing
> Oranges & Lemons. Pray to God to direct you for here (to deal
> ingeniously) my speech is very obscure.

This mocking passage lifted from Starkey obviously cannot be taken to support a soteriological goal for alchemy, be it his own or that of Newton. The American chymist's point is that his peers lack a proper comprehension of the technical, laboratory processes required for the *arcana maiora* of alchemy, and that their only hope is to pray for a better understanding.

A more central passage for Dobbs's linkage of Newton's alchemy to his religious quest is found on folio 4v of Newton's manuscript "Of Natures obvious laws & processes in vegetation," which contains in passing a brief consideration of the limitless possibilities of the creation:

> Of God. what ever I can conceive wth out a contradiction, either
> is or may ~~effected~~ [bee made] by something that is: I can conceive all
> my owne powers (knowledge, activating matter, &c). without
> assigning them any limits Therefore such powers either are or
> may bee made to bee.
>   Example. [All the dimensions imaginable are possible.] A body by
> accelerated motion may ~~becom infinitely long or~~ trancend all
> ~~space~~ distance in any finite tim assigned [also it may becom infinitely long.]
> This if thou denyest tis because thou apprehendest a contradictiō
> in the notion & if thou apprehendest none thou wilt grant it [to the]
> pour of things.

According to Dobbs, Newton inserted this discussion into an alchemical manuscript text in order to explain how God could circumvent the mechanical order of the cosmos by means of "the nonmechanical laws of vegetation."[19] In her theocentric analysis of Newton's alchemy, this was part of an attempt on his part to demonstrate "divine activity in the world."[20] But in fact there is nothing alchemical about this passage, and its linkage to the rest of the text is obscure. It is in fact much closer to the Cartesian-inspired jottings found in Newton's early commonplace book *Certain Philosophical Questions* than it is to his alchemical sources. A related passage can be found there, at the end of Newton's notes on Descartes's *Meditations* and his *Responses*:

> Ax: ~~That thing~~ Tis a contradiction to say, that thing doth
> not exist, ^wch^ ~~may bee conceived~~ whose existence implys no
> contradiction, & being supposed to exist must necessarily exist.
> The reason is y^t an immediate cause and effect must be in ye same
> time & there fore ye præexistence of a thing ~~must~~ ^can^ bee no cause
> of its post existence (as also because y^e ~~former~~ after time depends
> not on ye former time). Tis onely from the essence of it that a
> thing ~~can by it owne~~ perpetuate its existence w^{th}out extrinsicall
> helpe. Wch essence being sufficient to continue it must bee
> sufficient to cause it there being ye like reason of boath.[21]

The editors of *Certain Philosophical Questions* assert that this is a Newtonian gloss on the ontological proof for God's existence in Descartes's "Fifth Meditation." Newton was probably thinking of other portions of the *Meditations* as well, and the "Second Set of Objections" in particular, where the following criticism is raised against the ontological proof – "From this it follows not that God really exists, but only that he ought to exist if his nature is something possible or non-contradictory."[22] It is in the light of this criticism that one should approach Newton's emphasis on non-contradiction. The concerns expressed in *Certain Philosophical Questions* are an outgrowth of the criticisms of the ontological proof found in the *Opera philosophica* of Descartes that the young Cantabrigian studied as a student.[23] Similarly, Newton's passage "Of God" in "Of Natures obvious laws" testifies to his encounter with Descartes's ruminations on the existence and nature of God: it is not the affirmation of non-mechanism that Dobbs asserts. What then is this passage doing in the midst of Newton's heavily alchemical text? "Of Natures obvious laws" is itself a sort of commonplace book, organized around topical entries that need not be closely related. The passage "Of God" looks more like a digression than a thought that grew integrally out of Newton's text on alchemical vegetation. Newton himself seems to have acknowledged its outlier status by leaving the rest of the page after the entry blank in his manuscript.

In short, a close inspection of this passage and indeed of most of the evidence used by Dobbs in support of her theocentric reading, does not support her interpretation. Rather than seeing, then, Newton's chymistry as somehow more religious in orientation than his physics, one should view it as arising from the same desire to penetrate behind the appearances and to arrive at the most general possible explanation of reality. In the hands of Newton, both chymistry and physics were tools for arriving at fundamental truths about nature and its operations.

A final claim, namely the position that Newton was only interested in a positivistic quest for chemical knowledge in the modern sense, can be dispensed with in short order. This assertion was presented forcefully by Rupert Hall and Marie Boas Hall in a long article that appeared in 1958.[24] Despite their careful and valuable analysis of Newton's laboratory notebooks in the Cambridge University Library, the Halls were shackled by a tacit definition that equated alchemy with fraud. Thus the Halls asserted that "Alchemy was never disinterested chemical research," and they adopted the goal of showing that "there is no evidence that any of <Newton's> processes are of the kind necessarily preliminary to the Great Work, or that he ever hoped to fabricate a factitious gold." These assertions are clearly belied by the obviously alchemical character of Newton's "Of Natures obvious laws & processes in vegetation," a text that the Halls seem not to have known in 1958. More than this, the Halls' interpretation is challenged even by Newton's experimental notebooks. CUL Add.

Ms. 3975, for example, reveals Newton's quest for such mysterious alchemical desiderata as the Green Lion, the Caduceus of Mercury and the Scepter of Jove. These *Decknamen* come right out of Johannes de Monte Snyders and Eirenaeus Philalethes, authors whom no sane person today would deny to be alchemists. Nor can it be argued that Newton was using the materials represented by these *Decknamen* in a way that was somehow unalchemical. CUL Add. Ms. 3975 contains numerous pages devoted explicitly to chrysopoeia, such as "Of ye work wth common ☉"on 123r–123v (continued on 132r). The entry on the work with common gold follows a course of action that is above all dominated by *The Marrow of Alchemy*, *Secrets Reveal'd*, and *Ripley Reviv'd*, all works written by the famous chrysopoetic author Eirenaeus Philalethes (George Starkey). Newton's process for "common gold" carefully describes procedures for making a sophic mercury that was supposed to lead to the traditional *summum bonum* of alchemy – the philosophers' stone. The recapitulation and attempted decipherment of similar processes in fact make up the bulk of Newton's alchemical *Nachlass*, but the fact that they appear here in his own experimental notebook gives them particular cogency. In a word, the idea that Newton rejected the goals of the alchemists while appropriating their techniques and accidental discoveries can only be described as wishful thinking.

NEWTON'S CHYMISTRY AND ITS RELATION TO HIS SCIENCE AS A WHOLE

Having completed this essential exercise in ground clearing, we are now in a position to raise the questions that must occupy any researcher of Newton's alchemy. What was the real significance of chymistry over the course of Newton's career? Or to phrase it another way, what did he hope to attain from alchemy and how did it fit with his other scientific research? These are very serious questions, and they cannot receive full answers at the moment. But thanks to the online publication of several key Newton manuscripts by the *Chymistry of Isaac Newton* project, we are now in a position to make some preliminary steps towards answering these questions. What we are beginning to see is that Newton himself had very diverse goals for alchemy. In the remainder of this chapter I will briefly describe some recent discoveries pertaining to Newton's alchemical multi-tasking, while focusing on his use of chymical analysis and synthesis. As we shall see, paired chymical analysis and synthesis were immensely fruitful models in Newton's mind that allowed him to reason out processes ranging from the realm of optics to what I have taken to calling Newton's "theory of everything."

The publication of CUL Add. Ms. 3975, Newton's most comprehensive laboratory notebook, has made it possible to place his early optical discoveries in an entirely new context.[25] This substantial manuscript of 348 pages contains a collection of reading notes and experiments extending from at least 1669 to 1693. Most of the reading notes come from Robert Boyle and George Starkey, two authors who were pivotal in directing the young Newton's alchemical interests. The vast majority of the experiments and notes concern chymistry. But imbedded in this overwhelmingly alchemical manuscript one also finds the second version of Newton's most famous optical discovery, his experiments demonstrating that white light is actually a heterogeneous mixture of unaltered spectral colors. Now in this version, "Of Colours," unlike its earlier predecessor in Newton's student notebook, *Certain Philosophical Questions*, is the very first Newtonian document to clearly state that the spectral colors separated out of white light by a prism are completely immutable. Earlier, he had thought that the speed of light-corpuscles hitting the surface of the eye could vary, and that a corpuscle producing the sensation of red could be slowed to produce the sensation of blue. In other words, Newton's earliest experiments with prisms showed him that white light can be divided into spectral rays of differing refrangibility, but did not provide him with evidence that the spectral rays producing different colors were immutable. Hence, the Newton of *Certain Philosophical Questions* was still a believer in the mutability of colors. In other words, he still belonged in the camp of those who believed that colors could be mutually "transmuted," not wholly unlike the alchemical transmutation of metals.[26] All of this changed some time in the second half of the 1660s, and this change is reflected in "Of Colours," the treatise found in CUL Add. Ms. 3975. By the time of this treatise, probably composed between 1666 and 1669, Newton had performed new experiments that completely revolutionized his optical theory, and thereby overturned some 2,000 years of theorizing about the formation of colors.[27]

What did these new and revolutionary experiments consist of? In a word, by the time he composed "Of Colours," Newton had figured out that he could not only *analyze* white light into its spectral components, but that he could subsequently *resynthesize* the white light back out of the previously separated components. At the same time, other experiments described in "Of Colours" revealed that the red and blue produced by a prism could *not* be analyzed into other spectral colors or indeed changed in any way. It followed that the resynthesized white light itself is merely a compound of unaltered spectral colors that produce an illusion of homogeneity when seen by the eye of man. Newton still thought of light as composed of minute material corpuscles, but now the behavior of these corpuscles was fixed among rays of a given type – one spectral color could no longer turn into another, and the whiteness that resulted from their combination was no more innate to the components of sunlight than the redness of cinnabar is innate to *its* ingredients, mercury and sulfur (though Newton himself does not draw this comparison).

Now anyone conversant with the historiography of alchemy over the last ten years will immediately begin to feel a sense of recognition. Recent work has shown that the analysis and synthesis of chemical compounds had a well-developed history in alchemy. Early seventeenth-century chymists such as Daniel Sennert and Joan Baptista Van Helmont were able to draw on a medieval tradition of analysis that helped to bring a decisive end to traditional scholastic theories of mixture, thus setting the stage for the mechanical philosophy.[28] The Thomistic theory of perfect mixture, whereby the ingredients were thought to lose their identity and meld into a perfectly homogeneous substance, was debunked by alchemical experiments that showed exactly how those supposedly lost ingredients actually retained their robust identity all along. An extensive alchemical tradition extending from the High Middle Ages up to Robert Boyle's immediate predecessors had long used the analytic retrievability of the constituents of compounds to argue for the permanence of the ingredients that went into them.

But what about the *resynthesis* of components acquired by chymical analysis? Recent research has shown that Van Helmont was a key figure in converting Paracelsian *spagyria*, which had initially focused mostly on analysis, into a genuine art of analysis and synthesis. Van Helmont famously performed quantitative analyses and syntheses of glass and other materials which served as models for later alchemists.[29] But it was Robert Boyle who first brought these techniques explicitly into the mechanical philosophy and hence into the purview of the young Newton before he began his intensive reading of chrysopoetic texts in the late 1660s. By showing that naturally occurring compounds could be analyzed into their unaltered parts and then reassembled like the components of a watch, Boyle would cast doubt on the need for scholastic substantial forms. Thus Boyle used analysis and synthesis as supports for the corpuscularian basis of the mechanical philosophy, thereby attacking Aristotelian hylomorphism head on. And in his *Certain Physiological Essays* of 1661 and his *Origin of Forms and Qualities* of 1666, Boyle brought chymical analysis and synthesis to the attention of the young Newton.

Boyle's *Certain Physiological Essays*, for example, describes an experiment for what he calls the "redintegration" of saltpeter or niter – the chemical that we now refer to as potassium nitrate. "Redintegration" here refers to resynthesis after analysis – the dissolution of saltpeter into its ingredients and the subsequent recombination of those ingredients to arrive once more at saltpeter.[30] In simplest terms, Boyle's experiment worked by injecting burning charcoal into molten saltpeter, and thus igniting it. This resulted in the release of nitrogen and carbon in combination with oxygen, leaving a non-volatile residue of "fixed niter" that resembled salt of tartar (potassium carbonate – in reality it *was* potassium carbonate). Knowing that spirit of niter (nitric acid) could be produced by the thermal decomposition of niter, Boyle then added spirit of niter to the tartar-like residue, and acquired a product that resembled the original saltpeter in all its significant properties. He was then able to conclude that niter itself is merely a compound of two very different materials, namely spirit of niter and fixed niter, which we would today call an acid and a base.[31] Boyle would expand on this experiment in his 1666 *Origin of Forms and Qualities*, where he described additional experiments for the redintegration of amber, turpentine, and stibnite.

Let us now pause for a moment and consider chronology. In the same year as Newton's famous *annus mirabilis*, 1666, the year in which he later claimed to have begun experimenting with prisms, Boyle had published his *Origin of Forms and Qualities*. The very manuscript in which Newton recorded his first experiments with the resynthesis of white light from the spectral colors – the chymical laboratory notebook CUL Add. Ms. 3975 – also contains extensive notes drawn from Boyle's *Origin of Forms* on the redintegration of stibnite and turpentine.[32] Although the order in which this document was composed remains unclear at present, it is at least likely that Newton had read about Boyle's experiments with chymical redintegration at the time when he composed "Of Colours." Chymical redintegration was a phenomenon that clearly interested the young Newton, and one that he could easily have adapted to his optics from his reading in Boyle's chymistry.

Is it just coincidence that a mere five years or so separated Boyle's devastating attack on the homogeneity of scholastic "perfect mixture" by means of chymical analysis and synthesis from Newton's attack on the scholastic view of white light as a perfectly homogeneous mixture by means of prismatic analysis and synthesis? Boyle had introduced his redintegration experiments in 1661 and

Newton's resynthesis of white light dates from the period between 1666 and 1669. What are we to make of this? In addition to the fact that we know Newton was reading Boyle at the time of writing "Of Colours," there are numerous terminological clues to support a theoretical borrowing by Newton. In Newton's lectures given between 1669 and 1672 as Lucasian professor, called the *Optica*, he explicitly argues that it is the *"redintegration"* of the white light that proves beyond any reasonable doubt that it is actually composed of a mixture of colorfacient rays.[33] Newton speaks of the sunlight reconstituted from spectral colors as being an *albedo redintegrata* – quite literally a redintegrated whiteness.[34] In classical Latin, the term *redintegrata* or "redintegrated" means primarily "renewed" or "restored," as when one's powers are restored by rest after the fatigue of battle.[35] But the English term "redintegration" has a long history in alchemy as well, where the meaning is quite different. George Ripley, for example, uses it to refer to the recombination of the volatile and fixed components of a material after their analysis in the laboratory, in his fifteenth-century *Compound of Alchymy*.[36] This is precisely the sense in which Newton uses the term *redintegrata*, and he was the first in the field of optics to employ it in that fashion. It appears that Newton's use of the term is a direct appropriation from chymistry, most likely stemming from Boyle's chymical redintegration of niter, stibnite, turpentine, and other substances.

NEWTON'S "THEORY OF EVERYTHING"

One could continue with further terminological evidence linking Newton's analyses and syntheses to those of Boyle, for there are a number of cases where Newton transfers Boyle's peculiar corpuscular terminology to light and colors.[37] But for the sake of completeness, it is better here to give a sense of the diverse and wide-ranging character of Newton's chymistry. He did not stop, of course, with the transfer of chymical concepts and practices to optics. Indeed, Newton went so far as to develop a "theory of everything" that would explain organic life, the origin of heat and flame, the mechanical causes of gravitation, cohesion, the generation of metals and minerals, and so forth, by making an appeal to circulatory processes involving the interaction of metallic vapors, the atmosphere, and various forms of ether. This comprehensive theory emerges already in Newton's early interpretation and summary of chymical theory, "Of Natures obvious laws & processes in vegetation," where it is heavily indebted to early modern alchemists such as Michael Sendivogius and Johann Grasseus.[38] Indeed, Newton's already described idea of a circulatory process involving air and ether is largely an attempt to combine mechanical theories of gravitation with the Sendivogian "aerial niter" theory according to which a nitrous component of the air (related to but not identical with ordinary saltpeter) circulates between the core of the Earth and the outer reaches of the atmosphere. In Sendivogius's *Novum lumen chemicum* (1604), the aerial niter is a universal principle of life and also a cause of combustion. Newton similarly says in "Of Natures obvious laws" (fol. 2r) that there is an atmospheric spirit bearing an affinity with niter that is "yᵉ <illeg.> ferment of fire & all vegetables." The Earth, being like "a great animall," undergoes continual revitalization from inspiring this nitrous spirit as its "dayly refreshment" and breathing it forth again in altered form (fol. 3v). Similar ideas recur in Newton's "Hypothesis of Light," sent to Henry Oldenburg in 1675, although Newton tried to erase any open debt to the aerial niter theory there.[39] Given this emphasis on niter, it is perhaps unsurprising that Newton would also refer to the redintegration of saltpeter in "Of Natures obvious laws." Nonetheless, the phenomenon of redintegration plays a remarkably central role in that text, just as it did in Newton's optical theory, and this is a fact that has escaped scholars up until the present.

In "Of Natures obvious laws" one finds Newton trying to distinguish between purely mechanical processes and those that he links to a principle of "vegetation." This distinction was a key one for Newton, since even in his undergraduate days he was already searching out the flaws in Cartesian physics, a system that of course left no space for vegetation as a non-mechanical process. As we shall see, the mechanical–vegetable demarcation relied in part on redintegration as a test-case for distinguishing mechanical from vegetative processes. Those materials that could be analyzed and synthesized fit Newton's criterion for mechanical products, whereas substances produced by vegetation were not fit products for redintegration.

"Of Natures obvious laws" begins with a comparison of generative processes across the three kingdoms of nature – animal, vegetable, and mineral. Newton focuses on the idea that metals grow, putrefy, and regenerate themselves within the Earth, much after the fashion of trees on the Earth's surface. But he soon takes the discussion in a different direction. He launches into an apparently quite original treatment of the formation of sea-salt and niter by means of a putative interaction between water and the metallic fumes that rise up from the Earth's depths.

It is likely that Newton's introductory lines about saline generation are loosely inspired by Bernhard Varenius's discussion of sea-salt in the latter's *Geographia generalis*, a work that Newton edited and published in Cambridge in 1672.[40] Indeed, Newton's words (fol. 1v) betray the direct influence of Varenius's assertion that seawater contains both a fixed and a volatile salt. As Newton says, "Because the sea is perpetually replenished wth fresh vapours it cannot bee freed from ^{a} salin tast by destillation, that salt arising wth ye water wch is not yet ~~indurated~~ concreted to a grosser body." This passage surely recapitulates a section from Varenius where the latter asserts that tiny saline atoms of light weight are found mingled in with larger, heavier ones in seawater; distillation merely separates the two types of particles by raising the smaller and leaving the bigger behind.[41] Hence it is possible for the smaller atoms of the volatile salt to ascend while the larger, fixed ones remain behind, making it impossible, supposedly, to completely remove the salinity of seawater by distillation. The same ideas linking subtlety to volatility and grossness to fixity pervade Newton's reasoning as well, and it is quite possible that Varenius's influence in "Of Natures obvious laws & processes in vegetation" extends well beyond the discussion of mere sea-salt.

But Newton differs markedly from Varenius in bringing niter into his discussion of salts. Probably stimulated in a general way by Varenius's claim that sea-salt contains components of varying volatility, Newton asserts that niter is a looser, less fixed salt than sea-salt, and that the difference between the two salts arises not from a chemical diversity between their ingredients, but rather from the fact that the niter is made when metallic fumes combine with "subtile invisible" water vapor, whereas sea-salt originates from the combination of the volatilized metals with liquid water or mist. A preponderance of water causes the fumes to be "overwhelmed & drowned," which results in the immediate formation of sea-salt.

What is Newton's first evidence for the claim that physical modes of combination alone, such as solution in liquid water versus solution in water vapor, can produce such different salts as niter and sea-salt? Once again, Newton turns to chymical analysis and synthesis. He points to Boyle's famous redintegration of saltpeter, which we described earlier in this chapter, where niter was first analyzed into its components and then resynthesized. As Newton puts it on fol. 2r of the manuscript: "Nor is it strange y^t so slight causes should produce so <*illeg.*> different salts as ⊖ & ◐ if wee consider y^t ye fixt salt <*illeg.*> left in ignition returns to ◐ by dissolution." "The fixt salt left in ignition" is the potassium carbonate produced by Boyle's injection of burning charcoal into hot niter. The product, Newton says, "returns to <niter> by dissolution." Interestingly, Newton here seems to focus solely on the *physical* features of the experiment – the fact that the fixed salt left by ignition is "dissolved" into saltpeter, without considering the *chemical* fact that the solvent has to be nitric acid. The omission on Newton's part is a calculated move intended to bring the experiment into conformity with his theory, whereby the looser, more subtle niter is formed by mere "dissolution" of the more fixed and impassible potassium carbonate. In other words, he interprets the redintegration of niter as a purely mechanical process resulting in the conversion of one salt into another by a change of gross texture alone. Newton then launches on folios 2r and 2v into a detailed comparison of niter and sea-salt in the world at large in order to confirm his idea that the latter is merely a more fixed version of the former.

As we have seen, Newton wants to locate the essential distinction between sea-salt and niter purely in the mechanical property of texture. Niter is more volatile and subtle, whereas sea-salt is more fixed and gross, and this distinction arises from the respective combination of the same metallic fumes either with water vapor on the one hand or with liquid water or dense mist on the other. Although Newton's reputation lies mainly in his work as a physicist, this is not an empire-building move on the part of a reductionist natural philosopher intent on leading all change back to physical principles such as brute, passive matter and motion. To the contrary, Newton is keenly aware of the fact that not all chemical phenomena can be reduced to what he calls "gross mechanical transposition of parts." Indeed, in the section on niter and sea-salt, Newton is already setting up a discussion of vegetation.

To Newton, as to Robert Boyle and many early modern chymists, vegetation implied a goal-directed process guided by tiny *semina* or "seeds" implanted deep within matter.[42] The processes of salt-production that we have analyzed so far are manifestly *not* instances of vegetation, since they involve only a mechanical change in texture brought on by corpuscular interaction between metallic fumes and water. Newton classifies these changes with such purely mechanical operations as the mixing of differently colored powders to produce new colors (as when jumbled blue and yellow granules give the appearance of green), the dissolution of metals in mineral acids, and the separation of cream into butter, curds, and whey by churning. As for vegetation, Newton defines it in the following terms in "Of Natures obvious laws" (5r):

Natures actions are either ~~seminall~~ ^vegetable or ^purely mechanicall (grav. flux. meteors. vulgar Chymistry <|>

> The principles of her vegetable actions are noe other then the ~~seeds~~ ^{seeds or seminall vessels} of things those are her onely agents, her fire, her soule, her life,
>
> The seede of things that is all that substance in them that is attained to the ~~full~~ _{fullest} degree of maturity that is in that thing <illeg.> so that there being nothing more mature to act upon them they acquiesce.
>
> Vegetation is nothing else but ye acting of w^t is most maturated or specificate upon that wch is <illeg.> less specificate or mature to make it as mature as it selfe And in that degree of maturity nature ever rests.

In drawing this sharp distinction between mechanical and vegetative processes, Newton had to confront an obvious potential objection. Although the artificial operations employed by a laboratory technician in cases of "vulgar chymistry" might be purely mechanical, there are plenty of instances where a hidden, indwelling nature may actually be driving operations that seem to our senses to be mere mechanism. This seminal "vegetable substance," acting as a latent "invisible inhabitant," may direct grosser particles to take on the structure of bones, flesh, wood, fruit, and other materials subject to growth. As Newton clarifies on folio 5v:

> So far therefore as ye same changes may bee wrought by the slight mutation of the textures of bodys in common chymistry & such like experi ments ~~may~~ may judg that ~~there is noe other cause that will~~ such changes made by nature are done ye same way that is by ye sleighty transpositions of ye grosser corpuscles, for upon their disposition only sensible qualitys depend. But so far as by ~~generation~~ ^vegetation such changes are wrought as cannot bee done w^thout it wee must have recourse to som further cause And this difference ~~is seen clearest in fossile substances~~ is vast <illeg.> & fundamental because nothing could ever yet bee made w^thout vegetation wch nature useth to produce by it. [note ye instance of turning Irō into copper. &c.]

The point of this passage is that even seemingly mechanical operations in nature can be directed by hidden, seed-like entities that occupy an "unimaginably small" portion of matter. How then can we distinguish between the purely mechanical operations of ethereal gravitation, fusion, meteorology, and vulgar chymistry and the vegetative processes employed by nature?

Newton responds by asserting that any laboratory process that allows one to retrieve the initial ingredients from what we would call a "chemical compound" or recreates the compound from its ingredients reveals that the compound in question was a mere mechanical mixture rather than a product of vegetation. A similar ideology underlay Newton's experimental analysis and synthesis of white light, and the use of decompounding followed by recompounding as an index of mere mechanical change in "Of Natures obvious laws" probably also had its sources in Boyle's work.[43] As Newton puts it in "Of Natures obvious laws" (5v):

> all y^e operations in vulgar chemistry (many of wch to sense are as strange transmutations as those of nature) are but mechanicall coalitions $^{\wedge\text{or seperations}}$ of particles as may appear in that they returne into their former natures if reconjoned or (when unequally volatile) dissevered, & y^t wthout any vegetation.

In other words, all the ordinary reactions that Newton groups within the realm of "vulgar chemistry" are mere mechanical interactions, and this is demonstrated by the retrievability of their unaltered ingredients by analysis or their recombination by synthesis. As we have already seen, Newton used the redintegration of niter as a paradigmatic case of such purely mechanical recombination earlier in "Of Natures obvious laws." It is likely that he has the same process in mind here, though the reference to unequal volatility suggests that he has broadened his scope to include compounds that can be separated by mere sublimation or distillation rather than combustion. Like earlier alchemists, Newton viewed such separations and recombinations as a sort of change that took place between "the grosser corpuscles" of bodies. Real transmutation, which Newton has in mind when he speaks of vegetation, had long been thought of in alchemy as something that occurs at a deeper microstructural level of matter.[44]

To the young Newton, who had not yet embraced the principle of action at a distance that marked his mature *Principia*, the phenomena exhibited by falling bodies, melting materials, changes in the atmosphere, and inorganic chemical reactions were all explicable by means of micro-level particles acting mechanically on one another. Vegetation, on the other hand, is a goal-directed process whereby a more mature seed leads a less mature material into a state of maturity equivalent to its own. In other words, vegetation is the procedure whereby generation and growth occur in the natural world. In Newton's mind, it is clearly the operation by which nature retains and replenishes the species of the world around us. Even if the phenomenal world may *appear* to operate by purely mechanical means, nature employs vegetative processes at a deeper level to drive the corpuscular interactions that result in generation and growth. Hence in reiterating the distinction between mere mechanism and vegetation, Newton says (5v) "And this difference ~~is seen clearest in fossile substances~~ is vast <*illeg.*> & fundamental because nothing could ever yet bee made w^{th}out vegetation wch nature useth to produce by it."

CONCLUSION

We have seen, then, that Newton's use of alchemy spanned markedly diverse areas in his scientific work ranging from optics to his theory of everything. Yet chymical analysis and resynthesis were particularly fruitful concepts for him throughout. On the one hand, a transfer of chymical analysis and synthesis to the realm of optics allowed Newton to resynthesize white light out of its analyzed components or to "redintegrate" it in the Boylean language that he uses. This provided conclusive evidence to him for the fact that no transmutation of spectral colors had occurred. Alternatively, analysis and synthesis provided Newton with a marker differentiating the mechanical from the vegetable in the generation of salts. It was the fact that particular substances such as niter could be taken apart and put back together again that demonstrated their immediate origin to be purely mechanical rather than involving the intimate transmutational processes of vegetation. Hence we have seen how Newton used analysis and synthesis both in the realm of optics and the genesis of salts to supplant transmutational processes with mechanical ones. It does not follow, of course, that Newton did not believe in transmutation, but like many alchemists of the time, particularly Van Helmont and George Starkey, he was trying to distinguish genuine transmutation from mere transfer and apposition of gross particles. It is a peculiar irony of history that alchemists, in their undying quest to transmute the products of nature, became the first experimental proponents of the fixity of chemical species in the form of corpuscles that retained their chemical identity throughout their association and dissociation.[45] Like Starkey and Van Helmont, Newton saw the possibility of real transmutation only at the extreme nano-stage of corpuscular hierarchy, well below the level of gross corpuscles that made up the Lego-blocks of vulgar chymistry. Seeing Newton in the light of the longstanding alchemical emphasis on analysis and synthesis provides a new window on the thirty-plus years that he devoted to the aurific art and allows us to discern little explored connections between his chymistry and the scientific work for which he is more famous.

To conclude, then, it is time to abandon the outworn positions adopted by the early pioneers of Newton's alchemy. The roles for alchemy advocated by Westfall and Dobbs and now viewed as matters of fact by large swaths of the public and scholarly communities alike arose in part from the absence of edited texts, which encouraged these scholars to rely on selective core-samples extracted from Newton's large and diverse *Nachlass*. Perhaps even more significantly, these scholars were working during a period when the historical study of alchemy was, to borrow a term from Nathan Sivin, "moribund."[46] It was only natural for Dobbs and her predecessor Mary Churchill to see Newton's alchemy as primarily a religious phenomenon at a time when the dominant interpretation of alchemy as a whole was that of Carl Jung. Similarly, the claim of Westfall and the early Dobbs for the influence of the "hermetic tradition" and alchemy on Newton's concept of gravitational attraction was partly due to the influence of Frances Yates, whose work encouraged the view that the so-called occult sciences made up a homogeneous group characterized by the quest for mysterious and secret sympathies in nature.[47] Over the last two decades a Renaissance in the historiography of alchemy has taken place, however, and the influence of Jung and Yates has accordingly declined. At the same time, the *Chymistry of Isaac Newton* project is well on its way to producing a complete online edition of Newton's alchemical writings. Although many problems remain, particularly the relationship between theory and practice in Newton's records of his alchemical experimentation, we are now in a uniquely favorable position to make sense of his long engagement with the aurific art. The complex picture that is emerging reveals at once a textual scholar intent on disentangling the riddles of alchemical encipherment, an experimental scientist keen on replicating the deepest arcana of the art, and a theorist determined to incorporate chymical explanations into his own theory of nature at large.

NOTES

1 David Brewster, *Memoirs of the Life, Writings, and Discoveries of Sir Isaac Newton* (Edinburgh: Thomas Constable and Co., 1855), vol. 2, pp. 374–5.

2 J. M. Keynes, "Newton the Man," in *Newton Tercentenary Celebrations, 15–19 July 1946* (Cambridge: Cambridge University Press, 1947), p. 27.

3 J. E. McGuire, "Force, Active Principles, and Newton's Invisible Realm," *Ambix* 15 (1968), 154–208; see 166–7. John Henry has already drawn attention to this passage in his "Occult Qualities and the Experimental Philosophy: Active Principles in Pre-Newtonian Matter Theory," *History of Science*, 24 (1986), 335–81; see p. 369, n. 7.

4 Richard Westfall, *Force in Newton's Physics* (London: MacDonald, 1971). See, for example, p. 369: "Neither in the 'Hypothesis' nor in the letter

to Oldenburg did Newton attempt to reduce the 'secret principle' of
sociability to mechanical terms, although he employed it in mechanical
contexts where it aided the power of mundane factors such as size.
Redolent of hermetic tradition, it refused to be made sociable to the
mechanical philosophy and stood out starkly against its background.
In the case of the principles of motion or of activity mentioned in the
'Hypothesis,' Newton asserted their mechanical nature, although
he did not venture to interpret how that might be. With their immediate
Helmontian forebears, they too suggested the lingering presence in his
thought of a tradition alien to the mechanical. His intensive study of
alchemical literature during the latter years of the 1670s may well have
intensified these influences."

5 Richard Westfall, "Newton and the Hermetic Tradition," in A. G. Debus,
Science, Medicine and Society in the Renaissance (New York: Science
History Publications, 1972), vol. 2, pp. 183–98; see pp. 193–4. Westfall
goes on to argue that Newton only gradually "rejected the specificity of
force" thus eventually arriving at the position that gravitational force is
universal. Nonetheless, Westfall reasserts at the end of the article that
Newton's concept of immaterial attractions originated in "the Hermetic
tradition."

6 Betty Jo Teeter Dobbs, *The Foundations of Newton's Alchemy*
(Cambridge: Cambridge University Press, 1975), pp. 211–12. Dobbs
later acknowledged the demonstration by William R. Newman that the
"Clavis" was actually by George Starkey rather than Newton, and even
backed away somewhat from her claim that alchemy was responsible for
Newton's move to an immaterial gravitational force. See *Janus Faces*,
pp. 15 (for the "Clavis") and 207–8, where she admits that "the story
no longer seems quite so straightforward." But her partial recantation
has escaped the public eye entirely, as may be seen from a passage in
Wikipedia's entry "Isaac Newton" (accessed April 7, 2013), which is
the very first hit encountered when one searches "Isaac Newton" via
Google. According to *Wikipedia*, Newton "replaced the ether with occult
forces based on Hermetic ideas of attraction and repulsion between
particles . . . Had he not relied on the occult idea of action at a distance,
across a vacuum, he might not have developed his theory of gravity."

7 William R. Newman, "Newton's 'Clavis' as Starkey's 'Key'," *Isis* 78
(1987), 564–74.

8 See the *Chymistry of Isaac Newton* site (www.chymistry.org). "Of Natures obvious laws" can be found at http://webapp1.dlib.indiana.edu/newton/mss/dipl/ALCH00081/ (accessed April 21, 2013).

9 J. E. McGuire and Martin Tamny, *Certain Philosophical Questions: Newton's Trinity Notebook* (Cambridge: Cambridge University Press, 1983), p. 362.

10 *Ibid.*, p. 288. I am less convinced by McGuire and Tamny's suggestion that Newton's main source was Boyle's *Spring of the Air*, for which see *Certain Philosophical Questions*, p. 426 n. 122.

11 A. Rupert Hall and Marie Boas Hall, *Unpublished Scientific Papers of Isaac Newton* (Cambridge: Cambridge University Press, 1962), pp. 302–8.

12 Isaac Newton, *Optice: Sive De Reflexionibus, Refractionibus, Inflexionibus & Coloribus Lucis. Libri Tres* (London: Samuel Smith and Benjamin Walford, 1706), pp. 343–4.

13 I have argued elsewhere that Starkey's speculations about layered corpuscles endowed with forces may have influenced Newton's views on the microstructure of particles and their dynamic interactions in the realm of chymistry. See pp. 228–39 of my *Gehennical Fire: The Lives of George Starkey* (Cambridge, MA: Harvard University Press, 1994).

14 John Henry, "Occult Qualities and the Experimental Philosophy: Active Principles in Pre-Newtonian Matter Theory," *History of Science* 24 (1986), 335–81. Henry has reiterated this point with further evidence in a much more recent article where he also addresses the vexed problem of dating Newton's *De gravitatione et aequipondio fluidorum*. See Henry, "Gravity and *De gravitatione:* the development of Newton's ideas on action at a distance," *Studies in History and Philosophy of Science* 42 (2011), 11–27, esp. 19–23.

15 The important use that Newton made of magnetism in the *Principia* is described by Domenico Bertoloni Meli in his *Thinking with Objects* (Baltimore, MD: Johns Hopkins University Press, 2006), p. 263.

16 B. J. T. Dobbs, *Janus Faces*, p. 13. See also pp. 243–8, where she again stresses the role of "the alchemical vegetable spirit" as a mediator between God and man and associates this with "the Arian Christ."

17 Mary S. Churchill, "The Seven Chapters, with Explanatory Notes," *Chymia* 12 (1967), 27–57; see p. 38: "In alchemical writings, Newton must have believed, lay hidden a religious expression stripped of sacerdotal dogmas, which was very close to his own belief. To him

the Roman Catholic Church had usurped authority. It had abused
and degraded Christianity by its drive for power, its use of confession,
absolution, and indulgences, and by the corruption of the clergy. To him
the alchemists must have represented the true unsullied wisdom of the
past. They were the preservers of the teachings of the ancient wise men
and of the earliest Christian Church. They kept in its true form the
secret of salvation, regeneration and immortality, a matter of individual
growth and conscience, not to be legislated by popes or bishops." For the
part played by Carl Jung in Churchill's argument, see her p. 36.

18 Churchill, "The Seven Chapters," pp. 38–9. Dobbs originally criticized
Churchill, but in *Janus Faces* Dobbs explicitly endorsed her views and
went so far as to offer Churchill an apology for her earlier scepticism.
See *Janus Faces*, p. 18, n. 42.

19 Dobbs, *Janus Faces*, p. 115.

20 *Ibid.*, p. 116.

21 This passage is found on p. 464 of the McGuire and Tamny edition of
Certain Philosophical Questions. As Tamny and McGuire point out,
this is inspired by Descartes's "Fifth Meditation." I have compared the
transcription to the digital scan posted by the Cambridge University
Library (cudl.lib.cam.ac.uk/view/MS-ADD-03996/170; accessed April 4,
2013). The term "post existence," altered by McGuire and Tamny to
"past existence" in their normalized version of the text, is not a slip
of the pen on Newton's part. The point is that if existence is implied
by essence, as in the Cartesian ontological proof for God's existence,
then cause and effect must be simultaneous. Apparently unaware of the
Cartesian background to the related passage in "Of Natures obvious
laws," Dobbs links it to voluntarism and tries to give it an alchemical
significance. See Dobbs, *Janus Faces*, pp. 113–17.

22 I owe this reference to an extended discussion with Roger Ariew.
The translation is from René Descartes, *Meditations, Objections
and Replies*, edited and translated by Roger Ariew and Donald Cress
(Indianapolis, IN: Hackett, 2006), p. 74. Gideon Manning has also found
echoes of the third Meditation in Newton's comments, a fact that he has
kindly related to me in a personal exchange.

23 Roger Ariew has kindly pointed out to me that Leibniz made great use of
a "contradiction clause" quite similar to Newton's. In his *Monadology*,
for example, Leibniz says: "Thus God alone (or the necessary being) has
the privilege, that he must exist if he is possible. And since nothing can

prevent the possibility of what is without limits, without negation, and consequently without contradiction, this by itself is sufficient for us to know the existence of God *a priori*" (translation by Roger Ariew and Daniel Garber in G. W. Leibniz, *Philosophical Essays* [Indianapolis, IN: Hackett, 1989], p. 218). Moreover, the main elements of this argument already appear as early as 1676 in Leibniz's *De summa rerum*. Ariew has also provided me with the references for these: see G. W. Leibniz, *De summa rerum* (New Haven, CT: Yale University Press, 1992), pp. 47–9, 63, 91–107.

24 Marie Boas and A. Rupert Hall, "Newton's Chemical Experiments," in *Archives internationales d'histoire des sciences* 11 (1958), 113–52.

25 This new interpretation of Newton's early optical discoveries was first expounded in William R. Newman, "Newton's Early Optical Theory and its Debt to Chymistry," in Michel Hochmann and Danielle Jacquart (eds.), *Lumière et vision dans les sciences et dans les arts* (Geneva: Droz, 2010), pp. 283–307. A preprint version of the article may also be found on the Chymistry of Isaac Newton website, at www.chymistry.org.

26 Significantly Newton himself later uses the term "transmutation" for the theory that is usually referred to by historians as "modification." For example, his *Lectiones opticae* contains the following sentence – "Quemadmodum si desideretur ut sensui planissimé pateat quòd prisma convertit lucem in colores non transmutando proprietates ejus intrinsecas, sed segregando tantum radios . . ." The same language occurs in the closely related *Optica*. See Alan Shapiro, *The Optical Papers of Isaac Newton, Volume I, The Optical Lectures 1670–1672* (Cambridge: Cambridge University Press, 1984), pp. 165, 472, and 520. The term "transmutation" appears also in Newton's "New Theory about Light and Colours" of 1672.

27 Shapiro, *Optical Papers*, pp. 12–13, says the following: "Sometime between the beginning of 1666 and 1669, but most probably closer to the former than the latter, Newton wrote up the experiments from his 'age of invention' in an essay again entitled "Of Colours" [= CU Add. 3975, fols. 2v–11v.] There is no statement of the theory and little theoretical interpretation, but cautiously reading backward from the later accounts, especially the *Optical Lectures*, it is clear that he already had the main features of his theory, since the essay contains many of the fundamental experiments of the *Optical Lectures*."

28 For a full account of this tradition up to the time of Boyle, see William
    R. Newman, *Atoms and Alchemy: Chymistry and the Experimental
    Origins of the Scientific Revolution* (Chicago, IL: University of Chicago
    Press, 2006).

29 William R. Newman and Lawrence M. Principe, *Alchemy Tried in the
    Fire* (Chicago, IL: University of Chicago Press, 2002), ch. 2.

30 See Newman and Principe, *Alchemy Tried in the Fire*, ch. 5, for
    Worsley. See also John T. Young, *Faith, Medical Alchemy and Natural
    Philosophy: Johann Moriaen, Reformed Intelligencer and the Hartlib
    Circle* (Brookfield, VT: Ashgate, 1998), pp. 183–216, esp. pp. 198–200.

31 The experiment is clearly described by Boyle, *Certain Physiological
    Essays*, in *The Works of Robert Boyle*, ed. M. Hunter and E. B. Davis
    (London: Pickering and Chatto, 1999–2000), vol. 2, pp. 92–6.

32 Newton, CUL Add. Ms. 3975, fol. 32v, from The Chymistry of
    Isaac Newton, http://webapp1.dlib.indiana.edu/newton/mss/norm/
    ALCH00110/:

> The purenesse of this ^redintigrated Antimony seemed to proceede
> from ye recesse of so much Sulphur wch is not at all necessary to
> ye constitution of Antimony though perhaps too ye vitrum a top
> might proceede from ye avolation of two much Antimony from y^e
> superficiall parts. pag 265
>   But redintegration of Bodys succeeded best <*illeg.*> in
> Turpentine for a very cleare liquor being distilld from it <*illeg.*>
> was againe put to ye caput Mortuum (wch was very dry brittle
> Transparent sleeke & red but purely yellow when poudered) it
> was immediatly dissolved part of it into a deepe red Balsome. And
> by further disgestion in a large well stopt Glasse became perfect
> Turpentine againe ~~both~~as all men judgd by ye smell & Taste. pag 268
> of for<ms>

33 Shapiro, *Optical Papers*, vol. 1, p. 504: "Et eadem ratione constat
    reflexam albedinem similiter compositam esse, siquidem (ut dixi)
    redintegrata est . . ."

34 Shapiro, *Optical Papers*, vol. 1, p. 162, line 9; and p. 516, line 16.

35 *Oxford Latin Dictionary*, ed. P. G. W. Glare (Oxford: Clarendon Press,
    2003): see the entries for "Redintegro" and "Redintegratio" *sub vocibus*.
    The meanings given for "Redintegro" are "to restore physically" in the

sense of refreshing, "to replenish," and "to revive"; "to revive, renew"; and "to say over again" or "repeat in full." For "Redintegratio," one finds nominal forms of these meanings followed by "Reiteration, repetition."

36 George Ripley, *The Compound of Alchymie*, in Elias Ashmole, *Theatrum Chemicum Britannicum* (London: Nath: Brooke, 1652), p. 176.

37 Some further instances of Newton's terminological borrowing from Boyle may be found in Newman, "Newton's Early Optical Theory," pp. 305–6.

38 For a more complete description of these themes in Newton's "theory of everything," see William R. Newman, "Geochemical Concepts in Isaac Newton's Early Alchemy," in G. D. Rosenberg (ed.), *The Revolution in Geology from the Renaissance to the Enlightenment* (Boulder, CO: Geological Society of America, 2009), pp. 41–9.

39 See A. Rupert Hall, "Newton and the Aerial Nitre," *Notes and Records of the Royal Society of London* 52 (1998), 51–61, esp. 57.

40 On Newton and Varenius, see William Warntz, "Newton, the Newtonians, and the Geographia Generalis Varenii," *Annals of the Association of American Geographers* 79 (1989), 165–91. For the relationship of "Of Natures obvious laws & processes in vegetation" to Varenius, see Newman, "Geochemical Concepts," pp. 41–9.

41 Bernhardus Varenius, *Geographia generalis*, ed. Isaac Newton (Cambridge: Henricus Dickinson, 1672), p. 112 (translation by William R. Newman): "Even if salt is left behind in the bottom of the vessel in both distillation and decoction (which are the same) nonetheless the water separated by distillation or decoction is still found to be salty, so that it is not fit for human drink, which seems a wonder to those ignorant of the cause. But chymistry, that is, true physics, has taught this, by whose help it is known that there is a double salt in bodies; or two genera of salts, which even if they agree in taste yet differ greatly in <their> other qualities: the artificers call one <of them> "fixed" salt, the other "volatile." The fixed salt is not elevated in decoction and distillation on account of its weight, but remains in the bottom of the vessel. But the volatile is a spiritual salt, and is nothing other than a very subtle spirit, which is raised by a very mild fire, and hence it ascends with the sweet water in distillation, and is tightly united <to it> on account of the subtlety of <its> atoms."

42 For Boyle's rather conflicted thoughts about seminal principles, see especially Peter R. Anstey, "Boyle on Seminal Principles," *Studies in History and Philosophy of Biology and Biomedical Sciences* 33 (2002), 597–630.

43 For a discussion of combined analysis and resynthesis as a way of distinguishing mechanical from non-mechanical processes in the work of Robert Boyle, see William R. Newman, "How Not to Integrate the History and Philosophy of Science: A Response to Chalmers," *Studies in History and Philosophy of Science* 41 (2010), 203–13, esp. 206–7.

44 For a discussion of this corpuscular tradition in medieval and early modern alchemy, see Newman, *Gehennical Fire*, pp. 92–114 and 141–69.

45 This argument is made at length in Newman, *Atoms and Alchemy*, particularly pp. 23–44.

46 Nathan Sivin, "Research on the History of Chinese Alchemy," in Z. R. W. M. von Martels, *Alchemy Revisited* (Leiden: Brill, 1990), pp. 3–20; see p. 4.

47 This view of the occult sciences has largely gone out of style in recent decades, but is still upheld by Brian Vickers. See Vickers, "The 'New Historiography' and the Limits of Alchemy," *Annals of Science* 65 (2008), 127–56. See also the response to Vickers in William R. Newman, "Brian Vickers on Alchemy and the Occult: A Response," *Perspectives on Science* 17 (2009), 482–506.

12 The religion of Isaac Newton

Rob Iliffe

From early in Newton's scholarly career to the end of his life, he displayed a deep interest in prophecy and Church history, and they remained the core elements of his faith. He knew a great deal about Christian doctrine, though his method of study – fueled by a fierce hatred both of Roman Catholicism and the doctrine of the Trinity – was primarily empirical and historical. His approach was also predominantly negative in that he was overwhelmingly concerned with what he took to be the corruption of the simple, original faith preached by Christ and his apostles. He was also fascinated by the history of pre-Christian religions, and in the earliest phase of his work in this area he assumed that there had been one rational religion that had been dispersed around the globe in the wake of the Flood. As Mordechai Feingold shows in his chapter in this volume, in the last three decades of his life Newton devoted a vast amount of time to reconciling different histories of the world in the centuries before the birth of Christ.

Newton's theological writings also tell us a great deal about the man himself. Not only did he believe that he had a special talent, namely his intelligence, but he also believed that he was one of the Elect, part of a chosen saintly remnant that would reign with Christ during the Millennium. For now, as the Bible showed, the gifted Christian had a duty to make use of his superior reasoning facilities to determine what was true and what was false in whatever he chose to study. This confidence in his own understanding was closely related to his view that a truly godly man such as himself had to find his own way in his studies. Newton's belief in the need for the free and independent study of religious topics was also bound up with his support for a broad religious toleration, a position that was particularly pertinent in his own case because of the extreme

485

views that he held. The brave decision he made in 1674 to avoid taking holy orders, and thus to remain a layman in the Church of England, was almost certainly because the formal demands of the ministry would curtail his freedom to engage in research, rather than because Anglican doctrine clashed with his radically heterodox private beliefs. Indeed, there is no evidence that Newton had arrived at his radical opinions by this time, though he had certainly developed a profound antipathy towards the doctrine of the Trinity by the end of the decade.

A STUDENT OF THEOLOGY

The sheer scale of Newton's religious investigations demonstrates that his theological research was central to his life. Although little evidence from his early religious study remains, a list of confessions of various offences that he compiled in 1662 demonstrates that he was a devout individual who took his duties to God extremely seriously. His uncle, stepfather, and first major patron were all Church of England clergymen, though as a teenager during the Cromwellian Protectorate (1653–8) he was exposed to powerful Presbyterian influences.[1] His pronounced puritan moral attitudes were deeply ingrained, and were not shaped by any particular religious upbringing, but he needed serious training to give form to his studies. At the Grantham Free School he attended from 1655 to 1661, pupils were required to attend and take notes on sermons on a daily basis, and they were also taught Greek and Latin to a good level. This provided Newton with the skills both to read original printed sources and, in due course, to compare these sources with manuscript originals. At Trinity College Cambridge, where he arrived in the summer of 1661, he studied the Greek New Testament in much more detail and learned many of the exegetical techniques that formed the bedrock of his independent theological studies from the 1670s. Although divinity was not part of the curriculum, religious discipline and devotion saturated his existence at the college as it had done at school. He and all other students had to regularly attend the college chapel and the university church (Great St. Mary's), take notes on sermons, and be present at disputes on theological topics.[2]

The opportunity for serious theological study was limited by the famous projects in the exact sciences that Newton undertook in the decade following his introduction to the most pressing problems in mathematics and his discovery of the "new" philosophy in 1664. Within a short time of beginning his intensive theological research programme he had focused his ire on the doctrine of the Trinity, viewing it as a pagan and diabolical fiction that had been introduced early on in the history of the Church. There is no evidence that his extreme position arose as a result of meeting anti-Trinitarians, or of reading anti-Trinitarian texts. Rather, it seems to have been motivated by holding fast to core Protestant values that engendered an extreme dislike both of Roman Catholicism and of idolatry in general. While Newton's pronounced anti-Catholicism did not distinguish him from many of his countrymen, the combination of his heightened sensitivity to idolatry and his view that he should follow the dictates of his understanding gave raise to the belief that the doctrine of the Trinity was a particularly pernicious form of polytheism. Nevertheless, this catastrophic contamination of the true religion had left numerous footprints in the historical record, and he made it his Christian duty to detect them.[3]

Newton was unconcerned with many of the issues that exercised contemporary writers, and blank entries in his theological notebook on the topics of freewill, justification, and the remission of sins are indicative of a broader lack of interest in these subjects. Because Scripture gave no definitive answer to questions about these doctrines, Christians could not know the truth about them with any certainty and should not speak or behave as if they did. Learned and mature people could discuss such topics, but, unless such conversations were conducted in an appropriately charitable manner, they could lead to fundamental disagreements between Christians and even to schism. In particular, Newton condemned those aspects of religion that were redolent of what contemporaries called "enthusiasm." He showed no sign that he was concerned with attaining the sort of inner spiritual regeneration or "paradise within" that was desired by other puritans such as Bunyan. As he saw it, speculative metaphysical theology, the fraudulent and imaginary fictions of the Roman Catholic Church, and the quest for an emotional brand of inspiration were all examples of religious corruption. In natural philosophy, the same tendencies manifested themselves in the penchant for developing over-ambitious, incredible, and subjective systems of thought, and in the reliance on unsubstantiated hypotheses.

As was true for all other natural philosophers of the period, Newton's cosmology was bound up with his views on the being and attributes of God. In his undergraduate notebook he drew from and built on the ideas of René Descartes, Henry More, and others to devise some preliminary statements about the relationship between God and his Creation. From the start he believed that almost all of the infinite cosmos was empty of matter, and that God (being an "infinite spirit") was present in these vacuous spaces as well as in material objects. At some point in the 1670s, as various contributors to this volume have noted, Newton wrote a lengthy attack on Descartes's *Principia Philosophiae*, whose philosophy had been the target of the infinitist cosmology and vacuist ontology offered by More. In this text, now known as "De gravitatione," he argued that the Cartesian equation of substance with extension was a pathway to atheism because it left no room for God to operate in the cosmos. Extension (which for Newton and More was space that was empty of matter) was an "emanative effect" of God, that is, something that existed necessarily as a result of God's nature, while substantial objects (i.e., material bodies) were separate from God. Newton also attacked Descartes's claim that the size of the cosmos was "indefinite," proposed (according to Newton) on the grounds that if space were infinite it might be identified with God. Empty space was really extended to infinity, and in a novel argument, probably based on the views of Isaac Barrow (the first Lucasian Professor), Newton stated that empty space was made up of interpenetrating mathematical objects. Unlike Barrow, who had suggested that such entities were potential only, he argued that they were real (if invisible), and constituted an infinite space on the grounds that some mathematical objects were infinitely long.[4]

In the second half of Newton's essay he argued that God had created material objects by a mere act of will, and that this was accomplished by making objects accessible to "the senses and fancy" of perceiving subjects. This, he said, both eradicated unnecessary objects (such as unknowable substances) and removed redundant procedural steps from the divine act of creation. It also opened a pathway towards understanding God's activity through an analysis of the way in which humans moved their own bodies. Newton emphasized that this link was warranted by the numerous Scriptural references to the fact that humans were created in the image of God. Humans did not possess the same creative power as that of the Almighty, but their capacity to engage in freely undertaken self-motion was a "delineation" of that power. It followed from this, he suggested, that we could learn about the Creation by empirically investigating the physical processes by which we moved our own bodies. Newton undertook such a research programme early in his career, and the question of how human self-motion was related to divine power remained of central importance to him throughout his life.[5]

The analogy between the human frame and divine creation formed a key part of the (extremely brief) account of Newton's religious beliefs that he published in his lifetime. These ideas were outlined in his *Optice* (1706) (the Latin edition of his *Opticks* [1704]), and in the "General Scholium" to the second (1713) edition of the *Principia Mathematica*. In a series of "Queries" appended to the main text of *Optice*, he argued that the universe was the divine analogue of the physical part of the brain that allowed humans to think and to be aware of the outside world, while in the "General Scholium" he gave a highly influential account of his conception of God. Newton emphasized that the latter was omnipotent and had created a world that was both exquisitely designed and benignly superintended. God was worthy of worship not because of his infinite perfections but on account of his power and his eternal, omnipresent dominion. His attributes, and indeed his incorporeal substance, were inaccessible to humans as mere finite creatures ("as a blind man has no idea of colours") but could be discussed allegorically. Two issues, however, gave Newton hope that we could know God to a limited extent. Firstly, in the Queries to *Optice*, he rehearsed his claim in "De gravitatione" that we were created in the Image of God and that therefore we could make some inferences about his being from the proper analysis of our own minds and bodies. Secondly, we could understand God, and make inferences about his actions and intentions, from looking at the way he had crafted the natural world. "To discourse of God from the appearances of things," Newton concluded the "General Scholium" to the third (1726) edition of the *Principia*, "does certainly belong to natural philosophy."[6]

THE CORRUPTION OF THE TRUE RELIGION

Newton's protracted historical critique of Trinitarian Christianity marks him out as a radical anti-Trinitarian rather than a milder non-Trinitarian. From his scrutiny of the voluminous writings of pagans, the Church fathers and later historians, he produced a detailed picture of the terrible fate that had befallen the true Church in the fourth century. Although there had been many heresies before this, it was at this point, as he saw it, that all the major features of the most terrible heresy, the Great Apostasy, were put in place. These included relic-, image-, and saint-worship, the adoration of the Virgin Mary, and the introduction of the doctrine of the Trinity. Monks, who practiced increasingly bizarre mental and corporeal regimens that Newton examined at length, disseminated this false religion far and wide, and under Theodosius the Great it became the official religion of the Roman Empire at the end of the fourth century.

At the heart of Newton's account of the way that Christianity had been corrupted were the events during and after the great Council of Nicaea, held in 325 CE. In terms of doctrine, the vast majority of attendees of the council subscribed to the view that the Son was "homoousios" with the Father. What this word actually meant, that is, whether the Greek prefix "homo" should be translated into Latin as "same" or "similar," and whether "ousia" should be translated as "person," "nature," "essence," or "substance," exercised Newton for the rest of his life. Like everyone else, he knew that the term was not found in the Bible, and for that reason alone he considered that it ought to be rejected. However, the term had acquired a much darker resonance in the aftermath of Nicaea, for the Latins in the West had translated *homoousion* as "consubstantial" in order to rebut subordinationist claims that made the Son a creature, or a semi-god. For Newton this was a false definition that made the Son not just equal to God, but composed of the same physical substance (and thus numerically identical). The "physicalist" account of their relationship was a gross and obnoxious perversion that lay at the heart of the demonic debasement of pure Christianity. In reality God was completely different from and infinitely superior to the Son, but graciously allowed the Son various powers by effecting a union of their wills.

Although Newton downgraded the status of Jesus Christ in comparison with the position attributed to him by the orthodox, he had a sophisticated understanding of his nature and office. Christ had come to restore the true religion, as Moses had done before him, and he was truly the divine Son of God who had a unique redemptive mission. Newton denied the Socinian claim that Jesus was merely a man, and he held that Christ had pre-existed his incarnation as the created *logos* mentioned in John 1:1. For this reason, his views were very close to what his contemporaries understood as Arianism (named after the fourth-century priest Arius), a view that was seen as the most potent heresy in orthodox Christianity. Newton also denied the orthodox position – designed to avoid the implication that part of the divine godhead had died on the Cross -- that it was only the human part of Jesus Christ, joined to the *logos* by some obscure "hypostatic union," that had suffered and perished. Rather, for Newton Jesus Christ was the intelligent, homogenous incarnate *logos* whose humility, obedience, and crucifixion had prompted God to elevate his status in such a way that he was entitled to be worshipped as the Lamb of God and as the Messiah.[7]

The architect of the great perversion of Christianity was Athanasius. Newton held him responsible not merely for introducing many of the most idolatrous practices and doctrines into official Christianity, but for rewriting and indeed fabricating the history of the Church so as to produce the version now held in common by orthodox Protestants and Catholics. Athanasius's religious misdeeds were immense, but Newton also noted that he and his henchmen were repeatedly punished by civil authorities for crimes such as sedition, immorality, and murder. He helped pervert the Council of Nicaea and other councils that followed, introduced a range of deviant views and ceremonies into orthodox Christianity, and persecuted the godly exponents of the original Christian religion. According to Newton, during a long exile in the Egyptian desert between 356 and 362 Athanasius fabricated a vast array of sources in order to give a Trinitarian tenor to the writings of the most authoritative Church Fathers. At the end of the 350s he also wrote a florid life of Antony, who founded the monastic order in the Egyptian desert. Athanasius was banished from Alexandria by emperors that Newton considered wise and godly (primarily on the basis that they were anti-homoousian), but aided and abetted by his friends, and by the devil himself, he always came back into positions of seniority and influence. His greatest crime against the true religion was to ensure that Trinitarian Christianity became the orthodox version of that religion.[8]

Newton used standard scholarly analytic techniques to bolster his claim that Athanasius had rewritten history. He used primary accounts composed by pagan and Christian writers, and he used heterodox sources such as those composed by the fourth- and fifth-century

Arian chronicler Philostorgius, and the modern historian Christopher Sand. However, for more details he scoured major sources such as those he located in the *Annales Ecclesiastici* of Cesare Baronius. One line of argument was to point out that the decision at Nicaea had been by no means unanimous, and that some attendees had subscribed with mental reservation. Another tack was to claim that others present had subscribed willingly, but had understood *homoousios* differently from the way it was later portrayed by Athanasius. The so-called argument "from silence" was also crucial to his approach. Athanasius's much later accounts of Nicaea and the events that followed could not be verified by independent documents. As a result of this, Newton was able to read as true all the stories propounded by Athanasius's enemies, which the latter, along with all subsequent orthodox historians denounced as corrupt or absurd. These referred to Athanasius's sedition, lying, immorality, subversion of ecclesiastical practices, and even murder. Orthodox accounts written in Newton's lifetime, which were based on Athanasius's own writings, wasted no opportunity to dismiss such stories as the work of evil and demented Arian heretics, but they provided Newton with a coherent and detailed counternarrative with which he could run. And he did so with gusto, ploughing through Baronius and other sources to add a tremendous degree of detail and colour to his anti-Athanasian history. For over half a century he worked on this remarkably daring and innovative project, inverting and rebutting the orthodox Protestant and Catholic accounts.

On the topic of the bodily regimens of early Roman Catholics, Newton offered an idiosyncratic and original account that was at least partly autobiographical. In one lengthy diatribe, he lambasted the assumptions that underlay the monks' efforts to grapple with and conquer their sexual fantasies as a means towards attaining a life of perfect celibacy. Drawing on earlier work on the nature and deceptions of the imagination, he detailed the failures of the great founders of monasticism to discipline their lustful tendencies by engaging in dubious spiritual techniques and bizarre corporeal regimens. Taking on the imagination in this way, and indeed, thinking about celibacy

the Trinitarian and other Romanist "inventions" of Athanasius at the heart of the Great Apostasy. Not only did Newton bring forward the origins of the Great Apostasy by a few decades in contrast with Mede, but he emphasized that these much earlier events, and not the battles between Protestants and Roman Catholics in his own day, were the most significant episodes in sacred history.[10]

With characteristic ambition, Newton attempted to generalize the technique of synchronisms far beyond what Mede had accomplished. In a burst of creativity in the late 1680s he wrote down the outlines of a five-book treatise, the first of which concerned the language of the prophets, and the second of which concerned the allusions to the Apocalypse in the law, history, and religious ceremonies of the Jews. Drawing on Maimonides's *De Cultu Divino*, Josephus's *Antiquities of the Jews*, John Selden's *De Synedriis & Praefecturis Iuridicis Veterum Ebraeorum*, and John Lightfoot's "Prospect of the Temple Service," as well as a wealth of other primary and secondary sources (many reproduced in Bryan Walton's *Biblia Sacra Polyglotta*), Newton proceeded – as Mede had done earlier – to show how the events described in Revelation were set in the Tabernacle, and how its architecture and ceremonies foreshadowed the structure of the true (Judæo-Christian) Church, its division of offices, its proper forms of worship, and its future fate. As he launched into an analysis on the architecture of the Temple described in the first few chapters of Revelation, he gave increasingly detailed accounts of its dimensions, noting that he felt minded to give a "fuller" account elsewhere since other commentators had made so many mistakes.[11]

At some point he did just this, writing an account of Solomon's Temple based both on the claim that it was the same as that described in Ezekiel chs. 40–3, and also on certain assumptions about its connections with the Second Temple that was constructed by Zerubbabel, completed by Herod, and destroyed by the Romans in 70 CE. Newton built on the work of the previous commentators he had criticized, especially Lightfoot, Juan Bautista Villalpando (Villalpandus), Benito Arias Montanus, and Louis Cappellus. Although reliant on these analyses,

Newton's treatment was an original, erudite, and critical examination that drew on and reconciled as many different and independent sources as he could find. He made extensive use of Josephus's description of the Second Temple, took notes on the Talmud, and compared Hebrew, Greek (Septuagint) and Latin versions of Ezekiel – with the Septuagint version usually being preferred. To aid him in his task of correcting and harmonizing these sources, he made his own calculations of the optimal form of the Temple by deriving the lengths of both ordinary and sacred cubits (the ancient units of measurement). Newton's restoration of the exact dimensions of the Temple was accompanied by his account of its typological import for the future history of the Church. Solomon's Temple had been built with an inner and an outer court, the first being reserved for the priests, and the second for the people. The fact that gentiles were able to move around the outer court when it was rebuilt was an indication that idolaters had been allowed to pollute the Church (Ezek. 46:2); the account of gentiles treading down the outer court in Revelation 11 thus portended the great perversion of the Christian religion.[12]

Prophecy was not only written by way of allusion to the religious practices of the Jews, but it also took into account what Newton took to be a "figurative" language in which references to natural disasters referred to epoch-making social and political events in the human realm. This language had been written and spoken by a number of learned people who had lived in India, Egypt, and Persia at the time the prophecies were written down. He followed Mede and Henry More in listing a number of "definitions" based on this esoteric Indo-Egypto-Persian language, which had supposedly been decoded in the so-called "Chaldee" paraphrases found in the Targums (Jewish Aramaic translations of the Hebrew Scriptures) and in the early medieval work on dream interpretation (the *Oneirocriticon*) written by a Byzantine Christian known as Achmet. Based on the Medean assumption that the prophets spoke in this figurative language, Newton understood the frequent apocalyptic references to natural objects such as the Sun, Moon, and stars, and to hailstorms, earthquakes, floods, meteors, and comets, as accounts of historical political episodes. Indeed, it was a grave hermeneutical error to understand such references as real natural events. In one early version of his book on the language of the prophets, he followed the "definitions" with an extended section entitled the "Proof," which invoked a number of passages from the Old Testament to justify the claims made in Achmet. Newton was so conversant with the figurative language that he was able to immediately understand prophetic phrases as references to political events.[13]

Newton made use of his notion of the figurative language in a letter to Thomas Burnet in 1681 on the nature of Creation described in Genesis. Burnet, who had just written the first of two parts of his *Telluris Theoria Sacra* (Sacred Theory of the Earth), had asked Newton whether his own account of the creation of the Earth was not a suitable and plausible replacement for the narrative given by Moses. Newton admitted that Burnet's theory, which explained the origins of the solar system in terms of natural causes, was ingenious, but balked at Burnet's over-confident claim that his work gave the true account of Creation. Newton also took umbrage at the suggestion that Moses had propounded a fictitious story or "hypothesis," which he knew to be false, and which was designed to appeal to the imaginations of his unlearned audience. Although Newton agreed that Moses had "accommodated" his discourse to the capacities of the vulgar, he argued that Moses had described the visible or "sensible" creation, and had crafted his story to convey what ordinary people would have seen (rather than what they could currently imagine) if they had been present during the first few days of creation. Thus, although the Mosaic narrative bore no relationship to the physical development of the cosmos, it was not false. Moses, who was writing as a prophet rather than as a philosopher, could have given more detail about other features of the universe, such as the existence of other star systems (where Newton believed there was life on orbiting planets), but had decided not to, conversing instead in the figurative language of Asia and the Middle East.[14]

Newton rehearsed this division between what was appropriate to the Bible, and what was relevant only to natural philosophy in the *Principia Mathematica*. In the Scholium to Definition VIII, he distinguished between "absolute" and "relative" notions of space and time, claiming that the techniques described in his own book would make it possible for scientifically sophisticated users to derive true and absolute accounts of the world from a number of different measures. By contrast, ordinary people were stuck with "sensible" or "relative" conceptions of things because they were governed by their sense-experiences. For example, their inability to abstract from their sensory information left them unable to determine what was truly at motion and truly at rest in the case of two objects moving relative to each other. According to Newton, the so-called "common" sensory referents of terms such as "space," "place," and "motion" were to be understood when interpreting Scripture, but not when dealing with the natural world. Just as people corrupted natural philosophy when they dealt only with sensible or relative measures, so interpreters perverted the meaning of biblical terms when they understood Scriptural terms as referring to true or absolute quantities. Because such words concerned only what ordinary people could sense, nothing about the real nature of the physical cosmos could be gleaned from the Bible.[15]

The figurative language was key to applying prophetic terms to real-world geopolitical events but further justification in the form of "Propositions" or "Positions" was required to link various images to each other. In a major break from Mede's system, Newton synchronized each successive vial with its "correspondent" trumpet, the variant descriptions in the corresponding vials and trumpets presenting a different view of the specific historical event in question. He also broke with Mede by making the key period of 1260 years (42 prophetic months) of apocalyptic time begin with the onset of the fifth vial and trumpet, and terminate with the close of the sixth, rather than (as Mede had argued) with the start of the Great Apostasy in the fourth century. There was intense prophetic activity in the time marked out from the first vial and trumpet to the end of the fourth, but it was the fifth and sixth trumpets/vials that were synchronized with a number of other key images in Revelation. These included the 42 months of the beast making war against the saints, the reign of the Whore of Babylon, and the treading underfoot of the holy city by the gentiles. Although this placed Newton's own time firmly within the 1,260-year period, his scheme emphasized the significance of those events that had taken place during the first four vials and trumpets. It expressed his view that the pouring of the vials should not be reserved for the heroic triumphs of Protestantism, and implied that nothing of any prophetic significance whatsoever had taken place since the Reformation. Mede's work had promised both his Puritan and Anglican readers a millennium whose start was imminent, but Newton's system deferred the expected date of the Second Coming (the start of the seventh trumpet and vial) many hundreds of years into the future.[16]

For his historical interpretation of prophecy, Newton pored over a vast number of sources, dwarfing the research efforts undertaken by Mede and others. He made slight changes to the dates Mede gave for the early development of the Great Apostasy, but retained Mede's general view of how specific events constituted "fulfilments" of various prophecies. The fourth century witnessed the gradual setting up of the religion of the beast on Earth, soon after the latter had been expelled from heaven. Trinitarian ("homoousian") emperors took over the Christian world, and a swathe of demonic corruptions polluted Christian doctrine and practice. All this came to a head at the end of 380, when the 7th seal was opened, and in 395 (after fifteen years of silence), the sounding of trumpets, and pouring of vials began. Despite the multitude of terrible events that befell the Church in the fourth and fifth centuries, things worsened at the start of the seventh century CE, with the strengthening of Roman Catholicism and the advent of Islam.

Newton's counter-orthodox history of the Church contained a number of remarkable features. For example, he argued that the

Newton's belief in the great intellectual accomplishments of the Ancients was inextricably linked to what he thought the *Principia* was, and what he took to be his role as its author. He believed that, by publishing the *Principia*, he was recovering the actual knowledge that had been known to the Ancients, and his proposals to add references to this Ancient wisdom in various guises of the *Principia* were not mere "glosses" to a scientific text. He accepted the notion that the ancient priests of nature had amused the vulgar by revealing their precious mysteries in the form of obscure allegories and concentric hieroglyphs, the latter representing the true planetary order within the solar system. Ultimately, however, knowledge of these philosophical and religious truths had been corrupted by a misguided literalist hermeneutics that resulted in idolatry and – in the case of the concentric signs – by the acceptance of Aristotelian geocentrism. For this reason, the *Principia Mathematica* functioned in part as a tool with which Newton could decode the poetic allegories that the Ancients had supposedly used to hide their own knowledge. Similarly, the relationship between the technically forbidding *Principia* and its readers mirrored the much older association between the knowledge held by the elite philosopher–priests and the ignorant common people.

SCRIPTURAL EXEGESIS

Newton's knowledge of the Bible was acknowledged as extraordinary by many of his contemporaries. He knew extended passages by heart, and had memorized a vast number of textual interconnections, holding the standard protestant belief that various passages of Scripture "interpreted" each other. This was a propitious moment to study the origins of the Bible. From the middle of the seventeenth century, various polyglots and critical editions of the New Testament proliferated, providing further fuel for both defenders and critics of orthodoxy. Increasingly drawn into the Republic of Letters, Church of England divines found themselves having to devise new methods to defend the sanctity of their preferred versions of Scripture against attacks by deists, anti-Trinitarians, Spinozists, and Roman Catholic exegetes such as Father Richard Simon. Simon, whose works on the critical history of the texts of the Old and New testaments were translated into English in the 1680s, was particularly disturbing for Anglican scholars. He made an extensive survey of ancient manuscripts in various European libraries, especially those of the Vatican and Louis XIV, and his work eroded confidence that any particular Greek manuscript of the New Testament could serve as the basis for an authoritative version of Scripture. In England, disputes over the meaning, authenticity, and Scriptural basis for the doctrine of the Trinity came to the fore in the wake of the Glorious Revolution of 1688–9.

Newton was keenly aware of these debates, and made copious use of the rich textual resources at his disposal. By the 1680s he was in contact with a number of other scholars at Oxford and Cambridge who were interested in examining the oldest surviving manuscripts of the Greek New Testament, and he subjected the human record of the word of God to the same type and degree of scrutiny with which he examined the documents relating to the history of the Christian Church. By removing what he took to be false interpolations from the accepted text of the Bible, he was able to reconstruct what he took to be the original and authentic version. Unsurprisingly, the bulk of his exegetical energies were devoted to examining the doctrine of the Trinity. In the spring of 1690, having just completed his stint as MP for Cambridge University in the first parliament after the Glorious Revolution, Newton was invited by his new friend John Locke to consider the pedigree of two central Trinitarian proof-texts, 1 Tim. 3:16 and 1 John 5:7–8 (which contained the so-called "Johannine comma"). These passages had long been subject to criticism from heterodox writers, and many Anglican divines were also hesitant to appeal to their authority.

In November 1690 Newton sent Locke a lengthy discussion of the two texts in question, arguing that both were examples of forgery. Unlike Simon, he was not prepared to consider them as the harmless actions of over-enthusiastic Catholic scribes, nor could they be excused by having been introduced to counter obvious heresies. In the case of the Johannine comma, Newton undertook a lengthy treatment of how and why the text had been introduced. Early scribes had glossed the original text in margins of various manuscripts in order to make it more clearly support the doctrine of the Trinity, and in time the gloss had "crept in" to the main text. He performed the same analysis on 1 Tim. 3:16, using evidence from Walton's *Biblia Sacra Polyglotta* about the readings of these passages in other bibles, along with references in secondary literature to the oldest extant Greek manuscripts. He told Locke that his essays were merely neutral pieces of textual criticism, though his argument was clearly aimed at eroding the authority of the major texts used to support the doctrine of the Trinity. All the evidence, he concluded, showed that the texts were missing from the oldest manuscripts, and thus they had been added in much later. He complained to Locke that it was hypocritical of Protestants to condemn Catholics for interfering with the authentic Word of God when their own bibles contained such perniciously false readings.[22]

As he had done with the writings of Athanasius, so Newton used conventional forensic techniques to demonstrate when, how, why, and by whom the original text of the New Testament had been corrupted. The man responsible for introducing the Johannine comma was Jerome, the fourth-century translator of the Vulgate (the "common" Latin version of the Bible used by the Catholic Church after the Council of Trent). In a "Preface" to the Epistles allegedly written by Jerome, the latter had claimed that the older Latin version of 1 John had wrongly omitted the comma, which could be seen in the oldest Greek versions. He defended his inclusion of the text in his own translation, firstly because it was in the Greek manuscripts, and secondly because it confirmed the true faith. For Newton, who accepted that Jerome was the author of the Preface, the first claim regarding the presence of the text in the oldest Greek manuscripts was patently false. It was not in the oldest surviving texts (as Richard Simon confirmed), nor was it cited by any of the Church Fathers in the great Arian controversy. Claims by modern editors of various bibles to have personally witnessed ancient manuscripts containing the text were inventions of the "popish clergy," Newton argued, and similarly, Jerome's admission that it ought to be included because it corroborated the true faith showed that his action was not that of a disinterested translator. Ultimately, he told Locke, the non-Trinitarian reading made much more sense than the standard verses did.[23]

Newton used the same approach to the passage on "the great mystery of godliness" in 1 Tim. 3:16, and some weeks later he drafted another letter to Locke in which he subjected a number of other texts to the same type of scrutiny. Locke went to some lengths to get the text translated into French and published by the Genevan scholar Jean le Clerc. Le Clerc – with Newton's blessing – suggested that the unknown author bolster his argument with evidence from the writings of Richard Simon and Gilbert Burnet. The facts that the pieces were cast as examples of textual criticism, that they were anonymous, and that they would be translated into a different language, would all have made Newton's authorship impossible to detect, but for various reasons his enthusiasm for the project had dimmed by the end of 1691 and he successfully prevented its publication. Perhaps, despite the appearance of being a mere piece of criticism, it was obvious what the author's leanings were – and perhaps he feared that a determined detective could unmask his identity. As Scott Mandelbrote shows elsewhere in this volume, despite Newton's best efforts to suppress the text, it had a complex afterlife that led to its belated appearance in print in 1754.

THE DIVINE COSMOS

Like every other English natural philosopher, Newton assumed that the degree of order and beauty visible in the cosmos was *prima facie* evidence of the existence of an intelligent designer. In late 1692, he answered pertinent questions sent to him by the classical scholar and clergyman Richard Bentley regarding the implications for natural theology of the doctrines in the *Principia*. Bentley, who was preparing to deliver the first Boyle lectures aimed at defending religion against atheists and deists, forced Newton to confront the fact that references to God were almost entirely absent from the work, and his questions prompted Newton to extend "divine design" arguments to astronomy and physics. The current nature and structure of the solar system, especially the fact that the Sun had just the right amount of heat and light to support life, could not have arisen by chance. The direction, speed, and mass of the planets also revealed a divine hand, since only a supremely intelligent being could have calculated and effected all these parameters in such a way that the result was the stable system we now witnessed. Bentley also forced Newton to think more deeply about the possibility of giving a physical explanation for Universal Gravitation. Although he told Bentley that he would accept a plausible account of that kind, or even a "spiritual" explanation, the evidence from the "Classical Scholia" and other sources suggests that he believed that the only direct or real cause of motions in the universe was God.[24]

Nevertheless, Newton was also privately committed to the notion that God made use of secondary or physical causes to effect great changes in the cosmos, though he also apparently believed that these events were occasionally superintended by angels. Soon after his correspondence with Bentley, Newton told David Gregory that he thought that the satellites of Jupiter were held in reserve by God for a new creation, and a few years later he told Gregory that the material agent that would probably effect the destruction of those planets closest to the Sun was the Great Comet that had appeared at the end of 1680. In 1725 Newton repeated this idea to John Conduitt (the husband of his half-niece Catherine), saying that the supernovae of 1572 and 1604 were examples of the same process happening in other solar systems. After a number of further orbits, the 1680 comet would be directed by a group of "intelligent beings superior to us" to crash into a waning Sun, causing its heat to increase dramatically. It would destroy any do after the Day of Judgment, were all questions that Christians could discuss and should endeavor to understand, but about which they should not condemn each other. In the same way, "disputable" questions concerning the nature and origin of matter, the production of the world by natural causes, free will, providence, the nature of angels, the state of the dead before the resurrection, forms of Church government, the question of whether the dead would rise with physical bodies, were all topics for Christians to study privately and to debate, but not subjects over which to divide the Church. Indeed, at one point Newton stated that disputing to this extent was to become "carnal" (following 1 Cor. 3:1–2). Similarly, philosophical opinions, such as whether the Earth went round the Sun, and whether there were many habitable worlds, had no place in religion; it was the introduction of such elements into religion that had helped to corrupt it. The discussion of all human opinions, doctrines, and theories potentially led to strife, and such issues could be studied in the proper way by philosophers but not by divines.[28]

For Newton, the issue of how to deal with disagreements between sincere Christians demanded an understanding of how the Christian polity was to be ordered. As with every other religious issue, he believed that this question could only be resolved by having recourse to the study of the early Church. This body of believers contained many sorts of people with very different opinions, and every member was allowed to remain in the state he was, whether circumcised or not. However, in these first ages of Christianity, Newton claimed, there were already two sorts of people who greatly troubled the "Churches of the uncircumcision." These were the Jews who tried to impose upon them the ceremonies of the law "and the traditions of their Doctors," and those gentiles who tried to force onto them the opinions of the heathen philosophers (discussed in the following section). For as long as different groups did not attempt to impose their own practices on others, the early community was truly Christian. At this time there existed two groups of Jewish Christians, the Nazarenes and Ebionites, who differed from each other in key elements of their doctrine and practice but who did not condemn each other (at least initially) despite disagreeing over doctrine. While the former lived peacefully with the uncircumcised Christians, the Ebionites became overly zealous of the law after the siege of Jerusalem and endeavored to impose it on the converted (uncircumcised) gentiles. For this, Newton complained, they should be considered schismatics. His extensive analysis of the wide variety of views present in the early Church, and of the charitable attitudes each group apparently adopted towards each other, clearly underpinned his commitment to religious toleration in his own age.[29]

THE ARACHNID ORIGINS OF HERESY

In a new and extended project begun in the last two decades of his life, Newton devoted substantial efforts to grasping how pristine apostolic Christianity had been corrupted. As stated in 2 Thessalonians 2:7, a central text for radical Protestants, the early Church was troubled by the "Mystery of Iniquity," an apostasy that would gradually erode the integrity of the Church until its wicked author was revealed as the Man of Sin. For Newton the Mystery of Iniquity consisted of the "metaphysical theology of the heathens & Cabbalists," a bundle of absurd doctrines regarding the transmigration of souls, celestial intelligences, and, above all, the notion that the cosmos had been created by beings that were physical emissions of God. This evil force began in the Apostles' days but was successfully held in check; however, after a while it "broke into" the true Church, revealing the true nature of the Man of Sin. As Newton and others saw it, the miscreants, whose leaders were termed gnostics on account of the pretended knowledge that they professed, were true heretics, "Antichrists or enemies to ye true Church of Christ." They were surpassed in their pernicious historical influence only by the Roman Catholics, who in due course would perfect the most egregious elements of gnostic doctrines.[30]

His pupil Valentinus awarded God two wives Ennoia and Theleus, or Understanding and Will, calling them the affections of the unknown father. Both of these men, Newton claimed, had lived in Alexandria and had conceivably learned these views from Egyptian Cabbalists.[33]

Newton divided up the progressive contamination of Christianity by gnosticism into four distinct periods. The first age lasted until the date conventionally given for the end of the Age of the Apostles, which lasted until the death of John in c. 100 CE. Based on the testimony of Irenaeus, Newton asserted that the first heretics were either Jews or Samaritans, such as Nicolas (allegedly the founder of the Nicolaitans condemned in Revelation), Simon, Cerinthus, and Menander, "but these being checkt by the authority of Apostolick men who had conversed with Christ, [they] made no progress." The second age of heresy lasted until the death of Polycarp, teacher of Irenaeus and disciple of the apostle John, in 169 CE. Gnostics such as Saturninus, Basilides, Carpocrates, Valentinus, and Marcion now began to spread their poison in Christian communities, but the Church maintained the unity of its doctrine and the mutual respect of its followers, and so avoided being contaminated by the heresies.[34]

At the end of this period the "false prophets" Montanus and his female supporters Prisca and Maximilla, became extremely powerful, and the third age of heresy set in. According to Newton, their heresy "being a more refined sort of Gnosticism then any of the former spread much faster & within the space of twenty <or thirty> years insinuated it self into the Church of Rome." Montanism (or Cataphrygianism) was exceptionally dangerous, since it was carried out under the guise of tradi-tional Christianity. During their celebration of the Eucharist, the heretics offered sacrifices to a god composed of the Bythos (the first being) and two Aeons, termed by them the Father, the Son, and the holy ghost. So seduc-tive was this doctrine that it gained adherents such as Victor, bishop of Rome, and Tertullian. Irenaeus and a few others attempted to thwart their superstitious beliefs, divisive practices, and metaphysical wranglings, but to no avail. Victor claimed that the Word of God was "the λόγος ἐνδιάθετος of the father from all eternity," and this inward word (*logos endiathetos*) or wisdom emitted from the Father as a ray of light was emitted from the Sun. This explicit denial that the *logos* was a separate being with its own authentic will and understanding constituted the first formal introduction of emanationism into the Roman Church. Newton considered it to be equally reprehensible that Victor had introduced into the Church the practice of excluding Christians for opinions deemed to be heretical, excommunicating a tanner named Theodotus for affirming that Christ was a mere man born of the virgin by the power of the holy ghost.[35]

Newton dated the onset of the fourth age to 255 CE, in the days of Pope Stephen. The groups comprising the gnostic heretics now recognized each other's baptisms as authentic, and as Newton learned from Basnage, in the time of Stephen, the Church of Rome accepted the baptism of heretics and recognized their sacraments. It excommunicated the righteous African and Eastern Churches for forbidding the same, and thus gnosticism contaminated the original doctrine of the Church to its core. Allowing these heretical sacraments was, Newton noted, "the greatest step that could be made towards a reconciliation <with the mystery of iniquity>," and it gave rise to a terrible division within the Church. As ever, he understood that the degradation of the Church into parties was inevitably accompanied by the embrace of really (and not nominally) heretical doctrines and idolatrous practices. Auricular confession and corporal penance were now introduced into the life of the ailing institution, and with the rise of popery it disintegrated into parties. Finally, Newton returned to the source of the great perversion of religion that had blighted the Church in the fourth century. The notion of *logos endiathetos* led inexorably to the concept of *homoousios* and its physicalist and emanationist Latin rendition as "consubstantial," which – as we have seen – underpinned the orthodox doctrine of the Trinity.[36]

A PRACTICAL RELIGION

Rumors of Newton's heterodox opinions began to circulate soon after the publication of the second edition of his *Principia* in 1713, although already in 1705 he had been attacked by a large crowd of students as an "occasional conformist" (i.e., as a dissenter who only worshipped publicly for show). It is unclear to what extent he was a sincere member of the Church of England, that is, whether he exercised some sort of mental reservation when he publicly professed his allegiance to articles of faith that he privately denounced. According to Humphrey Newton, he worshipped regularly at the university church, Great St. Mary's, in the mid to late 1680s, though Humphrey also remembered that Newton's attendance at the college chapel had been perfunctory. Here, and on those occasions when Newton took public office, he publicly subscribed to the doctrines of the Church of England, although this must have caused him serious concerns. In his only explicit comment on the matter, penned at the end of his life, he argued that it was a strength of the Church of England that it allowed as broad a swathe of opinions as possible (such as his own). Radically, as ever, Newton insisted that it could impose on its members only those doctrines and statements that had Scriptural warrant, a view that excluded the Nicene and Athanasian creeds as well as a number of Articles.[37]

Newton always insisted that Christianity was a practical and useful religion, and he noted that "as faith without works is dead, so doctrines or opinions which do not tend to good works are unprofitable & useless." According to John Conduitt, he condemned the irreligious tendencies of late Stuart and Georgian society and was especially moved by stories of cruelty to animals. He lived by the Mosaic-Christian values he espoused in his writings and often displayed extraordinary acts of charity. His avoidance of "dead works" was primarily aimed at religious idolatry but a related and equally dangerous aspect of Christian backsliding was undue attention to the fictional products of the mind and the eye. Newton's abstinence from sexual relations, and from "inordinate desires of the flesh" – the wrong kind of love – was also a primary religious duty. Like his other Cambridge colleagues, his vocation as a scholar prevented him from getting married or engaging in carnal relations. Nevertheless, his lengthy critique of the lustful thoughts and practices of the first monks shows that his commitment to chastity lay at the heart of his life of faith. Thinking about relations with women, or about women at all, was a distraction from his godly mission and an ever-present temptation that could only be avoided by hard work.[38]

In his later career, Newton consistently assailed the introduction of "metaphysicks" into religion, and he criticized those who turned religion into a set of theories rather than realizing that its most fundamental tenets were moral and practical truths. The acceptance by allegedly orthodox Christians of the strange "metaphysical" doctrines of the heathen philosophers, the Cabbalists and latterly, the schoolmen, was the "grand occasion" by which the "moral and monarchical" meaning of Scripture had been turned into an unintelligible, "physical" sense. This contrast between false and idolatrous "metaphysical" or "physical" religious systems, and the true "moral and monarchical" version of Christianity lay at the heart of Newton's religious faith. God was the "supreme monarch of the universe," and he was worthy of being worshipped not because he was infinitely good or intelligent – although he was – but because he exercised infinite power and dominion. Fraudulent priests might convince the ignorant to believe in vanities, or "imaginary ghosts or Demons," but neither the priests nor the supposed supernatural entities had any real power. For Newton, it was the inability to exercise this power that bound together the idolatrous products of the imagination and the (false) consubstantiality of the Son and the Father: "'Tis not consubstantiality but power & dominion wch gives a right to be worshipped." This was the defining characteristic of God, though in his wisdom he occasionally allowed Jesus Christ to exercise some of that power and dominion.[39]

Newton's religious studies formed the most significant part of his life, and they were not completely separate from his other intellectual pursuits. Although he adopted very different approaches to problems that arose in separate academic fields, his theological writings were governed by the same general standards as those that operated in his scientific and mathematical work. Reason, hard work, and the disciplined use of the senses were always to be preferred before hypotheses, premature systems and, in general, to the figments of the imagination. It is because these principles guided his theological studies for more than half a century that they cannot be considered as the half-baked musings of a dilettante. Whatever credence we give to his religious researches today, they were the products of the same brilliant and intellectually daring analyst who contributed so much to science and mathematics.

NOTES

1 Newton's maternal uncle William Ayscough, his stepfather Barnabas Smith (d. 1653), and the Trinity College fellow Humphrey Babington (brother of the best friend of Newton's mother) were all Church of England clergymen. His landlord while in Grantham was William Clarke, a staunch parliamentarian and Presbyterian Alderman (mayor) of Grantham in 1650–1 and 1656–7.

2 Newton's confessions are in Sheltonian shorthand in the Fitzwilliam notebook, Fitzwilliam Library, fols. 3r–4v.

3 Newton's religious writings are published at www.newtonproject.ox.ac.uk.

4 See A. R. Hall and M. B. Hall, *Unpublished Scientific Papers of Isaac Newton* (Cambridge: Cambridge University Press, 1962), pp. 132–4 and 137–41.

5 Hall and Hall, *Unpublished Scientific Papers*, pp. 141–4.

6 Newton, *The Mathematical Principles of Natural Philosophy* . . . translated into English by Andrew Motte, 2 vols. (London, 1729), vol. 2, pp. 389–92.

7 Socinus's views, by no means accepted by all "Socinians," are detailed in S. Mortimer, *Reason and Religion in the English Revolution: The Challenge of Socinianism* (Cambridge: Cambridge University Press, 2010); for the history of Arianism see M. Wiles, *Archetypal Heresy: Arianism through the Centuries* (Oxford: Oxford University Press, 2001). For similarities between Newton's position and those of leading Socinian writers, see S. Snobelen, "Isaac Newton, Socinianism and 'The One Supreme God,'" in M. Mulsow and J. Rohls (eds.), *Socinianism and*

Arminianism: Antitrinitarians, Calvinists, and Cultural (Leiden: Brill, 2005), pp. 241–98.

8 Accounts of Athanasius's misdemeanors can be found in numerous locations in Newton's papers. National Library of Israel, Yahuda Mss. 2.3 and 2.5 detail the spread of Roman Catholicism in Europe, Asia, and Africa, while the text entitled "Paradoxical questions concerning the morals and actions of Athanasius," now in the William Andrews Clark Memorial Library, Los Angeles, contains a number of impassioned reflections about Athanasius's general behavior and his rewriting of history, as does Yahuda Ms. 19.

9 The most extensive treatment of the deviant corporeal regimens of the early monks is Yahuda Ms. 11.

10 Newton's first major attempt at a systematic account of the internal order and historical meaning of prophecy is Yahuda Mss. 1.1–1.8, composed in the late 1670s or early 1680s.

11 Yahuda Ms. 9.2, fols. 1r and 8r, dated to the late 1680s on the basis that it is in the hand of Humphrey Newton.

12 Huntington Library, Babson Ms. 434, fols. 3r–6r, and 39r–40r and 58r (for Newton's own description of his harmonizing strategy); Yahuda Ms. 2.4 (an earlier version of the Babson Ms.); Yahuda Ms. 13.2 fols. 19r–22v (notes from the Talmud). More generally, see R. Delgado-Moreira, "'What Ezekiel Says': Newton as a Temple Scholar," *History of Science* 48 (2010), 153–80.

13 Yahuda Ms. 1.1 fols. 20r–23r (draft at 24r–27r) and 28r–55r (for the "Proof," with another version at Yahuda Ms. 1.1a).

14 Newton, *Correspondence*, vol. 2, pp. 323, 326, and 331–2.

15 Newton, *The Principia: Mathematical Principles of Natural Philosophy*, translated by I. B. Cohen and A. Whitman (Berkeley, CA: University of California Press, 1999), pp. 408–15, esp. pp. 411 and 413–14.

16 See Yahuda Mss. 1.1–1.5 passim.

17 Yahuda Ms. 1.6, fols. 35r–44r.

18 Newton, *Correspondence*, vol. 3, pp. 193–4, 338, 384, and 386; David Gregory, *Astronomiae Physicae & Geometricae Elementa* (Oxford, 1702). The original "liber secundus" is now CUL Add. Ms. 3990.

19 Yahuda Ms. 41, fols 1r–12v (esp. fols. 5r–7r), a work entitled "The Original of Religions" that was probably written at some point in the early 1690s (with drafts at Yahuda Ms. 17.3).

20 See Yahuda Mss. 16.2, fols. 3r–v and 17.2, fols. 15r–19v.

21 Yahuda Ms. 41, fols. 5r–7r.

22 Newton, *Correspondence*, vol. 3, p. 83.

23 Newton, *Correspondence*, vol. 3, pp. 88–92.

24 Newton, *Correspondence*, vol. 3, pp. 233–56.

25 King's College Cambridge, Keynes Ms. 130.11.

26 Yahuda Mss. 15.2, fols. 23r, 24r; 15.3, fols. 43r–46r; 15.7, fol. 116r.

27 Yahuda Ms. 15.6, fols. 100r–v and 102v; and Keynes Ms. 7, fol. 1r; 3,
    fols. 1r–3r, 9r, 17r, 27r, and 33r–34r.

28 Yahuda Mss 15.3, fol. 45r (for falling out over religious matters as an
    example of carnality); 15.5, fol. 79r (and esp. fol. 80r); 15.6, fol. 100v and
    15.7, fols 134r–b.

29 Yahuda Mss 15.4, fols. 68v–69r; 15.5, fols. 77v–79v; 15.6, fol. 97r, and
    15.7, fols. 122v, 123r–v, 126r, and 176r. See in particular Yahuda Mss.
    15.6, fols. 100v–103v for an analysis of the gradual corruption of the
    Apostles' creed. The Nazarenes, according to Newton, did not believe
    in Christ's pre-existence, nor did they believe that Christ had created
    the world, while the Ebionites believed that Jesus was a mere man, born
    the natural son of Joseph and Mary, and onto whom the divine nature
    of Christ descended. Newton considered the two groups separately,
    but understood the Ebionites to be schismatic Nazarenes; see Yahuda
    Ms. 15.7, fols. 171r–172r. The major source for the knowledge of the
    Ebionites was Epiphanius's *Panarion*.

30 Yahuda Mss. 15.4, fols. 53r–55r; 15.5, fols. 77v, 79r; 15.6, fols. 110r–114v;
    15.7, fols. 120v, 131v, and 138r–139v.

31 Yahuda Mss. 15.5, fols. 77r–80r; 15.6, fols. 110r–111r and 116r–117r;
    15.7, fols. 137r–139r.

32 Yahuda Mss. 15.7, fols. 120r, 127r–128r, and 137r–138r. For the sources
    of Newton's analysis see M. Goldish, *Judaism in the Theology of Isaac
    Newton* (Dordrecht: Kluwer Academic, 1998), 141–54. Newton seems
    to have been interested in the *Kabbalah Denudata* from the early 1690s,
    and he owned the 1708 English translation of Basnages's work.

33 Yahuda Mss. 15.5, fols. 83r–85r; 15.6, fols. 108r–111r; 15.7, fols.
    127r–131r. For the confrontation of Irenaeus and Epiphanius with
    the early heresies of the Church (many of the details of which were
    undoubtedly hatched in their own imaginations), see J. G. A. Pocock,
    Barbarism and Religion, 6 vols. (Cambridge: Cambridge University
    Press, 1999–2015), vol. 5, *Religion: The First Triumph*.

34 Yahuda Mss. 15.4, fols. 68v–70r and especially 15.6, fols. 105r–107r.

35 Yahuda Mss. 15.4, fols. 70r–71r; 15.5, fols. 77r–82r; 15.7, fols. 116r–v, 121v–123Av, 126r, 139r, 170r.

36 Yahuda Mss. 15.4, fols. 71r–72r and 75r–76r (for Basnage); 15.6, fols. 109r and 112r, and esp. 15.7, fols. 130r–v, 139r, and 170r–177v.

37 Keynes Ms. 3, fols. 51r–52r (for Newton's account of the Church of England); Humphrey's reminiscences are at Keynes Ms. 135. For an accurate account of Newton's private beliefs published soon after his death, see William Whiston, *A Collection of Authentic Records* (London, 1728), pp. 1076–7. Larry Stewart gives an excellent account of the rumors surrounding Newton's heterodoxy in his "'Seeing through the Scholium': Religion and Reading Newton in the Eighteenth Century," *History of Science* 34 (1996), 123–65, while Richard Westfall produces clear evidence that Newton was the target of accusations of "occasional conformity" at Cambridge in the first few years of the eighteenth century in *Never at Rest: A Biography of Isaac Newton* (Cambridge: Cambridge University Press, 1980), pp. 623–6. For the general techniques Newton used to hide his own views, see S. Snobelen, "Isaac Newton, Heretic: The Strategies of a Nicodemite," *British Journal for History of Science* 32 (1999), 381–419.

38 Yahuda Mss. 15.4, fol. 68v; Keynes Ms. 6, fol. 1r.

39 Yahuda Mss. 15.3, fol. 47v; 15.5, fols. 98r–99r; 15.6, fol. 115r and 15.7, fols. 154r and 176r.

13 Isaac Newton, historian

Mordechai Feingold

For nearly a century following its publication in 1728, the *Chronology of Ancient Kingdoms Amended* proved to be Newton's most widely read work. Such celebrity, however, did not imply conversion to Newton's ideas: far from it. The book engendered controversies as fierce as any triggered by Newton's other works. Nor was the wide readership of the *Chronology* simply a function of its greater accessibility, compared to the *Principia* or even the *Opticks*. The fascination with Newton's posthumous publication attested instead to the centrality of chronology to contemporary scholarly and religious concerns – argued and defended passionately. In contrast, modern scholars have found it difficult to appreciate such passion, in part because they are aware that efforts to ground universal history on a Scriptural timeline are futile, and in part because they find the subject matter itself dreary. Richard Westfall articulated this aversion when he sought to excuse his own disinclination to accord the *Chronology* more than fleeting attention: "A Work of colossal tedium," it "excited for a brief time the interest and opposition of the handful able to get excited over the date of the Argonauts before it sank into oblivion. It is read today only by the tiniest remnant who for their sins must pass through its purgatory."[1] This chapter seeks to recapture some of the vitality of a long-forgotten discipline by demonstrating both the enormous intellectual effort Newton invested in chronology over the last four decades of his life, as well as his remarkable ingenuity – commensurate with his ingenuity in other domains – in rewriting universal history.

The present article supplements considerably the analysis of Newton's writings in Jed Buchwald and Mordechai Feingold, *Newton and the Origin of Civilization* (Princeton, NJ: Princeton University Press, 2013). Readers are invited to consult it for a broader perspective.

Newton's turn to antiquity was motivated in the first instance, by his growing distaste for Cartesian mathematics. As Niccolò Guicciardini has demonstrated, by the late 1670s Newton had become convinced of the superiority of the Greeks' method of analysis over Descartes's method, and he embarked on a meticulous study of ancient mathematics to substantiate his belief.[2] Several years later, as he immersed himself in the composition of the *Principia*, Newton extended his anti-Cartesian crusade to include natural philosophy. He now convinced himself both that the Ancients possessed a perfect understanding of "the true frame of nature," and that their cosmology had been integral to the true (original) religion. As he delved deeper into the nature of primitive religion, however, Newton's focus shifted. He now sought to explore how and why that religion had been corrupted – with the concomitant perversion of the genuine system of the world – as well as to unveil the historical process that facilitated the spread of the resultant idolatry.

Egyptian history became the focal point of the investigation, since ancient writers were nearly unanimous in locating the origination of idolatry in Egypt, most notably, in the worshipping of the twelve major deities (*Dii consentes*). As Newton put it: "because Egypt was yᵉ oldest of kingdoms, its reasonable to beleive that yᵉ Egyptians were yᵉ first who worshipped such Gods, & by consequence that yᵉ 12 Gods were their ancestors." Elsewhere he expatiated: "in order that the people might worship such Gods more gladly, the Priests developed the notion that the Sun and the Stars were ensouled and understood all human affairs, and they composed various stories about them as acting freely in the persons of men. They also represented that the twelve gods were the first to rule in Egypt, then the Demigods." Eventually, these gods "were disseminated throughout the world from Egypt."[3]

Newton considered the "primitive religion" to have been the religion of the "Prytaneum or Vestal Temples," which Noah had transmitted to his sons following the Deluge, whence it "spread into all nations at yᵉ first peopling of the earth." Although it became quickly corrupted, Moses imparted to the Jews the true "religion of Noah purged from the corruptions of yᵉ nations."[4] Having spent some time in analyzing the content of the true religion, and its geographical distribution, Newton became engrossed with tracking its perversion – an inquiry that soon evolved into an all-out effort to establish the contours of post-diluvian history more generally. For evidence, he turned primarily to myth, since Scripture furnished only the barest outline of that history. Relying on myth never really bothered Newton. "[I]t is evident that a certain general tradition was preserved for a very long time among the Gentiles," he wrote, "of matters that were more distinctly passed down from Noah and the first men to Abraham, and from Abraham to Moses. Hence it is to be hoped that the history of the times which followed immediately after the flood can also be deduced from the traditions of the Gentiles not without a small element of truth."[5] Pride of place among those traditions he accorded to the myth of the Four Ages – as related by Hesiod and Ovid – which he believed to have been nothing short of an embellished chronicle of the great exploits of Noah's posterity, in recognition of which they were posthumously deified.

According to Newton, the "golden age lasted as long as all men lived in Babylon under the rule of Noah. The silver age began with the division of the Earth and the rule of Cham in Egypt. The bronze age begins when the sons of Cham left for the different lands which were later ceded to them by their father, and when they entered upon their new and separate reigns: in the fourth age reigned Belus, grandson of Cham, who was the first to make war with iron and, by involving the whole world in a many-sided war, founded the empire of the Assyrians."[6] The great upheavals contained in the final two Ages – the famous battles of the gods (or Titanomachia) – represented two consecutive attempts by Cham's sons to obtain political dominion. The first commenced when Phut, who ruled over Libya, murdered his brother Mizraim and usurped his Egyptian kingdom. Chus, the eldest brother, came to assist Mizraim's family and roundly defeated Phut and his allies. After consolidating his own rule over Egypt and northern Africa, Chus turned against the progeny of his uncles Shem and Japheth launching an epic military expedition, at the culmination of which he ruled over much of the inhabited world from Mauritania to India.

THE FOUR AGES

Informing Newton's investigation were the same principles that had previously guided him in interpreting Biblical prophecies. "For understanding the Prophecies," he asserted, "we are, in the first place, to acquaint our-selves with the figurative language of the Prophets. This language is taken from the analogy between the world natural, and an empire or kingdom considered as a world politic." Just as prophetic references to burning with fire stood for consumption by war, and references to floods stood for invasions, so the language of myth masked similar patterns:

> when the Giants rebel against heaven and Typho attempts to seize the kingdom of Jupiter, and the terrified Gods flee from there into Egypt, nothing more is to be understood than that Phut attempted to seize dominion over Egypt and that the Egyptians fled from their familiar haunts and their royal city into unknown parts of Egypt. For heaven is normally used by myth-writers and Prophets for Kingship and dominion. And the thunderbolt with which Jupiter struck down Typho is war. For fire and thunderbolt are used everywhere in the Prophets for war, and the Cyclopes and their father Vulcan who forged the thunderbolts for Jupiter are the first ironsmiths who made swords and instruments of war for Jupiter Belus.[7]

The details of this internecine conflict need not detain us here. No sooner did Newton arrive at a more or less coherent narrative of events than he felt compelled to discard it, primarily owing to considerations of population dynamics. He came to realize that it was inconceivable for mankind to multiply at such an exponential rate as to allow the existence of armies totaling several million men within two or three centuries after the Deluge. Instead of abandoning such a *jeu d'esprit*, however, the failure only reinvigorated Newton's forays into antiquity. Establishing a sound post-diluvian universal history proved a challenge, as intriguing and as demanding as establishing the physical laws of nature had once been. Newton remained convinced of the efficacy of the interpretative structure he had grounded on myth, with the proviso that its temporal application demanded placing it 1,200 years later. But, first, Newton needed to posit an evolutionary theory of societal growth in the aftermath of the Flood, which in turn would lead to the momentous events veiled in the ancient myth.

In Mesopotamia, ran his narrative, the "first men after the flood lived in caves of the earth & woods & planes well watered by rivers for feeding their heards & flocks . . . By degrees they cut down the woods & learnt to build houses & towns of brick in the planes & to live in society under laws & government." The early Egyptians too, had inhabited mountainous "syringes or subterranean vaults," not dissimilar to the labyrinth in Mount Ida in Crete, or the catacombs in Italy. As Newton possessed little information on the primitive conditions of Mesopotamia or Egypt, he undoubtedly extrapolated from the seemingly miserable circumstances of the early Greeks. When Cadmus arrived there, the "ignorant natives continued Canibals & lived in dens & caves of the earth like wild beasts & came not out thence but to mix with the forreigners & live in with them in houses & in towns but by degrees, as they could be induced to leave of their savage customes & become civilized." Similar conditions prevailed elsewhere in Europe, which "must have been in a very barbarous & uncivilized condition; even more barbarous & rude then the Americans were when we first discovered them."[8]

Newton viewed the process through which "forreigners" attained the degree of cultivation they brought to Europe as long and protracted. Noah's three sons followed their father's example by dividing their dominions among all their sons, and such a tradition continued unabated, "till the earth was planted with innumerable scattered families not subject to any other Lords then their own common fathers." Ultimately, the scarcity of land and the pressure of growing population engendered strife among tribes, so to thwart aggression tribes or neighborhoods found it necessary to: "consult together for their common safety & chuse out wise & valiant men to lead them against their enemies & fortify places with walls within which should be many houses for the people to resort unto . . . in time of danger." Eventually, those "fortified places became the first cities & the fathers of families became ye elders of the city composing a Council with ye same legislative & judicial power over the whole body of all their families wch every father had before over his own apart, & the captain of their forces being the most honourable & potent amongst the Elders became their King." The process of consolidation continued, with small kingdoms merging ("by conquest or by consent") into larger kingdoms, and ultimately empires. Crucially, however, the process of amalgamation did not begin "till after the days of Abraham"; for not before the time of Moses did the first major city-kingdoms emerge.

Newton continued to refine his scheme, which ultimately evolved into a sort of stadial model of societal evolution: the savage age – when mankind lived in the open or in caves, subsisted from hunting or from the fruit of the land – preceded the pastoral period. The agricultural stage followed, along with new forms of cohabitation and governance which, in turn, gave rise to towns and kingdoms as well as to the slow emergence of arts and sciences. On the heels of these three sociopolitical and economic stages followed commercial activity, which further enabled, and disseminated, early civilization.

As Newton developed his framework for post-diluvian universal history, considerations of time became imperative: not only in view of the centuries required for population growth, but in order to date with precision both individuals and events. Hitherto Newton had paid scant attention to duration. Since he had concerned himself with the exploits of a single branch of Noah's family over four generations, the length of each generation hardly mattered; only "that the ages are distinguished in such a way that a new age always begins with new kings and new Reigns." Thus, Hesiod's statement regarding the "wonderful longevity of human beings" during the Silver Age – "such that a child was nourished by the mother for a hundred years before reaching adulthood" – affected neither the structure of the argument nor the sequence of events.[9] In contrast, the exact structure of Newton's revised chronology could admit no temporal indeterminacy. A "generation of men" had to be understood to mean a third of a century. Thus, for example, "since Chiron was born in the golden age & lived till the Argonautic expedition or a little longer, the silver age & copper age could not exceed the length of ordinary generations." And since 134 years had elapsed between Cadmus's coming to Greece and the fall of Troy, the period "being divided into four equal ages allows about 33 or 34 years to an age." As for Hesiod's representation of longevity during the silver age, Newton now equivocated: "He makes the 2^d age of above 100 years duration but it is because he makes men live much longer in y^t age then in his own."[10]

THE RULES OF INTERPRETATION

With this structure in mind, Newton proceeded to fill in the historical details. He soon confronted the implications of Varro's celebrated tripartite division of Greek antiquity:

> Some of the *Greeks* called the times before the Reign of *Ogyges*, Unknown, because they had No History of them; those between his flood and the beginning of the Olympiads, Fabulous, because their History was much mixed with Poetical Fables: and those after the beginning of the Olympiads, Historical, because their History was free from such Fables. The fabulous Ages wanted a good Chronology, and so also did the Historical, for the first 60 or 70 Olympiads.[11]

Nevertheless, like Joseph Scaliger a century earlier, Newton was determined to render the middle period historically intelligible. The key to this was the era of Sesostris. Sometime in the 1690s he convinced himself that this great Egyptian conqueror was none other than Sesac (Shishak), who according to Scripture invaded Judaea in the fifth year of Rehoboam's reign with a huge army that included 1,200 chariots and 60,000 horsemen, and carried with him the treasures of the Jerusalem Temple. "This is no new opinion," Newton protested in the *Chronology*. Josephus had already "affirmed that *Herodotus* erred, in ascribing the actions of *Sesac* to *Sesostris*" (but only "in calling him *Sesostris*"), while "Our great Chronologer, *Sir John Marsham*, was also of opinion that *Sesostris* was *Sesac*."[12] Newton did more than rely on authority. Gradually, and painstakingly, he forged an elaborate interpretative framework that wove together a considerable body of textual evidence, skillfully deployed and laced with tightly argued reasoning into an ingeniously coherent historical narrative.

This broader framework was essential in view of the notoriously conjectural nature of Egyptian chronology. As Newton recognized, only a meticulous synchronization with Greek chronology could substantiate his radical reconstruction of Egyptian history. Scripture, despite its commanding authority, was of limited use here. True, the "Records of the Jews have above all others escaped the shipwrecks of time. They have been frequently in danger but by Providence have escaped tho not without some dammage." Yet, significantly for Newton, the authority of Scripture on historical matters derived from its antiquity, not its inspiration: "Samuel wrote before Cadmus brought letters into Europe & Ezra wrote before Herodotus & these authors extracted their histories and Records written long before their own days & therefore the histories composed by them are by far the oldest as well as the most authentic being originally written by Moses & the Prophets." Nonetheless, though sacred history "sufficiently conteins the affairs of the people of Israel down to the times of Darius Nothus king of Persia" – with additional "light" received "from the Chronical Canon of Ptolomy" – the history of all other Eastern nations, while receiving "some light from the scriptures . . . must chiefly be deduced from other authors."[13]

Hence the circumscribed role accorded to the Bible in the *Chronology*. Newton did put forth a Scripture-based argument for the impossibility of Sesostris being any one else but Sesac: "we do not read in Scripture, that any former King of *Egypt,* who Reigned over all those nations, came out of *Egypt* with a great army to conquer other countries. The sacred history of the *Israelites,* from the days of *Abraham* to the days of *Solomon,* admits of no such conqueror."[14] Likewise, since Sesac's army consisted of Libyans, Ethiopians, and Troglodites, he must have been their king, and Scripture mentions no other Egyptian king who had dominion over those nations. For positive evidence for Sesac's existence, however, Newton turned elsewhere, beginning with a concerted effort to establish the precise identity (and time) of the Egyptian king.

"Corruptions of names are frequent in history," Newton pronounced in the *Chronology,* as he sought to make order out of the various ancient accounts of Sesostris. He "was otherwise called *Sesochris, Sesochis, Sesoosis, Sethosis, Sesonchis, Sesonchosis.* Take away the *Greek* termination, and the names become *Sesost, Sesoch, Sesoos, Sethos, Sesonch*: which names differ very little from *Sesach. Sesonchis* and *Sesach* differ no more than *Memphis* and *Moph,* two names of the same city." Elsewhere he maintained that Sesostris had been "celebrated in several Nations by several Names. The *Chaldaeans* called him *Belus* . . . the *Arabians* called him *Bacchus,*" while the Phrygians and Thracians knew him as Mars. As for the Egyptians, before he ascended to the throne they called him Hercules, and after he died they deified him as "*Sihor, Nilus* and *Aegyptus;* and the *Greeks* hearing them lament *0 Sihor, Bou Sihor,* called him *Osiris* and *Busiris.*"[15]

Newton based such a conclusion on a careful (and selective) mining of multiple sources to produce a dazzling display of consistency. For example, whereas in *Jewish Antiquities* Josephus identified Sesac as the great conqueror whom Herodotus named Sesostris, in *Against Apion* the Jewish historian furnished alternative identities. There, Josephus cited Manetho's account of the exploits of Sethos and his brother Hermaeus, "the former of whom, [Manetho] says, took the name of Aegyptus and the latter that of Danaus" – he who ultimately fled to Argos.[16] Herodotus attested to Bacchus's being "the same God wth him whom all the Egyptians worshipped by the name of Osiris,"[17] while Diodorus Siculus cited certain mythologists who called "Osiris Dionysus & sirname him Sirius & particularly Eumolpus & Orpheus call him Dionysus." Furthermore, in Arrianus's *Anabasis Alexandri* Newton found that "the *Arabians* worshipped only two Gods, *Cœlus* and *Dionysus*; and that they worshipped *Dionysus* for the glory of leading his Army into *India*." Hence, Newton concluded, the "*Dionysus* of the *Arabians* was *Bacchus*, and all agree that *Bacchus* was the same King of *Egypt* with *Osiris*."[18]

Establishing the identity and era of ancient rulers lay at the heart of the Newtonian enterprise; and if elucidating the "historical age" could be thorny, how much more challenging would be the investigation into the fabulous or heroic periods? As Newton put it, owing to the diligence taken by Ezra and Nehemiah in collecting material preserved in ancient records, the historical books of Scripture – Samuel, Kings, Chronicles, along with Esther and Nehemiah – had rendered accurately "the history & chronology of the people of Israel down to the times of Ezra & Nehemiah." Those times were also "fully stated by Eclipses of the Sun & Moon mentioned by Thucydides & Ptolemy." Conversely, "the Records of other nations written before those times being all of them lost, it is very difficult to give a true account of the ancient affairs of those nations." Consequently, "the best way to come to any certainty" regarding their early histories "is to begin wth the later times where history & chronology is certain, & reccon upwards as high as we can proceed by any good arguments."[19]

In embracing such a procedure, Newton imported into his historical work a version of the methodology informing his scientific research: a seamless passage from the known to the unknown, and back again, in order to discover, and then validate, new results. As he outlined the methodology in a draft version of query 23 of the *Opticks* (1706):

> The business of Experimental Philosophy is to find out by experience & observation not how things were created but what is the present frame of Nature. This enquiry should proceed first

by Analysis in arguing from things more known to things less known & particularly from effects to causes & from compositions to their ingredients. And when we have found the Principles out & established any new causes or ingredients of things we may proceed by Synthesis from those causes & ingredients as Principles to explain their effects & compositions.[20]

Newton's manuscripts exhibit repeated utilization of this composite methodology. In an early manuscript, Newton felt it proper to gloat that having identified Sesostris to be Sesac – and having performed considerable work on ancient history – he had successfully "carried up the chronology of the Greeks as high as to the Trojan war[,] the Argonautic Expedition[,] & the invasion of the nations of Asia[,] India & Europe by Sesostris." He now envisaged carrying the chronology higher still, into "the ages reputed dark & fabulous by the ancient Greek historians," by comparing European history with the histories of other nations.[21]

The epoch he settled on as his signpost was the fall of Troy and, by implication, the time of the Argonautic Expedition which, by universal consent, had taken place a generation earlier. He chose the fall of Troy because it had been long recognized as the cardinal dated event in antiquity, with much subsequent Greek history contingent on it. Archbishop James Ussher had dated the event to 1184 BCE, following Eusebius's invocation of the testimony of Greek historians, who claimed the city fell 408 before the first Olympiad (776 BCE).[22] With this date in place, the return of the Heraclides into the Peloponnesus could be established too. For Apollodorus of Athens (c. 180–120 BCE) and Diodorus Siculus (first century BCE), following Thucydides (460–c. 395 BCE), figured eighty years between the fall of Troy and the return – and "from then to the First Olympiad three hundred and twenty-eight years, reckoning the dates by the dates of the reigns of the kings of Lacedaemon."[23] Dating the foundation of Rome at 753 BCE also had been reckoned in conjunction with Aeneas's flight from Troy some 430 years earlier. Drastically rectifying the era of Troy by undermining the validity of the Ancients' computations of Greek genealogies, therefore, became one focus of Newton's radical contribution to ancient history.

The Ancients themselves, Newton gleefully pointed out, acknowledged the great uncertainty of European chronology. Didn't Diodorus Siculus admit his inability to "define by any certain space the times preceding the Trojan War, because he had no certain foundation to rely upon"? Had not Plutarch noted the "great uncertainties in the Originals of *Rome*," and acknowledged that Hippias's list of Olympic victors could not be supported by any "certain arguments"?[24] Newton believed he knew the reason for such systemic uncertainty: the assumptions underlying Greek chronology were fundamentally flawed. Ephorus of Cyme (c. 400–330 BCE), for example, "formed a Chronological History of *Greece*, beginning with the return of the *Heraclides* into *Peloponnesus*, and ending with the siege of *Perinthus*, in the twentieth year of *Philip* the father of *Alexander* the great: But he digested things by Generations."[25]

Eratosthenes of Cyrene (third century BCE) and Apollodorus, in turn, continued the practice of computing regnal reigns by generations, despite the fact that Timaeus of Sicily (c. 345–250 BCE) had already introduced the method of reckoning time by Olympiads. Thus, well after the death of Alexander the Great, "Chronologers could frame nothing certain about times before the Trojan war, nothing more certain about the times between that war & the Olympiads then by computing the kings of the Lacedemonians": that is from their "making a reasonable allowance for the length of so many reigns." Hence their inflated reckonings. According to the calculations of these chronologers, the seventeen Spartan kings from the return of the Heraclides to the Battle of Thermopylae [480 BCE] reigned for a total of 622 years, and 328 years elapsed between the return and the first Olympiad (776 BCE). In such computations subsequent historians followed Eratosthenes and Apollodorus uncritically.[26]

Presuming regnal reigns to be "equipollent" to generations, and three generations to equal a century – a computation they borrowed from the Egyptians – proved to be "the fatal error" of Greek chronology, according to Newton. They credited the first twelve kings of Sicyon "to have Reigned 529 years, which is 44 years a-piece"; the first eight kings of Argos "to have Reigned 371 years, which is above 46 years a-piece"; and the first seven Roman kings "to have Reigned 244 years, which is 35 years a-piece." When not motivated by the desire to magnify the antiquity of their respective nations, however, such reckonings were grounded on "reasoning and conjecture." As proof, Newton introduced a quasi-law regarding the duration of regnal reigns, based on his analysis of dynasties for which reliable information existed. He pointed out that, as a rule, kings reigned on average 18–20 years, or slightly longer. Thus, he wrote in the early years of the eighteenth century, the 28 Kings of England between William the Conqueror and William III reigned for 635 years, averaging 22.6 per reign. The sixty-three French Kings that preceded Louis XIV reigned for 1,224 years, an average of 19 years per reign. The rule applied equally to antiquity: the ten Achaemenid Persian kings averaged 21 years per reign, while the ten Macedonian kings that preceded Alexander the Great averaged 15.5 per reign. In other words, Newton concluded, "since Chronology hath been exact, there is scarce an instance to be found of ten Kings Reigning any where in continual Succession above 260 years" – and such a conclusion established the rule to conform to "the ordinary course of nature."[27]

With such a rule in hand, Newton turned to systematically re-dating the chronology of the several Greek kingdoms, to establish a new era for the fall of Troy and for the Argonautic Expedition. According to Herodotus, Newton observed in late 1701 Leutichides, the commander of the Greek navy against Xerxes, was the twentieth in descent from Hercules, and "all the men in this succession were kings of Sparta except two. If to ye 18 kings be allotted 21 years a piece & to ye two private generations 33 years a piece the whole succession will take up 446 years wch counted back from ye 6th year of Xerxes when Leonidas was slain at Thermopylae, will place Hercules about 56 years after ye death of Solomon agreably to ye computations above."

Elsewhere he insisted that the seventeen Spartan kings reigned for a total of 340 years, not 622 years. Counting back from the Battle of Thermopylae, Newton dated the return of the Heraclides to the Peloponnesus to c. 820 BCE, the fall of Troy to 904 BCE.[28] The chronology of the Kingdom of Macedon lent itself to similar manipulation. Livy, Pausanias, and Suidas credited Caranus as the founder of the kingdom, prior to Iphitus's restoration of the Olympiads in 776 BCE. Newton demurred: "old Herodotus who lived nearest those times & was able to inform himself tells us that Perdiccas founded that kingdom & that from ye founding thereof reigned only these kings Perdiccas Argeus Philippus Aeropus Alcetas Amyntas Alexander, the last of wch was contemporary to Xerxes."[29]

Pheidon, king of Argos, came to play a central role in Newton's argumentative structure through the latter's exploitation of an error committed by Herodotus, who stated that Leocedes, son of Pheidon, had been one of the suitors of Agariste, daughter of Cleisthenes of Sicyon. Since this famous courtship was generally believed to have taken place c. 570 BCE, Pheidon must have been a near contemporary. Newton seized on this information in order to controvert several conflicting ancient reckonings of the dates of his rule. According to the Parian marble he reigned in 895 BCE, but Jerome placed him a century later. For his part, Syncellus thought Pheidon to be the seventh from Temenus, and the eleventh from Heracles, whereas Strabo believed him to be the tenth from Temenus. If with Herodotus we determined that Pheidon flourished in the 47th Olympiad, Newton suggested, and there existed nine intervals (ten generations) between him and Temenus, then – reckoning 28 years for an interval (or generation) – the return of the Heraclides had taken place 240 years earlier (c. 830 BCE). But, "Chronologers reccon about 511 years from the return of the Heraclides to the 47th Olympiad, & account Phidon the seventh from Temenus which is after the rate of 85 years to a generation & therefore not to be admitted." Consequently, Newton added in another version of the argument, "I had rather trust to Herodotus."[30]

THE ARRIVAL OF CADMUS

Synchronization of Egyptian and Greek myths furnished Newton with a potent chronological framework within which to situate the history of the entire Mediterranean basin (and beyond) before, during, and after the Four Ages. The arrival of Cadmus in Europe, and the beginning of the Golden Age – 1045 BCE according to Newton – stemmed from momentous events in the Near East. Twenty-five years earlier, Amosis, king of Egypt, had driven out the Shepherds. Fleeing east, they swelled the ranks of the Philistines in their battles with Samuel and Saul. The ascension of David to the throne [1059 BCE] witnessed the rapid expansion of the Israelite Kingdom, which resulted in the expulsion of the Philistines, followed by the conquest of Edom, whose inhabitants had long navigated the Red Sea. Some of the fleeing Edomites settled in Egypt while others, becoming known as Phoenicians, settled along the Mediterranean coast introducing the practice of deep-sea navigation wherever they went. Soon they began trading with Greece, and during one of these early voyages a group of Phoenicians abducted Io, daughter of Inachus, King of Argos. In retaliation, the Greeks abducted Europa, daughter of Agenor king of Tyre, and carried her to Crete, thereby instigating Cadmus's expedition into Greece in search of his sister Europa.

Newton based his narrative on Herodotus's Euhemerized version of Greek myth. Except that he regarded the purported rescue mission as a pretext for further territorial expansion by the Phoenicians: "they went with a great multitude, not to seek *Europa* as was pretended, but to seek new Seats."[31] Whatever the motive, the expedition played a crucial role in Newton's chronology. Apart from enabling him to attribute a fixed date to the expedition – midway through David's reign – the time-honored tradition accepting Cadmus's introduction of writing into Greece emboldened Newton to reject competing narratives of Greek history. As he never tired of pointing out, prior to the introduction of writing, "it is not likely that any thing done in Europe could be remembred above three generations before the use of

Letters." Indeed, he wrote emphatically on another occasion, "I allow no history of things done in Europe above 80 years before Cadmus brought letters into Greece."[32]

Following this seemingly sound premise to its logical conclusion, Newton felt sufficiently confident to conclude that the Greeks "have transmitted to posterity many things concerning the wars & actions of Sesostris, all wch must have been forgotten had those warrs been ancienter then ye use of letters brought in by Cadmus." To illustrate the point, he invoked Diodorus, who cited "ye history of Bacchus & the Amazons, the Argonautic expedition & the things done at Troy," written by Dionysius. This should mean, Newton glossed, that "he wrote the history of the Greeks beginning wth the expedition of Bacchus & the Amazons, proceeding to the expedition of ye Argonauts & ending wth ye destruction of Troy. & therefore this Bacchus flourished in the times next before ye Argonautic expedition & was contemporary to Sesostris. Had he been much older his actions would not have been remembered for want of ye use of letters."[33]

Newton applied the same line of reasoning to Egyptian history: "since the inhabitants of Thebais who drove the shepherds out of Egypt wrote in hieroglyphicks, & the shepherds who were driven out & came into Greece before Cadmus, namely Cecrops, Lelex & their contemporaries did not bring letters into Greece: it seems to me that letters were not in use in Egypt before the Edomites" arrived there. Consequently, the famed antiquity claimed for Egyptian dynasties could be rejected: "before the use of letters they could not write down the names of their kings. They could only represent them by Cyphers & write down their histories of the men represented by those cyphers." Hence he found it legitimate to follow Herodotus, and "omit the names of those kings who did nothing memorable" from consideration. The published *Chronology* presented Newton's final verdict on the matter: "there is no instance of letters for writing down sounds, being in use before the days of *David*, in any other nation besides the posterity of *Abraham*. The *Egyptians* ascribed this invention to *Thoth*, the secretary of *Osiris*; and therefore Letters

began to be in use in *Egypt* in the days of *Thoth*, that is, a little after
the flight of the *Edomites* from *David*, or about the time that *Cadmus*
brought them into *Europe*."[34]

Armed with this powerful argument Newton turned to set
the arrival of Cadmus in chronological perspective. According
to the Parian Marble, Deucalion's Flood occurred a decade before the
arrival of Cadmus in Greece. Such dating suited Newton's purposes
for two reasons: it allowed him to claim that the Flood preceded
the Four Ages, and to correlate, at least privately, mythical symbolism with historical events. Both assumptions proved problematic.
First, Newton's dating of the Flood differed from ancient accounts.
Ovid located it *after* the Four Ages, while Apollodorus represented
it as the instrument with which Zeus wiped out the Bronze Age.
Characteristically, Newton ignored such a disparity. Second, his
overriding conviction regarding the necessary correlation between
symbols and actual events appeared arbitrary.

The Egyptians – and by implication the Greeks – ran one version of the argument, "represent all things by symbols." And just
as "a man riding upon an eagle with a thunderbolt in his hand" represented "a great warrior soaring high in dominion," so did a flood
stand "for an invasion, & a new world after a flood for a new kingdom after an invasion." Specifically, Greece being "overflowed in the
days of Ogyges & Deucalion," meant it had been "overspread with
forreigners." Hence, the Four Ages after the Flood of Deucalion are to
be understood in terms of the creation of a new kingdom following
the invasion of Greece during the reign of Deucalion. It is noteworthy
that in one cancelled passage Newton proceeded to expound on how,
"in this sense a flood is used in scripture, waters being put for peoples
& multitudes & nations" – citing as authorities verses from Isaiah,
Jeremiah, Amos, and Revelation.[35] Unfortunately, here attachment
to the symbolism was at variance with the chronological structure.
Ancient myths recounted that Deucalion and his son Amphictyon
survived the Deluge by fleeing to Athens. Other sources described the
lavish entertainment that Bacchus received from Amphictyon upon

arriving in Attica. Newton proposed an ingenious interpretation: "the flood from which Deucalion fled I take to be the invasion of his kingdom by Bacchus. He fled with his son Amphictyon to Athens & there they made their peace with Bacchus. For there Amphictyon entertained Bacchus & his great men at a feast & erected an altar to him . . . And by these & such like practises the worship of the Dij magni majorum gentium was set on foot in Greece."[36] Regrettably, since Newton's scheme required the Flood to precede the Four Ages, Bacchus's (Sesostris's) invasion could not have been coeval with it, he being the luminary of the Bronze Age. Thus, without expressly saying so, Newton came to regard the Expedition of Cadmus – contemporaneous with Deucalion's Flood – as symbolizing an invasion by foreigners.

The dating of Cadmus permitted Newton to ascend as high as "the first memory of things." According to the Parian Marble, the reign of Cecrops in Greece had commenced some sixty-three years prior to Cadmus's arrival. The interval fitted squarely into Newton's chronology. According to his narrative, toward the end of the twelfth-century BCE – or "in the latter end of the days of *Eli*" – Misphragmuthosis, King of Thebes, waged war on the Shepherds that ultimately led to their expulsion from Egypt. Groups of Shepherds fled to Zidon, and thence to Greece, including the troupes of Pelasgus, Inachus, Lelex, and Cecrops. These founders of the Greek Kingdoms could not have flourished more than two or three generations before Cadmus for, as noted above, it was unlikely "that any thing done in Europe could be remembered above three generations before the use of Letters." The flood of Ogyges "might be two or three ages earlier then that of Deucalion," but not much older, "for among such wandering people as were then in Europe there could be no memory of things done among them above three or four ages before the first use of letters." We now, Newton concluded, "have already brought chronology almost as high as the first memory of things."[37]

The late invention of writing, combined with the slow process of population growth and political organization, therefore, helped

Newton to establish the twelfth century BCE as the upper limit of any meaningful historical investigation. Consequently, in view of the fact that all surviving records purportedly concerned individuals living (and events occurring) within the bounds of "remembered" time, Newton needed to compress as much of the evidence as possible into the period following "the first memory of things." For that reason much of the published *Chronology*, as well as Newton's private papers, read as if assembled by an obsessive genealogist and a minute antiquarian, who mistook the forest for the trees. Contemporaries, however, cognizant of the accumulative effect of such unprecedented inclusive sorting of data, were not fooled, and neither should we be. The potency of the chronology derived cogency not only from the efficacy of Newton's regnal years' rule and the argument from astronomy, but from the exhaustiveness of his mosaic. Sampling his forays into prosopography then, will reveal how his mastery of ancient myth and history facilitated a cast of thousands, each in their assigned place in the puzzle.

To begin with, Newton charted an interlocking network of familial relationships in order to corroborate the testimony of the Parian Marble regarding the proximity of Deucalion's Flood to the arrival of Cadmus, as well as to establish the reality of the ensuing Four Ages. Consider the era of Erectheus King of Athens. His daughter Creusa married Xuthus, son of Hellen, son of Deucalion. The Flood, therefore, occurred "a little before the reign of Erectheus." Their marriage helped to establish an approximate date for the arrival of Danaus in Greece, since two of his daughters married the sons of Achaeus, the son of Xuthus and Creusa. Danaus's daughters, therefore, "were three Generations younger than *Erechtheus*; and so was Theseus, "the son of *Aegeus*, the adopted son of *Pandion*, the son of *Erechtheus*." Theseus, in turn, linked the histories of Athens and of the Four Ages, for he had been, while "a beardless young man," part of the third tribute of youth delivered by Aegeus to the Cretan King Minos every seven years, in compliance with the terms of their peace treaty. Aegeus and Minos thereby ruled during the Silver Age – as did Ammon in Egypt – while Theseus and Sesostris ruled during the Bronze Age. The two were further connected through Ariadne, daughter of Minos. She helped Theseus kill the Minotaur and extricate himself from the Labyrinth, and joined Theseus in his voyage home only to be abandoned by him on the island of Naxos. Glaucus rescued her, but upon his return from India, Ariadne became Bacchus's mistress, bearing him two sons who became Argonauts.[38] Accordingly, Newton dated the reigns of Erectheus in Athens and Ammon in Egypt to commence c. 1035 BCE. Minos expelled his father Asterius two decades later, shortly before Sesac began his triumphant African conquests, while his father still reigned, finally ascending to the throne in 1002 BCE.

As Newton arranged and rearranged his data, a minor evidentiary complication prompted him to substitute the era of Troy with the era of the Argonautic Expedition as the focus of his system. The adjustment may seem innocuous for, by general consensus, Troy fell a generation after the Expedition. But it mattered to the argumentative structure of Newton's chronology. The first long ship built by the Greeks, he noted on the strength of Pliny's testimony was the ship Argo, and it was built "in imitation of the long ship in wch Danaus wth his 50 daughters fled from his returning brother Sesostris." Since Argus, Danaus's son, actually built the ship, and since Nauplius, son of Danaus's daughter Amymone – born shortly after her arrival in Greece – had been an Argonaut, Newton concluded the Argo set sail a generation after Danaus's escape from Egypt, in 937 BCE.[39]

The Expedition signified for Newton the conclusion of the Bronze Age, as it came on the heels of Sesostris's death and the ensuing turmoil in Egypt. The Greeks attempted to exploit such turmoil by dispatching the Argonauts on a diplomatic mission – the "golden fleece" served as a ruse – to persuade various rulers to revolt and deliver themselves from the Egyptian yoke.[40] This was followed by the "Heroic Age," which according to Hesiod ended with the war of the seven captains at Thebes, and the fall of Troy. He himself, Hesiod added, lived in the age that immediately followed; which for Newton meant about 30 or 40 years after the fall of Troy. He found further evidence to establish Hesiod's time in Herodotus's statement that Hesiod and Homer "were but 400 years older than himself": 870 BCE according to Newton's final estimate.[41] Dates may not have fitted precisely, or everywhere, into the prescribed contours of the Four Ages, but they proved sufficiently close. "I do not pretend to be exact to a year," was Newton's refrain; "there may be Errors of five or ten years, and sometimes twenty," but "not much above."[42]

ARGUMENTS FROM ASTRONOMY

Reflecting on the cumulative effect of his historical reconstruction of the "fabulous age" in the first decade of the eighteenth century, Newton sounded a note of triumph: "We have hitherto recconed by the genealogies & reigns of kings," for this sort of computation lay at "the foundation of ye Chronology for ye Greeks. And by shewing how erroneously the Greeks have recconed from thence & setting right the recconing we have brought Chronology nearer to the truth." Still, Newton recognized the insufficiency of myth-based interpretation to command assent. He searched for a more secure foundation for his revolutionary timeline: "And because arguments drawn from Astronomy are accounted the surest, we shall now confirm o^r recconing by an argument of that sort."[43] In the absence of recorded eclipses for deep antiquity – the sort of astronomical evidence his predecessors used for dating the more recent past – Newton resorted to a new, and equally powerful celestial phenomenon: precession of the equinoxes. A century earlier while attempting to determine the lengths of the tropical and sidereal years, Joseph Scaliger had already contemplated the potential inherent in precession, only to become disillusioned and turn violently against it. Standing on Scaliger's shoulders, Newton saw clearer and further.

He took his cue from a commentary written by Hipparchus of Bithynia (c. 190–120 BCE) on Aratus's celebrated didactic poem *Phaenomena*, into which Hipparchus incorporated material from a prose treatise that informed Aratus's account: the now lost

Phaenomena of Eudoxus of Cnidus (408–355 BCE). Eudoxus, Newton argued, described the sphere of the Ancients, furnishing the position of the constellations at the time of its formation. Ignorant of the phenomenon of precession, Eudoxus "made no allowance" for it, "but placed the Equinoxes & solstices in the middle of the Asterisms of Aries Cancer Chelae & Capricorn as they were placed by the ancients." However, Eudoxus's older contemporaries, the Athenians Meton and Euctemon, observed in 432 BCE the summer solstice, and found it to be in the eighth degree of the constellation Cancer: a shift of seven degrees from the position found on the ancient sphere. By the time Hipparchus made his observations (c. 146 BCE), it had reached the fourth degree of the constellation. Noticing the disparity between the observations occasioned Hipparchus's discovery of the precession of the equinoxes. Unfortunately, "great astronomer" though he undoubtedly was, Hipparchus's fidelity to "the Chronology of the ancient *Greeks* then in use" led him wide of the mark. Since contemporaries reckoned the Argonautic Expedition to be 1,090 years before his time, and since the equinox had "gone back eleven Degrees since," Hipparchus harmonized the two pieces of information by assigning a rate of 100 years to a degree. Yet Newton noted, if the correct rate of 72 years to a degree is applied, the Argonauts set sail only 792 years before Hipparchus's time.[44]

The "description of the colures set down by Hipparchus is but coarse," Newton acknowledged, and "the places of the fixt stars were but coarsely observed by the ancients." Nevertheless, these observations "suffice for determining the colures without erring above a degree in their Longitude." To substantiate the claim, Newton devoted considerable time and effort to astronomical computations – analyzed at length elsewhere – in order to prove that the ancient sphere actually existed, as well as to identify its inventor.[45]

Newton had paid some attention to the ancient sphere already in the 1680s, while pondering the westward transfer of astronomical knowledge and idolatry from Egypt. In that context he embraced the attribution of the role of mediator to Orpheus. In fact, he noted that, since Orpheus also authored the legend of the Argonauts, and that myth informed the imagery of the Greek heavens, "it is very likely that Orpheus, inspired by the striking Globe of the Egyptians, devised the aforesaid constellations, and depicted his own image without a name."[46] As noted above, considerations of time, which played no role in Newton's original scheme, became paramount after 1700. Hence the need to probe more fully into the nature and extent of astronomical knowledge in Greece, as well as the origination of the ancient sphere. Within this revised context, Orpheus had outlived his usefulness, notwithstanding his being the acknowledged purveyor of the Egyptian sphere to Greece, as well as an Argonaut. Newton grounded his revised scheme on the premise that only prose compositions could be accepted as trustworthy; yet Orpheus had been one of those philosophers who "delivered their Opinions in Verse," and hence was unreliable. As long as the Greeks continued writing in verse, Newton contended, "there could be no Chronology, nor any other History, than such as was mixed with poetical fancies." Disparaging comments by Lucian and Diogenes Laertius may have confirmed him in his opinion. While attesting to Orpheus's role in transmitting Egyptian knowledge to Greece in an early manuscript, Newton recorded that Lucian believed it came "in a confused fashion and wrapped in layers of fable and mystery." For his part, Diogenes Laertius "hardly knew whether [Orpheus] ought to be called a philosopher," given his predilection to impute to the gods human frailties and crimes. Whatever the motive, in the published *Chronology*, Orpheus is credited only with deifying in 942 BCE, "the son of *Semele* by the name of *Bacchus*, and [appointing] his Ceremonies."[47]

In Orpheus's stead, Newton placed Palamedes, son of the Argonaut Nauplius. He did so on the authority of Achilles Tatius, who cited a lost play by Sophocles, wherein Palamedes had been credited with several inventions, including the discovery of weights, measures, and numbers, as well as having "traced out / The spaces and the orbits of the stars, / Each in his rank, and the celestial signs."[48] As Newton initially chose the era of Troy as the focus of his new scheme, assigning Palamedes – who perished in the course of the war – the honor of discoverer appeared judicious. Concurrently, Newton entertained the possibility of a group effort: "Palamedes was a young man when he went to the war at Troy & not long before observed & measured the stars that is their situations one among another, & formed or reformed the signs & Asterisms. Musaeus might set the stars on the globe by viewing the heavens as a painter draws a face & Palamedes might rectify their places by his measures & form the signs & constellations more exactly."[49]

Eventually, as Newton determined that the globe had been prepared for the use of the Argonauts, Palamedes had to be dropped for reasons of age. And while still admitting Musaeus's contribution, Newton now singled out Jason's teacher, Chiron the Centaur. Clement of Alexandria furnished him with the crucial piece of evidence: he cited the author of a lost work on *Titanomachia*, who credited Chiron with having been the first to delineate the asterisms (σχήματα ὀλύμπου). Since the sphere depicted "nothing later then yᵉ Argonautic expedition," Newton felt certain "that the celestial globe was formed in the time of that expedition & most probably by Chiron & Musæus or one of them & that for the use of the Argonauts" because "Laertius tells us that Musaeus made the first sphaere & he was the Master of Orpheus & one of the Argonauts."[50]

In his manuscripts Newton wavered somewhat on the sources for Chiron's astronomical knowledge and competence. He even entertained one alternative route for the transfer of Egyptian astronomy to Greece. According to the historian Justin, the Libyan born Aristaeus, who married Autonoe, daughter of Cadmus, and became king of Arcadia, "was the first that observed the solstitial rising of Sirius." Newton imagined Aristaeus to have received his astronomical education in Libya, where he also served as tutor to Bacchus, eventually bringing "from thence into Greece the skill of observing & determining the solstices by the risings & settings of the stars," two or three generations before the Argonautic Expedition. Such a thread led Newton to deem it "probable that when Chiron & Musaeus formed the sphaere they did not observe the solstice themselves, but placed it where it had been found a little before by Atlas who made the first sphere or by Aristaeus & by the Egyptians or Greeks of their days." Alternatively, he thought that in order to settle the equinoxes and solstices, Chiron, Musaeus, and their assistants actually "observed the heliacal risings & settings of the stars as the Egyptians had done before."[51]

Either way, though Chiron and Musaeus copied Atlas's sphere, "the Asterisms of the Greeks were different from those of the Egyptians & Libyans," for the simple reason that "the sphere [had been] made for ye use of the Argonauts." Such wavering aside, what mattered to Newton most was not *who* devised the sphere, it was the need to establish the existence of sufficient astronomical sophistication during those "barbarous" times – "And least you should think that the solstices were not observed so long ago, the Greeks in those days had many famous Astronomers, Endymion, Aristaeus, Chiron, Linus, Musaeus, Atreus, Ancaeus, Orpheus, Palamedes."[52] The presence of a respectable degree of astronomical knowledge in Greece during the tenth century BCE served further to enhance the credibility of the astronomical information Newton attempted to extract from Hesiod's *Works and Days*: "*Hesiod* tells us that sixty days after the winter Solstice the Star *Arcturus* rose just at Sunset: and thence it follows that *Hesiod* flourished about an hundred years after the death of *Solomon*, or in the Generation or Age next after the *Trojan* war." Newton interpreted this as indication of precise observation, capable of being transformed into an actual date.[53]

During one of the periodic summations of his progress in expanding the bounds of the knowable past, Newton boasted of his success in carrying "up the chronology of the Greeks as high as . . . the first memory of things done in Greece"; namely, the reigns of Actaeus, Cecrops, Inachus, Lelex, Aegialeus, Pelasgus, and Deucalion. These "were the oldest kings of Greece of wch there is any certain memory," he asserted, and they all flourished three generations before Cadmus introduced writing into Greece. Hence, "it is not to be imagined things could be remembered wch were done above an hundred years before the use of letters." And yet, Newton marveled, Chronologers "make the kingdoms of Sicyon & Germany above 1000 years older then the first use of letters . . . that of Argos above 800 years older & that of Athens above 500 years older. But how come they know this? Could the history of Athens be preserved for 500 years together wthout the use of Letters?" Could any history? Undoubtedly, following the arrival of Cadmus, the Greeks committed to writing "as much of the antiquities of the several kingdoms of Greece as they could remember & thence it came to pass that the antiquities of all those kingdoms reach up to about 60 80 or 90 years before ye coming in of Letters & no higher."[54]

From a modern perspective, Newton's malleable use of the historical record is unmistakable. He approached the interpretation of ancient historical sources with the same assuredness he exhibited when deciphering the symbolisms of Biblical prophecies, or when presenting his new theory of light and colors. Remarking on the extent to which previous scholars had been confounded in their attempts to synchronize Persian "prophane history" with the narrative of Scripture, he declared: "I shall not stand to recite other men's opinions, but propose as shortly as I can what I take to be the truth."[55] Newton thereby reserved to himself the right to determine not just which historical sources were credible, but which parts of these credible sources were nevertheless untrustworthy and to be discarded. To a considerable extent, then, Newton followed the common practices of contemporary scholars. Yet his idiosyncratic, and exceptionally focused, chronology differed both in kind and degree from those of other historians – which partly explains the violent controversies that the *Chronology of Ancient Kingdoms Amended* generated upon publication in 1728.

These debates, discussed more fully elsewhere,[56] attest to the centrality of chronology to early modern intellectual life. Theologians of all stripes, as well as men of letters, vied with each other to erect systems of universal history, reacting violently to competing chronological schemes. Ultimately, however, all were doomed to failure, constrained as they were by Scripture timeline. As Louis Elisabeth de la Vergne de Tressan ruminated in 1776: "The obstinate and minute writer who wishes to probe more deeply into the darkness" of antiquity is destined to exhaust himself in a vain pursuit. Many have tried to establish systems of chronology and failed. "If anyone was worthy to succeed, it would have been the sublime Newton. But his chronology, the weakest work of this great man, appears to be the price to be paid for the feebleness of humanity. If even Newton was wrong, what could be hoped by those who labored after him, than to obscure more and more the order, or rather the appearance of order, of events and eras, which, it must be admitted, are almost entirely lost to us?" In 1812 Georges Cuvier still sought for the genius who would know how to "burst the limits of time" – just as Newton and his followers "burst the limits of space" – "and, by some observations, to recover the history of the world." It took many more decades, and the labor of numerous historians, archaeologists, naturalists, and theologians, before the contours of such an elusive dream were attained.[57]

NOTES

1 Richard S. Westfall, *Never at Rest: A Biography of Isaac Newton* (Cambridge/ New York: Cambridge Univerity Press, 1980), p. 815.

2 Niccolò Guicciardini, *Isaac Newton on Mathematical Certainty and Method* (Cambridge: Cambridge Univerity Press, 2009), pp. 79–107.

3 Yahuda Ms. 41, fols. 11, 26–7; Yahuda Ms. 17.2, fol. 21; Yahuda Ms. 16.2, fol. 2v.

4 Yahuda Ms. 41, fols. 1–5. On Newton and the Prytanea, see Rob Iliffe, "'Is He Like Other Men?' The Meaning of the *Principia Mathematica*, and the Author as Idol," in Gerald Maclean (ed.), *Culture and Society in the Stuart Restoration* (Cambridge: Cambridge Univerity Press, 1995); Raquel Delgado-Moreira, "Epistemology and Rhetorical Strategies in Newton's Theological Writings," Ph.D. thesis, Imperial College, London, 2006.

5 Yahuda Ms. 16.2, fol. 48.

6 Yahuda Ms. 16.2, fol. 18; Ms. 17.2, fol. 4v.

7 Isaac Newton, *Observations Upon the Prophecies of Daniel, and the Apocalypse of St. John* (London, 1733), pp. 16–19; Yahuda Ms. 16.2, fols. 62–3.

8 Yahuda Ms. 25.2f, fol. 35; New College Ms. 361.3, fols. 163, 230.

9 Yahuda Ms. 17.2, fol. 4; Hesiod, *Theogony, Works and Days, Testimonia,* trans. Glenn W. Most (Cambridge, MA, and London: Harvard University Press, 2006), p. 97.

10 Yahuda Ms. 16.2, fol. 18; New College Ms. 361.2, fol. 109; New College Ms. 361.3, fols. 5, 59v, 129v–130.

11 Newton, *The Chronology of Ancient Kingdoms Amended. To Which Is Prefix'd, a Short Chronicle from the First Memory of Things in Europe, to the Conquest of Persia by Alexander the Great* (London, 1728), pp. 44–5. For an earlier version, see New College Ms. 361.2, fol. 174v.

12 Newton, *Chronology,* p. 70.

13 New College Ms. 361.2, fols. 132–3, 88.

14 Newton, *Chronology,* pp. 69–70.

15 *Ibid.,* pp. 68–9, 98.

16 Josephus, *Works,* trans. H. St. J. Thackery, 8 vols., Loeb Classical Library (Cambridge, MA: Harvard University Press, 1926), pp. 203–5, 257, 299.

17 New College Ms. 361.3, fol. 255; Herodotus, *The Histories,* 4 vols. (Cambridge, MA: Harvard University Press, 1975), vol. 1, p. 327. Herodotus actually wrote Dionysus but as Newton commented elsewhere, citing Herodotus, "Osiris in the Greek tongue is Dionysus that is Bacchus." Yahuda Ms. 25.2b, fol. 20.

18 *Siculus Diodorus,* trans. C. H. Oldfather *et al.,* 12 vols., Loeb Classical Library (Cambridge, MA: Harvard University Press; London: W. Heinemann, 1933–67), vol. 1, pp. 39, 47; Arrian, *Anabasis Alexandri,* trans. F. Iliff Robson, 2 vols., Loeb Classical Library (Cambridge, MA: Harvard University Press, 1956), vol. 2, p. 271; Newton, *Chronology,* pp. 98–9, 125; Yahuda Ms. 25.2b, fol. 20. Newton gives a revealing and explicit account of the methods underlying his practice at Yahuda Ms. 10b, fols. 6, 10–10v and 12.

19 Yahuda Ms. 8.1, fol. 6; New College Ms. 361.2, fol. 133v.

20 CUL Ms. Add. 3970, fol. 242v, cited in Alan E Shapiro, "Newton's 'Experimental Philosophy'," *Early Science and Medicine* 9 (2004), 192.

21 New College Ms. 361.2, fol. 18.

22 James Ussher, *The Annals of the World Deduced from the Origin of Time, and Continued to the Beginning of the Emperour Vespasians Reign, and the Totall Destruction and Abolition of the Temple and Common-Wealth of the Jews* (London, 1658), p. 29; Eusebius, *Evangelicae Praeparationis*, ed. E. H. Gifford, 5 vols. (Oxford, 1903), vol. 3/2, p. 483.

23 Thucydides (1956 i. 23) *Diodorus*, vol. 1, p. 21.

24 Newton, *Chronology*, pp. 4, 47, 49.

25 *Ibid.*, pp. 2, 47; New College Ms. 361.1, fols. 103, 105–6.

26 New College Ms. 361.2, fol. 35; *ibid.*, pp. 7, 50.

27 Keynes Ms. 146, p. 15; *ibid.*, pp. 45, 51–4.

28 Herodotus, *The Histories*, vol. 4, p. 135; New College Ms. 361.2, fols. 20v, 36; Newton, *Chronology*, pp. 7–8.

29 New College Ms. 361.3, fol. 167. For the more nuanced position in the *Chronology* see *ibid.*, pp. 119–20.

30 Herodotus, *The Histories*, vol. 3, pp. 281–3; New College Ms. 361.3, fols. 1, 3–3v.

31 Newton, *Chronology*, p. 105.

32 New College Ms. 361.3, fol. 31v; *Chronology*, pp. 7, 200–1, 208.

33 New College Ms. 361.3, fols. 45, 6. *Diodorus*, vol. 2, p. 305. See also New College Ms. 361.3, fols. 51–2, 81, 101, 244, 256v; Ms. 361.2, fols. 21v, 104, 119.

34 New College Ms. 361.2, fol. 163v, 251v; Ms. 361.3, fol. 136, 187v; Newton, *Chronology*, p. 210.

35 New College Ms. 361.3, fol. 27.

36 New College Ms. 361.3, fols. 58–7v. In the *Chronology* Newton found it necessary to argue that a different (and later) Amphictyon entertained Bacchus; see *ibid.*, p. 18.

37 Newton, *Chronology*, pp. 10, 167–8; New College Ms. 361.3, fols. 81, 101–3.

38 New College Ms. 361.3, fol. 4; Newton, *Chronology*, pp. 67–8, 90.

39 New College Ms. 361.3, fols. 45, 51–3, 63, 115v, 129, 196, 244.

40 New College Ms. 361.2, fol. 42.

41 New College Ms. 361.2, fol. 107v; Ms. 361.3, fol. 249v; Newton, *Chronology*, p. 32.

42 Newton, *Chronology*, p. 8. Earlier he wrote: "The arguments hitherto used overthrow the Chronology of the ancient Greeks & bring us much

nearer the truth. If they determin the times within 10 or 20 or perhaps 30 years of the truth tis all we designed by them." New College Ms. 361.2, fol. 148.

43 New College Ms. 361.3, fols. 168, 166; Yahuda Ms. 25.2e, fol. 6.

44 New College Ms. 361.2, fol. 43v, 147–9; Newton, *Chronology*, pp. 82–3, 87–8, 93–4.

45 New College Ms. 361.2, fol. 157. For a fuller account, see Buchwald and Feingold, *Newton and the Origin of Civilization*, ch. 8.

46 Yahuda Ms. 17.2, fol. 15v.

47 Newton, *Chronology*, pp. 45–6, 25; Yahuda Ms. 17.2, fol. 6v. Diogenes Laertius, *Lives of the Eminent Philosophers*, vol. 1, p. 7.

48 Sophocles, *The Dramas*, trans. George Young (London: J. M. Dent, 1916), pp. 353–4.

49 New College Ms. 361.2, fol. 82v.

50 New College Ms. 361.3, fols. 246, 185; Newton, *Chronology*, pp. 83–4. Newton based the reversal of the relationship between Musaeus and Orpheus on Clement of Alexandria, not Diogenes Laertius. He undoubtedly sought thereby to further diminish from Orpheus's relevance.

51 New College Ms. 361.3, fols. 25v, 92, 184v–185v, 246.

52 New College Ms. 361.2, fol. 204.

53 New College Ms. 361.2, fols. 43, 107v; Ms. 361.3, fol 92v; Newton, *Chronology*, p. 95; Hesiod, *Theogony, Works and Days, Testimonia*, p. 133.

54 New College Ms. 361.3, fol. 256; Yahuda Ms. 25.2e, fol. 37.

55 Yahuda Ms. 25.1d, fol. 3.

56 Buchwald and Feingold, *Newton and the Origin of Civilization*, chs. 9–12.

57 Louis Elisabeth de la Vergne de Tressan, *Oeuvres*, 10 vols. (Paris, 1822–3), vol. 9, pp. 358–9; Martin J. S. Rudwick, *George Cuvier, Fossil Bones, and Geological Catastrophes* (Chicago, IL: University of Chicago Press, 1997), p. 185.

14 Newton and eighteenth-century Christianity

Scott Mandelbrote

You will be very able to deal with Sr Isaac, and I shall be glad to leave Him in such good hands. He is a man of such scope, and his Authority so justly celebrated in some things, that his name is of great weight in other matters, where He was plainly out of his element, and knew little of what He was talking about. Besides his countenancing Arianism, in the piece referred to, He has given too much encouragement to Popery by his large concessions, such as our best Protestant writers, att the time of K[ing]. James as well as before, would never make.[1]

Isaac Newton's *Observations upon the prophecies of Daniel, and the Apocalypse of St. John*, prepared for the press from his manuscripts by his nephew Benjamin Smith, was published in two editions in London and Dublin in 1733.[2] According to Richard S. Westfall, Newton's finest twentieth-century biographer, the author "had cleansed his *Observations*" and his heirs "could publish the manuscript without concern."[3] Yet one might be permitted to wonder whether either the actual or the intended reception of Newton's posthumous work was as uncontroversial as it has seemed to late twentieth-century eyes. The book was dedicated to Peter King, baron of Ockham, the Lord Chancellor, who had defended Newton's sometime disciple, William Whiston, during his trial for heresy in July 1713.[4] Although Whiston later fell out with King, he nevertheless continued to maintain that King's youthful writings on the primitive Church supported the Arian

I am grateful to Rob Iliffe, Tabitta van Nouhuys, and Steve Snobelen for their help with this chapter. In revising it, I have tried to take into account comments kindly provided by Mordechai Feingold.

position for which he had himself been condemned.[5] King was also the dedicatee of other works of dubious theological orthodoxy, such as Daniel Mace's attempted revision of the New Testament. Mace showed little respect for the authenticity of the two New Testament texts that most clearly upheld the orthodox doctrine of the Trinity, I John 5:7 and I Timothy 3:16. Listing ancient manuscripts which gave non-Trinitarian readings, he hinted strongly that their modern, orthodox variants were the product of interference with the primitive text of scripture.[6]

The young King's most significant friendship had been with his second cousin, John Locke. He was one of the philosopher's closest confidants towards the end of his life and an executor of his will, by which he inherited half of Locke's library and all of his manuscripts. He was also charged with "a little packet sealed up and directed to Mr Newton."[7] King had acted as an occasional intermediary between Newton and Locke, passing on information between the two men about matters concerning the Mint and about the interpretation of scripture. He conveyed chapters of the draft of Locke's *A Paraphrase and Notes on the Epistles of St. Paul* to Newton for comment.[8] Locke informed King that Newton was "really a very valuable man not onely for his wonderfull skill in Mathematicks but in divinity too and his great knowledg in the Scriptures where in I know few his equals."[9] As an acquaintance of Newton and a prominent whig politician, King may therefore have been a natural choice as the dedicatee of the *Observations*. But, as his earlier doctrinal sympathies, his knowledge of suspicions that had been voiced about Locke's orthodoxy on the matter of the Trinity, and his later patronage of heterodox Presbyterians such as Mace make clear, King was not a theologically neutral choice as a patron of a work of biblical interpretation.[10] Moreover, as the owner of Locke's manuscripts, King had access to evidence of Newton's heterodox beliefs about the Trinity, in the letters that passed into his keeping at Locke's death.[11] It is tempting to speculate that the "little packet" that King had been charged with returning to Newton might have contained a more incriminating piece of correspondence, sent by Newton to Locke in 1690 but no longer extant among Locke's papers: Newton's initial letters comprising "An Historical account of two Notable Corruptions of Scripture," I John 5:7 and I Timothy 3:16.[12] King was not displeased by the dedication of *Observations*, granting Smith a mediety of the rectory of Linton in Craven, Yorkshire.[13]

Smith had been ordained by a friend of Newton's twilight years, William Stukeley. Stukeley himself had been inspired by Newton to "[study] the Mosaic cosmogony seriously," suggesting that "Here is the Original Source of True Philosophy The Oracle of Nature, The Springhead of knowledge where Those that thirst after the *Newtonian Draughts* may drink largely at the Fountain."[14] He seems to have been only one of a group of those who met and were influenced by Newton who undertook to defend the accuracy of Moses's natural philosophy at one time or another.[15] His affection for Newton's theology extended to attempts to reconstruct the plan of Solomon's Temple, itself the setting for many of the prophetic events that Newton tried to elucidate.[16] However, Stukeley, like many of Newton's erstwhile disciples, doubted the accuracy of the calculations to be found in *The Chronology of Ancient Kingdoms Amended*, published by Newton's heirs from his manuscripts in 1728.[17]

The *Chronology* had been dedicated to Queen Caroline, an admirer of Newton who had encouraged his chronological writing and protected his closest theological disciple, Samuel Clarke, throughout the 1710s and 1720s. Even the Queen, however, was powerless to prevent debate about the historical accuracy and religious orthodoxy of Newton's writings. This had begun with criticism of the *Chronology* but soon spilled over into more serious attacks on *Observations*. Remarking on the plans for the publication of the *Chronology*, Stukeley's friend and Newton's physician, Richard Mead, commented that Newton "was a christian, believed revelation, though not all the doctrines which our orthodox divines have made articles of faith."[18] Following its publication, others were less generous to Newton's beliefs and intentions. The Bristol clergyman, orientalist, and moral reformer, Arthur Bedford observed that:

> When Sir Isaak Newton's Chronology was printed and extolled by many, which must absolutely have destroyed all the Scripture History, [I] first printed an Octavo against it, and afterward a Folio intituled, The Scripture Chronology demonstrated by Astronomical Observations, a Work recommended by Archbishop Usher in his Annals, but never attempted 'til then; the Consequence of which was the Establishing the Authority of the Hebrew Chronology, in so much that the other notions are now intirely disregarded.[19]

Bedford's comments might be dismissed as those of a disappointed rival, whose own mammoth chronology Newton had scooped. Indeed, the vituperative Jacobite antiquary, Thomas Hearne, did just this, remarking on April 18, 1728 that Bedford was "looked upon as a crazed man."[20]

Yet Hearne had his own reasons to be dismissive of low churchmen, and his opinion ignored the depth of continuing support for Bedford, whose writing was sponsored by the Society for Promoting Christian Knowledge, with which many of the hierarchy of the Church of England were associated.[21] Hearne ate his own words, noting two years later that Bedford's finished Scripture Chronology (1730) was "received very graciously" by the King, Queen, and Prince of Wales.[22] Bedford's initial criticisms were directed at the astronomical methods of dating that Newton's chronology had deployed. He pointed out that Newton's findings disagreed with those of the most prominent orthodox writers on chronology – James Ussher, William Lloyd, Richard Cumberland, and William Beveridge, all of whom were in agreement about the major dates in secular and sacred history.[23] But he soon identified his real target: "we live in an Age, when we cannot be too cautious . . . The Divinity of our blessed SAVIOUR is struck at by the Revivers of ancient and modern Heresies; especially that, which destroyed all the eastern Nations, and introduced *Mahometism* among them."[24]

Bedford was perceptive in noticing that Newton's conclusions about sacred history created doubts over the authority and antiquity of scripture.[25] He felt these were reminiscent of the beliefs of Newton's disciples, Whiston and Clarke, and therefore raised the spectre of Arianism. This heresy had swept through the Eastern Church in the early fourth century, weakening it both theologically and politically. Its beliefs about Christ's nature as the first of God's creations, rather than as God himself, seemed to people like Bedford the most blasphemous of the primitive heresies that were currently being revived by Whiston and, more cautiously, Clarke.[26]

In the months following Newton's death, speculation was rife that he had shared the heterodox beliefs for which Whiston and Clarke were pilloried. The Presbyterian minister and historian, Robert Wodrow, who was a friend of a number of Scottish Newtonians, received frequent reports about the publication of Newton's *Chronology*. As early as 1711, Wodrow had recorded rumours concerning Newton's influence on Whiston: "It is said he has not only much of his Mathematicks, but severall of his other errours from Sir Isaack Neuton, which I incline not to belive."[27] He was thus relieved to be informed in November 1727 that Newton's unpublished papers appeared at first to contain nothing about the doctrine of the Trinity. Wodrow's composure was shattered in May 1729 when he learned that Newton had agreed with Clarke about the subordination of Christ to God the Father and had had peculiar notions about the interpretation of the prophecies of Daniel.[28]

In the following year, Whiston excited speculation by writing that Clarke's interpretation of the prophecy of the seventy weeks (Daniel 9:24–7) was "only a Conjecture of Sir *Isaac Newton's*, and I think a Conjecture not well grounded neither." This prophecy was widely believed to have predicted the birth of Christ, the crucifixion, or the destruction of Jerusalem by the Romans as marking the end of a period of captivity for God's people. Whiston mischievously looked forward to the publication of "Sir *Isaac*'s own great work *upon the Scripture Prophecies* . . . which we expect this Summer," confident that it would provide information about Newton's unusual belief that the entire prophecy had not yet been fulfilled.[29] Others of Newton's former acquaintances also began to reveal details of his heterodox beliefs. John Craig privately observed that Newton's thoughts about religion "were some times different from those which are commonly receiv'd."[30] The Chevalier Ramsay was less discreet, suggesting to Joseph Spence that "Sir Isaac Newton and Dr. Clarke endeavoured to clear it [the doctrine of the Trinity] from its corruptions, but in their way 'tis as difficult and embarrassed as it was before." Ramsay had once been a pupil of Newton's closest friend of the early 1690s, Nicolas Fatio de Duillier, and shared his faith in the orthodox doctrine of the Trinity.[31] Once Newton's *Observations* was published in 1733, therefore, it was bound to become the subject of scrutiny from orthodox divines whatever protection might be provided for it by dedication to a prominent member of the ministry. The rumours that shocked Wodrow and that Whiston promoted were the same ones to which Voltaire drew attention in 1733, when he remarked that "this philosopher thought that the Unitarians argued more mathematically than we do."[32] The speculation that they raised about the validation of the Christian religion through prophecy fed into wider doubts about the meaning and implications of revelation. These were public topics for debate: the role of prophecy in testifying to the authenticity of Christ's claim to be the Messiah, for instance, was one of the subjects that Edmund Gibson, Bishop of London, chose for the first of his pastoral letters.[33]

Gibson did not reflect directly on Newton's works, but some of his allies did. Daniel Waterland, Master of Magdalene College, Cambridge, was perhaps the most indefatigable upholder of Trinitarian orthodoxy of the time. He was a veteran of numerous controversies, notably with Samuel Clarke, the deist Matthew Tindal, and Conyers Middleton. At first glance, Waterland's attitude to Newton's posthumous publications seems to have been ambivalent. His second in the duel with Middleton, Zachary Pearce, found Newton's *Chronology* a ready weapon in an argument about the relative antiquity of Egyptian and Israelite religious practices and hence about the reliability of the literal sense of the Bible as a historical source.[34] In this context, Newton was presumably one of the "men as learned and honest as *Spencer*, or *Marsham*" who had answered their arguments about ancient Egyptian religion.[35] Waterland advised Pearce in this opportunistic use of Newton's work: "And though I do not myself follow Sir Isaac Newton's Chronology, yet I am very well pleased to see it so strongly pressed upon one who perhaps does."[36]

Middleton, however, soon turned the use of Newton against Waterland and his ally: "I must take the liberty to dissent from you, and to declare, that for a thorough knowledge of Antiquity, and the whole compass of *Greek and Ægyptian* Learning, there have been, in my Opinion, and now are, many Men as far superior to him, as he within his proper Character is superior to everybody else." To hold Newton up as an authority on chronology was simply rash;[37] although this did not deter Waterland from again invoking Newton's authority in the preface published with the final part of his attack on Tindal, *Scripture Vindicated*. Here, Waterland referred admiringly to Newton's *Observations*, which, he claimed, "has given us some useful Hints for the better explaining such *symbolical* language."[38] It is, however, tempting to presume that this was a knowing attempt to set a thief to catch a thief.[39] Waterland and his allies were concerned about using the strong literalism and respect for the Hebrew Bible found in Newton's posthumous writings to combat the tendency of deist authors to read the Bible allegorically, and to offset historical and critical concerns about the reliability of the Hebrew text as a source. They wished to do this not because they were convinced of Newton's own orthodoxy, but because so many of their opponents either cited the work of Newton or his followers in some way, or could be expected to be awed by his example as a natural philosopher.[40]

Elsewhere, Waterland expressed much more straightforward opinions about Newton's theological writings and those of his allies. He attacked Clarke's duplicity with regard to the thirty-nine articles of the Church of England and the ambiguous language deployed in *The Scripture-Doctrine of the Trinity*.[41] He was equally damning about what he took to be Newton's lack of candor about the intentions and implications of his arguments in his *Chronology* and *Observations*. He thus wrote to Zachary Grey that he was "sorry that no one yet has undertaken a just *Answer* to *Sir Isaac Newton's 14th. Chapter* relating to the *Prophecies of Daniel*: in which he slily abuses the *Athanasians* . . . That *Prophetical* Way of managing this Debate on the Side of *Arianism*, is a very silly one, & might be easily retorted. But besides that, what *Sir Isaac* has said, is most of it *false History*. I have scribbled the *Margin* all the way . . ."[42] A particular excitement for Waterland and Grey was the possibility provided by Newton's *Observations* of catching the great mathematician out in his own calculations.[43] Since Waterland claimed he was too busy and too unwell for the task, Grey duly took up the cudgel on his behalf, thus enhancing his growing reputation as an apologist for the Church of England.[44]

The resulting attack on the fourteenth chapter of the *Observations* was unforgiving in its criticism of Newton's argument and intentions and unpleasantly insightful about his methods as a theologian and historian. Grey confronted Newton's chronology, logic, and use of sources and found all of them wanting. His target was particularly well chosen, since the chapter under review presented Newton's case for the growth of idolatry in the early Christian Church, itself a sign of Newton's broader point that the incarnation of Christ had not marked the fulfillment of Daniel's prophecies. Grey cannot have known that these had been the principal themes of Isaac Newton's theology since the 1670s, and it was only an inspired guess on his part to identify this passage as the key to the underpinning of Newton's Arian Christology in his interpretation of prophecy.[45] He argued that Newton had suppressed evidence demonstrating that respect was given to saints and martyrs in the primitive Church which was inconvenient to his prophetic scheme. He showed that Newton had distorted the Greek Fathers, to make it appear that the early cult of martyrs' graves constituted a form of idolatry and that the first monks had perverted true Christianity. He suggested that the accusations of furthering idolatry that Newton leveled at the orthodox, Trinitarian Athanasians ought properly to be directed at the Arians themselves.[46] An earlier attack on the *Chronology* by the Cambridge divine Arthur Young had also pointed out that Newton had placed the origins of the worship of saints too early. Young had been a subscriber to Bedford's *Scripture Chronology*, and, whereas Grey and Waterland were content to imply that Newton's works might give comfort to the deists, he explicitly associated Newton's publications with those of Tindal. He also argued that Newton's comments of figurative language and the preservation of the text of the Hebrew Bible, which had been disingenuously admired by Waterland, in fact "[could] not [be] more prejudicial to Christianity."[47]

For both Young and Grey, the commentaries of Symon Patrick, Bishop of Ely, and the *Connection* of Humphrey Prideaux, Dean of Norwich, provided the definitive treatments of the meaning of Hebrew prophecy.[48] They thus both upheld the authority of the classic biblical commentators of the time, whose works appealed to a broad spectrum of ecclesiastical opinion. Moreover, both critics argued that the only real beneficiary of Newton's attack on the reputation of the Fathers was the Roman Catholic Church. Grey suggested that Newton assisted its polemicists by falsely attributing corrupt Catholic doctrines to the pure, primitive Fathers.[49] Given Newton's own powerful history of anti-Catholicism, this was a remarkable conclusion. Because of the reputation of the theology of the early Church in English Protestant writing from the time of the Reformation, however, it was also justifiable.

Intellectually, one of the most powerful of Grey's criticisms of Newton's theological writings was that they distorted the meaning of the Greek Fathers. Grey noticed that Newton's quotations from writers like St Cyril of Jerusalem, St. Cyril of Alexandria, or St. Gregory of Nazianzus were often selective and that he was prone to making errors in citations (for example, confusing Sozomen with one of his sources, Socrates). Above all, the problem was that Newton often seemed to be using translations rather than the original text. This was most extreme in the case of St. Ephraem Syrus, where Newton appeared to be using a Latin translation made from a Greek version of the original Syriac text.[50] Grey had realized that Newton's method for his theological writings depended largely on the assimilation of works in English and Latin, many of which already seemed dated. Although he possessed several editions of patristic texts, Newton's Greek was probably not good enough to allow him to cope easily with the original versions of many of the sources on which he ought to have been most dependent for a history of the early Church. Where Newton did own the relevant Greek works, he did so in editions that also gave the text in Latin.[51] This tendency was even more marked with Newton's use of Hebrew works, where he quite shamelessly marked passages in the Latin parallel texts that later appeared as quotations in Hebrew in his own writings.[52] Newton's theological writings frequently appear to be little more than compendia of quotations; what is less apparent is that their copious citations were often constructed largely out of the compilations of previous critics.[53] Newton was not unusual among humanist scholars in employing this method of study, in which selective reading was rapidly converted into the appearance of mammoth erudition in pursuit of a particular, clearly defined goal. However, this technique worked best when the ideology informing it was an orthodox one, since, by definition, it was likely to be vulnerable to scrutiny.[54] Given the unusual nature of the case that Newton was trying to prove, it was unlikely that scholarly habits such as his would bear up well under examination.

Grey was by no means the only orthodox critic of Newton whom Waterland sponsored. In 1719, Waterland inaugurated a lecture series, to be delivered as sermons at St. Paul's Cathedral, in defense of the doctrine of the Trinity. These lectures were supported by Rebecca

Moyer, the widow of Sir Samuel Moyer, a Turkey merchant and sher-
iff of Essex. By her will, which was proved on 21 February 1723, Lady
Moyer endowed the sermons with twenty guineas a year for "an able
Minister of God's Word, to preach eight sermons every year on the
Trinity, and Divinity of our ever blessed Saviour, beginning with
the first Thursday in November, and so the first Thursday in the seven
sequel months, in St. Paul's, if permitted there . . ."[55] Waterland was
actively involved in the selection of many of the preachers at Lady
Moyer's lecture, several of whom acknowledged his aid. One of these
was Henry Felton, who preached the sermons for 1728–9, in which
he distanced himself from the "peculiar Notions, and Singularitys" of
"the incomparable Sir *Isaac Newton* . . . in the *Egyptian* Chronology,"
while praising Newton's "Principles of Gravitation and Attraction,
that Universal Magnetism of Nature, [which] tho' rightly assigned,
cannot yet themselves be accounted for but from the Virtue, and
Impression of the first great Mover."[56] Felton's juxtaposition of the
usefulness of the natural theology to be derived from Newton's
natural philosophy with the shortcomings of his writings as a biblical critic chimed with the characterization of Newton's work that
Waterland and his allies had been developing.

The Moyer lectures in general echoed Waterland's criticisms
of Samuel Clarke and often targeted the ideas of William Whiston.
William Berriman, for example, who preached the sermons for 1723–4,
had already cut his teeth in arguments with Whiston and used his
lectures at St. Paul's to advance an orthodox interpretation of the
patristic sources for the Arian controversy in the early Church.[57]
Joseph Trapp attacked the notion that "the Word *God* in these sacred
Writings denotes . . . but *Office* only, *Dominion*, or *Authority*," in the
process taking up one of Waterland's cudgels against Clarke and also
reflecting critically on the language used by Newton in the "General
Scholium" to the second edition of the *Principia* (1713). Trapp
revealed himself to be a subtle reader of Newton, alert to the chance
to turn a nuanced argument on its head. In the "General Scholium,"
Newton had suggested that God "rules all things, not as the world

soul but as the lord of all. And because of his dominion he is called Lord God *Pantokrator*." Some modern critics have seen in this passage evidence of Newton's exclusive view of the deity of God the Father and therefore covert signs of his Arian Christology. It seems likely that Trapp would have agreed with them, since he developed his own argument to suggest that the word *Pantokrator* had to be read in the context of Isaiah 43:10–44:6 and was properly an explicit reference to the power of "*governing, containing, supporting,* and *upholding* all things" exercised by Christ, rather than by God the Father.[58]

Waterland's protégés were not the only churchmen to criticize Newton's posthumously published theological works. Thus, both Samuel Shuckford and William Warburton (later Bishop of Gloucester) attacked Newton's *Chronology* and his attitude to ancient Egyptian history.[59] George Berkeley, newly appointed as Bishop of Cloyne, engaged in controversy over the metaphysical implications of Newton's mathematics. He found it necessary to deny that he wrote out of annoyance that "Sir *Isaac Newton* had presumed to interpose in Prophecies and Revelations, and to decide in religious affairs." Nevertheless, he asserted that "there are too many that deride Mysteries, and yet admire Fluxions; who yield that Faith to a mere Mortal, which they deny to *Jesus Christ,* whose Religion they make it their Study and Busines to discredit."[60] Although some authors defended Newton's writings in the course of the eighteenth century, they tended to be drawn either from the ranks of dissent, or from a noisy but embattled group of churchmen who were sympathetic to Newton's Arianism. The former group included some of those who had first welcomed Newton's *Chronology* and disseminated it, notably Philip Doddridge, who has been identified as the likely author of the summary of its conclusions in the journal *The Present State of the Republic of Letters.*[61] The latter included writers like Arthur Ashley Sykes, who had initially been a disciple of Samuel Clarke and who was much respected by later Unitarians, or the renegade Bishop of Clogher, Robert Clayton.[62] Although Sykes was able to gain access to Newton's unpublished papers through the patronage of the Conduitt family, he appears not to have consulted them until the autumn of 1755, shortly before his own death.[63] Edward Gibbon (1737–94) recalled his teenage study of Newton's *Chronology* as part of the retrospective account of his disillusionment with English theology and education that had set in prior to his brief conversion to Catholicism in 1753. Newton's ideas, and the quarrels they engendered, continued to play a role in Gibbon's thought as a mature historian, and Unitarian friends kept him abreast of what they knew about Newton's unpublished works.[64]

Thomas Secker (1693–1768), who had been brought up as a dissenter, embodied energetic and reforming churchmanship in his service as a bishop and, from 1758, as Archbishop of Canterbury. In 1767, he remarked:

> I do not see, what speculations can be built on the Doctrine of a vacuum to hurt the Doctrine of the Trinity; or that there is any Connexion between Newtonianism & Arianism. It is very unhappy that Newton chanced to be an Arian; for that hath tempted many Admirers of his Mathematics & Physicks to be so likewise. But he did not learn his System of Christianity from his System of Philosophy: nor was he the same great man in the Interpretation of Scripture as of Nature . . .[65]

During the whole of the eighteenth century, Newton's *Chronology* and *Observations* were not reprinted separately after their original publication. When the unsold sheets of the first edition of the *Chronology* were reissued in 1770, a letter was appended to them that had been written in 1754 by Zachary Pearce to Thomas Hunt, Regius Professor of Hebrew at Oxford and a friend of Arthur Bedford. This contained an account of Newton's revision of the *Chronology* in the weeks before his death, which made it clear that sections of the published *Chronology* had never been properly corrected, and that some of the problems which later authors had exposed were a product of confusion on the part of its editors.[66] Hunt himself may well have been responsible for introducing Benjamin Kennicott to Newton's work.

Kennicott, in turn, used knowledge of some of Newton's manuscripts (perhaps consulted among the papers of Jeffrey Ekins, Dean of Carlisle, who had obtained those borrowed by Sykes) in defense of his own project of the collation of variants in the text of the Hebrew Bible, calling on Newton's reputation to support the idea that the existing version might require scholarly correction.[67]

That Newton's reputation as an author who favored Christian belief grew during the eighteenth century depended largely on three things. The first was the steadfast maintenance of the story of Newton's own simple piety by friends like William Stukeley. This concealed the fact that Newton was only an occasional conformist for whom attendance at the worship of the Church of England was made considerably easier during his later years by life in Samuel Clarke's parish, where accommodations in the public liturgy could be made to ease his tender conscience.[68] Secondly, the general reception of Newton's natural philosophy, as presented by Richard Bentley's Boyle lectures, by Newton's own "General Scholium" to the *Principia*, and by the published correspondence of Leibniz and Clarke, was that it tended to promote Christianity and support the Church. This was perhaps more a reflection of a belief among Low Church divines that natural philosophy itself might be conducive to religion, and of the popularity of Locke's epistemology, rather than a wholesale endorsement of Newtonianism, but nevertheless it had powerful effects.[69] It was also the manner in which the cautious Newton had intended to present his system, apparently shorn of most of its clandestine heterodoxy. Even so, its appearance required the prompting of Bentley in 1692 and the careful direction given to the reader by Roger Cotes's preface to the *Principia* in 1713. Nor were the works in question, particularly the "General Scholium," in fact completely free of theological controversy.[70] Finally, there was the revival in eschatological prophecy in the last two decades of the eighteenth century, in whose vanguard came Unitarian readers of Newton's theology such as Joseph Priestley. This also paved the way for the widespread interest in Newton's *Observations* among nonconformists in the nineteenth century.[71]

This movement, however, returned Newton's theological works to controversy rather than saving them from it. Thus, Samuel Horsley, the High Church editor of Newton's *Opera Omnia* (1779–85), which reprinted the *Chronology* and the *Observations* and provided the first reliable edition (from the papers of Ekins) of Newton's letters on the corruption of scripture, took Priestley to task: "It is probable too, that after the pains which I have taken to examine the writings and authorities on which [Newton's] ancient chronology was founded, I am as well qualified, as Dr. Priestley, to judge of his talents in . . . subjects, which are not capable of demonstration. Now in these, I scruple not to say . . . that the great Newton went out like a Common Man."[72] For Horsley, as for many other orthodox divines, the printing of Newton's theological works was a way to reveal their inadequacy and thus to snatch away a weapon from anti-Trinitarian critics of the Church. While his unpublished notes on Newton's *Chronology* show respect for some of the corrections to historical dating that were made there, Horsley rejected Newton's fundamental reordering of Egyptian regnal dates and attacked his tendency to credit tendentious opinions without mention of more orthodox alternatives: "for the sake of doing credit to the Arian Doctrine by representing it as the oldest Christianity."[73] Some clerical authors felt it was acceptable to praise the style of Newton's interpretation of prophecy, but few argued for the validity of the resulting chronology. George Bingham, rector of Pimperne, Dorset, for example, who was sympathetic to the premillenarian interpretation of prophecy set out by Newton, nevertheless suggested that "Sir Isaac Newton has many notions which even his authority can never recommend" and repeated the view that "this great man confounds distinct periods, & died before he had revised his work."[74]

It was therefore unnecessary for eighteenth-century critics of Newton's theology to take refuge in the natural philosophy and scriptural exegesis of John Hutchinson, whose tenets seemed laughable to those, like Arthur Bedford, who had a competent knowledge of Hebrew. The Hutchinsonians, in any case, were more concerned with overthrowing Newton's natural philosophy than with bothering about his divinity and their arguments in favor of the Trinity were often less than incisive.[75] Nevertheless, the defense of the Trinity was essential to their arguments, which worried about "the sources of that strange indifferency & Laodicean lukewarmness with regard to the Divinity of our Redeemer, which threatens to destroy the western, as it did the eastern churches."[76] For many of Newton's readers, however, the principal attraction of his writings both in natural philosophy and theology lay in their anti-Trinitarianism. These included several leading figures in the Church of England, notably Edmund Law, Bishop of Carlisle, who themselves had doubts about the doctrine of the Trinity and for whom Newton's letters on "Two Notable Corruptions of Scripture," eventually published in 1754, proved irresistible ammunition in the campaign to institute a fresh translation of the Bible as part of the doctrinal improvement of the Church.[77]

Yet neither Newton nor Clarke ever risked their careers for such a reformation of the Church. According to Whiston, who was himself less cautious, the reason for this was that they believed that the prophecy of Daniel's seventy weeks remained unfulfilled:

> However, it is not impossible that such a Notion of a long future
> corrupt State of the Church soon coming on, according to the
> Scripture Prophecies, might be one Discouragement to Sir *Isaac*
> *Newton*'s and Dr. *Clarke*'s making publick Attempts for the
> Restoration of Primitive Christianity: as I confess my Expectation
> of the near approach of the Conclusion of the corrupt State,
> and by Consequence of the Commencement of the State when
> Primitive Christianity is, by those Prophecies, to be restored,
> greatly encourages me to labour for its Restoration.[78]

The reticence that led Newton to keep secret his views about the doctrine of the Trinity indeed did not derive principally from anxiety concerning publication of his ideas about the two notable corruptions of scripture. Other more orthodox critics also doubted the authenticity of the verses examined by Newton. Thus John Mill, to whose massive attempt to gather up variant readings of the text of the New Testament Newton had himself contributed during the 1690s, noted the paucity of authentic manuscript witnesses to I John 5:7 and rehearsed more briefly the problems associated with I Timothy 3:16.[79]

Richard Bentley, who perhaps knew of Newton's discussion of
I John 5:7, also questioned the authenticity of the received reading
of that verse without casting doubt on the doctrine of the Trinity
that it underpinned: "Arianism in its height was beat down without the help of that verse: and, let the *fact* prove as it will, the *doctrine* [of the Trinity] is unshaken."[80] Newton's concerns arose from
the fact that for him the corruption of the text of the Bible was one
aspect of a much broader perversion of the Christian religion, perpe-
trated by Athanasius and his followers in the fourth century. They
had spread calumnies against other theologians, notably Arius;
fomented sedition, and distorted the true meaning of the Nicene
Creed: "this Council [Nice] allowed the interpretation of homousios
by similitude & the fathers by way of caution exprest this interpretation in their subscriptions yet by the clamours of Athanasius & his
party it is since grown ye semiarrian heresy for any man to make this
interpretation. Whether Athanasius therefore & his friends have not
done violence to this Council I leave to be considered."[81] The false
religion and idolatry introduced during the fourth century had been
perpetuated by the Catholic Church and survived even in the reformed
Church of England of Newton's day. The Reformation had swept away
many of the aspects of Catholic religion that Newton most distrusted.
These included the invocation of saints and the institution of monasticism, which seemed to him to have fostered many of the errors of
the Church. But the critical elements of Athanasian corruption, in
particular the failure to acknowledge the full extent of God's dominion by attributing divinity to Christ and the Holy Ghost, persisted
in the Church of England. The exercise of political power by the priest-
hood, which Newton argued had helped to corrupt the early Church,
was also one of the distinguishing characteristics of the contemporary English Church.[82] Yet, despite the need for further reformation,
Newton believed that the lives of the faithful had to be governed by
the times of prophecy, not by personal whim. This may explain why
he waited for signs that the prophecy of the seventy weeks was being
fulfilled before taking action that might undermine lawful authority.[83]

Through his belief that he belonged to a remnant singled out to preserve the truth about the Church and his distrust of sacerdotal power, Newton revived concerns that were expressed earlier in the seventeenth century by numerous Independent divines, especially in the tumultuous years of the 1640s and 1650s. His suspicion of set forms in religion and his reluctance to subscribe to any of the accepted creeds of the Church are again reminiscent of the writing of that time, as are his convictions that the primitive Church had not practiced infant baptism and had worshipped God on a Saturday sabbath.[84] Like many writers of the mid seventeenth century, Newton approached issues of ecclesiastical and doctrinal history through the prism of a strict biblical literalism. One aspect of this attitude to the Bible was that the text of scripture both confirmed and interpreted itself.[85] These hermeneutical principles were borne out in the synchronism of the prophecies of Daniel and the Apocalypse which Newton proposed. They also helped to cast doubt on the authenticity of the doctrine of the Trinity, which depended for its scriptural authority largely on two verses, I John 5:7 and I Timothy 3:16.

For Newton, the notion of the divine Trinity represented the culmination of the human tendency to corrupt religion into idolatry. The survival of the true Church depended on the correct understanding of God, who ruled through his servants with undivided dominion over the created world, and its manifestation in an appropriate form of worship.[86] Much of Newton's unpublished theological scholarship was devoted to elucidating the history of that Church, from its reestablishment by Noah to its most recent corruption by Athanasius and his papal successors.[87] Traces of his conclusions about the pure, primitive religion of Noah can also be found in the published and unpublished queries to the *Opticks*.[88] It is possible that Newton derived some of his ideas about the corruption of scripture and the true nature of God from reading contemporary heterodox writings, in particular those of Socinian authors, yet it is equally likely that he reached his conclusions largely by himself, through the application of a sharp mind, intolerant of ambiguity, to the complexities of the Bible.

He was certainly unwilling to accept anyone as his master in the study of scripture and was thus representative of the most defiantly independent tradition of nonconformist biblical scholarship.[89] Newton's belief that the Christian religion consisted in a few fundamental truths (the worship of God and love of one's neighbor) found expression in his distrust of creeds that seemed to impose more than these essentials on the believer.[90] His concern to avoid excessive prescription in matters of faith may have been a reflection on his first experiences at Trinity College, Cambridge, where, within little more than a year of his arrival as an undergraduate, he would have witnessed bitter argument over the liturgy to be used in chapel and the expulsion of one fellow, the natural philosopher John Ray, for refusing to take the oaths under the Act of Uniformity in 1662.[91] Perhaps it was also a consequence of these events that Newton wanted to confine suffering for his faith to the private experience of his closet, even though his personal beliefs were quite different from those of ordinary members of the Church to which he nominally belonged.

Yet the burden of the prophecy of the seventy weeks might have forced Newton to intervene publicly in debate about the doctrines of the Church at two moments, in 1687–91 and in 1709–13. These were both times of tribulation for God's people when it seemed that the captivity of the Church might begin again.[92] In 1687, Newton broke cover to defend the legality of the University of Cambridge's refusal to admit the Benedictine monk, Alban Francis, to an MA without taking the oaths. This was Newton's first public act of defiance to the regime of James II and its policy of advancing the rights of Catholics. Following James's deposition in 1688, Newton took up a university seat in the Convention Parliament, which considered not only the succession but the right of the Church of England to persecute dissenters. Less than nine months after the dissolution of the Convention, when fears were already mounting about the religious and theological disorder that might result from the Toleration Act that it had passed, Newton sent the first of his letters to Locke about two notable corruptions of scripture, I John 5:7 and I Timothy 3:16.

For a brief few months, Newton dared to think of allowing Locke's friend, Jean Le Clerc, to publish a Latin or French translation of the work, before retreating under the mounting anxieties of the time.[93]

Le Clerc's copy of Newton's work, written in Locke's hand, was never returned. Le Clerc cited it anonymously in his contribution to Ludolf Küster's edition of Mill's work on the Greek New Testament, published at Rotterdam in 1710. Versions of it also circulated after Le Clerc's death in 1736, by which time the manuscript was incomplete.[94] One of these later became the basis for the first, inaccurate publication of the letters in 1754.[95] By then, reference to Newton's conclusions had been incorporated into John James Wettstein's great critical edition of the Greek New Testament, published between 1751 and 1752. This work was notable for its judgments about many of the manuscripts whose authority had been cited by earlier critics for establishing the text of the New Testament. Wettstein obtained information from a number of English informants, including those with Arian leanings, such as John Jackson of Leicester.[96] His distant cousin, Caspar Wettstein, who was librarian to the Princess of Wales, assisted in the search for manuscripts and spent some of his time trying to ferret out a complete text of Newton's letters on the corruption of Scripture, which for over a decade he had known might be found in the possession of the Conduitt family.[97] Although the efforts of the Wettsteins may have been linked to Catherine Conduitt's decision to approach Sykes to edit some of Newton's unpublished papers, they did not succeed in making public a complete version of the "Two Notable Corruptions of Scripture."

Overt critics of Newton's work were also alert to the possibilities provided by Le Clerc's copy in Amsterdam and their actions may have influenced the fate of plans for the publication of the letters. Thus John Berriman, brother of William, on hearing of the manuscript from a merchant in London in 1738, procured a copy of part of Newton's text via an intermediary in Amsterdam, from which he took a second copy that he deposited in the library at Sion College, London. The information that he gathered in this way was used to identify Newton's authorship of certain arguments more precisely and deployed in further attacks on his scholarship, in particular on his reliance on inaccurate Latin translations of Greek sources.[98]

There had also been a second occasion when Newton had considered publishing his letters to Locke. In around 1709, he commissioned Hopton Haynes, an employee at the Mint who shared his anti-Trinitarian sentiments, to translate what he had written about 1 John 5:7 into Latin. The manuscript title-page of this work bore the putative imprint "Amsterdam. 1709."[99] The years around the end of the first decade of the eighteenth century were difficult ones for Newton and his closest disciples. After the Tory election victory of 1710, the liberties that had been won for religious dissenters in 1689 seemed to be under increasing threat. Moreover, from 1708 Whiston began to draw attention to himself as a critic of the orthodox doctrine of the Trinity and a proponent of further reformation in the Church.[100] Whiston attempted to involve both Samuel Clarke and Newton in the debate that he conducted with Archbishops Tenison and Sharp and Bishop Lloyd during 1708 and 1709.[101] It seems likely that this exchange prompted Newton to reconsider the publication of his letters on the scriptural authority for the doctrine of the Trinity. Haynes later remarked of his translation that "I know Sr Isaac intended them for the Press, and only waited for a good opportunity,"[102] yet Newton hesitated. Both Whiston and Clarke knew of Newton's attack on the authenticity of 1 John 5:7 by 1719.[103] But although Whiston had obtained a copy of the letters by 1738, it seems unlikely that he had extensive physical evidence of Newton's beliefs during his mentor's lifetime.[104] John Berriman claimed that Whiston had told him that Haynes's translations would have been printed "if he had not blabb'd it out, [that Sir] Isaac was [the] Author of [them]."[105] Newton may have revealed hints of his heterodox ideas about God in the "General Scholium" that he added to the second edition of the *Principia* in 1713, in the process supporting Clarke's arguments, published in *The Scripture-Doctrine of the Trinity* during the preceding year.[106] Controversial though Newton's published views were, they stopped short of spelling out the implications for the Church of his beliefs about the nature of God.[107]

Newton therefore chose to keep his own counsel about the past and future of true religion, despite the dangers that confronted his friends and the threat of a return to the persecution of dissent. Curiously, the exposure of his genuine opinions was thus left largely to the divines of the eighteenth-century Church of England. Their rhetorical and intellectual triumph over the arguments favorable to Arianism in Newton's published works effectively consigned his treatment of the historical development of the doctrine of the Trinity to the margins of debate, where they have remained until very recently. They helped to ensure, as a consequence, that Newton's reputation as a theologian depended on the usefulness of his ideas for natural theology, rather than on his considerable skills as a textual critic.

NOTES

1 Daniel Waterland to Zachary Grey, c. 1735, British Library (hereafter BL), Ms. Add. 6396, fol. 14r.

2 See Richard S. Westfall, *Never at Rest* (Cambridge: Cambridge University Press, 1980), pp. 815–20, 872–3; Jewish National and University Library, Jerusalem, Ms. Yahuda Var. 1/ (Yahuda Ms.) 7.2b, fols. 1–9 and 7.2j, fols. 1–139; Yahuda Mss. 7.1, 7.2, and parts of 7.3 contain drafts which relate to the preparation of the book, see also Cambridge University Library (CUL), Ms. Add. 3989 (3); some surviving proof sheets can be found in the Hampshire County Record Office, Winchester, Ms. NC 10.

3 Westfall, *Never at Rest*, p. 817.

4 William Whiston, *Memoirs of the Life and Writings of Mr. William Whiston*, 2 vols. (London, 1749), vol. 1, p. 227; Eamon Duffy, "Whiston's Affair: The Trials of a Primitive Christian 1709–1714," *Journal of Ecclesiastical History* 27 (1976): 129–50.

5 Whiston, *Memoirs*, vol. 1, pp. 35, 362, 484; James E. Force, *William Whiston. Honest Newtonian* (Cambridge: Cambridge University Press, 1985), p. 99; cf. [Peter King], *An Enquiry into the Constitution, Discipline, Unity and Worship of the Primitive Church* (London: 1691), and King, *The History of the Apostles Creed* (London: 1702).

6 [Daniel Mace], *The New Testament in Greek and English*, 2 vols. (London: 1729), vol. 1, pp. iii–vii; vol. 2, pp. 772–3, 917, 921–35.

7 E. S. de Beer (ed.), *The Correspondence of John Locke*, 8 vols. (Oxford: Oxford University Press, 1976–89), vol. 8, pp. 412–17, 419–27 (quotation at p. 415); John Harrison and Peter Laslett, *The Library of John Locke* (Oxford: Clarendon Press, 1965), pp. 54–6; Maurice Cranston, *John Locke* (Oxford: Oxford Paperbacks, 1985), pp. 438–9, 449–82.

8 De Beer (ed.), *Correspondence of Locke*, vol. 8, pp. 404–6; John Locke, *A Paraphrase and Notes on the Epistles of St Paul*, ed. Arthur W. Wainwright, 2 vols. (Oxford: Clarendon Press, 1987), vol. 1, pp. 6–11; John Marshall, *John Locke* (Cambridge: Cambridge University Press, 1994), pp. 390–2.

9 De Beer (ed.), *Correspondence of Locke*, vol. 7, p. 773. For exchanges of information on the prophecies of Daniel and Revelation between Newton and Locke, see Bodleian Library, Oxford, Ms. Locke c. 27, fol. 88; Ms. Locke fol. 32, fol. 143v; *The Holy Bible* (London, 1648) [Bodleian Library, Locke 16.25], pp. 859, 866; *The Holy Bible* (London, 1654) [Locke 10.59–60], vol. 2, fifth interleaved page.

10 See de Beer (ed.), *Correspondence of Locke*, vol. 6, p. 522.

11 Peter, seventh Lord King (ed.), *The Life of John Locke* (London, 1829), pp. 215–33.

12 New College, Oxford, Ms. 361.4, fols. 2–41; printed in H. W. Turnbull et al. (eds.), *The Correspondence of Isaac Newton*, 7 vols. (Cambridge: Cambridge University Press, 1959–77), vol. 3, pp. 83–122; Newton had attempted to reclaim these papers as early as 26 January 1692, see Turnbull (ed.), *Correspondence*, vol. 3, pp. 192–3.

13 John Nichols, *Illustrations of the Literary History of the Eighteenth Century*, 8 vols. (London: 1817–58), vol. 4, pp. 33–4.

14 William Stukeley, *Memoirs of Sir Isaac Newton's Life*, ed. A. Hastings White (London: Taylor and Francis, 1936), p. 78; Library of Freemasons' Hall, London, Ms. 1130, p. 5.

15 For example, William Whiston, *A New Theory of the Earth* (London, 1696) or various comments by Nicolas Fatio de Duillier, in Bibliothèque Publique et Universitaire, Geneva (BPU), Mss. Français 602, fol. 85r; 605, fol. 12r.

16 See W. C. Lukis (ed.), *The Family Memoirs of the Rev. William Stukeley*, 3 vols. (Durham: Surtees Society, 1880–7), vol. 1, p. 78. Cf. Freemason's Hall, Ms. 1130, pp. 73–120; Isaac Newton, *The Chronology of Ancient*

Kingdoms Amended (London, 1728), pp. 332–47; Yahuda Ms. 14; San Marino, Huntington Library, Babson Newton Ms. 434; Matt Goldish, *Judaism in the Theology of Isaac Newton* (Dordrecht: Springer, 1998), pp. 85–107.

17 Lukis (ed.), *Family Memoirs*, vol. 2, pp. 262–3; for Whiston's reaction, see Frank E. Manuel, *Isaac Newton. Historian* (Cambridge, MA: Harvard University Press, 1963), pp. 171–7, and Whiston to Fatio, December 5, 1734, BPU, Ms. Français 601, fols. 270–1.

18 Lukis (ed.), *Family Memoirs*, vol. 1, pp. 424–5.

19 Wiltshire Record Office, Trowbridge, Ms. 1178/631. On Bedford, see Jonathan Barry (ed.), "The Society for the Reformation of Manners 1700–5," in Barry and Kenneth Morgan (eds.), *Reformation and Revival in Eighteenth-Century Bristol* (Bristol: Bristol Record Society's Publications, 1994), vol. 44, pp. 1–62; William Weber, *The Rise of Musical Classics in Eighteenth-Century England* (Oxford: Oxford University Press, 1992), pp. 47–56.

20 C. E. Doble *et al.* (eds.), *Remarks and Collections of Thomas Hearne*, 11 vols. (Oxford: Clarendon Press, 1885–1921), vol. 10, p. 7; Jed Z. Buchwald and Mordechai Feingold, *Newton and the Origin of Civilization* (Princeton, NJ: Princeton University Press, 2013), pp. 381–4.

21 Archives of the Society for Promoting Christian Knowledge (formerly held by the Society in London, recently deposited in CUL), Minute Book 12 (1726–8), p. 106; Abstract Letter Book 14 (1727–9), letters 9271 and 9288. Cf. Arthur Bedford, *The Scripture Chronology demonstrated by Astronomical Calculations* (London, 1730). The subscribers to this work included the President of the Royal Society, two Bishops, and more than forty clergymen, several of whom also became prominent critics of Newton.

22 Doble *et al.* (eds.), *Remarks and Collections of Thomas Hearne*, vol. 10, p. 305.

23 Arthur Bedford, *Animadversions upon Sir Isaac Newton's Book, Intitled the Chronology of Ancient Kingdoms Amended* (London, 1728), p. 5; see also Bedford, *The Scripture Chronology demonstrated*, pp. v–vi. Cf. James Ussher, *Annales Veteris Testamenti* (London, 1650); the chronological information which had been provided in large format English Bibles since an edition published by Lloyd at Oxford in 1701; Benjamin Marshall, *Chronological Tables*, 2 parts (Oxford, 1712–13), which were based on more detailed work by Lloyd; Richard Cumberland,

Sanchoniatho's Phoenician History, ed. S. Payne (London, 1720); William Beveridge, *Institutionum chronologicarum libri II*, 2nd edition (London, 1705). Newton's copies of these works, with the exception of Marshall, survive in the library of Trinity College, Cambridge, shelfmarks Tr/NQ.10.1; Tr/NQ.9.16; Tr/NQ.8.96; see John Harrison, *The Library of Isaac Newton* (Cambridge: Cambridge University Press, 1978). Cf. Marshall, *A Chronological Treatise upon the Seventy Weeks of Daniel* (London: 1725), which is highly critical of Newton's preferred source, Sir John Marsham, *Canon chronicus Ægyptiacus, Ebraicus, Graecus, et disquisitiones* (Leipzig, 1676).

24 Bedford, *Animadversions*, p. 143.

25 Manuel, *Isaac Newton: Historian*, pp. 171–7.

26 See Samuel Clarke, *The Scripture-Doctrine of the Trinity* (London, 1712); William Whiston, *Primitive Christianity Reviv'd* (London, 1712); Eamon Duffy, "Primitive Christianity Revived: Religious Renewal in Augustan England," *Studies in Church History* 14 (1977), 287–300.

27 Robert Wodrow, *Analecta*, ed. Matthew Leishman, 4 vols. (Glasgow, 1842–3), vol. 1, p. 325.

28 Wodrow, *Analecta*, ed. Leishman, vol. 3, pp. 205–6, 461–2; vol. 4, p. 59. For contemporary Scottish interest in Newton's religious beliefs, see also National Library of Scotland, Edinburgh, Ms. Wodrow Letters Quarto XXI, fols. 75r–77v (Andrew Grey to Wodrow, March 20, 1725); Stella Mills (ed.), *The Collected Letters of Colin MacLaurin* (Nantwich: Shiva Publications Ltd, 1982), pp. 179–80 (Robert Simson to MacLaurin, November 6, 1727).

29 William Whiston, *Historical Memoirs of the Life of Dr. Samuel Clarke* (London, 1730), pp. 156–7; cf. Newton, *Observations*, pp. 128–43. For the more orthodox interpretation, that the prophecy was completely fulfilled at the death of Christ, see Humphrey Prideaux, *The Old and New Testament Connected in the History of the Jews and Neighbouring Nations*, 2 parts (London, 1726–8), part 1, pp. 262–4; H. H. Rowley, *Darius the Mede and the Four World Empires in the Book of Daniel* (Cardiff: University of Wales Press Board, 1935), p. 135.

30 King's College, Cambridge, Keynes Ms. 132, fol. 2r (Craig to John Conduitt, April 7, 1727).

31 Joseph Spence, *Observations, Anecdotes, and Characters of Books and Men*, ed. James M. Osborn, 2 vols. (Oxford: Oxford University Press, 1966), vol. 1, p. 464; for Ramsay's views, see Bibliothèque Méjanes,

Aix-en-Provence, Ms. 1188, pp. 8–9, 33–9, 81–104; cf. G. D. Henderson, *Chevalier Ramsay* (Edinburgh: Thomas Nelson, 1952) and D. P. Walker, *The Ancient Theology* (London: 1972), pp. 231–63; Fatio's views on the Trinity may be found in BPU, Ms. Français 602, fol. 24r.

32 Voltaire, *Letters concerning the English Nation* (London, 1733), p. 48; Jean-François Baillon, "La reformation permanente: les Newtoniens et le dogme trinitaire," in Maria-Cristina Pitassi (ed.), *Le Christ entre orthodoxie et Lumières* (Geneva: Droz, 1994), pp. 123–37.

33 Edmund Gibson, *The Bishop of London's Three Pastoral Letters* (London: 1732), pp. 22–61.

34 [Zachary Pearce], *A Reply to the Letter to Dr. Waterland* (London, 1731), pp. 42–50, citing Newton, *Chronology*, pp. 186, 197 especially; cf. [Conyers Middleton], *A Letter to Dr. Waterland* (London, 1731), pp. 21–35. See also Pearce, *A Sermon Preached at the New Parish Church of St. Martin in the Fields* (London, 1727), which urged Newton to publish his revisions to ancient chronology in full.

35 The quotation comes from one of Waterland's annotations in his copy of [Middleton], *A Letter* [Bodleian Library, Oxford: Rawl. 8° 437, p. 27]; for Marsham, see note 23 above; cf. John Spencer, *De legibus Hebraeorum ritualibus et earum rationibus, libri III* (Cambridge, 1683–5) [Newton's copy is Tr/NQ.17.18].

36 Edward Churton (ed.), *Supplement to Waterland's Works. Fourteen Letters from Daniel Waterland to Zachary Pearce* (Oxford, 1868), p. 7.

37 [Conyers Middleton], *A Defence of the Letter to Dr. Waterland* (London, 1732), p. 70; cf. [Conyers Middleton], *Some Remarks on a Reply to the Defence of the Letter to Dr. Waterland* (London, 1732), p. 7.

38 [Daniel Waterland], *Scripture Vindicated*, 3 parts (London, 1730–3), p. xii; cf. Matthew Tindal, *Christianity as Old as the Creation* (London, 1730).

39 [Waterland], *Scripture Vindicated*, p. xii.

40 Tindal, *Christianity as Old as the Creation*, pp. 352–432, for example, is structured around a discussion of passages from Clarke's writings.

41 Daniel Waterland, *The Case of Arian-Subscription Considered* (Cambridge, 1721); BL, Ms. Add. 5831, fols. 173r–174r.

42 Waterland to Grey, 5 February 1735, BL, Ms. Add. 5831, fols. 172r–3r.

43 B. W. Young, *Religion and Enlightenment in Eighteenth-Century England. Theological Debate from Locke to Burke* (Oxford: 1998), pp. 37–8.

44 BL, Ms. Add. 6396, fols. 7–9, 14r; cf. Ms. Add. 5831, fols. 173r, 182r–3r; Zachary Grey, *An Impartial Examination of the Second Volume of Mr. Daniel Neal's History of the Puritans* (London, 1736); Grey, *The Spirit of Infidelity, Detected*, 2nd edition (London, 1735).

45 Zachary Grey, *An Examination of the Fourteenth Chapter of Sir Isaac Newton's Observations upon the Prophecies of Daniel* (London, 1736) [CUL, 7100 d.46, is Grey's own copy with his additions interleaved]. Many of Newton's unpublished theological manuscripts relate to these issues, most importantly: Keynes Ms. 5 and 10; Yahuda Mss. 1, 2, 8.2, 15; Fondation Martin Bodmer, Geneva, Ms. "Of the Church" (Bodmer Ms.); William Andrews Clark Memorial Library, Los Angeles, Ms. "Paradoxical Questions concerning yᵉ morals & actions of Athanasius & his followers" (Clark Ms.).

46 Grey, *Examination*, pp. 7–25, 35–58, 72–85, 103–17.

47 Arthur Young, *An Historical Dissertation on Idolatrous Corruptions in Religion*, 2 vols. (London, 1734), vol. 2, pp. 265–70, quotation at p. 269.

48 Young, *Dissertation*, vol. 2, p. 269; Grey, *Examination*, p. 3; cf. Symon Patrick, *A Commentary upon the Historical Books of the Old Testament*, 3rd edition, 2 vols. (London, 1727); Prideaux, *The Old and New Testament Connected*.

49 Young, *Dissertation*, vol. 2, p. 268; Grey, *Examination*, p. 1.

50 Grey, *Examination*, pp. 35, 56, 85, 109, 137, for example.

51 See Harrison, *Library of Isaac Newton*, pp. 128 (St. Cyril of Jerusalem), 153 (St. Gregory of Nazianzus).

52 Thus Newton's copy of Moses Maimonides, *De idololatria liber*, ed. Dionysius Vossius (Amsterdam, 1641) [Tr/NQ.8.46¹], at p. 168.

53 For example, Gerardus Joannes Vossius, *De theologia Gentili* (Amsterdam, 1641) [Tr/NQ.8.46²], in which Newton has frequently chosen to mark Vossius's Latin paraphrases rather than the original Greek.

54 Anthony Grafton, "The Humanist as Reader," in Guglielmo Cavallo and Roger Chartier (eds.), *A History of Reading in the West*, translated by Lydia G. Cochrane (Cambridge: Cambridge University Press, 1999), pp. 179–212.

55 Daniel Waterland, *Eight Sermons Preach'd at the Cathedral Church of St. Paul, in Defense of the Divinity of Our Lord Jesus Christ* (Cambridge, 1720); William van Mildert (ed.), *The Works of the Rev. Daniel Waterland, D.D.*, 10 vols. (Oxford, 1823-8), vol. 1, pp. 65–7, quotation at p. 65.

56 Henry Felton, *The Christian Faith Asserted against Deists, Arians, and Socinians* (Oxford, 1732), pp. ii, v–vi, lxxxvii. Others who explicitly

acknowledged Waterland's aid or example included William Berriman (1723–4) and Joseph Trapp (1729–30).

57 William Berriman, *An Historical Account of the Controversies that have been in the Church concerning the Doctrine of the Holy and Everblessed Trinity* (London, 1725); cf. [William Berriman], *A Seasonable Review of Mr. Whiston's Account of Primitive Doxologies* (London, 1719); Glocester Ridley, *The Good Christian Never Dies: A Sermon preached in the Parish Church of St. Andrew Undershaft, at the Funeral of William Berriman* (London, 1750). Berriman nevertheless shared Newton's belief that the triumphs of contemporary astronomy "great as they are, and prodigiously improved by an inimitable genius of our own nation" represented a revival of Pythagorean, Egyptian, and Patriarchal knowledge: see *Human Learning recommended from the Example of Moses* (London, 1727), p. 7.

58 Joseph Trapp, *The Doctrine of the Most Holy, and Ever-Blessed Trinity, Briefly Stated and Proved* (London, 1731), pp. 32–3; cf. Isaac Newton, *The Principia*, translated by I. Bernard Cohen and Anne Whitman assisted by Julia Budenz (Berkeley, CA: University of California Press, 1999), pp. 940–1. See also Stephen D. Snobelen, "'God of gods and Lord of lords': The Theology of Isaac Newton's General Scholium to the *Principia*," *Osiris*, 2nd series, 16 (2001), 169–208.

59 Samuel Shuckford, *The Sacred and Profane History of the World Connected*, 2nd edition, 3 vols. (London, 1731-40), vol. 2, pp. i–lv; William Warburton, *The Divine Legation of Moses*, 2 vols. (London, 1738–41), vol. 2, pp. 206–81; both works criticized Newton's *Chronology*. See also Buchwald and Feingold, *Newton and the Origin of Civilization*, pp. 384–6, 394–7.

60 [George Berkeley], *A Defence of Free-Thinking in Mathematics* (London, 1735), quotations from pp. 67 and 7.

61 See Buchwald and Feingold, *Newton and the Origin of Civilization*, pp. 386–7; cf. *The Present State of the Republic of Letters*, April 1728. This summary of Newton's *Chronology* was reprinted several times separately, in English and French, under the name of the journal's editor, the Scotsman Andrew Reid.

62 Arthur Ashley Sykes, *An Examination of Mr. Warburton's Account of the Conduct of the Antient Legislators* (London, 1744), pp. 222–364; John Disney, *Memoirs of the Life and Writings of Arthur Ashley Sykes* (London, 1785); Robert Clayton, *The Chronology of the Hebrew Bible Vindicated* (London, 1747); Nigel Aston, "The Limits of Latitudinarianism: English Reactions to Bishop Clayton's *An Essay on Spirit*," *Journal of Ecclesiastical History* 49 (1998), 407–33. Clayton

was not always positive about the conjectural nature of Newton's chronological arguments: see his *A Journal from Grand Cairo to Mount Sinai and Back Again* (London, 1753), pp. 53–4, 60–1, 74, 105.

63 New College, Oxford, Ms. 361.4, fol. 139.

64 Edward Gibbon, *Miscellaneous Works of Edward Gibbon, Esquire, with Memoirs of his Life and Writings composed by himself*, ed. John, Lord Sheffield, 2 vols. (London, 1796), vol. 1, pp. 31, 41, 74, 91–2; see also David Womersley, *Gibbon and the 'Watchmen of the Holy City'* (Oxford: Oxford Univeristy Press, 2002), pp. 100–46; J. G. A. Pocock, *Barbarism and Religion. Volume Five, Religion: The First Triumph* (Cambridge: Cambridge University Press, 2010), p. 362.

65 Pierpont Morgan Library, New York, Ms. Misc. Eng. Misc. Coleorton (B2 274B), Thomas Secker to [?] William Jones (January 6, 1767).

66 Newton, "An Account of what related to the Publishing of Sir Isaac Newton's Chronology of Antient Kingdoms, in 1728," in Newton, *The Chronology of Ancient Kingdoms Amended*, 2nd edition (London, 1770).

67 Benjamin Kennicott, *The Ten Annual Accounts of the Collation of Hebrew Mss. of the Old Testament* (Oxford, 1770), p. 57; on the history of Newton's papers, see also New College, Oxford, Ms. 361.4, fols. 141–51, 157–81.

68 See Stukeley, *Memoirs*, ed. Hastings White, pp. 69–71; Whiston, *Historical Memoirs*, pp. 98–9; Stephen D. Snobelen, "Isaac Newton, heretic: the strategies of a Nicodemite," *British Journal for the History of Science* 32 (1999), 381–419, esp. 396–412.

69 See John Gascoigne, *Cambridge in the Age of the Enlightenment* (Cambridge: Cambridge University Press, 1989); [Daniel Waterland], *Advice to a Young Student* (London, 1730), pp. 22–8.

70 Turnbull *et al.* (eds.), *Correspondence*, vol. 3, pp. 233–40; Larry Stewart, "Seeing through the Scholium: Religion and Reading Newton in the Eighteenth Century," *History of Science* 34 (1996), 123–65.

71 See Clarke Garrett, *Respectable Folly* (Baltimore, MD: Johns Hopkins University Press, 1975); John Arthur Oddy, "Eschatological Prophecy in the English Theological Tradition c. 1700–c. 1840," unpublished Ph.D. thesis, University of London, 1982; David S. Katz and Richard H. Popkin, *Messianic Revolution: Radical Religious Politics to the End of the Second Millennium* (London: Hill and Wang, 1999), pp. 107–204.

72 [Samuel Horsley], *Remarks upon Dr. Priestley's Second Letters to the Archdeacon of St. Alban's* (London, 1786), p. 20; cf. F. C. Mather, *High Church Prophet* (Oxford: Clarendon Press, 1992), pp. 45–8, 55–60.

73 Royal Society, London, Ms. 544, item 8, p. 4. Cf. Isaac Newton, *Opera Omnia*, ed. Samuel Horsley, 5 vols. (London, 1779–85), vol. 5, p. 3.

74 George Bingham, *Dissertations, Essays, and Sermons*, ed. Peregrine Bingham, 2 vols. (London, 1804), vol. 1, p. 267; [George Bingham], *A Dissertation on the Millennium* (London, 1772), manuscript additions by the author, facing p. 27 [library of All Souls College, Oxford, shelfmark X. 5. 18]; cf. the more extravagant praise of Newton's interpretation of the style of biblical prophecy in George Burton, *An Essay towards the Reconciling the Numbers of Daniel and St. John* (Norwich, 1766), which was devoted to proving the prophetic significance of the year 1764.

75 For example, George Horne, *A Fair, Candid, and Impartial State of the Case between Sir Isaac Newton and Mr. Hutchinson* (Oxford, 1753); Bristol Central Library, Ms. B 26063, correspondence of A. S. Catcott and John Hutchinson, letter 2; cf. Wiltshire Record Office, Ms. 1178/631.

76 George Horne to Deodotus Bye, 19 March 1756 (lot 277, Bloomsburg Auctions, 23 April 2009).

77 See Law's annotations interleaved in a copy of the Geneva Bible (London, 1606) [BL, C.45.g.13], especially vol. 3, facing sig. Mmm5v; Young, *Religion and Enlightenment*, pp. 45–119.

78 Whiston, *Historical Memoirs*, p. 157.

79 John Mill (ed.), *Novum Testamentum cum lectionibus variantibus* (Oxford, 1707), pp. 624, 738–49; Turnbull *et al.* (eds.), *Correspondence*, vol. 3, pp. 289–90, 303–4, 305–8 (Newton's "Specilegia Variantium lectionum in Apocalypsi," whose whereabouts are described as unknown [p. 308], may be found at The Queen's College, Oxford, Ms. 326, fols. 2r–4v).

80 *The Correspondence of Richard Bentley, D.D.*, ed. Christopher Wordsworth, 2 vols. (London, 1842), vol. 2, p. 530; cf. Whiston, *Historical Memoirs*, p. 101.

81 Clark Ms, fol. 73r and questions 1, 3, 9, 14, 15; cf. Keynes Ms. 10 and Yahuda Mss. 1.4, fols. 53–106; 1.5; 1.6; 15.1.

82 For these beliefs, see especially Bodmer Ms, fols. 36–40, 62–8, 98–102, 155–228, 260–367; cf. Yahuda Mss. 17.2, fols. 20v–21; 41, fol. 26.

83 Yahuda Ms. 1.1, fols. 1–3r.

84 Keynes Ms. 3, fols. 1–3; Yahuda Ms. 15.4; Bodmer Ms, fols. 36–40; Clark Ms, fol. 2r; cf. Bryan W. Ball, *The Seventh-Day Men* (Oxford: 1994); J. C. Davis, "Against Formality: One Aspect of the English Revolution," *Transactions of the Royal Historical Society*, 6th series, 3 (1993), 265–88.

85 Yahuda Ms. 1.1, fols. 12–18r.

86 Yahuda Mss. 14, fols. 25, 173; 15.5, fol. 90r; cf. Newton, *The Principia*, trans. Cohen, Whitman and Budenz, pp. 940–1.

87 Keynes Ms. 146, fols. 1–4; Yahuda Mss. 15.5; 15.7; 16; 17; 41; Bodmer Ms, chapter 1, fols. 5–30.

88 Isaac Newton, *Opticks*, 4th edition (London, 1730; reprinted New York, 1979), pp. 405–6; San Marino, Huntington Library, shelfmark Burndy 700873, p. 382.

89 Yahuda Ms. 1.1, fols. 1–10r; cf. Snobelen, "Isaac Newton, heretic," pp. 383–91, 406–7; Martin Mulsow, "Orientalistik im Kontext der sozinianischen und deistischen Debatten um 1700," *Scientia Poetica*, 2 (1998), pp. 27–57; Richard A. Muller, *Post-Reformation Reformed Dogmatics*, 2 vols. (Grand Rapids, 1985–93), vol. 2, pp. 465–543.

90 Keynes Ms. 3.

91 See James Fawket, *An Account of the late Reverend and Worthy Dr. George Seignior* (London, 1681), pp. 4–13; Charles E. Raven, *John Ray: Naturalist*, 2nd edition (Cambridge: Cambridge University Press, 1950), pp. 57–61; East Sussex Record Office, Lewes, Mss. Dan. 346–59.

92 Cf. Yahuda Ms. 10.2, esp. fol. 14v.

93 Jean Le Clerc, *Epistolario*, ed. Maria Grazia and Mario Sina, 4 vols. (Florence, 1987–97), vol. 2, pp. 50–2.

94 Leicestershire Record Office, Conant Mss, Barker correspondence, vol. 2, letter 123A (Samuel Crell to William Whiston, September 28, 1736); a copy made from Crell's copy of the manuscript survives at Bibliotheek der Rijksuniversiteit, Leiden, Ms. Semin. Remonstr. Bibl. 12.

95 *Two Letters of Sir Isaac Newton to Mr. Le Clerc* (London, 1754), pp. 13–14, recording that "the four first paragraphs of the Manuscript are lost."

96 On Wettstein, see C. L. Hulbert-Powell, *John James Wettstein 1693–1754* (London, [1938]); see also the references to Newton in Wettstein's edition of the Greek New Testament, 2 vols. (Amsterdam, 1751–2), vol. 1, p. 185; vol. 2, p. 335. For his contacts with Jackson and others, see Bibliotheek van de Universiteit, Amsterdam, Mss. A 158 and Q 97. Wettstein had preached Le Clerc's funeral sermon and his relative, James Wettstein, had overseen the sale of Le Clerc's books, see *Catalogus librorum . . . tum manuscriptorum. Doctissimi atque clarissimi viri Joannis Clerici* (Amsterdam, 1735). Wettstein may also have been responsible for placing Le Clerc's copy of Newton's letters to Locke in the library of the Remonstrant Seminary in Amsterdam, see Sir David Brewster, *Memoirs of the Life, Writings, and Discoveries of Sir Isaac Newton*, 2 vols. (Edinburgh, 1855), vol. 2, p. 338.

97 BL, Ms. Add. 32,415, fol. 388, Hopton Haynes to Rev. John Caspar Wettstein, 17 August 1736. Cf. Bibliotheek van de Universiteit, Amsterdam, Mss. A 168 (especially A 168(a), which mentions the search for a complete text of Newton's letters in March 1752), A 170, and J 97 (letters to J. J. Wettstein from England, 1748–52).

98 John Berriman, *A Critical Dissertation upon I Tim. iii. 16* (London, 1741). This book was the printed version of Berriman's Moyer lectures, delivered in 1737–8. A copy now in the British Library [shelfmark 1017 k. 17] has manuscript notes by Berriman, probably composed in 1761, which include the additional information about Newton's letters (at pp. 167–8). Berriman wrote up an account of his discovery in the transcription of Newton's "dissertation on I Tim. 3. 16" that he deposited at Sion College Library, London: Ms. ARC L 40.2/E 39, fol. 1r–v [now on deposit in Lambeth Palace Library]. He named the merchant as Peter Dobree and his intermediary as Rev. John Kippax. Elsewhere Berriman suggested that Wettstein had assisted Kippax while he was in Amsterdam: see his letters to J. J. Wettstein, March 26 and July 20, 1741, Öffentliche Bibliothek der Universität Basel, Ms. Mscr. Ki. Ar. 154, numbers 6–7. It may have been Daniel Waterland who communicated queries that were based on Berriman's work to another of his clients, John Mawer (see [Mawer], *Letters in Answer to Some Queries sent to the Author, concerning the Genuine Reading of the Greek Text, I Tim. iii. 16 . . . Now First Published on Occasion of Sir Isaac Newton's Two Letters to Mr. Le Clerc* [York, 1758]).

99 Yahuda Ms. 20.

100 BL, Ms. Add. 24,197; Gloucestershire Record Office, Lloyd-Baker Mss. [D 3549], box 74, bundle 9; Northamptonshire Record Office, Finch-Hatton Mss. 2623–5.

101 Whiston, *Historical Memoirs*, pp. 15–17.

102 BL, Ms. Add. 32, 415, fol. 388.

103 Whiston, *Historical Memoirs*, p. 100.

104 Whiston, *Memoirs*, vol. 1, p. 365; see also Isaac Newton, *Ecrits sur la religion*, ed. Jean-François Baillon (Paris, 1996), pp. 21–2.

105 Sion College Library, London, Ms. ARC L 40.2/E 39, fol. 1v.

106 Stewart, "Seeing through the Scholium."

107 See Newton, *The Principia*, translated by Cohen, Whitman, and Budenz, pp. 940–1.

15 Newton and the Leibniz–Clarke correspondence

Domenico Bertoloni Meli

INTRODUCTION

Between 1715 and 1716 Gottfried Wilhelm Leibniz and Samuel Clarke were engaged in a theological and philosophical dispute mediated by Caroline, Princess of Wales. Ten letters were exchanged, five on each side, before the controversy was brought to an end by Leibniz's death in November 1716. During the controversy those involved agreed to publish the texts, which were edited in 1717 by Clarke, who also translated Leibniz's letters into English. His *editio princeps* is considered to be both fair and excellent, and contains Leibniz's original French on facing pages, as well as a useful selection of additional explanatory materials. This extraordinarily influential controversy is among the most famous and heavily studied philosophical disputative texts of all times, and, in the words of a recent interpreter, its intellectual intricacies are reserved only for the very learned or the foolhardy.[1]

Despite the extent of interest and studies the correspondence has attracted,[2] however, we still lack a comprehensive critical edition taking into account all the relevant texts, including Caroline's and Clarke's. Interestingly, eighteenth-century editions did not include the private correspondence between Caroline and Leibniz, which was first made available in the nineteenth century, notably by Onno Klopp in the most complete form.[3] The private correspondence of the Princess of Wales was probably not available to Clarke and, even if it had been, publishing it at the time would have been highly

I wish to thank Daniel Garber, Andrew Janiak, Massimo Mugnai, and Richard Sorrenson for their help.

586

inappropriate. That correspondence, however, provides interesting perspectives on the exchange between Leibniz and Clarke. At times interpreters have assumed that Leibniz was writing to Clarke and Clarke to Leibniz, without taking sufficiently into account all levels of the exchange. Paying attention to Caroline's role and to the genre of the correspondence will help shed light on what was at stake.[4]

Besides the lack of a complete critical edition, some areas are still relatively unclear and little explored. For the purposes of this chapter, I wish to examine briefly two topics, namely the character of the exchange in terms of literary genre, and the level of Newton's involvement alongside Clarke in both defending his world-view and attacking Leibniz's. Although in the final section I will survey some of the main themes of the correspondence, this chapter should be read as an invitation to study it afresh.

THE GENRE OF THE CORRESPONDENCE

The correspondence between Leibniz and Clarke originated when Caroline, Princess of Wales, passed to Clarke an extract of a letter she had just received from Leibniz, an extract not originally intended for Clarke. She claimed that she was having a dispute with the English divine, gave him Leibniz's extract, and then passed on Clarke's reply to Leibniz. Caroline remained the mediator throughout the controversy. The documents that have survived consist of two parallel sets of exchanges, one between Leibniz and Clarke, and one between Caroline and Leibniz. In addition, we have records of Clarke's discussions with Caroline and Newton's visits to her, as well as her witnessing several experiments on colors and the void. Other parallel exchanges too have been considered relevant, such as that between Leibniz and Newton mediated by the Abbé Conti.[5]

Why did Leibniz and Clarke proceed inexorably, month after month, to exchange ever longer letters on the nature of space and time, the notion of miracle, and the cause of gravity? Are there literary precedents for such types of exchange? I shall start with the second question.

The first examples which spring to mind are the Leibniz–Arnauld and Leibniz–Pellisson correspondences, both dealing with theological and philosophical issues. The correspondence between Leibniz and French theologian and philosopher Antoine Arnauld was mediated by the Landgrave of Hesse-Rheinfels, a Catholic convert interested in Church reunion. The correspondence between Leibniz and Paul Pellisson, which also involved Church reunion, was instigated by, and conducted through, an interested aristocratic intermediary, Sophia, Duchess of Hanover. In both cases philosophical themes were interwoven with theological ones.[6] Incidentally, the issue of Church reunion was raised in the correspondence between Leibniz and Caroline early in 1716, at the time of the election of William Wake as Archbishop of Canterbury. In the dispute between Leibniz and Clarke, however, Church reunion was not mentioned, and the tone was more confrontational. Thus we need to look for a more appropriate precedent.

Another episode from earlier in the seventeenth century looks helpful, namely the affair involving scripture and Copernicanism at the Tuscan court in the mid 1610s. The exchanges between Benedetto Castelli and Galileo on one side, and the philosopher Cosimo Boscaglia on the other, with Grand Duchess Christina of Lorraine as patron and intermediary, share some analogies with the Leibniz–Clarke correspondence. Castelli had lunch with Christina, mother of Grand Duke Cosimo II, the Grand Duke himself, Boscaglia, and others. Apparently, Boscaglia had Christina's ear for a while. When Castelli left, he barely managed to get out of the palace before he was called back inside by Christina's porter. There, he was asked to reconcile passages from scripture with Copernicanism – notably where Joshua invoked God, asking him to stop the sun – a task Castelli accomplished brilliantly. This was a crucial episode in the attack against Galileo and Copernicanism, leading to his Copernican letters to Castelli, Piero Dini, and eventually Christina. Galileo's letter to the Grand Duchess was, at one and the same time, a continuation of the prior discussion after lunch when Copernicanism had been attacked and an appeal to an influential family member of Galileo's patrons.[7]

In the cases of both Christina and Caroline, one party used its contacts with a high-ranking female patron in order to launch an attack on the opposite side. In both cases the female patrons were not just spectators, but were known for their religious interests and orthodoxy, Christina on the Catholic side, Caroline on the Lutheran. Christina is described by the sources as a bigot in the hands of the papacy and, following Cosimo II's death in 1621, a regent possessed by religious zeal against state interests. By contrast, Caroline is depicted as an intellectual woman with a mind of her own. In her early twenties she showed sufficient independence of judgment to refuse to convert to Catholicism, thus renouncing marriage to the Emperor's son, in order to retain her Lutheran confession. Writing to a female patron, moreover, enabled Galileo, as well as Clarke and Leibniz, to reach a wider audience by addressing philosophical and theological issues in an intelligent, but not excessively technical fashion.[8]

On the philosopher's side, of course, Leibniz was a far more interesting and sophisticated thinker than Boscaglia, and his arguments are of incomparably greater philosophical import than the Joshua quotation from the Bible. Despite these important differences, however, the structure of the two events shows revealing similarities.

By appealing to such high-ranking patrons with such accusations as the claim that the Joshua passage in the Bible contradicted Copernicanism, or that Newton's and Locke's philosophies were detrimental to natural religion, philosophers were not just engaging in an intellectual debate. They were launching potentially devastating attacks with very serious consequences. Although Leibniz was not aiming at having Newton tried for heresy, he was certainly attempting to reduce him, together with his philosophical system, to the status of an intellectual pariah. Unable to reach an honorable settlement in the priority dispute over the invention of the calculus, Leibniz tried to undermine Newton and his allies through his contacts with the recently installed Princess of Wales.

Seen from this perspective, the correspondence between Leibniz and Clarke appears in a rather dramatic light. Leibniz's accusation of

Socinianism, a discredited religious sect, launched against Clarke, Locke, and Newton was an important step in this strategy.[9] The contenders were trying not just to explain their philosophies to each other, but to undermine the very credibility of each other's system. This partly explains the very selective nature of the exchange, the inclusion of some topics, and the exclusion of others. Readers of Clarke's dedication to Caroline will not fail to realize the high stakes involved, as well as how astutely Clarke used his theological prowess and proximity to Caroline against his rival.

By reflecting on the genre of the correspondence, we are drawn into paying more attention to Caroline's role. After the early events in her life mentioned briefly above, she became very close to Leibniz, whose *Théodicée* was one of her favorite readings. It is certainly not by accident that Leibniz referred to it so frequently in his dispute with Clarke. In the absence of a queen, since George I's wife remained in Germany relegated to the Castle of Ahlden, Caroline was the highest female royal.[10] Her role and theological interests made her particularly influential on religious matters. Some said that the election of the new Archbishop of Canterbury, William Wake, in December 1715 was due to her good offices. It is not difficult to grasp from this perspective a dimension of the dispute that would have been obvious in its significance to contemporaries.

NEWTON'S ROLE

The role Newton played in the correspondence has been a matter of debate. It seems appropriate here briefly to review both sides of the argument, assessing their significance in relation to the circumstantial and documentary evidence.

Manuscript evidence indicating Newton's involvement in the exchange does exist, but it is scanty, especially bearing in mind how obsessively he drafted and redrafted his works. Alexandre Koyré and I. Bernard Cohen forcefully stated that they had found no drafts of Clarke's replies in Newton's hand, no suggestions as to what those replies should be, and not even versions of Clarke's replies with Newton's emendations. There is, however, a copy in Newton's hand of Leibniz's "Apostille" to his fourth letter on atoms and the void, where Newton wrote "received of the Princess May 7th 1716, and copied May 8." The Princess must have made the text available to Newton immediately upon its arrival, and with good reason.[11] At that time, between April and May 1716, Caroline witnessed several experiments on colors and the void. The king set a special room aside so that they could be performed in front of his daughter-in-law. This may have been necessary for the optical demonstrations, requiring a space sufficiently long and which could be suitably darkened. It is difficult to imagine that Newton was not involved in these experiments, especially since Caroline referred to them as "les expérimens du chevalier Newton." Moreover, in the same letter where Caroline announced that she was going to witness the experiments, she referred to a visit by Newton and Clarke with Conti.[12]

Thus, despite the relative lack of manuscript evidence, what we have does suggest that Newton was kept abreast of the developments not just by Clarke, but by Caroline as well. In addition, Clarke and Newton were neighbors, and Clarke served at Newton's parish, St. James's, and was rector of the chapel in Golden Square, of which Newton was a trustee. Circumstances for meeting and discussing the exchange, without the need to pass written documents, would have been plentiful, and indeed we know that Caroline herself warned Leibniz that Clarke's letters were not written "without the advice of the Chevalier Newton." Moreover, we know from the diary of Mary Cowper, Lady of the Bedchamber to Caroline, that on 11 February 1716 "Sir Isaac Newton and Dr Samuel Clarke came this afternoon to explain Sir Isaac's System of Philosophy to the Princess."[13] Thus historians looking for signs of Newton's involvement exclusively among Newton's manuscripts may have cast their nets too narrowly. Evidence from a broader set of sources strongly points to his having been involved in the dispute.

Alongside these remarks, one should not forget that Clarke was a powerful intellect in his own right and an able controversialist.

His views were broadly, though not completely, in agreement with Newton's. Although he was clearly the material author of the letters on the English side of the dispute, his replies to Leibniz can be seen to some extent as the result of the collaboration between two minds working on the same wavelength.[14]

THE CORRESPONDENCE

These preliminary reflections are a useful springboard for a historicist reading of the correspondence, one taking into account circumstances of composition and authorship in conjunction with a number of themes interwoven with the religious and political events and debates of the day.

Unfortunately, we do not know what Leibniz wrote to Caroline in November 1715 in the letter that started the exchange. We know only the extract communicated by Caroline to Clarke, which seems to be cut out from a larger canvas, as the opening sentence and especially the word "itself" suggest: "Natual religion itself seems to decay." In the previous letter to Caroline of May 10, 1715, for example, Leibniz had outlined a sophisticated and effective argument on the doctrine of gravity and the Eucharist to embarrass the Newtonians. Topics related to other aspects of the decay of religion in England would thus have been at hand. Moreover, the extract from Leibniz's letter was selected by Caroline, and this is a significant feature. It seems at least plausible that Caroline selected for Clarke a portion she deemed suitable for an exchange. The fact that all subsequent exchanges went through her reinforces the importance of her role.

The opening words, "Natural religion," set the tone of the entire exchange. There was widespread belief in several quarters that the recent advancements of knowledge and the development of the experimental philosophy were going hand in hand with the strengthening of true religion. Leibniz's attack tried to put a devastating wedge between crucial points in Locke's and Newton's philosophies, on the one hand, and religious orthodoxy, on the other. This was a line of attack particularly suited to gaining Caroline's approval, and one Clarke had to reject thoroughly point by point. In his dedication to the Princess of Wales, he stated that "*Christianity* presupposes the Truth of *Natural Religion*. Whatsoever subverts Natural Religion, does consequently much more subvert Christianity: and whatsoever tends to confirm Natural Religion, is proportionably of Service to the True Interest of the Christian."[15]

The themes of the correspondence evolved from letter to letter. In some cases, such as Leibniz's attack on Locke's alleged opinion that the soul is material and perishable, Clarke did not see fit to mount a defense. In other cases, such as God's role in the universe, the exchange proceeded through all ten letters. Leibniz argued that in the Newtonian system God had to intervene from time to time in the mechanisms of the universe in order to repair it, as if God lacked foreknowledge to arrange them perfectly from the beginning. Clarke argued that Leibniz's system introduced materialism and fatality, in that the world continues by itself without any role for a deity. Other themes in the correspondence follow a similar pattern: for example, Leibniz's God has preordained the future course of events in the universe in the most perfect way, whereas Clarke's and Newton's God has to intervene every now and then to reach his purposes. Polemically, Clarke argued that Leibniz's God was *intelligentia supramondana*, emphasizing his detachment from the affairs of the world. The notion of miracle too is linked to this issue in that alterations to the normal course of nature were seen differently by the contenders. Clarke relied on the notion of what commonly happens in order to define a miracle. By contrast, Leibniz relied on the notion of laws of nature and what is not explicable by them in his definition. Thus attraction is obviously not miraculous according to Clarke, because it acts at each instant, whereas for Leibniz it is, because it transcends the power of bodies, which cannot act without being present.[16]

Probably the most heavily studied topic in the entire correspondence is the nature of space and time. The issue was raised in the first letter, when Leibniz accused Newton of having made space the *sensorium* of God. Indeed, Newton had unguardedly let this notion slip through his pen in two passages of his 1706 *Optice*, only one of which was removed in some copies, with an awkward cancel.[17]

The crucial point of the debate about space and time concerned again God's actions. In his attack Leibniz was able to construct an argument he had not previously put forward, although a similar line of reasoning can be found in the *Théodicée*.[18] He posited the principle of sufficient reason, namely that nothing happens without a reason, and argued that if space and time were something absolute and uniform, as Newton believed, the principle of sufficient reason would be violated. God could have created the universe in space, preserving the mutual situations among bodies, but changing for example West into East; similarly, he could have created the universe at a different instant. There could be no reason, however, why God could have chosen between two qualitatively identical situations, and thus in his act of creation he would have acted without a sufficient reason. Clarke's reply was that God's will was in itself a sufficient reason for his actions.

The existence of atoms too was attacked by Leibniz on the basis of a principle derived from that of sufficient reason, namely the identity of indiscernibles. Leibniz argued that if two qualitatively identical atoms existed, there would be no reason to place one of them here and the other there. God's wisdom would not allow him to create a world where he would have to make choices without reason, and therefore atoms do not exist. Later Leibniz argued that the existence of atoms would directly violate the other principle as well, because God would lack a sufficient reason to stop the divisibility of matter at one point rather than another.[19]

Caroline's presence as an arbiter between the contenders provided implicit guidelines for their correspondence, but this does not make the historian's task easier. Rather, it adds a dimension to the already complex field of Leibniz's, Clarke's, and Newton's theological and philosophical views.

NOTES

1 S. Shapin, "Of Gods and Kings: Politics and the Leibniz–Clarke dispute," *Isis* 72 (1981), 187–215, on 187. The most recent comprehensive account is E. Vailati, *Leibniz and Clarke: A Study of their Corresondence* (Oxford: Oxford University Press, 1997).

2 The main editions are the following: S. Clarke, *A collection of papers, which passed between the late learned Mr. Leibnitz and Dr. Clarke in the years 1715 and 1716: relating to the principles of natural philosophy and religion: with an appendix to which are added, letters to Dr. Clarke concerning liberty and necessity, from a gentleman of the University of Cambridge, with the doctor's answers to them: also, remarks upon a book, entituled, A philosophical enquiry concerning human liberty by Samuel Clarke* (London: James Knapton, 1717); H. G. Alexander, *The Leibniz–Clarke Correspondence* (Manchester: Manchester University Press, 1956); A. Robinet, *Correspondance Leibniz–Clarke présentée d'après les manuscrits originaux des bibliothèques de Hanovre et de Londres* (Paris: Presses Universitaires de France, 1957); V. Schüller, *Der Leibniz–Clarke Briefwechsel* (Berlin: Akademie Verlag, 1991), pp. 566–70. For editions of the private correspondence between Leibniz and Caroline see E. Ravier, *Bibliographie des œuvres de Leibniz* (Paris: F. Alcan, 1937).

3 O. Klopp, *Die Werke von Leibniz: Erste Reihe*, 11 vols. (Hanover: Klindworth, 1864–84), vol. 11.

4 The following reflections develop some of the themes explored in D. Bertoloni Meli, "Caroline, Leibniz, and Clarke," *Journal of the History of Ideas* 60 (1999), 469–86.

5 A. Koyré and I. B. Cohen, "Newton and the Leibniz–Clarke Correspondence," *Archives Internationales d'Histoire des Sciences* 15 (1962), 63–126.

6 E. J. Aiton, *Leibniz: A Biography* (Bristol and Boston: Hilger, 1985), pp. 171–2 and 180–6; R. C. Sleigh, *Leibniz and Arnauld: A Commentary on Their Correspondence* (New Haven: Yale University Press, 1990).

7 Joshua 10.12–13; S. Drake, *Galileo at Work* (Chicago, IL: University of Chicago Press, 1978), p. 222. The critical edition of the letter to Christina is in *Le opere di Galileo Galilei*, ed. A. Favaro, 20 vols. in 21 (Florence: Le Monnier, 1890–1909), vol. 5, pp. 263–78 and 308–48. See also J. Dietz Moss, "Galileo's *Letter to Christina*: Some Rhetorical Considerations,"

Renaissance Quarterly 36 (1983), 547–76; and E. McMullin, "Galileo on Science and Scripture," in P. Machamer (ed.), *The Cambridge Companion to Galileo* (Cambridge: Cambridge University Press, 1998), pp. 271–347.

8 On Caroline see Bertoloni Meli, "Caroline, Leibniz, and Clarke," pp. 471–4. On Christina see *Dizionario Biografico degli Italiani*.

9 This issue will be discussed below. On Socinianism see Nicholas Jolley, *Leibniz and Locke: A Study of the New Essays on Human Understanding* (Oxford: Clarendon Press, 1984), ch. 2.

10 Aiton, *Leibniz: A Biography*, pp. 177–8. For a discussion of Wake's election and its possible links to the dispute between Leibniz and Clarke see Bertoloni Meli, "Caroline, Leibniz, and Clarke," pp. 483–5.

11 Cambridge University Library, Add. Ms. 3968.36, fol. 517; Koyré and Cohen, "Newton and the Leibniz–Clarke Correspondence," p. 67; Richard S. Westfall, *Never at Rest: A Biography of Isaac Newton* (Cambridge: Cambridge University Press, 1980), p. 778.

12 Caroline to Leibniz, April 24, May 15, and May 26, 1716, in Klopp, *Leibniz*, vol. 11, pp. 90–1, 93 and 112, respectively. On April 24, Caroline wrote: "Après demain nous aurons les expérimens du chevalier Newton. Le Roy a donné une chambre pour celà. Je vous y souhaite comme aussi pour samedi, où le chevalier Newton, l'abbé Conti et Mr Clarke seront avec moy."

13 *Diary of Mary Countess Cowper, Lady of the Bedchamber to the Princess of Wales, 1714–1720* (London, 1864), p. 74.

14 Vailati, *Leibniz and Clarke*, pays attention to Clarke's intellectual abilities. On Clarke see *Dictionary of Scientific Biography*, *Dictionary of National Biography*, and L. Stewart, *The Rise of Public Science* (Cambridge: Cambridge University Press, 1992), ch. 3; M. C. Jacob, *The Newtonians and the English Revolution, 1689–1720* (Ithaca, NY: Cornell University Press, 1976), ch. 4.

15 S. Clarke, dedication, p. vii. On Leibniz and the Eucharist, see Robert Merrihew Adams, *Leibniz: Determinist, Theist, Idealist* (New York: Oxford University Press, 1994), pp. 349–60.

16 See especially Leibniz, iii, 17 and Clarke, iii, 17.

17 The details of this typographic and philosophico-theological case are reconstructed in A. Koyré and I. B. Cohen, "The Case of the Missing *Tanquam*: Leibniz, Newton and Clarke," *Isis* 52 (1961), 555–66.

18 Bertoloni Meli, "Caroline, Leibniz and Clarke," pp. 482–3.

19 Leibniz, iv, 1ff. See also the "Apostille" to Leibniz's fourth paper.

Bibliography

PART I NEWTON'S WORKS

All of Newton's papers on light and colors, all the printed editions of the *Principia*, and most of Newton's writings on mathematics are published on the Newton Project website.

1a Published in his lifetime

(i) Papers on light and colors

"A Letter of Mr. Isaac Newton, Professor of the Mathematics in the University of Cambridge; containing his New Theory about Light and Colors," *Phil. Trans.* 80 (February 1671/2), 3075–87.

"An account of a New Catadioptrical Telescope invented by Mr. Newton," *Phil. Trans.* 81 (March 1672), 4004–10.

"Mr. Newton's Letter to the Publisher of March 26, 1672, containing some more suggestions about his New Telescope," *Phil. Trans.* 82 (April 1672), 4032–4.

"An extract of another Letter of the same to the Publisher, dated March 30, 1672, by way of Answer to some Objections, made by an Ingenious French Philosopher [A. Auzout] to the New Reflecting telescope," *Phil. Trans.* 82 (April 1672), 4034–5.

"Mr. Isaac Newton's Considerations upon part of a Letter of Monsieur de Bercé printed in the Eighth French Mémoire, containing the Catadioptrical Telescope, pretended to be improv'd and refined by Mr. Cassegrain," *Phil. Trans.* 83 (May 1672), 4056–9.

"Some experiments proposed in relation to Mr. Newton's Theory of light, printed in Numb. 80; together with the Observations made thereupon by the Author of that Theory," *Phil Trans.* 83 (May 1672), 4059–62.

"Mr. Newton's Letter of April 13, 1672 . . . being an Answer to the foregoing Letter of P. Pardies," *Phil. Trans.* 84 (June 1672), pp. 4087–93.

"A Series of Quere's propounded by Mr. Isaac Newton, to be determined by Experiments, positively and directly concluding his new Theory of Light and Colours," *Phil. Trans.* 85 (July 1672), pp. 5004–7.

"Mr. Newton's Answer to the foregoing [second] Letter [of P. Pardies]," *Phil. Trans.* 85 (July 1672), pp. 5012–18.

"Mr. Isaac Newton's Answer to some Considerations [of Robert Hooke] upon his Doctrine of Light and Colors," *Phil. Trans.* 88 (November 1672), 5084–103.

"Mr Newton's Answer to the foregoing Letter [of Christiaan Huygens] further explaining his Theory of Light and Colors, and particularly that of Whiteness; together with his continued hopes of perfecting Telescopes by Reflections rather than Refractions," *Phil. Trans.* 96 (July 1673), 6087–92.

"An Extract of Mr. Isaac Newton's Letter, written to the Publisher from Cambridge April 3, 1673, concerning the Number of Colors, and the Necessity of mixing them all for the Production of White, [in further response to Huygens]," *Phil. Trans.* 97 (October 1673), 6108–11.

"An Answer to this Letter [of Franc. Linus]," *Phil. Trans.* 110 (January 1674/5), 150.

"Mr. Isaac Newton's Considerations on the former Reply [to Linus]; together with further Directions, how to make Experiments controverted aright," *Phil. Trans.* 121 (January 1675/6), 500–2.

"A Extract of another Letter of Mr. Newton, written to the Publisher the 10th of January 1675/6, relating to the same Argument," *Phil. Trans.* 121 (January 1675/6), 503–4.

"A particular Answer of Mr. Isaak Newton to Mr. Linus his Letter, printed in Numb. 121, p.499, about an Experiment relating to the New Doctrine of Light and Colours," *Phil. Trans.* 123 (March 1676), 556–61.

"Mr. Newton's Answer to the precedent Letter [of Anthony Lucas], sent to the Publisher" *Phil. Trans.* 128 (September 1676), 698–705.

(ii) Principia Mathematica

Philosophiae Naturalis Principia Mathematica (London, 1687; 2nd edition, Cambridge, 1713; 3rd edition, London, 1726). The second edition was reprinted in Amsterdam in 1714 and again in 1723. The third edition was reprinted in Geneva in 1739–42 (with an extensive commentary) and again in 1760, as well as in Prague in 1780–5 (Books 1 and 2 only); the third edition was also reprinted in Samuel Horsley's edition of Newton's *Opera* (London, 1779–85), 5 vols. Bibliographical details of these, the several *Excerpta* in Latin and in English, and translations into other languages are given in the Variorum edition of Koyré and Cohen, listed below, Appendix VIII, pp. 851–83.

Isaac Newton's Philosophiae Naturalis Principia Mathematica, the Third Edition with Variant Readings, ed. A. Koyré and I. B. Cohen, with the assistance of Anne Whitman (Cambridge, MA: Harvard University Press; Cambridge: Cambridge University Press, 1972).

The Principia, Mathematical Principles of Natural Philosophy: A New Translation, trans. I. Bernard Cohen and Anne Whitman, with the assistance of Julia Budenz, preceded by "A Guide to Newton's *Principia*" by I. B. Cohen (Berkeley, CA: University of California Press, 1999).

(iii) Opticks

Opticks: or, A Treatise of the Reflexions, Refractions, Inflexions and Colours of Light (London, 1704; Latin edition, London, 1706; second English edition, London, 1717/18).

Opticks: or, A Treatise of the Reflections, Refractions, Inflections and Colours of Light. Based on the Fourth Edition London, 1730, with a preface by I. B. Cohen, a forward by Albert Einstein, an introduction by E. T. Whittaker, and an analytical table of contents by Duane H. D. Roller (New York: Dover, 1952).

(iv) Other publications in Newton's lifetime

Bernhardi Vareni Med. D. Geographia generalis, In qua affections generalis Telluris explicantur, Summa cura quam plurimis in locis emendata etc. . . . *Ab Isaaco Newton Math. Prof. Lucasiano Apud Cantabrigienses* (Cambridge, 1672).

[Anonymously] "Epistola missa ad praenobilem virum D. Carolum Montague Armigerum, Scaccarii Regii apud Anglos Cancellarium, & Societatis Regiae Praesidium, in *qua* solvuntur duo problemata mathematica à Johanne Bernoullo Mathematico celeberrimo proposita," *Phil. Trans.* 224 (January 1696/7), 348–9. Reports Newton's solution to the problem of the curve of the fastest descent. (Reprinted in Whiteside [ed.], *The Mathematical Papers of Isaac Newton*, vol. 8.)

"Scala graduum Caloris," *Phil. Trans.* 270 (March and April 1701), 824–9.

"Theoria Lunae," an Appendix to David Gregory, *Astronomiae Physicae & Geometricae Elementa* (Latin edition, Oxford, 1702; English edition, London, 1715); English version published as a pamphlet in 1702 and reprinted in facsimile in *Isaac Newton's Theory of the Moon's Motion* (1702), introduction by I. B. Cohen (Folkestone, 1975).

"Tractatus de quadratura curvarum" and "Enumeratio linearum tertii ordinis," published as appendices to the first edition of the *Opticks*, 1704; English translations of the "Tractatus" and "Enumeratio" (under the heading "Curves") appeared in John Harris, *Lexicon Technicum* in 1710. (Reprinted in Whiteside [ed.], *The Mathematical Papers of Isaac Newton*, vols. 7 and 8.)

Arithmetica Universalis, ed. William Whiston (Cambridge, 1707; first English translation, 1720; second Latin edition, edited by John Machin, 1722). (Reprinted in Whiteside [ed.], *The Mathematical Papers of Isaac Newton*, vol. 5.)

"De natura acidorum" and "Some Thoughts about the Nature of Acids," in John Harris, *Lexicon Technicum: Or, An Universal English Dictionary of ARTS and SCIENCES: explaining Not only the TERMS of ART, but the ARTS Themselves*, vol. 2, Introduction (London, 1710).

"De analysi per aequationes numero terminorum infinitas," in William Jones, *Analysis per Quantitatum Series Fluxiones ac Differentias: Cum Enumeratione Linearum Tertii Ordinis* (London, 1711). (Reprinted in Whiteside [ed.], *The Mathematical Papers of Isaac Newton*, vol. 2.)

"Methodis differentialis," in William Jones, *Analysis per Quantitatum Series Fluxiones ac Differentias: Cum Enumeratione Linearum Tertii Ordinis* (London, 1711). (Reprinted in Whiteside [ed.], *The Mathematical Papers of Isaac Newton*, vol. 4.)

[Anonymously] "Problematis mathematicis anglis nuper propositi Solutio Generalis," *Phil. Trans.* 347 (January–March 1716), 399–400. (Reprinted in Whiteside [ed.], *The Mathematical Papers of Isaac Newton*, vol. 8.)

[Anonymously] "An Account of the Book entituled Commercium Epistolicum Collinii & aliorum, De Analysi Promota; published by order of the Royal Society, in relation to the Dispute between Mr. Leibnitz and Dr. Keill, about the Right Invention of the Method of Fluxions, by some call'd the Differential Method," *Phil. Trans.* 342 (1715), 173–224.

"Tabula refractorum," *Phil. Trans.* 368 (1721), 172.

[Anonymously] "Ad lectorem," in *Commercium Epistolicum Collinii & aliorum, De Analysi Promota*, 2nd edition, ed. John Keill (London, 1722).

[Anonymously] "Remarks upon the Observations made upon a Chronological Index of Sir Isaac Newton, Translated into French by the Observator, and Publish'd at Paris" *Phil. Trans.* 389 (1725), 315–21.

1b Published after Newton's death

The Chronology of Ancient Kingdoms Amended, edited by John Conduitt (London, 1728).

A Treatise of the System of the World, a translation of "De motu corporum liber secundus," the second of Newton's original two-book conception of the *Principia*, retitled by the translator (London, 1728).

De Mundi Systemate Liber, retitled publication of "De motu corporum liber secundus," (London, 1728).

A Short Chronicle from the First Memory of Things in Europe to the Conquest of Persia by Alexander the Great, first published in a French translation in 1725 and then in English, edited by John Conduitt (London, 1728).

Optical Lectures read in the Public Schools of the University of Cambridge, Anno Domini, 1669, translated from the Latin (London, for Francis Fayram, 1728).

Lectiones Opticae, annis MDCLXIX, MDCLXX, MDCLXXI (London, 1729).

The Mathematical Principles of Natural Philosophy, translated into English by Andrew Motte; to which are added, *The Laws of the Moon's Motion, according to Gravity*, by John Machin (London, 1729).

Observations upon the Prophecies of Daniel and the Apocalypse of St. John, edited by Benjamin Smith (London and Dublin, 1733). (Edited by W. Whitla as *Sir Isaac Newton's Daniel and the Apocalypse with an Introductory Study. . . of Unbelief, Miracles and Prophecy* [London, 1922]).

The Method of Fluxions and Infinite Series; with its Application to the Geometry of Curve-Lines, translated from the Latin (London, 1736).

A Dissertation upon the Sacred Cubit of the Jews, edited by Thomas Birch in *Works of John Greaves*, vol. 2 (London, 1737), pp. 405–33.

"A Description of an Instrument for Observing the Moon's Distance from the fixt Stars at Sea," *Phil. Trans.* 465 (October 1742), 155–6.

Newton's letter to Robert Boyle of 28 February 1678/9, reproduced in T. Birch (ed.), *The Works of the Honourable Robert Boyle*, 5 vols. (London, 1744), vol. 1, pp. 70–73.

Two letters of Sir Isaac Newton to Mr. LeClerc : the former containing a dissertation upon the reading of the Greek text, I John, v. 7 : the latter upon that of I Timothy, iii 16 / published from authentick MSS in the Library of the Remonstrants in Holland. (London : Printed for J. Payne, 1754).

Four Letters from Sir Isaac Newton to Doctor Bentley concerning Some Arguments in Proof of a Deity (London, 1756).

"An Hypothesis Explaining the Properties of Light," read to the Royal Society in December 1675/6, printed in Thomas Birch, *The History of the Royal Society of London*, 4 vols. (London, 1756–7), vol. 3, pp. 247–305.

1c Edited collections of Newton's papers

Cohen, I. B. and Schofield, Robert E. (eds.), *Isaac Newton's Letters and Papers on Natural Philosophy*, revised edition (Cambridge, MA: Harvard University Press, 1978).

Edleston, J., *Correspondence of Sir Isaac Newton and Professor Cotes, including letters of other eminent men, now first published from the originals in the Library of Trinity College, Cambridge; together with an appendix, containing other unpublished letters and papers by Newton* (London and Cambridge, 1850).

Hall, A. Rupert and Hall, Marie Boas (eds.), *Unpublished Scientific Papers of Isaac Newton: A Selection from the Portsmouth Papers in the University Library*, Cambridge (Cambridge University Press, 1962).

Herivel, John, *The Background to Newton's Principia: A Study of Newton's Dynamical Researches in the Years 1664-84* (Oxford: Clarendon Press, 1965).

McGuire, J. E. and Tamny, Martin (eds.), *Certain Philosophical Questions: Newton's Trinity Notebook* (Cambridge: Cambridge University Press, 1983).

Newton, Isaac, *Philosophical Writings*, ed. Andrew Janiak (Cambridge: Cambridge University Press, 2004).

Newton, Isaac, *The Preliminary Manuscripts for Isaac Newton's 1687 Principia, 1684–1685*, introduction by Derek T. Whiteside (Cambridge: Cambridge University Press, 1989).

Rigaud, Stephen Peter, *Correspondence of Scientific Men of the Eighteenth Century . . . in the Collection of . . . the Earl of Macclesfield*, 2 vols. (Oxford: Oxford University Press, 1841).

Shapiro, Alan E. (ed.), *The Optical Papers of Isaac Newton, Volume 1: The Optical Lectures 1670–1672* (Cambridge: Cambridge University Press, 1984).

The Correspondence of Isaac Newton, ed. Herbert. W. Turnbull, John F. Scott, A. Rupert Hall, and Laura Tilling, 7 vols. (Cambridge: Cambridge University Press, 1959–77).

Whiteside, Derek T. (ed.), *The Mathematical Works of Isaac Newton*, 2 vols. (New York, 1964, 1967).

Whiteside, Derek T. (ed.), *The Mathematical Papers of Isaac Newton*, 8 vols. (Cambridge: Cambridge University Press, 1967–81).

PART 2 SELECT WRITINGS ON NEWTON

(i) Biographies (in chronological order)

Hall, A. Rupert (ed.), *Isaac Newton, Eighteenth-Century Perspectives, a collection of early biographical memoirs* (Oxford: Oxford University Press, 1999).

Fontenelle, Bernard le Bovier de, *The Elogium of Sir Isaac Newton: by Monsieur Fontenelle, perpetual Secretary of the Royal Academy of Sciences at Paris* (London, 1728).

Stukeley, William, *Memoirs of Sir Isaac Newton's Life, 1752: Being some account of his family and chiefly of the junior part of his life*, edited by A. Hastings White (London, 1936).

Brewster, Sir David, *Memoirs of the Life, Writings and Discoveries of Sir Isaac Newton*, 2 vols. (Edinburgh, 1855).

More, Louis Trenchard, *Isaac Newton: A Biography* (New York and London: Charles Scribner's Sons, 1934).

Keynes, John Maynard, "Newton, the Man," in *Essays in Biography* (New York: W. W. Norton & Company, 1963), pp. 310–23.

Manuel, Frank E., *A Portrait of Isaac Newton* (Cambridge, MA: Belknap Press of Harvard University, 1968).

Cohen I. Bernard, "Newton, Isaac," *Dictionary of Scientific Biography*, vol. 10 (New York: Charles Scribner's Sons, 1974), pp. 41–103.

Westfall, Richard S., *Never at Rest: A Biography of Isaac Newton* (Cambridge: Cambridge University Press, 1980).

Christianson, Gale E., *In The Presence of the Creator: Isaac Newton and His Times* (New York: Free Press, 1984).

Gjertsen, Derek, *The Newton Handbook* (London and New York: Routledge and Kegan Paul, 1986).

Hall, A. Rupert, *Isaac Newton: Adventurer in Thought* (Oxford: Blackwell, 1992).

Hall, A. Rupert, *Isaac Newton: Eighteenth Century Perspectives* (Oxford; New York: Oxford University Press, 1999).

Gleick, James, *Isaac Newton* (New York: Vintage, 2003).

Higgitt, Rebekah, Iliffe, Rob, and Keynes, Milo (eds.), *Early Biographies of Isaac Newton 1660–1885*, 2 vols. (London: Pickering & Chatto, 2006).

Iliffe, Rob, *A Very Short Introduction to Newton* (Oxford: Oxford University Press, 2007).

(ii) Collections of studies

Bechler, Zev (ed.), *Contemporary Newtonian Scholarship* (Dordrecht: D. Reidel, 1982).

Beiner, Zvi and Schliesser, Eric (eds.) *Newton and Empiricism* (Oxford; New York: Oxford University Press, 2014).

Bricker, Phillip and Hughes, R. I. G. (eds.), *Philosophical Perspectives on Newtonian Science* (Cambridge, MA: MIT Press, 1990).

Buchwald, Jed and Cohen, I. Bernard (eds.), *Isaac Newton's Natural Philosophy* (Cambridge, MA: MIT Press, 2001).

Cohen, I. Bernard and Westfall, Richard S. (eds.), *Newton: Texts, Backgrounds, and Commentaries*, A Norton Critical Edition (New York: W. W. Norton & Company, 1995).

Dalitz, Richard H. and Nauenberg, Michael (eds.), *The Foundations of Newtonian Scholarship* (Singapore: World Scientific, 2000).

Durham, Frank and Purrington, Robert D. (eds.), *Some Truer Method: Reflections on the Heritage of Newton* (New York; Oxford: Columbia University Press, 1990).

Fauvel, John, Flood, Raymond, Shortland, Michael, and Wilson, Robin (eds.), *Let Newton Be! A New Perspective on his Life and Works* (Oxford: Oxford University Press, 1988).

Force, James E. and Popkin, Richard H. (eds.), *The Books of Nature and Scripture : Recent Essays on Natural Philosophy, Theology, and Biblical Criticism in the Netherlands of Spinoza's time and the British Isles of Newton's time* (Dordrecht: Kluwer Academic, 1994).

Force, James E. and Popkin, Richard H. (eds.), *Newton and Religion: Context, Nature, and Influence* (Dordrecht: Kluwer Academic, 1998).

Force, James E. and Hutton, Sarah (eds.), *Newton and Newtonianism* (Dordrecht: Kluwer Academic, 2004).

Greenstreet, W. J. (ed.), *Isaac Newton, 1642–1727: A Memorial Volume Edited for the Mathematical Association* (London: G. Bell and Sons, 1927).

Harman, Peter M. and Shapiro, Alan E. (eds.) *The Investigation of Difficult Things: Essays on Newton and the History of the Exact Sciences* (Cambridge: Cambridge University Press, 1992).

Janiak, Andrew and Schliesser, Eric, (eds.), *Interpreting Newton: Critical Essays* (Cambridge: Cambridge University Press, 2012).

King-Hele, D. G. and Hall, A. R. (eds.), *Newton's Principia and its Legacy*: *Proceedings of a Royal Society Discussion Meeting of 30 June 1987* (London: The Royal Society, 1988).

Palter, Robert (ed.), *The Annus Mirabilis of Sir Isaac Newton 1666–1966* (Cambridge, MA: MIT Press, 1970).

Theerman, Paul and Seef, Adele F., *Action and Reaction: Proceedings of a Symposium to Commemorate the Tercentenary of Newton's Principia* (Newark, NJ: University of Delaware Press; London and Toronto: Associated University Presses, 1993).

Thrower, Norman J. W. (ed.), *Standing on the Shoulders of Giants: A Longer View of Newton and Halley: Essays commemorating the tercentenary of Newton's Principia and the 1985-1986 return of Comet Halley* (Berkeley; Los Angeles, CA; London: University of California Press, 1990).

Sir Isaac Newton, 1727–1927: A Bicentenary Evaluation of His Work, a series of papers prepared under the auspices of the History of Science Society (Baltimore, MD: The Williams and Wilkins Company, 1928).

Newton Tercentenary Celebrations, the Royal Society (Cambridge: Cambridge University Press, 1947).

(iii) General works

Blay, Michel, *Reasoning with the Infinite: From the Closed World to the Mathematical Universe*, trans. M. B. DeBevoise (Chicago, IL: University of Chicago Press, 1998).

Blay, Michel, "Force, Continuity and the Mathematization of Motion at the End of the Seventeenth Century," in Buchwald and Cohen (eds.), *Isaac Newton's Natural Philosophy*, listed in Section (ii) above, pp. 225–48.

Cohen, I. B., *The Newtonian Revolution* (Cambridge: Cambridge University Press, 1980).

Cohen, I. B., *The Birth of a New Physics*, revised and updated edition (New York: W. W. Norton & Company, 1985).

Coles, Elisha, *An English Dictionary, explaining the difficult terms that are used in divinity, husbandry, physic etc.* (London, 1684).

Dobbs, Betty Jo Teeter and Jacob, Margaret C., *Newton and the Culture of Newtonianism* (Atlantic Highlands, NJ: Humanities Press, 1995).

Dry, Sarah, *The Newton Papers: The Strange and true Odyssey of Newton's Manuscripts*, (Oxford: Oxford University Press, 2014).

Feingold, Mordechai, *The Newtonian Moment: Isaac Newton and the Making of Modern Culture* (Oxford: Oxford University Press, 2004).

Gabbey, Alan, "Force and Inertia in Seventeenth-Century Dynamics," *Studies in History and Philosophy of Science* 2 (1971), 1–67.

Guerlac, Henry, *Essays and Papers in the History of Modern Science* (Baltimore, MD: Johns Hopkins University Press, 1977).

Guerlac, Henry, *Newton on the Continent* (Ithaca, NY: Cornell University Press, 1981).

Harper, William and Smith, George E., "Newton's New Way of Inquiry," in Jarrett Leplin (ed.), *The Creation of Ideas in Physics: Studies for Methodology of Theory Construction* (Dordrecht: Kluwer Academic, 1995).

Hesse, Mary B., *Forces and Fields: The Concept of Action at a Distance in the History of Physics* (London: Thomas Nelson and Sons, 1961).

Koyré, Alexandre, "An Experiment in Measurement," in *Metaphysics and Measurement* (London: Chapman and Hall, 1968), pp. 89–117.

Koyré, Alexandre and Cohen, I. B., "Newton & the Leibniz–Clarke Correspondence with Notes on Newton, Conti, & Des Maizeaux," *Archives internationales d'histoire des sciences* 15 (1962), 63–126.

Koyré, Alexandre, *Newtonian Studies* (Cambridge, MA: Harvard University Press; London: Chapman & Hall, 1965).

Lagrange, Joseph-Louis, *Analytical Mechanics* (Dordrecht: Kluwer, 1997).

Mach, Ernst, *The Science of Mechanics* (Chicago, IL: Open Court Publishing, 1960).

McMullin, Ernan, *Newton on Matter and Activity* (Notre Dame, IN: University of Notre Dame Press, 1978).

Robinson, Abraham, *Non-Standard Analysis* (Amsterdam, 1966).

Shank, J. B., *The Newton Wars and the Beginning of the French Enlightenment* (Chicago, IL: University of Chicago Press, 2008).

Truesdell, Clifford, *Essays in the History of Mechanics* (New York: Springer-Verlag, 1968).

Westfall, Richard S., *Force in Newton's Physics: The Science of Dynamics in the Seventeenth Century* (London: Macdonald; New York: American Elsevier, 1971).

Westfall, Richard S., *The Construction of Modern Science: Mechanisms and Mechanics* (Cambridge: Cambridge University Press, 1977).

Wilson, Curtis, "From Kepler's Laws, so-called, to Universal Gravitation," *Archive for History of Exact Sciences* 6 (1970), 89–170.

Yoder, Joella, *Unrolling Time: Christiaan Huygens and the Mathematization of Nature* (Cambridge: Cambridge University Press, 1988).

(iv) Studies of the Principia and related topics

Ball, W. W. Rouse, *An Essay on Newton's Principia* (London and New York: Macmillan and Co., 1893).

Bertoloni Meli, Domenico, "The Relativization of Centrifugal Force," *Isis* 81 (1990), 23–43.

Brackenridge, J. Bruce, "The Critical Role of Curvature in Newton's Developing Dynamics," in Harman and Shapiro (eds.), *The Investigation of Difficult Things*, listed in Section (ii) above, pp. 231–60.

Brackenridge, J. Bruce, *The Key to Newton's Dynamics: The Kepler Problem and the Principia*, with English translations from the Latin by Mary Ann Rossi (Berkeley, CA: University of California Press, 1995).

Chandrasekhar, S., *Newton's Principia for the Common Reader* (Oxford: Clarendon Press, 1995).

Cohen, I. B., "Hypotheses in Newton's Philosophy," *Physis* 8 (1966), 163–84.

Cohen, I. B., *Introduction to Newton's "Principia"* (Cambridge, MA: Harvard University Press; Cambridge: Cambridge University Press, 1971).

De Gandt, François, *Force and Geometry in Newton's Principia*, trans. Curtis Wilson (Princeton, NJ: Princeton University Press, 1995).

Densmore, Dana, *Newton's Principia: The Central Argument*, with translations and illustrations by William Donahue (Santa Fe, NM: Green Lion Press, 1995).

DiSalle, Robert, "Space–Time Theory as Physical Geometry," *Erkenntnis* 42 (1995), 317–37.

DiSalle, Robert, *Understanding Space–Time: The Philosophical Development of Physics from Newton to Einstein* (Cambridge: Cambridge University Press, 2006).

Dobson, Geoffrey J., "Newton's Problems with Rigid Body Dynamics in the Light of his Treatment of the Precession of Equinoxes," *Archive for History of Exact Sciences* 53 (1998), 125–45.

Ducheyne, Steffen, *The Main Business of Natural Philosophy: Isaac Newton's Natural-Philosophical Methodology* (New York: Springer, 2012).

Earman, John, *World Enough and Space–Time: Absolute versus Relational Theories of Space and Time* (Cambridge, MA: MIT Press, 1989).

Earman, John and Friedman, Michael, "The Meaning and Status of Newton's Law of Inertia and the Nature of Gravitational Forces," *Philosophy of Science* 40 (1973), 329–59.

Ehrlichson, Herman, "The Visualization of Quadratures in the Mystery of Corollary 3 to Proposition 41 of Newton's *Principia*," *Historia Mathematica* 21 (1994), 145–51.

Guicciardini, Niccolò, *Reading the Principia: The Debate on Newton's Mathematical Methods for Natural Philosophy from 1687 to 1736* (Cambridge: Cambridge University Press, 1999).

Harper, William L., "Isaac Newton on Empirical Success and Scientific Method," in John Earman and John D. Norton (eds.), *The Cosmos of Science: Essays of Exploration* (Pittsburgh, PA: University of Pittsburgh Press, 1997), pp. 55–86.

Harper, William L., *Isaac Newton's Scientific Method: Turning Data into Evidence about Gravity and Cosmology* (Oxford: Oxford University Press, 2011).

Herivel, John, *The Background to Newton's Principia: A Study of Newton's Dynamical Researches in the Years 1664-84* (Oxford: Clarendon Press, 1965).

Janiak, Andrew, *Newton as Philosopher* (Cambridge: Cambridge University Press, 2008).

Kollerstrom, Nicholas, *Newton's Forgotten Lunar Theory: His Contribution to the Quest for Longitude* (Santa Fe, NM: Green Lion Press, 2000).

Lakatos, Imre, "Newton's Effect on Scientific Standards," in *The Methodology of Scientific Research Programmes, Philosophical Papers*, vol. 1 (Cambridge: Cambridge University Press, 1978), pp. 193–222.

Maclaurin, Colin, *An Account of Sir Isaac Newton's Philosophical Discoveries* (London, 1748).

Nauenberg, Michael, "Newton's Early Computational Method for Dynamics," *Archive for History of Exact Sciences* 46 (1994), 221–52.

Nauenberg, Michael, "Newton's Portsmouth Perturbation Method and its Application to Lunar Motion," in Dalitz and Nauenberg (eds.), *The Foundations of Newtonian Scholarship*, listed in Section (ii) above, pp. 167–94.

Nauenberg, Michael, "Kepler's area law in the *Principia*: filling in some details in Newton's proof of Proposition I," *Historia Mathematica*, 30 (2003), 441–56.

Pourciau, Bruce, "Newton's Argument for Proposition 1 of the *Principia*," *Archive for History of Exact Sciences* 57 (2003), 267–311.

Pourciau, Bruce, "Newton's Interpretation of Newton's Second Law," *Archive for History of Exact Sciences* 60 (2006), 157–207.

Rigaud, Stephen Peter, *Historical Essay on the First Publication of Sir Isaac Newton's Principia* (Oxford: Oxford University Press, 1838).

Rynasiewicz, Robert, "By Their Properties, Causes and Effects: Newton's Scholium on Time, Space, Place and Motion," *Studies in History and Philosophy of Science* 26 (1995), 133–53; 295–321.

Smith, George E., "The Newtonian Style in Book II of the Principia," in Buchwald and Cohen (eds.), *Isaac Newton's Natural Philosophy*, listed in Section (ii) above, pp. 249–313.

Smith, George E., "Was Wrong Newton Bad Newton?" in Jed Z. Buchwald and Allan Franklin (eds.), *Wrong for the Right Reasons* (Dordrecht: Springer, 2005).

Smith, George E., "From the Phenomenon of the Ellipse to an Inverse-Square Force: Why Not?" in David Malament (ed.), *Reading Natural Philosophy: Essays in the History and Philosophy of Science and Mathematics to Honor Howard Stein on his 70th Birthday* (La Salle, IL: Open Court, 2002).

Smith, George E., "How Newton's Principia Changed Physics," in Janiak and Schliesser (eds.), *Interpreting Newton*, listed in Section (ii) above, pp. 360–395.

Smith, George E., "Closing the Loop: Testing Newtonian Gravity, Then and Now," in Biener and Schliesser (eds.), *Newton and Empiricism*, listed in Section (ii) above, pp. 262–351.

Stein, Howard, "Newtonian Space–Time," *Texas Quarterly* 10 (1967), 174–200.

Taton, René and Wilson, Curtis (eds.), *Planetary Astronomy from the Renaissance to the Rise of Astrophysics, Tycho Brahe to Newton, vol. 2, part A of The General History of Astronomy* (Cambridge: Cambridge University Press, 1989).

Weinstock, Robert, "Inverse-Square Orbits in Newton's *Principia* and Twentieth-Century Commentary Thereon," *Archive for History of Exact Sciences* 55 (2000), 137–62.

Whiteside, D. T., "The Mathematical Principles Underlying Newton's *Principia*," *Journal for the History of Astronomy* 1 (1970), 116–38.

Whiteside, D. T., "The Prehistory of the *Principia* from 1664–1686," *Notes and Records of The Royal Society* 45 (1991), 11–61.

Whiteside, D. T., (ed.), *The Mathematical Papers of Isaac Newton*, vol. 6, listed in Section (ii) above.

Wilson, Curtis, *Astronomy from Kepler to Newton: Historical Studies* (London: Variorum Reprints, 1989).

(v) Mathematics

Guicciardini, Niccolò, *The Development of Newtonian Calculus in Britain 1700–1800* (Cambridge: Cambridge University Press, 1989).

Guicciardini, Niccolò, *Isaac Newton on Mathematical Certainty and Method* (Cambridge, MA: MIT Press, 2011).

Pourciau, Bruce, "On Newton's Proof that Inverse-Square Orbits must be Conics," *Annals of Science* 48 (1991), 159–72.

Pourciau, Bruce, "Radical *Principia*," *Archive for History of the Exact Sciences*, 44 (1992), 331–63.

Pourciau, Bruce, "The Preliminary Mathematical Lemmas of Newton's *Principia*," *Archive for History of Exact Sciences* 52 (1998), 279–95.

Pourciau, Bruce, "The Integrability of Ovals: Newton's Lemma 28 and its Counterexamples," *Archive for History of Exact Sciences* 55 (2001), 479–99.

Pourciau, Bruce, "The Importance of Being Equivalent: Newton's Two Models of One-Body Motion," *Archive for History of the Exact Sciences*, 60 (2006), 157–207.

Pourciau, Bruce, "From Centripetal Forces to Conic Orbits: A Path Through the Early Sections of Newton's *Principia*," *Studies in the History and Philosophy of Science*, 38 (2007), 56–83.

Pourciau, Bruce, "Proposition II (Book 1) of Newton's *Principia*," *Archive for History of Exact Sciences*, 63 (2009), 129–67.

Turnbull, Herbert Westren, *The Mathematical Discoveries of Newton* (London and Glasgow: Blackie & Son, 1945).

Whiteside, D. T., "Patterns of Mathematical Thought in the Later Seventeenth Century," *Archive for History of Exact Sciences* 1 (1961), 179–388.

Whiteside, D. T., (ed.), *The Mathematical Papers of Isaac Newton*, 8 vols., listed in Section (ii) above.

(vi) Newton and Leibniz

Aiton, Eric, *Leibniz, a Biography* (Bristol: Adam Hilger, 1985).

Alexander, H. G. (ed.), *The Leibniz–Clarke Correspondence* (Manchester: Manchester University Press, 1956).

Bertoloni Meli, Domenico, *Equivalence and Priority: Newton versus Leibniz* (Oxford: Clarendon Press, 1993), including Leibniz's unpublished manuscript notes on the *Principia*.

Hall, A. Rupert, *Philosophers at War: The Quarrel between Newton and Leibniz* (Cambridge: Cambridge University Press, 1980).

Vailati, Ezio, *Leibniz and Clarke: A Study of Their Correspondence* (Oxford: Oxford University Press, 1997).

Whiteside, D. T. (ed.), *The Mathematical Papers of Isaac Newton*, vol. 8., listed in Section (ii) above.

(vii) Optics

Hall A. Rupert, *And All Was Light: An Introduction to Newton's Opticks* (Oxford: Clarendon Press, 1993).

Laymon, Ronald, "Newton's Experimentum Crucis and the Logic of Idealization and Theory Refutation," *Studies in History and Philosophy of Science 9* (1978), 51–77.

Sabra, A. I., *Theories of Light from Descartes to Newton*, 2nd edition (Cambridge: Cambridge University Press, 1981).

Schaffer, Simon, "Glass Works: Newton's Prisms and the Use of Experiment," in D. Gooding, T. Pinch, and S. Schaffer (eds.), *The Use of Experiment: Studies in the Natural Sciences* (Cambridge: Cambridge University Press, 1989), pp. 67–104.

Sepper, Dennis L., *Newton's Optical Writings: A Guided Study* (New Brunswick, NJ: Rutgers University Press, 1994).

Shapiro, Alan E., "The Evolving Structure of Newton's Theory of White Light and Color: 1670–1704," *Isis* 71 (1980), 211–35.

Shapiro, Alan E., *Fits, Passions, and Paroxysms: Physics, Method, and Chemistry and Newton's Theories of Colored Bodies and Fits of Easy Reflection* (Cambridge: Cambridge University Press, 1993).

Shapiro, Alan E., "The Gradual Acceptance of Newton's Theory of Light and Color," *Perspectives on Science* 4 (1996), 59–104.

Steffens, Henry John, *The Development of Newtonian Optics in England* (New York: Science History Publications, 1977).

(viii) Alchemy, chemistry, and the theory of matter

Dobbs, Betty Jo Teeter, *The Foundations of Newton's Alchemy, or "The Hunting of the Greene Lyon* (Cambridge: Cambridge University Press, 1975).

Dobbs, Betty Jo Teeter, *The Janus Faces of Genius: The Role of Alchemy in Newton's Thought* (Cambridge: Cambridge University Press, 1991).

Figala, Karin, "Newton as Alchemist," *History of Science* 15 (1977), 102–37.

Figala, Karin, "Die exakte Alchemie von Isaac Newton," *Verhandlungen der Naturforschenden Gesellschaft Basel* 94 (1984), 155–228.

Golinski, Jan, "The Secret Life of an Alchemist," in John Fauvel *et al.* (eds.), *Let Newton Be!*, listed in Section (ii) above, pp. 146–67.

McGuire, J. E., "The Origin of Newton's Doctrine of Essential Qualities," *Centaurus* 12 (1968), 233–60.

McGuire, J. E., "Force, Active Principles, and Newton's Invisible Realm," *Ambix* 15 (1968), 154–208.

McGuire, J. E. "Atoms and the 'Analogy of Nature': Newton's Third Rule of Philosophizing," *Studies in the History and Philosophy of Science* 1 (1970), 3–58.

Newman, William R., *Gehennical Fire: The Lives of George Starkey, an American Alchemist in the Scientific Revolution* (Cambridge, MA: Harvard University Press, 1994).

Priesner, Claus and Figala, Karin (eds.), *Alchemie: Lexicon einer hermetischen Wissenschaft* (Munich: Verlag C. H. Beck München, 1998).

Principe, Lawrence, "The Alchemies of Robert Boyle and Isaac Newton: Alternate Approaches and Divergent Deployments," in M. Osler, *Rethinking the Scientific Revolution* (Cambridge: Cambridge University Press, 2000), pp. 201–20.

Taylor, F. S., "An Alchemical Work of Sir Isaac Newton," *Ambix* 5 (1956), 59–84.

Thackray, Arnold, *Atoms and Powers: An Essay on Newtonian Matter-Theory and the Development of Chemistry* (Cambridge, MA: Harvard University Press, 1970).

Westfall, Richard S., "The Role of Alchemy in Newton's Career," in Maria Luisa Righini Bonelli and William R. Shea (eds.), *Reason, Experiment and Mysticism in the Scientific Revolution* (New York: Science History Publications, 1975), pp. 189–232.

(ix) Religion and chronology

Buchwald, Jed Z. and Feingold, Mordechai, *Newton and the Origin of Civilization* (Princeton, NJ: Princeton University Press, 2012).

Castillejo, David, *The Expanding Force in Newton's Cosmos as shown in his Unpublished Papers* (Madrid: Ediciones de Arte y Bibliofilia, 1981).

Cohen, I. B., "Isaac Newton's *Principia*, the Scriptures, and the Divine Providence," in S. Morgenbesser, P. Suppes and M. White (eds.), *Philosophy, Science, and Method: Essays in Honor of Ernest Nagel* (New York: St Martin's Press, 1969), pp. 523–48.

Copenhaver, Brian P., "Jewish Theologies of Space in the Scientific Revolution: Henry More, Joseph Raphson, Isaac Newton and their Predecessors," *Annals of Science* 37 (1980), 489–548.

Delgado-Moreira, Raquel, "Newton's Treatise on Revelation: The use of a Mathematical Discourse," *Historical Research* 79 (2006), 224–46.

Figala, Karin, "Ein Exemplar der Chronologie von Newton aus dem Besitz von Pierre des Maizeaux in der bibliothèque de la ville de Colmar," *Verhandlungen der Naturforschenden Gesellschaft in Basel* 84 (1974), 646–97.

Force, James E. and Popkin, Richard H., *Essays on the context, nature and influence of Isaac Newton's theology* (Dordrecht: Kluwer, 1990).

Force, James E., "Newton's 'Sleeping Argument' and the Newtonian Synthesis of Science and Religion," in N. Thrower (ed.), *Standing on the Shoulders of Giants: A Longer View of Newton and Halley* (Berkeley and Los Angeles, CA: University of California Press, 1990), pp. 109–27.

Gascoigne, John, "'The Wisdom of the Egyptians' and the Secularisation of History in the Age of Newton," in S. Gaukroger (ed.), *The Uses of Antiquity: the Scientific Revolution and the Classical Tradition* (Dordrecht and London: Kluwer, 1991), pp. 171–212.

Goldish, M., *Judaism in the Theology of Sir Isaac Newton*, International Archives of the History of Ideas Archives internationales d'histoire des idées (Dordrecht; Boston, MA: Kluwer Academic, 2010).

Hiscock, W. G. (ed.), *David Gregory, Isaac Newton and Their Circle: Extracts from David Gregory's Memoranda* (Oxford: printed for the editor, 1937).

Hutton, Sarah, "More, Newton, and the Language of Biblical prophecy," in Force and Popkin (eds.), *Books of Nature and Scripture*, listed in Section (ii) above, pp. 39–53.

Iliffe, Rob, "'Making a Shew': Apocalyptic Hermeneutics and the Sociology of Christian Idolatry in the Work of Isaac Newton and Henry More," in Force and Popkin (eds.), *Books of Nature and Scripture*, listed in Section (ii) above, pp. 55–88.

Iliffe, Rob, "Those 'whose business it is to cavill': Newton's anti-Catholicism," in Force and Popkin (eds.), *Newton and Religion*, listed in Section (ii) above, pp. 97–119.

Iliffe, Rob, "Prosecuting Athanasius: Protestant Forensics and the Mirrors of Persecution," in Force and Hutton, (eds.), *Newton and Newtonianism*, listed in Section (ii) above, pp. 97–119.

Iliffe, Rob, "The powers of demonstration: Simon, Newton, Locke and the Johannine comma," in A. Hessayon and N. Keene (eds.), *Scripture and Scholarship in Early Modern England* (Aldershot: Ashgate, 2006), pp. 77–110.

Jacob, Margaret C., *The Newtonians and the English Revolution 1689–1720* (Hassocks, Sussex: Harvester Press; Ithaca, NY: Cornell University Press, 1976).

Kubrin, David C. "Newton and the Cyclical Cosmos: Providence and the Mechanical Philosophy," *Journal of the History of Ideas* 28 (1967), 325–46.

McGuire, J. E. and Rattansi, P. M., "Newton and the 'Pipes of Pan'," *Notes and Records of the Royal Society* 21 (1996), 118–43.

McLachlan, Herbert, *Sir Isaac Newton's Theological Manuscripts* (Liverpool: Liverpool University Press, 1950).

Mandelbrote, Scott, "'A Duty of the Greatest Moment': Isaac Newton and the Writings of Biblical Criticism," *British Journal for the History of Science* 26 (1993), pp. 281–302.

Mandelbrote, Scott, "'Then this Nothing can be Plainer': Isaac Newton Reads the Fathers," in G. Frank, T. Leinkauf and M. Wriedt (eds.), *Die Patristik in der frühen Neuzeit* (Stuttgart: Friedrich Fromm Verlag, 2006), pp. 277–97.

Mandelbrote, Scott, "Isaac Newton and the Flood," in M. Mulsow and J. Assmann (eds.), *Sintflut und Gedächtnis* (Paderborn: Wilhelm Fink Verlag, 2006), pp. 337–53.

Mandelbrote, Scott, "Isaac Newton and the Exegesis of the Book of Daniel," in K. Bracht and D. S. du Toit (eds.), *Die Geschichte der Daniel-Auslegung in Judentum, Christentum und Islam* (Berlin: Walter de Gruyter, 2007), pp. 351–75.

Manuel, Frank, *Isaac Newton, Historian* (Cambridge, MA: Harvard University Press, 1963).

Manuel, Frank, *The Religion of Isaac Newton* (Oxford: Clarendon Press, 1973).

Pérez, Pablo Toribio, *Isaac Newton: Historia Ecclesiastica: de Origine Schismatico Ecclesiae Papisticae Bicornis* (Madrid: Consejo Superior de Investigaciones Científicas, 2011).

Schaffer, Simon, "Comets and Idols: Newton's Cosmology and Political Theology," in Theerman and Seef (eds.), *Action and Reaction*, listed in Section (ii) above, pp. 206–31.

Schaffer, Simon, "Newtonian Angels," in J. Raymond (ed.), *Conversations with Angels: Essays Towards a History of Spiritual Communication, 1100–1700* (New York: Palgrave Macmillan, 2011), pp. 90–122.

Snobelen, Stephen, "Isaac Newton, Heretic: The Strategies of a Nicodemite," *British Journal for the History of Science* 32 (1999), 381–419.

Snobelen, Stephen, "'God of Gods, and Lord of Lords': The Theology of Isaac Newton's General Scholium to the *Principia*," *Osiris* 16 (2001), 169–208.

Snobelen, Stephen "Lust, Pride and Ambition: Isaac Newton and the Devil," in Force and Hutton (eds.), *Newton and Newtonianism*, listed in Section (ii) above, pp. 155–81.

Snobelen, Stephen, "Isaac Newton, Socinianism and 'The One Supreme God'," in M. Mulsow and J. Rohls (eds.), *Socinianism and Arminianism: Antitrinitarians, Calvinists, and Cultural Exchange in Seventeenth-Century Europe* (Leiden: Brill, 2005), pp. 241–98.

Stewart, Larry, "Seeing Through the Scholium: Religion and Reading Newton in the Eighteenth Century," *History of Science* 34 (1996), 123–65.

Westfall, Richard S., "Newton's Theological Manuscripts," in Bechler (ed.), *Contemporary Newtonian Research*, listed in Section (ii) above, pp. 129–43.

(x) Newton at the Mint

Craig, John, *Newton at the Mint* (Cambridge: Cambridge University Press, 1946).

Craig, John, "Isaac Newton and the Counterfeiters," *Notes and Records of the Royal Society* 18 (1963), 136–45.

Haynes, Hopton, *Brief memoires relating to the silver & gold coins of England: with an account of the corruption of the hammerd monys, and of the reform by the late grand coynage, at the Tower, & the five Country Mints. In the years 1696, 1697, 1698, & 1699* (BL, Lansdowne Ms. DCCCI).

Levenson, Thomas, *Newton and the Counterfeiter: The Unknown Detective Career of the World's Greatest Scientist* (London: Faber and Faber, 2009).

(xi) Bibliographies

Gray, George J., *Sir Isaac Newton: A Bibliography, together with a list of Books Illustrating His Works* (Cambridge: Bowes and Bowes, 1907).

Harrison, John, *The Library of Isaac Newton* (Cambridge: Cambridge University Press, 1978).

Wallis, Peter and Wallis, Ruth, *Newton and Newtoniana 1672–1975: A Bibliography* (London: Dawsons, 1977).

Index

Note: Page numbers followed by '*f*' and '*t*' refer to figures and tables, respectively.